Dennis Potter

Dennis Potter

A life on screen

second edition

John R. Cook

Manchester University Press
Manchester and New York
distributed exclusively in the USA by St. Martin's Press

First edition published 1995 by Manchester University Press

This edition published 1998 by
Manchester University Press
Oxford Road, Manchester M13 9NR, UK
and Room 400, 175 Fifth Avenue, New York, NY 10010, USA
http://www.man.ac.uk/mup

Distributed exclusively in the USA by
St. Martin's Press, Inc., 175 Fifth Avenue, New York, NY 10010, USA

Distributed exclusively in Canada by
UBC Press, University of British Columbia, 6344 Memorial Road,
Vancouver, BC, Canada V6T 1Z2

British Library Cataloguing-in-Publication Data
A catalogue record for this book is available from the British Library

Library of Congress Cataloging-in-Publication Data applied for

ISBN 0 7190 5423 0 *paperback*

This edition first published 1998

05 04 03 02 01 00 99 98 10 9 8 7 6 5 4 3 2 1

Typeset in Great Britain
by Northern Phototypesetting Co Ltd, Bolton
Printed in Great Britain
by Bell & Bain Ltd, Glasgow

IN MEMORY OF
MY LATE MOTHER AND FATHER

CAVENDISH: I dislike strangers. I positively dislike young men. And I actively *hate* young men who claim to be writing. …

Dennis Potter, *Blade on the Feather*

Contents

Plates

Copyright for stills 1–5 held by the BBC Photograph Library.
Stills 6, 9 and 10 by courtesy of Kenith Trodd.
Stills 7 and 8 by courtesy of the author.

Plates appear between pages 174 and 175 and between pages 300 and 301.

Foreword to the first edition

Dennis Potter once inscribed a present to me 'with aggressive affection'. The phrase invokes not only the oddity of his relationship with me but also his general take on the world and its distillation in his works. No contemporary British dramatist has written more widely or more daringly than Potter. There is volume as well as vision to his output and, despite natural reclusiveness, he developed a strong public presence beyond his fictions (though often in ferocious defence of them). His audience 'knew' Potter the man, and they certainly did not know most of his peers. This pundit-Potter reached his elegant and charismatic apogee in the television programme he made shortly after receiving a death sentence from his doctor. As a personal goodbye and summing-up, it was a model of unself-pitying eloquence but also, like his best screen work, it managed to speak to, and for, countless people who were not dying, or male, or 59, had indeed nothing in common with him yet felt *his* insights were coming from inside *them*.

Many people will be writing about Dennis Potter in coming years – there may be more books than we, or Potter, deserve – but I am delighted that John Russell Cook's will be among the first. As a good researcher must, he has been everywhere – but everywhere – in Dennis's career, read everything, and talked to everyone with a good morsel to contribute. As a work of scholarship, his book makes it gratefully unnecessary for anyone else to go to so many sources because he has obviously done that job so well. However, what I admire most about his work is that the dossier is always at the service of ideas, that Cook's main drive is to make fair sense of Dennis's work, to tease out legitimate patterns and always be responsive to what Dennis's words and images are offering. Cook's conclusion, that the motor of Potter's writing is tension, may seem like a literary truism – but hard-earned insights have to be like that sometimes, and this was one of several from Cook which I would never have stumbled to on my own but which I will not now be able to do without.

Kenith Trodd

Foreword to the second edition

In the four years since Dennis Potter's death, dramatic cultural icons like him have effectively vanished from British television. As John Cook's Afterword to this new edition of his book shows, the appearance of Potter's last works *Karaoke* and *Cold Lazarus* in 1996 was treated more like the delayed and unwelcome echoes of a once noisy and obstreperous voice than in celebration of a great talent still to be prized. The genre in which Potter thrived, single drama genuinely meant for television, now struggles to exist and does so by being star- rather than writer-driven. When batches so appear, they tend to be umbrella-themed – *Love Bites* or *Obsessions*. It is perhaps also to the point that the high profile writer for the latter series (March 1998) should be Andrew Davies whom I first commissioned in 1967; a tribute to his durability, but not to the BBC's wish or ability to encourage 'New Potters', especially as this particular project was not even originally developed for them.

There is a consensus of practitioners that British television is in some transitional depression, from the slow decline of public service criteria through to whatever mix of niche, subscription, and bottom line the incoming multi-channel digital regimes will settle into. The 'Old Potter' wouldn't be enjoying the present moment – even polemically. Even he might struggle to make comforting ironic sense of his *bête-noir*, Rupert Murdoch, not only still expanding his small-screen global remit, but also being a major profiteer from both of the world's most currently lucrative movies: not only the prodigally budgeted *Titanic*, but also the exemplary 'small, British film', *The Full Monty*.

Stars for your crown you'd like for sure, but wool for the eyes maybe too, if you don't want to believe that Dennis's world is already a different time and place.

Kenith Trodd

Acknowledgements

Though the responsibility for the contents of this book rests entirely with one person, there are many people without whom it would never have been possible at all.

In fact, this project has been on the go for quite some time – long before Potter's tragic death from cancer in 1994. It began life, originally, as research for a Ph.D. thesis and was conducted under the auspices of the John Logie Baird Centre for Film and Television Research, based in Glasgow. Special thanks, therefore, must go to my Ph.D. supervisor, Tony Pearson of Glasgow University, for providing me with the time and the freedom to pursue what turned out to be a trail of clues as extraordinary as any in Potter's most famous TV serial, *The Singing Detective*. Thanks, too, to my Media Studies friends and colleagues at De Montfort University, Leicester, where the end of that trail was finally reached.

In terms of the field research that went into this book, there are many people to thank. The list of over twenty interview and corres-pondence sources cited in the Bibliography, attests to how many busy people were willing to devote not inconsiderable chunks of their time to having their memories ransacked in the name of research. Of these, special thanks must go to Kenith Trodd for his general approachability and help. Thanks are also due to Jon Amiel, Rick McCallum, Gavin Millar and Mark Shivas for providing me with access to scripts; Graeme McDonald and Philip Purser for doing likewise with press clippings, as well as to Clare Douglas and Lord Mayhew for important corres-pondence. Not just these names, however, but all the personal sources were generous with their time and remarkably open. I am indebted to them all.

In this regard, very special thanks must go to Dennis Potter himself for doing what he clearly did not have to do nor, as a reclusive character, did he particularly wish to do – that is, open himself up in interview to academic scrutiny. He had never done it before nor, to my knowledge, did he ever agree to it subsequently. There was nothing in it for him (and perhaps much to be lost). It was only out of sheer kindness in the face of my repeated invitations that he finally consented to an interview. This is why it seems extremely appropriate for me, here, in the acknowledgments, to pay my respects to the late playwright's memory.

Finally, a list of other thank you's: to former MUP staff Anita Roy and her assistant Michelle O'Connell for their solid editorial advice and support; to Jim McGuigan of Coventry University; to the staff at the British Film Institute Library and Viewing Service for their co-operation; likewise, to the staff at the BBC Television Script Unit (now sadly closed); to John Wyver for help and loans of archive Potter tapes; to Simon Reynolds of the BBC for arranging a screening of *Angels Are So Few*; to Caroline Cornish and Neil Somerville of the BBC Written Archives Centre at Caversham for providing invaluable Potter transcripts. Gratitude is also due to Bobbie Mitchell of the BBC Photographic Library for help in obtaining stills for the book, as well as to all those performers and their agents who kindly granted permission for these images to be reproduced. Finally, special thanks are due to Ian and Helena Farquhar for making their home available to me during my original research visits to London. Without them, none of the actual field research for this book could have been done.

Very lastly, thanks to my now late parents. It is they who were the most consistent supporters and encouragers of the project. It is to them that this book is dedicated.

Acknowledgements second edition

A very quick set of additional thank you's for the second edition: to new MUP staff, editor Matthew Frost and assistants Stephanie Sloan and Lauren McAllister for their encouragement and liquid camaraderie. Also in no particular order to: Clare Blick of MUP; Steve and Jennifer Kramer at Picpal; Jonathan Sarno; Humphrey Carpenter for providing information and justification concerning the 'official' biography; Roger Smith and Clare Douglas for recent help and insights; Vernon Gras and Dave Evans, two 'Potterites' who approached me after the first edition; Eckert Voigts-Virchow and Peter Stead for good information (and company) in Washington; to David Ryan, shamefully uncredited in the earlier edition; to students, past and present, on my Dennis Potter course for often helping me see things in a fresh light. Finally, special thanks must go again to Ken Trodd for his continuing help, support and goodwill as he (and I) struggle to make sense of the powerful 'legacy' his late friend has left behind.

Introduction

Aims and intentions: follow the yellow brick road

This book is about a screenwriter who, if not exactly hateful of the scrutiny of strangers, tended in his life not to welcome it, professing himself to be reclusive by nature. Nevertheless, Dennis Potter was perhaps the most instantly well-known and *scrutinised* of all British film and television writers. For more than a quarter of a century, millions watched, enjoyed or were outraged by his TV plays and serials. He was celebrated by the 'serious' newspapers as a 'genius', whilst excoriated in the British tabloid press, in relation to his sexual themes, as 'Dirty Den' and 'Television's Mr Filth'.[1] As the 'controversial playwright', he featured as the subject of innumerable press and television interviews – each time, always a willing (and outspoken) interviewee; a ready source for the good journalistic quote. There thus seemed to be a paradox – a disjunction between the writer's apparent willingness to act as public property and his own professed reclusiveness; his intensely private nature. It is precisely this realm of seeming contradiction – the gap between the private and the public face – which this book will seek to occupy and explore.

Moreover, it is a gap that becomes readily apparent in relation to previous criticism of Potter's work. Whilst each new play or serial was always greeted with a flurry of publicity and was much discussed in the press and on TV as the work of a 'major writer', it is significant that right up to his death, little sustained critical attention had been paid to Potter's work in its *entirety*. Television had conducted its own 'internal' reviews (notably *South Bank Show* and *Arena* profiles of the writer), yet aside from the many column inches that Potter generated over the years, no real substantial critical assessment of his work ever appeared in print during his lifetime.[2] It was almost as if Potter's very omnipresence – his courting of a high press profile; his ability to attract 'controversy' and willingness to act as 'celebrity' author – served as a deliberate means of dampening critical interest in his work, giving the false impression that there was nothing more to say about this 'recluse', he himself having said it all.

As this work hopes to show in abundance, nothing could be further from the truth. Its project is to demonstrate how for thirty years and over nearly fifty works, Potter's career was a conscious attempt to create a self-consistent *oeuvre* for television, through the weaving of an intricate web of theme and cross-reference from work to work. Behind this enterprise lay a deep desire on the writer's part to demonstrate that, far from its alleged ephemerality and domestic conditions of viewing being a handicap, television and its audience could be accorded the same degree of intelligence, 'seriousness' and respect by the practitioner as other cultural forms such as the novel, cinema film or stage play.

If, as subsequent chapters will show, underlying Potter's 'seriousness' about television was a deep desire to leap over cultural hierarchies in order to address the mass (working-class) TV audience from which he himself originally came, it can be seen how such intensity was the private face that motivated the partly reclusive writer to step out into the media limelight, promoting his work to the largest possible audience. Given that there is a complexity of 'authorial' themes running through the work, this public-private dichotomy in turn points up how much there is a need for a large-scale study of Potter's work to do what the profusion of individual interviews and articles were unable, by virtue of their very commodity form, to do during the writer's lifetime – namely, to tease out in extended detail the various thematic links between works; tracing through time, Potter's own personal progression as a television 'author': the private 'yellow brick road' he followed, step by step, for almost three decades.

As such a summary indicates, the appearance of this book could not be more timely. The typically very public events that surrounded Potter's death from cancer in June 1994 mean that for the first time a complete view of Potter's 'yellow brick road' is now available, given that the writer's own journey along it has sadly ended. Combined with an interpretive reading of 'authorial' themes, one of the other aspects of that journey which this book will try to map is the changing industrial conditions of British television drama in relation to which the writer increasingly had to struggle and adapt during his lifetime. Central, here, is the tracing of a history of the decline of the television studio play and the corresponding rise of all-film production which fuelled bitter creative struggles between the writer and various directors, producers and senior managers in television. An account of the key production aspects of Potter's career – from his early apprenticeship on *The Wednesday Play* right up to his death in 1994 – may hopefully serve to illuminate a wider story of the rise and fall of 'authored' drama on British television.

In so doing, the book relies heavily on primary sources. All Potter's extant plays were viewed and original unpublished scripts consulted (including those of productions for which videotapes of transmission no longer exist). Transcripts of important Potter television and radio interviews were collated, together with an extensive array of press clippings and magazine profiles. Many top film and television practitioners who worked with the writer were also sought out and specially interviewed for this project, with the result that the book is able to draw upon a unique record of over twenty first-hand accounts, covering all periods of Potter's life and career. Perhaps most important of all is a personal interview conducted with the writer himself – the only time he ever spoke at length about his work in an academic context. Here, it is important to note the use made of previous press and broadcast interviews with Potter, sometimes in contrast with the writer's own stated position on his work in interview. The aim is to suggest not only a sense of continuity but also a progression over time in the writer's thinking and pronouncements about his own work.

Ultimately, this book is therefore both textual investigation *and* excavation – an attempt to unearth the thematic continuities over three decades of a truly seminal and celebrated television 'author'. As all of this implies, its principal concern is with an analysis of text and production rather than of audience attitudes and pleasures, though sections of it *are* devoted to the critical and ratings reception of key Potter works, in acknowledgement of the fact that dramas such as *Pennies from Heaven* and *The Singing Detective* were as much social events as texts, with a discernible impact on both national and international culture. In each case, the object is not so much to conduct a detailed sociological analysis of the reception patterns of Potter's work, as to suggest the effect that the public impact of certain of his works had on *the author* himself and his subsequent career.

At the very outset, however, of such a journey along Potter's own 'yellow brick road', is it even possible to talk about an 'author' in television? Surely one must agree with the critic Rosalind Coward that at least in terms of film and television production, all such notions are media constructs – attempts to 'hide knowledge ... from us ... and make us complicit in the belief' that forms of mass communication can in fact be 'instruments of personal expression'?[3]

TV *auteur*? questioning 'authors' in television

Certainly, it has become conventional wisdom in media study that television production is an industry – the fruit of collaboration and *collective* endeavour. Writing in 1987, Rosalind Coward questioned press constructions of Potter as TV *auteur*, suggesting that these belied the industrial nature of the medium. Since film and television presented us with 'a complexity of production and division of labour', this, she argued, made the image of 'the transparent communication between one author and his or her audience hard to credit'.[4]

On closer inspection, however, this 'complexity of production' which Coward sees as rendering invalid notions of authorial expression on television, can be seen to resolve itself into a clear hierarchical system of creative power relations whereby traditionally in British television, the writer was privileged in drama production over other creative personnel (for example, over the director who was often relegated to the secondary role of interpreter or *réalisateur* of the writer's ideas). Particularly in the realms of the single television play where Potter's reputation as 'author' was first established, prioritisation of the writer was paramount – an emphasis and respect which derived in large part from British television drama's strong historical and cultural links with the theatre.

In this way, even after television drama evolved from the simple, live staging of theatre plays to the mounting of its own original productions, theatrical respect for script and writer remained, being translated into a desire to commission new scripts especially written for the medium. As the outsider commissioned by the broadcasting institution to feed it with original plays, the television playwright very much came to be regarded as the 'artist' and was given relative creative freedom by the institution to pick his or her theme and express an 'idea' (though always subject to ultimate veto from senior management, in terms of constantly shifting guidelines of public taste, decency or offence).

Meanwhile, in terms of their assigned institutional roles, the director and/or producer's task was to function largely as enabler or *metteur en scène* – realising the script technically in terms of production, whilst at all times endeavouring to facilitate communication between 'author' and audience by staying close to the writer's intentions and remaining faithful to the script. In turn, it was almost this very literary nature of the single television play which helped to signal its cultural seriousness – its difference from the rest of the evening's schedule and hence the need of the viewing audience to give it a different, closer sort of attention. In the listings guides as well as in their opening titles, television plays were headlined as 'by' the writer – Dennis Potter, David Mercer, Elaine Morgan and so on. This institutional privileging of the writer as 'author' not only determined how the plays were received and reviewed ('as the latest work from' Potter, Mercer and so on), it also typically had important effects on the nature of the productions themselves.

The precedence given to the script meant that directors and actors would often treat the 'serious' TV play as they would a stage drama – heavily rehearsing it, digging into the text in an attempt to extract the author's meanings. With the help of the director, leading actors would often strive to work up a more intense, theatrical performance than they would normally be able to give in the more popular TV serials and series where generic as well as tighter budgetary constraints made pressures on rehearsal time that much greater. In this aim, the performers were frequently aided by the predominantly studio-bound settings which were a feature of most British television plays up until the early nineteen eighties. With its wholly artificial lighting and boxed sets, the studio provided a far more theatrical environment for actors and directors (most of whom were recruited to television from the stage) than the alternative production method of location filming. Originally the result of production necessity, the studio play had become, by the nineteen sixties and seventies, its own *raison d'être*, surviving in the schedules despite the increased technical availability of film stock. Encouraged particularly at the BBC where senior management were keen that investment in studio space be put to good use (as well as, implicitly, that the theatrical connection of the 'well-made' play be preserved), the persistence of the studio TV play further reinforced the pre-eminence of the writer in the production process. With amounts of external location filming often strictly rationed, the confined domestic interiors of studio drama inevitably helped focus attention on the writer's themes and dialogue, as well as on 'theatrical' virtues of individual performance and character interaction.

It is for reasons such as these that John Caughie has suggested that the privilege given to writers and their ideas helps explain 'the astonishing formal conservatism' which marked mainstream single play production from the mid fifties to the early eighties. Despite sporadic attacks from television dissidents such as Troy Kennedy Martin and John McGrath, the connection between the theatre and the single play not only lingered on in terms of a cross-over of personnel from one to the other but according to Caughie in 'a resistance to theorisation' as well as experimentation in form. It was for this reason he concluded in 1980 that the 'theatrical' privilege given to the writers of TV plays 'was and is regressive'.[5]

On the other hand, with the hindsight of a decade and more in which the single play has been almost completely superseded by the growth of television film production, together with a resulting enhancement in the status of the director, the privileging of the writer which uniformly used to pertain in British single drama production can now be seen to have had its own advantages and progressive logic. Not simply a regressive throwback to the theatre, the single play, particularly at the BBC, had developed its own distinctive place in the television schedules by the sixties and seventies – becoming a kind of weekly free space on TV for novelty and experimentation, in addition to acting as a platform for new writing as well as new directing talent. As Caughie acknowledged in 1980, under the titles first of *The Wednesday Play* and then *Play for Today*, the BBC-1 single play slot came to function as some kind of 'cutting edge' for television, extending not only formal boundaries but what could be said and, more crucially, shown on television.[6] Tolerated and indeed tacitly encouraged by senior BBC management, the watchwords for *The Wednesday Play* and *Play for Today* were 'provocativeness' and 'controversy' – symptoms not only of an expressed desire by practitioners to challenge contemporary mores but also part of an institutional attempt to win large audiences for the single play.

In this aim, one of the strategies of the original architect of *The Wednesday Play*, BBC Head of TV Drama, Sydney Newman, was to encourage, through the foundation of a story editor system, the recruitment of as many new writers to television as possible. Following on from his successful policy at ABC's *Armchair Theatre*, the reason for the prioritisation of new writers was clear. Whilst with new directors there was the time and expense of training, new writers were the quickest and cheapest route of fulfilling the play slot's aim of trying to reflect life at the 'cutting edge' of social change in contemporary Britain. Drawn from a variety of different backgrounds, writers came to be privileged under Newman's story editor system because unlike directors, they were neither members of staff nor regular free-lancers. Outsiders to the broadcasting institution, they fitted in with the BBC's public service ethos of giving voice to a range of opinions and statements which otherwise would not or could not receive air-time. Single play writers had the advantage of being able to express controversial views or radical opinions which the institution and its own staff, operating under codes of political 'balance', could never allow to be aired uncritically in any other television form. The 'authored' single play thus fulfilled certain useful progressive functions in the television landscape of the sixties and seventies, bringing to it a freshness, energy and above all an element of personal address which could seldom manifest itself in the more machine-made, production line ethos of popular drama series and serials.

It was this sense of the BBC single play as a special space for the expression of the individual, dissident or questioning voice which Potter was able to exploit as one of the new playwrights recruited to television in the mid sixties. From his beginnings on *The Wednesday Play* right through to the nineteen eighties, he was able to embark upon the self-conscious construction of a television *oeuvre* of linked authorial themes because he knew that as a result of the single play's privileging of the writer, his scripts would never be rewritten or tampered with by the director but always faithfully rendered in terms, invariably, of a studio production. In this regard, he was by no means unique. The *system* of single play production which pertained at the BBC in the sixties and seventies implicitly encouraged the writer to think of him or herself as self-expressive artist. Where Potter stood out was that in keeping with his own aspirations, he took such notions much further than any previous television writer had done – exploiting the privileged status of the writer which was built in to the system in order to create authored thematic and stylistic continuities not only *within* a particular work but as his writing career progressed, *across* a large body of work as well.

Hence, in contrast to Coward's critiques of Potter as television author, individual thematic and stylistic continuities *can* be shown to exist and, as the rest of this study will attempt to trace in detail, *are* readable across the range and variety of Potter's writing for the medium. The reason that this should be so is not so much the result of any attempt by television to 'hide knowledge' of the collective nature of production from its audience, as the fact that in the period of the sixties and seventies when Potter first began to carve out a reputation for himself as a TV playwright, writers and their ideas were privileged in single drama production over all other aspects. Far from Coward's questioning of the 'author' in television, 'questioning' authors like Potter were able to exist at that time because the very structures of British television allowed and indeed encouraged them to do so.

First steps: outline of the early life and career of Dennis Potter

THE ARTIST

> Beauty is like the transcendent God
> whom earthly pilgrims never attain
> [...]
> There lies the purpose and the tragedy
> of the artist who seeks mastery
> Pity him walking an endless road
> like a pilgrim to a holy city.[7]

This poem, penned by Potter when he was just eighteen years old and still at grammar school, provides a quite definitive summary of his later writing career – in particular, his religious sense of authorship. The artist is characterised as 'the pilgrim' in search of 'a holy city': a 'transcendent God' he knows he is destined never to reach but for Whom he must keep striving. As subsequent chapters will argue, the progression of Potter's work is precisely that of a growing preoccupation with religious or spiritual themes. Moreover, as echoed by the title of his 1972 play, *Follow the Yellow Brick Road*, the image of life as a journey, with a shape and an ultimate destination – an 'endless road' along which the artist must keep travelling – was one Potter was frequently to evoke in his later writing career.

What is striking (and slightly unnerving) is why at eighteen, in making his first steps along that road, the young Potter should be thinking in such terms, since he never consciously set out to be a writer. Instead, progressing on to Oxford to study politics, philosophy and economics, it was the dream of entering the hard-nosed world of politics which consumed him in early adulthood. What the early poem suggests is that while at this time professing himself to be an atheist, underlying his intensely political nature was a religious sensibility – a personality formed by biblical teaching and imagery. Moreover, as the poem also attests, that religious background had already moulded the distinctive outlook which would come to mark the later plays. Hence the importance of Potter's early life to the subsequent work cannot be overstated. He himself once suggested that everything in his writing stemmed from his first fourteen years.[8] If this was an exaggeration, it was only a slight one. As Philip Purser has noted, with Potter, in terms of the upbringing that first shaped him, 'time and place and community conspired together with unusual attention to detail'.[9]

Dennis Christopher George Potter was born on 17 May 1935 in the village of Joyford Hill, off Berry Hill, deep in the Forest of Dean. He was the eldest child of a coal-miner. In many ways, these facts alone reveal a lot about him. As he himself put it, the Forest of Dean of his childhood was one of the most remote inward-looking districts of England, heaving up 'in half-hidden layers of grey and green between two rivers', the Severn and the Wye.[10] Bounded by the distant prospect of the Welsh mountains to the West and the blue hills of the Malverns to the North, the Forest was its own little enclosed world of villages scattered amongst woods and fields which were reachable only by steep and narrow country roads. To a child, it was a fairy tale realm yet also, as Potter attested in interview, a kind of 'Holy Land'. Being green and hilly and grey, the topography of the Forest seemed to him as a boy to be biblical – no different from any of the illustrations he had seen of the landscape of the Bible. Along with the pronounced rural dialect of the inhabitants, with their archaic use of 'thees' and 'thous', just as in the King James Bible, the very vividness and isolation of the Forest seemed to make it '*that* landscape': the land the scriptures depicted.[11]

Potter's upbringing was one steeped in the Bible. The remoteness of the Forest fostered a strong sense of community and one of the ways this was expressed was in terms of a fierce, almost evangelical devotion to religion. While not strictly Puritans, most of the Foresters were non-conformist Christian fundamentalists – chapel-goers who dutifully filed into cold stone buildings with names like Zion and Salem in order to be ignited, inside, by the hell-fire sermonising of the local preachers. As a child in

Berry Hill, Potter attended Salem chapel, a free church, twice every Sunday; joining in the hymn-singing from *Sankey's Book of Sacred Songs and Solos*.

This sense of a tightly-knit community with strong social values expressed itself in other ways too: in village brass bands; rugby football teams; packed and smoky working men's clubs, as well as a fierce sense of English patriotism (particularly *vis à vis* their Welsh neighbours over the border). Most important was the staunch commitment of the Foresters to socialism and the Labour Movement – a fact hardly surprising, given that the main industry of the Forest during Potter's childhood was coal-mining.

In many ways, the rest of Potter's early life and career can be summed up as a process of opening out – of being forced to open out – from this tight-knit closeness, into a world less familiar and secure than that which he had first come to know and love. The first signs of this came with the outbreak of World War II, as Prisoner of War Camps were built in the Forest – one for German, the other for Italian prisoners. Meanwhile, as a child growing up in the forties, the local village school became a principal focus of the young Potter's life. In interview, he stated he was 'cursed' with having a very high IQ which marked him out as different in the eyes of the teachers and his fellow pupils, in a way 'that no working class schoolboy *wants* to be different'. Not only did such 'complicity with those who made the chalk squeak on the blackboard' lead to bullying in the playground, it also meant that when the other children played in the Forest, the clever child would be left to climb trees on his own.[12]

This sense of separation was further compounded when in 1945, Potter was forced to leave his beloved Forest for the first protracted length of time, as part of an ill-fated attempt by his father to give up coal-mining. Originally a Londoner, his mother took the family to stay with her relatives in Hammersmith at the very end of the war. The traumatic effect this sudden wrench from the Forest had on her sensitive son cannot be overstated. It comes through strongly in his 1986 work, *The Singing Detective* (see Chapter 5). For a child who had only known trees and fields, the strange new world of the metropolis – with its noise, smoke and dank Underground system – was an alienating experience: a kind of Hell. After nine unsuccessful months, the family returned to the Forest but four years later they moved to London permanently 'as a whole attempt to leave the pit and everything'. Already separated from most of his original classmates in the village school, by virtue of passing the 11-plus exam, Potter now found himself switching schools from Coleford Grammar in the Forest to St Clement Danes in West London.

It was there that his ode to 'The Artist' appeared in an issue of the school magazine. As the evidence of these magazines suggest, Potter was able to be an academic success at St Clement Danes, unhindered by the guilt of being a clever scholarship boy within a rural environment. He acted in school plays and wrote articles for the school magazine: in one issue, editing its literary pages. In his final year in 1953, he won a private scholarship to study economics at the University of London but chose instead to take up a state one for PPE at New College, Oxford, in 1955.

In between, however, in common with all the males of his generation, he had two years compulsory National Service to do. Considered a bright squaddie, Potter found himself posted to the War Office in Whitehall where, at the height of the Cold War, he served as a Russian language clerk within the lower echelons of military intelligence (MI3). It was during this period he met Kenith Trodd – the man who would later produce many of his best known TV works, such as *Pennies from Heaven* and the spy drama *Blade on the Feather*. From similar working-class and religious backgrounds, the two became firm friends: both receiving postings to the War Office; both becoming even more politicised in terms of a mutual commitment to the Left, as a result of witnessing at first hand the Cold War antics of the upper-class majors and colonels under whom they served.

With political attitudes hardened, both moved on to Oxford. By this period, the university was entering a state of unprecedented political ferment, largely due to post-war reforms in education which had enabled far greater numbers of students from working-class homes to progress on to higher education, via the grammar schools, than had ever been the case before. Just as Potter and Trodd arrived at Oxford, working-class students had begun to come under the media spotlight, with national interest focused on the figure of the scholarship boy as a symbol of an old class order supposedly giving way to a new, more meritocratic classlessness. All of a sudden, working-class students found themselves thrust in front of microphones as spokesmen for a new post-war Welfare State generation. Sensing itself to be in the ascendancy, the Oxford network of working-class students into which Potter and Trodd quickly assimilated became more and more outspoken about the established political and social order. As Roger Smith, a friend and contemporary of both men at Oxford, recalls, what gave this grouping its voice was the impact of John Osborne's *Look Back in Anger*, in the wake of its premiere performance at the Royal Court in May 1956. As promulgated by the press to encapsulate the mood of a generation deemed to be in rebellion against a country riddled with class and still clinging to Imperial delusions, the phrase 'angry young man' quickly became attached to the Oxford scholarship boys. It served both as a media tag from without *and* a convenient focus for the expression of many of the real disaffections with fifties British life which that group undoubtedly felt.[13]

With Oxford seldom out of the press, flaunting your working-class credentials and your angriness was thus a valuable means of getting noticed. As Potter admitted much later: 'It was a time when being working class was fashionable and I exploited it'. Carrying the class war before him 'like a banner', he threw himself into the general mêlée of student life, rising quickly to become one of the most prominent of Oxford 'angries': Chairman of the Labour Club; frequent paper speaker at the Oxford Union; lead in various university dramatic productions and perhaps most importantly, editor of the distinguished undergraduate magazine, *Isis*.[14] Thus far from the plight of the working-class scholarship boy at Oxford being the anxious and forlorn one Potter would later portray in *Stand Up, Nigel Barton*, for him, as for many of that 'angry' Oxford generation, it ironically was the case that in Harold Macmillan's famous phrase of the period, they 'had never had it so good'.[15]

The sense of anxiety Potter would later communicate in *Stand Up* came not from Oxford life itself but from another source. As he himself made clear at the time, it arose from a sense of guilt over the far less privileged lives family and friends were leading back home. In 1958, he wrote that the working-class undergraduate 'cannot stomach the two languages that divide up the year, the torn loyalties and perpetual adjustments, the huge chasm between the classes'.[16]

These words are taken from Potter's first ever article to be published nationally – the ironically titled, 'Base Ingratitude', which appeared in the *New Statesman* in May 1958, during the term in which he edited *Isis*. It would lead to even greater opportunities that summer to protest against class in personal terms. That same month, Potter was invited to appear on BBC Radio to give 'a view of Oxford from *Isis*' – a broadcast which was quickly followed up by an invitation to appear on TV.[17] In the course of preparing a series of documentaries for BBC TV on social class in Britain, entitled *Does Class Matter?*, the Labour MP, Christopher Mayhew, invited Potter to appear on Programme Two – to discuss 'Class in Private Life'. Just as with his *New Statesman* article, the student's function was to talk personally about the 'torn loyalties and perpetual adjustments' of being working-class and yet at Oxford.

The interview was filmed in Potter's rooms at New College, Oxford. This was his first ever television appearance and he used it as an opportunity to discuss class in frank and personal terms. Especially significant was his admission of how class had affected relations with his family, particularly with his father who was now obliged to communicate with him second-hand, via his mother, almost with a kind of 'contempt'.[18] What is significant is that in Potter's famous 1965 play, *Stand Up Nigel Barton*, the central protagonist, Barton, also gives a highly similar TV interview on the topic of class which he is later obliged to watch at home with his mother and coal-miner father – all the time with a growing sense of guilt and betrayal (see Chapter 1). As Barton confesses to his girlfriend in the play, in talking so intimately about his family, he *used* them: 'I was acting it up a bit, over-dramatizing. I wouldn't mind a job on the old telly' (p. 70).[19] Sitting at home with his parents, Nigel hears himself say on TV: 'Yes. Class *does* matter to me. It matters intensely ... I even find my own father looking at me oddly sometimes, waiting to pounce on some remark, some expression in my face' (p. 72).

In the play, Nigel's confession that 'class *does* matter' hurts his miner father and exacerbates family tensions. In reality, according to Potter, the *Does Class Matter?* interview only served to strengthen family relations.[20] Like Barton, however, it did have negative consequences for him. He later wrote of the 'momentary bewilderment' on his father's face when on the following Sunday, *Reynold's News* led with the headline: 'Miner's Son at Oxford Ashamed Of Home. The Boy Who Kept His Father Secret'.[21] Moreover, private correspondence between Potter and Mayhew in the wake of the interview reveals that reaction to the student's TV appearance amongst villagers in the Forest of Dean was by no means complimentary. His father received jibes at work whilst Potter himself suddenly and mysteriously became quite ill. Prefiguring his later development of psoriatic arthropathy (a disease that is partially linked to stress), Potter confessed to Mayhew in 1958: 'I cannot seem to shake off my ill-health ... I think it is these things [the interview, the criticisms] that have set me back – if that doesn't sound too ridiculous.'[22]

Nevertheless, the experience of *Does Class Matter?* did not deter Potter in the following years from making something of a career out of broaching the sensitive subject of class in private life. As is well-known, when he came down from Oxford in 1959, he was offered a general traineeship with the BBC. What his correspondence with Mayhew reveals is that this was on the specific instruction of the then Director-General of the BBC, Sir Ian Jacob, who, immediately after seeing his TV interview, recommended that Potter be taken on staff.[23] Just as with the fictional Nigel Barton, it was precisely the quality of Potter's *performance* that landed him 'a job on the old telly'.

Having a pedigree in politics and student journalism, the young Potter was assigned to the Television Talks Department at Lime Grove where he was attached to various of its programmes in order to learn at first hand about television production and technique. He worked as an assistant to Robin Day on *Panorama*, watched how *Tonight* was put together and then in the winter of 1959–60, was assigned to work with Denis Mitchell – one of the BBC's most distinguished and innovative documentary film-makers.

This was significant because Mitchell's highly 'authored', pioneering style, which married recordings of 'real people talking' with impressionistic images of their environment (to give a stream-of-consciousness effect he called Think-Tape), did not have to conform to the requirements of 'objectivity' and 'balance' that characterised almost all the rest of the output of BBC Talks.

Potter's time with Mitchell was to be fruitful and decisive to his own career. In correspondence shortly before his death in 1990, Mitchell recalled how the young Potter was assigned to him for two or three months to learn by direct observation how films were made.[24] This was Potter's first encounter with film-making, as opposed to television cameras in the studio, and the whole process of how reality could be manipulated on film (particularly in the editing suite) fascinated him.[25] If not actually stemming from this period, his later explorations in television plays of the relationship between reality and illusion, his non-naturalistic interest in cross-cutting between objective and subjective versions of events, can at least be related to the experience of watching Mitchell, the 'God-like Artist', reshape the reality of his documentary footage in the editing suite. The virtue of being an expressive 'author', not a detached reporter; the desire to use television as a medium for tracing the movements of thought; above all, Mitchell's counterpoint style ('the stretch of tension between sound and picture', as Potter would subsequently label it)[26] – all of these find an echo in the writer's own later work, perhaps most strikingly in *Pennies from Heaven*'s famous concept of *counterpointing* the optimism of popular songs on the soundtrack with narrative depiction of the painful reality of life in the Great Depression.

As Mitchell recalled, Dennis, however, 'was first and foremost a literary man',[27] favouring scripts and actors over the other's preference for the cadences of real people's speech on the soundtrack. Shuttling back and forth between Lime Grove and the BBC's cutting rooms at Ealing, the pair would argue all the way, often talking about the films they would like to make. Potter's old tutor particularly remembered urging his apprentice to deal with subjects he knew from his own experience. By the spring of 1960, Potter would get his big chance to do just that. When the assistant head of Talks, Grace Wyndham Goldie, had a vacant half hour slot in the June schedules to fill, Potter was invited to make his own documentary film, under the supervision of Mitchell's fellow producer in the Talks Department, Anthony de Lotbinière.

The result was Potter's first original work for television: *Between Two Rivers*, transmitted by BBC TV on 3 June 1960. For his subject, the TV apprentice followed Mitchell's advice and turned to the place he knew best – the Forest of Dean. Moreover, his approach had distinct overtones of

Richard Hoggart's *The Uses of Literacy* for his chosen theme was the decline of traditional working-class culture in the Forest, in the face of post-war social change and the rise of a consumer society.[28] His title, *Between Two Rivers*, described not only the location of the Forest of Dean between the Severn and Wye but also the sense of being caught between old and new worlds. Implicitly, too, it indicated the plight of Potter himself – the working-class 'scholarship boy', caught in the chasm between the social classes; torn between home roots and the glittering worlds of Oxford and the BBC.

More an impressionistic rendering of the Forest and its people than a straightforward documentary description, the film also owed much to Denis Mitchell's style in its use of editing to counterpoint the thoughts of local people on the soundtrack with carefully selected images of Forest coal-mines, working men's clubs and pubs. These similarities belied one crucial difference, however. While Mitchell always preferred to let the subjects of his documentaries speak for themselves, the twenty-five year old Potter had no such qualms about inserting himself between subject and audience and talking directly to camera: making his opinions and personality pervasive in *Between Two Rivers*. Just as with *Does Class Matter?*, there seemed to be a strong need for him to speak intimately to the audience; to communicate his sense of a class divide in highly personal terms. Such a decision to ventilate his own feelings directly at the audience was one Potter would later come deeply to regret. *Does Class Matter?* may have set tongues wagging in the Forest of Dean but *Between Two Rivers* created outright hostility. As Potter recalled in interview, 'Christ, I thought they were going to lynch me'.

The reasons are not difficult to spot from the film itself. Potter stood before the cameras in his home village, telling viewers how, as a student, he had been glad to escape the 'drab and untidy' houses of his neighbours into 'a far more fertile and richer world' beyond the Forest of Dean. Also, whilst making heavy use of interviews with the Foresters themselves, he would frequently undercut what they had to say. Introducing footage of 'a friend', his voice-over announced that the ambitions of getting on in life which this person was about to express on camera had in fact been 'channelled off into mere status-seeking by all the pressures … of our status-ridden society'.[29] Even before the subject himself could be heard on film, Potter's voice-over had already tainted all his hopes and ambitions as those of a 'status-seeker'.

It was in this way that the film aroused deep hostility in Potter's village. As the scholarship boy fresh from Oxford and newly returned with a camera crew in tow, it seemed as if he had pronounced upon and patronised the Foresters, adopting a position of superior knowledge as to what they were and worse, what was good for them. In turn, there is no doubt this experience had a profound effect upon Potter, colouring the nature of his subsequent career and writing. Looking back nearly ten years later, he would castigate himself as a 'yob' down from Oxford: 'Saying it's this way and that, drawing lines and hard distinctions, betraying and being cruel and hurting people'.[30]

Underlying the opinionated nature of his voice-over commentary, it had been the strength of his own feelings about his home roots, together with his anxiety about being separate from them, which had caused the problems. Moreover, far from bringing him into a closer relationship with the Foresters, the making of the documentary had merely served to increase his sense of isolation from them. Certainly, *Between Two Rivers* seems to have engendered in Potter strong feelings of having betrayed his own roots, of being a traitor to his class: themes which would carry on into the later plays. From the evidence, the climax of *Stand Up Nigel Barton* in which the central protagonist realises he has betrayed his working-class roots and his father by appearing on television, seems less a dramatic retelling of a single autobiographical event (*Does Class Matter?*) and more a composite: the circumstances of Barton's TV appearance resembling *Does Class Matter?*; the virulent reaction of Barton's father more closely in tune with the degree of local hostility which greeted *Between Two Rivers*. As Chapter 1 will examine more closely in relation to such plays as *A Beast with Two Backs* and *Where the Buffalo Roam*, another strong theme which runs through Potter's work of the sixties is that of the outcast, hounded by the local community as a result of others' innate prejudice and desire to persecute those who do not conform. With *Between Two Rivers*, one finds a real-life echo of this theme of a community which threatens those who are different.

If the documentary created feelings of betrayal and guilt, it also taught Potter much about the nature of television. He summed the experience up in a 1987 interview for BBC TV's *Arena* arts programme:

> Seeing how those scenes with the clapperboard in front of them got turned into that and seeing what was on either side of the camera and wasn't on the film and the way my own voice-over had diminished what this person was saying or what this person was about to say, which was worse, taught me how easy betrayal is, compared to … 'art' which is not concerned with betrayal. … 'Art' cannot betray in that sense.

Between Two Rivers taught Potter how in contrast with 'art' or drama, 'facts' could be 'lies'. The 'reality' of documentaries and current affairs could paradoxically conceal the truth. From the experience of constructing his own film and voice-over commentary, the young Potter had learned that far from being 'the window on the world' of fifties' and sixties' broadcasting mythology, television could manipulate the truth and distort the audience's view of that world. As he put it in the same *Arena* interview: 'The process fascinated me and the lies fascinated me and the way in which [*Between Two Rivers*] failed to deal with what I knew to be there'.

Potter's work with Denis Mitchell, culminating in the production of his own documentary, was thus a crucial stepping stone in his development as a writer – beginning his disenchantment with the factual worlds of journalism, politics and current affairs; leading him towards an interest in the other kind of 'truths' of fiction or drama. As Chapter 3 will explore in more detail, the notion of most television as 'lies' seems crucial to his later development of a distinctive 'non-naturalistic' dramatic style which consciously sought to draw the audience's attention to the artifice of television. The theme of 'facts' as 'lies' is also central to a number of key Potter works, particularly his first novel, *Hide and Seek* (1973) and his famous 1986 TV serial, *The Singing Detective* (see Chapters 3 and 5).

Indeed, almost Potter's entire writing career can be viewed as an attempt to atone for the damage caused by *Between Two Rivers*, through devotion to the very medium, the 'people's medium' of television, on which he felt he had betrayed his own people. If the experience of the documentary taught him how powerful television was and how easy it could be in the wrong or untutored hands, to distort reality and hurt others, the world of drama and fiction did not carry such heavy consequences because it could not offend in quite the same way ('art cannot betray in that sense'). In *Stand Up, Nigel Barton*, it allowed Potter to show what was on 'either side of the camera' – the tensions and pressures on a 'scholarship boy' which motivated his television appearance and his burning need to communicate personally with a working-class audience. Hence it was only with his third attempt that Potter was finally able to say, in drama, all he had wanted to say about the class divide in his two previous current affairs outings but which the very form of factual programming had prevented him from doing.

Given his disillusionment with current affairs and eventual switch to writing, it is perhaps telling that the last major assignment of Potter's BBC traineeship involved him not with the world of facts but with fiction. From October 1960 to June 1961, he worked on a Sunday afternoon books programme called *Bookstand*. It was he that proposed the original format to Grace Wyndham Goldie: namely, a programme that would try to introduce the world of books in a way accessible to a mass television audience. If its project of cultural dissemination meshed perfectly with his own need to reach out to the working class from whom he felt estranged, the *way* in which *Bookstand* did this was to prove highly significant for the future direction of his career. As Potter recalled, his suggestion was that instead of relying on the conventional TV format of an interview with an author, the themes of a particular book might be better brought alive if the audience were provided with brief dramatisations of extracts from it.

It was in this way that Potter became *Bookstand*'s Script Associate – dramatising scenes from the various books under review each week, which fellow BBC trainee, John McGrath, would then invariably direct. Anticipating his debut on *The Wednesday Play* by five years, these brief dramatisations were very instructive in terms of familiarising Potter with the process of writing scripts and constructing dialogue.

By this time, however, he had been forced to resign his BBC traineeship, after only one of his two years had been completed. This was because he had begun to combine his TV training with writing for the left-wing newspaper, the *Daily Herald* – a situation which offended BBC strictures that its employees publicly observe political balance at all times. Refusing to give up writing for the *Herald*, Potter's resignation left him as a freelance, without financial security for his wife and young family. In February 1960, however, he had had his first book published.[31] Its title an oblique echo of Richard Hoggart's description of post-war consumer society as 'shiny barbarism', *The Glittering Coffin* was an amalgam of all Potter's views on social class and 'the affluent society' which he had previously expressed on television, radio and in print journalism.[32] Written quickly in late 1959 to satisfy an offer by Gollancz, the book was, as his close friend, Roger Smith, recalls, something of a 'rehash' of all Potter had said before on the subject of class – consciously ticking off its targets in the tone of the 'angry young men' of the day: Oxford; the Conservative Party; advertising and so on.[33] Nevertheless, being written in frank autobiographical terms, it does provide a unique snapshot of the life and opinions of the young Potter, years before his fame as a television playwright, illustrating once more how deep his need was to speak intimately in a heavily 'authored' mode.

Certainly, Potter used the book opportunity as a means of getting himself noticed – in one chapter, listing his achievements at Oxford almost as if it were a curriculum vitae. His reward would come in August 1961 when, having left the BBC, he was appointed as a feature writer on the *Daily Herald*. An ailing left-wing daily, desperate to stem its fall in circulation and shake off its thirties cloth-cap image which had seemed to be rendering it obsolete in the age of apparent 'affluence', the *Herald* employed the 'angry young' Potter as part of its strategy to attract a younger, more upwardly mobile readership. From 1961 to 1964, Potter joined the ranks of Fleet Street, carrying out a variety of assignments for the *Herald*. Significantly, he also managed to retain one foot in broadcasting. Still a frequent invited speaker on BBC Radio (most notably *Woman's*

Hour), in 1962, he joined forces with fellow *Herald* journalist David Nathan to form one of the many new writing partnerships that were needed to provide scripts for the launch of BBC TV's new late night satire show, *That Was the Week That Was* (*TW3*).

Allowing him a platform for motivated political comment without the kind of 'balance' he had previously found so irritating at the BBC, Potter, in conjunction with Nathan, became a regular free-lance contributor to *TW3* throughout the show's famous run from late 1962 until it was finally taken off air in December 1963. As he was later to recall, however, he never felt happy working in tandem with someone else.[34] Hence it is perhaps significant that during this period, his second major writing activity outside the *Herald* was a solo one. As part of a Secker and Warburg series on the regions of Britain (called 'Britain Alive'), Potter was commissioned to write *The Changing Forest* – an account of contemporary life in his native Forest of Dean. In essence, this second non-fiction book (published in 1962) was an extension of the examination of working-class decline in the Forest he had previously conducted in *Between Two Rivers*, though here, in book form, with the luxury of many chapters' worth of analysis, Potter was able to seem less strident in tone, more measured, than the condemnatory voice-overs which had caused him so much trouble with the documentary.[35]

A glittering Fleet Street career as a journalist, political wit and social commentator seemed to lie ahead for Potter in 1961-62. Then, suddenly and unexpectedly, disaster struck. In the winter of 1961–62, whilst covering a Young Conservatives conference for the *Herald*, Potter suddenly felt the first twinges of the mysterious illness which was to dog him for the rest of his life. Listening to the delegates from his position at the press table, he suddenly felt extremely ill. Thinking 'the speeches couldn't be that bad', he tried to get up and found he was unable.[36] His knees had locked and one of them was swelling up like a balloon. Later, when he had managed to get outside and was crossing the road, he found, to his horror, that his legs had locked again.

These were the first symptoms of what would eventually be diagnosed as psoriatic arthropathy – as its name suggests, a combination of psoriasis and arthritis which enflames the skin and cripples the joints. Though affecting many people in a mild form, Potter's was an extreme case in which his whole body could become one hundred per cent psoriatic – with purple scales and deep lesions forming on the skin, as well as intense arthritic pain affecting the joints. At its peak, the illness could leave its victim unable to walk, talk, even move, while the body's temperature soared out of control. In turn, this could lead to hallucinations. From the time it struck him down at the age of 26, Potter had to cope with periodic bouts of this disease. Originally, these came twice a year and even later, when treatment with the most sophisticated new drugs became available, he always knew there would be at least six weeks in any one year when he would be completely incapacitated. In the course of his life, he saw countless specialists and tried a succession of different drugs in his attempts to keep the illness at bay, all with varying degrees of success and often very unpleasant side-effects. There was never any complete cure. All medical science could do was to try to hold the disease for as long as possible, until eventually it had to erupt once more on to the skin.

Such an affliction and the acute personal suffering he undoubtedly experienced as a result of it are thus crucial facts in trying to understand Potter. The play-writing career upon which he later embarked in some ways became his attempt to come to terms with the pain and stress which illness caused. As he himself suggested in interview, having had a childhood steeped in the Scriptures, it was very easy for him, when the disease first struck, to make the connection with the biblical leper. Assumptions that the sick person was a sinner and that the poisons of the mind had erupted on to the body were all too easily lodged.

Undoubtedly biblical in its intensity, Potter's battle to contain his illness came to be seen by him as not only a physical but a spiritual struggle – a war against himself. In many ways, the plays became the terrain upon which this battle was waged. As subsequent chapters will trace, Potter's dramatic writing engages far less with social and political concerns about the 'real' external world and much more with the inner lives of central protagonists racked by personal tensions and inner conflict, struggling not only against that outside world but with their own natures. Potter often described his disease as a 'shadowy ally' – indeed in several interviews, he went further to suggest that far from being a completely alien intrusion into his life, he in fact chose his illness.[37] In other words, the nature of the affliction which befell him was in accord with his own personality. Disease forced him to turn inwards; its unpleasant eruptions transformed him into something of a recluse, with a preference for withdrawing from the wider world into the private realms of home and hospital. As a product of the remote inward-looking district of the Forest of Dean, he maintained the event of illness suited his *already* reclusive, introspective personality.[38]

In turn, this reclusiveness through illness suited the life of a writer. Disease took him out of the 'real' world of politics and current affairs (a world with which, as we have seen, he had already become disillusioned) and made him more concerned with the inner life of the individual and ultimately, with spiritual questions about the nature of personal suffering, death and God. In that sense, though terrible in its physical nature, Potter's disease performed a useful function for him. Issues of politics and social class which had preoccupied him as a young man paled into insignificance beside the need to survive and to look into himself in his attempt not only to cope emotionally with the fact of illness but by so doing, possibly to find a cure. It was in this way that the disease could be said to be his ally for without it Potter the writer might never have emerged to find his voice. The fact of disease was literally the making of both him and his career.

Not only that but its physical effects meant that much of the work was also literally born out of pain. Because of the crippling effects of disease on his hands, Potter, as a professional writer, could never type, but instead had to write physically on paper, with a great deal of difficulty and pain. To write at all, let alone to be as prolific as he would later prove, thus required an extraordinary effort of emotional strength, courage and, above all, perseverance. The very difficulty involved in the act of writing meant it was an activity to which he attached the very greatest value. Particularly in the darkest days of his illness, from the early to mid seventies, writing became not only a job to him but a passion. With the illness biting deeper and deeper, his TV plays increasingly came to represent his life-line to the world outside: a 'way of measuring [his] own dignity' in terms of a refusal to bend the knee to illness.[39]

Certainly, when it struck at the age of 26, the advent of illness knocked all his immediate plans and ambitions sideways. In terms of his work for the *Daily Herald*, it meant he had to be taken off his existing duties as a feature writer in order to become TV critic, since this was a job he could do from home. Potter would later be disparaging about this, describing the role of TV reviewer as the newspaper equivalent of a refuge for the sick and the crippled.[40] Nevertheless, perhaps because it suited his reclusive temperament, it was the one job in newspapers he most enjoyed. As he was later to recall, when the first crippling effects of illness more or less rendered him housebound, he immersed himself in watching television and not only because it was his job: 'The thin-legged box in the corner had indeed become a "window on the world" '.[41]

The two years (from 1962 to 1964) which Potter spent watching TV as a critic are undoubtedly important in terms of his later writing career. Following his basic apprenticeship as a BBC trainee, this period allowed him to engage in a measure of theoretical reflection on the nature of the medium – on what worked well on it, what did not – which undoubtedly helped inform the nature of his subsequent TV writing, particularly the first few plays. For example, the ideal which he carried into his writing of trying to create a common culture through television seems to have had a strong foundation in the particular two-channel situation which prevailed when he was a full-time reviewer in the earlier half of the decade (see

Chapter 1). Similarly, the distinctive 'non-naturalistic' style which characterised his dramatic work right from the very beginning, appears to have had much to do with the condition of the television play, as he found it as a critic in the early sixties. Writing in 1967, Potter recalled how, as a reviewer for the *Herald*, the days of the studio play had always seemed to him to be numbered because it was too closely wedded to 'kitchen-sink' naturalism. With television continually widening its technical frontiers in the early sixties by means of satellite link-ups, the introduction of lighter-weight filming equipment, increasing use of video-tape and so on, who needed a 'slice of life' from the boxed-set studio play, when live by Tel-Star it was possible to see 'Gagarin being effusively embraced by his leaders in Red Square'?[42]

In this light, Potter's subsequent 'non-naturalism' became an attempt to revive the single play by disentangling it from the 'naturalism' which, as a critic, he had seen was threatening its very survival. Moreover, a response he wrote in the theatre magazine *Encore* in 1964 (only a year before his debut as a TV playwright) illustrates how he was not alone at this time in wishing to progress beyond boxed-set naturalism. As TV critic of the *Herald*, Potter was one of the prominent figures invited by *Encore* to reply to writer Troy Kennedy Martin's polemical attack against naturalism, 'Nats Go Home', which the magazine had published in April 1964. Significantly, in the light of his own development of an alternative dramatic style, Potter was enthusiastic about Kennedy Martin's assault against naturalism, voicing his own conception of what a 'non-naturalistic' TV drama should be concerned with – namely, 'to present all sorts of evidence, constantly infiltrating all our defences ... attack[ing] from all sides at once, out of a mosaic of objects, details, moods and memories and conversations. Pictures in a real fire. Pictures ablaze.'[43]

If this is what he himself would attempt a year later in his own dramatic work, an old dream first had to die. In September 1964, in a last desperate attempt to attract a new, younger readership, the *Daily Herald* relaunched itself as the *Sun* newspaper and made Potter its leader-writer. A month later, he resigned from the paper. Taking advantage of a period of remission in his illness, Potter had made one last desperate attempt of his own at pursuing his old dream of entering politics – by standing as a Labour candidate in the 1964 General Election. Unfortunately, for him, the seat he was chosen to contest (East Herts) was one with a rock-solid Conservative majority.

Nevertheless, Potter went on the campaign trail: an experience which would prove completely disillusioning to him and provide much of the material for his television play a year later, *Vote, Vote, Vote for Nigel Barton*. According to Potter's then close friend, Roger Smith, who accompanied him for several days on the campaign, real-life electioneering was very close to the experiences the TV play would later describe. As the days of the campaign wore on, Potter became more and more sick and chastened by the reality of the political process – the falseness of slogans such as 'Let's Go With Labour' and the utter futility of canvassing housing estates and kissing babies. Far from party politics being, as he had once believed, the means of putting one's ideals into practice and changing things, all he encountered amongst voters was apathy, suspicion and prejudice.

As Smith puts it, the experience of the campaign 'really was the end of a dream' for Potter. He vowed never to stand again and indeed never even bothered to vote for himself on polling day. Needless to say, when the results were announced, the Conservatives, in the shape of candidate Derek Walker-Smith, held firmly on to the seat. At the same time, any further lingering hopes of a political career had been knocked sideways for Potter by the exhausting effect the campaign had had on his health. In February 1964, however, his friend Roger Smith had found himself appointed story editor of a new BBC slot for single plays and was desperately seeking fresh new writers to fill the weekly gaps that were looming in the television schedules. As Chapter 1 will trace in more detail, it was Smith who effectively launched Potter's career as a television playwright, persuading him to adapt a novel he had begun writing into a television play since a play would earn quicker returns, both financially and critically, in terms of building up his reputation as a writer. Suddenly, having abandoned one dream, Potter found himself with a new one to pursue. He grabbed this opportunity with both hands, adapting the novel *The Confidence Course* into his first television play and writing three more, all of which would be produced within the space of a year: *The Nigel Barton Plays* (*Stand Up, Nigel Barton; Vote, Vote, Vote for Nigel Barton*) and *Alice*, based on the relationship between Lewis Carroll and the 'real' Alice of *Alice in Wonderland.* From having no clear future, Potter suddenly found himself with a new vocation as a television playwright, involved in what would prove to be a landmark event in the history of British television drama: the birth of *The Wednesday Play.*

1

The confidence course: Dennis Potter and *The Wednesday Play*

Vote of confidence

DIRECTOR: Perhaps once, and ONCE ONLY, in your life, Opportunity comes … and with it, Redemption … You trudge life's thorny path.

BLACK: Unsure of your destination.

JONES: Unaware of your potentialities.

DIRECTOR: But then. Ah, then. The breakthrough comes.[1]

These opening lines from *The Confidence Course* may well have had a special significance for Potter himself by the time his first play was transmitted on 24 February 1965.

The Wednesday Play was to prove a breakthrough not only for him but for the whole sixties' 'counter-culture' in Britain. Originally conceived of as a popular strand of single plays on BBC-1, *The Wednesday Play*, in its first season under producer James MacTaggart, quickly established itself as a prominent forum for political dissent and bold experimentation in TV drama. Viewing figures climbed as millions tuned in each week to see the latest play trailed as 'controversial' in the press and condemned as 'filthy' by Clean-up TV campaigners such as Mary Whitehouse. With its reputation for 'permissiveness' and general anti-Establishment bias, the play slot soon became bound up with the fortunes and progress of the 'swinging' sixties. There was a sense, amongst practitioners and critics who championed it, that *The Wednesday Play* was important: a vital television platform which not only aired but actively promoted the values of the new 'counter-culture' to a mass (predominantly working-class) audience.[2]

The very first play commissioned by Roger Smith set the trend for 'controversy' and 'challenge' that later works would follow. Written by a convicted murderer and depicting the cynical progress of a villain from gangster to baronet, *A Tap on the Shoulder* (wr. James O'Connor; tx. 6.1.65) marked a conscious break with the conventions of the polite, 'well-made' play. Its determination to break new ground came to characterise *The Wednesday Play* ethos as a whole – from the first crucial season in 1965 to the last in 1970. The slot also acted as a showcase for new talent. Many well-known practitioners gained their first big breaks working on *The Wednesday Play*: not only Potter but others like Simon Gray, Kenith Trodd and Ken Loach whose directorial contributions to the slot eventually came to include some of the most celebrated TV plays of the sixties: the documentary dramas *Up the Junction* (wr. Nell Dunn; tx. 3.11.65), *The Big Flame* (wr. Jim Allen; tx. 19.2.69) and *Cathy Come Home* (wr. Jeremy Sandford; tx. 16.11.66).

If, by providing him with the chance to write for this brand new slot, Roger Smith was the 'angel' who brought 'Opportunity' and 'Redemption', it did not take Potter too long to sense the possibilities.[3] As he was later to recall:

> I'd been concerned with forms of television for two years [as a TV critic]. So I didn't want to write just like something that I'd seen. I wanted to use where possible as much of television and certain narrative techniques like addressing the audience directly which seemed to me a possibility in a political play. All these things I thought about for at least four years and I just needed the event.[4]

It was Smith, however, who had to persuade him to seize that event. Despite his previous script-writing experience on *Bookstand* and *TW3*, Potter was initially sceptical about his ability to write for *The Wednesday Play*. As Smith recalls: 'He said, "No, I can't write plays" ... He had to be persuaded.' It was only when Potter came back to the story editor with the more modest suggestion of adapting the novel he had half-written, that Smith was finally able to secure from him a script of *The Confidence Course*, set out in his own 'meticulous handwriting'.[5]

The resulting play fitted well with the developing *Wednesday Play* ethos of challenge and controversy. Explicitly political, it mounted an attack on 'the Admass society', with all of its promises of success through self-advancement. In that sense, it dramatised themes and anxieties which Potter had already expressed in his non-fiction writing: his two 'political' books, *The Glittering Coffin* and *The Changing Forest*:

Directed by Gilchrist Calder, the plot of *The Confidence Course* hinges on three confidence tricksters who succeed in luring a dozen victims to a hotel, on the strength of a poster advertising a course in self-assertiveness. There, by a mixture of ruse and rhetoric, the chief fraudster called 'The Director' (played by Dennis Price) sets about trying to persuade his audience of the necessity of their enrolment on the course. Unfortunately, a mysterious thirteenth member of the audience is also present. Calling himself William Hazlitt, this self-styled reincarnation of the famous critic and essayist begins to attack all the values of the consumer society espoused by the Director, until eventually he is bundled out of the room by the Director's two helpers. By suppressing freedom of speech in this way, the Director has given the lie to his own professed philosophy of the individual. The audience begins to get restless and when, in his attempts to pacify it, the Director lets slip, 'I have to be ruthless sometimes. You see, any business that sets out to help the weak and life's failures', he sews the final seeds of his own destruction (p 60). Preferring the freedom to remain unconfident, his victims quickly desert him until at the end of the play, the Director is left alone and abandoned – himself 'a failure' (p. 61).

If, in its denunciations of 'Admass', the play was the kind of work one might expect from any angry young writer given his first break in TV drama, it also exhibits several features highly distinctive of Potter. Most important is the mysterious figure of Hazlitt – the outsider who enrols on the Confidence Course only in order to disrupt and destroy it.

By 1965, the idea of the outsider as dark destroyer of established values had become almost a cliché amongst the post-Anger generation of British writers. If Colin Wilson began the trend in 1956 with his key 'angry' text, *The Outsider*, Harold Pinter, in his 1963 screenplay for the film, *The Servant*, had portrayed a working-class outsider reversing traditional master-servant relations in the home of his upper-class employer. Meanwhile, David Mercer, in his TV play of that same year, *For Tea on Sunday* (tx. BBC 17.3.63), had portrayed a polite upper-class tea party being wrecked by the arrival of an outsider wielding an axe, intent on destroying all it stood for.

Taken in relation to the wider social and cultural currents of the period, it is not difficult to see why this plot device should be so common. It provided a perfect metaphor for what was perceived during this time to be the breakdown of the English class system at the hands of a new post-war generation, alienated by persistent structures of inequality and radically opposed to dominant values through the articulation of an alternative 'counter-culture'.

In *The Confidence Course*, Potter, too, attacks the notion of a society based on class and money yet significantly he does so not in terms of a coherent alternative vision of the future but rather in the name of the past. In particular, it is the one-hundred-and-fifty-year-old essays of William Hazlitt which are invoked: 'If you'd read any of my essays', Hazlitt's apparent reincarnation tells the other course members, 'you'd know that there are other and superior values to this shabby little gospel of greed and gain' (p. 57).[6]

A similar progressive–regressive uncertainty is also evident in Hazlitt's characterisation. If, on the one hand, he is clearly Potter's hero speaking out against Admass, on the other he is a duplicitous Judas figure who infiltrates the group of twelve only in order to undermine it and destroy its leader. Indeed, Potter's script likens him to an invading demon escaped from hell. When he first appears outside the hotel conference room, he is described as 'a shadow-with-eyes, standing in a pool of gloom' (p. 8)[7]. Moreover, running through the play is the suggestion that he may be a lunatic escaped from an institution – though whether an asylum, prison, hospital or even Hell itself, we are never told. When the Director asks him, Hazlitt replies, 'I've escaped from the bondage of time' (p. 56).

In many ways, this use of an ambiguous 'mad outsider' as central protagonist articulates the dilemma of those from the working class, like Potter, who had been helped to prominence by post-war social and educational reform. Given unprecedented opportunities by the 'Establishment' to achieve academic and material success, many nevertheless felt obliged to attack continuing iniquities, on behalf of those to whom the system had been less kind. The dilemma which the leaders of the new counter-culture faced was precisely whether they were mad to attack the established order – to bite the hand that had effectively helped to feed them. Was it they who were mad or society? Was the 'sickness' of society they railed against as much a product of their own psychic dislocation and feelings of separation, as the result of any political cause? Such anxieties link *The Confidence Course* with other 'mad outsider' works like Mercer's *For Tea on Sunday*.

At the same time, perhaps the most distinctive feature of *The Confidence Course* is the fact that it exhibits the first tangible signs of the famous 'non-naturalistic' style ('the concern with forms of television') which would become such a hallmark of Potter's writing. Most important here is the play's use of an off-screen narrator who, intervening at key points in the action by means of voice-over, 'addresses the audience directly'. This allows the play's political message to be explicit – for example at the very end, when the narrator urges the viewing audience to recognise its power to overturn the existing social order:

> NARRATOR: The party's over and the game is done. The weak have become strong and the strong weak. Soon it will be time to turn out the lights and the Director will walk out into the rain … a failure.
> (*He begins to laugh*) (p. 61)

What is striking is how closely this device resembles some of the 'expressionist' techniques first pioneered by Roger Smith and others on earlier BBC play strands such as *Storyboard* (1961) and *Studio 4* (1962). Undoubtedly these experiments in 'non-naturalistic' TV drama helped shape the style and approach of many of the subsequent *Wednesday Plays*, including Potter's first few works.

'Nats Go Home': a question of style

To understand this history, it is useful, briefly, to consider the twin dramatic styles of 'naturalism' and 'realism' against which the term 'non-naturalism' has often been defined. According to Raymond Williams, realism and naturalism were originally used to refer not to stylistic conventions in drama but to 'changed attitudes to reality itself': the replacement of a view of the world as governed by supernatural or irrational forces, with a new emphasis on the presentation of actions rooted entirely in human and secular terms.[8] Gradually, however, in this fundamental shift in representations of reality (which Williams traces to the economic rise of the bourgeoisie in the eighteenth century), a theoretical distinction between naturalism and realism began to emerge. Naturalism as a description of character formed by environment eventually came to be perceived as a passive form. People were felt to be stuck where they were in a kind of trap, with no possibility of changing their social lot. As a result, a counter-sense of realism emerged in the second half of the nineteenth century which insisted on 'the dynamic quality of all 'environments' and on the possibility of intervention to change them'.[9]

At first glance, this might seem to complicate definitions of style in TV drama for if 'realism' can be opposed to 'naturalism', then surely it should, strictly speaking, be seen as a form of 'non-naturalism'. Such a confusion over terms has frequently dogged debates on TV dramatic style amongst practitioners as well as critics. In many ways, the uncertainty can be traced back to Troy Kennedy Martin's 'Nats Go Home': the 'manifesto' for a new TV drama which Potter so enthusiastically endorsed in 1964. Its importance for *The Wednesday Play* cannot be overstated for, appearing less than a year before the launch of the new play slot, it undoubtedly had an influence over the latter's stylistic direction.

In 'Nats Go Home', Kennedy Martin attacked naturalism as definitely the wrong form for TV drama. For him, this meant telling a story through dialogue and following a strict sequence of natural time (where the time span of the play equalled real time, with very few lapses or jumps in narrative chronology). It was this unhealthy dependence on 'theatrical naturalism' which, in his view, had made the television play 'a makeshift bastard born of the theatre and photographed with film techniques' – its directors invariably reduced to 'photographing faces talking and faces reacting'.[10]

In its place, Kennedy Martin called for a 'new TV grammar' based upon image rather than word: a release of dramatic structure from the constraints of real time and from the tendency to accord dialogue more importance than *mise en scène*. Lighting, sound and design, he asserted, would all play their part in this new drama; the old boxed sets of naturalistic TV plays would be replaced by 'new designs leading to maximum fluidity in the studio'.[11] The net result would be a 'narrative form of drama' in which 'visuals [would] not supplement nor restate information, they [would] in fact distil it'.[12]

Despite his conscious attempt to make a break with the past, Kennedy Martin's ideas on 'visual narrative' were simply theorisations of techniques that he and a number of other BBC writers and directors, including Ken Loach, John McGrath and Potter's friend, Roger Smith, had pioneered over three successive play slots between 1961 and 1963: *Storyboard*, *Studio 4* and *Teletale*, respectively. Together with the 1964 six-part serial, *Diary of a Young Man* (co-written by Kennedy Martin), these were all varyingly successful attempts to put into practice the 'Nats Go Home' principle of telling 'a story in exciting visual terms'.[13]

Crucially for the subsequent history of *The Wednesday Play*, not only was Smith involved but this loose coalition of 'anti-theatre' dissidents was led and inspired by *The Wednesday Play*'s first producer, James MacTaggart. As Smith acknowledges, it was MacTaggart who pioneered stylistic experiment in the early sixties, launching *Storyboard* and *Studio 4* as a conscious attempt to exploit the resources of the television studio to the full. Though very much influenced by the earlier Langham Group of TV drama experimenters, the live studio plays of *Storyboard* and *Studio 4* were much more populist in emphasis. As Smith confirms, 'We took over popular forms. We wrote more available stories.'[14]

It is not only the emphasis on popular 'visual narratives' and 'maximum fluidity in the studio' which makes these early play slots the direct forebears of 'Nats Go Home' and the subsequent *Wednesday Play*. A number of neo-Brechtian techniques later advocated in Kennedy Martin's 'manifesto', such as characters directly addressing the audience and the reminder that 'we are constantly being told a story', were devices also employed by these early experimental play strands.[15] As Smith recalls, *Studio 4* dramas used to signal their artifice by deliberately revealing their studio settings and the attendant cameramen. Meanwhile, direct address to the audience via voice-over narration was pioneered as a means of surmounting the problem (inherent in naturalistic TV drama) of how to convey plot detail without reducing the pace of the visual narrative. In contrast to conventional TV dramatic naturalism which conveyed the bulk of dramatic information through dialogue with visuals remaining supplementary, *Storyboard* and *Studio 4* plays reversed the relationship – visually distilling dramatic information, in Kennedy Martin's terms, rather than restating what had already been rendered through dialogue.[16]

It is thus possible to trace a history and continuity of stylistic experiment, stretching from the early *Storyboard* and *Studio 4* dramas through 'Nats Go Home' and on towards the various innovations of Potter and others on *The Wednesday Play*. The waning of the 'post-Anger boom' of naturalistic 'kitchen sink' drama helped put the ideas of dissident experimenters like MacTaggart, Smith and Kennedy Martin into the mainstream as one of the few hopes for the reinvigoration of the single TV play within the schedules. The crucial year was 1964: the new Head of BBC TV Drama, Sydney Newman, appointed James MacTaggart to produce *The Wednesday Play*, whilst Troy Kennedy Martin launched his strategically timed 'manifesto' at that same moment.

It is significant that a few months after the publication of 'Nats Go Home' and in response to critical reaction from his fellow practitioners, Kennedy Martin went on to identify what he thought would be the two styles that would replace theatrical 'kitchen sink' naturalism. Restating his belief that visual narrative was the best way forward, he also acknowledged there was:

> interest in moving away from naturalism to a kind of expressionism … [which] presupposes the existence of the TV studio at the beginning of the show. In this way it does not lie to its audience, pretending that it is a 'slice of life' … Once having shown the studio, the expressionist director brings together the actors, scenic form, sound and light and builds up a dramatic structure within it.

While indicating this style was, for him, too close to the theatre 'as many … have [said] … 'narrative' draws too much from the cinema', Kennedy Martin nevertheless predicted that TV plays would 'develop along these two lines: narrative and expressionist'.[17]

It is striking that these two approaches which Kennedy Martin sought to oppose in 1964 had already co-existed on *Storyboard* and *Studio 4*. Hence when the loose 'anti-theatre' coalition of experimenters such as MacTaggart, Smith and Ken Loach, progressed to *The Wednesday Play*, it is possible to see a continuation yet also a divergence of approach, as techniques pioneered on the early play slots were allowed to develop into fully fledged alternative TV dramatic styles. For example, as Raymond Williams has argued, the documentary dramas of Ken Loach, though often judged the epitome of descriptive naturalism, are actually much closer to the 'dynamic' qualities of realism insofar as they constantly insist upon the possibility of social change.[18] Such an emphasis inevitably dictates a 'narrative' (as opposed to a wholly 'descriptive') dramatic style and Loach's increasing moves in his *Wednesday Play* work away from the television studio towards location shooting on 16mm film can perhaps be seen as symptomatic of this desire for a greater realism in representation, through ever more 'visual narratives'.[19] Certainly, Troy Kennedy Martin, scourge of descriptive naturalism, was later able to write in praise of Loach's *Up The Junction*, suggesting it had lifted 'drama out of the rut' by making 'nonsense of the idea that television is only a poor relation of theatre or film'.[20] Directly descended from *Studio 4* and *Teletale*, a filmic strain of 'narrative' realism therefore became one of the clearly marked styles of *The Wednesday Play*.

It is also possible to relate Potter's 'non-naturalistic' style on *The Wednesday Play* back to the 'expressionist' experiments of the early *Storyboard* and *Studio 4* plays. Rather than an evasion of the real, as critics have sometimes described it, the armoury of 'non-naturalistic' techniques which Potter later developed to represent the inner life of his protagonists (flashbacks, adult actors as children, characters' direct address to camera and so on), can simply be seen as an alternative means of 'expressing' reality.[21] Here it is again useful to refer to Raymond Williams' work on the history of realism and naturalism and his observation that towards the end of the nineteenth century

> new methods and conventions were developed *to take more account of reality, to include 'psychological' as well as 'external' reality, and to show the social and physical world as a dynamic rather than a merely passive and determining environment*. Between 1890 and 1920 these were often described as breaks 'from naturalism' or 'beyond realism' but the confusing irony is that most of them were attempts to realise more deeply and more adequately the original impulses of the realist and naturalist movements.[22]

Applying this to *The Wednesday Play*, it is possible to argue that in seeking to represent 'what goes on inside people's heads', Potter's non-naturalism was also paradoxically an attempt at a greater realism in television drama.[23] Akin to Loach, there was the same concern to go beyond 'surface' naturalism in order to explore the deeper, more dynamic 'reality' that was thought to underlie it. Williams describes the particular modernist impulse to articulate the real in terms of the psyche as a kind of 'psychological expressionism', and such a label seems useful in relation to Kennedy Martin's distinction between 'narrative' and 'expressionist' styles.[24] All such innovations, according to Williams, were concerned to represent more fully the 'true' movements of a dynamic, underlying reality. It was simply the methods which differed.

The 'documentary realism' of Ken Loach and the 'non-naturalism' (psychological expressionism) of Potter can therefore be traced to the same basic concern of a whole group of practitioners at this time to question received notions of the real, particularly those of habituated TV naturalism. When stylistic differences became more pronounced on *The Wednes-*

day Play, a shared concern to be 'anti-theatre' nevertheless continued. As Smith makes clear, the shifts in emphasis took place as *The Wednesday Play* progressed. Under MacTaggart and Smith, the first season of 1965 was more 'expressionist' in style than in later years when, with Loach's chief collaborator, Tony Garnett, as story editor and then subsequently one of the producers, 'it became much more documentary'.[25] Prior to the trend for filmed documentary-style narratives, however, those first productions, which included *The Confidence Course*, were more akin to the attempts of the earlier *Studio 4* and *Teletale* to exploit studio space.

As story editor, Smith states he encouraged Potter in his first play to experiment with 'expressionist' techniques such as the use of a narrator who would be able to distance the audience from naturalistic empathy with the characters, whilst at the same time rendering essential plot information in the 'visual narrative' without recourse to additional establishing scenes of dialogue between characters. The influence of the 'Nats Go Home' tendency was therefore evident in the techniques Potter used to transform for television material which had started life as prose fiction.

What does appear to be Potter's own contribution is the use of the narrator in *The Confidence Course* not only as an expositor of information but as a Chandleresque cynical commentator with his own opinions to offer on the action. For example, near the beginning of the play:

> NARRATOR: The Director is already speaking. Every phrase has been considered. Every pause is calculated. Every attack meaningful. It might almost be a party political broadcast (p. 12).

Here one can detect the origins of the similar narrator figure in Potter's subsequent *Vote, Vote, Vote for Nigel Barton*, even down to the reference to party political broadcasts.

Such comparisons, however, are difficult to test with any great conviction as nothing now remains of Potter's first television play as it was broadcast. While the script still exists at the BBC, in common with no less than three other of Potter's sixties TV plays, the videotape of the production was wiped long ago in order to make room for other material. Though now regarded by bodies such as the National Film Archive as an almost criminal act of vandalism, this destruction was justified at the time by the high cost of videotape which meant that if a tape was reusable it was reused. Potter, however, did survive as a playwright: *The Confidence Course* was judged a very sharp piece by *The Wednesday Play*'s production team, and on the strength of it he was commissioned to write more for the new play slot. In fact, three further Potter *Wednesday Plays* followed in 1965 alone – *Alice* (tx. 13.10.65) based on the life of Lewis Carroll, as well as two thematically linked works which helped seal his reputation, not to mention his new 'vocation', as a writer: *The Nigel Barton Plays*.

Class comics

> Mr Dennis Potter, being an atheist said: 'I think the Gods must be with me at the moment.' He was very careful about the plural for he is a good atheist.
>
> And religious questions aside, he seems to be right. Clearly, somebody is with him. Mr Potter, aged 30, a miner's son and an Oxford graduate, stands at present like a study in suspended animation – poised to hurtle, or be hurtled, through a doorway marked 'Success'. Behind him, last Wednesday, is *Stand Up, Nigel Barton*, for my money one of the best plays the BBC has presented this year. Ahead, next Wednesday, is the sequel *Vote, Vote, Vote for Nigel Barton* which, if it lives up to expectations, should put him in the forefront of TV playwrights.[26]

If, as Barry Norman's article suggests, 1965 was the *annus mirabilis* for Potter, it was indeed *The Nigel Barton Plays* (tx. 8.12.65 and 15.12.65) which hurtled him 'through a doorway marked 'Success'', earning him no less than three top writers' awards.[27] Truly, a major talent seemed to have arrived – one that was all the more significant because it was entirely a *Wednesday Play* discovery.

The central theme of *Stand Up, Nigel Barton* – miner's son (Barton) wins a scholarship to Oxford, only to be confronted with class prejudice at home and university – was nothing new, however, for the period or for Potter. The plight of the scholarship boy, physically and emotionally uprooted from his class through education, had become a media commonplace by 1965. As long ago as 1957, Richard Hoggart had devoted a whole section of his *The Uses of Literacy* to a problem which had become one of the unforeseen consequences of the 1944 Butler Education Act.[28]

Similarly, the plot of *Vote, Vote, Vote*, in which Nigel finds his political idealism as a Labour candidate undermined by the lies of vote-catching, can not only be related to Potter's experience of the 1964 General Election. It also dramatised left-wing fears of the time that Harold Wilson's Labour Government was selling out its traditional principles in a vain attempt to win over an electorate that had voted it into power by only the slimmest of majorities. In the play, Nigel's disillusionment with vote-catching springs from the need to appeal to what his political agent identifies as 'the floating voter with his house, his car, his 2.8 children' (p. 107).[29]

If familiarity of theme contributed to the plays' success, what undoubtedly generated a favourable critical response was their highly 'authored' quality: the feeling that television drama was being used as a vehicle for personal expression by a writer who deeply identified with the struggles of his central protagonist. Barry Norman in his *Daily Mail* article focused almost exclusively upon the fact that 'interestingly, both plays are about Dennis Potter', whilst other critics praised this 'exciting new playwright' for his 'passion and narrative power'.[30] What distinguished *The Nigel Barton Plays* from previous television drama was their almost complete concentration upon a single central protagonist (as indicated, even, by the title of each play). Whilst earlier TV plays, such as David Mercer's *Generations* trilogy and Alun Owen's *Lena, Oh My Lena*, had dramatised political or class anxieties, the conflict of Potter's plays seemed less an external one between the individual and family or society and more an internal dilemma of self.[31]

In both works, Nigel Barton (played by Keith Barron) is portrayed as a torn hero – 'I remember, I remember the school where I was torn', his voice-over intones near the beginning of *Stand Up* (p. 33). A clever child, uprooted from his working-class background through education, he finds himself cursed in adulthood by 'his blasted conscience' (p. 112) which refuses to abandon old ties, demanding that some attempt be made to build a bridge 'between the two rivers' of his own past roots and his present success. His quest is to heal the social and psychological divisions he feels in his life; his dilemma, how best to do it – is politics the answer or perhaps a career in the new mass communication 'miracle' of television ?

Over the two plays, Nigel tries both. In *Stand Up*, his debating prowess at the Oxford Union comes to the attention of a BBC producer who invites him to appear on a television programme on 'Class in Britain'. Nigel is easily persuaded, yet as the transmission date of the interview looms he begins to grow worried about what he has said. As he tells Jill, his upper-class girlfriend at Oxford: 'I was acting it up a bit, over-dramatizing' (p. 70). By discussing his relationship with his own father and mother, he realises he used them: 'I damn well, bloody well, *used* them!' (p. 66). As outlined in the Introduction, he later has to watch the interview at home with his parents, wincing all the time as he hears himself say:

> NIGEL (*on TV*): Yes. Class *does* matter to me. It matters intensely … I travel between two utterly different worlds … Yet I even find my own father looking at me oddly sometimes … Watching me like a hawk. I don't feel at home in either place. I don't belong. It's a tightrope between two worlds and I'm walking it.
>
> HARRY (Nigel's father): You bloody liar, Nigel! (*He is addressing the screen*) (pp. 72–3)[32]

The truth hurts. Far from bridging the class gap between Nigel and his miner father, frankness only serves to underline it: 'Watch you like a hawk ... What'll they say at work? Here comes the bloody hawk, they'll say! With his son on a tightrope' (p. 73). Father and son are later shown heading off together to the local working man's club, yet as Potter is at pains to emphasise in his script, there can be no private reconciliation after the damage of the interview, merely a public show of solidarity. As they walk away from camera in the final shot, his script directions indicate the pair should be 'separated by a mutual anxiety' (p. 75).

The bitter lesson Nigel learns at the end of *Stand Up* is that the truth does not pay. To some extent, this has already been anticipated by an earlier flashback scene (one Potter would rework twenty years later for *The Singing Detective*). In it, Nigel is seen as a child back at the village school where he first became isolated from his peers. Partly to assuage feelings of loneliness on account of his over-eager cleverness, he steals a daffodil from the classroom window sill and is later challenged by the disbelieving teacher. Under great pressure to confess his crime, he tells a lie, putting the blame on the 'class comic', Georgie Pringle, whom the play has earlier identified as one of those who bullies Nigel in the school playground. Though Pringle protests his innocence, the teacher is more inclined to believe her favourite, Nigel. As she begins to question others in the class, seeking to corroborate Nigel's story, Potter's script directions indicate the other children 'sense blood and start to get nasty' (p. 64). One by one, they all join in the chorus of blame against Pringle – their malice vindicating Nigel but ensuring that his innocent victim is severely caned for a crime he did not commit.

In *Vote, Vote, Vote*, Nigel also learns that the real world prefers lies to truth. This time, the pivotal scene is at an Annual Council Dinner which the Labour candidate is obliged to attend. With the local mayor, assorted dignitaries and the rival Conservative candidate present, Nigel decides to 'stand up' for his 'blasted conscience', launching an outspoken attack on the Tory myth of 'a hitherto prosperous, classless, opportunity-free Britain basking in a rare contentment' (p. 120). He goes too far, however. When the Tory audience starts to jeer, he turns in a sudden spasm of anger to the Conservative candidate and gives what Potter's script directions coyly term a 'two-fingered salute at its most emphatic' (p. 123). Flash-bulbs go off, as the once-proud 'man of principle' finds himself 'crucified in every paper as the poor fool who made a filthy gesture at a public function' (p. 125). Not only has Nigel finished with politics, politics have finished Nigel.

Together, the twin climaxes of *Stand Up* and *Vote, Vote, Vote* both suggest the inevitable consequence of honesty is humiliation. As with the daffodil scene, the implication is that truth is punished while lies are rewarded. This is not to suggest that Nigel Barton is simply a hapless victim of the class divide. Running through the plays is a definite subtext which seeks to implicate this 'working-class hero' as a self-publicising fraud who is a traitor to his class. Punning here is rife: Nigel's 'class' becomes not only the social grouping of which he is painfully aware in the present but also the one which he literally sat in at school as a child. Even the very title of *Stand Up* is ambiguous. It refers not only to the adult Nigel, 'standing up' for one class against another but also to the command barked out by the authoritarian teacher at school when she wished to interrogate a suspected wrong-doer or, worse, from Nigel's point of view, humiliate him in front of his peers by holding him up to the class as a paragon of virtue. Heroic class rebel or humiliated class puppet, the injunction 'Stand Up, Nigel Barton' embraces both possibilities and holds them in taut suspension across the entire play.

Ambiguity is even present in the name Potter gives his 'hero'. If the upper-class connotations of the Christian name Nigel contrast with the working-class surname Barton (thus instantly indicating the class tensions within the character), it is also important to recognise that the name 'Nigel Barton' is a corruption of 'Nye Bevan'. Throughout both *Barton Plays*, Bevan is implicitly held up as the epitome of radical protest against which Nigel is found to be lacking. In *Vote, Vote, Vote*, the compromises of Nigel's election campaign are unfavourably juxtaposed with edited newsreel footage of Bevan's famous Trafalgar Square speech during the Suez crisis. Similarly, in *Stand Up*, Nigel's father, on learning his son is to wear a dinner-jacket at the Oxford Union, grumbles to his wife: 'Nye Bevan always refused to wear a dinner-jacket, you know that?' (p. 47).[33]

On one level, 'standing up' for his class whilst simultaneously betraying it in his haste to get on, makes Nigel as much a 'class comic' as Pringle. This reading is strengthened by a scene in which Barton, on holiday from Oxford, accompanies his father to the local village working man's club. There, he watches the club comic on stage, who turns out to be the adult Georgie Pringle. Once more, an implicit connection is made between Nigel and Pringle, as the play cuts back and forth between two scenes: one, with the stand-up comic Pringle, in the warmth of the club, telling a joke about 'university boys' to uproarious laughter; the other, showing Nigel in his dinner-jacket at the imposing Oxford union, 'standing up' to make a speech on his working-class origins and being jeered from the gallery (p. 57). As the juxtaposition helps to emphasise, Nigel is every bit as much a 'class comic' as Pringle, except that his position is made even more ludicrous by the fact that unlike the real comic, he is accepted neither by his native class nor by his Oxford audience.

A subsequent Potter *Wednesday Play*, *Where the Buffalo Roam* (tx. 2.11.66) helps explain why the writer should choose to forge this symbolic link between Barton and Pringle. Coming less than a year after *The Nigel Barton Plays* and having the same director, Gareth Davies, *Where the Buffalo Roam* can be seen as the follow-up to an earlier success. In terms of theme and style, it is certainly a companion piece for, as in *Stand Up*, its hero is also a social outcast, ostracised by his working class community on account of his educational ability. Unlike Nigel, however, he does not have the luxury of escaping from his background to university since the reason for his isolation is not intelligence but backwardness, as manifested by his painful inability to read. Laughed at by his 'class-mates' in school and later at the adult literacy centre he attends for reading lessons, Willy Turner (played by Hywel Bennett) takes refuge in his imagination where he dreams of being a Wild West outlaw. The richness of his fantasy life forms a stark contrast to the desolate reality of his existence as a young, unemployed labourer in Swansea.

Where the Buffalo Roam therefore investigates the flip side of *The Nigel Barton Plays*: Turner, laughed at by his peers, is another of Potter's 'class comics'. Like Georgie Pringle in *Stand Up*, he is unfairly persecuted for something he cannot help – a victim of the sins of the wider group. Unlike Pringle, however, who succeeds in adult life by exploiting his status as the village 'idiot', Turner fails to find acceptance within his native community. This closely associates him with Nigel Barton and in turn helps to explain the Pringle-Barton link of *Stand Up*. By having the chief character of *Where the Buffalo Roam* function as a mirror image of the 'hero' of *Stand Up*, Potter makes a direct symbolic link between the clever child and the backward child as the same type of outcast from the community.

As with *Stand Up*, there is a similar structure of ambiguity in *Where the Buffalo Roam*. The play questions whether Turner, like Barton, is a victim or a villain: are his dreams of being a Western outlaw a way of escaping a constricting social environment or simply the delusions of a psychotic? Popular culture (the Western genre) becomes the centre of a conflict in the play between progressive and regressive attitudes to Willy's plight. On the one hand, there is the view expressed by Black, Turner's tutor at the Adult Literacy Centre, that the youth is a 'young thug', even a 'potential psychopath'. This is counter-balanced by the opinion of Jenkins, a liberal probation officer, who discovers that Turner was the victim of physical abuse as a child (at the hands of his late father). Jenkins rejects the black and white moral absolutes of the 'genuine hero' and the 'genuine villain' which Westerns promote, telling Black: 'You know, I've often thought that the traditional Western hero would be categorised as a squalid delinquent nowadays.'[34]

In Potter's updated Western, the regressive stereotype of the outlaw as 'genuine villain' must prevail, however, if generic conventions are to be satisfied. In what has been labelled an 'awful descent into early-MGM techniques',[35] *Where the Buffalo Roam* ends with a cowboy shootout in which Willy goes on the rampage with a loaded gun. After he kills one of their own, he is mercilessly pursued by armed police. Eventually, they trap him on the roof of a warehouse and while this seems to act as a form of shock therapy, curing Willy of his cowboy fantasies ('My name isn't Shane. It's William John Turner', he cries to the watching crowds below), it is too late for any reversal of fortune. A police marksman fires and while Jenkins looks helplessly on, Willy falls from the roof into a dam below. Later, as the dead hero is fished out in a straitjacket, 'Streets of Laredo' plays on the soundtrack, with its plangent chorus: 'For I am a cowboy and I know I've done wrong'. In Potter's 'Western', the liberal approach of Jenkins gives way to a violent cycle of transgression and retribution which has to be followed through to its inevitable tragic end.

Not only does such a violent dénouement satisfy the generic conventions of the Western, it also accords with Potter's theme (raised in *Stand Up*) of the persecution of the individual at the hands of the wider community. If, as the 'village idiot' who falls prey to the 'blood-lust' of his peers, Turner resembles Georgie Pringle, he is also much like Nigel Barton – the social outcast who, in his failure to conform to community norms, is marked out as different and punished accordingly. Despite the reactionary triumph of the values of the Western over more 'progressive' attitudes to Willy's problems, the villain-victim ambiguity, noted with *Stand Up*, is also present at the end of *Where the Buffalo Roam*.

In common with both its sister works, *Vote, Vote, Vote*, too, exhibits a definite ambivalence towards its working-class hero. 'Oh, come on now', says Nigel's wife, Anne, when he declares he is standing for Parliament as an act of public duty. 'You quite enjoy it in a way. There's a little bit of the charlatan in you' (p. 83). Unlike *Stand Up* which leaves it up to the viewer to decide the true extent of Nigel's guilt, *Vote, Vote, Vote* aids judgement through the authority of a narrator figure: Nigel's political agent Jack Hay, who directly addresses the audience near the end of the play, claiming 'There's a lot of good in him. But you'd never vote for a Nigel Barton in a million years' (p. 125). Hence while *Vote, Vote, Vote* also ends with its torn hero racked by guilt and anxiety as a result of his public 'crucifixion', narratorial intervention finally absolves him of all blame. Instead, it is all the fault of the system – the electoral machine which turns honest men into charlatans – and as Hay's closing statement implies, the fault ultimately of us, the audience, who countenance it.

That *Vote, Vote, Vote* should be a less complicated play than the others, both in tone and structure, is hardly surprising for although finally transmitted a week after *Stand Up* (on 15 December 1965), it was actually the first to be written and recorded. According to Roger Smith, because *The Confidence Course* was felt to be so sharp and exactly the sort of piece *The Wednesday Play* was looking for, it was immediately decided to commission another play from Potter, for a projected transmission date of April 1965. In common with other *Wednesday Plays* of the period, *Vote, Vote, Vote* was recorded on 35mm film stock a month before it was due to go out. However, a technical flaw which had spoilt alternate reels in the film necessitated reshooting for a revised screening date of Wednesday 23 June. Transmission details were printed in the *Radio Times* for that week, yet, as Potter complained two years later in his introduction to the published scripts, 'Seven hours before it was due to go out on the air, the BBC announced that the play was being withdrawn. It was, they said, "not ready" for transmission.'[36]

Not for the last time in his career, Potter found himself embroiled in a censorship battle, which also cost Roger Smith his job as story editor of *The Wednesday Play*. After a huge argument with the Head of BBC TV Drama, Sydney Newman, Smith resigned over the issue.[37] Although certainly not alone amongst BBC management in his reservations about the play, Sydney Newman admits in interview that he was particularly uneasy about *Vote, Vote. Vote*. It had to do with certain 'Canadian prejudices' he had about naming real political parties in a work of dramatic fiction:

> It posed a problem for me because it was about a Labour Party candidate ... I was terribly worried about this and I had some of it modified and maybe incurred the wrath of Potter ... The word 'censor' is lousy but if you're running a department, you're making judgments. You can call these judgments censorship or you can call them judgments. My judgment was that we would get into trouble if we alienated the Labour Party ... I brought that to England with me, my Canadian, puritanical stuff ... And of course I never had it with [Potter] directly – I had the big fight with Jimmy [MacTaggart] and Jimmy defended Potter which was good and so did the story editor defend Potter.[38]

In the end, though changes were insisted upon, they proved not to be too substantial. After much negotiation, the savagery of the political agent's cynicism was toned down somewhat and the character given more 'balance' through motivation. As Potter sarcastically put it in 1967, 'his benumbing, politically degenerate cynicism was, visibly, to gurgle out of a broken heart ... Sob, sob.'[39] In addition, Potter rewrote the last ten minutes of the play, making it, in his opinion, 'more powerful. But because it didn't actually say it in one sentence they could pick on, it was let through.' According to Potter, the difference between the first drafts and the second drafts of the play were in fact minimal.[40]

As outlined previously, *Vote, Vote, Vote*'s use of a cynical narrator commenting directly on the action, was an idea developed from *The Confidence Course*. This time, however, the narrator is an on-screen character in the drama. In that sense, the device is a marked progression for as Potter made clear in 1967, Hay's comments, in close-up and to camera, are designed to be so cynical as to make even the most hard-hearted viewer instinctively recoil.[41] This is clear from an example near the end of the play, when Hay describes his reasons for taking Nigel canvassing round an old folks' home: 'All's fair in love and politics ... After all, some of them still had strength enough left to put an ex on a ballot paper ... It's about the one thing left which gives them any importance. My job was to [*bares his teeth*] *make sure they realise it*' (p. 113).

Viewers are supposed to *judge* the savagery of Hay's cynicism and find it wanting, yet equally the intention is they should recognise some of the attitudes he expresses about the political process as their own, albeit heightened and made grotesque. This seems to be why Potter was so scathing about being forced to provide motivation to explain the character's behaviour, since in one sense it lets the audience off the hook. Hay's cynicism is reduced to the level of personal psychology rather than used as a vehicle to unsettle the audience with questions about its own political attitudes. As the playwright argued in 1967, this was the point of the play – to portray a political campaign from the candidate's view in order to indicate that 'party politics in Britain has ... almost ceased to be about real issues'.[42] The intention was to show that disillusion with party politics was not the same thing as total political cynicism 'which is surely a dangerous and disreputable position to maintain'. A vigorous assertive attitude, Potter maintained, could step 'over the tub-thumper's little box or tear down the big bright poster'.[43]

The progression from *The Confidence Course* to *Vote, Vote, Vote* is therefore the *exposure* of such cynicism by bringing into view its founding source, the authorial narrator, in order that the audience can question his authority and motives. Faced with a biased unreliable narrator, the viewer is forced out of passivity in order to *work* to understand the play and produce meaning. If it is possible to trace the non-naturalistic device of a dramatic narrator back to the neo-Brechtian techniques of *Studio 4*, it can also be seen how clearly Potter was influenced by the Brechtian concept of an active, rather than passive, spectator, politically engaged in the production of meaning. His advance was to extend the *Studio 4* device, drawing upon techniques pioneered by literary modernism – replacing an objective, omniscient 'third-person' voice with a subjective, unreliable narrator. Potter's introduction to television of the fractured perspectives of modernism was not confined, however, to undermining the 'dangerous and disreputable' position of total political cynicism in *Vote, Vote, Vote*. Both the *Nigel Barton Plays* and also *Where the Buffalo Roam* employ a range of non-naturalistic techniques, all of which serve to highlight the 'interior' qualities of the dramas and their highly 'authored' nature.

In *Stand Up*, for example, the emphasis on subjectivity is even greater than in *Vote, Vote, Vote*, the later play clearly having evolved in terms of technique from its sister work. By this time, Potter had clearly learned how to *interiorise* his plays, constructing them around the memories and emotions of a central protagonist.[44] Rather than being structured, as in the past, by a cynical, distancing narrator, both *Stand Up* and *Where the Buffalo Roam* are designed as 'memory plays' in which the audience is given direct access to the memories and fantasies of the central male protagonist. Frequent flashbacks lend both plays a highly fluid structure in which changes of scene and location are governed less by narrative chronology than associative psychological connections. A good example is the very beginning of *Stand Up* when Nigel is first seen accompanying his miner father to the pit gates. Watching his father head off for another day at the coalface, the son murmurs, 'There but for the grace of God and the eleven-plus' (p. 31)[45]. Suddenly, the scene switches associatively to the village school where Nigel was first separated from his 'class'.

Even more strikingly, Potter shows Nigel's memories of his village school to be inherently subjective by specifically indicating in his script that all the children in the class (including the central protagonist) be played by adult actors. Not only does this technique magnify the 'pains and terrors' of childhood, so aiding adult identification with events in the classroom, it also reinforces the scene's status as memory filtered through the adult's knowledge of how his former 'class-mates' have progressed to maturity.[46]

Together, the techniques of unreliable narrator, flashbacks and adults as children can all be seen as variants of Raymond Williams' label, 'psychological expressionism'. They all derive from the modernist impulse to 'express' individual subjectivity as more significant and 'real' in many ways than external reality itself. Potter's chief achievement in *Stand Up* was to show, more or less for the first time, that television could be mobilised as a space for this kind of 'interior drama'. In 1976, he summed it up this way:

> I'm much more concerned with interior drama than with external realities. Television is equipped to have an interior language ... It seems to me very important that television should be concerned with that because the people watching it are watching it in a very peculiar way, with all their barriers down.

> You've got a huge audience on the one hand and yet it's also a series of very informal, very tiny audiences, multiplied X times and the interior drama, if you like to call it such, can work in those conditions almost better than anything. Most of us bob around the streets with a whole boxful of fantasies, which are actually central to the way we see ourselves and other people.[47]

Lost apprenticeship

As his statement suggests, Potter, no less than Troy Kennedy Martin, had his theories on the television play and its audience. Occasionally, in his career, these were set down in print. One important example is an article, 'Cue Teleciné – Put on the Kettle', which first appeared in *New Society* a few months prior to the transmission of *Where the Buffalo Roam*.[48] The piece is important because it not only gives a contemporary insight into Potter's ideas, it also sheds light on why, throughout the sixties, he continued to write exclusively for television.

In the article, Potter maintains, in contrast to Kennedy Martin, that there should be no hard and fast definitions of television drama since these always tend to stultify. Instead, he states his own approach, which is that drama 'takes its zest and colouring and technical proficiency from the news, documentaries, sports, entertainments and sermons which surround it' in the TV schedule. Viewers watch TV drama as 'a television programme like the rest' and no-one bothers much about artificial boundaries in the evening's 'flow'. Much of the exhilaration and purpose of writing for the medium springs from this: 'Television drama does not even have to generate its own specific breath of 'experiment' or novelty. Since it takes its colouring from the programmes encasing it in the evening's viewing, the TV play can plunder at will.'[49]

Styles can be parodied: the 'horrible confessions' of Vox Pop can be mimicked; 'the direct-to-camera burblings of clergymen and politicians' sent up. Potter cites the use of narration direct to camera in *Vote, Vote, Vote* as an example of a parody of the party political broadcast (and notes his great good fortune that on the night the play was finally transmitted, it was preceded by a party political broadcast from Edward Heath: 'I could never have had such a gift in the theatre or cinema').[50] It is also possible to see *Where the Buffalo Roam*'s parody of the Western genre as feeding off the popularity within the schedules of old cowboy films and Western series such as *Wagon Train*. Each of these styles 'give different layers of response and different patterns of dramatic conflict as and when needed'. As a result, Potter asserts the television play should be seen to be 'as flexible as the whole thing around it'. In marked contrast to Kennedy Martin, he states: 'I would rather work on the assumption that [the TV play] does not exist in its own right at all'.[51]

Even more important in Potter's optimistic sixties' gospel of 'anything goes' is the special relationship he sees between the writer and the TV audience. He takes *Stand Up* as an example:

> In the theatre – or at least, in the West End – the audience [for this play] would have been largely on only one side of this particular fence. If it had worked at all in the cinema, the sort of tensions which any play creates in an audience might have compromised the effectiveness of the story, which attempted to use the specially English embarrassment about Class in a deliberately embarrassing series of confrontations. But with television, I knew that, in small family groupings, both coalminers and Oxford dons would probably see this play. To know this in advance, when actually getting the dialogue down on paper, is to feel the adrenalin slopping about inside yourself.[52]

The gulf between don and coal-miner, of course, is exactly the theme of *Stand Up, Nigel Barton*. To Potter, in the mid sixties, the desire to write for television was therefore so strong because of the potential it gave the author to leap over established hierarchies and bridge the class gap which Barton (and he) had had to face. Television could reintegrate the social outcast. In short, it offered the possibility of a common culture.

Potter ends his article by declaring that television gives the writer an awesome sort of freedom: '"thank you for letting me into your homes" oozes the comic and the fool doesn't realise the terrible truth of what he has just said as a public-relations cliché'.[53]

Aside from the *Barton Plays* and *Where the Buffalo Roam*, this almost evangelical vision of the possibilities of the medium can be seen at work in a number of plays from the mid to late sixties which, together, may be termed Potter's 'lost apprenticeship'. The scripts survive but, as with *The Confidence Course*, the videotapes of the original productions were long ago wiped to make room for other material.

Emergency Ward 9 (tx. 11.4.66) was one such piece. Again directed by Gareth Davies, it was written for *Thirty Minute Theatre*: a series of half-hour plays which went out live on BBC-2 every year from 1966 to the end of the decade. As Potter's title suggests, the action takes place in hospital and indeed within a single set: 'a large, long, rather shabby iron-bedsteaded and battle ship grey radiatored general ward (male) of a ramshackle London hospital' is how the setting is painstakingly described in his original script (p. 2).[54]

Much of the play's comedy (for it is largely a comedy) rests on the dilemma of Padstow (played by Tenniel Evans), a liberal teacher and lay preacher, who finds himself in the next hospital bed to Flanders (Terence de Marney), an irascible old working-class Londoner who exhibits deep racial prejudice against another patient in the ward, a black man called Adzola.

The preacher tries to convert Flanders to the cause of racial equality. He finds it difficult but eventually his message of brotherly love seems to hit home when the old man is delegated to deliver tea to all the patients and hands Adzola a cup, with a smile. His parting words, however, cause a storm: 'Here y'are then, Sambo!' (p. 32). Furious, Adzola lunges at the old man who in turn is flabbergasted. As he later explains to Padstow:

> FLANDERS: I was only trying to be friendly. Give him a nice cup of tea. Little Black Sambo, that's what it said on the wall at school. Children of all countries. Little Black Sambo. With cokynuts and bananas and the Union Jack. I thought all niggers was called Sambo. I was only trying to be ... *good* (p. 35).

If Flanders' attitudes are shown to be the product of a bygone age of Empire and institutional racism, Padstow, far from leaving well alone, feels he must try to retrieve the situation. He calls Adzola over and begins to apologise for the old man's behaviour, stressing his is only a minority view. He is in for a shock, however, with Adzola's reply:

> ADZOLA: Oh don't worry, man. I take no notice of a thing like him ... He's a very common man. Working class ... He's low class ... I don't work with my hands, like he does. I'm my own boss, I am. He's just scum. I've just got me a new E-type, man, and that man there, he's got *nothing*, you know that? Nothing! (*He bows slightly*) Thank you for your good wishes (p. 37).

He walks away, leaving Padstow's liberal conscience more confused than ever. Who has been the victim of greater prejudice: Flanders or Adzola? Which was worse – the days of the British Empire with its institutionalised racial prejudice, or the 'glittering coffin' of the new post-war consumer society that holds out the possibility of success, regardless of colour and background, yet creates a new social pecking order based on money and possessions? By wrestling in a humorous fashion with this dilemma, Potter's play uses its hospital setting as a metaphor for British society in the 1960s and the idea that increased social mobility may mask a continuing (if transformed) structure of inequality. The ramshackle 'battle-ship grey' hospital comes to symbolise a Britain in terminal decline from an Imperial past; a microcosm in which to observe the contemporary social mix – the liberal teacher/preacher, the aspirant immigrant, as well as the older generation who fought in two World Wars at great personal cost but who now see themselves as disenfranchised. This is indicated not only by the name of the old man, 'Flanders' but also his constant complaints to Padstow: 'I don't know what we fought the war for' (p. 7).

Potter's appropriation, for his play's title, of a familiar name from the world of popular culture can also be seen in this light. If the intention of his *Thirty Minute Theatre* offering is clearly to parody the half-hour soap opera format, the reduction by one, of the numeral in *Emergency – Ward 10* indicates a view that 'reality' in 'Britannia Hospital' never quite measures up to the ideal world of the soaps.[55] Likewise, the ideal of racial and social harmony, it is implied, never quite works out in practice as intended. Padstow, the site of liberal values in the play, attempts to impose his ideals of brotherly love on Flanders but his own good intentions bring latent prejudice (on both sides) to the surface and help to make it worse. Another of Potter's 'torn' heroes, he is described at the end as being more 'confused and unhappy' than ever (p. 37).

Message for Posterity (orig. tx. 3.5.67), another 'lost' Potter play, also explored the social implications of the decline of Empire.[56] This was a full-length *Wednesday Play*, with the same production team as *Where the Buffalo Roam* (Gareth Davies the director; Kenith Trodd the story editor; Lionel Harris the producer). Moreover, because of its 'controversial' theme, *Message*, like *Vote, Vote, Vote* before it, had been subject to a censorship wrangle within the BBC prior to transmission. The reason this time was the similarity of Potter's fictional situation to real-life characters and events.

The play deals with Sir David Browning, an ex-wartime Conservative Prime Minister who has his portrait commissioned by the House of Commons as a tribute. The artist who is chosen to paint it, however, is a political radical who hates all that Browning stands for. James Player agrees to the commission, telling his daughter that his portrait of Browning 'will be – *must* – be brilliant. An indictment of the whole British Establishment. The sag of [Browning's] ageing flesh will be quite clearly the disintegration of a facade' (p. 55).[57]

It was this which set alarm bells ringing within the BBC for, as one commentator put it, 'you don't need to be overgifted to come up with the conviction that the story has a remarkably strong bearing on the life of Sir Winston Churchill.'[58] Akin to the fictional Browning, Churchill, too, had had his portrait commissioned to mark his eightieth birthday, yet the finished painting by Graham Sutherland had so displeased him in its depiction of him in old age that the portrait was never shown in public (and in fact was later destroyed). With Churchill dead less·than two years, his funeral a state occasion matched only by the death of royalty, this Potter play was inevitably going to be the source of some Corporation unease.[59]

In retrospect, Potter's script is chiefly interesting not so much for this fact but rather for its uncertainty of response to its subject matter. Like *Stand Up* and *Where the Buffalo Roam*, there is a definite ambiguity running through it, yet in this case, it is not entirely clear whether this is the product of the sophistication of the writer or simply bad dramatic construction.

For example, the play incorporates numerous flashbacks to stirring wartime speeches in which Browning is seen urging Britain to cleanse the world of 'the Nazi plague' (p. 22). At the same time, the play stigmatises its Churchill figure for his actions in the 1926 General Strike. Though he comes to respect (even feel affection towards) Browning, Player can never forgive him for having sent in troops to break up a miner's meeting 'on some common ground in the middle of the Forest of Dean' (p. 78). With this reference to Potter's own birthplace, it is not difficult to perceive a similar ambivalence towards Churchillian values on the author's part to that experienced by his fictional artist in *Message*.

As a whole, the play seems undecided as to whether it should be a celebration of the power of the artist to transcend both political and physical barriers or a hard-edged political drama. On the one hand, there is an emphasis on the artist as an omnipotent god able to manipulate others on a timeless canvas – Player at one point quotes Leonardo da Vinci: 'The painter is *lord* of all types of people and of all things' (p. 18).[60] On the other, Potter finally opts for a highly political attack on the power of the Establishment to suppress the freedom of the artist.

This occurs in the penultimate scene when, 'as if suddenly possessed by a demon', Player violently assaults Browning after the old man falls asleep while posing for his portrait. 'I'll 1926 you, you bastard!' Player cries (p. 91). Order is quickly restored. In the final scene, Browning is shown propped up in bed, apparently well, as he is told by his granddaughter and private secretary that no-one will ever see the painting again. Player, too, will 'never paint another picture ... Not with his arms strapped behind his back ... He won't trouble us again.' In response, Browning mumbles the last words of the play: 'We always win in the end ... Always win ... in the end' (p. 107).

The play at its close therefore deals with the ability of the British Establishment to move against any challenges to its authority, demonising the attacking artist as 'mad'. As such, its pessimism (mirrored in the real-life suppression of Sutherland's portrait) contrasts with *The Confidence Course*, where a similar challenge to the dominant order by a 'mad' hero, though defeated on the personal level, nevertheless achieved its objective of reversing the *status quo*.

It is just this despair about the capacity of political protest to effect change which makes *Message for Posterity* important in terms of Potter's development as a writer during the sixties. In many ways 'torn' between being a play about art and a play about politics, the work marks a moment of transition in Potter's concerns, coming as it does (in terms of chronology of composition) between the treatment of particular social issues such as class in his first few plays and explorations of more universal themes in later dramas like *A Beast with Two Backs* or *Son of Man*. The fact that in *Message* Potter lurches away from an exploration of the relationship between the artist and his subject, towards his usual *Wednesday Play* territory at this time of an attack on the political Establishment, seems to explain why it is only at the play's end that class loyalty is finally shown to supersede admiration of Churchillian wartime leadership. As in *Where the Buffalo Roam*, only then, it seems, does the author decide the weight of a repressed past necessitates a violent dramatic dénouement.

This need to attach (however incongruously) a violent climax to each of his plays was a characteristic Potter trait during the sixties. His first two ITV plays, for example – *The Bonegrinder* (tx. 13.5.68) and *Shaggy Dog* (tx. 10.11.68) – both exhibit this feature, almost as if the author knew that particularly on a commercial network, his plays would have to fight every second they were on air to satisfy a mass audience reared on a diet of police, Western and adventure series. Though a recording of it still survives, *The Bonegrinder* (written for Associated Rediffusion) was a critical disaster (see Chapter 2). If *Shaggy Dog* was greeted with marginally less venom by reviewers, nevertheless it was the work which became the victim of wiping.

Produced by Stella Richman for London Weekend Television (and again directed by Gareth Davies), *Shaggy Dog* is perhaps the most bizarre of all Potter's single plays. A man called Wilkie (played by John Neville) goes for an interview with the Restawhile Organisation, unaware that the company has decided to enlist the services of a management consultant who specialises in testing out interviewees' ability to cope with unexpected situations. This takes the form of his meeting each candidate, wearing a large bulbous clown's nose! Wilkie goes into the interview and is startled by the clown's nose, yet not as startled as his potential employers when later on in the interview, he produces a shotgun and threatens to kill them all. This he subsequently does. As he emerges from the office, a young female receptionist goes in, sees the carnage and faints. Returning, Wilkie places the unconscious girl on the window ledge of this, the top floor of an executive tower block, and begins to tell her about 'the Rarys': mythical creatures of non-violence and innocence that were hunted to extinction by 'the bloody, bloody hunters, management consultants, doctors' (p. 29).[61]

Finally, the last known Rary was trapped by 'the hunters' on the edge of a cliff: 'The little thing looked down and knowing they were going to push, it said IT'S A LONG WAY TO TIPPERARY.' With that, Potter's script states that 'in the way ... one might react to a shaggy dog story', Wilkie jumps from the top floor, whilst on the soundtrack, a 'brass band oompahs "Tipperary"' (p. 31).

As both the script and this truly awful pun make clear, *Shaggy Dog* should be taken at face value – as simply a shaggy dog story. Potter seems to have borrowed the theme of William Golding's 1955 novel *The Inheritors* and used it as a metaphor to criticize the absurdities of capitalism.[62] Both at the beginning and at the end of the play, the script specifies that shots of executive blocks should be counterpointed on the soundtrack with jungle noises. If the implication is of capitalism as a jungle in which it is either kill or be killed, Wilkie's reversal of power relations through violence recalls not only Hazlitt's reversal of the *status quo* in *The Confidence Course* but also Player's in *Message*. In common with the latter, however, there is evidence of increasing pessimism in the possibilities of that victory of the mad hero being ever anything but temporary. As Wilkie makes clear in his own shaggy dog story, there can be no escape from the hunters and as if in proof, he, like the Rary with whom he so identifies, has to jump off the edge of Restawhile's temple to capitalism before he is effectively pushed. Pessimism is even built in to the very structure of the play for by definition a shaggy dog story is one that can never happen in reality.

It is in this pessimistic light that Potter's subsequent work for the BBC should be evaluated. Although his final *Wednesday Play* dramas of the sixties, *A Beast with Two Backs* (tx. 20.11.68) and *Son of Man* (tx. 16.4.69), differ considerably from *Shaggy Dog* in that they grapple with more universal 'grand themes', both, also in varying degrees, continue the thread of pessimism and political disillusion which *Message* and his ITV work had begun to make visible.

Who killed the bear?

A Beast with Two Backs (dir. Lionel Harris) tells a real-life tale, familiar to the writer from his childhood. In April 1899, some miners from Ruardean in the Forest of Dean stoned to death two Russian dancing bears owned by a party of Frenchmen, after they had heard a rumour that one of the bears had allegedly mauled a child. In Potter's hands, this basic source material is expanded and reworked into an exploration of the prejudice, repression and fear that can fester within a closed community. This was the first time the playwright had set one of his plays in 'home' surroundings (a setting which would come to loom large in his later work).

The play begins with Joe (played by Patrick Barr), an Italian who brings a dancing bear into the Forest of Dean with a view to entertaining the children of a nearby village. In the village pub, however, some of the local miners are engaged in their own grotesque parallel entertainment: drunkenly baiting the village idiot, Rufus, who is the mentally handicapped son of the local hell-fire preacher. Meanwhile, in the Forest near to Joe, two lovers hide in the undergrowth. Michael Teague (Laurence Carter) is carrying on an adulterous affair with the local 'whore' Rebecca but when she announces she is pregnant and threatens to tell the whole village, repressed fears surface. Michael pounds her head repeatedly with a rock and runs off, leaving her for dead.

When Joe and his bear, Gina, arrive in the village, word spreads fast among the locals that 'There's a beast about the place.'[63] In the meantime, Michael, the real beast, slinks back to his wife. Rufus is also dragged home by Ebenezer (Denis Carey), the Old Testament-like patriarch who guiltily fears his son's handicap is a punishment from God. Later, the son succeeds in escaping his clutches and flees the village, just as several hours before, those other outsiders, Joe and Gina, were forced to head for the Forest in the face of the racial taunts of the villagers.

Under cover of darkness, Ebenezer goes into the Forest in search of his son and discovers him by Rebecca's body. Immediately, all his Old Testament fears and prejudices against women and his son's condition bubble up to the surface to take concrete form: 'My God, I knew this would happen … Thou slut, Rebecca! Thou slut!' Rebecca, however, is still moving, not quite dead. Fearing the consequences if she should live, Ebenezer tries to repress what he believes is his son's crime by taking its burden upon himself. It is he who finally kills her, lifting up a rock and bringing it crashing down upon her skull.

Word spreads around the village of a murder in the Forest, as 'a detective', a police inspector from nearby Coleford, is dispatched to investigate. Acting on a tip-off, he is led to Michael's house but Michael's wife covers for her husband by providing him with a concrete alibi. Someone must pay for the crime and later, in the village, Michael tries to divert suspicion away from himself by suggesting the killing may all have been the work of the dancing bear. Rather than face the fact of a beast within their midst, his fellow coal-miners acquiesce in this more convenient solution.

The drama reaches its climax, as all of the God-fearing villagers pack into the local church to hear their preacher's view of events. Ebenezer, burdened with guilt, climbs into the pulpit and announces 'This is the last time I shall be speaking to you. I'm not worthy to be your minister.' He then begins a sermon which constitutes the message of the play, as he publicly attempts to wrestle with his conscience, telling the congregation: 'Be not easy. There is a beast inside each and everyone of you … Satan … was walking here about last night … Was it a man? Or the beast that is inside every man?'

Michael, in the congregation and also guilty, refuses to acknowledge Ebenezer's agonised implication of a 'beast within'. He tries to displace the monster by calling out to the assembly: 'The beast … Aye, the bear!' Eager to embrace this less disturbing possibility, the villagers leave the church to hunt down and kill the bear, as Ebenezer, sensing a way of purging himself of personal guilt, calls out fanatically from the pulpit: 'The Lord said an eye for an eye and a tooth for a tooth. Let us get rid of the beast that festers inside us … Use the evil to get rid of the evil … Hunt down the beast that lurks within! … Hunt it down and burn it out! Curse it and *cleanse* thyselves!'

A lynch party of miners, led by Michael, then heads for the nearby quarry, where they overwhelm Joe and club the bear to death. At that moment, down in the village, Rufus listens puzzled from behind a door as Ebenezer prays before hanging himself: 'No, Lord. Rufus is a babe at arms. Do not punish him, God.' Entering the room and seeing his father hanging, the boy runs panic-stricken out of the house and out of the village, meeting, to his horror, the returning lynch mob. As he speeds past them in the final shot of the play, one of the miners is heard to remark: ''Tis as if Devil himself was on his tail.'

As Philip Purser suggested at the time, *A Beast with Two Backs* is 'a powerful piece of myth-making' which, although set in 1890s Forest of Dean, has 'the quality of being transposable to any other place' in respect of its allegorical theme of the beast that lurks just beneath the exterior of civilised man.[64] As such, the play shares with its immediate predecessor, *Shaggy Dog*, a strong similarity with the work of William Golding, in this case Golding's famous first novel, *Lord of the Flies* (1954).[65] On first transmission, many reviewers objected, however, to the play's unrelieved pessimism: 'Blackest Wednesday', cried Henry Raynor of *The Times*[66] whilst a puzzled Stanley Reynolds wondered in the *Guardian* why Potter had bothered to write this *Wednesday Play* at all:

> The story of an Italian bear trainer who comes to a little village where his dancing bear is falsely accused of murder is loosely based on fact. But for some reason Potter abandoned the … real French bear trainers and their two bears and turned the dead child of the true story into a grown woman who is killed by her married lover when he finds she is pregnant.[67]

In retrospect, these changes, whilst perhaps puzzling at the time, are explicable in the light of Potter's later work. Indeed they are what make this play a highly significant entry in the Potter canon, for in *A Beast* themes and motifs are introduced which much of the later writing would seek to explore and unravel.

On the surface, the play's topicality springs from its preoccupation with race and the characteristic British fear of the foreigner. Though a theme which Potter had touched on before, for example in *Emergency Ward 9*, by 1967–68, this had come into much sharper focus as fears about immigration began to dominate the political agenda. In interview, Potter described how *A Beast* fitted into this context:

> So I just turned [the story] into the one bear: the Italian; the one man; the intruder; the image of the intruder. The image – the way we see blacks, foreigners, is an animal. Like the Hartlepool people hanging the monkey as a French spy … I remember I wrote a very angry piece about Enoch Powell in the pre-Murdoch *Sun*. So that was very much in my head … because I'm aware myself of having certain racist tendencies. I know it … because I think it's instinctive … That Race Relations stuff is a lot of crap: a lot of it, a lot of the time. And people are entitled to feel defensive … – if you were brought up in a street in Wolverhampton and you went back and it was full of mosques and people in saris … You don't have to be a racist to feel pity about that. Well, I don't. Maybe I *am* a … racist! I *am* in some ways. But then I distrust anyone who says they're not. I distrust people who have pure feelings, automatically and spontaneously. I don't believe it. I believe we have to *struggle* to get those.[68]

A Beast can be seen as part of Potter's struggle to confront (and condemn) 'instinctive' racism by literally writing about it on his own doorstep: his native Forest of Dean. The behaviour of the isolated, backward Foresters towards the Italian and the bear symbolises the Little Englander attitudes of Enoch Powell and others, who were seeking at the time to place the blame for their country's own post-war malaise upon a convenient external target.

Important though it is, there is much more to *A Beast* than this theme, however. The play's title hints at these other concerns for it is in fact a quotation from Shakespeare's *Othello* ('I am one, sir, that comes to tell you your daughter and the Moor are now making the beast with two backs', is how the villainous Iago reports to Desdemona's father at the beginning of the play).[69] If, like Shakespeare's work, *A Beast* deals with the tragedy of 'colour' as well as of misplaced suspicion, the appropriation of Iago's bawdy phrase would seem to suggest that at least part of Potter's project is an exploration of sexual themes. It is this aspect which makes the play the direct ancestor of such later works as *The Singing Detective* and Potter's first novel, *Hide and Seek*. If *A Beast* is indeed 'a powerful piece of myth-making', an examination of the play in the light of these subsequent works allows that 'myth' to be at least partially decoded.

The key motifs of the play are:

An Italian (with a 'beast') who intrudes into the Forest of Dean.
'The crime': adultery and assault in the Forest plus a 'detective' who goes on the trail of the killer.
Uneasy relationship between father and son – Old Testament patriarch and his 'crippled' charge; attendant guilt and repression.
The sermon on 'the beast within' that leads to the killing of the bear.

As Stanley Reynolds wondered, why should Potter change the real-life story of the Frenchmen into the single 'image of the intruder', the Italian in the Forest? His first novel, *Hide and Seek* (written in 1972 and published a year later), suggests an answer. In it, the main character remembers a brutal encounter with an Italian prisoner of war when he wandered alone, as a child, into the Forest of Dean:

> Behind him the grass slithered quietly, and he closed his eyes. He could hear breathing, slow and heavy, the sweet breath of God, which made all things come alive.
>
> A hand came down upon his shoulder and he opened his eyes again.
>
> 'You with anybody?' asked the voice, a soft purr of gentleness in it.
>
> 'No', said the boy whispering.
>
> 'You wanta see nice ring ?'
>
> … Something was wrong. He turned, bewildered and saw a big man with spiky grey hair, a tanned skin and eyes that later always seemed to be the colour of phlegm.
>
> 'But you're not God !' he said, almost shouting, relieved and disappointed.
>
> … They looked at each other without moving. They were alone in the middle of acres of oak, hundreds of yards away from the nearest path. It would have been a sensible place to have encountered a loving creator, but it was a wretched spot for a pale and spindly child to fall victim to the predatory hunger of an Italian prisoner of war with a tobacco tin filled with metal rings made in the camp workshop three miles away across the woods.[70]

'I was … sexually assaulted when I was ten years of age. That is true. I was', Potter admitted in interview. He added: 'People endure what they endure and they deal with it. It may corrupt them. It may lead them to all sorts of compensatory excesses in order to escape the nightmare, the memory of that.' In terms of his work, however, he stressed this traumatic real-life event should not be seen as the main *raison d'être* but only a side-note: 'It's important but it's not *that* important [because still] you're left with your basic human strivings and dignity.'[71]

In *A Beast*, it is an event that is important to acknowledge since the crime for which the Italian becomes the innocent scapegoat is a 'sex crime': namely, Michael's adultery which blurs into assault. In turn, this casts light on why Potter should choose to replace (as well as equate) the assumed mauling of a child in the real-life incident, with the actual murder in the play of a pregnant woman. Sex and death are consistently linked in Potter's writing – for example, in *The Singing Detective* where the Forest adultery of *A Beast* is reworked into a famous scene in which the main protagonist recalls surreptitiously witnessing his mother commit adultery with his father's best friend, around the time of VE Day in 1945, when he was 10 years old. His subsequent revelations to her about what he has seen become linked in his memories with her death. Moreover, in trying to piece together these clues from the past, the central protagonist, Philip Marlow becomes a 'detective', akin to the similar figure in *A Beast*. In both works, too, the 'crime' of adultery is specifically couched in dialogue which evokes imagery of the Fall (see Chapter 5). In the 1968 play, Rebecca is cast as Eve the temptress, holding out the forbidden fruit of adulterous sexuality to Michael, who in turn replies:

> MICHAEL: I do feel like a snake every time I look at thee.
>
> REBECCA: Snake's right. Snake in the grass. Who do you want? Her down there with her red neck and her dolly tub? Or me up here with my back in the grass?

Michael is characterised as both the wicked serpent and the tempted Adam: torn between spirit (loyalty to his wife) and flesh (the forbidden fruit of his lover). As in the Genesis story, this functions as a metaphor for Man's supposed dual nature – the competing claims of animality and spirituality between which he must choose. If he chooses the former (the 'beast'), he transgresses God's law, automatically forsaking access to divinity and heaping eternal damnation upon himself. A form of spiritual death will ensue. He will be literally shut out of Eden. As the fallen Ebenezer makes clear to his congregation at the climax of *A Beast*: 'Man is but an airy beast if he does not walk in the ways of the Lord, your God.' Similarly, the child in *Hide and Seek*, believing he is approaching union with God in his own Garden of Eden (the Forest of Dean), turns to find himself staring into the eyes of a beast – another 'snake in the grass' who brings what the boy of the novel, with his intense Bible upbringing, can only ever see as a spiritual Fall from grace, from God.

In the 1968 play, the source of Ebenezer's despair is therefore that he cannot approach divinity because he is afflicted with this same 'beast' of human sexuality. Finishing what the other started, his murderous assault of Rebecca links him with the adulterer Michael as one of the 'fallen'. By virtue of the equation of sex with death which runs right through Potter's work, Ebenezer's becomes a symbolic sexual act for which he will later feel remorse.

Crucially, however, while perpetrating this act, he is watched by his son Rufus – just as the young Marlow watched a similar parental 'sex crime' in *The Singing Detective*. If Michael and Ebenezer are linked by deed, Rufus, as maligned victim, is implicitly related to the slaughtered bear, both in terms of his Latin name and the blame heaped upon him as a consequence of others' guilt. By virtue of his status as the village idiot, scorned by the wider community and falsely accused by Ebenezer of a crime he himself later commits, Rufus resembles Georgie Pringle in *Stand Up*. Moreover, the classroom scene in *Stand Up*, which showed a lie becoming a truth for the sake of another's persecution, is echoed in the scapegoat theme of *A Beast*. Just as Potter in *Stand Up* equated the backward child with the clever child as the same type of outcast from the community, so too does the uneasy relationship between father and son in *A Beast* seem to echo that between Nigel and his father in the 1965 play. As the repository of Old Testament values, Ebenezer the patriarch literally functions as God to his 'crippled' son. This intricate web of connections becomes revealing when set out schematically:

Joe and bear → related to Italian POW of *Hide and Seek* = *'beast'*
Rebecca → pregnant 'whore' in forest → related to dead Mrs Marlow of *The Singing Detective* = *dead 'mother'*
Michael → adulterer/murderer → linked by physical deed to Ebenezer → Old Testament patriarch = *God-like father*
Rufus → 'cripple' → outcast/victim → related to Pringle → linked in *Stand Up* to *Nigel Barton* = clever *child*

This allows an interpretation of the *Beast* 'myth' for what the play seems to be exploring in coded form is a version of the Fall – the end of childhood 'innocence' through the child's shock of realisation of how it came it be, as the product of sexual intercourse between its parents. In the play, a symbolic sexual act is depicted between a symbolic mother and God-like father which is witnessed by a 'child'. This discovery of forbidden knowledge literally brings death in its wake – to the 'mother' but also to the child's 'guilty' father. A bond of trust and belief in a God-like father is shattered and to the now alienated child, the resulting loss of integration and security represents the end of Eden: an expulsion from the Garden and the arrival of 'a beast' in his midst. God has gone out of his life and a God-like father, with his set of patriarchal absolutes, evaporates to become nothing but 'an airy beast'.

If that beast is ultimately linked to the one brought by the Italian, the play absolves the latter, however, of all blame. The Italian is shown to be a false scapegoat – simply a 'bogeyman'. The real beast is revealed to be much closer to home, within the hearts of the Foresters themselves. Erupting into brutality, it is their repressions that are shown to be the real cause of the 'crime' in the play and it is from their Old Testament world of an eye for an eye and a tooth for a tooth that Rufus, the 'outcast', 'cripple' child must flee at the end, if he himself is ever to confront and deal with his own beast inside, as Ebenezer's sermon urged. The message behind the play's bleak ending seems to be that Old Testament bloodshed must give way to genuine Christian forgiveness and toleration, if a taming of the real beast is ever to take place.

Double-edged, therefore, with regard to its themes – a surface concern with racial prejudice, an exploration of a whole cauldron of hidden demons underneath – this play is itself 'A Beast with Two Backs'. One question surely remains. Why should Potter choose to link his sexual themes with the real-life story of the bear? What prompted the connection in the first place?

Newspaper research may provide an answer. During the nineteen forties, *The Ross Gazette*, a newspaper covering the Ross-on-Wye/Forest of Dean area, revived local interest in the bear story. It delved into its files to retell the bear story of fifty years before, under the headline, 'Who Killed The Bear?'[72] It is the date of this article which provides (at the very least) a remarkable coincidence for the story appeared one week after VE day, on 17 May 1945 – that is, on the date of Potter's tenth birthday.

End of apprenticeship

In many ways, *Son of Man* (dir. Gareth Davies) was a natural progression from *A Beast* in terms of themes and subject matter. This was Potter's final *Wednesday Play* (the slot gained a new time and title in 1970) and it undoubtedly sealed his reputation as a major playwright, winning praise and, perhaps even more significantly, many column inches in the British press.

The reason for the publicity was Potter's controversial retelling of the Gospels in which Jesus (played by Colin Blakeley) is presented as a wild man: an outcast fasting in the wilderness who is racked by doubts over his own divinity. Like many other Potter protagonists, this Jesus is a 'torn' hero, caught between the demands of the everyday world and those of his spirit. God 'burns inside', making him no longer sure he is simply the son of a carpenter.[73]

As the action of the play widens to examine the historical context of the

Roman occupation of Judaea, it becomes clear there are many 'agitators and terrorists' claiming to be the Messiah amongst the persecuted Jews who long for such a figure. When Jesus emerges from the wilderness to gather disciples, his claims to be 'the One' are greeted initially with derision by Andrew and Peter who brand him a 'looney'.

Soon, he convinces them to join in his mission, yet as he goes preaching amongst the people Potter's Jesus performs no miracles. The nearest the play comes to one is when he is seen calming one of his audience who has fallen into a fit. Significantly, this is presented as no supernatural event but simply a tried and tested psychological technique popular in the nineteen sixties: the Warrendale technique which involved the therapist physically grappling with the victim in order to calm him or her. To Jesus' dismay, his superstitious onlookers do take it as a miracle.

As indicated by its title, the central assertion of the play, therefore, is that Jesus was less a supernatural entity and more a 'son of man', with all of a man's doubts and fears. This is encapsulated by lines of dialogue which Potter added to the subsequent stage version of the play. When Jesus is asked by Judas if he is from God, he replies: 'The son of man must be a man. He must be all of a man ... He cannot be other than a man, or else God has *cheated*.'[74]

By demythologising the life of Christ, the play in this way emphasises how much more remarkable his martyrdom must have been, given that he was essentially a human being, opposing his will over his own physical fears and 'animal' instincts for self-preservation. If he had been anything other than a man, Potter seems to be saying, his mission to be a role-model for the rest of humanity would have been an empty one – a divine deceit.

This links the play with *A Beast* for if that work emphasised the 'animal' in man, *Son of Man* foregrounds the ability of the human 'spirit' to overcome the demands of the physical body, body and spirit clearly representing for Potter the dual nature of humankind. While *A Beast* dramatised the terrors of an Old Testament logic and world-view, *Son of Man* emphasises in opposition Jesus' New Testament message of love and forgiveness. This is made explicit in Potter's handling of the Sermon on the Mount which concentrates almost exclusively upon Christ's injunction to 'Love thy enemies' (Matthew 6: 44). As Potter's Christ puts it: 'An eye for an eye. A tooth for a tooth ... So our forefathers have spoken ... Love your own kind. And *hate* the enemy ... Love for your enemies. That is what I have come to tell you ... Love – your – enemy!'

Rather than promising Heaven in the after-life, Potter's Jesus is thus a revolutionary idealist seeking it in this one, opposing the 'eye for an eye' view of the Old Testament patriarchs (such as Ebenezer in *A Beast*) with an identifiably socialist vision of a brotherhood of man. This in turn links in with Potter's treatment of Judas (Edward Hardwicke) who is characterised in the play as one of the Temple Police (laymen who enforce the law of Judaism). Sympathetic to Christ's message of love, Judas is sent as a spy by the devious Caiphas, High Priest of the Temple, to infiltrate the disciples and note down any of Christ's 'blasphemies'. Rather than for thirty pieces of silver, Potter's Judas betrays Christ to the authorities in the mistaken belief this will help clear his name and establish his credentials to the Temple Court as the true Messiah. To his horror, he finds Christ is resigned to the inevitability of the sacrifice he must make. Maintaining his silence in front of Caiphas, he refuses to help himself. Condemned as a blasphemer, he is handed over to Pilate (Robert Hardy) who is shaken by Christ's eerie calm in the face of death. In a clear reversal of roles, Christ tells him not to be afraid. Frightened by what he cannot understand, Pilate immediately orders Christ's crucifixion. As Potter's directions in the stage version then make clear, 'the biblical account follows in all its brutality': Christ is beaten, stripped, whipped and crucified by a mob of Roman soldiers.[75]

Reminiscent of the ending of *A Beast* in its emphasis on the blood sacrifice of the innocent to appease collective guilt, the television *Son of Man* concludes on a similar bleak note. Christ is seen on the cross shaking with rage. His final words are: 'Father! Father! Why have you forsaken me?' The play finishes there at the moment of death and extreme despair, with no depiction of the subsequent supernatural resurrection portrayed in the Gospels. That Potter should end his play this way might seem puzzling given the view expressed earlier that *Son of Man* is in many ways more optimistic than *A Beast* in terms of its vision of the triumph of the human spirit over 'animal' instincts for self-preservation. One reason is hinted at in an interview Potter gave to the *Radio Times*, in which he dwelt upon Jesus' message of Love thy enemies: 'The thought behind that leaps 2000 years. Today we have war after war, race riot after race riot. We are still no nearer loving our enemies.'[76]

If the purpose of the television version was therefore to underline that, in terms of the subsequent path of human history, Jesus' sacrifice was in vain, when the BBC decided to repeat the play only two months later as a result of favourable critical reaction to its first showing, the *Radio Times* ran a follow-up piece examining earlier responses. It recorded the opinion that many Christians 'could only be distressed at the play ending with words of despair … instead of the defiant and victorious "It is accomplished. Father into thy hands".'[77] Significantly, when Potter came to adapt his play for the stage, he modified the ending to take account of these objections. After Jesus dies a realistic death on the cross with words of despair on his lips, Potter's stage directions indicate:

The Lights fade, leaving a spotlight on the cross. Calm. Jesus is still, finished. Then he lifts his head in sudden triumph.

JESUS: It – is – ACCOMPLISHED!

His head drops. It is all over. The spot slowly fades. Darkness. No sound.[78]

If a supernatural emphasis is therefore put on Christ's life and death in the stage version, unusually, Potter seems to have been striving in his TV play for a believable naturalism. The use in the script, for example, of anachronistic colloquialisms like 'flaming' and 'shut up', together with the casting of Colin Blakeley as an iconoclastic, fiery Christ, underline the fact that Potter was clearly seeking to lend the Gospels an earthy reality for contemporary audiences. Indeed, the request for the Northern Irish, 'barrel-chested' Blakeley to play Christ was the writer's own, after he had seen him as De Stogumber in a BBC Plays production of *Saint Joan*.[79] As Potter put it, Blakeley's performance exhibited such pent-up hatred and aggression: 'It was the pent-up quality that I wanted, not of hatred this time but of this other, unprecedented thing that was pent up.'[80]

The resulting portrayal of Christ made Potter and *Son of Man* a news event, setting a precedent that later works would follow. The play was heavily previewed by the press prior to transmission and prominent slots were set aside on television for analysis and discussion with critics and theologians. If the net effect of all this hype was further to confirm the reputation of *The Wednesday Play* discovery of four years before, the expected post-transmission controversy never came. Despite some newspapers' best attempts ('Storm over TV Christ' – *Daily Mail;* ' "Tough Guy" Christ Shocks Viewers' – *Daily Mirror*), most were forced to concede with the *Guardian*, a 'Quiet Reception for New *Son of Man*'.[81] As the play's producer Graeme McDonald recalls, much of the reaction to the play was supportive, with only a minority protesting that a Christ with a Northern Irish accent was 'obscene'.[82] Several churchmen praised the portrayal as 'rightly desentimentalised' and 'moving' whilst most of the (not outstandingly high number of) viewers' telephone calls to the BBC post-transmission, were critical not so much of the play's 'blasphemous' reworking of the Gospels, as the violence of the Crucifixion scenes.[83] TV reviewers, on the whole, were also extremely kind to the play. Julian Critchley in *The Times* thought the play a 'considerable achievement', whilst James Thomas of the *Express* described it as 'one of the most compelling pieces ever put out by that controversial vehicle *The Wednesday Play*'. It was perhaps the *Daily Sketch*, however, which put its finger on the real reason for the play's success, with its headline 'This Gospel of our Times'.[84]

Potter's Christ is indeed a Christ of the late sixties. A long-haired drop-out who wanders into Judaea preaching a message of love and peace, he is not only a hippy but, as Peter and Andrew make clear, a 'looney' if he genuinely believes he can change things.[85] If a determination to overturn the established order links him with other 'mad' outsiders like Mercer's axeman in *For Tea on Sunday* or Potter's own Hazlitt in *The Confidence Course*, it also makes him, as the son of a carpenter, very much like Nigel Barton: a working-class hero who feels himself different from his class and who sets out to challenge the occupying power in the name of the poor and oppressed. Moreover, like Barton, he, too, has doubts about his own upward mobility. In one famous scene, widely commented upon by reviewers, Jesus approaches one of the crucifixion crosses scattered across the Judaean landscape and strokes the wood, commenting, 'Good timber, this ... I could fill a room with tables and chairs with wood like this.' For a moment, the anguished Messiah becomes a simple carpenter again, forgetting the terrors of the cross on which he knows he will die. Later, out of earshot of his disciples, he smacks the wood and mutters 'Ach! You should have stayed a tree ... And I should have stayed a carpenter.'

Potter's portrayal of Christ's age as one of violent revolutionary fervour also carries clear echoes of the period, in this case the year of the play's composition, 1968. As the writer made clear in contemporary interviews, he decided to write the play, after having come into contact with some of the notable student revolutionaries of the period:

> I was staying in a flat in London when Danny le Rouge came over that time. All the left-wingers met there one evening – Tariq Ali, everyone – debating away. I listened and felt very lonely and out of it. The same old hates, the same old dogma, the same belief that if only the systems of the world could be changed everyone would be happy. No concern for the sick and the bereft and the lonely and the suffering. Jesus was *their* man. He was their man the instant he asked himself the terrible question: 'Am I He? am I the Messiah?'

It was his reaction against the violence of sixties revolutionary politics which prompted Potter to make the 'love your enemies' passage from the Gospels the central message of *Son of Man*:

> This was something completely the opposite of the vengeful Judaic creed of 'an eye for an eye, a tooth for a tooth'. This is what was really revolutionary about Jesus. I suppose the play represents a retreat from political positions I previously held.[86]

In turn, it was this notion of violence begetting violence that gave *Son of Man* its topicality. Christ is portrayed as the genuine revolutionary (amongst many false ones) on account of his truly novel message to 'Love your enemy'. It is fear of this which makes the political Establishment of his day plot against him. As some contemporary reviewers spotted, Judas, caught in a larger conspiracy he cannot understand, very much represents the 'anguished liberal' figure within the drama.[87] Sympathetic to the aims of the 'revolution', he betrays it in the end through his earnest attempts to intercede on its behalf with the devious authorities.

Just as with *A Beast*, public and personal themes also mingle in *Son of Man*. As Potter's statement makes clear, the play was a conscious movement away from political concerns towards a grappling with more private issues of religious faith. Again, this is most apparent in Judas' relationship with Christ which resembles the villain–victim relationship of Barton and Pringle in *Stand Up*. This symbolic link first becomes clear when Judas arrives amongst the disciples, claiming he wants to join Christ's mission. In both the television and stage versions, there is instant electric rapport between traitor and Messiah to the exclusion of all the other disciples (as Potter's directions for the stage play indicate, 'The others are out of it; this is between Jesus and Judas').[88]

Such a relationship puzzled some contemporary reviewers who correctly identified that 'in the Gospel according to Potter, Judas is gentle and Christ violent. A reversal of roles … more topical than true.'[89] In contrast to the angry, scruffy Christ, Judas 'looked for all the world like an SPCK Jesus, all gently waving locks and sad benevolence'.[90] Given the link between 'traitor' and 'victim' made in previous Potter works, this becomes explicable in terms other than a simple reversal of stereotypical representations. Judas is given sympathetic treatment because he is not only a traitor but a victim of his ideals who closely resembles Christ in intention if not in deed. What makes him a traitor is, as for Nigel Barton, his desire that his beliefs should 'stand up' in the Temple Court and be publicly validated. Just like Barton in his relationship with his father, Judas, by proudly seeking to 'broadcast' his ideals, betrays both himself and the site of all his values: Christ his 'master'.

In marked contrast, Potter's Jesus maintains a humble, dignified silence throughout interrogation and thus fails to betray. Judas may *appear* like a Messiah both in appearance and in his wish to campaign publicly on behalf of others but, like Nigel Barton, he is revealed to be a traitor because while apparently sincere in intentions, he belongs more to the enemy than with those he seeks to represent. True authenticity in the play resides in the earthy working-class Jesus who will not betray his peers because he remains part of them – as Potter put it, 'He was *their* man'.

If the correspondence with *Stand Up, Nigel Barton* helps explain the links between Judas and Jesus, it also indicates why both characters are torn by inner conflict. This is true, too, of the play as a whole. On one level, the portrayal of Christ in relation to his time may unite religion with politics but the play itself seems torn between these conflicting concerns. This is underlined by Potter's two alternative endings for it: on television, a humanistic and politically 'authentic' enactment of the Crucifixion, ending with Christ's cry of despair as he dies; on stage, a greater emphasis on the religious significance of the act ('It is accomplished').

In a number of contemporary interviews, too, it is possible to detect an ambivalence in Potter's response to the Christian story. If, on the one hand, he could describe himself as an agnostic and not religious at all ('I went to chapel as a kid but as soon as I grew up I stopped'); on the other, he could assert he wrote the play as a free thinker who 'would like to believe' and who shared a 'yearning for there to be something else'.[91] The play itself, it seems, was a grappling with his own personal faith; an attempt to reconcile adult agnosticism with a childhood Christian upbringing, using drama to create a Christ in which he, personally, could believe. This seems to be what he meant when he described how, out of his own doubts and longings, he had tried to create a 'real man' and to write a play 'about a man questioning himself'.[92] Potter's Christ was made in the author's own image: his uncertainty about his faith became, in the play, Christ's uncertainty over his divinity.

Even at the time, Potter could therefore recognise *Son of Man* as marking a sea change in his work. In a 1969 interview with the *Sunday Telegraph*, he described how he had written most of the play whilst in hospital, after having undergone a period of illness and depression. Significantly, he concluded:

> Everything I've done till now I see as an apprenticeship. Every time I've seen one of my plays I've felt twinges of shame. With [*Son of Man*] I think the apprenticeship is over. I begin to say something which I really feel, without the awful barriers and the cheats and the deceits and the deceptions. The feeling that you've done something at last gives you a sense of emancipation. Actually, it somehow got me out of hospital.[93]

Conclusion

As Potter recognised at the time, *Son of Man* marked the end of his 'confidence course' on *The Wednesday Play*. The 'atheist' of Barry Norman's 1965 profile had turned out to be like his fictional creation, Nigel Barton, after all: 'An atheist who is fond of hymn tunes', as Barton describes himself at one point in *Stand Up* (p. 61).

If Potter's move to more spiritual themes is clearly detectable in his later contributions, as this chapter has tried to indicate, it had already been foreshadowed by the earlier plays. *All* of his *Wednesday Play* work was distinguished by a fusion of the political and the personal, in which topicality of subject matter often served only to half-obscure the cauldron of private anxieties, embodied by a succession of 'torn' male central protagonists, that was seething underneath.

Outside, in the wider television world, times were changing, however. The Head of BBC TV Drama Sydney Newman had quit his job in 1968 to become a feature film producer with Associated British Pictures. That same year, James MacTaggart, Tony Garnett and Kenith Trodd had departed the BBC to form their own independent TV production company: Kestrel Productions. Thus many of the protagonists who had made *The Wednesday Play* possible and helped facilitate Potter's success had left the BBC by the end of the sixties. As a result, some newspaper pundits questioned the survival not only of *The Wednesday Play* but of the single television play itself. If, by the close of the sixties, its golden age was certainly over, the BBC's original play slot continued on into the seventies as *Play for Today* and Potter continued with it. As Chapter 2 will illustrate, if times got tougher, so, too, did Potter's writing and attitudes. Though consistently engaging with contemporary society, his plays of the seventies became less openly 'political' and more introspective in tone and content. Their author had begun consciously to create an *oeuvre* rather than (as had perhaps been the case for much of the previous decade) seeking to attack the world.

2

Angels are so few: the *Play for Today* era

Wednesday Play rebels: Kenith Trodd and Kestrel Productions

'They thought they were buying *The Wednesday Play* lock, stock and barrel', reflected Kenith Trodd in 1970.[1] He was recalling the rise and fall of Kestrel – British TV's first independent drama production company, formed long before Channel Four helped establish the notion of the independent TV producer. 'They' were London Weekend Television – the ITV company which three years earlier had promised to revolutionise commercial television. Both had become victims of their own ideals.

The brainchild of TV presenter David Frost and his business partner Clive Irving, LWT's original aim had been to bring the values of the sixties counter-culture to television. The ambition was to shake up the existing ITV network with a new company that would reflect the more anarchic, anti-Establishment mood of the times. In order to win a franchise to broadcast, Frost set out to persuade the Independent Television Authority (ITV's regulatory body) that LWT stood for programme quality, rather than simple money-making. He did so by boldly going to the heart of public service broadcasting and poaching some of the BBC's top programme-making talent. Seduced by the vision of a Trojan horse that was going to breach the walls of ITV, bringing 'culture' to the masses, many famous Corporation figures, including Humphrey Burton, Frank Muir and BBC-1 Controller Michael Peacock, were persuaded to join Frost in his latest television venture.

In terms of drama, LWT looked no further than *The Wednesday Play*. Both Trodd and Tony Garnett were approached separately at the end of 1967 and asked whether they would like to defect to 'the other side'. Meeting over a drink, the pair tried to work out a joint response. Ardent left-wingers, neither wished to work for a commercial company. Hence why not embarrass LWT by saying they would not come individually but only as part of an autonomous collective? Both thought this would put an end to LWT's wooing. To their amazement, they found the new company was only too happy to oblige and suddenly what had started as a dismissive riposte became a serious business proposition. As Trodd stated in 1970, 'LWT were vulnerable at that time – new and knowing very little about drama.'[2] Thinking they were 'buying' the prestigious *Wednesday Play*, they were glad to accept any terms that he and Garnett cared to demand.

To an extent, the company was right to believe it had bought *The Wednesday Play*. In order that LWT could promote itself in its franchise application as a champion of quality drama, Trodd and Garnett enlisted two more distinguished *Wednesday Play* practitioners, David Mercer and James MacTaggart, to act as partners in their new drama collective. Thus swelled to four, this group, together with Clive Goodwin (Trodd's and Potter's agent at the time), formed Kestrel. Appropriately named after a small bird of prey, its principal task was to service LWT with television plays.[3]

Over the next two years, Kestrel produced seventeen plays for the new ITV company, including works not only by Potter but Jim Allen, Roger Smith and Colin Welland. Trodd and Garnett's collective became a haven for fellow refugees from *The Wednesday Play*: an apparent oasis of freedom and autonomy from which drama practitioners could cock a snook at what they felt to be the constraints of working at the BBC. In practice, 'the *Wednesday Play* rebels' (as the press dubbed them) encountered just as many restrictions at LWT as they had at the BBC. These were chiefly economic and logistic. As the TV critic T.C. Worsley complained in 1969, one of the defining features of *The Wednesday Play* work particularly associated with Garnett had been its location shooting on film. The Kestrel plays, however, were ham-strung by their need to be recorded on videotape within the confines of LWT's studios – 'In the studio', Worsley wrote, 'it has proved impossible to capture that very breath and taste of contemporary life which the film plays specialised in.'[4]

At the same time, the rebels found censorship pressures were not unique to the BBC. In the course of its two-year association with the company, a number of Kestrel's productions became embroiled in controversy with LWT management. The very first play Trodd produced for LWT aroused deep unease, being a satire on the ITV franchise race which the company had so recently won.[5] Similarly, when Kestrel commissioned a work from the celebrated French director, Jean-Luc Godard, this, too, ran into trouble. Immersed in the revolutionary politics of Paris 1968, Godard delivered *British Sounds* – an 'anti-Image' film, consisting almost entirely of polemical voice-overs expressing solidarity with British workers. When Humphrey Burton, LWT's Head of Arts, deemed it untransmittable, he provoked a huge, very public, row.

The *British Sounds* affair was undoubtedly Kestrel's and LWT's greatest failure. As Trodd put it, 'It did show … the limitations of LWT's liberalism, even in their honeymoon period.'[6] It also underlined the difficulties which a left-wing collective faced in attempting to operate within a commercial TV environment. In September 1969, both sets of problems came to a head when, confronted with dwindling audiences, falling advertising revenue and pressure from the other ITV companies, the LWT Board decided to sack its Managing Director, Michael Peacock.

Furious at this *coup d'état*, many programme-makers, including Trodd and Garnett, expressed their solidarity with Peacock by tendering their own resignations, arguing that LWT would never have won its franchise if it had not been for its staff. Appeals to the ITA to intervene fell on deaf ears since the latter did not wish to embroil itself in the internal affairs of an ITV company. Meanwhile, the LWT Board hired an Australian newspaper tycoon to become the company's troubleshooter – one Rupert Murdoch. With his help, new schedules were drawn up to appease advertisers. These were approved by the ITA and LWT's flirtation with the sixties' counter-culture was over.

Looking back on the Peacock crisis, Trodd asserted in 1970 that Kestrel's was a straight choice between survival and honour. He and Garnett felt there was no honour in survival at LWT.[7] With offers of work elsewhere, both decided to go their separate ways. Prior to this dissolution, however, Trodd managed to commission and produce two Potter plays for Kestrel/LWT. Both are interesting in their own right. One is crucial for understanding the writer and his work.

Happy Days ...

Moonlight on the Highway (tx. 12.4.69; dir. James MacTaggart) marked a watershed in Potter's writing. The first Potter play to be produced by Trodd (for Kestrel), it was also the first to articulate a number of key themes which the writer would come to explore in more detail in his most famous works, *Pennies from Heaven* and *The Singing Detective*. Above all, *Moonlight* was the first play to foreground what would become a Potter trademark: a fascination with the popular music of the nineteen thirties and forties.

The play revolves around David Peters, a journalist who shares not only the same initials as Dennis Potter but also an obsession with thirties' pop music, particularly the songs of the legendary thirties' crooner, Al Bowlly. One Bowlly song haunts the play's soundtrack, a 1938 tune called 'Moonlight On The Highway', with its plaintive lyric: 'Moonlight on the Highway / ... Turn your light on my way / Through Memory Lane.'[8]

Counterpointed with the music are Peters' own memories. There are flashbacks to a funeral, intercut with a child's eye-view of 'being sexually assaulted by a man with spiky hair and eyes the colour of phlegm' in a narrow lane, near his home, when he was 10 years old. As with clues in a detective story, it is the significance of these images and their connection with Bowlly which the rest of the play then begins to unravel.

Moreover, the way this is done is highly reminiscent of *The Singing Detective*, in which the central protagonist, Philip Marlow, is forced to confront his own repressed past with the help of a hospital psychotherapist (see Chapter 5). In *Moonlight*, Peters also goes to hospital and encounters Chilton – an urbane psychiatrist who believes he has the answer to all problems. He establishes that Peters' mother died only six weeks before and that somehow this event has become mixed up in the patient's mind not only with the terrifying childhood assault but with the death of Bowlly, who was killed in the London Blitz by a buzz-bomb, right at the peak of his career. Convinced by his own diagnosis, Chilton dismisses the patient with two small bottles of tablets, believing he will eventually open up to someone – a friend or a relative. As the psychiatrist tells two of his medical students, the NHS does not have the bed-space and besides he, Chilton, is not God. Significantly, however, he is *God-like* in his certainty about what ails Peters:

> CHILTON: It's very simple, very common, very ordinary ... He has a longing for an Eden, before the bomb, before the alley ... before that fateful age of ten. The paradisial Eden does not in fact exist but he dreams that it might have done – before the bomb, before the war. Why, this singer, this Bowlly. ... He's a thirties figure! He sings of the dreams ... They're the songs [Peters] might have heard on the radio downstairs while drifting off to sleep [as a child]. ... Six weeks ago, his mother dies ... Grief is the trigger – the depressive is in the tunnel.

Thus Peters is left alone to solve his own problems. At the end of the play, he is found typically pursuing his obsession – this time at an Al Bowlly convention where ageing music fans gather every year to commemorate 'that fateful day' (17 April 1941) when the singer was wiped out in the Blitz. As the young editor of a Bowlly fanzine, Peters makes his way on to stage to deliver a speech to the faithful but, drunk and troubled, his oration turns out to be far from the expected eulogy. He describes how all the songs from the thirties are about love: 'Sweet love. Innocent love ... But what about *making* love?' None of the songs discuss sex. Suddenly he is screaming hysterically: 'Wicked wicked thing – bodies on top of each other. Horrible bodies. Painful bodies.' He ends: 'I have to tell you. I have slept with 136 women. Prostitutes! Yes, you can't buy love ... Why are you running away?'

With the elderly crowd stunned at this mention of what can never be mentioned in their favourite songs, pandemonium breaks out in the hall. Peters, however, is sublimely happy: 'It's out now! … I've said it! I've said it!' he shouts. In the final shot of the play, he turns to a poster of Bowlly, whispering eternal gratitude to his saviour: 'Good old Al!'

Psychiatry thus gets its come-uppance at the end of *Moonlight*. The most immediate source of Peters' guilt is revealed to lie not so much in childhood trauma or the death of his mother but in a sexual predilection for prostitutes. Clearly, this 'addiction' can be linked to the nightmare of sexual assault (that 'fateful age of ten' which Chilton correctly identifies) but in contrast to the professional certainties of the psychiatrist, the play suggests the individual cannot be reduced mechanistically to the level of a few biographical events over which he or she has no control. The implication is that each person has the power to take control over their own life – to cope with their own problems in their own way and as best they can.

Crucially, in this replacement of a view of the patient as victim with an assertion of the power of the individual to transform his or her own destiny, popular music plays the enabling role. The songs of Al Bowlly offer the keys to self-knowledge, unlocking a repressed past. Thirties' crooner destroyed in the Blitz, Bowlly represents a vanished innocence which the central protagonist longs to recapture. Perceived to be the source of his Fall from this earlier innocence, sexuality comes to embody Peters' sense of separation from an idyllic past. It is a 'wicked wicked thing' – to be repressed and practised covertly (in an implicit relationship of dominance) with prostitutes. There are clear links here with *A Beast with Two Backs* where a similar Fall from innocence coincided with a child's estrangement from its symbolic parents (a dead mother and guilty father). In *Moonlight*, memories of sexual assault are also directly linked to permanent estrangement from a parent – namely, the death of Peters' widowed mother six weeks before.[9]

Likewise, the final scene of the play (in which the central protagonist embarrassingly bares his soul in public) has much in common with the endings of both *Nigel Barton Plays* – though with one major difference. In those earlier plays, public honesty always led to disaster for the central protagonist. In *Moonlight*, it becomes the key to psychological redemption. The central character may still be a social outcast who is persecuted by a hostile audience, but now 'broadcasting' the truth becomes a means of unyoking the burden of a repressed past: 'It's out now! … I've said it! I've said it!' cries Peters at the end. No longer at the mercy of psychiatrists, he discovers a new sense of autonomy, thanks to the songs and 'Good old Al'.

Popular culture (the music of the thirties) thus intertwines with the main themes of the play – of Peters' regret for a vanished era, for a loss of innocence. On one level, such nostalgia marks the protagonist out as an absurd figure: a man out of time. On another, it lends him a nobility as he attempts to use the past to come to terms with his life in the present. Such ambivalence is also present in another Potter play which Trodd produced for ITV: *Paper Roses* (tx 13.6.71; dir. Barry Davis).[10] Like *Moonlight*, it examines the impact of popular culture upon the psyche of a central protagonist who is at once both pathetic and heroic.

Set in the world of tabloid journalism, the play deals with Clarence Hubbard – an ageing hack; once the pride of his paper for his ability to find 'human interest' stories but now consigned to writing the obituary columns as he waits out his last days before retirement. Increasingly out of step with the sex, sin and sleaze mentality that sells newspapers in the seventies, the knowledge that he is about to be pensioned off from the profession to which he has devoted his life is driving him progressively insane. A memory play, *Paper Roses* takes the audience inside Clarence's head, charting his final day at the office as he plunges towards complete mental breakdown. In so doing, it deploys a formidable array of non-naturalistic techniques.

First, there are flashbacks to past glories. The play frequently returns to the image of Hubbard as he once was: 'Ace human interest reporter', dictating stories from telephone kiosks. As these flashbacks recur, it becomes clear that Hubbard's past copy has something to say about his present:

> HUBBARD: She added – colon, quote – 'It will break my heart to give up Paddywhack'. Stop. 'He is very faithful and I hope the council will show some human feeling' ... A council spokesman said yesterday quote 'The breed of the dog does not matter. Paddywhack must go.' (p. 13)[11]

Meanwhile, in the present, Hubbard's exchanges with his journalistic colleagues are repeatedly punctuated by sequences of headline graphics. Accompanied on the soundtrack by the strains of 'Happy Days Are Here Again', these not only satirise the values of the tabloids but provide oblique comment on Clarence's own situation. For example:

> BLADDY (on phone): Newsdesk – er, Bladdy. Anything for me?....
> HUBBARD: It's all go.
> (*Headline Captions*: ... PARDON MISS, YOUR SLIP IS SHOWING
> BRR! BRITAIN FREEZES ...
> FAITHFUL DOG FACES EVICTION) (p. 19)

These devices come together at the end of the play when Clarence orders all his old cuttings from the press library. To the astonishment of his colleagues, he goes to the window of his top-storey office and throws all of his life's work out on to the breeze. Then, striding out of the office for the last time, he heads for the lift shaft, despite the fact that no lift is there. Ignoring the shouted warnings of others, he steps out into thin air and falls headlong down the shaft; his progress significantly accompanied by a series of headline graphics: 'DOWN! DOWN! DOWN!' 'WHEEEEE!' 'NECKLINE PLUNGES AGAIN!' Haunted to the last by his tabloid headlines, 'THE END' superimposes itself on screen as Clarence hits the ground (p. 97).

It is not quite the end, however. The play has two codas which serve to underline the pathos of Hubbard's passing. First, there is a scene with one of the feature editors of Clarence's old paper. He is seen on the telephone to a colleague, adamantly stressing that the paper can only spare two paragraphs for Clarence's obituary. Still, he remarks, at least the old man's fall might make the bosses do something about 'that damn lift-shaft' (p. 99). Then, he quickly moves on to discuss a feature on topless barmaids. Clarence has already become yesterday's news – forgotten by the transient profession to which he devoted his life.

The second coda is even more telling. At various points throughout the play, *Paper Roses* featured shots of a mysterious viewer, apparently watching the drama of Clarence unfold on his TV screen. Bored and inattentive, this spectator seemed as if he would rather be doing anything than watch the play – at one point, even practising his golf swing in his livingroom. Who is this indifferent viewer? All is made clear in the play's final scene, when he is seen on the telephone dictating a few hastily scribbled notes. He is none other than a television critic for one of the national newspapers and the programme he is reviewing is the play which we, the audience, have just been watching – *Paper Roses*. The critic delivers his verdict:

> Last night's TV play, *Paper Roses*, gave us about as true a picture of popular newspapers as a funfair distorting mirror ... We are told the author used to work in Fleet Street but if this led any viewer to think that the sour caricature on the screen was based on real experience of real journalists, he has only to open this morning's newspapers to see how ludicrous the idea really is. Full stop. End. (p. 103)

By the end of *Paper Roses*, the joke is on newspapers and the casual nature in which TV is reviewed by the press. The ironic last sentence of Potter's fake review invites the audience to measure the truth of the fictitious critic's opinions, in terms not only of the playwright's attested knowledge of Fleet Street but also of the viewer's own experience of reading popular newspapers.

Each of these twin codas also invites the audience to judge the significance of Clarence's passing. In this way, *Paper Roses* is structured like a Shakespearian tragedy. Like some latter day King Lear, Clarence is an old man who loses his 'kingdom' and slides into madness – in the process gaining a measure of self-knowledge. Like Shakespeare's tragic hero, his realisation is that 'nothing can be made out of nothing';[12] that his life in newspapers has essentially been an empty one, fit only for the breeze. Structurally, the twin codas at the close of the play perform a task similar to the supporting players at the end of a Shakespearian tragedy: the lesser mortals who comment upon the protagonist's passing, pointing up its significance by pointing to the hero's 'greatness' and tragic stature.

The 'tragedy' of *Paper Roses*, however, derives not from recognition of the protagonist's greatness but from the *indifference* with which others treat his demise. The tragedy is one of insignificance, in terms both of the central character and, more widely, of the values of the throwaway newspaper culture he represents. Akin to *Moonlight*'s lament for a lost Eden, *Paper Roses* mourns the superficiality of a tabloid press culture. This elegiac feel is best summed up by Kenith Trodd who sees the play as 'a rather sad, neurotic story about ... an old *Daily Herald* journalist who can't survive the onset of *The Sun*'.[13] As the Introduction noted, Potter himself was literally such a person: an old *Daily Herald* journalist who resigned in 1964 after only one month working on the *Sun*. In this light, Hubbard's demise (demoted from 'ace reporter', just as illness forced Potter to switch from feature writer to TV critic of the *Herald*) becomes symbolic of the demise of an older tradition of popular journalism in the face of a new tabloid culture that saw Potter's old paper, the leftist *Daily Herald/Sun*, transformed into an aggressive right-wing daily, after its takeover by Rupert Murdoch in 1969.

As all of this illustrates, Potter was thus highly adept at taking elements of his own life and embroidering them into elaborate fictions which also functioned as wider social metaphors. Nowhere was this more apparent than in two Potter 'spy' plays that were also transmitted in the early seventies: *Lay Down Your Arms* and *Traitor*.

Spies like us

Lay Down Your Arms (tx. 23.5.70; dir. Christopher Morahan) was the second Potter play that Trodd produced for Kestrel. Significantly, it draws on material which Potter would rework over twenty years later for his Channel 4 serial, *Lipstick on Your Collar*. *Lay Down Your Arms* is set in 1956, at the height of the Cold War, and revolves around Bob Hawk – a clever working-class youth who is doing his two years' National Service as a private in the British Army. The drama begins with his arrival at the War Office in London, his progress across the Whitehall courtyards accompanied on the soundtrack by the most popular song of that summer of 1956, Anne Shelton's 'Lay Down Your Arms'.

Assigned to the War Office as a Russian language clerk, Hawk's task is to assist MI3 translate intelligence on Russian troop movements. Significantly, this is no mere fiction but based on fact. As the Introduction noted, both Potter and his producer, Trodd, worked for MI3 in the early fifties. In interview, Potter recalled their time at the War Office as simply a farce:

> It was the height of the Cold War – the Korean War had just ended, Hungary was about to begin. MI3's job was basically to draw up the Soviet battle order – where are they, where they move from, where are they going to ... – personnel, troop movements; by all the varieties of information that came in ... [Trodd] was in another section, MI3 C or something. I was in MI3 D on the ground floor of the War Office, in this huge office with just the majors and the colonels and a service sergeant who was like a sort of office administrator.

In the play, memories of national service are linked to wider historical change. Potter moves the action on a year or so to 1956 in order that events coincide with the Suez Crisis and the era of the 'angry young man'. The political and social upheavals of the period are in turn given symbolic expression through the personal dilemmas of the central protagonist. Like Nigel Barton before him, Hawk is a 'torn' hero – caught between the stuffy upper-class milieu of the War Office and his own working-class roots, particularly his uneasy relationship with his coal-miner father.

Like other Potter protagonists (such as Ebenezer in *A Beast with Two Backs*), Hawk is also torn between the contradictory pulls of flesh and spirit. This is made clear by a key sequence in which he is seen nervously approaching a prostitute in Soho and following her to a dingy room at the top of some narrow stairs. Through cross-cutting, the play explicitly counterpoints this scene – Hawk's first ever submission to the desires of 'the flesh' – with his first ever visit to the theatre that same night. Attempts to nourish his soul with high art are contrasted with and undercut by his more basic hunger for sex. Significantly, Potter incorporates within his own play a scene from the play Hawk goes to see: a production of Chekhov's *The Seagull*. Perched awkwardly in the gods, the soldier hears Chekhov's writer character, Trepliov, make a declaration of love to Nina; one which seems to echo his own plight: 'I am lonely ... I feel as cold as if I was in a dungeon ... I want you'.[14]

In this way, art (the 'fiction' of the play) comes to dramatise the essential truth of Hawk's own situation, allowing him to see his own plight more clearly. The inclusion of the Chekhov play within the play thus marks a turning point for Hawk and the drama as a whole. Permitting him to recognise, for the first time, the often blurred lines between reality and fantasy, 'truth' and 'lies', the experience of drama enables him to begin to come to terms with his own inner conflicts.

He does this by transforming himself into a kind of Billy Liar figure. Alone in a London pub, Hawk finds himself the centre of attention when he mischievously decides to use his knowledge of Russian to re-invent himself into the goalkeeper of the visiting Moscow Dynamo football team: 'I Russkie footballist. Dynamo ... I like drink,' he announces to the local pub regulars. It is only when his friend Pete unexpectedly arrives in the bar from Yorkshire and calls him by his real name that his lies are exposed. The soldier nevertheless remains unrepentant. As he later tells Pete, 'It's know your place ... That's what keeps people down. Keeps them like they are.' Telling tall tales has become his liberation, in which everything can be 'kicking away' inside his head.

Imagination (or 'lies') is thus presented as the key to resolving all the conflicts – class, political, generational, sexual – which dog the protagonist in the play. Leaping over the rigidities of each of the battle-lines that separate individuals and 'keeps them like they are', allowing the protagonist to reinvent himself into whomever he chooses to be, it becomes, in Potter's drama, the means to bridge all oppositions – the way to *Lay Down Your Arms*.

From 'the turning point' of the Chekhov scene on, Hawk discovers the power of being a writer. This is made clear at the climax of the play when, amongst assorted low-grade intelligence material at the War Office, the soldier discovers a letter from a Russian tank driver written to his father – a coal-miner in Magnitogorsk. Insisting on reading the letter out to his superior officers, Hawk tells them it is about the relationship between a son and a father who 'obviously haven't gone on too well in the past'. The son, however, has come to realise 'what it must mean and what it must do to your hopes and dreams to be entombed in black tunnels for all your waking life'. The soldier looks up at his superior officers: 'Sometimes, sir, you don't know what you feel until somebody writes it down for you.'

'Writing' becomes the means of revealing 'truth' in the play. Not only does it finally demonstrate to Hawk the absurdity of fighting a Cold War against an enemy who is just like him, it also expresses what he himself could never say to his own father face to face. Allowing identification with an opposing point of view, it heals wounds and resolves divisions, urging enemies everywhere to 'lay down their arms' and make their peace.

Hawk's personal exploration of the blurred lines between reality and fantasy also connects with the drama's historical backdrop insofar as there seems a clear parallel between the private's 'lies' and the wider 'truth games' of the Cold War. Just like a real spy, Hawk has to learn to move easily through a number of different worlds and disguises – soldier in the War Office, working class lad in Yorkshire, even Moscow Dynamo goal-keeper in the London pub – reinventing or fictionalising himself at will. As the closet Red who, by education and accident, finds himself infiltrating the British Establishment and working for MI3, he shares much in common with a double agent.

On one level, this 'infiltration' seems symbolic of the position of the working-class scholarship boy who, given unprecedented opportunities to rise up the Establishment ladder, nevertheless often felt himself to be in a kind of secret rebellion against it. On another, however, it directly relates to the actual infiltration of British Intelligence during the nineteen forties and fifties, particularly its utter compromising at the hands of KGB mole, Kim Philby. Near its close, the play provides a humorous reminder that Philby was still very much active during Hawk's (and Potter's and Trodd's) time at MI3. Bamboozled by all the information on the Suez crisis coming into their office, Hawk's superior officers at least take comfort from an imminent counter-intelligence briefing. Who is giving it, one officer asks? 'Oh, a chap from the Foreign Office,' replies another. 'Fellow by the name of Philby. Kim Philby.'

The reference is significant in the light of *Traitor* (tx. 14.10.71; dir. Alan Bridges), Potter's celebrated BBC *Play for Today* which followed *Lay Down Your Arms* a year later. It, too, exhibits a fascination with the Cold War and in particular the idea of the double agent as metaphor for the crossing of ideological battle-lines of class and politics in English society.

The 1971 play opens not in England and the War Office but in a dingy Moscow apartment where Adrian Harris, the Philby-like traitor of the title – former high-ranking controller in British Intelligence, now defected to the Soviets – awaits the arrival of a group of Western journalists who have obtained special permission to interview him for their newspapers back home. Harris (played by John le Mesurier) is a haunted man – tormented by unhappy memories of public school, guilt over his involvement in the murder of a Russian defector and above all his relationship with his father, an eccentric archaeologist who literally believed in the legend of King Arthur and who instilled in his young son a dream of Camelot which, the play suggests, may be one explanation for the adult's betrayal of his country.

A memory play like *Stand Up, Nigel Barton*, *Traitor* unfolds through a series of flashbacks and, like *Stand Up*, it seeks to build up a convincing psychological dossier on the motives of its central character. In this light, Harris betrays his country because he is chasing his father's vision of Camelot – a dream of perfection which leads him in adulthood to embrace extreme political ideologies that seem to offer a similar panacea to all the world's problems. Fitting into this picture are the flashbacks to the traitor's time at English public school where he is shown humiliated in class by his teacher on account of his bad stutter. Counterpointed with the adult's wincing remembrance of it in the present, this again seems to point to a possible reason why, in his quest for the Camelot of his father, Harris should choose to go against the interests of his own upper class.

Typically for Potter, no such easy explanations of betrayal in terms of personal psychology will quite do, however. Rather, as the play digs deeper into the life of its main protagonist, a series of ambiguities emerge. Constantly interrupting the action of the play is newsreel footage of the Jarrow Hunger Marches – images which seem to suggest that Harris betrayed his class for communism because he believed in the workers' struggle. At the climax of the play, completely drunk, he starts to sing a garbled version of 'I Belong to Glasgow'. He begins to ramble to the disbelieving press men: 'It was an awful shock when I saw for the very first time ... saw for the very first time ... what people lived like.'[15] One possible implication, therefore, is that Harris betrayed England and the upper class for communism when he saw the slums of Glasgow for the very first time.

Characteristically, Potter draws no hard and fast conclusions in *Traitor*. As he suggested in a BBC *Late Night Line-Up* interview, transmitted the same night as the play, perhaps he should 'have put a question-mark' after the title *Traitor*.[16] Not only does the play suggest a complexity of motives driving the central protagonist, it also raises the question of whether Harris's betrayal of his country was really a betrayal at all. Asked by the journalists if he is a traitor, Harris replies, 'To my class, yes. To my country, no ... Not to ... the England of the watermill and ... gentle faces.'

In the play, patriotism is thus wrested away from its normal associations with the Right and ironically shown to be one of the possible underlying causes of an idealism on the Left. Harris' treason is linked to too much patriotism, not too little of it – the idealism of his politics arising from the idealism of his vision of his 'motherland'. He is demonstrably, like Hawk in *Lay Down Your Arms*, a torn hero, caught between the opposing ideologies of the Cold War, pulled by contradictory demands of flesh and spirit. Potter sets up a clear opposition in the play between capitalism as a function of the material and communism as a function of the spirit. On the one hand, there is Harris' view of the 'capitalist press' as being only interested in judging 'a man by his material possessions rather than his mind.' On the other, there is the journalists' observation that all Harris' 'dreams and hopes of a better world' have been reduced to an 'uncomfortable room in an uncomfortable block ... in the biggest soul-destroying bureaucracy the world has ever seen!'

By extension, what Harris seems to symbolise is all things spiritual –

communism, the need for belief and a search for Paradise (Camelot), even at the cost of personal self-sacrifice. In this light, the 'traitor' ironically resembles Potter's Jesus in *Son of Man* – a heroic spiritual seeker after truth, eschewing the temptations of the material world and the physical self in order to follow to its inevitable lonely conclusion, his own private vision: the vision of a better world.

Comparison with *Stand Up, Nigel Barton* is also instructive in this regard. Both it and *Traitor* are memory plays, taking place largely inside one character's head and tracing an emotional trajectory which involves a central male protagonist being uprooted from and betraying his original social class. If the trajectory of *Traitor* is the precise inverse of that of *Stand Up* (away from rather than towards the upper class), both plays nevertheless reveal that journey to be a one-way ticket to alienation and anxiety. There is the same guilty introspection and the same suggestion that the protagonist's actions may be motivated by an emotional need to keep faith with a father who is the site of all his values. There is also, in each play, a similar pivotal classroom scene in which the main character, as a child, learns of the wrongful persecution of those who are different from the dominant group – a persecution which fuels his subsequent rebellion against his 'class'. Finally, as in *Stand Up*, there is the same need for Harris in *Traitor* to 'broadcast' his ideals (and separation from his native origins) to the world, in this case through an interview with Western journalists. Just as with *Stand Up*, that world is shown as a hostile one which does not want to hear the truth. The journalists are largely out to humiliate the turncoat and to tell their readers what they want to hear, namely that the traitor is wretched and unhappy in Moscow. As a result, all attempts by Harris to have his reasons understood merely increase his isolation, leaving him, like Nigel at the close of *Stand Up*, more anxious and unhappy than ever.

If in *Traitor*, the externals of Harris' life and career seem to approximate to the life of Kim Philby, for the 'internals' it can be seen that Potter has drawn on a source much closer to home. By structuring his 1971 play so that it provides a striking inverse symmetry to that of *Stand Up*, he is suggesting that whether upper-class or working-class, betrayal is the inevitable product of crossing the heavily fortified battle-lines which traditionally have separated one class from another in English society.

As the final few shots of the play make clear, however, there is one crucial difference between *Traitor* and *Stand Up*, for Harris, unlike Nigel Barton, is unable even to reveal to others the burden of his guilt. After the climactic scene in which he has drunkenly told of his shock at seeing, for the first time, 'what people lived like', the play cuts back to its beginning, repeating the same sequence of shots of him alone in his apartment, awaiting the arrival of the journalists, which the audience saw in the opening moments. Things, however, are not quite the same – Harris is seen searching amongst the objects in his apartment, as if looking for something. Eventually he finds it: a KGB bugging device stuck to the bottom of a table. The doorbell rings and once more he is seen opening the door of his flat to the Western journalists. As he does so, this time the image freezes and his voice is heard insistent on the soundtrack: 'Remember the microphones and be careful ... For God's sake remember the microphone!'

Unlike Barton, Harris, at the end of *Traitor*, has to keep all of his feelings bottled up inside, in peril possibly of his life if he reveals too much. All of the events in the play, including the supposedly real interview with the journalists, have, in fact, been taking place inside his head, as he waited anxiously for them to arrive. What he allegedly told them is what he would like to confess but in reality will have to repress. Distrusted and unwanted by both sides in the Cold War, his rebellion has come to nothing – even more than Nigel Barton, his great 'stand' has dwindled down to anxiety and paranoia. If the entire play has been a wrestling with himself over whether he should speak out to journalists and what it might be like if he did, the conclusion he finally arrives at is that the truth would only hurt him. With no mechanism of expressing and hence easing his guilt, Harris is fated to replay the events of his past over and over again in his head, perpetually awaiting the knock of 'the strangers outside his door who are really inside his head'.

Outsiders knocking on doors

The phrase is one of Potter's own (the 'stranger outside the house who's really inside your head') which he has used to describe a number of his plays that turn on this same basic plot device: the arrival of a visitor whose appearance triggers off intense introspection within the central protagonist.[17] The development of this motif can be traced across a number of Potter plays of the late sixties and early seventies. In this way, it is possible to see how it evolved from basic origins into a fully elaborated structural feature of the work, present for its own sake as a marker of the single play *oeuvre* Potter was consciously trying to create during this period and which culminated, arguably, in his controversial 1976 play, *Brimstone and Treacle*.

As Chapter 1 noted, the ambiguous outsider who disrupts and overturns established hierarchies was a key sixties' archetype: one which Potter exploited fully in his *Wednesday Plays*, *The Confidence Course*, *Message for Posterity* and *Son of Man*. In a number of his other works of the period, one finds, however, a very different conception of the outsider – namely, as in *Emergency Ward-9* and *A Beast with Two Backs*, the outsider as foreigner, the 'intruder'.

Both of these conceptions are combined in *The Bonegrinder*: an ITV play from the same year as *A Beast*, which was almost universally savaged by the TV critics.[18] In retrospect, however, this work takes on new interests, when viewed against other Potter plays. *The Bonegrinder* (tx. 13.5.68; dir. Joan Kemp-Welch) revolves around George King, a respectable English middle-class gentleman who nevertheless decides one day to visit a seedy London pub in search of prostitutes, whilst his wife is absent caring for her dying sister. There, all he succeeds in doing is meeting Sam, a loud American seaman with a bitter hatred of the English. Immediately, uninhibited 'Uncle Sam' realises he has the perfect target in repressed 'King George'. He quotes some lines from *Jack and the Beanstalk* that shed light on the title of Potter's play: 'Fe-fi-fo-fum / I smell the blood of an Englishman / ... Be he alive or be he dead / I'll grind his bones to make my bread'. Ominously, he adds: 'It'll be nice visiting you and your little wife. Very nice.'[19]

True to his word, Sam soon succeeds in blackmailing his way into the King household where he begins to take over, ordering the guilty Englishman to fetch and carry for him. As 'Uncle Sam' starts to make life impossible for them, George and his wife Gladys are seen sitting up in bed wondering what to do. It is Gladys who appeals to English national pride, urging her husband that the only way to get rid of the intruder is to kill him. George is eventually persuaded to creep downstairs where he bludgeons Sam to death with a coal-hammer – all the time repeating the rhyme: 'I'll grind his bones to make my bread.' When Gladys appears, however, she immediately calls the police, as her husband realises he has been the victim of a cruel trick. The very last scene of the play reveals why, like Sam, she too can never be happy with life in suburbia beside George: 'And you thought you'd go whoring on the very night [sister] Emma choked to death ... Daddy always said the worst thing a gentleman could do ... was to let the side down'.

While clearly a comic allegory on the post-war decline of England and the corresponding global rise of the USA ('King George' versus 'Uncle Sam'), this drama, like *A Beast with Two Backs*, works on a number of other levels too. In a 1973 *Guardian* interview, Potter claimed the idea for his play had come from seeing 'a crazy Canadian sailor in a pub one afternoon in Ladbroke Grove.'[20] The situation he develops from this is significant: repressed George goes in search of sexual relief from a prostitute and ends up bringing home what he fears most. Insinuating his way into middle-class suburbia, Sam embodies all the uninhibited values of the sixties counter-culture, with its challenge to traditional hierarchies and social hypocrisies. Akin to the 'mad' outsider heroes of Pinter's *The Servant* and Potter's own *The Confidence Course*, this 'crazy' working-class sailor succeeds for a time in reversing normal power relations (literally making middle-class George his servant), before his rebellion is finally crushed.

Comparison of *The Bonegrinder* with *A Beast with Two Backs*, is also instructive. In *A Beast*, one finds a similar intrusion into an insular English milieu by a *foreigner* (the Italian), which is also fiercely resisted. As noted previously, the play directly linked this suppression to that of the 'beast' of human sexuality. In *The Bonegrinder*, the invasion of the intruding foreigner is also strongly linked to sexuality, in this case George's desire for prostitutes. It becomes the same guilty secret, the nightmare of its exposure literally arriving on his doorstep in the shape of an uninhibited American. The embodiment of all George's worst fears, Sam is almost willed into life as a consequence of the other's sexual guilt. The resulting problem is one that both husband and wife have to deal with – significantly, in their bedroom in the middle of the night as their uninvited 'guest' plays havoc with their lives and relationship.

Hence what *The Bonegrinder* seems to be dramatising, in coded form, is the difficulties of accommodating male sexual desire within marriage. For the sake of respectability, George tries to repress the 'beast' (kill Sam) but the damage to his marriage has already been done. However hard he tries to make amends to Gladys for his furtive whoring, normality cannot be restored to their relationship, with the result that she finally abandons him (to the police), just as he abandoned her. As at the close of *A Beast*, the message is that the logical consequence of repression of the 'beast inside' is isolation and disaster for the male protagonist. Just as Sam represents the new sexual openness of the counter-culture, the suggestion is that if a marriage relationship is ever to work, guilty sexual secrets must be aired in the first instance, rather than allowed to fester until their inevitable discovery.

Two years later, Potter was to return to the 'problem' of sex in suburbia in *Angels Are So Few* (tx. 5.11.70; dir. Gareth Davies) – the first of his dramas in the BBC *Play for Today* slot.[21] This time, the problem is presented not through the perspective of a middle-class husband but a suburban housewife.

Bored and sexually frustrated, Cynthia Nicholls one day receives a visit from a strange young man, Michael Biddle, who announces on her doorstep that he is an 'angel'. Seemingly filled with a sense of wonder at Creation, he begins to tell her of wondrous things – how 'we are free … with a great bag full of images … choices … chances … free to remember, free to change our memories, free to be or to do what we want.' (p. 32)[22]

On one level, this gospel of hope echoes the speeches of Jesus in *Son of Man* and recalls remarks Potter made during pre-publicity for that earlier play about how he had wanted to write 'about a man who thought that he might be Christ.'[23] Also similar to *Son of Man* is the initial scepticism with which others treat the ramblings of the 'mad' outsider. In *Angels*, Cynthia ushers Biddle quickly out of the door. As Potter suggested in 1969, 'if Jesus came today ... we would want to shut the door on him.'[24]

If this is the inspiration for *Angels* (how would a would-be Messiah fare today?), in contrast to Jesus in *Son of Man*, the audience is left in no doubt that Biddle is indeed quite mad. This emerges in a subsequent scene in which he is seen taking tea with an elderly couple, the Cawsers, who live on the same street as Cynthia. A Welsh lady with a strong religious upbringing, Mrs Cawser begins to tell Biddle of a pulpit banner she remembers from chapel-going days as a child long ago. Embroidered on it was a picture of two little children picking flowers, poised right on the very edge of a precipice: 'And this golden-haired little boy ... was stretching out his arm to try and pick [one]. It was obvious that [he] was going to fall' (p. 43). Miraculously, however, a beautiful angel was on hand – a hovering guardian to protect the child from falling.

The 'golden-haired' child in peril as a result of its own curiosity and desire; the imminence of a fall from a great height; a protecting angel – the metaphor is of a Fall from grace and a loving God which, as with *A Beast* and *Hide and Seek*, can be connected to the idea of a loss of sexual innocence and acquisition of 'forbidden knowledge'.[25] In *Angels*, the sexual connotations become clear through Biddle's shocked response to Mrs Cawser's assertion that the angel was a lady angel: 'You mean with tits? No, no ... There is no sex in heaven.' Besides, he remarks: 'I'm protected ... I am *safe*. I am an angel ... A celestial being' (p. 47).

As this makes clear, Biddle has fantasised himself into an angel as a means of avoiding his own sexuality. The scene is set for the climax of the play in which Cynthia frustratedly decides to make a pass at him when this 'angel' shows up at her house once more. Potter's original script directions for the seduction scene are revealing here since the imagery evoked is that of the biblical Fall. Cynthia is the tempting serpent: 'she coils her hands together' (p. 70); 'he watches her like a man watches a snake slithering inexorably towards him' (p. 73). Biddle, meanwhile, is 'like a man going to his execution' (p. 69), until finally and literally stripped of all illusions of being an angel, he runs away from her after the seduction: 'a man stripped of all his magic ... all his charisma' (p. 87).

In *Angels*, sex does not bring 'counter-culture' liberation but a kind of blankness and despair. Not for nothing did Potter subtitle his play a 'fable for television' for in its ending *Angels* has a strong moral resonance.[26] As the writer suggested to the *Radio Times*, the play is about 'the way we manipulate our fantasies to protect ourselves and what happens to us when they are ripped away.'[27] On one level, having his 'wings' ripped off and being forced to shed his illusions might seem a healthy act, a 'cure' for Biddle. The same could be said for both characters' liberation from sexual repression. Through his ending, however, Potter suggests that the stripping away of old beliefs is invariably a painful rather than a redemptive process. Forced to recognise his own mortality, Biddle feels only spiritual emptiness at the close. His world has been drained of the 'wonder' he earlier felt – a process in which sex has played the crucial role and which the script explicitly likens to a Fall.

How to recapture that lost sense of wonder is very much the theme of *Schmoedipus* (tx. 20.6.74; dir. Barry Davis), a subsequent Potter *Play for Today* and the third in his 'outsiders knocking on doors' cycle. The title comes from the comic Jewish exclamation: 'Oedipus Schmoedipus, what does it matter so long as he loves his mother!' As this suggests, the play dwells upon the relationship between a mother and a long-lost 'son', in a kind of psychodrama which, in the eighties, Potter would subsequently rewrite as a movie: *Track 29* (see Chapter 6).

The setting for the TV play is once more repressed English suburbia, the focus on a dissatisfied housewife. Elizabeth Carter is sexually frustrated and bored, not least by her husband Tom's obsession with model railways. One day, when he is out at work, she discovers a strange young man on her doorstep – a Canadian called Glen, who announces that he is her abandoned 'baby boy' from an unwanted teenage pregnancy long ago.

Schmoedipus thus rings the changes on aspects of *The Bonegrinder* – the 'crazy' Canadian, the intruding outsider – as well as of *Angels* – the bored suburban housewife, the doorstep revelation of a strange young man. Here, however, the outsider has arrived for a specific purpose. As he tells his 'mother', he wants to have his English childhood since he is fed up with being a grown-up: 'There's no fun in it. No magic ... Nothing' (pp. 50–1).[28]

The 'magic' or 'wonder' which Biddle felt in *Angels* is here explicitly connected with childhood. Childhood is portrayed as the 'angelic' state which, as with Biddle, all adults must lose when they become sexually aware but which they yearn to recapture. In the 1974 play, this is dramatised through the figure of Elizabeth's husband Tom and his obsession with toy trains: 'Probably the happiest time of my life,' he sighs, as he swaps childhood memories of train-spotting with a friend from work (p. 62).

Juxtaposed with these scenes of Tom at work is the depiction of Glen's suckling behaviour towards his supposed 'mother'. On one level, this functions as a humorous magnification of Freud's notion of the Oedipus Complex, here emphasised by the fact Glen is a fully grown adult: 'I spy with my little eye something beginning with B,' he whispers flirtatiously to Elizabeth at one point, staring through her blouse (p. 23). As with *Angels*, the final scenes of the play make clear, however, that such seduction attempts are the product not of male but of female desire: an attempt by Elizabeth to escape the dreariness of her suburban existence.

This is made apparent when, after Glen has given a schmaltzy rendition of the sentimental old song 'Mother', Elizabeth falls asleep, only to wake much later to find her 'son' gone. Alarmed, she calls over her next-door neighbour Dorothy and slowly the story of her teenage pregnancy begins to unravel. She confesses to Dorothy how she was seduced at a fair by the man who ran the dodgem cars, in an encounter that became a rape. Suddenly, she looks up, as she seems to hear a door closing: 'He's gone. Gone away,' she whispers (p. 88).

Glen has gone because Elizabeth has at last brought out into the open what she had 'kept inside herself for so long' – namely, that he was the product of a rape trauma (p. 84). As husband Tom arrives unexpectedly from work and begins to take control of the situation, she starts to ramble: 'I put the pillow over his face. His little pink wrinkly face … It didn't hurt him or anything … He was only two days old, you see' (pp. 94–5).

To Dorothy's dismay, Tom is completely unconcerned about these revelations, muttering it is only a 'game'. Panic-stricken, the neighbour runs out of the house, leaving the couple to their private world. Tom quickly becomes stern, telling Elizabeth she simply must not involve other people in their games. She, however, is sure Glen will return: 'He's bound to come back.' As long as he does not break the trains, warns Tom, adopting the role of a stern father. Potter's final script directions are significant: 'Smiling, he goes out to the kitchen. She chews her nails' (p. 99).

Elizabeth's fantasising of the 'outsider who is really inside her head' has not been an aid to psychological recovery but, as for Harris in *Traitor*, part of an endless mental replaying of past trauma and guilt. Glen is 'bound to come back' because her problems as a bored and frustrated housewife remain. Her attempts through fantasy to escape from her domestic prison have ironically become part of her husband's own ritualised retreat from the adult world into a kind of deluded infantilism; part of the very 'game', that is, from which she is trying to flee.

Taking all three of the 'outsider' plays together, it is possible to see how each mounts an attack, in the name of the sixties' and seventies' counterculture, on middle-class English suburban values. As suggested by the theories of R. D. Laing, the entry of the 'mad' outsider hero exposes the real madness as lying at the very heart of the 'bourgeois' home and family (see

Chapter 1). Each work focuses on the problems of marriage – boredom, frustration, sexual repression – and presents these as almost an inevitability for both spouses. Adultery features in all three plays: explicit in *The Bonegrinder* and *Angels Are So Few*; implied and suggested at certain points in *Schmoedipus*. Each, however, presents sex with a stranger as disastrous. George's (attempted) whoring brings havoc to his home in *The Bonegrinder* while *Schmoedipus* and *Angels* present two different versions of sexual assault – the fairground rape that haunts Elizabeth; the 'male rape' of Biddle by Cynthia which the drama equates with a Fall.

Common to all three plays is the figure of the outsider – the long-haired drifter who is by turns lover, child, intruder. In *The Bonegrinder* he is principally a combination of the first and third of these – a manifestation both of guilt over a desire for prostitutes and the 'foreigner' who can be linked to the Italian in *A Beast*. In *Angels*, the stranger's initial wonder and innocence link him more with a child; one who 'falls' in the course of the play to become a reluctant lover. Finally, in *Schmoedipus*, the outsider is the memory of sexual assault – the phantom seducer who nevertheless longs to recapture the wonder of childhood and rekindle a 'dead' mother-son relationship. The fact that each of these plays shares the same plot device ('the outsider who is really inside the head') would seem to imply linkage between these respective themes: connections in the work, therefore, between childhood wonder, the fall and sexual guilt in marriage.

Storms of faith

'It is Eros and not Thanatos who mostly cavorts upon our screens and I do not doubt that it is more entertaining to see someone pretending to make love than someone else pretending to die,' wrote Potter in 1983 of *Joe's Ark* (tx. 14.2.74; dir. Alan Bridges).[29] First transmitted as a BBC *Play for Today* only several months before *Schmoedipus*, this play in many ways functions as Thanatos to the other's Eros, providing a detailed on-screen exploration of the experience of dying (as opposed to the medium's more normal territory, the excitement of violent death). It is also a very difficult work to view now in the light of Potter's own death since this is a play about cancer. Eerily, it was transmitted exactly twenty years ago to the day (St Valentine's Day) before Potter would learn he was dying of the disease. Like *Schmoedipus*, it too begins with an outsider knocking on a door.

The play opens on Joe, the embittered owner of a pet shop in a Welsh town. Upstairs, Lucy, his only daughter, is dying of cancer. Meanwhile, far from home, his estranged son, Bobby, tours the working men's clubs with his stand-up comedy act and stripper girlfriend, unaware of his sister's illness. Suddenly, there is a knock on the door and Joe finds a strange young man, John, on his doorstep. Announcing that he is a friend of Lucy's from her time at Oxford University (where she had spent only two terms before illness struck), he tells Joe he has hitched all the way to Wales because he is in love with the dying girl. As the play unfolds, a variety of other characters are introduced – each converging on Joe and the little shop, each reflecting and being reflected by their attitudes to the same central event, death. Finally, having been contacted at Lucy's request, Bobby arrives just a minute too late to see his dead sister.

As Potter himself suggested, such a scenario in summary 'sounds like a winning entry in a *New Statesman* Competition parodying gloomy pretension',[30] and it was generally as an exploration of family trauma, illness and death that the play was received and reviewed on first transmission. Potter subsequently observed that few seemed to notice at the time that he was really 'writing about religious themes.'[31]

In fact, what the play is dramatising is a crisis of faith caused by the effects of serious illness. This finds its clearest expression in Joe, Lucy's chapel-going father, who cannot reconcile literal belief in a loving God with the physical reality of his daughter's dying. As with Biddle in *Angels*, simple child-like faith in a divine order has been ruptured by personal adult experience. This is most starkly represented through Joe's quarrels with Watkins, the local preacher. When the latter visits his shop in an effort to restore his faith, Joe is contemptuous of the other's argument that the variety of animal species in the shop is proof of a benign 'pattern' or 'overall purpose'. As a pet shop owner, Joe is all too aware of the Darwinian, 'survival of the fittest', ruthlessness of the animal kingdom. One cichlid in amongst that tank of fish, he points out, and it would 'gobble them up in two seconds flat. Snap! Swallow!' (p. 110)[32]

Meanwhile, in chapel, Joe literally 'stands up' and quarrels with the preacher during his sermon. Reflecting on the Old Testament story of Noah, the one just man saved from the flood, Watkins declares humanity to be no less wicked today than it was before the Great Flood: 'We are none of us good enough for this earth.' Suddenly, Joe is on his feet, shouting: 'No! That's not true!... You've *had* your life, Daniel ... You've got no right' (p. 99).

Joe's protest is thus against the notion of an avenging Old Testament God (the ruthlessness of 'an eye for an eye, a tooth for a tooth', noted in *A Beast*) that could permit such suffering as that of his own daughter, with no possibility of salvation or redemption. It is the assumption that she does not deserve to live with which he takes issue; that the sick person is a sinner (see Introduction).

If Joe embodies 'spiritual' questions about death, Lucy, stripped of all the 'details' of life and reduced to the bare bones of mortal survival, undoubtedly represents the physical. The two protagonists thus resolve themselves into a familiar Potter dichotomy: a division between flesh and spirit. Ironically, however, it is Lucy who signals the potential *spiritual* turning-point in the drama – the beginnings of a movement away from despair which helps set in relief some of her father's most crushing religious doubts. Receiving a visit from her doctor, just as earlier Joe had received one from his preacher, she begins to ask what happens to people at the exact moment of death. After some hesitation, the doctor replies that he has never seen a person die who, knowing what was happening, did not accept it in peace. Lucy, however, has to know: 'you mean – something natural – takes over' – like the dying animals she has seen in her father's shop? The doctor's response is significant: 'Yes, I think that's one of the very few reasons why I personally believe in – well, God' (p. 125).

Ironically, through its observation of the processes of the flesh, medical science provides a more convincing reason for the existence of God than orthodox religion in the shape of Watkins, since it seems to gesture at the existence of something universal, beyond the individual self. It is here that *Joe's Ark* begins to move towards a tentative resolution of the fundamental flesh-spirit dichotomy which runs through Potter's writing, for in this scene 'spiritual' is linked to 'physical' through the notion of 'instinct'. This, in turn, helps shed light on the very end of the play when, summoned upstairs by the doctor, Joe gazes 'astonished, unbelieving' at Lucy's face, 'placid, dead' (p. 129).

Spontaneously sinking to his knees, he mutters a prayer in Welsh whilst 'from below, like an answer', Potter's script directions specifically indicate the viewer should hear the cry of a big, brightly coloured cockatoo that Joe keeps in his shop. Coming downstairs, Joe meets Bobby, his prodigal son returned: 'She's with your mam,' he tells him. 'A minute ago ... I was with her ... She sent her love and said she was going home ... *As though to a child* That's where your Mam is, see' (p. 130).

Having *apparently* witnessed his daughter go to her death 'placid', Joe's simple child-like faith in God has *apparently* been restored. As a result, he is able to express to his son, 'as to a child', his old simple belief in Heaven, having offered up a prayer to God: a prayer that while clearly an expression of grief and loss nevertheless seems to find its 'answer' in the cry of the cockatoo, the cry of instinct. It is this notion of an instinctive child-like faith, unclouded by adult doubts and questions, which in turn seems to nudge at a resolution to the spiritual crisis explored in the play. Instinctive faith takes over from intellectual doubt at the end, with childhood functioning as the site of natural belief. The implication is that one has either to believe or not believe in an ultimate good (God), choosing whether to trust adult intellect or one's original childhood instincts.

What is significant about *Joe's Ark* is that the play does not so much come down on one side or the other as hold both possibilities in taut suspension. Its ending is almost completely ambiguous, full of questions. Did the doctor simply fool Lucy into accepting her death in peace ? Did Lucy appear to die peacefully in order to help shore up her father's faith?[33] Is Joe's return to his old faith simply regressive delusion – an easy means of self-comfort, a father's attempt to console his other 'child', Bobby? Or has he, like some latter-day Noah, genuinely weathered the storms of faith, glimpsing from the storm-tossed 'ark' of his pet-shop an apparently greater good moving behind the rain-clouds?

Joe's Ark sustains all these possibilities. In keeping with its questioning religious perspective, it finally leaves it up to the viewer to find significance or otherwise in the events it portrays. On one level, Lucy's death represents the defeat of every human hope insofar as all her struggles eventually come to nothing. As if cursed, brother Bobby arrives a minute too late to satisfy her final wishes. On another, however, it stands for precisely the opposite. Out of her passing comes good – father and son are reunited, both in their own ways having instinctively returned to a natural childhood 'home' of belief and values.

Ironically, behind the 'gloomy pretension' of this 1974 drama, it is therefore possible to discern a more optimistic view shining through. As Potter suggested in 1983, the play in its resolution 'makes more than a wry nod at possibilities which can comprehend pain or disgust or the implacable presence of death itself.'[34] It is for this reason that *Joe's Ark* occupies a crucial place in an *oeuvre* that by the mid seventies was beginning to shift ground in terms of its attitudes and outlook. To understand why, the play has to be looked at in the perspective of Potter's next three single TV plays – all of which had been earmarked for transmission by the BBC in the same month, April 1976. In the event, one, *Brimstone and Treacle*, was famously banned; but before the history of this is examined in detail, it is worth attempting to resituate it within the context of the sequence of work of which, originally, it was intended to be just one part.

1976 'trilogy'

In his 1978 Introduction to the published stage play version, Potter wrote of *Brimstone and Treacle*: '[it] came at the end of a particular sequence of work which was taking me clear of an in-turned spiritual nihilism and on towards a new and (for me) startling but exhilarating trust in the order of things'.[35] Citing *Joe's Ark* as a predecessor, he went on to indicate how such plays were born not only out of his physical struggles with a painful and debilitating illness but in tandem, out of a number of 'unresolved, almost unacknowledged 'spiritual' questions'.[36] If these are clearly evident in *Joe's Ark*, Potter explores them in much further depth in his 1976 plays, advancing the 1974 drama's qualified optimism to a more settled conclusion.

Where Adam Stood (tx. 21.4.76; dir. Brian Gibson) is perhaps the most immediately close of the three 1976 works to *Joe's Ark*. A period drama, screened not in the BBC-1 *Play for Today* slot but on BBC-2, it is credited as being 'based on' an external source – Edmund Gosse's famous autobiography, *Father and Son*.[37] In fact, Potter centres his play around only one incident from the Gosse book: a choice which offers significant clues to his own preoccupations at this time and the direction in which they were moving.

The play focuses upon Gosse's account of the ill-fated attempts of his naturalist father to reconcile fundamentalist belief in the book of Genesis with Darwin's emerging theories of evolution in the mid nineteenth century. Like *Joe's Ark*, the drama thus portrays a crisis of faith in a patriarchal figure, brought about when a literal belief in the Bible is contradicted by adult experience. Moreover, in both cases, Darwinian notions of survival of the fittest are revealed as instrumental in shaking faith. Both widowers, Phillip Gosse and Joe, find their belief coming under severe pressure as a result of observing the processes of the natural world.

While for Joe such a crisis of faith brings only despair and disillusion, Phillip Gosse's response is one of dogged defiance. Refuting the import of Darwin's theories, he invents a theory of his own – the 'Omphalos' theory which is explicitly designed to counter the fossil evidence that seems to contradict accounts in Genesis of the spontaneous creation of Man.[38] Gosse's clinging to religious dogma in the face of the scientific evidence is paralleled in the play by his blindness to the true reality of his son's needs. Edmund is an ailing child, afflicted by a severe cough which acts as a metaphor for his suffocation under his father's piety. Gosse senior is unconcerned, however, commenting merely that 'if it is the Lord's will' that Edmund should be taken to be beside his dead mother, then so be it. As with *Joe's Ark*, the assumption which the child has to struggle against is that the sick person is a sinner: 'all our pains and ailments … are sent by the Lord to chastise us for some definite fault,' asserts his Old Testament patriarch of a father, urging his son to pray.

Edmund's father and his fundamentalist beliefs are thus potentially life-threatening to the boy, endangering both his health and survival through a fatalism which, in its desire to be gathered up 'in the arms of Jesus', becomes almost a death-wish. Oblivious to the fact he is the cause of the nightmares, Gosse senior cannot understand why the boy wakes up at night, screaming, 'I don't want to!' Instead, he urges yet more prayer, suggesting the child's troubles may all be God's punishment for having coveted a toy ship in the window of the local village shop. An image of desire as well as of freedom from the restrictions of his father, the ship is implicitly linked in the play with the boy's yearning for his dead mother. Cut into sequences depicting Edmund's dreams are shots of a painting of his mother in which, clearly visible in the background, is a sailing ship. The desire for the toy ship is really a symbol of the child's longing for his mother who has departed for the 'far shore'; something which his father, whose Puritanism forbids toys, cannot comprehend.

The ship also stands for another kind of desire in the play. As Edmund stares at it in the shop window, Mary Teague, a mad woman of the village, approaches him. Asking if he likes the ship, she tells him to come along with her to 'Paradise'. Curious, the child is led into some nearby woods where, muttering 'ship, ship, ship', she attempts to interfere with him. The motif is the familiar Potter one of sexual assault which, as in *A Beast* and *Hide and Seek*, can be seen as a version of the Fall.[39] If like the Fall in *A Beast*, the image of the ship seems to link the motifs of a dead mother, 'guilty' patriarch and an awakening from childhood innocence, the crucial difference with *Where Adam Stood* is that the victim resists and escapes. Crying out, 'you're mad', Edmund throws a stone in the mad woman's face and succeeds in fleeing her clutches. The child is able to survive and cope with his trauma; a fact which marks a progression both in Potter's work as a whole and within the play, provides the precedent by which Edmund can begin to resist that even greater threat to his health and survival, his father.

This is made clear at the very end of the drama when, after more nightmares, his father again urges his son to pray. Earnestly entreated to say what the Good Lord has advised, Edmund's reply to his father is devastating: 'The Good Lord says I am to have the ship.' Stunned but unable because of his dogmatic belief to broach any argument with the judgements of 'the Lord', Gosse senior exits, troubled, from the room. Having gained the measure of his father and his religion, Edmund can sleep peacefully at last. His final actions in the play are telling. Getting out of bed, he carefully wedges a chair against the handle of his bedroom door. No more will his well-being be threatened by his father as, on the soundtrack, the voice of William Brackley (one of the proponents of the new Darwinism to which Gosse senior is so implacably opposed) is heard, spelling out the first principles of the theory of natural selection:

> Any creature, any life-form, which can, by however small a degree, adapt to the harshness of its own environment is the one that is going to persist. Extinction awaits those creatures which cannot meet the complexity of the

conditions under which they live. The fit survive. The unfit perish.

The proof of Darwin's theories is ironically to be found in the home of one of its staunchest enemies. Edmund has found a way of coping with his environment and will persist. His father, unable to take account either of his son or of the wider discoveries of science, is doomed to extinction. As in *Lay Down Your Arms*, imagination or 'lies' is shown to be the key to survival. Gosse senior cannot adapt because he believes in the absolute, literal truth of the Bible. In contrast, by using his imagination and telling 'lies', his son takes the first step away from literalism – becoming a storyteller, a writer.

Central to the drama is the idea that events in the Book of Genesis are not literally true but at best, metaphor. It is this which helps explain the Fall that does not happen in this play. Unlike previous Potter protagonists, Edmund cannot truly 'fall' because the play demonstrates such a concept not to be literally true. 'Where Adam Stood' once, notions of a Fall into irredeemable sin are replaced with an emphasis on the centrality of 'storytelling' and metaphor. It is this rejection of the Old Testament assumption of a literal and irrevocable Fall from God which seems to mark a progression in Potter's writing towards a new 'trust in the order of things'. As he put it in interview, *Where Adam Stood*, like Gosse's *Father and Son* memoir, represents the throwing off of 'other people's interpretation' of religion – the fact that 'you have to assert something about yourself in order to be yourself. When the child put the chair against the door, that said what the whole book had said – 'I will be me', said the child.'[40]

In his banned play *Brimstone and Treacle* (originally to have been transmitted on 6 April 1976; dir. Barry Davis), Potter takes both the consequences of escape from under the shadow of a permanent Fall and the revolt against 'other people's interpretation of religion' to their logical conclusion. As its title suggests, the remedy which *Brimstone and Treacle* prescribes is old-fashioned, albeit one sugared for popular consumption.[41] Potter deploys the familiar plot device of the 'outsider knocking on the door' – only in this case, in a conscious inversion of *Angels Are So Few*, the young man knocking outside believes himself to be a demon not an angel.

As the play progresses, the visitor begins to transform the suburban household into which he has insinuated his way. His hosts, Mr and Mrs Bates, have a daughter, Pattie, left severely brain-damaged after a horrific car accident. Ostensibly because of his daughter's 'vegetable' condition, Mr Bates is a man who has lost all faith: 'there is no God and there are no miracles' that will bring Pattie back, he tells his wife. Mrs Bates, by contrast, is a woman who believes simply and absolutely: 'I'd sooner be dead than think like that,' she replies.[42]

For Martin, the demonic visitor, this unhappy household is the perfect breeding ground for evil. When husband and wife are both out, he seizes the opportunity he has been seeking: the rape of helpless Pattie. On returning, her mother, however, senses a change in her daughter, not for the worse but for the better. 'There is a definite *light* in her eyes', she tells Martin. 'A real sense of – of something trying to speak to us.'

To the demon's astonishment, Mrs Bates asks him to help her pray to God for Pattie. The result is 'a purple-prosed prayer' by Martin, 'ranging through various styles and accents' (Cathedral English, Irish Catholicism, American Evangelism) in 'a ghostly reflection of clerical voices we have all heard'. In this way, parodying 'certain familiar forms of faith', the play tries to draw a clear moral – namely, that a religion which becomes ritualised into cant and dogma provides a perfect camouflage for evil.[43]

Martin's prayer for Pattie prepares for the climax of the play when, in the dead of night, the demon sneaks downstairs to the girl's divan – a second rape on his mind. This time, his assault seems to shock her into speech. The whole household having been awakened, the Bates rush downstairs to find Martin gone but their screaming daughter apparently 'cured'. Turning to her father, Pattie asks 'What happened – ?' By way of reply, the TV version of *Brimstone* reveals in brief flashback what really did happen on the night of her accident – the night she discovered her father in bed with her best friend, Susan. The accident followed as a direct consequence. Running tearfully out of her friend's flat on to the road, Pattie was struck by a passing vehicle. As the play returns to the 'present', a family tableau is revealed: Pattie stares up, confused; Mrs Bates turns to her husband overjoyed, the long-prayed-for 'miracle' a reality at last. Bates simply stares down at his daughter – unhappy, guilty.

Brimstone and Treacle's cure is thus an unorthodox one: sexual assault as a form of shock therapy. As such, it is a direct inversion of *Angels Are So Few*, for here the supernatural outsider is the attacker not the victim and the forced seduction becomes a kind of Redemption, not a Fall. Exact mirror images, the two plays function as book-ends for the crisis of faith – the 'unacknowledged spiritual questions' – which Potter admitted in 1978 he had been exploring in other works in between.

In interview, Potter called his play 'an inverted parable' – the inverted moral of which is that out of evil can come good.[44] If sexual assault is the 'evil', the play shows it has the capacity to work its own kind of 'good' in terms of releasing repressed memories and guilt. It is symbolically significant that it is only when Martin rapes Pattie a second time that she is 'awoken' from her catatonic spell. As the flashbacks make clear, the girl relives at the end not Martin's first assault but the sexual trauma involving her father. There is a causal connection between Pattie witnessing this and her subsequent accident and illness. As with the similarly handicapped Rufus in *A Beast*, Pattie is the victim almost of an Old Testament logic of transgression and retribution in which she has been 'struck dumb' by the shock of exposure to a parent copulating. This is the secret 'forbidden knowledge' which has had to be locked away inside her head.

In turn, the fact that Pattie's illness arises as a direct consequence of Mr Bates' sexual desires is related to the notion of the sins of the father being visited on the child. Moreover, that the 'sexcrime' should be committed with the daughter's 'best friend', yet the sexual trauma revolve around Pattie herself, suggests a metaphor for incest. Martin the rapist becomes Bates' secret demon self: the embodiment of his incestuous desires for his daughter. Like Sam in *The Bonegrinder*, he is a projection of guilt: the intruder from the streets who is also inside the head.

If the play shows the demon to be literally at the heart of suburbia, at the same time it also indicates him to be functioning in the name of a greater good. When Martin thinks he is doing evil, he is actually changing others' lives for the better. The demon lover is paradoxically a transforming angel and, while blissfully ignorant of the true import of the actions and motives of those around her, the prayerful Mrs Bates is the only one of the characters who is able to sense this.

Brimstone and Treacle thus ultimately affirms a simple instinctive faith 'in the order of things'. While Martin and Mr Bates go through the play with a variety of hidden motives which finally prove to be their undoing, Mrs Bates simply prays to God for a 'miracle' and is granted one in the end. As Potter suggested in interview:

> The weakness of the play was maybe that I caricatured her too much but I knew what I was trying to do which was to make the one genuinely good person in it a fool so you couldn't get a handle on it. Just like with religion, you can't get a handle on it. You just have to know or not know. People either believe or they don't believe.[45]

Martin's knowing parodies of religion and Mr Bates' nihilism are both exposed as inadequate in the face of Mrs Bates' child-like faith which wins through in the end. Sophisticated or worldly adult attitudes thus blind religious truth. According to Potter, true religion is

> the world behind the world that these forces, Evil, Good, contend. And they don't contend where the Good has all the good lines. It is a mix which is what I believe it is like, occupying a religious sensibility ... Contending forces fight within and they're not recognisable. You don't know which is which except she knew, Mrs Bates knew, in some odd way.[46]

'Good' can come out of 'Evil' because to Potter, these are not such rigidly defined moral categories as much organised religion would have us believe. On one level, this is a liberation, for like Edmund in *Where Adam Stood* it allows escape from 'other people's interpretations' of religion and a throwing off of old Fall notions of sexual guilt and sin. On another, however, a collapse in conventional moral categories and an attendant moral relativism bring new sets of problems. As with Pattie's return to speech (and accusation) in *Brimstone*, there are consequences to be faced.

Double Dare, Potter's third 1976 play (tx. 6.4.76; dir. John McKenzie), points to the dangers that attend a collapse of conventional categories and distinctions, moral or otherwise. As with so many Potter plays, the title is from an Al Bowlly tune, 'I Double Dare You' and the song reflects the themes. In this case, the 'double dare' is first, how far will an actress go in the pursuit of her profession and second, how far will a writer go in blurring the distinctions between his fictions and his own life?

Helen, a beautiful young actress, agrees to meet Martin, a television playwright, in a large London hotel because she has been told he wishes to write a part for her in his next play. As they talk, both, however, cannot help glancing across to another table where a corpulent client is plying a girl from an escort agency with dinner and wine. Martin is very nervous. He has been ill and is suffering from a writer's block. The object of the meeting, he tells Helen, is to 'release' him from this block since the tension in their real encounter will be 'merely anticipating the kind of tension between a man and a girl' he sees in his new play. When Helen points out that the client at the next table tried to pick her up, Martin spills the contents of his glass over the table: 'That's what I'm writing about – a girl from an escort agency comes along to meet a client.' And it is Helen he has in mind for the part of the girl, Carol.[47]

The actress grows increasingly uneasy at these too unlikely coincidences and Martin's line of questioning. As a writer, he is obsessed with the border-lines between reality and fantasy and the question, 'how real are invented things?', yet he is also obsessed with her and where she draws the line as to 'how far she will go in the pursuit of her profession'. He cites some examples of her past work, including a commercial (a parody by Potter of a real seventies' commercial) in which she is seen sucking seductively on a chocolate bar, called a 'Fraggie Bar'. 'All I want to know', asks Martin, is whether 'the director of that commercial ... explicitly [said] ... this chocolate is a penis'. Martin is questioning the boundaries between public and private acts. Should the line turn out to be blurred, what would that make a woman whose profession means she has to 'perform' anywhere, any time, with anyone – a prostitute?[48]

If this explains the linking of Helen and Carol, the arrival of Martin's producer friend, Ben, sheds light on the other half of the 'Double Dare' – how far a writer will go. 'Can't you guess?' the producer asks Helen. 'He's in love with you'. Helen is sickened, even more so when Ben insists she will get a good part out of it. 'Whore, actress, yes?' she retorts. 'They get mixed up, don't they, Martin?' For her, it is simply the 'sneaky way ... that writers, directors ... want to think about actresses ... The logical consequence of the way our society looks at ... women.'[49]

This prepares for the ending of the play when, after Ben has left, Helen tells Martin, 'Well, you did want to know where I drew the line.' She and the apologetic writer leave the bar to collect some baggage she has left in his room upstairs, yet, as they head up in the lift, the play cuts between two different scenes – one of Martin and Helen in the lift, the other featuring the client and the prostitute, Carol. Back in his room, Martin suddenly becomes tense, pressing his ear against the wall. Next door, a murder appears to be taking place: the client, frustrated by his sexual impotence, is strangling the prostitute. Martin turns away from the wall to look at Helen. The play follows his gaze, cutting to reveal Helen lying on his bed, her eyes wide open. Though the director, John McKenzie, frames the shot in such a way it could almost be a seduction pose, there is no doubt Helen has been strangled.

As with the similar crime in *A Beast*, the murder in *Double Dare* is a sex crime. This is made clear by Martin's final actions in the play which are almost post-coital: he lights a cigarette, switches on the radio, lies beside his 'sleeping love'. The play serves as a warning for it ultimately demonstrates that if 'reality' can cross into the imagination, then so too can imagination cross into 'reality'. As a writer, Martin takes figures from life (such as Helen) and fantasises them into fictitious characters (the prostitute) for the TV play he is writing inside his head. In turn, these fictions begin to express deeper 'truths' about himself than the surface reality of the mild-mannered persona he presents to Helen, to such an extent that they *become* reality.

Imagination or fiction is more 'true' than everyday surface reality. The theme has emerged before in Potter's writing, particularly in *Lay Down Your Arms*. *Double Dare*, however, takes the logic of this much further, for whilst in the earlier play Hawk was 'torn' between reality and fiction, life and art, flesh and spirit, the lesson Martin learns in the 1976 drama is that there are no such clear distinctions. The writer and client, actress and whore are one and the same here, not the conflicting impulses of Chekhov and Soho with which the young soldier wrestled in the 1970 work. Though, as *Brimstone* and *Where Adam Stood* showed, such a collapse in old categories of thought can be a liberation, *Double Dare* illustrates that it also carries certain dangers. With no clear-cut boundaries, it is up to the individual to decide where he or she draws the line between reality and fantasy and how far to go in crossing that line. Potter rams that point home in *Double Dare* by portraying a television playwright, like himself, who goes too far. Failing to keep his own dark fantasies in check, Martin blurs them with external reality to such an extent that he becomes his own fictional villain. In so doing, he forces the actress, Helen, to cross the line that she *had* drawn in deciding how far she would go – finally making her act out her sexy screen role for real, by virtue of a sexual assault which, as with his namesake in *Brimstone*, sees Martin assume the role of demon.

Taking the three 1976 plays together, it is finally possible to see what Potter meant, when, in response to the banning of *Brimstone and Treacle*, he insisted that although not 'a formal trilogy', all three plays had to be seen together because they all 'occupy the same territory'.[50] What this loose 1976 'trilogy' seems to represent is precisely that movement from spiritual nihilism to a new trust in the order of things which Potter was later to record in his 1978 introduction to the *Brimstone* stage play. Each play reflects aspects of that movement. *Where Adam Stood* traces the collapse of the belief, stemming from the Old Testament, of having somehow experienced a Fall from God. In its place is an assertion both of the natural instinct for survival (learning to cope with a hostile environment) and of literature or 'story-telling' which displaces organised religion as a much healthier outlet for spirituality in a relativistic, increasingly secular society. In one sense, both of these bring the individual much closer to God. *Brimstone and Treacle* extends the collapse of belief in traditional moral thinking and takes it to its logical conclusion. Conventional definitions of right and wrong are shown to be not only inadequate but frequently a convenient cover for evil which finds its natural breeding ground in the unctuousness and sanctimoniousness of many forms of organised religion. A simple child-like faith is instead advocated as the means to God since through it the individual is able instinctively to feel what reason cannot – namely, that behind all the apparent evil in the world there may be a greater good shining through. Realisation of this becomes a liberation. *Double Dare*, however, shows that even liberation has its consequences and dangers. A collapse in conventional categories and distinctions begs the question of how you order your universe and where you draw the line. If the answer is that it is up to each individual to decide for him or herself, the play also shows how imperative it is that that personal choice be rigorously self-policed. Fiction may be the ideal outlet for 'the spirit' but unless properly controlled, the road to heaven can all too easily, as Martin learns at the end of *Double Dare*, become the gateway to hell.

Banned!

Given the links between them, it was thus unfortunate that Potter's three 1976 plays were never transmitted close together, as had been originally intended. As *Brimstone*'s director, the late Barry Davis, expressed it: 'It's that lovely Zen concept of two hands clapping and you don't make sense of two hands clapping if one of them is not there.'[51]

The irony is that *Brimstone and Treacle* was there. Having been commissioned and recorded by the BBC, it was 'pulled' from the schedules very close to transmission on the orders of Alasdair Milne, then Director of TV Programmes with the Corporation. This was the aspect of the whole affair which most annoyed and hurt Potter at the time – the fact that the BBC had had the play since early December 1974 and yet vetoed it only at the eleventh hour, without any consultation or discussion with the writer.

Why was the play banned, having been so long in the BBC system? To understand the reasons, states the 'censor' Milne in interview, one has to understand how, on a day-to-day level, the Corporation functions largely through a delegation of responsibility. A system of referral operates: if any BBC executive becomes nervous about a particular sequence or scene in a drama, he or she is expected to refer the matter up to a superior. With *Brimstone*, the finished play was referred to the then Controller of BBC-1, Bryan Cowgill, who in turn referred it to Milne because he could not make up his mind about the play's 'general tone' – the relationship between the demon and the girl; the central rape scenes but also the 'funniness' of the play. 'Was this actually going to outrage people? Was it going right over the top? ... The incantation scene – is that going to be blasphemous?'[52]

Despite the fact that, as the play's producer Kenith Trodd later claimed to the press, BBC management had seen a script of *Brimstone* as long ago as summer 1975, Milne only decided to ban the play on the morning of Friday 19 March 1976, having viewed the finished tape for the first time – less than three weeks before it was due to be transmitted.[53] This caused him some problems. The *Radio Times* was due to go to press the following Tuesday with a substantial feature in which theatre critic Robert Cushman discussed ten years of Potter's work at the BBC and offered the view that of the three 1976 plays, *Brimstone and Treacle* was the most interesting. It was the pressure of the *Radio Times* deadline, claims Milne, which necessitated an instant decision on the play that morning, with no time to consult Potter on changes or cuts before transmission.[54]

Why, instead of banning it outright, did Milne not suggest a postponement of transmission to allow for discussion with the producer, director and writer? What was it that he found so offensive in the play that precluded even the possibility of cuts or rewrites for a new transmission date? According to Milne, it was 'the actual central construction of the plot' – the rape of a mentally handicapped girl which 'cures' her – that he thought would cause outrage, not 'details of amelioration' here or there: 'I thought ... actually out of the depth of his own psyche and the depth of his own suffering at the time ... [Potter] had written a tortured piece which I thought would outrage people ... I just thought it was too much, actually.'[55]

Milne subsequently wrote to Potter and told him so. In a famous letter, widely leaked to the press by its offended recipient, the only justification the writer ever received for the ban was contained in one brief paragraph:

> I found the play brilliantly written and made, but nauseating ... I believe that it is right in certain instances to outrage the viewers in order to get over a point of serious importance but I am afraid that in this case real outrage would be widely felt and that no such point would get across.[56]

A cause célèbre was in the making. As there was no right of appeal within the BBC against a Controller's decision, all the aggrieved Potter and Trodd could do was to try to generate as much publicity for their cause as possible. To the great chagrin of the BBC, reviews started appearing in the press of a play that had never been broadcast. As Barry Davis made clear, this was because he and others used to invite TV correspondents round to their flats to view smuggled copies of *Brimstone* – it was 'our sad little revenge,' he recalled.[57] One important result, however, was that critics like Peter Fiddick of the *Guardian* and Sean Day-Lewis of the *Daily Telegraph* were able to argue against the ban from direct personal knowledge of the play.

Meanwhile, Potter conducted his own crusade, consulting with lawyers to see if an injunction could not be sought, preventing the BBC transmitting the other two plays in his loose 'trilogy'. He and Trodd also both asked for their names to be removed from the credits of *Double Dare* and *Where Adam Stood*. Both moves came to nothing. In banning *Brimstone* less than three weeks before it was due to be broadcast, Milne had to find a play to fill the vacant *Play for Today* slot on 6 April. Also weighing on his mind was the special *Radio Times* feature on Potter's work. Consequently, with no other new plays ready for transmission, he decided to move *Double Dare* a week forward into the transmission slot that had been originally intended for *Brimstone*.

To Potter, this decision merely added 'insult to injury'.[58] The fine thematic strands he had carefully woven between the three plays had been obliterated at a stroke by the blunt instrument of Milne's rescheduling. By the end of that April, with the prospect of any reversal of the ban fast receding, he resorted to using his position as occasional TV critic of the *New Statesman* to make one last appeal. In his column of 23 April, he described the BBC as 'an uneasy confederation' of different interest groups, 'each pushing and concealing its product' until the moment of transmission – a place where 'memoranda drift up from one floor to another' and programmes get made 'in the spaces between'. The Corporation was, in short, a 'ramshackle anachronism' that offered marvellous opportunities to the artist if 'the game' was played with skill. Occasionally, however, a controller would 'lose his head, froth at the mouth and expose himself and the whole system to ridicule'.[59]

In many ways, this is how the *Brimstone and Treacle* affair should be interpreted in hindsight – as an instance where the mutually self-sustaining 'game' that the free-lance artist must always play with the broadcasting institution broke down. John Caughie has touched on the nature of this 'game' in his 1980 article, 'Progressive Television and Documentary Drama.' In it, he states that the single play or play series functioned in many ways 'as some kind of cutting edge' for British television in the nineteen sixties and seventies, testing the limits (socially, politically, sexually) of what its regulators would allow to be shown or said on screen.[60] Despite its gradual disappearance from commercial television, the single play survived in BBC schedules during the nineteen seventies because, as Caughie puts it, it conferred 'a certain cultural prestige, a 'seriousness' on television as a whole'.[61]

It did other things too. By providing an outlet for the expression of a plurality of voices and opinions independent of the Corporation (in practice, almost always those of white male writers), the single play allowed the BBC to proclaim itself as a public servant in touch with contemporary opinion and tastes and free from any Government bias or control. The dramas shown as *Wednesday Play*'s and *Play*'s *for Today* were not only important to the creative personnel who worked on them (the writers, directors, actors), they were valuable to the Corporation too – a point which the former Director-General Milne concedes with reference to Potter: 'He was very important to us, not least for causing trouble,' he states. 'I have always believed people should be stirred up and shaken by somebody of that calibre writing in his own way.' Potter was as valuable to the BBC, he agrees, as the BBC was valuable to Potter.[62]

The tensions between broadcaster and artist which the *Brimstone and Treacle* affair exposed revolved almost entirely around Caughie's notion of the single play as marker of cultural 'seriousness'. Uncomfortably for both sides, it showed there were limits to the licence which the institution was prepared to give to the 'troublesome' artist of 'calibre'. It demonstrated that, however distinguished his reputation, the artist, far from having complete creative freedom on TV, was actually only free to move within a certain limited territory which the institution had *prescribed* for him.

Thus *Brimstone* was banned by Milne because he failed to detect any 'serious' point behind the notion of a demon raping a mentally handicapped girl for the sake of an ultimate good – as he wrote to Potter, 'I believe that it is right in certain instances to outrage the viewers in order to get over a point of *serious* importance' (emphasis added). In interview, Kenith Trodd states his impression of the whole affair was that much of the problem resided in the fact that most of the BBC Controllers during this period 'had come from anywhere but drama'. He believes many in BBC management at the time were uncomfortable with dealing with drama, particularly 'if it spilled over into current affairs or moral issues in a way that forced it out of the television viewers' page and on to the front page. That was a problem and they didn't want those kind of problems.'[63]

Clearly, Milne, a former current affairs producer, was simply 'nauseated' that any writer could present an audience with the spectacle of the rape of a mentally handicapped girl. Failing to see any 'serious' point or metaphor behind it, he applied journalistic criteria and viewed the piece as an expression of the suffering of its writer (ironic if one considers that the play in many ways deals with a liberation from suffering). This seems to explain why no cuts or rewrites were acceptable to him. It was not so much the depiction of the rape scenes themselves but the very idea of them to which he objected.[64]

As Caughie argues, an explicit act of censorship is always anathema, not only to the artist but to the broadcasting institution as well since 'it disturbs its view of itself: a confusion arises between the role of guardian and the role of public servant.'[65] It is out of just such uncertainties and contradictions, he states, that television drama is created: 'the lines between "conviction" and "excess", between the "talented" and the "less talented", between "provocation" and "offence"'. It is also along those lines that 'the skirmishes take place'.[66]

As regards *Brimstone and Treacle*, if Potter and Trodd asserted the right of the artist to be 'provocative', Milne spoke of 'offence'. If it was held up to be a work of great moral 'conviction', the Director of Programmes accused it of 'excess' – 'too much', 'over the top'. Only on the question of 'talent' did both sides seem to agree; yet that could only help to fuel rather than diminish anger over the ban. As Caughie puts it, there are always two discourses circulating in television drama production: the 'creative' and 'the official'.[67] On the one hand, there is the broadcasting institution: always trying to curb and restrain; mindful of 'the family viewing context' and insistent on 'referral up'. Policing the schedules, its managers regard themselves as the true 'professionals' of broadcasting, confident in their assumption of what is good and bad for *their* audience. On the other, there are the drama producers, free-lance writers and directors whose aim (at least in the case of *The Wednesday Play* and *Play for Today*) was to attempt to challenge conventional television thinking, extending the boundaries of what was permissible on screen. It is important to note that this was an aim which the institution itself tacitly *invited* and supported – it set aside prominent slots in the schedules for the single play; it poured time and resources into bringing new writing and innovative drama to screen because it perceived it as being in the best interests of its own health and long-term survival to do so.

As Potter hinted in the *New Statesman*, the 'game' for the individual writer or drama producer in the nineteen sixties and seventies was thus to manoeuvre controversial single play work successfully through this BBC system, 'pushing' and 'concealing' it, 'until the moment it gets on the air', from all the managers and monitors within the institutional hierarchy whose task it was to 'control' precisely the kind of 'challenging', 'dangerous' work which the *Wednesday Play* and *Play for Today* slots had been specifically set aside in the schedules to promote. In other words, the struggle between creative and official was a struggle enshrined within the BBC system itself: the game, in many respects, a veritable 'double dare'. Akin to Potter's own play, the question the individual artist faced in negotiating the system was, having been implicitly 'dared' by the institution to be controversial, how far did one go? When would the blind eye stop being turned and the line drawn?

This seems to explain why Milne only got to see *Brimstone and Treacle* less than three weeks before transmission. According to Barry Davis, those involved with the play always sensed it might be 'controversial'. He remembered Kenith Trodd urging him to get the play through the BBC editing suites as quickly as possible, in case of trouble.[68] It seems the play was still being worked on so close to its transmission date because this offered a means of protection from prying eyes, a chance almost to smuggle it on air before any manager would need to see it. It was, in other words, all a legitimate part of the 'game' between artist and institution. When Milne banned the play, much of the anger and incomprehension may well have sprung not so much from the fact that the 'creative' had been caught out by the 'official' but that this mutually beneficial game of cat and mouse which the two sides had grown accustomed to playing had, to all intents and purposes, broken down. As Potter put it in the *New Statesman*, 'a controller had lost his head', deciding to draw his own personal, arbitrary line.[69]

Blacklist

There is another perspective to the *Brimstone and Treacle* affair, however. According to Kenith Trodd: 'In 1976, there was a very murky but undoubtedly existing attempt to purge the BBC of some of the "Lefties" ... and the only producer "Lefty" they could actually get was me.'
In September 1976, Trodd's free-lance contract as producer on *Play for Today* was terminated, despite having been annually renewed for the previous four years. Immediately, his friends and colleagues suspected that the decision was 'political'. As Trodd puts it:

> Throughout quite a lot of this period, I and some of the people I worked with, including Roger Smith, [Tony] Garnett in a different way but certainly [Roy] Battersby were all to different degrees flirting with the WRP: the Workers' Revolutionary Party ... And there was ... quite a lot of media penetration by members of that party of television and the theatre.

Despite attending meetings, Trodd asserts he was never a member of the party, just 'one of the sort of in and out fellow travellers' who shared some of the goals and aspirations of active members like the director Roy Battersby.[70]

Unconvinced by reassurances that the system of free-lance contracts was simply being reorganised to phase out one-year renewals, many of Trodd's colleagues and friends urged him to confront the Corporation head-on and demand some answers. This need became particularly pressing after supporters unearthed a 'Deep Throat' – an ex-BBC mandarin who was prepared to confirm there was indeed a hidden agenda behind the whole affair. Trodd remembers his repeated visits to Alasdair Milne and Ian Trethowan (Managing Director of BBC TV) in his quest to find out the truth. The latter told him he was 'overattached to the conspiracy view of history'. With Milne, however, something curious happened. As Trodd was leaving Milne's office, having been subjected to more stonewalling, he was urged to stop worrying: 'You've always stood up for your beliefs', Milne said. 'You've gone for Parliament'. Puzzled by the nature of this small-talk, it was only once Milne's office door had closed behind him that Trodd states he realised: 'They think I'm Roy Battersby. They think I'm somebody else!'

As Trodd puts it, it was one thing for BBC managers occasionally to tolerate a 'controversial' figure like Battersby being invited in to direct the odd play, quite another for them to have on the staff someone they believed was a full-time revolutionary. But how to persuade the Corporation they had got their wires crossed and that he was not a fully paid-up party worker? Trodd states he found a 'circuitous' route to get the message across. The problem was finally sorted out and his contract renewed.

In *Blacklist*, their 1988 account of political vetting within British institutions, Mike Hollingsworth and Richard Norton-Taylor describe how the recently appointed Head of Plays, James Cellan Jones, fought with Ian Trethowan against sacking Trodd. Trethowan had suggested removing Trodd because there were 'security problems'. The producer was a 'trouble-maker and suspected by the security people'.[71] Though Trethowan eventually backed down in the face of Cellan Jones' protests, what this episode illustrates is that the *Brimstone and Treacle* affair was only part of a much wider backlash in the mid-seventies against the so-called left-wing 'radicals' within BBC drama. Moreover, like allegations of 'dirty tricks' campaigns against the Labour Government of the time under Harold Wilson, that reaction was ultimately instigated by the Security Services in the shape of MI5.

As Hollingsworth and Norton-Taylor show in *Blacklist*, far from being a delusion of left-wing paranoiacs, highly secretive political vetting of a large number of its employees had indeed been practised by the BBC – from Graduate Trainees through to directors and producers in every department – since 1937. This was done by MI5 via the BBC's Personnel Department, where the Corporation employed a 'Security Liaison Officer'. In the mid nineteen seventies, however, during a period of great political turmoil, a special desk was set up within MI5 itself to look at 'subversives in the media'. One of the targets the Security Services were especially gunning for was BBC Drama.[72] It was an obvious target to choose.

As Alasdair Milne puts it, by that time, a general feeling had been ventilated by right-wing newspapers such as the *Daily Express* that the entire Plays Department of the BBC was run by 'Workers Revolutionary Party people' and that consequently all of its output was slanted to the Left. There was 'a certain tension', Milne confesses, between management and staff concerning this issue. He recalls telling Christopher Morahan, Head of Plays prior to Cellan Jones, that there was an 'anxiety here. Keep an eye on it'.[73] This edgy, volatile climate of the mid-seventies is perhaps the context in which the *Brimstone* affair should be understood.

Though still unrepentant about the ban, Milne admits, 'there was no doubt the climate in '76 was difficult … and to some extent that might have coloured my judgment'. He cites the pressures the BBC was under at the time because of accusations of too much TV sex and violence. Government had picked up on the possible connection between what was on screen and trouble in the streets, inviting the Chairmen of both the BBC and the IBA to discuss new curbs with the Home Secretary. In addition, the Annan Committee was due to report to Parliament in 1977 on the future of TV. Hence there was, states Milne, 'that sort of pressure going on round about the time of *Brimstone*'.[74]

Certainly, when the play was banned, many TV commentators and practitioners detected a loss of confidence and a gradual undermining of the BBC from within. Potter himself decried the ban as a loss of nerve and an indication 'of the changing nature of the BBC.'[75] In the week following the ban, the *Daily Mail* reported that Milne faced 'an open revolt' from top producers angry at the introduction of a new wave of censorship. This was a reaction not only to *Brimstone* but also to *The Naked Civil Servant* – a dramatisation of Quentin Crisp's autobiography which the BBC had turned down yet which subsequently went on to win many top awards for ITV. At a heated meeting, the verdict of producers was that 'we are in a climate of frightening conformity. Plays which would not have raised an eyebrow five years ago would not be tolerated today. We have capitulated to Mary Whitehouse.'[76]

Given this context of blacklist and backlash in the mid-seventies, is it conceivable that *Brimstone* was banned not merely out of personal taste but as an attempt by management to be *seen* to be having teeth in dealing with the tide of 'subversive' drama? Was banning the work of perhaps the most distinguished television playwright to emerge from that 'radical' *Wednesday Play* generation an attempt to set an example to others, particularly the suspected 'troublemaker' Trodd? As indicated earlier, Milne denies the wider context of the time did anything more than 'colour his judgment'. Trodd, however, believes the events were connected, even though he states he never realised it at the time: '*Brimstone* was not a subject I don't think I accused … [as having] to do with that but clearly, it was part of that.'[77]

Certainly, Potter's three 1976 plays formed the climax of his single play work and association with *Play for Today*. Only one more BBC play would follow: *Blue Remembered Hills* in 1979 (see Chapter 3). Was this relative paucity in single play output the result of disillusionment with BBC censorship and management? At the time of the *Brimstone* ban, Potter lamented that 'a generation of second-rate bureaucrats' was 'leading the BBC down from the heights'.[78] He saw the writing on the wall for the single play: 'It will soon all be done on film and it'll be a director's medium like the cinema. It only remains an author's medium at the moment because of British anachronisms.' In the same breath, however, he could add: 'But before it ends, I want to make a few defiant noises.'[79]

Paradoxically, the *Brimstone* ban seemed to sting him into life, fuelling rather than diminishing his desire to write for television. By May of 1976, he could tell the *Daily Express*: 'Strangely enough, the [*Brimstone*] argument has made me realise afresh the importance of television … If I can get that kind of reaction to a play, maybe it is saying something important.'[80] He also admitted to the *Daily Telegraph*: 'This has reawakened my appetite. I have got to make some kind of reply.'[81]

In many ways, that 'reply' would come two years later with his highly acclaimed six-part serial, *Pennies from Heaven* (see Chapter 4). Potter's lack of single play output was thus because he was increasingly turning his attention towards other TV dramatic forms. If, in retrospect, this seems an astute move in view of the subsequent decline of the single play, it was one which his earlier work in the seventies had foreshadowed: the 1976 'trilogy' of thematically connected plays but also his occasional forays into the realm of the 'classic serial'. In 1971, Potter had written *Casanova* – an original six-part serial, based on the memoirs of the famous eighteenth-century lover (see Chapter 4). Also, as an established TV figure, he was consistently being commissioned during this period to adapt a number of 'classic' literary works for BBC TV.

His remote rural upbringing in the Forest of Dean and his perspective as a writer guiltily educated out of his class made him a perfect candidate to tackle the works of Thomas Hardy. The first of two such adaptations during the seventies was a single filmed drama for BBC-2, *A Tragedy of Two Ambitions* (tx. 21.11.73; dir. Michael Tuchner).[82] Three years later, Potter was commissioned to do another Hardy adaptation for the BBC, only this time of a much larger work: Hardy's famous 1886 novel *The Mayor of Casterbridge*. The idea emanated from the Serials Department of the BBC where script editor Betty Willingale had suggested Potter's name for the task of transforming the tragic novel into a seven-part 'classic serial' for BBC-2.[83] The resulting dramatisation of the rise and fall of Michael Henchard (played by Alan Bates) – a man who sells his wife at a fair and by this act brings about his own downfall twenty years later – was widely praised on its first showing on BBC-2 between 22 January and 5 March 1978. Indeed some of the novel's themes may be seen to connect with Potter's own, most notably the idea of a single fatal lapse from grace and the 'commodification' of women by men.[84] In many ways, however, the process of adapting *Mayor* in the summer of 1976 was much more a chance for Potter to return to writing again after the death of his father in November 1975. As he told Joan Bakewell in an interview the following November, during the year since the loss he had written no original work: 'The grief has been so pitiless I didn't want to turn myself to anything but that.'[85] Begun in February 1977, it was *Pennies from Heaven* which would mark his return to original writing for television.

There was one other work which Potter adapted for TV during the seventies: Angus Wilson's 1964 novel, *Late Call*. Transmitted between 1 and 22 March 1975 on BBC-2, this portrayal of life in the emerging New Towns of post-war Britain seemed perfect material to offer to the writer of *The Nigel Barton Plays*. Interviewed in the *Radio Times*, Wilson himself claimed as much. Mapping a changing social landscape and class structure, the novel dealt with 'a senior citizen watching young people in the late fifties and early sixties – the years of coffee bars, New Towns and CND.' As Potter 'was in his twenties then … he [seemed] just the man to do it for television.'[86]

In the TV version, Dandy Nichols plays Sylvia Calvert, an elderly woman who gives up her life as a hotelier to spend her retirement in a New Town, living with her widower son Harold (Michael Bryant) and his grown-up family. A working-class woman with unpleasant memories of a brutal childhood incident, she finds herself a displaced person in the new 'classless' Britain, as she wanders around the New Town alone with many hours to fill. After rescuing a young girl from lightning, she gradually, however, begins to discover a new *raison d'être* and sets about rebuilding her life on her own terms. Her private salvation as the saviour of others is extended to helping Harold and his family deal with their own personal traumas (see Chapter 3).

In each of his TV adaptations in the seventies, Potter was invariably content to remain faithful to the literary source, not seeking to impose his own personal authorial stamp, as he did with original work. One reason for this comes from his comments to the *Radio Times* about his dramatisation of *A Tragedy of Two Ambitions*, which he said 'demanded all of one's technique to remain faithful to the mood and tone of the story … If you're tackling something of that stature, you feel some presence looking over your shoulder. And the more skilful the writer, the more difficult the adaptation.'[87]

One consequence, however, of fidelity to the text was that, in spite of winning praise for his adaptations, there was always some dissatisfaction that these were poor substitutes for the original work on which his reputation was based. This was certainly the case amongst BBC management. Alasdair Milne asserts: 'I don't think adaptation is his game … *The Mayor of Casterbridge* [was] a well-crafted piece but … there's a 'zing' about Potter's work which is not in adaptations of books he does.' He remembers asking the Head of Drama, Shaun Sutton, about Potter and his state of health during the writing of *Pennies from Heaven*. Was this remorse over the *Brimstone* ban? Milne replies: 'There was no feeling of guilt. Just an anxiety to see what came next.'[88]

If this illustrates how much the institution needed a celebrated playwright like Potter in the difficult climate of the seventies, it also explains why the BBC was so 'badly shaken' (according to Milne) when the writer unexpectedly departed for Independent Television at the end of the seventies. At a press conference held in May 1979, Michael Grade, then

Director of Programmes at London Weekend Television, announced that Potter's and Trodd's recently formed independent production company, Pennies From Heaven Limited, had signed a major deal to provide LWT with six Potter plays.

To the astonishment of journalists, Potter declared at the same conference that the only reason he had allowed himself to be 'poached' in this way was to get back at the BBC. In terms of drama, he asserted, it was the BBC that was really the place to be. The adventurous mood of the sixties had disappeared, however, to be replaced by a 'crisis of management' as a result of which, to many working there, the present time was the worst period they had ever known. The future of television, he concluded, lay not with the established broadcasting institutions but with 'small production companies [which] are going to break up these monoliths we have'[89] (see Chapter 5).

Though in reply Alasdair Milne asserts there was not a word of truth in these very public attacks against the BBC (Potter and Trodd departed for more money, he states), by the close of the seventies there could be no doubt that events had come full circle.[90] Ten years after Kestrel, the 'independents' were back at LWT.

Conclusion

From *Moonlight* in 1969 to Pennies From Heaven Limited in 1979, Potter's progress had thus been inexorable throughout the *Play for Today* era. Some measure of the extent to which his own preoccupations as a dramatist had shifted and matured over this period is provided by an interview he gave in 1977 to the BBC TV religious affairs programme, *Anno Domini*. Looking back on *Son of Man* eight years before, he commented, 'nothing could be easier than to write a humanistic, I think rather evasive picture ... of Jesus, in which really many of the central claims were evaded. I am aware of that evasion now though I wasn't then.'

He stated that at the time it was written he was beginning to orientate himself towards the 'awesome, formidable claims' of the Christian faith but denied that the play was an example of religious television. It was the same assumption, he said, as television's general treatment of religion: 'because *Son of Man* is about Jesus, it is a religious play. That is exactly what the 'God slot' does, you see. It makes you look for religion in the obvious places.'[91]

In his 1978 introduction to the *Brimstone* stage play, Potter expands on this notion, commenting that few critics realised that *Joe's Ark*, for example, was a play with 'religious themes'. At first, he states, he was puzzled and then pleased because 'at least I was avoiding the label-sticking which ... assigns religion to its special little enclave ... the so-called "God-slot"' – the protected hour in the Sunday schedules which British television traditionally had been obliged to devote to religious programmes. To Potter, 'a religion that is diminished into a special time and a special (i.e. narrow) form of address is not much more than a scandalously privileged pressure group' – the inevitable consequence of a materialist secular society and a natural breeding ground for banality, sentimentality and sanctimoniousness.[92]

By contrast, Potter asserted in his *Anno Domini* interview that it was religion which was increasingly occupying 'the central territory' of what he was doing as a writer. The very act of pigeon-holing his work as 'God-slot', he went on, would destroy the 'openness and receptivity' of television which had allowed him to communicate these ideas to a public increasingly hostile or indifferent to traditional forms of religious expression.[93] If this makes Potter a 'religious' dramatist, it is not religion in the conventional sense familiar to the television schedulers: 'The sort of "religious drama" that I want to write,' he stated in his 1978 introduction to *Brimstone*, 'will not necessarily mention the word 'God' at all. Perhaps too, it will be based on the feeling that religion is not the bandage, but the wound.'[94]

For 'religion' in Potter's work, read spirituality: the totality of an individual's personal response to existence and a desire, not necessarily satisfied, for there to be something beyond 'the suffocatingly dead materiality of things'. Doubt, for him, is 'part of the provenance if not the language of faith.'[95] It is in 'the tension between those two, the yearning ... in the deepest ligaments of my being ... and a detached view saying 'Come, come' ... religion is there in that tension'.[96]

Such views leave little room for the Church and established forms of worship. As *Brimstone and Treacle* showed, religion as public practice can become distorted ritual can become the perfect breeding ground for evil. In a 1976 radio talk, Potter went further, stating that:

> Religious people are often horrifyingly dishonest in the way they use concepts because so many of them seem to feel compelled to use one system of signs, one means of knowing, to commend and sustain a different category of discourse. I once wrote a play, using a few chapters of Edmund Gosse's *Father and Son* to show to myself as much as to others how crippling and ultimately doomed an enterprise it is to subborn and discountenance the facts which our proper search for knowledge will keep bringing into the light. The agony which the theories of evolution brought down upon many Christians showed, as so often before, the frightened contortions and moral dishonesties which

> follow when the love of God is subverted into worship of a fading shadow.[97]

Just as in *Where Adam Stood*, literal belief in a system of symbols must give way to an understanding of the centrality of metaphor in the expression of faith. It is this perhaps which marks the fundamental shift in Potter's writing during the seventies.

As Chapter 1 noted, *Son of Man* was an attempt to create a version of Christ that could be believable to modern audiences (and the writer himself). In a 1977 interview for BBC TV's *Tonight* programme, Potter stated: '[it was] written from an agnostic point of view but in the very writing of it I was suddenly aware that my attention was being fixed too strongly upon something which I could therefore not evade and would have to examine and pay attention to'.[98] The distinction between religion and politics was blurring – an overtly socialist outlook on the world was beginning to reveal a wider set of spiritual questions underlying it.

An early indication of Potter's move to a new 'religious drama' was *Moonlight on the Highway*, a play where neither God nor religion is mentioned. Instead, popular songs function as the outlet for the spirit: not only the 'bandage' for the hero's 'wound' but the means by which he can shape his own destiny and free himself from the deterministic formulations of the psychiatrist Chilton. As noted previously, there is ambiguity in the outcome but according to Potter in the *Anno Domini* interview, that is what gives life its 'edge':

> Doubt is a very double-edged weapon and it ought ... to be turned against the mechanistic and materialistic visions of life which predominate where there really is, if we take that materialistic view, mechanistic view of life, there is no area left at all for individual freedom. I mean we are just programmed genes ... And that to me in my response to life, in my feelings about my own self, is an absurdity ... At very barren times I feel ... it is also an absurdity to believe in God. It is a choice between absurdities. That is what gives human life its particular poignancy and pain and edge.[99]

The heroes of the two 'spy' plays, *Lay Down Your Arms* and *Traitor* both make their choice between absurdities and both, significantly, opt to forsake the material world for freedom of the spirit. In Hawk's case, it is implied that this will take the form of a career as a writer; for Harris, it is a dingy flat in the 'largest, most soul-destroying bureaucracy the world has ever seen'. The question which *Traitor* begs is whether absolute unquestioning belief in ideology or creed can ever be the right way. If the answer is no – that doubt is 'the language of faith' and what it is to be human – *Angels Are So Few* demonstrates that a child-like literal belief in absolutes nevertheless still 'tears'. To lose that belief is in a sense to drain the world of some 'wonder'.

Can that 'wonder' be recaptured? Glen in *Schmoedipus* wants to become a child again, yet like Sam in the earlier *Bonegrinder*, he is ultimately shown to be a symptom of sexual guilt: 'the outsider knocking on the door' who exposes the rot at the heart of suburbia. Only in *Joe's Ark* does one begin to get a sense of some kind of resolution to the 'unacknowledged spiritual questions' which Potter admits he was wrestling with at this time. By the 1976 'trilogy', as we have seen, the assertion of an instinctive faith expressed not in literal but metaphorical terms is what finally renders *Son of Man*'s questioning of the reality of the historical Christ redundant.

If imagination and 'narrative' are the keys to faith, can these be used to recapture the 'wonder' of childhood? As Chapter 3 will show, that was the other spiritual question which Potter's work in the seventies tried to resolve. In fact, the two questions are two sides of the same coin – to re-experience the lost wonder of childhood is to reaffirm a faith in the order of things and vice versa. Each, however, has different implications within the work: 'Angels Are So Few' does not *quite* mean the same as 'Only Make Believe'.

3

Only make believe: tales for children and adults

Lost lands

> I am trying to go back into a strange and all but lost land that cannot be traced by any cartographer, but which can suddenly – and sometimes unexpectedly – yield up a few of its shapes, colours, smells and mysteries. I refer, of course, to the land – no, the *continent* – of our own childhood.[1]

These are the opening lines of *A Christmas Forest*: a 1977 radio talk in which Potter tried to recall childhood Christmases in the Forest of Dean. As we have seen, from *Nigel Barton* through *Moonlight* to *Schmoedipus*, recollections of the past and of childhood are integral to Potter's writing. His central protagonists yearn to recapture the 'wonder' of a lost Eden from which they feel in permanent exile, tracing the roots of their present anxiety back to a single fatal lapse in the past. With his 1976 'trilogy', however, Old Testament notions of a Fall from grace were discarded for a new faith 'in the order of things'. Where, then, does that leave the felt reality of exile from a childhood Eden?

Though an adaptation, Potter's 1975 dramatisation of Angus Wilson's *Late Call* indicates the direction in which his own writing was heading at this time. Of particular note is his treatment of the novel's Prologue in which the main character, Sylvia, is first introduced to the reader as a child, wandering the East Anglian countryside with her friend, Myra, in the long hot summer of 1911. Encouraged by Myra's middle-class Edwardian mother to be 'free spirits', the little girls decide to take off their dresses when it gets too hot, enjoying the freedom of wandering around in their underclothes. When they are caught by their respective mothers, middle-class Myra's 'free spirit' is tolerated. Sylvia, however, is only the daughter of a poor farmer. Accused of not knowing her place, she is beaten by her father ' 'Till the blood run'.[2] This class oppression sets the pattern for the rest of her life. Chapter 1 of the novel finds her in old age, a lifetime having been spent in domestic service and the hotel business, catering for her 'betters'. As she retires to a dull New Town existence beside her son, it seems the 'free spirit' she once experienced as a child has gone forever.

In Potter's version, however, Sylvia begins to re-experience the 'wonder' of that day in 1911 through the power of memory and imagination. By rendering 'The Hot Summer of 1911' as a series of flashbacks and counterpointing them with depiction of Sylvia's New Town present, he makes central to the drama what was simply a prologue in Wilson's novel. What the novel implied was a psychological wound from childhood is grounded in the serial as the deepest root of the protagonist's current ills. Akin to his own original plays, Potter's *Late Call* becomes a kind of psychodrama in which the heroine resolves her troubled present by confronting her own repressed memories, searching back to the fatal moment in her past when she was physically abused out of the innocence and wonder of childhood.

In turn, this provides Potter with a structure for dramatising events from the novel. The first two episodes of the TV serial contrast scenes from 1911 with Sylvia's deadening experience of retirement in the New Town, introducing the audience both to her and to the events which have shaped her life. By Episode 3, the gulf between past and present has become so marked, the intrusion of memory so insistent, it triggers off in Sylvia an intense psychological crisis. Breaking the shell of passivity which retirement in the New Town has induced, she begins to take long solitary walks in the countryside that surrounds the town. In the TV version (as opposed to the novel), Potter emphasises how this sudden activity is as much psychological as physical. Walking through some woods, memories of another woodland adventure begin to intrude:

> YOUNG SYLVIA: Let's go back through the wood. It'll be cooler there ...
> MYRA: We'll never get the dirt off, you know.
> YOUNG SYLVIA: We're going to feel free.[3]

In Potter's version, Sylvia's walk through the woods becomes symbolic of her mental retracing of a path that leads to the 'lost land' of her childhood. As suggested by the additional dialogue he writes for the flashbacks, she is trying to shake off 'the dirt' of the past, cleansing herself of its pain in order to try and recapture the wonder of that one day in 1911 when she was able to feel free. Long obscured by the drudgery of her adult life which began with her father's abuse, it is only through remembering the wonder of childhood that she will be able to overcome her present crisis and rediscover what it means to be free.

Her reward comes at the end of this crucial third episode of the TV serial. Caught in a thunderstorm, she rescues a child from under a tree just before it is struck by lightning. In both versions of *Late Call*, this acts as a kind of baptism of renewal for the heroine. The TV serial, however, explicitly links present with past. The thunderstorm is cross-cut with flashbacks to 1911, the screams of the terrified child she rescues becoming mixed on the soundtrack with the screams of young Sylvia as her father beat her.

The lightning scene in Potter's version thus not only functions as a rite of passage for Sylvia (propelling her, as in the novel, into a new existence by bringing new friends in the shape of the child's grateful parents), it also brings her in touch with her lost childhood. Through the flashbacks and sound mixes, the serial suggests that Sylvia relives the terror of her beating during the terror of the thunderstorm – this time, not as a helpless child but as the rescuer of a helpless child. Similar to the rape in *Brimstone and Treacle*, the lightning acts as a form of shock therapy: an intense moment of danger in which a repressed memory returns to consciousness to be purged forever. Also as in *Brimstone*, a present terror cancels a past one. Sylvia's good act (the rescue) negates the bad that was committed against her. The psychological barrier which had separated her from the free spirit of childhood is at last removed.

The 1975 TV version is therefore a subtle reworking of the original novel. Though remaining faithful to Wilson's text, Potter uses his familiar flashback techniques to explore his own interests in the 'lost land' of childhood. Not so much obscuring the novel, this highlights what was implicit within its structure – namely, the progress of a character from childhood wonder in the Prologue through adult despair in the middle sections to psychological freedom at the close. The importance of *Late Call* within Potter's own *oeuvre* is thus that it provides an early model for the 'redemption sagas' which would be a hallmark of his work in the eighties. The mental journey of Philip Marlow in *The Singing Detective* – from a trough of illness and despair through to recovery and personal redemption – is echoed in Sylvia's own in *Late Call*. Both have a positive destination that is reached only through the power of memory and imagination (see Chapter 5).

Such themes, however, have long been present in Potter's writing. In only his second transmitted TV play, he was already beginning to explore the relationship between childhood, memory and the imagination. Unlike his other *Wednesday Play* dramas of the period, *Alice* (tx. 13.10.65) was a costume drama based on historical record. Directed by Gareth Davies and produced by James MacTaggart, it dealt with events surrounding the publication of Lewis Carroll's *Alice in Wonderland*, exactly a century before, in 1865.

The play opens in a 'dark tunnel'. The Reverend Charles Dodgson (the real author behind the 'Lewis Carroll' pseudonym) is on a train, travelling to an unknown destination. Suddenly, a young woman, Ellen Rance, recognises him as someone from her childhood who used to enchant her with his stories. When she tells the white-haired old writer she is soon to be married, he grows hostile, retorting that he is not the least bit interested in her affairs. As it unravels in flashback, the rest of the play reveals why.

Alice explores the relationship between the young Dodgson (played by George Baker) and the eponymous Alice Liddell – daughter of the Dean of Christchurch, Oxford, and real-life model for the heroine of *Alice in Wonderland*. Afflicted by a terrible stammer which renders him inarticulate in the company of adults, Dodgson takes solace in the nonsense world of childhood: riddles, rhymes and above all the company of 10-year-old Alice. To the adult world, this is a source of worry. Mrs Liddell grows suspicious of a man who prefers the company of little girls, especially when her daughter says Dodgson 'loves' her. The spectre of child abuse hangs over the play: is Dodgson's affection for the girl 'pure' or could it be that *Alice in Wonderland* is the English equivalent of Nabokov's *Lolita*?[4] Potter sets up an area of sexual doubt. On the one hand, Dodgson may be channelling his repressed sexual desires into his friendships with little girls. On the other, perhaps the refusal to ascribe any innocent motive to his love of children is an indication not of *his* corruption but that of the 'fallen' adult world. This is hinted at one point when Mrs Liddell looks out of a window and tells her husband: 'I've never liked looking from a lighted room into the dark. You have to be all dark yourself to see into the black out there.'[5]

The play reaches its climax with a picnic on the River Thames – one that parallels an earlier trip Dodgson and Alice made six years before. The previous expedition had been the 'golden afternoon' when he had first entertained the 10-year-old with the story of *Alice in Wonderland*.[6] In Potter's play, that event becomes like Sylvia's 'golden' day in *Late Call* – a childhood moment of Eden which almost seems to defy time and any natural laws. 'I wish this could go on forever and ever and ever,' Alice tells Dodgson. 'Perhaps it will,' the author replies.

Six years on, after the publication of *Alice in Wonderland*, time has its revenge. The second picnic finds Alice 16, almost a woman and with eyes only for Hargreaves – a young undergraduate amongst the party which sets sail up the river in 1868. The onset of adolescence means she has no time for the childish stories of Dodgson, a fact of which he is all too painfully aware. Asked to recite one of his nonsense rhymes, Dodgson gives up, stammering, while Alice and her friends snigger. An embarrassed silence falls over the party. Then, suddenly, Lorina, Alice's sensitive elder sister, takes a copy of *Alice in Wonderland* from her picnic basket and begins to read from the closing paragraph:

> LORINA: Lastly, she pictured ... how this same little sister of hers would, in the after-time, be herself a grown woman; and how she would keep, through all her riper years, the simple and loving heart of her childhood ... remembering her own child-life, and the happy summer days.

The reading becomes a cue for reconciliation. Moved by an awareness of the passing of childhood, Alice kisses Dodgson on the cheek, but as she does so the picture freezes, takes on sepia tones and disappears down the dark tunnel through which the older Dodgson's train is moving. By these visual effects, *Alice* returns to its beginning, with a final image of the bitter old writer hiding behind his newspaper, as Ellen Rance looks pitifully on.

Dodgson's train journey thus functions as a metaphor for the journey of life: one that for Potter in 1965 grows increasingly 'dark' as it hurtles away from the 'wonderland' of childhood. His second transmitted TV play becomes a meditation on the passing of time, an expression of regret that childhood must always fade into a 'lost land' in the face of encroaching adulthood. Note that it is sexuality which marks the end of the child's world: Dodgson's platonic relationship with the young Alice, already precarious through the dark suspicions of others, is finally broken by the onset of adolescence. The only hope the play offers for the preservation of 'wonderland' lies in the immortalising qualities of art, yet as the final image of a bitter, aged Dodgson seems to ask, can that ever be enough?

Significantly, when Potter came to rework his play into a movie script eighteen years later, it was just this question which was addressed and resolved. *Dreamchild*, a feature film directed by Gavin Millar and released in January 1986, retains many of the scenes and much of the dialogue of *Alice* (see Chapter 5). Importantly, however, events are rendered in flashback – not from Dodgson's perspective but that of Alice as an old woman of eighty, recalling her childhood of seventy years before.

The premise is based on fact. In 1932, to mark the centenary of Dodgson's birth, the real Alice set sail from England to the USA in order to receive an honorary degree from Columbia University. Dodgson's 'dreamchild' had grown up to become respectable Mrs Hargreaves.[7] In the film, 80-year-old Alice (played by Coral Browne) is the 'perfect Victorian' and as out of place in twentieth-century America as it is possible to be.[8] In an echo of Potter's 1982 movie version of *Pennies from Heaven*, she finds an America reeling from the Depression (see Chapter 4). As she soon learns, 'All of Me', the song playing on board the ship which brings her to the New World, sums up the mood of the time – a time in which everyone must sell all of themselves if they are to survive. Despite her years, the old lady quickly sees the profit potential of exploiting her connections with Lewis Carroll; yet as she begins to sell 'all of herself', she finds this conscious manipulation of her past forcing her to confront hitherto repressed memories of her childhood and of Dodgson.

The memories of Victorian childhood which *Dreamchild* then renders in flashback are essentially the events of *Alice*: the 'golden afternoon' on the river; Mrs Liddell's suspicions; scenes between young Alice and Dodgson (Ian Holm). There is one crucial difference, however, between the film and the TV play of twenty years before. In keeping with the clear progression in Potter's writing, noted with the 1976 plays, life and art do not merely come to reflect each other in *Dreamchild*, they *intersect*. As in *Double Dare*, fantasy and reality blur and merge. Alone in her New York hotel room, Mrs Hargreaves begins to hallucinate scenes from *Alice in Wonderland* in which she herself becomes the fictional 'Alice'. Suddenly in *Dreamchild*, it is an old woman, not a young girl, who is debating 'change' with a caterpillar:

> CATERPILLAR: So you think you've changed, have you?
> MRS HARGREAVES: I'm afraid I am, sir. Very changed ... I – I can't remember things ... Perhaps – perhaps they are things best not gone into. Best forgotten. (pp. 93–4)[9]

The nonsense world of Lewis Carroll becomes the only way the old woman can make sense of her memories. Inserting herself into the imaginative world Dodgson created for her as a child, she confronts her guilt about using the author for commercial gain, her own fears about her senility and, above all, the suspicion of her mother that the writer's feelings for her were less than pure. As with Sylvia in *Late Call*, the film suggests it is only the adult self which can make sense of what the child could not properly understand. In an echo of the lightning scene of the 1975 serial, the elderly Alice has to relive her childhood if she is ever to come to terms with it. As this suggests, *Dreamchild* bears more than a passing resemblance to *Late Call* – not only in its choice of an old woman as heroine but in this central concern of an individual trying to find a shape to her life by mentally returning to the lost wonderland of her childhood.

The film reaches its climax at Columbia University where Mrs Hargreaves is to be honoured. As the university choir gives a musical rendition of one of Dodgson's nonsense poems, the old woman's mind drifts back to the picnic where she and her teenage friends had sniggered at his stammering. As with the 1965 play, Lorina's reading of the closing paragraph of *Wonderland* prompts the teenage Alice to kiss Dodgson. When the film returns to 'the present', Mrs Hargreaves begins reading out the same paragraph to her Columbia audience, and tells them: 'At the time, I was too young to see the gift whole, to see it for what it was, and to acknowledge the love that had given it birth. I see it now. At long, long last. Thank you,

Mr Dodgson. Thank you' (p. 137).

After seventy years, Alice finally makes her reconciliation with Dodgson, acknowledging the depth of the genuine love which had gone into *Alice in Wonderland.* In marked contrast to the 1965 *Alice*, the teenager's kiss becomes not a parting regret for the end of childhood but a symbol for the psychological recapturing of that 'lost wonderland'. Like Sylvia in *Late Call*, the elderly Alice comes to terms with the past; in this case by confronting and then dismissing a dark suspicion about Dodgson which she had long repressed. In so doing, the mental journey back to her childhood allows her to see the shape of her life anew. This seems to be 'the gift' for which she thanks him so profusely at the end. By immortalising the wonder of her childhood in literature, Dodgson has provided her with the chance to remain permanently in touch with her childhood, undergoing a perpetual spiritual renewal.

This is why, as her speech indicates, such a gift can only be properly appreciated in later life, not as a child. Echoing *Late Call*, it always has to be the adult who rescues the child from within. The progression from *Alice* is marked. In *Dreamchild*, the journey is not away from the light of childhood into a permanent 'dark tunnel' of old age and death but, in keeping with the more optimistic tone of *Late Call* and the 1976 'trilogy', towards a fresh light at the other end. When Alice's ship docks in the New World, it symbolises her own spiritual journey to a renewed 'wonderland'. Triggered off by the pressure of her new surroundings, her inner search for meaning unearths a cure for her own 'Depression blues': one found not amongst the glitter of her sudden status as media personality but behind, in another land from which she thought she had departed forever:

> That is the land of lost content,
> I see it shining plain.
> The happy highways where I went
> And cannot come again.[10]

These lines from A. E. Housman are quoted at the very end of *Blue Remembered Hills* – Potter's famous final *Play for Today* (tx. 30.1.79) which is also perhaps his most definitive evocation of the lost land of childhood. Produced by Kenith Trodd and directed by Brian Gibson, it remains Potter's best-known single TV drama: the winner of a 1979 British Academy Award and his most often-repeated play. Its success is partly due to its simplicity. There are no flashbacks; fantasy sequences or even long speeches – nothing 'to ripple the surface of "naturalism"' very much.[11] Instead, it deals sparely with one summer afternoon in the lives of seven West Country children in 1943: a 'golden day' that will end in tragedy.

Potter permits only one 'ripple' to the surface naturalism of the drama and that is to insist each of the children be played by adult actors. It is the same device he used for the classroom scenes in *Stand Up* and the effect here is similar. Just as the device in *Stand Up* reinforced the classroom scenes' status as memory filtered through an adult imagination, so, too, in *Blue Remembered Hills* are events made to seem mediated yet also immediate. Adult actors underline the 'remembered' quality of the title and the fact that in memory it is always the present self which is superimposed upon the past. They also help magnify the world of the child and make it identifiable to an adult audience.

In a 1979 interview, Potter hinted at another important reason why the play has to have adults as children when he asserted: 'I don't believe the common adult assumptions about the world of children.' He stated that for him, childhood is the 'adult world writ large, not small'. It is 'adult society without all the conventions and the polite forms which overlay it'.[12] In *Blue Remembered Hills*, childhood is presented as but a magnified reflection of the adult world, with all its imperfections. This can be related to the progression in Potter's writing, noted with the 1976 'trilogy', where Old Testament notions of a Fall from grace were discarded in favour of a general blurring of moral categories and distinctions. In *Blue Remembered Hills*, similarly, no clear Fall from childhood is depicted. Instead, there is a general blurring of distinctions between the child's and the adult's world. To Potter in 1979, the 'fallen' nature of adults is there right from the very beginning in their child selves. In contrast to much of his earlier (pre-1976) writing, childhood in *Blue Remembered Hills* becomes not a pre-lapsarian state but one of original sin.

The play makes this clear right from the very start, as it opens on 7-year-old Willie (played by an adult, Colin Welland), who is seen meandering through some woods, pretending to be a spitfire shot down in flames. 'Them be all dead … Burnt to nothing,' he mutters of his imaginary air crew, as he bites into a large cooking apple (p. 41).[13] Sin is thus present in the child's Garden of Eden right from the very outset. As symbolised by the biting of the apple, it is already a 'fallen' world of temptation and death which the child inhabits. There is no real innocence in him at the start from which the rest of the play could trace a lapse. World War Two is raging in the adult world outside and he knows it. His behaviour reflects this as he revels in the excitement of the destruction.

The significance both of the apple and of 'burnt to nothing' becomes more apparent as the rest of the play unfolds. Soon Willie is joined by his mates, Peter, Raymond and John, and together the four trap and kill a squirrel in the woods. The scene recalls the killing of the bear in *A Beast with Two Backs* – the persecution of an innocent animal serving only to highlight the real 'beast' inside the boys. Crucially, this killing is juxtaposed with a scene in a nearby barn where two girls, pretty Angela and plain Audrey, are teasing a '*timid* [and] *anaemic looking*' child, on account of his nickname: Donald Duck (p. 51).

As the play progresses, details about the 'weakling', Donald, begin to emerge from the conversation of the other children. His father is a prisoner of war under the Japanese. He is also literally an 'abused child' since his mother beats him with a poker (p. 51). Though unaware of the significance of the remark, John reports he has overheard his mother say the bedsheets of Donald's mother 'could tell a pretty tale' (p. 57). Ostracised by the other boys, Donald is always going off on his own, 'like a looney' (p. 69).

Comparison here with the other child protagonist of *Blue Remembered Hills* is instructive. Though he never appears in the play, the name 'Wallace Wilson' is mentioned frequently by the other children. He is the 'cock of the class' – the cleverest child of their year in school (p. 45). He is also the best athlete: he can 'pee' the highest and punch the hardest. In stark contrast to Donald Duck, he is 'Number One', yet like Donald he, too, has a tendency to voluntary reclusiveness. Asked by Peter where Wallace is, Willie replies: 'Down the quarry, I'll bet. Mooching about' (p. 46). Like *Stand Up* and *Where the Buffalo Roam*, *Blue Remembered Hills* makes a link between the clever child and the backward, 'abused' child, seeing both as the same type of displaced person *vis à vis* the dominant group.

This is important in helping to understand the climax of the play. Left alone in the barn by the other children, Donald begins to vent his frustrations by striking matches from a box of 'England's Glory'. Suddenly, a flame catches the straw and a little fire begins. Meanwhile, the other children are hatching a cruel practical joke. A few minutes earlier, a siren had sounded through the woods, filling them all with fear for it had seemed to signal the escape of an Italian prisoner from the nearby POW camp. This ultimate image of childhood terror quickly gives way to a desire to take out their fear on the weakling, by pretending the Italian is outside the barn, with a knife. Mimicking his accent for the benefit of Donald inside, they slam the barn door shut. Only as flames begin to gut the barn, do they realise, too late, the consequences of their actions. When they re-open the door, the last image of their victim is of him 'briefly glimpsed through the flames, gesticulating, then wholly engulfed' (p. 84).

The killing of the squirrel and the girls' baiting of Donald have just been rehearsals for a much more horrific persecution at the end of the play. As in *A Beast with Two Backs* (as well as Golding's *Lord of the Flies* which this play echoes in theme), the 'beast' is shown not to be outside in the Forest but within all of the children. It is the children themselves who become what they fear most: the 'bogeyman' Italian, the physical reality of whose threat is revealed as illusory in this play. As with *A Beast*, the real danger is shown to lie much closer to home, within the hearts of the Foresters themselves.

The play's links with *A Beast* are thus tangible: the threat of an Italian roaming the woods; a remote rural setting evocative of the Forest of Dean; a 'remembered' quality that suggests an Edenic 'mythic land'. As persecuted outcast, Donald Duck also bears a strong resemblance to Rufus, the 'looney', 'cripple' child of *A Beast*. Both significantly have an adulterous 'mother' and an 'airy' father. A prisoner-of-war like the elusive Italian, Donald's father has also, like the Italian, vanished into thin air. As Peter tactlessly asks Donald at one point: 'Your Dad's *missing*, ent he?' (p. 70).

The difference between the two plays is that in keeping with the progression in Potter's writing and thinking, noted with the 1976 'trilogy', *Blue Remembered Hills* depicts no clear Fall from innocence into permanent exile from Eden. Like Rufus, Donald may be finally separated from his peers and his background, consumed in a kind of hell-fire but, as the play makes clear, this is brought about by the fault of others' actions *and his own*. The child sows the seeds of his own destruction. External events (an Italian with 'a knife', symbolically linked to his father, who turns out to be an illusion) may contribute to Donald's downfall but he is shown to be no angelic innocent. Instead, he shares with the other children a natural propensity to sin. Constantly putting themselves and each other in danger, each of the children is always threatening to destroy their own Eden. This is what the play means by 'original sin' – not that Man is 'irredeemably corrupt' but that in its very intellectual curiosity and capacity to get embroiled in trouble, 'the human animal is potentially extremely dangerous'.[14] However serious his persecution, it is Donald himself who helps bring about his own exile from his childhood Eden, significantly with a box of 'England's Glory'. Through the final image of the burning barn which separates him from his peers forever, Potter suggests that in spite of the mitigating circumstances, it was his own curiosity and mischief which made the child play with fire and get burned.

The play ends with Potter (or is it Wallace Wilson?) inserting himself into the drama by means of voice-over to read the lines from Housman quoted earlier. Given that the play portrays the many cruelties of childhood, such nostalgia for a 'land of lost content' may seem ironic. Certainly, *Blue Remembered Hills* does not romanticise children and its demonstration of how the 'fallen' world of adults reflects the 'original sin' of childhood might render any notion of it as a 'lost land' inherently suspect. In interview, however, Potter asserted childhood is to everyone a 'lost land':

> The loss of Eden is experienced by each and everyone of us as we leave the

> wonder and magic and also the pains and terrors of childhood ... Whereas the discipline is imposed by an adult, when children are amongst themselves, it's all continual fidget and movement, exploration, speculation, wonder, which in a sense to lose that is to lose Eden, is to be expelled from the Garden. And I only use that metaphor as a continuous one because I believe that ... when Jesus said 'Be as little children', that is what is meant. In other words, be as open as you like ... The knowledge that we have about what it is to be human that we have as a child is something that we necessarily must lose but we don't have to lose it totally if we can remember. We remember an Eden even though it wasn't perfect ... but it was an Eden in terms of its possibilities and potentialities.[15]

The loss of Eden becomes universal rather than denoting a unique, individual lapse from grace – a metaphor for a general fading of 'wonder', common to all. Importantly, that 'Eden' comes to encapsulate not only the joys of childhood but, as in *Blue Remembered Hills*, its terrors as well.

In short, for Potter, the wonder of childhood that is Eden is the ability of children to experience life intensely (both the pleasure and the pain), without the staleness of custom and habit that corrodes adult responses to the world. To lose that ability to see the world as if for the first time is, for Potter, to lose Eden. In a 1978 radio talk for Lent, *The Other Side of The Dark*, he expanded on this, suggesting that children's ability to live in the present tense presupposed an 'immense trust in the order of things'. Apply this to an adult, he suggested and you would immediately notice 'the immense degree of concentration and *attention*' required in which once again all things would be 'as new'.[16]

This echoes the 'dark tunnel' out of which Sylvia and Mrs Hargreaves travel in *Late Call* and *Dreamchild*. Old women, staled by habit and convention, they come to a different sort of 'attention' by remembering the long summer afternoons of their childhood. By recalling how it was to live in a moment that seemed to go on forever, they learn once more to look at their lives as if for the very first time. In *Blue Remembered Hills*, it is an imperfect world which is remembered. Nevertheless it is an Eden too 'in terms of its possibilities and potentialities'. All of the children may be afflicted with original sin but they are never cynical or jaded. Each of them experiences life (and death) as if for the very first time and each possesses the childhood wonder of living in the moment. In *The Other Side of the Dark*, Potter went on to suggest that:

> It was from a starting point something like this, pieced together with an urgency rather too close to panic out of the need to do more than dumbly endure or complain about what I took to be a particularly humiliating illness that I found that I was able, in time, to concentrate or pay attention to what

> was happening to me and in me and in front of me. I sought to inhabit the present and the actual sting of the moment became a point of such unexpected clarity that I could use it, if not as a window, then certainly as a widening chink of light through which I could look. I was attempting simply to deal with the distortion of pain and what I admit to be a considerable amount of anger and fear – the predictable old 'Why me?' of the afflicted – and I found instead that I was facing something other than my own beleaguered self and gradually experiencing something other than an introverted locked-in anguish.[17]

In terms of his writing, Potter's first novel, *Hide and Seek* (published in 1973) can be seen as that 'starting point': the beginnings of his attempt to arrive at the different sort of 'attention' which is clearly evident in his work from the mid-seventies onwards. Written at the time of his own greatest crisis of illness, this novel is undoubtedly worth emphasising and exploring in depth. In a very real sense, it is the pivot upon which the entire body of Potter's work turns. *Hide and Seek* provides the crucial clues as to how and why Potter's writing for television began to shift – from despair to hope.

Into the woods

According to Potter, *Hide and Seek* is 'an obsessive piece of work'. It was completed in January 1972, and the author was to experience his worst period of illness a month later. His hands became so buckled and twisted that to the end of his life he only had the movement of four fingers in one hand. 'There was a torrent of *something* moving through me,' was Potter's verdict on that time.[18]

As Chapter 2 noted, this was the period when previously unacknowledged spiritual questions were beginning to surface in the work. *Hide and Seek* reflects those. There is a spiritual nihilism, a despair and disgust with the world which the writer would later attribute to illness: 'the spreading of my own disease, so to speak'.[19] The novel, however, is also a highly *self-aware* piece of writing. Importantly for his subsequent television work, it manipulates its despair and takes it to a kind of resolution.

The book is divided into six sections. Part One ('Into the Forest') introduces Daniel Miller, a character with a problem. As he tells his psychiatrist, he *knows* he is a character in a novel. Moreover, it is a dirty novel, written by 'a malignant and sex-obsessed Creator'.[20] He is trying to escape this feeling of 'being written about, pinned down, by some vastly superior force or person' (p. 38). It is the 'Author', Miller believes, who has made his wife leave him; who makes him use pornography and prostitutes; who has caused his illness (psoriatic arthropathy) and cost him his job as lecturer at a London polytechnic. His only hope is to retreat to the Forest of Dean of his childhood – to a place where 'the Author *was not there*' (p. 28).

The religious parallels are clear. Like Joe in *Joe's Ark*, Miller is a character whose own experience of suffering has led him to question the reality of a loving Creator. Childhood belief in a benign presence has given way to an adult view of Man tormented by a ruthless Old Testament God. The return to the Forest becomes an objective correlative for a mental retracing of the lost land of his childhood. If Miller can recapture the wonder of that past, perhaps he can recapture the sense of a loving God too.

As he drives round the Forest in circles, memories of childhood churn in his mind: 'An Italian showed him a tobacco tin filled with chunky rings. A boy cried alone in the bracken' (p. 16). He recalls his shy coal-miner father and the name, 'Rumpelstiltskin', which he used to mutter like an incantation whenever he found himself frightened and alone in the Forest as a child. Now, the Forest seems like a fairy-tale wood, exactly the place 'a sour hobgoblin sang and danced round his evening fire of spitting branches' (p. 29).

It is one of Miller's oldest memories which occupies a crucial place in the novel. He recalls the words of an old dance band song he heard playing on the radio when he was four years old: 'When deep purple falls / Over sleepy garden walls'. This puzzled the boy. How can a colour fall over a wall? And do walls go to sleep? The child realises the words are about something else. They mean more than they say. They are not the same as chairs, tables and other objects: 'The song hinted at words with disguises in them ... words too complex ... the thing grown-ups whispered about together, heads leaning in towards each other as though he was or should not be in the room' (p. 33).

Emerging from his reverie, the lecturer realises he has come upon his country cottage retreat: the external object of his night's drive and search. Switching off his headlights, he is plunged into darkness once more. He recalls lashing out violently at his wife. Touching his cheek, he discovers it to be 'as cold as a corpse, as when he had last touched his mother's flesh'. In his head, Miller begins to mix up dead mother, separated wife and his furtive liaisons with prostitutes: 'How many times had he woken with the wrong name in his mouth? How many, many times had he stretched out alongside the wrong woman in the wrong bed?' (p. 37).

Part One is undoubtedly the most important section of the novel. Each of the other five sections unravels the implications of 'Into the Forest'. In Part Two ('Acid and Lollipop'), the reader learns that Miller is far from mad. There is indeed a malevolent Author. At the beginning of this second section, he even introduces himself.

Addressing the reader directly in the first person, this Author asserts that he has decided to emerge from behind 'the misleading radiance' of third person omniscience for the sake of literary honesty (p. 38). As his narrative proceeds, however, it becomes clear that he has sent Part One of his first novel (the 'Daniel Miller' narrative) to his literary agent. Now, he fears the outside world will assume Part One is autobiography and that Miller is him.

It is for this reason he has decided to devote Part Two to a long apologia, listing the differences between himself and Daniel Miller, in order to try and distance himself from his 'sick' character. He begins to list the points of similarity and difference between himself and Miller, yet as he does so, his own assertions are constantly undermined by the weight of the evidence he presents. Like Miller, he was born in the Forest of Dean; is the son of a coal-miner; went to Oxford University and had ambitions to write a critical biography of Samuel Taylor Coleridge. He denies, however, that he suffers from the same illness as Miller: psoriatic arthropathy. The reason he wears gloves and uses a walking stick, he claims, is habit: not because of a crippling skin disease.

It is when he turns to comparing Miller's attitude to women with his own that the Author's status as an unreliable narrator becomes increasingly exposed. His defence turns into a kind of confession: 'Women. They are the root or the flesh of the problem' (pp. 56–7). He recalls seeing a beautiful black-haired girl in a seedy coffee bar called 'The Lollipop' and asks who would want to 'soil' such a figure:

> I am disgusted by the thought of spoiled human flesh. Mouth upon mouth, tongue against tongue, limb upon limb, skin rubbing at skin. Faces contort and organs spurt out a smelly stain, a sticky betrayal. The crudest joke against the human race lies in that sweaty farce by which we are first formed and given life. No wonder we carry about with us a sense of inescapable loss, a burden of original sin and a propensity to wild anguished violence … We are implicated without choice in the catastrophe of the copulations which splatter us into existence. We are spat out of fevered loins, or punctured rubber and drunken grapplings in creaking beds.[21]

He asserts that he adores women: 'It is a holy impulse in me to worship and to cherish them.' Echoing the familiar flesh-spirit dichotomy of other Potter works, the Author asks how such a 'soul' as he could possibly have fornicated with prostitutes? 'I could not have done these things any more than I could have killed my mother', he asserts (p. 83).

By the end of Part Two, having got all this down on paper, the Author is rewarded by a strange feeling of an 'indefinable presence of something greater than or beyond myself and my body, something sustaining me, feeding me, encouraging me' (p. 86). His thoughts return to Daniel Miller, still stuck in the Forest where he had left him. He decides he will allow his character to enter the fictitious cottage he had reached at the end of Part One because he does not 'lack mercy'. As for the other 'presence' he feels in the room, all the Author can say is that 'it or he or He is not *hostile*' (p. 87).

After Part Three ('A Sort of Ending') in which the Author finally allows Miller to retreat into his cottage, Part Four ('Oak and Attic') shifts from the character's to the Author's point of view once more. Now, however, it is not only Miller but the Author himself who is being 'written about' – his thoughts rendered in the third person. Hence is the Author himself the creation of that non-hostile presence he felt at the end of Part Two and if so, does this mean this new 'meta-Author' is as similar to him as he so clearly was to his fictional Daniel Miller ?

What is certain is that detached third-person omniscience enables the reader to judge the veracity of the Author's first-person account in Part Two. It is true he worships women and places them on a pedestal but what he did not tell the reader was that while sitting in 'The Lollipop', he had wondered how much it would have cost to 'buy' the beautiful black-haired girl. As this makes clear, the allegedly factual first-person account of Part Two is in reality a heavily edited series of lies and evasions. Part Four reveals that the apparent spontaneity of the Author's confessional prose has masked a careful process of rereading, rewriting and erasing. By contrast, it is the Author's fiction (his Daniel Miller narrative), not his factual writing, which communicates the 'truth'.

As he looks across at the girl in the café, the Author begins to remember how as a boy in the Forest of Dean, he would perch on top of the oldest oak in the Forest and stare out over the tops of the trees.[22] Up there, the Forest seemed 'a Holy Land' – a complete integrated world in which the boy was aware of 'a protective grace, moving above, beyond and yet within itself'. The child realised God was not a great figure in the sky but 'in and of things, every sort of thing, breathing through them' and that if you took that presence away there would be '*no point*'. The thought almost makes him 'fall' out of his tree until, steadying himself, he 'put God back into the world, holiness back into the Forest' (p. 110).

Experiencing a 'total illumination', the boy thinks he can hear God walking below on the forest floor. When he climbs down from the oak, it is not, however, a loving God he discovers but an Italian prisoner of war from the nearby camp. As previously indicated, he 'falls' victim to the adult's 'predatory appetites', with 'an innocence never to be reclaimed, a shock which changed even the ways of looking at the ferns and fox-gloves'

(p. 115).[23]

The 'trust in the order of things' which he had experienced up in the oak vanishes to be replaced by disgust for a malevolent deity that could perpetrate such a cruel trick on a boy. Tormented by the thought that at the very moment he had turned to face a loving God, he 'fell' instead 'into the hands of the Devil', he comes to think that what he had once felt in the tree were only 'mocking illusions and treacherous visions of grace' (p. 120). This is why he had made his character, Daniel Miller, try and escape from a malevolent Author in Part One. The memories of the Italian and the boy crying in the bracken were his own.

As the Author sits in his flat, rereading his apologia, the question he now faces is whether he can recapture that sense of unity with the 'presence' he had once felt in the Forest and which now seems to be with him in the room, 'sustaining, feeding him, encouraging him' to write (p. 120). He begins writing again, this time giving an account of his liaison with his one hundred and fifty-sixth prostitute. Significantly, the third-person narrative states the Author is 'getting nearer to himself, travelling on a long loop of bumpy path through the trees' (p. 136).

In Part Five ('The Education of Children'), the reader learns how the Author/Daniel Miller (the two are now synonymous) followed a black prostitute back to her attic room, only to discover, with horror, that a child was sleeping in the corner. Immediately, the Author/Miller felt he must protect the child from suffering the same psychological scars which had led him to the mother's room, yet as he turned back to the prostitute, ready to vent his indignation, he saw her standing naked. Biology took over: 'Of course I forgot about the sleeping child. Of course I did' (p. 141). How, his narrative asks, 'can a man do such a thing' as 'jerk up and down' on a naked woman within a few strides of a sleeping child? (p. 145) The narrative abruptly switches from first to *second* person as the Author begins to address his wife, Lucy: 'You do not know about these things' (p. 152). His apologia becomes an apology as he confesses how for long periods the only way he could make love to her was by secretly pretending she was 'a tart ... picked up ... on a street corner'. He cites the evening he picked up the black prostitute as a concrete example of this fundamental flesh–spirit, sex–love schism in his life. It was also the night Lucy left him, tired of his preference for reading Coleridge in bed rather than making love. Part Five of *Hide and Seek* closes with the Author's description of his sexual climax with the black prostitute. At the moment 'where exultation turns to disgust, the moment of spilling, of defilement', he had shouted:

> A shout loud enough to wake the child. The child began to scream ... Did you expect me to tell you *that*, Lucy? You, who wanted me to enter you on

> the same night, with the same sound still in my head, a sound that I knew I had somehow, somewhere heard before (p. 159).

As this implies, the screaming of the prostitute's child recalls his own screams during the sexual assault he underwent as a boy. The past victim has become a kind of abuser but has one 'bad act', as in *Brimstone and Treacle*, purged another? Has the moment of 'release', both physically and on the page (as he confesses this), enabled the Author to let go at long last his repressed guilt and fear?

In Part Six ('Trying To Begin'), the Author stares down at his night's work. He has ripped it to shreds. He thinks again of his character, Daniel Miller, and wishes he, too, could be out of London and in the Forest of Dean: 'Better … if it could be. Better to be his own character.' Suddenly, his own wish makes him realise this need not necessarily be beyond his grasp:

> He could make Miller wake up now. He could heal Miller's skin … Bring back his wife. He could do anything with, to or for this fictional character, simply by lifting up his pen … Why not ? What were novels *for*? He was the narrator. The Author. Creator of All! (p. 163)

He starts to write: 'It is, of course, no accident that redundant theological speculation about the death of God should run parallel with an equally tedious literary preoccupation with the death of the novel'. A thrill runs through him as he prepares to take the only way he knows how to escape to the Forest of Dean. For him, this is the 'beginning … and starting here he was both fucking *and* getting back into the tree' (p. 164).

With that, the novel, at its close, playfully returns to its opening (Part One) as a character announces to his psychiatrist that the Author 'knows I am trying to escape'. This time, however, events are recounted in the first person. The character declares it ought to be 'wholly forbidden to children'. What should, he is asked? 'Sexual assault' is the reply (p. 165).

Now that he has got out the hitherto repressed facts about his sexual assault and liaisons with prostitutes, the Author feels a liberation from guilt, as he reaches 'the open air on the far side of the back of the cover' (p. 166). Note that it is fiction which has played the enabling role. As a lecturer and literary critic, he has spent most of the novel worrying about the relationship between his fictions and the 'facts' of his own life. Suddenly, in Part Six, he begins to think about the value of fiction for the first time: 'What were novels *for*?' As the close of *Hide and Seek* makes clear, the answer is that they allow the imagination free play, enabling the Author to become his own God – 'the Creator of all'. This is how he can transform himself into his own character at the very end and how, too, a character can finally escape from an Author, disappearing off the page into 'the open air on the far side of the back cover'. Through fiction, the Author suddenly realises he can do anything he wants. He can reshape reality. The implications of this are worth exploring in detail for they are important not only in terms of understanding *Hide and Seek* but also the later *Singing Detective* and *Blackeyes* TV serials, both of which draw heavily on the themes of this first novel (see Chapters 5 and 6).

There are three key questions which *Hide and Seek* explores and finally resolves. In Part One, Miller is terrified by an omnipotent Author – a relationship which clearly functions as a metaphor for that between Man and God. As Part Two indicated, there is another presence, however, behind the Author-God, feeding and encouraging him in his act of creation. Hence if 'God' Himself is a creation, who created God and in turn, who created His Creator? The answer to the question simply throws up the same question at a deeper level. It is a recursion which goes on *ad infinitum*.

The other dilemma involving God has to do with a loss of integration. As a child, the Author had experienced a sense of harmony between God, the world and the self. On top of his favourite oak, the child felt he was God – a part of all things through which His Spirit breathed. The intrusion of sexuality, however, brought about a Fall from this position of divine grace, draining his world of 'wonder', until there seemed nothing and no point. Related to this are the numerous references in the text to a dead mother. As with *A Beast*, acquisition of the forbidden knowledge of sexuality breaches the child's sense of absolute security and trust in his parents, resulting in the 'death' of the special bond with his mother.

By the end of the novel, discovery of the possibilities of fiction has resolved both the recursion dilemma and the loss of integration. As the novel progresses, it becomes clear that character and Author are the same. In terms of religious metaphor, *Hide and Seek* collapses the distinctions between God and Man. This is why the Author finally writes that the death of God can only ever be 'redundant theological speculation'. Suddenly, through fiction, he has discovered he can be his own God ('the Creator of All'). This solves the recursion problem. By its close, the novel shows the chain of recursion (character, Author, 'meta-Author' and so on) is not infinitely linear but circular. The character is his Author; the Author can become his character. Man is a part of God. God is a part of Man. God creates Man. Man creates God.

Potter's various radio talks during the seventies help throw light on the religious conundrum. Describing his journey back from despair to a different sort of 'attention' (a journey in relation to which *Hide and Seek* is clearly pivotal), he indicated in 1978's *The Other Side of the Dark* the importance of the belief that 'the world is being made right in front of us

… and in living out our lives [we] give back piece by piece what has been given to us to use and work with and wrestle with. We shape our own lives.' Two years earlier, in his Christmas broadcast, *And with No Language but a Cry*, he stated that what is given back is 'what is given in the minute upon minute in which the mystery I call myself is making and being made'.

To Potter, the world is 'made' but so too are we making it minute by minute. Man is his own Author. There is a God without but also a God within and He is completely dependent upon Man for survival. Man creates Him. This, Potter asserted in 1977, was the true meaning of the Nativity, with its image of the helpless baby Jesus, through which God is 'seen as utterly dependent and completely helpless, manifest in human culture'. The cradle song of Christmas 'celebrates the birth of God in the hungering soul'.[24]

In *Hide and Seek*, the Author likewise comes to realise that the death of God is greatly exaggerated. He learns that, far from having disappeared, God and 'the truth' have been there in front of him all the time. Both are waiting in himself to be born. By rediscovering this, the Author can begin to reshape his own destiny. Recognition of a God within as well as without, restores the sense of integration he thought he had lost forever. As Part Six indicates, he feels a heightened 'attention' can be permanently his: it is both 'fucking and getting back into the tree'. The world of the adult and the world of the child, separated by a Fall, are brought together again through a renewed intensity in the perception of experience.

In this way, notions of a Fall become redundant. As the reference to 'fucking and getting back into the tree' indicates, the idea of sex as the means of separation from God is discredited by the end of the novel. Just as in *Where Adam Stood*, the implication is that this Fall which the Author thought he had experienced was really the product of a strict Bible upbringing and literal belief in the Old Testament. As a child in the Forest, the Author had convinced himself he was about to meet God as an external object or person. Disgust and disillusion set in when, instead, all he encountered was the brutality of an Italian POW. Implicit in this is the suggestion that it was not so much a cruel cosmic trick but the failed expectations of his own literal belief which made him think God had disappeared from his life.

This seems to be the significance of the 'deep purple' passage in Part One. Listening to the lyric 'When deep purple falls …', what the child discovers is the distinctness of language and *metaphor*. It hints at an unknown world behind the material world of objects. The idea of a non-material 'spiritual' realm is territory which the child's curious mind feels he has to explore. A quest for knowledge – for God – has begun, one that culminates at the end of the novel, with the Author's triumphant discovery that far from being a literal entity, God is a metaphor of his own making. In contrast to Old Testament accounts of Adam's Fall, the novel finally vindicates desire for hidden knowledge as not sinful. Words, language, metaphor – the original reason for his quest – become the Author's salvation.

If metaphor reduces the death of God to 'redundant' speculation, it also solves the parallel problem of the death of the novel. Part of *Hide and Seek*'s enquiry is clearly the question which the Author articulates in Part Six: 'What were novels for?' By making him a lecturer and literary critic, Potter allows his 'Author' character not only to conduct a quest to find out about himself and God through his own writing but also to discover the nature of fiction. In this way, by scrutinising his own life and work, the critic eventually succeeds in transforming himself into a writer ('The Author. The Creator of all!').

In interview, Potter stated much modernist and post-modernist innovation in literature is concerned with asserting the idea 'that creative writing has its own category and its own right and its own truth' in a world where old moral certainties have been displaced in favour of a greater relativism of values. Certainly, this seems to be one of the reasons Potter chose to write *Hide and Seek* as a first novel, rather than a TV play. Having a longer pedigree of formal experimentation than TV drama (as well as a smaller audience), a novel meant there was less danger that the 'truth' of the fiction could become confused in the public mind with the writer's own life. In *Hide and Seek*, Potter chooses to live dangerously by creating a tormented Author character who shares many of the biographical details of his own life – illness, Forest of Dean upbringing, Oxford education – 'facts' which by 1973 were in the public domain, not only through countless TV and newspaper interviews but also Potter's own use of them in dramas such as *The Nigel Barton Plays* and *A Beast with Two Backs.* In *Hide and Seek*, is Potter therefore playing his own game with the reader? Is this first novel 'art' or autobiography?

Potter, in interview, vigorously denied any direct similarity between his life and fiction, insisting that *Hide and Seek* 'is a novel ... It's all about characters. They only live between those pages.' At the same time, he asserted 'autobiographies are a complicated series of lies', full of self-justifications and evasions. This is borne out in the novel by the Author's apologia which is exposed as fraudulent. It is important to note the metaphor behind this – that it is always through fiction that 'truth' is revealed. When the Author claims to be putting down the 'facts', he is shown to lie. Only through his Daniel Miller narrative does he tell the 'truth'. In Potter's hands, fiction becomes more true than fact. Implicit is the message that one must always look to the work of the writer for truth, not to what he says about it.[25]

Indeed the whole dynamic of *Hide and Seek* is the possibility of using fiction in order to discover the truth about oneself. The novel portrays a writer, fearful of the connections between his fictions and the facts of his own life, who begins to probe those links, delving down through layers of fact and fiction and by so doing, gradually 'getting nearer to himself'. Crucially, relief from guilt comes only with his discovery of the power of fiction to *liberate* him from the facts. This is made apparent when, having transformed himself into a fictional character at the close, he freely admits his sexual assault to his psychiatrist. Suddenly the facts he had previously wanted to conceal become an irrelevance. He can casually confess the most intimate details of his own life because his discovery of the deeper 'truths' of fiction has made the 'facts' redundant. In *Hide and Seek*, truth is unyoked from fact and reassigned to fiction. As the 'Creator of all', the Author realises he can re-invent himself and so change the 'facts' of his own life.

Prefiguring *Double Dare, Hide and Seek* thus blurs all distinctions between fantasy and reality at its close. Suddenly, the Author discovers that the transformation of fact into fiction, which he has spent the rest of the novel worrying about, is actually a *two-way process* and that fiction can be turned into fact. In this way, he discovers the possibility of altering his own situation and reshaping reality. *Hide and Seek* itself therefore answers the question of whether it is autobiography or artifice. Like the question of the death of God, it does so by rendering it redundant through an emphasis on the power of metaphor. Wilfully blurring the boundaries between autobiography and fiction, the novel suggests such distinctions are ultimately meaningless beside the deeper spiritual truths which imagination and metaphor can access.

In turn, this throws light on Potter's use of the 'facts' of his own life in his work (including the 'fact' of sexual assault). In interview, he claimed the reason his own biographical details frequently appeared in the work was because they lent the writing 'a present tense kind of immediacy'. They make things come 'across as true, as characters you can't beat off … like somebody coming up to you.' The autobiographical genre, he asserted, is an 'extraordinarily powerful one' because of 'audience expectations of a certain ritual form of behaviour about 'the narrative'.' By playing with the conventions of autobiography, the writer can make the audience believe "This must be the truth'. And of course it isn't.'

Seen in this light, *Hide and Seek* lives up to its title. Its intimate confessional tone manipulates the reader's expectations that a first novel should be autobiographical. The work seems more self-exposing than it actually is: 'I'm a reclusive character and I don't expose myself. I appear to', was Potter's own view. The external biographical 'facts' which seem so revelatory are really part of a literary ruse, hiding a complete fabrication. The 'facts', as his Author character discovers at the close of the novel, are an irrelevance. They only conceal 'lies'.

Such a position seems unsatisfactory on several counts. *Hide and Seek*'s obsession with autobiography and self-exposure; the fraudulence of the Author's public apologia as opposed to the private truth of his fiction; his clear identity with Daniel Miller – all of these seem to cast doubt on the notion of Potter as *wholly* divorced from the products of his own imagination. He himself hinted there was something more by quoting Nabokov: 'Of course, it's not me but if what I was writing was not in some sense true other than my imagination, it wouldn't come across as true.' Facts may conceal fiction but fiction expresses the truth. This is one of the manifestations of the religious sensibility which informs Potter's writing. Akin to *Hide and Seek*'s recursive narrative strategy, the idea is of delving down through layers of surface fact and underlying fiction in order to reach a deeper truth and so get nearer to oneself. This seems to be why the writer was always so keen in his life to distance himself publicly from the autobiographical resonances in his own work. Because of his use of details from his own background, he faced the constant danger in a contemporary media culture ever more obsessed by journalistic 'facts', that his work would be reduced to the level of simple autobiography, thus obscuring its fictionality and the deeper 'truths' he saw as underlying it. As he expressed it in interview: 'People want to know "Is this true?" which is a very curious question to ask in that sense about a play or a novel. It should be true in another sense: ... I mean "art" and "truth".'

Hide and Seek is therefore not simple autobiography. Potter certainly weaves his own biography into the novel, blurring it with fiction to such an extent that, like Martin's experience in *Double Dar*e, it becomes almost impossible to decide where 'fact' ends and fantasy begins. This, however, is precisely the intention, for the aim is to show that such distinctions are irrelevant beside the deeper truths fiction can access – 'the truth of the content, the truth emotionally, the truth socially' in Potter's own terms. It is only at this deeper level of 'truth-telling', where events described in the novel may or may not be *literally* true but nevertheless express a genuine feeling or longing on the part of the writer, that the work can be labelled autobiographical (a sort of emotional or spiritual autobiography). For Potter, 'creating ... obsessed and tormented people means there must be some truth in one's own imagination that is complicit with that.' The tormented Author in *Hide and Seek* is not him yet at a deeper level it is him. Potter was always constantly aware, however, of the dangers of creating characters who mirrored the 'externals' of his life so closely:

> The closer writing approaches to therapy, the worse it becomes. I believe that passionately. So you've got to have that ruthless discipline about whether you're doing this to ease and soothe or as a balm to your own soul – I mean I've destroyed lots of things where I felt that was happening ... because [of] the very delicacy, the very danger, of both dealing and not dealing with what are certainly medically, geographically, age terms, socially, all those things true of myself and also some of my fantasies which I believe every adult person has which is a mix. Your head is a kind of warring with and battling with all sorts of things that the normal social self represses which a writer cannot or can only do so at a great cost. On the other hand, 'just letting it out' is one of the definitions of bad art. So there's always that monitoring eye.[26]

Double Dare is a warning of what can happen when that 'monitoring eye' is not used and a writer allows his own dark imaginings to take control of him. *Hide and Seek*, on the other hand, demonstrates the advantages of creating characters who are so 'close' to the writer. According to Potter, every writer instinctively weaves 'emotional truths and ... actual geographical facts, certain real things' into their own work but by *choosing* to do so in such a self-conscious way he allows connections to be forged, not only with his own life but with 'everyone's lives'.[27] A personal voice emerges from the work, creating the impression that the audience is being directly addressed in intimate confessional tones. It is a voice with which they are invited to identify.

If *Hide and Seek* is the most definitive example of this intimate voice, it seems highly appropriate it should have been in the novel that Potter first chose to experiment seriously with the conventions of autobiography since his manipulation of the genre is essentially an extension of the standard self-reflexivity of much modern literary fiction. In Potter's case, however, not only does his first novel deal with itself (the writing of a novel), it deals with the personality of its 'Author' who becomes its main character. In this way, the novel about a novel becomes a novel about the Author of a novel, searching for the 'truth' about himself and hence a pathway out of his spiritual crisis. As he eventually comes to realise, fiction is that pathway. It enables him to create a new reality for himself, propelling him on to a different sort of 'attention'.

'The play we're in'

Potter's first novel is so important because the legacy of its experimentation is tangible within his TV work. Indeed two contemporaneous television plays, *Follow the Yellow Brick Road* and *Only Make Believe*, share many of its themes, techniques and even plot devices. Together, they function almost as a televisual equivalent of the novel.[28]

Like *Hide and Seek*, *Follow the Yellow Brick Road* (tx. 4.7.72; dir. Alan Bridges) opens with a tormented character visiting his psychiatrist. As with Daniel Miller, fading actor Jack Black (played by Denholm Elliott) believes he is a character in a work of fiction – in this case, a television play. Moreover, it is a dirty play in which the cameras constantly hound him, zooming into big close-ups at all the wrong moments. His psychiatrist, Whitman, wonders if his talk of 'The play I am in. The play you are in' has anything to do with God (p. 329).[29] He coaxes the patient into revealing how, as a child, he had been riding a tricycle near his home one day when suddenly the clouds seemed to take on a '*radiance*'. The child sensed 'God was *too near*' (p. 331).

The description echoes the Forest scene in *Hide and Seek* where the 'Author' once sensed God walking nearby. In the TV play, however, Black proceeds to describe a much more recent spiritual encounter. Kneeling down one morning to pray, he had waited for 'the word' to drop into his mind. The word was: 'Slime! … That was the message I got. No God … nothing else but slime' (pp. 332–3). He rushes from the psychiatrist's room, choking back the vomit.

In his 1983 Preface to *Waiting for the Boat*, Potter admitted the writing of this scene to be his own personal 'low point':

> Naturally, no-one who gasped out such things in such a manner in such a place would be capable of one modicum of the detachment, let alone the discipline, needed to write such a scene … And yet I am afraid to concede that the excess of disgust jerking out from Jack Black's mouth more closely represented what I felt about the cold or faithless world, and its suffocating materiality, or my cold and faithless self.[30]

In the play, Black's own spiritual crisis is translated into disgust with television drama. 'Filth', he declares to Whitman, is what oozes out of all the television plays: 'They turn gold into hay, these people. Angels into whores. Love into a s-s-sticky slime – and Jesus Christ into an imbecile bleeding and screaming on a cross' (p. 324).

As the allusion to *Son of Man* indicates, *Follow the Yellow Brick Road* is partly a self-referential play about television. This becomes clearer as Jack contrasts the plays with the commercials. These are 'clean'. No one mocks goodness or wallows in vice: 'There's laughter … and sunshine and kids playing in the meadows' (p. 322). As Whitman realises, his patient is himself an actor in these commercials, having significantly tried but failed to get work on the single plays. In his own play, Potter illustrates Jack's work, punctuating the action with mock TV commercials.

Thus the audience is treated to the spectacle of Jack acted off the screen by a Great Dane, eager for its can of Waggy Tail Din Din. He is also seen creeping downstairs in the dead of night where a packet of Krispy Krunch biscuits lies behind a kitchen door. Recurring throughout the play, these mock adverts gradually come to reflect Jack's real-life worries and concerns. For example, the second time he is seen creeping downstairs, it is not Krispy Krunch he finds behind the door but his real wife in bed with a younger man. The fantasy of the commercials and the reality of his life become mixed up inside his head as he tries to deal with the domestic crisis which has finally led him to a psychiatrist. His wife has left him, as the Author in *Hide and Seek*, was left, because of his disgust with sex. It was his refusal to make love to her which led to her adultery.

Later, as the play progresses, Black learns that his actress wife Judy (Billie Whitelaw) has also committed adultery with his agent Colin. Contemplating revenge, Jack arrives at the latter's flat, only to discover Colin's beautiful young bride Veronica there all alone. Potter uses their encounter to explore Jack's sexual tension. Veronica becomes an image of purity in a fallen world – a living embodiment of the 'radiance' Jack had once felt gazing at the clouds. This is made explicit when he tells her of the many letters he has written to her but never sent. He weeps: 'I was writing to God' (p. 368).

As this makes clear, despite the most secular of themes – advertising, 'filthy' TV plays, the sight of an attractive woman – *Follow the Yellow Brick Road* is really a religious play. The title hints at this tension: is the 'Yellow Brick Road' material or spiritual? Is it the capitalist route of the commercials the hero is following, the road to Heaven or both? The title also carries a whiff of despair. At the end of the original 'Yellow Brick Road', Dorothy found no Wizard of Oz, simply a watery-eyed old fraud. Does the same apply here, in the case of either God or Mammon?

Looking back on the play in 1978, Potter asserted that organised religion differs little from the 'Holy City' of perfection which Jack glimpses in the commercials. Both offer 'New and Improved Pie in the sky'. Nevertheless, he maintained that he had wanted:

> half mockingly, and with an extremely grudging acknowledgement of what I was myself beginning to understand, to show how the human dream for some concept of 'perfection', some Zion or Eden or Golden City, will surface and take hold of whatever circumstances are at hand – no matter how ludicrous. Even in a future land of Muzak, monosodium glutamate and melamined encounters, the old resilient dreams will insist on making metaphors and finding illumination in the midst of the surrounding dross. There is, then, no

place where 'God' cannot reach.[31]

Whether in the false promises of the commercials or simply in the image of a beautiful woman, the 1972 play implies that spirituality – a yearning for something better than the present – will always outcrop. The theme is that of *Hide and Seek*: God, 'radiance', grace are all metaphors for the same 'human dream for *some* concept of "perfection"'. We create our own Wizard of Oz.

This is borne out by Veronica's actions in the play. She is not the 'angel' Jack has created in his imagination. When he tells her he loves her, she, a child of the permissive society, mistakes it for something else, replying 'O.K. we've got an hour ... Unzip me, Jack' (pp. 370–1). Black's spiritual yearning is immediately consumed by the flames of his own sexual desire. Like the Author in the room with the sleeping child, he finds, to his own disgust, that he has to submit to that desire.

By the end of *Follow the Yellow Brick Road*, Jack's disgust with the world (that is also the play) is thus complete. His only recourse is a return to his psychiatrist, yet this time it is not Whitman he encounters but a younger man, Bilson, a new breed of psychiatrist who is far more certain of the answer to Jack's problems. It comes in a bottle and is called Mogabrium. Bilson tells him no one today needs to be burdened with a sense of disgust: 'If Mogabrium had been available two thousand years ago ... I can think of at least one wild man who would have stuck to carpentry' (pp. 376–7).

As this second *Son of Man* reference indicates, the brave new world of 'happiness' pills cannot be the answer to Black's problems. They may cure him of depression but they will probably steal his soul at the same time. The clear implication is that it is better to recognise and be disgusted by the filth of the world than to blot it out by chemicals. As in *Moonlight on the Highway*, a deterministic solution to emotional or spiritual problems is rejected by the play. Significantly, however, it is not rejected by the central protagonist himself. Jack's mental torment is so great he will try anything to gain peace of mind. Swallowing the capsules, he asks Bilson if they are 'like the ads?' (p. 379).

The play's final scene suggests that they do indeed offer the same false paradise. Jack is seen acting in yet another advert. This time, it is not dog food or biscuits he is selling but Bilson's panacea – Mogabrium. He quotes from the Bible (Epistle to the Philippians 4: 8): 'Whatsoever things are true, whatsoever things are honest, whatsoever things are lovely', stumbling, as he does so, on his lines. The camera pulls back to show the wider scene, as a voice cries, 'Never mind, Jack. Try again. Keep it punchy!' (p. 382). Pulling back still further, the camera reveals all the electronic paraphernalia of the TV studio in which the actor has been performing, while the final credits roll.

As this self-referential final image makes clear, Jack's convictions were absolutely right. It was indeed a TV play he was in (and by implication a filthy world). Thanks to Mogabrium, however, he will never know. At the end of the play, life for him has become one big long commercial. As also indicated by the Biblical quotation, the false paradise of capitalism (advertising) is shown to be the same as the false promises of established religion. Both eschew complexity of thought, preferring the simplicity of selling 'New And Improved Pie In The Sky'. Sweeping the 'dirt' and pain of the world under the carpet, they are the same sort of 'lies'.

The ending of this play about TV plays also hints at Potter's changing attitudes towards television itself. In his introduction to the published edition of the play a year later, he wrote:

> The once-named 'window on the world' of brave old promise (or dishonest prospectus prose) is now much more like a silvered mirror sending back features we already know and do not wish to change. It sells aerosoled reassurance during the programmes and aerosoled deodorants in between.[32]

This casts light on the final image of Jack peddling his wares in a TV studio. Just as the pills have purged him of independent thought, so too, it seems, has television been purged of any honest engagement with the world. Even the TV plays (including the very play Black is in) have become one long commercial, selling false dreams. The window on the world has given way to the yellow brick road of consumer capitalism which prefers to reassure the public with lies than disturb them with the uncomfortable truth about the filth of the world. The view offered by this 1972 play is thus a bleak one – despair and disgust with a world which has become a veritable 'glittering coffin'. Undoubtedly, *Follow the Yellow Brick Road* marks Potter's lowest point in terms of his desire to write for the medium.

If it was not until 1976 and the *Brimstone* controversy that that desire would be fully reawakened, *Only Make Believe* (tx. 12.2.73) highlights the problems which Potter clearly felt in the early seventies as a writer who had made television his chosen medium. Directed by Robert Knights and produced by Graeme McDonald, this *Play for Today* is in many ways a companion piece to *Follow the Yellow Brick Road*. It deals with the second major narrative strand of *Hide and Seek* – not a character who knows he is a character but an ill writer, beset with problems and searching for creative inspiration in his dingy London flat.

The play opens on Christopher Hudson, a TV playwright who is hard at work on his latest play for the BBC. Much to his frustration, he has burned his right hand which means that instead of writing in his usual longhand, he has been forced to employ a secretary to type the lines as he 'composes'. This frustrates him. The presence of another person in the room feels like someone sharing his private fantasies. Even more frustratingly, he is attracted to the demure girl sitting at the typewriter. She, however, is interested neither in him nor his play. To her, the process of writing is not a personal act, simply a mundane job for which she is paid by the hour. Essentially, this is the drama – an exploration of the sexual and creative tensions between these two very different personalities as they find themselves locked up in a room together, bound only by the need to finish the all-important play. Where Potter creates added interest is by interpolating dramatised extracts from this TV play into the action of his own, for it soon becomes clear that the play Hudson is dictating is none other than one of Potter's own, his 1970 *Play for Today*, *Angels Are So Few*.

As with *Follow the Yellow Brick Road*, the self-reference is partly an opportunity for Potter to explore attitudes to television itself. Pouring all his energies into the writing of *Angels*, Hudson begins to experience doubts about the whole enterprise. As he tells Sandra, his secretary, it is only a *Play for Today*: 'Just today … Something easy, undemanding. It's all part of the commercial! It's all 'pass the time'!'[33]

The sentiments are those of *Follow the Yellow Brick Road* – television (and even life itself) has become one big commercial. Sandra's attitude only adds to Hudson's misery. She tells him she never watches TV plays. They are always too 'gloomy'. He, however, does not give up writing *Angels* in despair. The very disadvantages of the medium become a challenge to him to create characters who 'come up close' and cannot be shaken off so easily. As previously noted, the vividness of characters 'you can't shake off so easily' was one of Potter's own reasons for playing with the conventions of autobiography. In turning his plays in on themselves and having them *seem* to be about his own life, his aim was clearly that of his character, Hudson – to make a distracted TV audience sit up and take notice.

The connections with *Hide and Seek* are thus palpable, not only in terms of the self-reflexiveness and manipulation of autobiographical conventions but also in the recursive narrative strategy: the idea of a play about a writer writing a play. Exploring the links between Hudson's life and his TV play, Potter, in *Only Make Believe*, teases the audience with questions about the links between his own life and work (especially when it is realised Hudson's play is one of Potter's own). Like the novel, the 1973 play also offers the audience apparent insights into the creative process: the thoughts and feelings, stops and starts of a writer as he writes.

There are other links too. Like the Author in *Hide and Seek* (and Jack

Black), Hudson has been deserted by his wife for another man. This is the source of his sexual angst and the reason he starts to beg Sandra to have sex with him. A stranger 'hired' for the purpose of helping him to write, she becomes like Helen was to Martin in *Double Dare* – a kind of prostitute, holding out the possibility of 'healing release' not only creatively but sexually as well. Sandra, however, spurns all the writer's advances, telling him flatly: 'I'm only here to do some typing'.

As with the Author and Jack Black, Hudson is a figure racked by his own sexuality. A flesh-spirit dichotomy runs deep through his life, impelling him to seek sexual 'release' with 'hired' figures like Sandra, whilst being unable to make love to his own wife. This helps to explain the significance of the play within a play. If, as Chapter 2 noted, *Angels* can be read as a metaphor for the moment of a Fall from sexual innocence and the loss of a child-like faith, *Only Make Believe* portrays life 'after the Fall'. Biddle, the male victim of *Angels*, contrasts with the male manipulator or abuser, Hudson – the writer who pushes his fictional characters into bed, sexually harasses his secretary yet who is torn by a guilt that can be connected to feelings of a loss of unity with God. Stripped of his own wings, he burns in a kind of hell. This is the symbolism behind his damaged hand. In a series of short recurring flashbacks, Potter shows how Hudson came to injure it; how he deliberately mutilated himself by pressing his hand down on to a hot gas ring. Far from being an innocent in his own Fall, the symbolic inference is that, like Donald Duck in *Blue Remembered Hills*, Hudson was a victim of his own curiosity and desire for self-destruction.

By the end of the play, it is clear the writer is searching for the integration he feels he has lost – a way back from the Fall. His TV writing and his attempted seduction of Sandra are simply manifestations of his desire to reach out towards some greater communication or union beyond the isolation of himself. This is made evident in the climactic speech of the play in which, dictating furiously to his secretary, Hudson strips away all pretence of writing *Angels*, leaving only his own very personal memories of childhood:

> When kids cry out at night ..., there comes a big tall teetering adult with a light to say 'shoosh', it's alright ... It's only a dream ... But what if it's not only a dream? What if everything's not alright. Sandra? ... Who is going to come with the light and say it's alright? ... Only God Himself. Only God. And he won't. He can't. Too late.

Reaching out towards Sandra, he breaks down as she comforts him. With the *Angels* play within a play complete, she has been his 'ideal audience', allowing him to unburden his feelings of having 'fallen' from God.

As she leaves his flat, closing the door behind her, he mutters the last words of the play: 'It's alright. It's only a dream. Everything's alright.'

The question which the play begs at its close, however, is whether everything *is* alright? Is there a loving God and a benign order or is it all, like the play itself, 'Only Make Believe'? Conversely, with its self-referential quality and autobiographical connections, can this play really be said to be 'Only Make Believe', or could it be that like Hudson's notion of God and a Fall from God, drama and fiction contain their own hidden kinds of 'truth'?

The uses of enchantment

> If we hope to live not just from moment to moment, but in true consciousness of our existence, then our greatest need and most difficult achievement is to find meaning in our lives ... Like many other modern psychological insights, this was anticipated long ago by poets. The German poet Schiller wrote: "Deeper meaning resides in the fairy tales told to me in my childhood than in the truth that is taught by life".[34]

This is the opening of *The Uses of Enchantment*, Bruno Bettelheim's famous study of the meaning and importance of fairy tales. First published in 1976, the book argued that stories such as 'Sleeping Beauty' and 'Snow White' had survived and been passed down through the generations because they contained their own wisdom and their own truth. Implicit in the argument was the idea that modern psychological insights were only restatements of old truths about humanity, long ago recognised and embedded within the tales themselves.

Significantly, Potter was aware of the Bettelheim book and of the potency of fairy tales:

> Bruno Bettelheim's book about fairy tales and the archetypal structure of the fairy tale [shows] how powerful, potent they can be ... As a structure in the back of my mind, some of those stories ... first hit me, whether ... Jesus' parables or the Brothers' Grimm or Hans Christian Andersen (all of which of course become almost the same thing in the mind of a child), as structures of narrative ... Though I'm not going to tell you if you haven't found them – I'm not going to tell anybody – there are some of my plays that follow the structure ... or that started with the structure of some of those Grimm stories. So as a source, what one first reads and broods and thinks about becomes terribly important. What is it that made one want to be a writer? It's exactly that response to those things – those myths and stories and parables. And they itch in your brain in some odd sort of way. In another sort of way, they tell you how to live.[35]

Looking back on the work which this and earlier chapters have covered, it is possible to see the influence of the fairy tale structures which Potter hints at here. In *The Uses of Enchantment*, Bettelheim argues that one of the key fairy tale motifs is that of 'the usurper [who] succeeds for a time in seizing the place which rightfully belongs to the hero'.[36]

The Bonegrinder, *Angels*, *Schmoedipus* and *Brimstone* all feature such usurpers. As Chapter 2 indicated, they are the intruding strangers who take over the bourgeois suburban home, displacing its male head. Indeed both *The Bonegrinder* and *Brimstone* employ fairy tale endings in their dénouements. The 1968 play is a version of 'Jack The Giant-Killer' in which brave little 'King George' stands up to the mighty invader, 'Uncle Sam', with an axe at the very end. Meanwhile, *Brimstone and Treacle* closes with a variation on the 'Sleeping Beauty' story. If Pattie is the sleeping princess, Martin is the black Prince who awakes her from the spell of her passivity, not with a kiss but with what the original tale meant it to symbolise – rape.[37]

Schmoedipus, too, is a variation on 'Sleeping Beauty'. As her demon son and lover, Glen 'awakens' Elizabeth at the close, releasing what she had 'kept down' for so long – the memory of rape and an unwanted child. Though in all three plays, a release from guilt is shown to bring its own problems, nevertheless confronting fears and repressions, 'naming the demon', becomes the key to resolving the central dramatic problem of the 'outsider who is inside the head'.

In this respect, one fairy story stands out as crucial to Potter's writing: 'Rumplestiltskin'.[38] As previously indicated, it features in *Hide and Seek* – when Daniel Miller, driving through the Forest, imagines a 'sour hobgoblin' singing and dancing around a fire of twigs and branches.[39] Grimms' fairy tale of a miller's daughter forced to spin straw into gold connects not only with Miller's surname but with the plight of the Author, locked up in his London flat, trying desperately to turn the straw of his memories into literary gold. Similarly, the attempts of the heroine in the tale to banish the demon by trying to name him, echoes the Author's own delving down through layers of fact and fiction in *Hide and Seek*, as he tries to name and banish his own demons of sexual assault and sexual guilt. As in the fairy tale, the very *naming* of evil takes away its threat. In *Hide and Seek* words – writing – are the means by which the Author eventually liberates himself from the 'sour hobgoblins' of his past.

Fairy tales are thus a powerful ingredient in Potter's work. By making them the narrative foundation of many of his plays, Potter lends his writing an emotional power and a quality of universal truth. Covert use of archetypal plot structures allows audiences to identify with characters and situations more easily – hooking their interest in stories which seem both powerful and familiar. At the same time, Bettelheim's insistence on the struggle for meaning is enacted in Potter's own modern fairy tales. In works like *Schmoedipus* and *Brimstone*, the 'wonder' of a child's way of seeing the world (the fairy tale) is transposed on to the very epitome of the reined-in conventions of adult living (suburbia). Potter's message to his predominantly adult and suburban TV play-watching audience is clearly that of Biddle's to Cynthia in *Angels*: namely, that in order to see the truth of one's own life and so live it properly, the world has to be perceived anew with the eyes of a child.

Aside from fairy tales, there are other common structures running through Potter's work. What may be termed a '*Hamlet* structure' recurs in a number of plays. Determined to 'stand up' for his working class roots, Nigel Barton is haunted, like Shakespeare's tragic hero, by the 'ghost' of his father. As Chapter 1 indicated, both his climactic speeches (on TV in *Stand Up*; at a council dinner in *Vote, Vote, Vote*) revolve around the figure of his miner father and the stunting effect that social class has had on the older man's life and relationship with his son. As the idealistic young student 'prince', Barton's quest is to set the world to rights in the name of an injustice done to his father. In so doing, he is, like Shakespeare's tragic hero, torn by doubt. Should he stand up in the name of conscience or simply acquiesce to the *status quo*? His problem is exactly that of Jesus in *Son of Man* – is he mad to want to change things 'in the name of the Father', or is it the rest of the world that has gone mad?

Across a range of Potter plays, this common *Hamlet* structure of a 'torn' hero, opposed to the *status quo* in the name of an older set of paternal values, can be seen to recur – not just in *The Nigel Barton Plays* and *Son of Man* but also *Traitor* and *Lay Down Your Arms* (see Chapter 2). To this list can also be added *Where the Buffalo Roam* in which the main protagonist is literally haunted by the 'ghost' of his dead father. Inhibited from learning to read by the memory of his father's taunts, the torn young hero 'take[s] up arms against a sea of troubles' in order to try to alleviate his situation.[40] Transformed from a victim into a villain, he is led by his ghost from the past to a tragic end.

Significantly, these connections with *Hamlet* are only part of a much wider structural relationship which links together many Potter plays. What many have in common is their concentration upon a single male central protagonist who is torn by conflicting impulses – whether they be home and Oxford, reality and fantasy or more generally, flesh and spirit. Around this agonised Hamlet figure flutter two main supporting players, one male, one female, who, pulling him in different directions, embody his own inner conflicts. In *Stand Up*, Nigel's tensions between home and 'selling out' at Oxford find expression in the competing claims of his miner father and his upper-class girlfriend Jill, who keeps urging the student not to worry so much about the class divide. In *Double Dare*, Martin's inner conflict between reality and fantasy (the real world and that of his own imagination) finds an external echo in the figures of Ben and Helen: one, the worldly-wise producer 'pimping' for a friend; the other the source and inspiration for all his deepest fantasies as a writer. Meanwhile, in *Traitor*, though tormented by journalist interrogators in the present, the real source of Harris' inner flesh-spirit conflict is shown to lie in the past. What haunts him is the incompatibility between chasing his father's dream of Camelot and leading a 'normal' life, embodied in the play by his mother's more down-to-earth concerns for his development.[41]

The dilemma is that of Hamlet's: follow the airy vision of a ghostly father or conform to an unhappy *status quo*; cling to a spiritual ideal or compromise with the material world. The *Hamlet* comparison also shows how frequently Potter employs trios of characters: like that of the son, torn between the claims of a fleshly mother and ghostly father in Shakespeare's tragedy.[42]

In his film version of the play, Olivier famously described Hamlet as 'the tragedy of a man who could not make up his mind'.[43] Another common feature of Potter plays is their ambiguity. Many of the plays (particularly the early ones) are decidedly ambiguous towards their own central characters, making it unclear, for example, as to whether Nigel Barton is a rebel or a fraud, Willy Turner a victim or a villain (see Chapter 1). When quizzed about this aspect of his writing, Potter asserted: 'It's out of ambiguities that we make choices. But there's something very cruel about a choice that's made without doubt.' He related this to the distinction he saw between political writing and 'art':

> It's easier to show political drama if you're naturalistic or if you're an issue writer – ... and you say this is a scandal and so on. I believe that is the role of journalism and the essay and political polemic ... It's difficult to put into words but I don't believe that that is the category [of] ... 'art' ([in] quotation marks). The truth-finding – for example, in *Brimstone*, using the woman [Mrs Bates] whose prayer is answered as an absolute suburban canting humbugging fool and yet right. Now if you had made that a political drama, you would be tempted to make your message explicit and I don't believe 'art' (again [in] quotation marks) can be explicit. All it would do is buck up and cheer up those who support your side and it will not drop an ounce of the alternate view into those who oppose.[44]

The early plays in particular were so ambiguous because, though far more concerned with political issues than some of his later work, Potter wished to avoid didacticism, believing it to be inappropriate for drama. This is why in both *Stand Up* and *Vote, Vote, Vote*, Nigel Barton's inner conflict is mirrored in the plays' wider conflict of attitudes towards him. His dilemma is explored from two contradictory points of view rather than any simple solution being proffered or made explicit. For Potter, 'truth-finding' in 'art' is complex and not reducible to a single political stance.

This, too, is why, in many Potter plays, there are always two different versions of the central protagonist struggling to get out – the hero and the villain; the victim and the fraud. Not only are the audience left to make up their own minds which version to embrace, so, too, are the protagonists themselves. Indeed it is the root of their inner conflict. If this is so for *The Nigel Barton Plays* and *Where the Buffalo Roam*, it is also the case with *Son of Man* and *Lay Down Your Arms*. Jesus' struggle with himself is in order to decide whether he is the Messiah or mad. Similarly, Hawk may be a liar, user of prostitutes and a traitor to British Intelligence but his inner struggle to remain true to his (and his father's) ideals shows him to have genuine moral courage.

Potter's protagonists are never all good or all bad but always both and. Each always has to confront a moral dilemma, one that is invariably a variation on the central flesh-spirit dichotomy which runs through much of Potter's writing up until the mid seventies. Their choice is always whether to capitulate to the material world (the 'animal' half of their own natures) or else to try to struggle against it in the name of a higher spirituality (the 'angel' side). This is so whether that struggle takes the form of a political or religious ideal or simply, as with *Where the Buffalo Roam*, an assertion of the freedom of the individual to fantasise escape.

Since each work is about the conflict that goes on 'inside a person's head', there are always two versions of the same character, struggling within for dominance. One is the public self the protagonist presents to the external world; the other, the inner or secret self which inhabits its own private spiritual domain. The flesh-spirit dichotomy that each of Potter's protagonists has to confront is *internalised* as a battle between warring aspects of the same personality. For example, in *Where the Buffalo Roam*, there are two Willy Turners – the young unemployed Welshman which the external world sees and the Wild West outlaw he dreams of being inside his head. Each version of the self is shown to be incompatible with the other. In *Stand Up*, there are two opposing Nigel Bartons – the heroic working-class rebel at Oxford versus the swot of the village school who, as a child, once sneakily betrayed a fellow 'class-mate'. If the first is the present-day public persona, the other is a private self living within: a 'secret friend' capable of being reawakened when an object or event in the present triggers off a sudden renewal of feelings from childhood. When the adult Nigel watches his miner father head for the pit gates at the very beginning of *Stand Up*, he murmurs, 'There but for the grace of God and the eleven-plus' as the scene associatively flashes back to the village school, where, as a child, he was first emotionally separated from his class background and his father.[45]

The events of *Stand Up* are triggered by an external event impinging upon the consciousness of the central protagonist. The rest of the play takes place inside his head as a series of flashbacks, alternated with scenes depicting him in the present. This is a characteristic trait of Potter plays. In *Traitor*, Harris' memories of public school and England are triggered by the arrival of a group of well-heeled Western journalists to his Moscow flat. In *Paper Roses*, it is the prospect of imminent retirement which prompts Clarence Hubbard to look back on his life. The 'outsider' cycle of plays presents a variation on this insofar as it is the intrusion of a stranger within the suburban home that triggers a conflict within the central protagonist between the public or domestic self and a secret, private one. Morally upright husbands like George King and Mr Bates, as well as the seemingly conventional wife Elizabeth Carter, are all forced to confront old guilts. The outsider represents an externalisation of what is inside their heads and will not go away until that private truth has been more closely reconciled with the public lie of the domestic facade.

This holds generally true of the single plays: external events trigger memories in the central character at a moment of personal crisis, when the disparity between the public and the private self has grown too wide. Taking place largely inside their main characters' heads, the plays chart the attempts of protagonists to bring external reality closer to their own internal reality so that these two conflicting aspects of the self may be reintegrated. This is clearly what lies behind Nigel's attempts in *Stand Up* and *Vote, Vote, Vote* to 'stand up' for his class. His deep desire to change the political realities of class in Britain springs from his need to bring the external world more in line with his own internal reality, in terms of the disjunction he feels between his new life as an upwardly mobile student/politician and his own working-class roots. Triggered off by the realisation of the widening status difference between himself and his father, his drive in *Stand Up* is to heal the division he feels between his life in the present and the way it once was in the past.

Similarly, at the close of *Where the Buffalo Roam*, Willy's rampage as a cowboy can be seen as one last desperate attempt to reconcile a fertile inner life with the grim reality of his existence in Swansea. Becoming a real outlaw is the only way he can see of bridging the gap between the richness of his own imagination and the poverty of his external world. If, as Chapter 1 indicated, Potter's plays of the sixties suggest that the world ultimately does not want to know of the struggles of protagonists to reconcile themselves honestly with it, his later works demonstrate that such a reconciliation between material reality and the spiritual self need not necessarily manifest itself in overtly political attempts to change the external 'facts'. Barton and Turner both fail at the end of their respective plays and are left worse off than before, yet as the later *Hide and Seek* makes clear, such a transformation can be achieved internally, through the power of memory, imagination and fiction.

Hence because it offers the possibility of new ways of seeing and being, it is the 'enchantment' of fiction – myth, fairy tales and other cultural archetypes – which has, for Potter, many 'uses'. Certainly, these are present in his writing, hidden deep within its structures. The writer himself, in a 1979 interview with the *Radio Times*, summed up one reason why:

> Human beings are story-telling creatures. We need – myth is the noble word for it – we need myth to contend with the absurdity of being here. The most beautiful part of being alive is our capacity to shape our lives by language, by stories. We can't live without them. We tell them to each other all the time. The world is full of the murmur of human beings trying to reshape reality.[46]

'Style is truth'

Because they offer other ways of seeing, stories provide us with the ability to reshape our reality. Nowhere is this more clear than in relation to Potter's distinctive non-naturalistic *style* which is inextricably bound up with his personal beliefs. In Chapter 1, it was suggested a more precise label for this 'non-naturalism' was 'psychological expressionism'. The phrase, borrowed from Raymond Williams, seemed to encapsulate Potter's concern with 'expressing' the mental life of his protagonists ('what goes on inside people's heads'). It also fitted Williams' view that since the eighteenth century the broad trend of drama history has been towards greater representation of the 'real'. As a form of 'psychological expressionism', Potter's style could be classed as an offshoot of realism – one more way of taking 'account of reality … to include 'psychological' as well as 'external' reality'.[47]

While such a view seemed ideal for locating the early work within a broader *Wednesday Play* context of 'agitational contemporaneity', it cannot so easily be extended to Potter's later exploration of spiritual themes.[48] As Williams points out, characteristic of a greater dramatic emphasis on 'reality' is that the actions of plays become not only contemporary but secular. 'Realism', he states, was originally conceived as a conscious reaction:

> against the characteristic presentation of the world in 'romance' and 'myth' – seen as including extra-human, supernatural and in these terms irrational

> (non-comprehensible) forces. It was also an emphasis against 'theatricality' and 'fictionality': against the presentation of 'substitute worlds', based on earlier writing and on the past, on the separation of 'fancy' from 'fact'.[49]

Clearly, the presence in Potter's later plays of angels and demons; his use of myth and fairy tale; his probing of the realms of 'fancy' and 'fact', all mean that arguments about style have to be extended somewhat from Chapter 1.

It is perhaps ironic that the key to making sense of the problem lies not with Raymond Williams but in a second paper entitled 'Realism and Non-Naturalism', which was also delivered at the Edinburgh International Television Festival in 1977. This was by Potter himself.

In it, the writer spells out his reasons for preferring a 'non-naturalistic' TV dramatic style. He also sketches a view of television far removed from his upbeat vision of the sixties. Licenced like a dog, the task of TV, Potter asserts in the paper, is to supply a constant flow of images into the home. Much of that output is designed merely to pass the time. One programme trickles into another until it comes to feel that the same sort of 'experience' is on offer. There is also a complex exchange of mutual values between types of programmes. The best analogy, he maintains, is with 'the yellow brick road' of the commercials. Not only do most programme styles ape those of the commercials (and vice versa), it also feels as if they are all *selling* something. That is, just as the effect of more competition in the market-place paradoxically narrows choice rather than widening it, so the need of producers to have their programmes stand out from the crowd as more distinctive and exciting results in each of their offerings coming to look more and more like any other part of the schedule. Potter states: 'The reason, I think, is that they are selling much the same thing – a particular view of Reality'.[50]

Faced with all this, the writer has a choice – either to confirm and strengthen the prevailing values of society or else to let 'the movements of his imagination take him in the opposite direction'. In television drama, the problem is particularly acute since a play can be sucked into the general context of the programmes surrounding it in the schedules and so be drained of much of its meaning. According to Potter, much discussion about TV drama is characterised by the need to mark it out as separate and special from the news, entertainment and ads which surround it. Unfortunately, the debate amongst practitioners tends to reduce itself to the relative merits of various technical aspects of production. The result is that TV plays and drama series come to merge with the rest of the programmes – trying to 'sell' themselves as technically innovative or exciting and in the very process, losing all sense of distinctiveness from the rest of the schedule.

By contrast, Potter asserts there should be a genuinely alive debate not about *styles* of production but about the choices between 'naturalism' and its alternatives.[51] The distinction is highly significant. For Potter, the choice between 'naturalism' and 'non-naturalism' is not simply a question of which dramatic style to use but between two fundamentally different ways of *seeing*.

If this suggests a connection between the deeper truths perceived in creative writing and his own 'non-naturalistic' style, Potter goes on in his paper to define the relationship as being that between 'the word and the world'. Advocates of 'realism' and 'naturalism' confidently assume that there is a stable and generally agreed idea of external reality – of the world 'out there'. In their work, they seek to represent that world, holding it up for the audience's inspection and telling them this is how things are. As a television writer, Potter states he feels increasingly drawn towards other modes. Importantly, he relates this not only to his view of television but to his own personal beliefs:

> [and] my need to relate the changes and the anxieties and the yearnings of my own personal belief to the world as I now apprehend it. I am not yet sure whether I love God or the idea of God, and I am not going to stand up here and baldly announce all the force that makes me translate the human need for order, for justice, mercy, pity and peace into a yearning for God. But that is what haunts me.

He also sets his choice of 'non-naturalism' against a wider historical context of modernist thinking and practice: 'As the still underrated H. G. Wells put it, the frame within which the writer sees 'reality' has splintered and got into the picture'.[52]

'Naturalism' has come under pressure from the awareness of a relativity of perspective – that 'reality' is as much a question of the observer as that which is observed. Extending his argument to television, Potter asserts the single play 'is virtually the last place on the box where the individual voice and the personal vision is central to the experience.' This is important because amongst TV's bombardment of images and messages, most of which serve to reinforce rather than challenge the habits and attitudes of society, a play has 'the chance to show that the world is not independent of our making of it and, more, that the other programmes, too, are engaged in making the world even as they purport merely to reflect it'. Hence the first task of a TV play is to be a play, not an imitation of something else: 'It can step out of the flow and back on to the bank only by drawing attention to its status as drama and by demonstrating its own workings.'[53]

Potter ends his paper by suggesting that television practitioners should concentrate more on the activity of drama rather than just take 'realist' or 'naturalist' forms for granted. By definition, he thinks the 'non-naturalist' writer is inevitably going to be more wary of those forms and conventions because 'he often wants to examine them and lay them bare, in the structure of his play. He wants to show the workings. He wants to look at our way of looking even as he is looking.' Potter closes with a summary of his arguments for 'non-naturalism':

> Most television ends up offering its viewers a means of orientating themselves towards the generally received notions of 'reality'. The best naturalist or realist drama, of the Garnett-Loach-Allen school for instance, breaks out of this cosy habit by the vigour, clarity, originality and depth of its perceptions of a more comprehensive reality. The best non-naturalist drama, in its very structure *dis*orientates the viewer smack in the middle of the orientation process which television perpetually uses. It disrupts the patterns that are endemic to television and upsets or exposes the narrative styles of so many of the other allegedly non-fiction programmes. It shows the frame in the picture when most television is busy showing the picture in the frame. I think it is *potentially* the more valuable, therefore, of the two approaches.[54]

The implications of this are important for understanding Potter's commitment to TV drama. A 'non-naturalistic' style disorientates because it disrupts television's habitual 'naturalism'. Potter's purpose is to make the viewer sit up, take notice and attend to his play. He is also, however, trying to raise questions about the view of 'reality' which the bulk of television offers its viewers for passive acceptance.

In many ways, it is possible to trace the roots of this challenge to received TV wisdom all the way back to his *Between Two Rivers* documentary. As a BBC General Trainee, Potter learned how the 'facts' of current affairs could be 'lies' (see Introduction). Television – the transparent 'window on the world', allegedly offering direct access to things as they are – was actually a thoroughly manipulated medium. If this prefigured his move to drama five years later, it also links in with the 'fact', 'fiction', 'truth' distinction which runs through much of the work: the idea that 'facts' not only can be 'lies' but that 'fiction' can express deeper 'truths' than 'fact'.

As a predominantly 'naturalistic' medium, purporting to reflect the world, television has traditionally tried to conceal its own conditions of manufacture. Writing TV plays became Potter's way of challenging the 'particular view of Reality' which he felt the medium was 'selling' to a mass audience. For much of the sixties, this linked him with Ken Loach, Tony Garnett and other prominent *Wednesday Play* practitioners, all of whom were trying to depict on television areas of experience which had hitherto been neglected or underrepresented: the problems of social class, sexuality, homelessness and so on. Extending the limits of what could be portrayed on screen, they were all trying to question received notions of 'reality' (bourgeois reality), in the name of a more 'comprehensive' vision of a world that was dynamic and could be changed.

Right from the very beginning, however, Potter's alternative reality was not so much external as internal. His 'psychological expressionism' challenged television's conventional view of the world by suggesting that what went on inside the head was just as important as anything that went on outside it. This modernist emphasis carried a political edge: not only did it introduce an intimate 'interior' drama to television, it also implied that the 'facts' which other programmes offered were inherently subjective and could be changed. As a current affairs documentary, *Between Two Rivers* had carried the ring of 'factual' authenticity. As a drama taking place inside its main protagonist's head, *Stand Up* made sure its view of social class in Britain could never be construed as anything other than personal.

As Potter's work progressed, however, his broadly 'political' themes deepened into explorations of the 'unacknowledged spiritual questions' which had been underpinning them. The fact that we make our own world and can reshape reality could be emphasised by having a play reveal its own manufacture (and by implication that of the rest of television). In *Follow the Yellow Brick Road*, *Only Make Believe* and *Double Dare*, self-reflexive devices were used to emphasise that a play in the TV schedules had its own special category and 'truth'. This was something which 'realist' and 'naturalist' dramas by definition could not do. However radical their challenge to orthodox views of the world, they had to share with the rest of television a concern to present their version of the 'facts' and so conceal their own manufacture.

Potter's desire to be a television 'author' can also be seen in this light. Not only does heavily 'authored' drama underline a personal subjective vision, it also draws attention to this manufacture of television and the idea that we make our own world and can reshape reality. Potter's style is thus inextricably linked to his vision of the world. Just as stories provide other 'ways of seeing', so too does 'non-naturalism'. In interview, the writer asserted this view that dramatic style is indivisible from 'truth':

> I mean you can tell a writer who is a liar not by the events but by the style. It is style that is truth ... If you get a piece of overwrite or flatulent writing and you know that it is *emotionally* untrue, it is the style which tells you, while the event may well be [*factually* true] I mean, somebody could sit down and write their life and be absolutely factually accurate and the style would be a lie if it was pompous or if it was fickle or if it just played with the truth in

that way. That is the truth to me. It's a far more important area of truth-telling than saying "well did X actually happen and was that followed by Y or did Y actually precede it?"

Mere 'facts' are not the 'truth'. There are deeper 'truths' which fiction can access. In one way, this emphasis on the primacy of 'art' and an inner as opposed to an outer world makes Potter a television modernist. In another, however, it also connects with much older narrative traditions of myth and fairy tale, insofar as it adheres to the idea that however fantastic or outlandish the form in which it is contained, fiction can reveal 'truths' about life.

It is this which seems to separate Potter from Raymond Williams' notion of 'psychological expressionism' as a kind of 'realism'. As Chapter 1 indicated, Williams' argument was that many of the modernist innovations of early twentieth-century drama were part of the broad dramatic trend towards 'realism'. They were a kind of 'psychological realism'. In the same paper, however, he was also forced to make a somewhat awkward distinction between drama which focuses on an inner 'psychological' world and that which deals with 'spiritual' or metaphysical themes. In the latter category, he cited the plays of Eliot, Yeats and 'some Beckett', asserting these were:

based on attempts to restore the world-views which realism and naturalism had attacked: the deliberate reintroduction of supernatural or metaphysical forces and dimensions controlling or operating on human actions and character, or the less easily recognisable introduction of forces above and beyond human history and 'timeless' archetypes and myths.[55]

Because of his view of (and ideological commitment to) 'realism' as the main historical trend of drama since the eighteenth century, Williams, here, is forced to hive off as regressive an important strand of modernist writing which does not fit his definition of drama as increasingly contemporary, socially extended and above all, secular. The latter, to him, deals with the 'real' world; the former does not.

By contrast, what the example of Potter shows is that far from being an offshoot of 'realism', it is possible to relate an emphasis on 'interior drama' to a fundamentally different way of seeing. The preoccupation of 'naturalism' and 'realism' is with external reality – describing its 'surface' or depicting the underlying social, historical and political forces which both shape it and can change it. Potter's 'non-naturalism', on the other hand – which includes 'psychological expressionism', self-reflexive devices, use of myth and fairy tale – is concerned with an inner world; with what, as an increasingly self-conscious religious dramatist through the nineteen seventies, he came to regard as the 'spirit'.

Conclusion

This is why, in 1977, Potter was able to label art 'the inheritor of religious acts'.[56] Because it allows other ways of seeing, art provides a way for individuals not only to order but to reorder their world. It can restore the 'wonder' and recapture the lost lands of childhood. It also has the power to reshape reality. As *Hide and Seek* showed, not only can Authors shape characters, characters can shape their own Author. An Author can become his character and through this, find a way of resolving his own personal problems. In this way, writing becomes an act of faith. It inherits the power of religion to transform lives.

As an Author, too, the individual can become a kind of God – the true Author of his Fate. Indeed Potter pushes the metaphor further. For him, the world is both made and being made. God waits within us: hence we are our own God. The world of stories – 'Only Make Believe' – opens up and reveals the sovereignty of the 'spirit'.

If it was this recognition which resolved the crisis of faith that haunts *Follow the Yellow Brick Road* and *Hide and Seek*, it also has implications for a number of recurring features in the plays: the self-reflexivity; the 'uses' of the enchantment of fairy tales; the 'non-naturalistic' style. Each is a way of asserting the power of fiction or drama and of a different way of seeing. Ultimately, they are Potter's challenge to the materialist secular thinking that dominates contemporary society.

Hence his continuing choice during the seventies to write plays for television was not merely expedient or accidental. As his broadly political attacks became superseded by spiritual themes, TV became even more important to him as not only the most potent medium but the one which most authenticated prevailing attitudes. To write for TV was in a sense to attack materialist secular thinking from within.

There was, however, one problem. As early as his 1973 Introduction to *Follow the Yellow Brick Road*, Potter had pinpointed it. Writing of why he first chose to be a television playwright, he commented:

> And so while most of my original reasons for choosing to write for television are – if suitably rephrased – still valid, they leave out something crucial: the quality of *response*. Bullets on one side and football on the other … [mean] the life of a play so doubly boxed can be sucked away in the surrounding flow. Worse, a panel game, a plastic-prairied Western, a hard-eyed news bulletin, Wimbledon, a detective melodrama and an original play eventually submerge together into the same *kind* of experience. It is this landscape of indifference,

so hotly lit, which in the end defeats the pride and passion of the writer.[57]

In *Only Make Believe*, Potter illustrates the point through the figure of Hudson's secretary, Sandra. People tend not to watch TV plays. The mass audience – the coal-miners and other working people from whom Potter had escaped yet whom he now wanted to reach through television – had little or no interest in one of the medium's most traditionally prestigious and 'high-brow' forms: the single play. It was series and serials like *Z-Cars* and *Coronation Street* which got the high ratings. Despite Potter's best attempts to make an audience sit up and take notice of his work by means of his 'non-naturalistic' style, the very title *Wednesday Play* or *Play for Today* before each of his plays, was always going to be a cue for 'half the bloody audience to switch over or switch off' (as Christopher Hudson puts it, in *Only Make Believe*). It was not the coal-miners but the dons and the TV critics who would be guaranteed to keep on watching.

It is in this context that Potter's move to the more popular serial format should be seen. The highly successful 'serials with music', *Pennies from Heaven* and *The Singing Detective*, were both attempts to use this format as a vehicle for the exploration and expression of 'authored' themes, normally associated with the single play or TV film. As Chapter 4 will examine in more detail, Potter's intention with the extended format was not simply to gain ratings or even enhance his reputation as a 'major' TV writer. It was also to challenge prevailing (materialist secular) attitudes by challenging prevailing TV forms. If the original play and 'the detective melodrama' tended after a while to merge into the same landscape of indifference, then it would only be through colonising those other forms (as with *The Singing Detective*) that Potter would be able to challenge viewer indifference.

It is therefore no coincidence that the appearance of *Pennies from Heaven* should coincide with an upward curve of optimism in Potter's work, together with a renewed interest, after the *Brimstone* banning, in the possibilities of writing for the medium. Aside from adaptations like *Late Call* and *The Mayor of Casterbridge*, *Pennies*, however, had been by no means Potter's first foray beyond the single play. Transmitted seven years earlier, his first original 'authored' serial was *Casanova*.

4

Sex, lies and videotape: *Casanova* and *Pennies from Heaven*

Magic moments: *Casanova* and the evolution of the 'authored' serial

First transmitted on BBC-2 between 16 November and 21 December 1971, *Casanova* makes it possible to trace the ways in which Potter began to experiment with 'authored' drama beyond the single play. A forerunner of *Pennies from Heaven* and *The Singing Detective*, it helps explain why these works are not easily categorisable in terms of conventional television forms.

In 1971, Potter suggested to the *Sunday Times* that far from being a serial or a series, *Casanova* was 'a single play divided into six episodes'. Based on the memoirs of the famous eighteenth-century lover, the idea of a six-hour play had arisen because he 'wanted to do an accumulative portrait; something that wasn't swallowed up as soon as the screen went dark'.[1] Potter was thus seeking to overcome the anxiety he would later express in the Introduction to the published *Follow the Yellow Brick Road* – the fear that all too often the single play could 'be sucked away in the surrounding flow of television', so defeating 'the pride and passion of the writer'.[2] A longer work, stretched out over weeks, might make more of an impact. It could stand out from the 'flow'.

On one level, such a desire was only part of a growing trend amongst BBC dramatists to extend 'authored' drama beyond the confines of the one-off play. If David Mercer's *Generations* trilogy had provided an early illustration of how 'authorial' themes could be spread across a number of related works, in 1966, John Hopkin's *Talking to a Stranger* had demonstrated the possibilities an extended format could offer the TV playwright. Characterised by the narrative continuity of the weekly serial, this work, examining the breakdown of a suburban family, employed the kind of formal experimentation normally associated with the one-off 'authored' play.[3]

'Authored' drama in an extended format thus evolved largely from the direction of the single play. It arose from the desire of writers to explore single play themes in greater depth than the temporal constraints of the single play form would allow. Conventional serials, being generally 'unauthored', could offer only narrative continuity from week to week.[4] Writers like Hopkins and Potter were seeking *thematic* continuity as well. Right from the very outset, however, these episodic dramas created a confusion in production categories. Originating not within Series and Serials but the Plays Department of the BBC, they blurred the distinction between what constituted a *serial* and a *series* of related *plays*.

In the case of *Casanova*, this confusion was further complicated by its links with the historical or costume drama. Having entirely self-generated the *Casanova* project in the manner of his single play work, Potter completed the scripts over a period of thirteen months and delivered them to Gerald Savory, the Head of BBC Plays, who then invited Mark Shivas to produce them.[5] This was a significant choice, revealing how *Casanova* was perceived within the BBC. In the early seventies, Shivas was a producer of BBC-2 plays who had gained a reputation for lavish costume drama, following the considerable success of his *The Six Wives of Henry VIII*. Like *Talking to a Stranger* this was a series/serial that nevertheless emanated from the Plays department of the BBC: a group of six historical plays which sought to exploit audience fascination with the private life of royalty. First transmitted in January 1970, they attracted an average of four million viewers per episode – record audiences at the time for a BBC-2 drama. Winner of the Prix Italia and many other awards, the plays subsequently went on to become highly lucrative for the BBC in terms of programme sales overseas.[6]

What is evident from its production history is that in *Casanova*, the Plays Department spied a suitable follow-up to its last big costume success. Shivas reassembled many of the team he had worked with on *Henry VIII*: director John Glenister, designer Peter Seddon, costume designer John Bloomfield and so on. Also like *Henry VIII*, the production was considered too large for one director to handle alone. The six *Casanova* plays were divided equally between two directors – Glenister and Mark Cullingham – who each had their own individual crew.

By the time of its transmission the following November, Potter's drama had become a major new costume production for the BBC's autumn season. The *Radio Times* gave it prominent space, putting its 'star', Frank Finlay, on the front cover, dressed in full eighteenth-century garb as Casanova.[7] It is here that a marked divergence begins to appear between the BBC's promotion of the drama and Potter's own in various interviews he gave at the time. While the writer described his latest work as a single play over six episodes, to the Corporation it was 'a six part series'. Where the *Radio Times* stressed *Casanova*'s 'historical accuracy' and the fact that several of its production team had worked on 'the award-winning *Six*

Wives of Henry VIII', Potter told the *Sunday Times*: 'To me, the term 'costume drama' means something totally pickled'.[8] Not only did he claim *Casanova* was a work of 'contemporary relevance', he also insisted it was completely lacking in historical authenticity. The memoirs on which it was based were fraudulent: 'They're vain and egotistical ... they are about a man who is hunted by what he is hunting – and that is freedom, expressed in sexual terms.'[9]

So what was the motivation behind the drama? There is evidence that part of Potter's intention was to subvert the trend in costume drama which had become increasingly dominant in BBC drama, following the worldwide success of *Henry VIII* and the earlier *Forsyte Saga*. Though long a staple of its schedules, by the early seventies a number of factors had helped the historical or costume drama to thrive at the BBC. The departure of Hugh Carleton Greene from the post of BBC Director-General in 1969 had seemed to many in British television to mark the end of a regime which had actively encouraged adventure and experiment in programme-making. As Chapter 1 noted, by 1970 there were fears that a new wave of 'middlebrow' reaction had set in against 'controversial' single play subjects: a determination on the part of management to crack down on the freedoms programme-makers had enjoyed under Carleton Greene. The advent of colour television in 1967 had also created new pressures within the BBC to justify the additional cost to the audience of installing colour equipment and buying a new licence. With its meticulously designed costumes and sets, historical drama was one way of satisfying the viewer that all the extra expenditure to watch television in colour had been worthwhile. Given all these factors, it was little wonder that by 1970, prominent single play practitioners like Kenith Trodd could complain that in this new post-Carleton Greene era, you could do 'anything you like[d] at the BBC so long it [was] about three girls in a flat or the six wives of Henry VIII!'[10]

In this light, *Casanova* can be seen as Potter's response to changing TV fashions – an attempt to subvert the trend away from contemporary single play subjects by means of a costume drama which portrays not a king or an aristocrat but one of history's most notorious rogues, Giacomo Casanova. In marked contrast to the typical protagonist of costume drama, Potter's Casanova is depicted very much as a deviant on the margins of society whose quest of the senses becomes an attempt to escape from all its suffocating moral codes.

Episode 1 (titled 'Steed in the Stable') illustrates this point well. It opens with the stereotypical image of Casanova as great lover – in bed with one Barberina, whilst an anonymous voice on the soundtrack lists his many vices: 'Seducer of countless women ... Corrupter of youth ... *Unbeliever*.'[11] Suddenly, the door of his apartment bursts open, as Casanova is caught *in flagrante delicto* by Messer Grande, the Chief of Police. Acting on behalf of the State Inquisition of eighteenth-century Venice, Grande informs the libertine that he is to be arrested 'for impiousness, fraud and fornication' (Ep. 1, p. 14). The 'steed' is to be 'stabled' under the lead roof of the Doge's Palace, where he will have 'cause and time to reflect upon his wickedness and *amend* it' (Ep. 1, p. 17).

In Potter's version of the story, State repression becomes synonymous with sexual repression. The anti-hero pitted against dark forces of reaction, Potter's Casanova embodies some of the key 'counter-culture' slogans of the sixties and early seventies: 'sexual liberation', 'dropping out', 'doing your own thing'. In various interviews of the time, the writer himself made the link with the 'permissive society' and the threat of reaction against it. In the *Sunday Times*, he explained that what had first attracted him to the subject was the 'myth' of Casanova:

> Everyone's heard of it ... But what does it mean? You hear about the office Casanova, the small-town Casanova, the shop-floor Casanova. He was what we describe as a libertine: but he was concerned with religious and sexual freedom, and these are things we have to address ourselves to now ... He lived in a time very much like our own. The same fear of sex as a liberating agent is abroad now: we even have our own Inquisition.[12]

If this was Potter's argument against considering the drama a 'mere' costume romp, what is also clear is that he was no innocent party to the BBC's decision to produce *Casanova* as an historical drama in the *Henry VIII* mould. In many ways, that choice had already been determined by the nature of his scripts, which parallel *Henry VIII* in several key respects. Aside from the fact that both are a series of six plays dealing with the private life of a historical figure, *Casanova* mirrors *Henry VIII* by presenting a shifting view of its subject. In Shivas's earlier production, each of the six plays had concentrated on the relationship between Henry and one of his six wives. Scripted by a different writer, each had illuminated 'different facets of Henry's character'.[13] In *Casanova*, the extended format is also used to present a complex portrait of a man seen at different phases of his life. Over the six plays, Casanova is variously portrayed as archetypal Italian lover, wretched prisoner of the Inquisition, European traveller, as well as practitioner of black magic. Finally, in the last play, he is discovered in old age, cloistered within a German castle, where he has found employment as the librarian of a Count. It is at this point he begins to write down the memoirs of his various exploits: the memories which have formed the basis of the other five plays.

Like *Henry VIII*, Casanova's relationships with women are, for obvious reasons, a principal focus of the drama. Though many appear and disappear over the six plays, Potter chooses to focus on three whom it is implied haunted the libertine all his life: first, a black-haired black-eyed country girl, Cristina, whom Casanova almost marries in Episode 1; second, Anne Roman-Coupier, the god-daughter of a friend in Grenoble, whose heart Casanova breaks in Episode 4 ('Break A Window'); and finally Pauline, a melancholy 'English Rose' he encounters in London in Episode 5 ('Fevers of Love'). As implied by the title of this fifth play, it is Pauline whom Casanova comes closest to loving, after she replies to the offer of a room he has advertised in an English newspaper. She, however, has a husband and a mysterious past and is simply seeking a place to hide. His declarations of love rebuffed, the libertine for the first time is forced to deal with a broken heart. Even worse is his dawning recognition that having seduced and abandoned so many women in the past, he may no longer be capable of love. As he tells Pauline, even he is unsure whether his declarations of love to her are sincere or not: 'I've used up all the words ... Everything bounces back to times ... I have used *exactly the same phrases*, with *seemingly exactly the same kind* of sincerity' (Ep. 5, pp. 80–1).

As with Henry and his wives, each of Casanova's three main 'loves' allows different aspects of the central protagonist to be explored from week to week. In the case of Cristina, it is the spiritual longing which Potter sees as underpinning Casanova's quest of the senses. This is most clearly illustrated in Episode 1 when Casanova first glimpses her: an image which is to haunt him throughout the rest of the six plays. Standing by the edge of a Venetian canal, he gazes across an expanse of shimmering water into the face of a beautiful young girl, sitting in a gondola with her uncle, a priest. In his original script, Potter's directions indicate Cristina should be seen 'as in sweet memory, in a haze of light almost' (Ep. 1, p. 36).

The image is really a vision, heavy with religious symbolism – the girl with the name of Christ, attended by a priest. As with the Author in *Hide and Seek*, the sight of the raven-haired beauty becomes a moment of epiphany for the male protagonist: a Paradise spied from the far shore. She comes to embody all his spiritual longings for perfection, for God. The paradox of this goes to the heart of Casanova's dilemma in the plays. If, as the drama suggests, all of his relationships with women are the product of a desire to express his deep spiritual longing, to approach the religious vision of purity he spies from afar, he knows only one way to do this – through his own sexuality. In the case of Cristina, she is a virgin who agrees to be 'deflowered' by him in return for a promise of marriage. Matrimony, however, is out of the question for a libertine. As he worriedly confesses to his 'patrone', it is 'a lifetime's sentence' (Ep. 1, p. 70).

It is here that Potter begins to link the two main plot strands which dominate *Casanova*. As previously indicated, the drama begins with the arrest of the main protagonist and his imprisonment under 'the Leads' of the Doge's Palace. A man who has lived only for the senses, the experience is literally hell on earth for Casanova. Stripped of all material comforts, he is locked away in a tiny dark cell with only the rats for company. In this way, the drama begins a narrative experiment, revolving around the flesh-spirit dichotomy so central to Potter's work. The story of Casanova's imprisonment is used as a means of exploring how a man who has lived all his life only for the flesh would cope with a situation in which he was placed at the opposite extreme; where, stripped of everything, all he had to rely on was the strength of his own 'spirit'.

Reduced in prison to the bare essence of being, Potter's Casanova begins to look inwards for the first time in his life, towards his 'spirit': 'Think ... think ... think', he mutters as he paces about his cell (Ep. 1, p. 58). Only by this means will he find escape from his present condition. As his prison doctor warns him when he contracts fever, if he wants to survive, he must 'abandon *despair*' (Ep. 1, p. 86). Counterpointing scenes of his prison 'present' with memories of his freedom as a libertine, Episode 1 portrays Casanova in a 'fury of recollection', pacing about his tiny cell (Ep. 1, p. 90). Frustrated at his lack of freedom, he kicks at a pile of rubbish on the floor and in so doing, suddenly dislodges an old bolt which has been buried in rags. With a cry of joy, the prisoner realises he has a ready-made tool with which to engineer escape. Significantly, within the logic of the drama, this comes as a reward for the intensity of his recollection. The moral is clear – by turning inwards and confronting his own spirit, Casanova has found a means of escape. Following his doctor's advice, he has turned despair into hope.

With great determination, he begins to dig his way to freedom, using his 'bolt' to pierce 'a hole' in his cell floor from whence he hopes to escape out into the world he knows lies just beyond. As this implies, the enterprise abounds with a sexual symbolism which in many ways encapsulates the drama's view of its protagonist. Potter's Casanova is a man who tries to use sex as a means of transcendence to a spiritual nirvana which he knows lies just beyond his reach, yet which in his everyday experience he finds impossible to grasp. If the image is the same as that of Cristina – the religious radiance he seems fated only to glimpse from a distant shore – so, too, is the strength of his desire to 'penetrate' that world; to possess it.

Casanova's dig for freedom becomes a kind of religious travail: one which is eventually rewarded when, pushing his thumb through the bottom of the hole he has dug, a tiny chink of light appears. From the darkness of his present world, the prisoner earns a glimpse of the next. At the very moment of triumph, however, comes defeat. Lorenzo, Casanova's jailer, enters the cell and informs the prisoner he is to be moved to a new cell: 'Bigger ...

Cleaner. With windows' (Ep. 1, p. 104). Episode 1 ends in an air of absurdist black comedy as Casanova is forcibly dragged from the tiny cell which, previously, he would have given anything to leave. Defeated by the material world, he seems fated only ever to glimpse the light of spiritual 'grace', never to get at it. At the very moment when escape seems possible, the material world with its compromise and temptation – 'Bigger. Cleaner. With windows' – steps in to separate him from it.

In many ways the benchmark for the other five plays, Episode 1 reveals Potter's attitude to the Casanova story. Far from prison or marriage being the 'stables' which confine 'the steed', it is shown to be his own sexuality. Potter's Casanova is a prisoner of his desires. His yearning is for spiritual transcendence which he tries to achieve through the flesh. It is for this reason, the plays imply, he always fails, for even when eschewing the material world and concentrating hard, he seems destined never to escape it. In this way, Potter universalises the Casanova myth, audaciously transforming a particular historical rogue into a general metaphysical hero: a kind of spiritual everyman, struggling for something better yet always unable to attain it. Instead, Casanova has to settle for the temporary Paradise of a string of sexual encounters – a series of 'magic moments'.

This transformation of the lewd memoirs of a libertine into a spiritual work for television is made clearer through the structure of subsequent episodes – each of which follows Episode 1's pattern of counterpointing scenes from Casanova's life with details of his experience in prison. In Episode 2 ('One at a Time'), Casanova seduces each of the three siblings of his landlord in Geneva, yet the result merely brings post-coital depression and spiritual dissatisfaction. As he gazes out over the river Isère, he mutters to himself, 'Poor Isère. Even you are confined to your banks. All your life confined to your banks' (Ep. 2, p. 65). The suggestion is that, even when free, Casanova, as pathological womaniser, was always in prison. By Episode 3 ('Magic Moments'), his attempt to trick a greedy judge in Mantua through black magic has begun to raise serious doubts in his mind about the path he is on. Pretending to conjure up the devil, he succeeds instead in conjuring up a real thunderstorm and flees for his life, fearing his behaviour has incensed the gods.

By Episode 4 ('Break a Window'), the 'sinner' and unbeliever is fated, it seems, never to achieve escape from the life that confines him. Attempting through his affair with Anne Roman-Coupier to break the window that separates him from the spiritual nirvana he longs to reach, all he succeeds in doing is breaking her heart. By the end of Episode 5 and his rejection by Pauline, his imprisonment appears complete. As he watches the 'English Rose' leave, he presses his forehead against the window pane of his London apartment in what is clearly a symbolic gesture.

Ironically, it is only in the final episode of *Casanova* that the libertine finds escape. The play's title, 'Golden Apples', indicates how a cherished wish can often be fulfilled in the most unlikely circumstances and against all the odds. It forms part of a quotation from Virgil, heard on the soundtrack as the final episode opens: 'Let the hard oak bring forth golden apples. Let narcissus bloom in the elder ... Ah! If the last days of my life could only be prolonged to see the whole of creation rejoice in the age that is yet to come' (Ep. 6, p. 2). The voice is that of Casanova in old age, and as the play begins he is seen shuffling about amongst all the books he looks after in the castle library of the German Count Waldstein. As librarian to the Count, he is engaged in an almost constant battle with a retired warrant officer, Herr Feldkirchner (played by Graham Crowden) – a strict military type whose demeanour contrasts markedly with that of the far less orderly old Italian.

Casanova's reputation as a libertine has thus brought him little reward or freedom in old age. This is emphasised by shots of him labouring up some stone stairs to his room at the top of the castle. In an elaborate montage sequence, the old man's progress is cross-cut with images from Episode One of the young Casanova being led through a maze of corridors to his prison cell in the Doge's Palace. Not only does the old man parallel his younger self in being confined by his environment, he, too, is a prisoner of the body. While the young libertine was trapped by his desires, the old man is painfully aware of the fading of his senses. As he confesses to Feldkirchner, he is a prisoner of 'this defunct body with its withered appetites, faded tastes, deadened senses ... and – defunct organs' (Ep. 6, p. 53).

Episode 6 shows him at work on the story of his life – an ageing scribbler sifting through his many papers and memories. In his script directions, Potter states this image of 'his gnarled, swollen old hands shuffling through page after page of his own handwritten memories' should be 'the concrete image which sums up and perhaps justifies the method behind the whole series' (Ep. 6, p. 22). In other words, *Casanova*'s counterpointing of different episodes from a life – the flashbacks and flashforwards to the libertine's life before and after prison, coupled with the use of prison as an objective correlative for the protagonist's psychic state – are all justified by this image of an organising mind, sifting through memories in old age, making connections between disparate events. As in John Hopkins' *Talking to a Stranger*, the extended format of six plays is used by Potter not only to portray different aspects of a personality from week to week (as with *Henry VIII*) but also to show the same event from a variety of different perspectives. Throughout the drama, events from other episodes are replayed and juxtaposed with new scenes in such a way that they take on fresh meaning or significance. The final effect is of a kind of 'narrative montage' in which dramatic meaning is conveyed not so much through the action and dialogue of any one scene but through a *combination* of scenes that together take on a significance greater than the sum of the constituent parts. As Potter himself suggested at the time, he was trying to create:

> a portrait ... that accumulated, that sifted through layers of various incidents and how they changed perspective like the things we think about ... We're walking compendiums in a way of memory and previous instincts embalmed by present states of mind and we know that we change perspective as we mature or decay.[14]

All of this is neatly encapsulated by Potter's dramatisation of the famous story of Casanova's escape from 'the Leads'. Forming the climax of the six plays, this is the suspended enigma towards which the rest of the 'serial' has been building – the gap in the text which had separated the audience's knowledge of Casanova's life before prison from that of his life after. Rather than giving a simple narrative account, however, Potter chooses to juxtapose the escape scene with Casanova's perspective on it from old age, thus resituating it within the context of the aged libertine's desire to 'escape' his withered body.

Crucial in this respect is the central role Potter gives to writing. In flashback scenes to his incarceration under 'the Leads', the libertine is shown being provided with a basket of mulberries by his jailer Lorenzo and, later, some books borrowed from a prisoner in a neighbouring cell, a defrocked priest called Father Balbi. Suddenly, with the books and the juice of the mulberries, Casanova realises he has paper, ink and a ready-made postman, in the shape of Lorenzo, through which to smuggle out messages to Balbi. Aware that since the discovery of his own previous escape attempt (in Episode 1), it is impossible for him to use the bolt he still has hidden in his possession for a future break-out, he decides to conceal it in a large Bible and smuggle it out via Lorenzo to Father Balbi, under the pretence of an exchange of books. If Balbi can use the tool to dig his way out of the ceiling of his own cell, then perhaps he can come and fetch Casanova too.

In the course of this sequence of events, Potter emphasises, through juxtaposition of past with 'present', links with the elderly Casanova. If prison has become a metaphor for Casanova in old age, writing is also shown to function as the means of escape. As the prisoner told Lorenzo in justification of his request for more books: 'When I open a book I also open that door. For a moment' (Ep. 6, p. 63). Likewise, in recording the history of his life, the elderly Casanova is able to open the door, if only temporarily, to that other world of the 'spirit' which he had tried so hard as a young man to reach through sex. The symbolism of Casanova's prison escape emphasises this. On the one hand, if the hiding of a 'bolt' in the Bible mixes images of the sacred and profane, freedom only comes for the libertine when his 'tool' is contained within the covers of a book. On the other hand, true escape through the 'hole' in the ceiling – the desired transcendence to another world – is achievable in the end only through the aid of a priest. Similarly, whilst writing offers a temporary door to that other world of the spirit for the libertine in old age, it cannot recompense him for the withering of his body and the fading of his senses. As a consequence, he decides to take to his bed, announcing, 'I am trying to escape.' His doctor, Rasp, tries to argue against Casanova's death-wish and despair, urging him to 'engage [his] mind in some project!' (Ep. 6, p. 73). As he confesses to Feldkirchner, he fears Casanova will die unless he can be encouraged to 'care about something'. Significantly, it is writing, the doctor thinks, which holds the key: 'Get him *involved* again with the writing ... Let the past rekindle flames in the present, so to speak' (Ep. 6, p. 80).

At Rasp's instigation, Count Waldstein's mistress, Caroline, is dispatched to the dying Casanova's bedside to read his memoirs to him and so, with luck, raise his spirits. The aged libertine is more interested, however, in acquiring something else from her before he dies. As he tells her: 'A suck ... That's all. At your nipples. Can't manage much else' (Ep. 6, p. 92). With this last faint rekindling of the flames which consumed much of his life, the drama ends. As Caroline unlaces her dress, exposing her 'golden apples', the old man dies. The final image is the drama's most telling. In a last flashback, the young libertine is seen emerging triumphant on to the roof of the Doge's palace, having escaped his prison cell. As Potter describes his actions in the original script: 'Italianate, he kisses the air and starts his slither down the moon-polished slope ... Pan across to the rooftops of a sparkling moon-lit Venice, shining almost like the "holy city"' (Ep. 6, pp. 109–10).

As this final flashback makes clear, the libertine has been released in death from the prison of his passions and has reached the 'holy city' which all his life was a struggle to achieve. Despite its portrayal of all his so-called 'sins', the drama ultimately vindicates Casanova's striving for spiritual perfection which, it is suggested, was the source of his compulsive desire for women.

Far from being a 'mere' costume romp, *Casanova* can thus be viewed as a religious work, one which draws its spiritual themes from a most unlikely source. In this respect, the drama has a number of interesting links with the contemporaneous *Traitor*. If Adrian Harris was a figure who eschewed the material world in order to chase his dream of Camelot, Potter's Casanova functions as an exact mirror image. A man of the senses, he embraces that world to extremes, yet at the same time his life is portrayed as a similar search for a 'holy city'. The flip side of Harris (material versus non-material man), he is possessed of the same spiritual yearning. Transmitted close together in the autumn of 1971, the two dramas can be seen as related examinations, from either side of the flesh-spirit dichotomy running through Potter's writing, of the same underlying spiritual questions which were beginning to surface in his work of the early seventies. Utterly secular, even profane, in their actions and settings, both smuggle spiritual themes out to a mass viewing audience, under the guise of the spy play and costume drama respectively. As such, they embody Potter's view that religion has to be taken out of its special 'God-slot' and rooted in the everyday – including the everyday television schedules.

Casanova has resonances with other Potter works too. Cut off from the pleasures of the outside world in a kind of 'hell' under the Leads (a 'hell' in which he runs a high fever and has to be attended by doctors), Casanova's predicament echoes Philip Marlow's hospital 'hell' in *The Singing Detective* (see Chapter 5). There is the same medical advice that if the patient wants to get well, he must abandon despair and acquire a more positive mental outlook. Like Marlow, it is only by looking into himself that Casanova discovers the rudiments of escape. Also strongly echoing *The Singing Detective* are the scenes of Casanova in his 'prison' of old age. Like the psychiatrist Gibbon in the 1986 serial, Dr Rasp realises that the clues to the protagonist's defiance of doctors and insistence on finding his own means of 'escape' lie within the pages of the book he is writing. Behind the mask of apparent despair, the old man does care about something: his writing. If his mind could be 'engaged in some project', then perhaps he could get well again.[15]

Written during a bad period in Potter's illness, *Casanova* provides an early prototype for *The Singing Detective*. Both main protagonists find themselves in a position where, stripped of everything, they have to search deep inside themselves in order to understand and deal with their current predicament. In both cases, too, the drama moves between the agonies of their confinement and their memories of the world outside. Like the 'two' Marlows in *The Singing Detective*, there are 'two' Casanovas: one, the clean-shaven expensively dressed libertine, out in the sensuous world of eighteenth-century Venice; the other, the bearded wretched victim of the Inquisition, locked up in prison. These alter egos correspond exactly to the flesh-spirit dichotomy Potter explores in the drama. They are the visible manifestations of a 'torn' hero, caught between the atheism of the unbeliever and the prisoner's need for there to be something more.

For all its links with other more celebrated work, Potter's *Casanova* was not well received in 1971. As the writer recalled in interview: 'People hated it. It was voted the worst series of the year by the critics … and I felt the same grief I felt about *Blackeyes*.'[16] Misleadingly promoted by the BBC as a historically accurate costume drama, *Casanova* was quickly condemned by Mary Whitehouse and other 'Clean-up TV' campaigners for its 'lewdness and gross indecency'. Potter quickly retorted that Whitehouse was 'an ignorant and dangerous woman', incapable of grasping that the drama was in fact 'a moral work'.[17] This very public sparring would set a precedent for later works like *The Singing Detective* and *Blackeyes*. It was with the 1971 drama, however, that the first real equation was made in the popular and press mind between 'sex on TV', 'controversy' and 'Dennis Potter'. The history of Potter drama as 'media event' had begun in earnest.[18]

Aside from these public attacks, another and perhaps more fundamental reason for the drama's relative unpopularity was its very complexity for audiences and lack of overt narrative 'signposting'. This was hinted at by Christopher Dunkley in a review for *The Times* in which he observed that it was a pity the BBC would probably never allow *Casanova* what it needed – a marathon showing of two three-hour episodes on successive nights. That way, he suggested, 'the repeated flashbacks and allusions … would … acquire infinitely more significance than … when seen at weekly intervals, where they tended towards confusion.'[19]

Three years later, when *Casanova* gained a repeat showing, this is exactly what the BBC did. With Potter's approval, the plays were re-edited into two ninety-five-minute episodes and shown on consecutive nights. He himself suggested how the new structure of *Casanova* should go: the scenes of Casanova in old age were to be used as 'book-ends' at the beginning and end of the drama, between which the rest of the protagonist's exploits (his life as a libertine and in prison) were to unfold in flashback.[20] In other words, the 'method' of the plays which it had taken Potter six episodes to reveal in 1971 was immediately foregrounded in the repeats, allowing the audience to grasp more easily the non-chronological structure of the narrative.

What this new version also did was to bring *Casanova* much closer to being a single play. It showed that what was described as a serial had originally been written by a writer of single plays who had not paid much attention (because previously he had never had to) to the conditions under which episodic narrative operates in television: that is, the need to maintain a strong central narrative thread from episode to episode, allowing the audience 'space' each week to refamiliarise themselves with characters and events. In his next venture into the 'authored' serial, *Pennies from Heaven*, these lessons would be learned and put to use. It is perhaps significant, however, that it would be another seven years before Potter again attempted to extend his original, 'authored' drama beyond the single play.

Pennies from Heaven

Origins

Next time, the results were to prove far more conclusive. *Pennies from Heaven* (first transmitted on BBC-1 between 7 March and 11 April 1978) not only became one of the most celebrated dramas in British television history, it also rejuvenated Potter's career, setting him on a path that would lead eventually to Hollywood.

The idea for *Pennies* only arose after much discussion between Potter and his now regular producer, Kenith Trodd, as to what their next project together should be. As Chapter 2 noted, the banning of *Brimstone and Treacle* had paradoxically strengthened Potter's desire to write for television: if drama could have that kind of impact, then some kind of response from him was needed. There were other pressures too – the death of his father in November 1975 had meant that, unusually for this prolific writer, he had submitted no original work to the BBC during 1976. The autumn of that year had also seen the fuss surrounding the renewal of Trodd's contract. By the winter of 1976 events had thus created a need for some new major Potter work to appear – both as a response to the past and as a commitment to the future. The question was, what should it be?

From the BBC, Trodd managed to secure a commission for Potter to write a *Casanova*-type series of six original plays, to be transmitted in the regular Tuesday *Play for Today* slot: that is, prime-time BBC-1. Six plays rather than one would provide Potter with a broader canvas, perhaps enabling him to create the equivalent of a television novel. Trodd believes the BBC were so generous in their donation of eight hours of screentime because in the wake of *Brimstone* and the other events of 1976, controllers were feeling 'guilty and permissive' towards both him and Potter.

Having secured copious amounts of prime-time, the problem for Potter and Trodd was then how to fill it. A number of ideas were mooted and rejected – one, about children, later became the basis for *Blue Remembered Hills*. The most consistent theme, however, in these discussions involved the thirties' dance band music which had been used atmospherically in past Potter plays and in which Trodd is also an acknowledged expert. Though this music had furnished the titles for such past Potter works as *Angels Are So Few*, *Only Make Believe* and *Double Dare*, it was the use of thirties' songs in *Moonlight on the Highway* which became the inspiration for *Pennies*. The desire once more to counterpoint the sentimental tunes of Al Bowlly with the sordid 'reality' of a protagonist's life led to the idea of a drama revolving around the exploits of a thirties' crooner – a Bowlly figure who was also a Casanova type, seducing his way through the six plays. As Potter put it in interview, this, however, was 'too on the nose'. It might have embroiled him in all sorts of unwanted controversy over the life of the real Al Bowlly.[21]

A drama revolving around a protagonist at the very top of his profession would also have made it difficult to evoke the specific historical context out of which the popular music of the thirties had emerged: the reality of Depression-hit Britain, in relation to which the romantic hopes and dreams expressed in the songs seemed to function as some kind of necessary antidote. To convey this gulf between the poverty of most working lives and the richness of the aspirations expressed through the music, it would be necessary to create a character who was not on top but on the margins of society – a 'wannabe' high on dreams yet low on cash. Eventually this led Potter to the idea of making his central male protagonist a sheet music salesman: someone who lived by the songs (indeed lived for them), yet at the same time could not make his living *from* them. Along the way to this conclusion, however, ideas ebbed and flowed. According to Kenith Trodd:

> There was talk of a provincial loser who'd failed to pull off the perfect murder and the music receded. So, in these discussions did the adrenalin, especially when I suggested we might be advised to call off the songs and think instead of a Lawrence novel Potter had tinkered with adapting. There was no relish for that; the music would not go unheard and eventually the dangerous breakthrough came, ending the dither and guaranteeing funk and terror. Potter announced he would start the series in a bleak suburban bedroom with a man bursting into early morning song. He would be miming to a fuzzy '78 and the record was by a woman. He told me the song and I said there were good versions of men singing it. NO, he said, I want the audience to be as disoriented as possible. Primetime BBC-1, it would be crazy. But of course it was that craziness that made it work and provided the pitch of tension and peculiarity which *Pennies from Heaven* needed to express its attitudes to the music.[22]

Above all, therefore, it was the songs themselves, rather than any specific idea about a singer or a murderer, which determined the shape of *Pennies from Heaven*. The plays evolved as an attempt to express 'attitudes to the music' rather than the other way round. As Potter suggested in interview, 'the voice synching concept' of characters miming to original thirties' recordings arose from a desire for the songs to be 'upfront' rather than 'background' to the narrative.

In fact, such a TV dramatic innovation had a precedent. At one point in *Moonlight on the Highway*, David Peters is shown sitting alone in his bedsit, staring at himself in the mirror, whilst Al Bowlly's 'Lover Come Back To Me' plays on the gramophone (see Chapter 2). As the camera pans around the room and towards the mirror, the protagonist is discovered miming the words of the song. Quickly, his own imitation is overwhelmed by the emotion of Bowlly's rendition. Finding he can no longer hold back the tears, he guiltily switches off the record as a knock on the door jolts him back to reality.

If this is the origin of the miming device in *Pennies* (the idea that songs can mirror emotions to such an extent that individual identification with the singer becomes complete), it also emphasises the fact that the drama was not explicitly conceived as a musical. The decision to have characters burst into song was arrived at only gradually and always through a wish to foreground the original recordings. At the same time, having achieved this, Potter's drama then uses it to evoke images of the film musical. Thus in Episode 1, as the central protagonist, Arthur Parker, mimes to the first musical number (a 1932 recording of 'The Clouds Will Soon Roll By'), Potter's script directions indicate 'he appears to sing – and in a woman's voice ... and he does it wholly in the conventions of a musical – as though totally in earnest for a moment, Arthur and [his wife] Joan are in a film musical' (Ep. 1, p. 10).[23]

What is also clear is that *Pennies* is informed by the film musical's inherent optimism – its typical narrative trajectory of the triumph of hope over experience, faith over defeat. The drama not only contrasts the upbeat tunes of the time with the 'reality' of the Depression, it also snatches the unlikeliest of happy endings from the jaws of an otherwise bleak dénouement. The final episode (Episode 6, 'Says My Heart') ends with Arthur Parker turning up 'like a bad penny' on Hammersmith Bridge, after the audience has just seen him hanged for a murder he did not commit (Ep. 6, p. 115). As he turns to face the camera, he gives a cockney smirk: 'Couldn't go all through that wivaht a bleed'n happy endin' now, could we?' (Ep. 6, p. 116). If the self-reflexive gesture is a familiar Potter technique, the need for a happy ending resolutely conforms to the generic conventions of the film musical. This, however, confounds audience expectations of how the narrative should end. (The central protagonist has just been hanged. It should be a gloomy conclusion. Why is he still alive?) The result is thus a foregrounding of the basic tension upon which the whole of the drama rests – the disjunction between depiction of the 'reality' of the Depression and the rose-hued saccharine world celebrated by the songs. As with the Hollywood musical, the power of music is finally shown to win through. Resurrecting Arthur, it defies and disrupts the 'realist' narrative that had portrayed his execution. At the same time, if it is a sentimental intercession by the 'Author' which finally saves Arthur from the gallows and delivers the happy ending of the musical ('Says My Heart'), this is heavy with ambiguity and tension for it implies that in the real world beyond the musicals, the protagonist would have been allowed to hang. In *Pennies*, a careful balance between optimism (the songs) and pessimism (the 'real' world) is preserved right to the very end, albeit with one major qualification. Since it is the dreams and hopes expressed in the songs which ultimately triumph and are celebrated in the plays, this necessarily undercuts many of the doubts and ambiguities troubling the narrative. In the final scene, pessimism is transcended by the power of the music, in a manner that carries clear religious connotations. Like *Brimstone and Treacle*, *Pennies* asserts the existence of a greater or ultimate good: a world of the 'spirit' behind that of 'gloomy realism' which the songs both recognise and express.

Such inherent optimism not only permeates the ending but much of Potter's original *Pennies* scripts. Even the execution scenes are written with a mischievous black humour – as Arthur goes to the scaffold, for example, he tells his jailers, 'Hang on a bit – I got an itchy conk. I said, hang on will you?' (Ep. 6, p. 112). To understand the reasons for this perceptible lightening of tone as compared to most of Potter's single play work, it is worth considering briefly the personal circumstances out of which the *Pennies* scripts emerged. As the writer recalled in interview, in February 1977 he was admitted to Guy's Hospital in London for the first clinical trials of a new drug for his illness. Called razoxane, this was hailed at the time as a 'miracle' cure for psoriatic arthropathy (though later its unpleasant side-effects would result in its withdrawal). In 1977, however, it looked as if Potter's long-standing illness had finally been beaten for good. For a few years after that, he was virtually free of the illness, with no arthritic pains or skin lesions. He himself made the connection with the changing mood of his writing: '77, as they were administering Razoxane and I was at Guy's, I started *Pennies*. I see that as the change.'[24]

Just how much of a change is illustrated by an interview which Potter's wife Margaret gave to the *Daily Mail* in April 1977. She stated that the moment she arrived at the hospital with her husband's clothes:

> I noticed the incredible difference. He wasn't just walking normally – he was pacing furiously up and down like a caged animal. I saw years and years of pent-up energy in that pacing … I saw a lightness of spirit … It was almost a relief when he stopped dashing madly around and picked up his pen … He wrote a new play in hospital, *Pennies from Heaven* … Today he set off gaily to London with a second play he's just whizzed through in the past eleven days.[25]

As this shows, *Pennies* was written at a time of great optimism in Potter's own life. It would thus be surprising if the sense of hope in the face of despair which the scripts communicate were not directly attributable to Potter's changed situation at the time. What these biographical details also indicate is that, from February 1977 on, *Pennies* was written extremely quickly and with a sense of great freedom. The serial's director, Piers Haggard, testifies to the speed: episodes, he recalls, were delivered to him at an average of one a fortnight.[26]

Given this frenetic creativity, searching for possible sources that inspired the drama might seem a fruitless quest, yet there is evidence that the murder for which Arthur is hanged in *Pennies* was based on an actual case. In interview, Potter pointed to the 1990 film *Chicago Joe and the Showgirl* as having been drawn from the same factual source which provided him with the inspiration for the murder plot of *Pennies*. *Chicago Joe* is based on a notorious real murder that occurred in Hammersmith in 1944. According to Potter:

> That murder during the war was something I'd been playing with in my head and I think was ... the obscure origin for the idea of a murder set at the time – because thinking about that led to me think of the music of the time; of the forties. So an aborted start on that ... eventually dropped a decade and changed nature ... Just before going to Guy's and starting on the Razoxane ... I went to the BBC with that idea and that gradually ... became *Pennies*.[27]

In the real-life case, Karl Hulten, a deserter from the American army, was tried at the Old Bailey and sentenced to hang in January 1945 for the casual murder of a taxi driver. Also found guilty and sentenced to death (but later reprieved) was his lover Betty Jones, a runaway from the Welsh valleys who had come to London in search of the bright lights, only to end up as a 'showgirl' – a dancer cum stripper. Together, the pair had lived out a mutual fantasy of a gangster and his moll, escaping from the reality of war-torn London into their own private world saturated with images from popular culture. It was their attempt to enact their 'Bonnie and Clyde' dreams for real which eventually led to murder.[28]

Considered in the light of his later *Singing Detective* serial, it is possible to see what attracted Potter to the case – autobiographical resonances of Hammersmith and 1945; a 'crime of passion'; the power of popular culture; a blurring of fantasy and reality.[29] Despite his eventual decision to use the music of the thirties, the influence of the 'Chicago Joe' case can still be traced in Potter's construction of *Pennies*.

For example, the image of the lovers on the run, flouting the restrictions and the repressions of their society, is clearly echoed in Arthur's involvement with Eileen Everson – a demure girl from the Forest of Dean (on the Welsh border) who, like Betty Jones, leaves for the bright lights of London and is gradually transformed into a tough self-reliant prostitute. After Arthur finds he is wanted for the murder of a blind girl, both he and she become desperadoes, fleeing London for the countryside where she casually guns down a farmer. Of particular note in this 'fatal attraction' is the place of fantasy and popular culture in sustaining their relationship. If Arthur dreams of a world 'where the songs come true', this is the very quality which Eileen most admires in him (Ep. 4, p. 95). As she tells him in Episode 5, 'you acted as though the songs were real ... as though they *allowed* you to – to – get away with ...' Arthur completes the thought for her: 'No – I draw the line at murdering people, love' (Ep. 5, p. 24).

The conversation of the fugitive lovers is also peppered with references to popular culture. As with Hulten and Jones in the forties, popular culture functions for Arthur and Eileen as a means of temporary escape from the oppressive social structures of thirties' England. Even when they are in hiding from the law and have their first lover's quarrel, they realise they are fighting just 'like in the pictures' (Ep. 6, p. 50). Arthur, however, longs not just for temporary escape but for a complete break with class-ridden English society. As he tells Eileen, 'I'd rather be a Yank ... They got the best songs (Ep. 4, p. 95). By Episode 6, he is suggesting they ought to head for 'Chi-ca-go ... I like the sound of it. You can roll it in your mouth, can't you? Chi-ca-go' (Ep. 6, p. 42).

As with the Hulten-Jones case, the freedom to dream of this 'Chicago Joe' proves short-lived, however. Society in the form of the law catches up with the rebels trying to escape it and punishment is meted out. In the process, it emerges in court that Arthur is not only a social fugitive but, like Hulten, a military one as well. The court prosecutor reveals that as a young soldier in World War One, he was 'court-martialled for cowardice and narrowly escaped being shot as a deserter' (Ep. 6, p. 90). Convicted of murder (whilst Eileen is let off free), Arthur is sentenced to hang. In the real 'Chicago Joe' case, society exacted the ultimate price from Hulten for his devil-may-care attitude and his attempts to turn fantasy into reality. In the drama, as noted earlier, Arthur and his dreams are finally rescued from the scaffold. What seems clear, however, is that while the actual details of the murder case are much transformed, the themes of fantasy and rebellion, embodied in the 'Chicago Joe and the Showgirl' story, provided Potter with the basic plot model for his own *Pennies from Heaven.*

Production

Production on *Pennies* commenced on 26 August 1977 and lasted right through to 30 March 1978 (three weeks into the serial's first transmission) under the stewardship of director Piers Haggard. The choice of Haggard as director was a significant one, revealing how the drama was originally conceived. Though having a long track record in TV drama, he was picked after Potter saw his BBC-1 production of *The Chester Mystery Plays*, transmitted during Easter 1976. This adaptation of fourteenth-century texts was nothing less than the history of the world in two and a half hours: a portrayal of life as medieval people saw it, from the Creation to the Last Judgement. It was widely praised on transmission, chiefly because of its use of colour separation overlay (CSO) which portrayed real actors against painted backgrounds.[30]

Undoubtedly, the 'non-naturalism' of this appealed to Potter. The *Pennies* scripts contain directions for graphic and 'caption sequences' that are designed to exploit the range of effects available for videotape drama at this time. Throughout the six plays, CSO is used whenever the drama needs to evoke a thirties, period backdrop. Thus Episode 1 opens with what the script specifies should be 'detailed, slightly idyllic paintings of [a] leafy suburban street (Metroland), early nineteen thirties' *in front of which* 'a man with a trilby hat is walking his dog' (Ep. 1, p. 2). The effect is of nostalgic pastiche. Drawing attention to the plays' artifice, the use of real actors in front of painted backgrounds allows Potter to emphasise his depiction of the thirties as 'non-naturalistic' – not verisimilitude but a backward glance from the present, a subjective collage of received images and stock motifs.[31]

If Haggard's experience on *The Chester Mystery Plays* equipped him well for this aspect of *Pennies*, it seems above all to have been his ability to handle religious drama which made him ideal for Potter's purposes. With his proven track record on *The Mystery Plays*, he was able to bring to *Pennies* the techniques he had developed of treating 'spiritual' themes in ways that would be visually interesting to an overwhelmingly secular TV audience.

Related to this was the problem of how to work the musical numbers into the drama in a manner that would be visually stimulating. Potter's scripts seldom provided an image of what should happen during each song and simple miming would soon bore the audience. Thus the director saw it as one of his main tasks to connect each song with the action of an individual scene, in such a way that even if the actual performance were spare and simple (as BBC finances would inevitably dictate for most of the numbers), the audience would still feel the narative had been advanced or some new insight into the characters gained. For this purpose, Haggard enlisted the help of BBC choreographer, Tudor Davies, and it was with his assistance that many of the musical numbers were transformed into the shape in which they appear in the finished production.

Another example of collaboration lay in casting. Suggestions for who should play Arthur Parker had come from a number of different directions. As Kenith Trodd recalls, Potter had his own off-beat ideas, suggesting the comedian Roy Hudd for the part, together with Spike Milligan as his *alter ego*, the 'Accordian Man' (the real culprit of the murder for which Arthur is eventually hanged).[32] Bizarre as this may sound, it indicates Potter's sense of *Pennies* as black comedy – of Arthur's exploits being those of a tragi-comic hapless figure, whose belief in 'the songs' is as absurd as it is touching.

Though never seriously taken up, the writer's suggestion also emphasised how important it was that the central role be played by someone whom the audience could empathise with as the epitome of the flawed, sentimental hero. Haggard tested a number of different actors for the part. Hywel Bennett (Willy in *Where the Buffalo Roam*) read for it and was a real possibility. Eventually, he was given the part of Tom: a villain who seduces Eileen when she first arrives in London in Episode 4. The actor to whom Haggard was really on the point of offering the central role was Michael Elphick – a versatile character actor who would have made a convincing cockney.[33]

Three to four weeks into casting, however, Trodd suggested one other possibility – a then relatively unknown cockney actor called Bob Hoskins who at that time was only really familiar for his role as Alf, an illiterate removal man, in the BBC TV adult literacy series, *On the Move*.[34] Though Haggard knew nothing of his work, he agreed to see Hoskins. It was not, states the director, that the actor read the part incredibly well which led to him being offered the role of Arthur. Rather, it was that while Elphick was a very good and proven performer, there was a quality to Hoskins: 'something about him that might be extra special'. Nevertheless the director recalls that the decision to cast him was something of a gamble for the production – one that could have easily backfired, given that he was relatively so inexperienced.

By the autumn of 1977, work on the £800,000 Plays Department production was well under way. One of the most noteworthy aspects of the actual production process was the amount of rehearsal time the actors received. A very precise director who works with his actors until he gets exactly what he wants, Haggard persevered especially long and closely with Hoskins, until there were times when the other man (who is more of an instinctive performer) despaired of ever pleasing him. If credit for the strong performances in *Pennies* is partly due to directorial tenacity, Haggard asserts this was in no small part aided by the fact that the drama was recorded mainly on videotape within the multi-camera studio – with only its exterior scenes shot on 16mm film. As the dominant mode of BBC drama production at this time, such a mixture of taped scenes with filmed inserts ensured that the production benefited from copious amounts of rehearsal time very close to the actual recording/filming dates – to such an extent that the material became second nature to cast, crew and director.[35]

At the same time, Haggard took steps to minimise the inevitable 'textural' contrast involved in such a mixed media approach of cutting between scenes shot on film and those recorded on tape within the multi-camera studio. Borrowing from soft-focus techniques in cinema, he developed a way of softening the distinction between the aggressive sharpness of the videotape image and the more grainy texture of film. His technique was to fit the studio cameras with light fog filters for the recording of the dramatic scenes, whilst using double fog filters for the musical numbers. The effect was to give the studio scenes a much more 'hazy', painterly look which also helped visually emphasise *Pennies*' view of the thirties as being that of cultural memory: of the past seen from the vantage point of the present and filtered through a haze of recollection.

This device was not simply a director's annoyance at having to mix tape with film. Haggard felt a heavy clash between taped and filmed scenes would distract from the real stylistic distinction he wished to make in the drama – that between the saccharine world of the songs and the 'normality' of life in the Depression. To this end, the director worked closely with *Pennies*' lighting man, Dave Sydenham, to ensure that just as the 'naturalism' of the dramatic action was disrupted by characters bursting into song, so too would the 'normal' studio lighting change to various different colours to fit the mood of the music (for example, as in the obvious choice of blue for the song, 'Blue Moon' in Episode 1).[36]

On the way to achieving this, however, one significant experiment was tried and abandoned. In an attempt to highlight the distinction between the musical numbers and the drama, Haggard tried having all of the dramatic scenes in the first two episodes of *Pennies* recorded in black and white, only switching to colour for the musical numbers. The effect was a bold contrast: the drab black and white world of the Depression was counterpointed with the world of the songs that literally brought a splash of colour into the lives of the protagonists. Haggard showed the results to both Potter and Trodd. While both the director and the producer quite liked the idea at first, the writer was less sure. The repetition of the device over sixty songs in six episodes would become a tiring gimmick, he maintained: whenever there was music, in would come the colour. Trodd and Haggard also became less sure. As the latter puts it, it would have been too much of 'a sledge-hammer device', too literal a metaphor. Instead, a change in lighting was felt to be a slightly less obvious (if more theatrical) means of signalling that through the songs the protagonists were being transported into another realm.

What this aborted experiment also shows is the degree of consultation that went on between director, writer and producer during the actual production of *Pennies from Heaven*. As Haggard attests, this was in part due to certain nervousness as to whether *Pennies* would actually work. By 1977, both Potter and Trodd had large reputations to maintain and the drama's miming device *was* unusual. Without careful thought as to its execution, it might well have been disastrous. Haggard recalls that Potter was worried 'whether he was going up a blind alley, whether he was going to make a fool of himself'. It was only after the writer had seen the rehearsal tape of the first scene in which Arthur bursts into song, that he felt able to declare 'It's going to work.'

Such nervousness about *Pennies* was not confined to those behind the camera. While its cast today may, in the light of its subsequent success, declare that everyone knew the drama was going to work, many at the time were worried about the damage it might do to their careers.[37] In the event, none needed to be. The production received very good, though not rave, reviews on first transmission. Peter Buckman in the *Listener*, for example, called 'the plot banal and the behaviour of the central characters frequently incredible ... it was irresistibly funny to see them break into mime.'[38] Others, however, were much more kind. Michael Ratcliffe in *The Times* praised *Pennies* as 'the televisual equivalent of the serialised Victorian novel'.[39]

Significantly, it was in the popular press that *Pennies* made its biggest impact, in this way bringing Potter's work out of the *Play for Today* ghetto and to the attention of a mass public. James Murray in the *Daily Express* called the serial 'a magical welding together of popular music, trenchant humour, high drama and all the tricks of television technology. It's all so refreshing, I think it will galvanise the whole country.'[40] On the strength of such eulogies, twelve million viewers tuned in to the first episode – the drama having also been heavily trailed in the *Radio Times*.

In this fashion, *Pennies* became elevated to the status of 'instant classic' and was quickly repeated by the BBC the following Christmas. As Piers Haggard makes clear, this was less for audiences to have 'another chance to see', however, than to nudge voters in their nominations for the British Academy awards the following March.[41] In the event, though nominated for many, the serial won only two awards – Potter picked up the Best Writer's award while the drama itself won the award for most Original TV Production. To the disappointment of many, Hoskins did not win the Best Actor's prize.

As this summary indicates, though *Pennies* is now looked back upon and celebrated as a significant event in British television history, opinion at the time was somewhat mixed. It won some awards, not others; it was lauded by some reviewers, not by others. Perhaps the key to understanding why lies in Piers Haggard's opinion that: 'Amongst discerning audiences, the media and otherwise, it has an impassioned following. Amongst the general public, I don't know.'

What this indicates is that the drama found its most ardent champions amongst a quite narrow élite of 'opinion-formers' within metropolitan media circles – journalists, TV critics, fellow TV practitioners – whose views of *Pennies* as 'pioneering' drama were then disseminated to the wider audience via the press, as well as weekly journals like *Time Out* and the *Radio Times*. In this way, *Pennies* quickly became a byword for 'quality' television drama. It was held up within media discourses as an example of what British televison could do or be.

In the absence of rigorous sociological investigation, what the bulk of the general audience thought of *Pennies* can only be guessed at (for example, from the letters columns of the *Radio Times*). One clue, however, comes from the fact that an EMI soundtrack album of songs from *Pennies* became such a best-seller that a second album had to be quickly released.[42] At the close of the seventies (just prior to the election of a Conservative Government under Margaret Thatcher), *Pennies from Heaven* had unearthed a hugh British nostalgia market, waiting to be tapped.

By 1990, when the drama was next repeated on British television, though Potter feared it might not stand the test of time, it hardly seemed to matter any more if the serial seemed somewhat overlong or employed too many songs.[43] It was the songs themselves that mattered now. BBC Enterprises, sore at losing out to EMI in the seventies, used the occasion to launch its own heavily promoted soundtrack album, complete with sleeve introduction by Trodd. *Pennies from Heaven* by this time had become not only a byword for 'quality' but part of the BBC's very own marketing strategy.

Interpretation

In many ways, the central dramatic conflict of *Pennies* is that between freedom and repression. Arthur and Eileen are characters who go on the run from their own society – attempting to flee all its various repressions and demands for conformity, as symbolised by the forces of law and order pursuing them for a crime Arthur did not commit. At the start of the drama, both protagonists are shown imprisoned within domestic routines from which they crave distraction: for Arthur, this is life in suburbia and a dull marriage to the petit-bourgeois Joan; for Eileen, it is being surrogate wife and mother to her coal-mining family in the Forest of Dean, whilst holding down a day job as teacher in the local village school.

Each protagonist finds their own means of temporary escape from this domestic drudgery. In the village school, Eileen enchants her pupils with the fairy story of Rapunzel: a tale that expresses her own secret longings for escape – of the princess locked up in a tower who is rescued by a handsome prince. Arthur's escape, meanwhile, is sex. As is made clear right from the very first scene of *Pennies*, in which he pleads to Joan for 'a bit of the other' as he is 'going to be away from home for the next four days', sex is shown to be Arthur's way of dealing with the frustrations of his life as a salesman (Ep. 1, p. 7). Not for him the sexual repression of a Jack Black, nor even the spiritual angst of Casanova: instead he is earthy and sensual; an unrepressed working-class Londoner who even admits to Joan at one point that given half the chance he would 'fuck [his] own grandmother!' (Ep. 3, p. 12).

The key to understanding this shift in characterisation from previous male protagonists lies in the collapse of the flesh-spirit dichotomy noted in Potter's writing, with the 1976 'trilogy' (see Chapter 2). With Old Testament notions of a Fall from Eden shrugged off, the way is open for Potter to create a protagonist for whom sex is not just an empty act. On the contrary, it is when Arthur is deprived of sex that he feels empty. Sitting at the breakfast table in Episode 1, after Joan has denied him his conjugal rights, he points to his heart and tells her 'I'm empty – blank – I've got nothing *here*' (Ep. 1, p. 14). Sex is not the source of Arthur's spiritual imprisonment (as it was for Casanova). Rather, it is one of his few means of gaining spiritual *sustenance*. The previous Potter divide between 'spirit' and 'flesh' has been blurred irrevocably. In *Pennies*, it is impossible to separate out Arthur's need for sex from his need for love, the demands of his 'flesh' from those of his 'spirit'.

The inner conflict which had haunted previous Potter protagonists is gone in *Pennies*. Instead, it is *externalised* and shifted on to Arthur's relationship with his frigid wife Joan. Their marriage is dramatised as a constant battleground between desire and repression – 'liberated' Arthur versus puritanical Joan who denies him sex, calling him a 'filthy beast' (Ep. 1, p. 10). Unlike his counterparts in previous Potter plays, *Pennies*' central protagonist is completely free of sexual hang-ups. All of the forces of repression now come from without – from society at large which extends itself right into the home in the form of his morally upright wife Joan and her pretensions to bourgeois respectability.

Domestic and sexual repression are only symptoms of a much wider oppression from which Arthur and Eileen both eventually flee. The chief battleground within the plays is ultimately that of the individual versus society – of the desire for personal freedom and self-expression set against a society characterised as wholly reactionary and oppressive. Crucial in this respect is the historical setting of thirties' England. Forming a constant backdrop of economic despair and exploitation, the Depression of the thirties becomes synonymous in the plays with repression.

As Ian Colley and Gill Davies have pointed out, the period setting of *Pennies* has little to do with the real nineteen thirties: it 'eclipses the 'documentary' decade of wars, slump, mass unemployment and open class conflict.'[44] Potter draws instead upon a few stock motifs – music, Metroland, a salesman in the Depression – in order to offer a pastiche of the thirties, one that belongs more to general cultural memory than any real historical past. If explanations for this are familiar from past Potter works – 'non-naturalism', a distrust of 'fact' as opposed to 'fiction', a desire to subvert the historically accurate costume drama – one other reason suggests itself. The past is presented as memory because the drama wishes to draw attention to its own relationship with the present.

Written in 1977, a Jubilee Year that was a time of economic crisis, *Pennies* is also set in a Jubilee Year that was a time of economic crisis.[45] It is 1935, the twenty-fifth year of George V's reign and the country 'is going to the dogs', according to Arthur's fellow salesmen (Ep. 2, p. 78).[46] As the little man struggling in the face of economic crisis and decline, the character of Arthur Parker invites audience identification. His exploits seem explicitly designed to touch a popular nerve about the state of Britain in 1977–78. At the same time, it is important to note how such contemporary resonances intersect with more personal 'authorial' links. 1935 was not only a Jubilee year. It was also the year in which Potter was born. In court, accused of murder, Arthur fails to produce a convincing alibi for where he was on the night of the crime, 17 May 1935 (Potter's own date of birth). Later, condemned to hang, he is asked where it had all gone wrong. 'The day I was bleed'n born' is his reply, playing on suggestions not only of his own but of Potter's birthday – that is, the date of the 'crime' (Ep. 6, p. 105).

Through this linking of 1935 with 1977, the period of Potter's own lifespan, the implication seems to be that nothing has changed very much in Britain. The same old repressions are still there – economic, social, political. The more personal 'authorial' links with Arthur also suggest that the 'Depression' portrayed in *Pennies* is as much psychic as economic. This is made clearest in the figure of the Accordion Man: the real culprit in the murder of a blind girl for which Arthur eventually hangs. An epileptic stammering tramp, this figure makes his living playing hymns on his battered old piano accordion. He is first encountered by Arthur in Episode 1, thumbing a lift on the highway from London to Gloucester. Both on the same road, Arthur and the Accordion Man are both in a sense 'commercial travellers' – each in his own way trying to interest an indifferent public in the 'songs' he peddles. Despite the surface 'naturalism' of their differing social status, *Pennies* suggests an equivalence at some deeper 'non-naturalistic' level – a psychic or symbolic world behind the world in which relative economic positions become irrelevant, beside both men's similar struggle for survival in the Depression. Like the Accordion Man, the implication is that Arthur, too, is at the bottom of the social heap, fighting against poverty and despair.

Plate 1 'Opportunity and Redemption': Dennis Price and Yootha Joyce in *The Confidence Course*, 1965 © BBC Photograph Library

Plate 2 The devoted couple: Dennis Potter and his wife, Margaret, *c*. 1978 © BBC Photograph Library

Plate 3 The greatest lover: Frank Finlay as *Casanova*, 1971 © BBC Photograph Library

Plate 4 Singing for your supper: Bob Hoskins in *Pennies from Heaven*, 1978 © BBC Photograph Library

Plate 5 A view from Hammersmith Bridge: Michael Gambon as *The Singing Detective*, 1986 © BBC Photograph Library

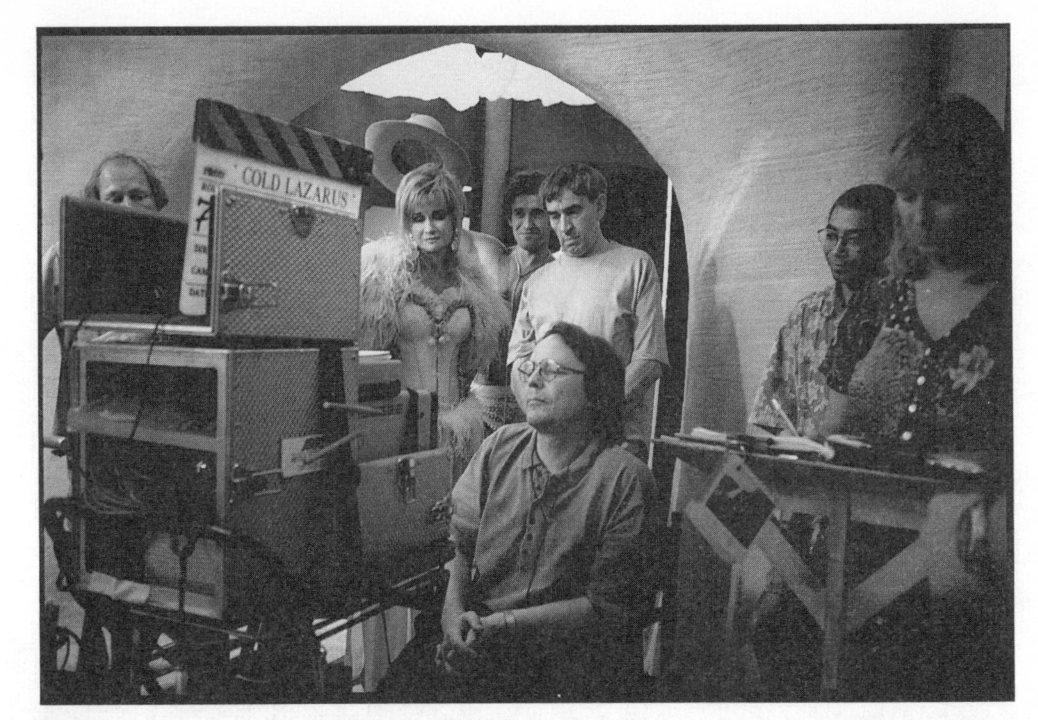

Plate 6 'Keepers of the Flame': producer Kenith Trodd (standing) and director Renny Rye with star Diane Ladd on the set of the 1996 posthumous Potter production, *Cold Lazarus*

In turn, these links are reinforced by the number of times the Accordion Man reappears throughout *Pennies*, haunting each of the main protagonists. In Episode 2, Joan sees him standing on a street-corner and for a moment experiences the 'queer sensation' that he is her husband, Arthur (Ep. 2, p. 96). Stripped of the surface 'lie' of material difference, she spies Arthur's spiritual 'essence' in a surrogate – a beggar trying to interest passers-by in his 'hymns', literally pleading for 'pennies from heaven'.

Even more significantly, Eileen encounters the Accordion Man in Episode 5. As he passes her in a London street, he suddenly shouts: 'I thought you were dead! ... The d-devil had put out your eyes. He told me to – to – No. It couldn't be you' (Ep. 5, p. 39). Later that episode he is found dead in the Thames, having jumped off Hammersmith Bridge. If this case of mistaken identity illustrates his guilt over the murder of the blind girl which subsequently induces his suicide, it also symbolically links Eileen with the murder victim. Crucial, here, is the fact that earlier his *alter ego*, Arthur, had also encountered the victim on his travels. Having parked his car at the side of a country road in Episode 2, he had met the blind girl walking alone through a field. Transfixed by her strange vulnerable beauty, he had offered to escort her home, yet though she had declined, he could not help shouting emotionally, 'I shall never forget this! Not ever! ... I think you're the most beautiful young lady I've ever seen!' Out of earshot, however, he had whispered: 'I'd cut off my right arm if I could make you see again ... I dunno what I'd do if I could only – *take your knickers off*' (Ep. 2, p. 48).

Suddenly, a potentially darker side to Arthur's errant sexuality is revealed. As the cockney Casanova carrying on an adulterous affair with Eileen, he may seem the lovable rogue; but could it be that his sexual desires border on the pathological? Running through *Pennies* is a villain-victim ambiguity which plays with notions of Arthur's guilt. By way of the symbolic link with the Accordion Man, it raises the question of whether at some 'deeper', 'non-naturalistic' level, Arthur is not indeed guilty of the crime for which he eventually hangs. As the drama unfolds, a case gradually forms against him. Not only does he lust secretly after the blind girl but later, like the stereotypical murderer, he returns to the scene of the 'crime' – the spot where he had desired her and where, in an improbable coincidence, she is later found raped and murdered. It is because of his return to the scene that the police first come to suspect him of the crime.

Moreover, it is a sex crime – the work of a 'sexual maniac', according to the puritanical Inspector who leads the police investigation (Ep. 5, p. 29). Given his sexual peccadilloes ('outrageous' for the period), Arthur becomes a suitable candidate on whom to pin the murder. The result is an echo of the scapegoat motif of *A Beast*, *Stand Up* and *Where the Buffalo*

Roam. The individual is punished by the wider community not so much because of his guilt as his failure to conform to the narrow set of behaviour codes that constitute the socially acceptable 'norm'. The individual is persecuted for *being* individual.

At the same time, the villain-victim ambiguity of Nigel Barton and Willy Turner is also present in Arthur's characterisation. The salesman may not have literally killed the blind girl, but is his sexuality in some way aberrant? Is the murder to which he is symbolically linked not somehow an expression of his own forbidden desires? Throughout the six episodes, Pennies maintains a careful balance in its portrayal of Arthur as everyman hero and Arthur as social/sexual 'criminal'. On the one hand, he is shown to be a common liar and cheat, two-timing not only his wife but also Eileen. As the 'prince' unlocking her from the tower of her virginity, he seduces Eileen on the promise he is unmarried, yet later abandons her when she becomes pregnant. It is this which in turn symbolically connects her with the blind girl and helps account for her meeting with 'the murderer' (and likewise Arthur's with 'the victim'). An 'innocent', metaphorically blind in terms of her lack of worldliness, Eileen is led by Arthur to her downfall via a forced seduction that parallels the Accordion Man's sexual assault of the blind girl. Discovering her own pregnancy in the same episode as the police discover the body of the blind girl (Episode 3), she is forced to resign from her teaching job in the Forest of Dean and head to London in search of a new life. Once more, however, she finds herself exploited by men, as she is forced into prostitution to survive. Only by the end of Episode 4 does she finally get to be reunited with Arthur, her 'prince', at which point the pair decide to cut the ties of their previous lives and go on the run.

On one level, Arthur is therefore extremely guilty in *Pennies*: a metaphorical 'murderer' who 'kills' off Eileen's old life in the Forest of Dean, forcing her to become a prostitute in London. By virtue of his past misdeeds, his dramatic fate is to 'become' the Accordion Man – literally hanging in his place at the end of Episode 6.

At the same time, *Pennies* complicates the simple virgin-whore dichotomy in its presentation of Eileen's transformation into a 'fallen' woman. Moreover, it does so in a way that helps to redeem Arthur, suggesting a more positive view of his actions. Thus Eileen is no mere victim of Arthur's seduction. As she admits to him in Episode 3, 'I wanted you, you see' (Ep. 3, p. 72). From her shy passive role serving her father and brothers, her liaison with Arthur forces her out of the Forest of Dean and turns her into a strong independent woman of the world who learns to look after herself.[47] Ironically, by Episode 5 when they go on the run, it is she who has to protect Arthur, resisting his calls to give up prostitution; calculating instead that the selling of her sexuality is their one hope of economic advancement in Depression-hit Britain. As Arthur tells her, 'I ain't got no guts at all', to which she replies, 'Don't worry. I've got enough for both of us (Ep. 4, p. 102).

The development of Eileen's characterisation in *Pennies* is a further illustration of the blurring of the flesh-spirit dichotomy in Potter's work as a whole. Rather than as a simple victim of a 'fall' from sexual innocence, she is portrayed as no innocent at all but a willing party to Arthur's seduction. Having been exploited by men, she later begins to turn it to her advantage in Episode 5. There are clear parallels with *Blue Remembered Hills* (see Chapter 3). The abandonment of the notion of an innocence from which one can lapse leads to more complex Potter characterisations – a world of blurred categories rather than simple stereotypes of 'good' and 'evil', 'innocence' and 'experience', 'virgin' and 'whore'.

In turn, this blurring of categories helps redeem Arthur. As suggested earlier, sex is one of his few means of spiritual sustenance and expression. If his sexuality verges on the pathological, it is also a sign that he *cares* – a spontaneous overflow of his emotions. Thus *Pennies* sustains two completely opposite readings of his character: one, that he is the self-centred 'sexual maniac' which the law believes him to be, deserving of the punishment he receives; the other, that his strong sexuality is simply the sign of a warm-hearted, highly emotional man. In this light, his desire to remove the blind girl's knickers becomes but the comic manifestation of his wish that she could be made to see: 'I'd cut off my right arm if I could make you see again. I'd – I dunno what I'd do if I could only *take your knickers off* ... Take care! Take care!' (Ep. 3, pp. 48–9).

If by way of the title of Episode 6 ('Says My Heart') Potter hints at his own verdict, it is left mainly to the audience to decide the true extent of Arthur's 'guilt'. In the final episode, the protagonist is literally put in the dock. After his arrest, lengthy scenes follow, depicting his trial at the Old Bailey. In this way, *Pennies* sums up the evidence for and against him. At the same time, its theme of the individual versus society is starkly dramatised. Sentenced to death, Arthur, the 'little man', finds himself powerless against the full weight and authority of the British State. He is finally seen being hanged, just as the screen goes black.

Hence, although he apparently turns up 'like a bad penny' on Hammersmith Bridge after he has been hanged, it is decidedly unclear as to whether his resurrection is in body or simply in spirit. Turning to camera, Arthur and Eileen both say, 'The song is ended but the melody lingers on' (Ep. 6, p. 116). *Pennies* finally leaves it up to each viewer not only to decide whether Arthur is guilty but also to choose the version of events they most wish to believe: either that Arthur has been granted a reprieve at the last possible moment and that he has raced to be beside Eileen, or that his 'song' has indeed ended, even if his 'spirit' (the dreams he lived for) does still linger on. If the tension is very much that of the happy endings of musicals as opposed to the 'real world', it is also exactly the struggle between optimism (freedom) and pessimism (repression) which informs all of *Pennies*. In other words, it is a struggle of probabilities, of the defiance of 'improbable' optimism over pessimism: the more predictable, 'realistic' world-view.

It is this which clearly motivates the ambiguity in Arthur's characterisation. Neither purely a victim of circumstance nor quite a villain, he is both in *Pennies*. While the law is portrayed as deterministic in its search for convenient solutions and simplistic absolutes (complete innocence *or* utter guilt), the drama itself offers a more complex world-view. It is not 'either or' but '*both and*': Arthur is profoundly guilty yet so, too, is he an innocent. Crucially, this is what separates the villain-victim ambiguity in his characterisation from that of previous Potter protagonists like Nigel Barton and Willy Turner. The central male protagonists of earlier Potter plays were always 'torn' heroes, hovering uneasily between contrasting possibilities of guilt or innocence. This uncertainty was as much internal as external to their construction: flashbacks, fantasy sequences and other 'psychological expressionist' devices helped emphasise how much the guilt and tension that racked the plays emanated from inside their own heads.

With Arthur Parker, there is no such angst. As previously noted, all of his problems are *external*, lying in the disparity between the 'real world' of the Depression and the vision of a better world he senses in 'the songs'. There is therefore no need for elaborate flashback sequences to dramatise his inner conflict and private guilt. He has none. His struggle is with an outside world that does not measure up to the confidence of his dreams. If this helps explain the 'naturalistic' simplicity of his characterisation in *Pennies* – the fact that aside from the musical numbers, he is portrayed wholly from 'the outside', the viewer never being taken inside his head to be shown his memories – it also accounts for why it is finally left to the audience to judge the true extent of his guilt. The strength of Arthur's own dreams rules out any great degree of private angst or self-awareness on his part. In keeping with the shift of emphasis, noted with the 1976 'trilogy', there is no longer a sense of a male Potter protagonist being torn between irreconcilables. Arthur is much more of an integrated personality in whom guilt and innocence, flesh and spirit mingle and blur. In the very simplicity of his character and desires, he resembles the children in the contemporaneous *Blue Remembered Hills*: a sinner who at the same time is innocent because he is unaware.

Like the 1979 play, *Pennies* also contains an underlying movement towards an instinctive faith in an ultimate Good ('God'). Sitting in a cheap hotel in Episode 2, listening to his fellow salesmen air their Depression woes, Arthur suddenly tries to articulate the feeling he himself can only half-consciously grasp through the songs – the sense that behind all the immediate evil and misery in the world, everything is ultimately *alright*:

> ARTHUR: Blimey, I can almost taste it! It's looking for the blue, ennit, and the gold. The patch of blue sky. The gold of the, of the bleed'n dawn, or – the light in somebody's eyes – Pennies From Heaven, that's what it is. And we can't see 'em, clinking and clinking, all around, all over the place ... just bend down and pick 'em up! (Ep. 2, p. 90)

The realisation that there is an ultimate purpose and Good is simply a feeling. It can be expressed 'with no language but a cry'. Nevertheless, Arthur perseveres with his depressed fellow salesmen in this key scene, telling them: 'Somewhere the sun is shining – And do you know where? Inside yourself! Inside your own head! ... Put[s] the real meaning into them songs' (Ep. 2, pp. 90–1).

It is the strength of his own spiritual yearning rather than any special qualities of the tunes themselves which makes the thirties' songs so potent for Arthur. As his cynical colleagues are quick to remind him, the songs of Tin Pan Alley were really just 'a business ... dreamed up in a back-office by a couple of Jew-boys with green eyeshades' (Ep. 2, p. 91). This is the idea Potter first fully articulated in *Follow the Yellow Brick Road*: namely, that the power of the human spirit, 'the human dream for *some* concept of 'perfection', some Zion or Eden or Golden City', will always outcrop in some form, no matter how secular the context or how 'ludicrous' the object through which this basic religious impulse is expressed.[48] As a result, *Pennies* holds out the tenuous possibility that unlikely as it may seem, the schmaltzy songs of Tin Pan Alley may just have had it right after all – namely, that if one acquires a spiritual faith, believing positively enough that 'somewhere the sun is shining', the storm-clouds may indeed soon all roll by, banishing the 'Depression blues' which, within the drama, are as much psychological as economic. In this way, the optimistic assurances of the songs become either extremely trite or boldly emancipating. As with Arthur's ambiguous characterisation, it all becomes a matter of from which perspective one chooses to look.

The salesmen scene thus functions as an important microcosm of the drama as a whole – a drama in which the viewer is invited to choose between 'predictable' pessimism ('Depression' and repression, culminating in Arthur's legalised murder) and 'improbable' optimism (faith in the songs which leads to his miraculous resurrection). What is important to note is that this pessimism/optimism duality exactly corresponds with 'naturalism' and 'non-naturalism'. Both the narrative and characterisation of the drama conform to the familiar conventions of habituated TV 'naturalism'. As previously noted, there is none of the interior drama or psychological expressionism of other Potter plays: Arthur's characterisation is wholly external in relation to the world of the Depression whilst the drama itself takes the form of a simple linear plot. It is chiefly in the musical numbers which constantly interrupt the narrative that *Pennies*' 'non-naturalism' resides. In their sheer number (eighty-two in all), the songs offer a constant *alternative* to 'naturalism' – the brightness and happiness of the melodies and choreography contrasting with the gloomy depiction of 'real life' in the Depression. In turn, this connects with the drama's religious view for if, as Chapter 3 suggested, Potter's 'non-naturalism' is ultimately an assertion of another way of seeing, beyond 'naturalist/realist' modes, this is precisely the function of the songs in *Pennies*. When the music begins, the gloomy 'naturalism' of the dramatic narrative is disrupted or transcended. The different, brighter fictional space which the miming and the lighting changes announce becomes an assertion of the existence of an inner realm of the spirit; one where dreams of perfection reside, in stark contrast to the depressing reality without.

It is this which seems to lie behind Potter's desire that the audience be as 'disorientated as possible' by *Pennies*' very first musical number, 'The Clouds Will Soon Roll By'. The phrase recalls his comments in his 'Realism and Non-Naturalism' paper of that same year, in which he claimed the best 'non-naturalist drama, in its very structures *dis*orientates the viewer smack in the middle of the orientation process which television perpetually uses' (see Chapter 3). Suddenly, with a male character miming to a woman's voice several minutes into a 'serious' drama, viewer expectations are undermined. The habitual 'naturalism' of TV drama – the fiction whereby audiences are invited to collude in the belief that what is taking place on screen is real – is disrupted. Audience engagement and identification with the central protagonist is momentarily suspended and received notions of 'reality' thrown into question. The incongruity of a man singing in a woman's voice makes it impossible for the audience to deduce anything other than that this is an actor in a TV studio miming to a recording on the soundtrack. In this way, the manufacture of 'naturalism' and of drama in general is exposed. After only a few minutes of conventional acting and plot exposition, the normally concealed realm of production is opened up to the viewer, revealing 'naturalism' to be a pretence. The result is a perfect dramatic metaphor for *Pennies*' assertion of the existence of a realm of the spirit – of a world behind the world, underlying everyday surface 'naturalism', a place where individuals retain the freedom to dream of other possibilities and so perhaps the power to shape their own destiny.

It hardly seems coincidental that many of the songs used in *Pennies* are those which Potter first heard in early childhood. He has written that they were the songs you used to 'hear coming up the stair [from the wireless]. When you're a child. When you are supposed to be asleep.'[49] They are thus indelibly associated with the wonder of childhood – the child's way of seeing the world for the first time that for Potter is religious and which he was clearly trying to invoke in his audience with the 'disorientation' of the very first song in *Pennies*. This seems to be why, in interviews of the time, he suggested the songs in the drama were like 'psalms':

> [The songs] represent the same kinds of things that the psalms and fairy tales represented: that is, the most generalised human dreams, that the world should be perfect, beautiful and loving, and all of those things ... I believe that there is a sort of religious yearning that the world shall be whole, and what I want people to recognise by the end of the plays is that the songs are only diminished versions of the oldest myths of all in the Garden of Eden.[50]

It is therefore the songs which, standing in opposition to the pessimism and 'repression' of the central narrative, constitute the optimism in *Pennies* – part of a simple assertion of belief that 'the world shall be whole'; the triumph of hope over experience. In this light, *Pennies* can be seen to abound with Christian symbolism. The trial and persecution of the innocent Arthur, his hanging and subsequent inexplicable appearance on Hammersmith Bridge, all carry echoes of Christ's Crucifixion and Resurrection. At the moment of extreme pessimism, when it seems brutality and death have triumphed, the 'miracle' happens. Like the equivalent one with Pattie in *Brimstone and Treacle*, it does so through the power of an instinctive faith. Just as with Mrs Bates, Arthur believes in something. In the face of other's cynicism and all the evidence of experience, he clings to his conviction that the songs (the 'psalms') are true and it is this which sees him through, even to the bitter end. His reward for his trials is salvation through God: that is, through the God-like 'Author' who, in deciding he should live, expresses his own instinctive belief, the gut reaction or emotional choice of 'Says My Heart'.

The songs as 'psalms' ultimately become the expression of a desire for emotional justice. In keeping with this theme, it is highly significant that, reunited on Hammersmith Bridge at the very end of the serial, the final song to which Arthur and Eileen mime is called 'The Glory of Love', its title echoing the Christian conception of love as the means to spiritual rebirth. The two characters who believe most in the songs, Arthur and Eileen, literally embody this Eden dream – as the initials of their Christian names suggest, they are Adam and Eve. Combining innocence with original sin, they resemble the children in *Blue Remembered Hills*. Naive and reckless, they are also in some sense the children of God, with the capacity to achieve salvation at the very end because they believe in Him.

Also implicit within this salvation is transformation. It seems no coincidence that Arthur should be resurrected on the same bridge (Hammersmith) from which the Accordion Man jumped in Episode 5, suddenly appearing there after his execution.[51] As noted earlier, the Accordion Man's suicide was motivated by his burden of guilt over the murder of the blind girl. Unlike his salesman *alter ego*, he therefore conforms to a more familiar type of Potter protagonist, one torn between the demands of spirit and flesh: the spiritual yearnings he expresses through the hymns he plays versus his own physical compulsions which lead him eventually to sexual assault and murder. In this way, he seems to embody the old flesh-spirit dichotomy of previous Potter plays, as opposed to the new more 'integrated' personality of Arthur in whom such categories blur. The difference ultimately seems to be that between despair and hope. Poor, marginalised, racked by guilt, the Accordion Man can see no way out of his dilemma other than suicide. Arthur, however, has something to believe in (the songs). His instinctive faith gives him the 'spiritual' power to confront death and finally the miracle which allows him to cheat it. Completely unrepressed and child-like through his proximity to the songs, the difference between Arthur and his *alter ego* is like that between a new and an old self. If this explains Arthur's resurrection at the spot where the Accordion Man died, it also, in turn, suggests *Pennies* as a work depicting psychic transformation: of old attitudes jettisoned in favour of new, of an old self dying in order to live again in new form.[52]

In that sense, *Pennies from Heaven* can be seen as a drama about the overcoming of spiritual trials which culminates in an eventual reward of personal transformation. Again, it is through the figure of the Accordion Man that this is made clearest. It is he who sings the title song to Arthur in Episode One, with its lines: 'Every time it rains / It rains Pennies From Heaven / ... If you want the things you love / You must have showers' (Ep. 1, p. 74). The fact that Potter takes the title of his drama from this song indicates the centrality of the idea that, although every life 'must have showers', all the apparent trials and storm-clouds may be for a greater good. The metaphor is clear: those 'Pennies From Heaven' (literally, the rain) may seem to be of little value and bring no cheer and yet they are everything. They are what brings life to the earth – hope and renewal. The implication is that, wrapped up in the cares of day to day living (for example, the need to earn money, symbolised in the plays by the harsh materialism of the Depression), it is all too easy to forget or become habituated to this essential truth. Only by a different way of seeing, the drama asserts, can we perceive afresh all the 'pennies' lying around us every day. In that recognition, it is implied, comes a spiritual transformation and renewal – the development of an instinctive faith in an ultimate Good. Or as an enraptured Arthur puts it to his fellow salesmen in Episode 2, 'Pennies From Heaven ... clinking and clinking all around, all over the place ... Just bend down and pick 'em up!'

Pennies, however, finally leaves it up to its audience to choose whether they wish to do so or not. An avowedly religious work, written from a Christian perspective, the drama is ultimately a struggle between probabilities, between different ways of seeing – the 'predictable' pessimism of 'naturalism' (the 'real' world of the Depression which hangs Arthur as a villain) versus the 'improbable' optimism of 'non-naturalism' (the realm of the 'spirit' and songs, belief in which finally resurrects Arthur as a hero). Balanced on the knife-edge between optimism and pessimism, *Pennies* permits both views to be tenable – Arthur may be innocent or guilty, alive or dead. God and salvation may exist or they may not. If Potter indicates his own choice ('Says My Heart'), the drama, by sustaining both possibilities, finally leaves it up to each viewer to decide, ultimately as a matter of personal faith. In *Pennies*, Potter's own Christian optimism may be palpable but it has to be left open-ended. As he suggested in 1978:

> I think optimism is open-ended, you see. I don't think it's a blind assertion of things. And I'm more and more inclined to the opinion that drama should be open at all points of access so that you can take even the opposite sometimes of what is intended. You should be able to use it as sort of working material for what you are responding to, and take from it a lot of things that I wouldn't want people to take from it. But they will, and that's good ... All politics and all religion and all social aspirations ought to be about allowing, encouraging, searching for people to be given the chance of being other than they are seen to be, other than the way they are going. When predictability is built into drama or drama-documentary and it seems to be asserted that C follows B follows A, and there's no way out, there's no surprise left, and I think that's pessimism and when I use the word, optimism, I use it against that grain.[53]

Pennies from Hollywood

Fuelling his own increased optimism, the success of *Pennies* led to a period of frenetic activity in the late seventies and early eighties which saw Potter transform himself from reclusive BBC playwright into 'self-confessed hustler', determined to negotiate his own production packages and to challenge traditional orthodoxies and working practices not just in television but in film as well.[54] By 1981, he had written his own American movie (a big budget cinema version of *Pennies* for MGM) and for a time he was reputedly the highest paid screenwriter in Hollywood, after Neil Simon – all of this from a man who had spent the previous twenty years ill, as a virtual recluse and who had never ventured out of England until he was 41.[55]

After the British success of *Pennies*, approaches were made from both Bernard Delfont and Joseph Janni to adapt the plays for cinema. An option on the movie rights was finally given, however, to Greg Smith, a British film producer then setting up business in Chicago, a city which had promised to invest heavily in film.[56] By the end of 1978, Potter had produced a draft screenplay for him, with all of Arthur Parker's exploits relocated from England to Chicago in the American Depression of the thirties. Despite this obvious targeting of the American market, the *Pennies* screenplay could find no financial backers in Britain. It was at this point Potter began to realise 'what goes on ... [when] someone hopes to make a movie' in Britain and he vowed to do something about it.[57] The formation of his own independent production company, Pennies From Heaven Limited (PFH), was partly the result (see Chapter 5). Not only were he and his partner Kenith Trodd keen to challenge traditional broadcasting structures, their move into independent production was also an attempt to give a boost to the ailing British film industry by trying to generate enough money and prestige to produce 'an annual British movie, without fees or commissions'.[58] By autumn 1980, Potter announced that the first of these projects would be a feature film version of the banned *Brimstone and Treacle* – to be produced in Britain by PFH, with shooting scheduled to start the following spring.

The idealism behind PFH had also to be backed up by substantial financial resources. Ironically, it was Potter's rejected *Pennies* screenplay which would give the company its biggest economic boost. Whilst in Britain, working on his film *Nijinsky*, Hollywood director Herbert Ross became acquainted with Potter's work and approached him with a view to scripting his next project: a follow-up to the director's 1977 film about ballet, *The Turning Point*. Travelling to America, ostensibly to discuss this project with Ross, Potter (now the self-confessed 'hustler') produced the *Pennies* screenplay from his pocket.[59]

A director at the peak of his career in both commercial and award terms, Ross had reached a point where he was in a position to build a reputation as a major Hollywood artist, taking risks with daring material that might lead to critical acclaim. *Pennies* seemed to fit the criteria. Having a background in musicals and choreography, he and his producer wife, the late Nora Kaye, also had the expertise to realise the musical numbers on film.

With Ross and Kaye's support behind it, *Pennies* was offered to the major Hollywood studios. Paramount (with whom Ross had just made *Nijinsky*) turned it down. Things, however, were different at Metro-Goldwyn-Mayer. By 1980, the erstwhile home of the Hollywood musical was a studio in decline, its last major film having been *Straw Dogs* nearly ten years before. MGM, however, was under new management. David Begelman, a former executive at Columbia, had taken over the reins with a brief to turn the studio around in one year and restore it to somewhere near the pre-eminence it had once enjoyed. Hence, just as *Pennies* was being offered, he needed to get ten or twelve major projects quickly into production in order to signal a decisive break with the previous decade of decline. What better way to announce MGM was back from the grave than with the production of a big-budget 'musical', the genre with which the studio had once been so successfully associated? If not a financial one, at least Ross's picture might be a critical and Oscar success, thus putting MGM back on the map as a bold, adventurous studio which encouraged talent and innovation.[60]

For these reasons, MGM and Begelman decided to back *Pennies* where other studios had turned it down. Importantly, there were two conditions attached to the agreement. The first was that a major star play Arthur Parker. After many top Hollywood actors (including Dustin Hoffman, Robert Redford and Al Pacino) had turned the *Pennies* script down, a Hollywood agent, John Gaines, succeeded in contriving a meeting in Las Vegas with Ross, Begelman and the movie's young executive producer, Rick McCallum. According to the latter:

> What we didn't know was that [Gaines] represented Steve Martin and that Steve Martin was performing live in Las Vegas ... We were invited to meet Steve during the half-break of the show and as we were walking down the corridor, the sound of 'Pennies From Heaven' started to come up and there was Steve lip-synching to the Arthur Tracey version. And that was it. We had the movie. We were ready to go.

Within a week of his unorthodox 'audition', a deal had been signed with Martin as Parker, together with Bernadette Peters (Martin's co-star in his previous movie, *The Jerk* and also at the time his off-screen partner) in the role of Eileen. On the film's release, many criticised the casting of a comedian in the central role. Though the choice of Steve Martin recalls Potter's suggestion for the BBC *Pennies* that Arthur be played by a comic, the reason in the case of the Hollywood version was simple economic pragmatism. *The Jerk* had been the highest grossing comedy ever ($92 million). Thus MGM thought they had at last found an Arthur Parker who was a proven box office draw. For his part, Martin now had the chance to establish himself as a premier Hollywood star by tackling his first 'serious' dramatic role.

The Hollywood version of *Pennies* was thus born out of a number of expediencies: Ross wanted a critical success; Martin wanted to become a major star; MGM needed a big-budget production to restore its credibility as an important Hollywood studio. Meanwhile, Potter himself wanted to use some of the money and kudos of having worked on a big American movie as a way of realising his own ambitions of reviving film production at home. In this last aim he came partly unstuck as a result of the second important condition MGM attached to the *Pennies* deal. This was an insistence that all further international sales of the original BBC drama be halted, in case box office interest was drained away by American TV stations buying up the serial and screening it at the time of the movie's release. As a consequence, Potter's agent (Judy Daish) was forced to go to the BBC to ask them to stop any further sales effort, aware that if the Corporation refused the whole MGM deal would collapse. The BBC exacted a high price for its compliance, demanding $100,000 plus half Potter's further profits from the film. Considering the writer's fee for the *Pennies* screenplay was $250,000, these were terms which could only further sour relations between the BBC and Potter – already at an all-time low after his departure to LWT the previous year. Though the Corporation has always refused to comment, undoubtedly Potter's going played a part in its dealings. The consequent suppression of the TV *Pennies* for the sake of Hollywood also resulted in much bad feeling being directed towards Potter from those involved with the original drama.[61]

In the event, neither Potter nor the BBC managed to profit highly from the $19 million MGM version. Through 1980 and 1981, the writer became a regular transatlantic commuter between Britain and the MGM set in Los Angeles, as his script went through successive drafts in which lengthy scenes and stretches of dialogue from the original version were pared down to fit the constraints of a ninety-minute Hollywood movie. On the film's release, this abridgement drew fire from many British critics familiar with the TV version who felt that the heart and soul had been cut out of *Pennies*: 'Dennis Potter made simple (and painless)', as one reviewer put it.[62] In fact, closer inspection reveals that the pared-down version contains its own structure and did not result simply from across-the-board cutting. Many of the revisions are made in the service of a much darker and bleaker vision than that of the original TV plays.

This is tellingly illustrated by the movie's treatment of the scene in which the Accordion Man sings the 'Pennies From Heaven' title song to Arthur. Whilst in the original TV drama the Accordion Man's performance took place in a café to which Arthur had taken him for a meal, the film version moves the character beyond these confines in order to have him sing and dance against a stylised backdrop featuring images of the homeless and dispossessed. In this way, the Accordion Man is transformed from the *unique* character he was in the television version (the specific *alter ego* of Arthur) into a *general* representative of all the suffering victims of the Depression. De-emphasising the specific 'murderer/rapist' symbolism of Arthur's relationship with the Accordion Man, the Hollywood version refashions the link as one of fellow sufferers unable to escape the Depression.

This seems to be why, in 1982, Potter suggested that the movie version was 'even more bleak in a way' than the original BBC drama.[63] Its general outlook and tone is unusual (even remarkable) for a big-budget Hollywood film and clearly has much to do with the combination of a British writer's playful enjoyment of the possibilities of critiquing capitalism from the very heart of the American Dream (Hollywood), together with an American director's desire to take risks and create an artistic success. As Potter suggested in 1982: 'I wanted to use the musical convention that this film tells you everything is fine, even while I'm saying everything is NOT alright, that there is something, a piece of imagination that says everything is not alright.'[64]

It is to this desire to create a genuine 'Depression' musical that most of the differences between the Hollywood and TV versions of *Pennies* can be attributed. In marked contrast to the irony, ambiguity and playfulness of the TV drama, the film concentrates instead on an exploitation of genre. Traditionally the escapist form *par excellence*, the musical is used in the MGM *Pennies* to suggest that there is no escape for those, like the central protagonists, caught up in the Depression.

A clear example of this comes in one of the few genuine rewrites to Potter's original movie screenplay when, near the end of the film and while on the run, Arthur and Eileen escape into a cinema. Sitting in the dark, they watch a scene from the 1936 Astaire-Rogers musical, *Follow The Fleet*. On screen, Fred Astaire is singing 'Let's Face the Music and Dance'. Suddenly, silhouetted against the large image on screen, Ross's film shows the small figure of Arthur, miming the song and mimicking Astaire's gestures exactly. Then, just as suddenly, the spectator is metaphorically taken 'in' to this film within a film in order to be shown the dance sequence from 'Let's Face The Music' reconstructed in detail – with Eileen and Arthur (Bernadette Peters and Steve Martin) temporarily 'becoming' Ginger and Fred. If the aim is to illustrate how important the escapist dreams of the musicals were to those struggling in the Depression era, the MGM *Pennies* also emphasises the impossibility of complete identification with the image. Dancing as Ginger and Fred in an ornate ballroom setting, the lovers are joined by a male chorus, all of whom are dressed in top hat and tails and carrying shiny black sticks. Foregrounded as the pair dance behind, the chorus slowly raise their sticks vertically until these come to seem prison-like: 'like huge bars tightly surrounding seemingly miniature Arthur and Eileen', as Potter's final script draft puts it.[65] If the effect is to suggest there is no escape for Arthur and Eileen from the Depression, it also implies that no matter how hard they try to submerge themselves in dreams, those dreams will never be realised. Their fate, instead, is to 'face the music' of the Depression and Arthur's murder charge. Poor and on the run, they can only glimpse Paradise from the cinema stalls. They are mere spectators, ultimately shut out of the image.

The American Dream of success lying within the grasp of everyone is thus undermined in the film. In turn, this helps shed light on how the musical numbers work within the Hollywood version. Whilst the performance of the songs in the BBC drama was always dramatically motivated by the sheet music Arthur peddled, the MGM version exploits its production context in order to pay homage to the screen musicals of Hollywood's past. Counterpointing the dark tableaux of the Depression scenes, most of the songs are realised as lavish 'white set' production numbers which, as with 'Let's Face The Music', come to reflect not only Arthur's particular dreams but the collective fantasies of cinema audiences of the period. Where, then, does all this leave the 'religious' element of the Hollywood *Pennies*? While the use of songs in the context of a 'serious' BBC Drama was formally unique, representing an alternative realm of the 'spirit', surely the very capacity of the musical numbers to be assimilated within the traditions of the American screen musical must nullify any religious theme in the MGM *Pennies*. Potter, in 1982, disagreed:

> I don't think that's true. I mean, the film is more difficult by being, on the surface, easier to assimilate in the musical numbers ... [It] is ... mentally, more difficult and challenging because the realisation of the dream is less tacky ... When you're dealing with the dreams of uneducated, naive and apparently simple people, you use irony, a slight distancing of yourself from the substance of their dreams. Whereas I maintain that the substance of their dreams is as real as the Psalmist's cry. I'm using a Busby Berkeley sequence as a found artefact to illustrate what Arthur would actually see and relate to.[66]

For Potter, the religious element in the Hollywood *Pennies* is actually strengthened by comparison with the BBC version, ironically because greater amounts of money have been lavished on the production of the musical numbers. The film is thus more 'difficult' because audiences cannot so easily adopt a position of detached or ironic amusement at the 'tackiness' of the realisation of the songs (as they might have done with performances in the BBC studio). The very strength of the songs' production means the nature of Arthur's dreams cannot be dismissed so easily.

In this way, the MGM *Pennies* provides both a critique and a celebration of the American Dream. The Dream, as refracted through the screen musicals, ironically becomes Arthur's means of surviving the American Dream gone wrong of the Depression. As in the *Follow the Fleet* scene, the bleak impossibility of most individuals ever achieving the capitalist dream of success is indicated in the disjunction between fantasy and reality, whilst at the same time the persistence of that 'old human dream' for something better than one's present lot – of which the American Dream is but one manifestation – is celebrated. The American Dream is thus turned in and against itself. The film celebrates the resilience of dreams and the power of individuals to hold on to a vision of something better even *against* the implacable odds of the American capitalist system.

All of this has important effects for the end of film. It means that the optimism of Arthur's final 'miracle' escape from the hangman becomes even more hard-won and improbable than in the BBC drama. This is suggested by the final 'Glory of Love' song which, unlike the TV version that showed Arthur and Eileen miming alone on Hammersmith Bridge, is a big Busby Berkeley-like production number, featuring chorus girls dancing against a gloomy backdrop of Chicago in the Depression. Far less ambiguously than the TV drama, the unlikely optimism of the MGM version cannot be as the result of a change in material conditions (Arthur's bodily resurrection; an end to the 'Depression'). It must be 'spiritual'. It can only be the defiance of belief and optimism in the face of an otherwise bleak landscape; a final assertion of hope over pessimistic experience. This is undoubtedly why Potter described the religious element in the Hollywood *Pennies* as being 'more accomplished': 'I know it's more difficult to get to but maybe this is perverse of me, I wanted to cheat the studio people over there, as I've learnt to do at the BBC.'[67]

With American audiences, however, Potter's attempt to smuggle religion into Hollywood backfired. The religious element of the original TV conception may well have been enhanced (as he claimed) but the very fact that the production numbers could be so easily assimilated within the traditions of the Hollywood screen musical also meant they could be easily dismissed.

Mindful of the amount they had spent on it, MGM previewed the finished film in Denver, Colorado, just prior to its release at Christmas 1981. The studio's publicity department went into overdrive, advertising the film as a 'musical extravaganza' and even, 'Coming for Christmas, the funniest film you'll ever see.' As a consequence, half the audience walked out, so unprepared were they for a film which, given the publicity and the casting of Steve Martin and Bernadette Peters, they had presumed would be a comedy along the lines of *The Jerk*.[68]

When the film subsequently went on general release – in the USA just before Christmas 1981, in Britain on 20 May 1982 – reaction was also violently mixed. In Britain, the film was inevitably compared with the BBC serial and found wanting.[69] In the US, however, the movie found favour with some well-known reviewers. Pauline Kael called it 'the most emotional movie musical I've ever seen ... There's something new going on – something thrilling – when the characters in a musical are archetypes yet are intensely alive.'[70] The general returns across America, however, were a disaster. The film cost almost $20 million to make but took only $7 million at the box office – not only a record-making loss for MGM which helped to accelerate the studio's decline, but figures that made *Pennies* one of the biggest loss-makers in Hollywood history.[71] If there were clearly many reasons for the film's financial failure – a Christmas release for a broadly downbeat 'Depression' movie; false expectations generated by the casting of Steve Martin; the general unfashionability of musicals in 1981 – neither was the film the decisive artistic success which had been hoped for (though Potter's screenplay *was* nominated for an award at the 1982 Oscars ceremony).

As a result, after a brief fling during which time he wrote a number of (mainly unproduced) screenplays, Potter was no longer quite the flavour of the month in Hollywood any more. As he himself put it, the Americans came to view him as a 'black' writer and recoiled from his alleged 'savagery' and 'bleakness' – little realising, of course, that if it had not been for the very strength of his own *optimism* at the end of the seventies, Potter would never have made it to Hollywood in the first place.[72]

Conclusion

Certainly, the writer had come a long way from the religious introversion of his work in the early seventies. The difference is clearly signalled in the respective treatments of sex in *Casanova* and *Pennies*. In the 1971 drama, the 'vacuity' of living for the flesh was embodied in the figure of the eighteenth-century libertine: an Italian prisoner, desperate to escape the material world for a 'higher' spiritual realm that he knew lay on the other side of his cell yet which, despite all his efforts, he seemed fated never to reach. Death paradoxically became the moment of ultimate triumph for Casanova, when he was finally able to leave the pains and passions of his body behind, freed at last from the material world.

Compare this with *Pennies*, only seven years later. The transformation of his personal life in 1977 by an apparent 'miracle' cure for illness only helped fuel the new optimism which, as with the 1976 'trilogy' of single plays, was becoming tangible in Potter's writing. In *Pennies from Heaven*,

Arthur Parker's 'spirit' does not express itself in a desire to flee the body but rather *through* the body. Sex is no longer seen as 'vacuous' but along with 'the songs', as one of his main spiritual outlets. Arthur's material aspirations have become inseparable from his spiritual yearnings.

As a consequence, in sharp contrast to *Casanova*, death in *Pennies* paradoxically marks the moment of the drama's most confident endorsement of life. Whilst in the 1971 drama, the death of the protagonist signalled his *escape* from the physical world, in the 1977 plays it marks the moment of *defiance*: an assertion of the power of belief and of the 'spirit' to cheat death. Arthur's 'spirit' returns to the world to live again; to live through it. He does not reject material reality. He embraces it.

Potter's return from reclusiveness in the late seventies and his adventures in Hollywood can be seen in much the same terms. If it is too negative and reductive to say the writer went there simply for the money, it would also be naive to attribute his motives purely to an idealistic aim of reviving the British film industry. Rather, like his central character in *Pennies*, material aspirations and 'spiritual' ideals interpenetrated each other: a desire to try and change the way films were made in Hollywood and Britain mingled with the legitimate financial desires of a professional writer with self-professed 'ambitions, inevitable anxieties and a fair measure of what used to be called avarice', coupled with a clear need to expand his own personal and career horizons.[73] In 1982, he expressed it in this way:

> I went to Hollywood for a clutch of differing and sometimes contradictory reasons. One was simply to do with curiosity. Another was to do with getting the longer perspective about what I want to do and in order to do it, I need to get hold of the money. And a third is more or less precisely the same reason that I wanted to write for television sixteen years ago. Biographically, it may be because I come from the English working class and because I can't swallow the cant about High Art easily, and because I have a partly hostile, partly eager, partly complicit relationship with so-called Popular Art. I don't find it easy to step away from and say that's not my field … I think the place for me is in the middle of it.[74]

A few years later, in 1985, he also admitted that he had desperately needed a few years out of British television: 'I was digging a hole for myself. How long can a writer write without any external stimulus?'[75]

Potter's new entrepreneurism in the late seventies and early eighties was thus in one sense a desire to escape the reclusiveness of his past – not only that of his illness but also the career he had developed in tandem with it as a writer for television. Originally, he had taken up writing because it was one of the few jobs he could do, given the nature of his illness. It suited an enforced reclusiveness. By the late seventies, however, when temporarily free from illness, becoming a businessman – an active media 'hustler' – was one way for Potter to make a decisive break with that past.

The problem now confronting him was whether this new extroversion would affect the work, perhaps for the worse. Would his sudden rash of activity across a range of different media disperse his energies, making the writing suffer? In 1980, Sean Day-Lewis hinted at the dilemma in a *Daily Telegraph* profile which appeared the day after the first of Potter's new TV plays for LWT had been transmitted. 'The good news', Day-Lewis stated, 'is that he does not want to desert. He still considers himself a ... television playwright ... The less good news is that [he] is plainly enjoying his distracting new role as a businessman, a very active partner in his Pennies From Heaven independent production company.'[76] In tune with the free-market ethos of the newly elected British Conservative Government under Margaret Thatcher, Potter had transformed himself into an Arthur Parker figure – a salesman for his own work. In terms of television drama, it was the three play package for LWT in October 1980 which provided the first test of whether, in purely creative terms, that transformation had been for the best.

5

Singing for your supper: Potter in the eighties

Cream in My Coffee: the PFH/LWT deal

As Chapter 2 noted, Potter and Trodd had some harsh words to say about the BBC when they made their much-publicised defection to LWT in May 1979. They argued that an illiberal climate of censorship and bureaucracy had stifled the creative freedom which BBC programme-makers had enjoyed in the sixties. It was undoubtedly the attraction of a future outside established broadcasting structures which had led them to form their own independent production company, Pennies From Heaven Limited. In turn, their subsequent 'partnership' with LWT was watched closely by the rest of the television industry as a timely example of what the future might hold – particularly through 1980, as Margaret Thatcher's Conservative Government began to push through Parliament legislation which would lay the foundations of Channel Four.[1]

For Potter, the PFH/LWT deal was particularly significant. Not only was it a specific riposte to the BBC over the banning of *Brimstone*, it also seemed to signal the fact that important changes were on the way for both him *and* British television. After years of 'wistful dreaming about the possibilities' of his chosen medium, remission of illness had at last seemed to put him in a position where he could turn his dreams of wresting creative control away from the broadcasting 'bureaucrats' into reality. As he put it in 1979, 'I vowed to myself ... there would be a few bloody changes. And now that I've got the power ... and the opportunity, I can do something.'[2]

It was the BBC's lack of flexibility in the face of these aspirations which led to Potter and Trodd's final break with the Corporation. The specific issue centred around both men's difficulty in reconciling a new desire for independence with their own long-standing commitment to public service broadcasting and the BBC. PFH Ltd had been formed in 1978 whilst the pair were still at the Corporation. For their first project Potter and Trodd had been ambitious – deciding to mount a television adaptation of all of Anthony Powell's thirteen novels in the sequence, *A Dance to the Music of Time*. Independently of the BBC, they approached the novelist and succeeded in persuading him to sell the TV rights to his books. Then, with no choice in these pre-Channel Four days but to co-operate with a traditional broadcaster, they took the project to the BBC, with a view to inviting it to commission Potter to adapt the novels into a drama serial. It was at this point that the problems began, as Potter and Trodd found all their work in wooing Powell and making the project possible reduced to the payment of a flat format fee by the BBC. Further confirmation that the Corporation begrudged the notion of working with 'independents' came at the end of 1978 as Potter was working on the scripts. Suddenly, without prior consultation, the BBC told him that due to financial constraints, what had been agreed as six seventy-five minute episodes would have to be reduced to five of fifty minutes each. The proportion of drama to be shot on film (as opposed to studio-recorded on videotape) would also have to be diminished. As Potter later recalled, 'That sort of news is very depressing when you are actually in the middle of working on scripts.'[3] Coupled with this were the threats to his producer: namely that if the plays were not done as required, Trodd would no longer be given a slot in the schedules and his contract would not be renewed.[4]

Immediately, Potter asked for indefinite postponement and with Trodd and his agent, Judy Daish, began to look for a home for his work beyond the BBC. Finally, after a number of 'euphoric lunches followed by disconsolate silences' with several interested parties, PFH Ltd fetched up at LWT in May of 1979, with a deal to supply it not with *A Dance to the Music of Time* but a package of nine plays to be delivered over a notional two-year period – six of them by Potter.[5]

For the writer, it seemed a 'cracking deal.'[6] LWT – in the shape of Director of Programmes Michael Grade, Controller of Drama Tony Wharmby and Managing Director Brian Tesler – had agreed to finance an expensive package in which every play would be shot wholly on location on film, with a workable average of twenty-three days shooting per film, plus a quota of free-lance cameramen of Trodd's choice. Acknowledging the 'independent' principle, LWT undertook to pay PFH overhead and script development costs and, on delivery of each script, to take full responsibility for the costing of the production budget. It all seemed a brave move. Here was a commercial company prepared to support the new breed of 'independent' that one day might break up the cosy television duopoly which ITV had shared with the BBC for over twenty years. The writer and producer also hoped the deal could be used as leverage to achieve what they had really wanted all along – to get back to the BBC 'on proper terms', as acknowledged 'independents' working *within* the Corporation.

It was only after this honeymoon period had ended and PFH became immersed in the practical production details that serious problems began to emerge. Once the first three Potter scripts were in, the company discovered there had been a fundamental misunderstanding about costs. It transpired that prior to delivery of the scripts, Michael Grade had presented the LWT Board of Directors with budget projections for the first three films that were badly underestimated: £100,000 per film as opposed to Trodd's own base-line projection of £200,000.[7] With no experience of this type of high-cost filmed drama (LWT's previous output in this area having always been highly studio-based), the company had not done their homework. They had apparently failed to make adequate comparisons with the budgets of films produced by other TV companies.

In order to compensate for these financial miscalculations, LWT asked Trodd whether he would mind making the first Potter script, *Rain on the Roof*, more cheaply as a studio play rather than as a film on location. Trodd refused, responding that he was unwilling to help bail out the company for its own financial mistakes. LWT eventually backed down. Each of the three Potter scripts, it agreed, would be shot on film. Accordingly, new budgets, totalling £832,000, were drawn up in line with the spending of other ITV film-making subsidiaries.[8] The Potter films would be made back-to-back throughout the first half of 1980 for transmission dates in the autumn. By February, location shooting on *Rain on the Roof* had already begun under the direction of Alan Bridges.

The problems, however, were not over. As Trodd puts it, Grade's relationship with the LWT Board never recovered from his initial miscalculation. By the time the last Potter play, *Blade on the Feather*, was being shot in June 1980, relationships between PFH and LWT were deteriorating fast, as a difficult wet shoot on the Isle of Wight played havoc with the budget, resulting in a £150,000 overspend. After his initial (mis)calculation of a total of £300,000 for the three films, Michael Grade now had to tell the Board that close to £1 million had been spent on Potter and Trodd.

In the meantime, Trodd was preparing his next project for shooting: a two-part Jim Allen film, entitled *The Commune*, which had been budgeted at a total of £675,000. Just prior to the start of filming on 15 July 1980, Grade announced that he was postponing the project indefinitely. Alleging 'cash flow problems', he accused PFH of letting the budget drift up by £35,000, even before shooting had started.[9]

By the summer of 1980, suspicions were growing that LWT was looking for a pretext to abandon its commitment to the remaining films in the package. It had not escaped Potter's and Trodd's attention that the franchises of the ITV companies were up for reconsideration by the IBA at the end of the year and that one of the most important factors in determining whether, in the face of possible competition, LWT would retain its licence to broadcast, would be a judgment on the 'quality' of its programmes. Perhaps this had been the real motive behind LWT's deal with PFH all along and of Grade's recent actions. As Trodd put it that July: 'If LWT can get three window dressing films by Dennis Potter on the air before franchise time, then the PFH deal will have served its main purpose for them. They might then be happy to loose us quietly as an unnecessary thorn in their side.'[10]

His words were to prove prophetic. On Monday 28 July, Michael Grade issued a statement to the press, announcing that the partnership between LWT and PFH was dissolved. He cited 'irreconcilable differences' whereby PFH had found it very difficult to work within 'normal budgeting constraints and disciplines'.[11] Generous budgets, he alleged, had been heavily overspent. The statement concluded: 'It is now clear that there are likely to be insurmountable difficulties when an independent production company of this kind comes to work inside a major broadcasting organisation, whether ITV or BBC.'[12]

Potter and Trodd were enraged by the statement – particularly after they discovered that Grade had authorised both it and a formal letter to PFH, prior to disappearing from the country on a month's holiday to California. Worse, the press had received news about the deal's collapse before PFH had received their letter. Having got to the press first to put his side of the case, Grade had succeeded in putting PFH on the defensive regarding allegations of overspending. Moreover, there was nothing the 'independents' could do to prevent the deal's collapse. As LWT were quick to point out, the PFH contract, in accordance with normal practice, had specifically been for the supply of *scripts*. Whilst the ITV company had intended to produce them, legally it was under no obligation to do so.[13] Despite subsequent press coverage in which both men tried to put their side of the case, there was nothing in real terms which Potter and Trodd could do. The PFH/LWT deal was dead.

In retrospect, it is possible to see that there were faults on both sides. As Trodd admits today, there was, during shooting, 'an uncontrollable tendency to let costs rise'. This was not simply a question of the ill-advised choice of the Isle of Wight as a location for *Blade on the Feather*. He recalls a clear example during the shooting of the second Potter film, *Cream in My Coffee*: a play set in the Grand Hotel, Eastbourne, which alternates between the 'present' and the thirties. In the course of shooting one of the period scenes, Trodd and his director, Gavin Millar, suddenly noticed one of the leading actors was wearing an old-fashioned thirties' wristwatch – an item which no-one had requested. On investigation, it transpired that the LWT costumes department had spent hundreds of pounds on the watch in order to give the production an authentic period feel. Trodd claims that in the absence of adequate LWT production controllers (due to the company's inexperience in filmed drama), it was impossible for him to police every area of the production to cut down on such lavish spending. Besides, he states: 'there was a feeling we were doing the posh stuff [on film] … There was a certain scale of production value and that was what we were going to do.'

At least some of the budgetary problems of which Grade later complained therefore resided within LWT itself. They were a product of the *enthusiasm* amongst the company's staff for having been given the opportunity to work on 'posh' drama, which manifested itself in a desire that every aspect of the production look and feel right. Coupled with this was Trodd's own preoccupation with making TV drama expensively on film. As a figure who had worked predominantly at the BBC, he had little experience or indeed desire to act as a line producer, with both eyes permanently fixed on the budget. It was these factors which helped create pressures on the budget that in turn were magnified ten-fold by the inexperience of LWT management in dealing with the costs of filmed drama. Rather than any conspiratorial move connected with the franchise, the dropping of PFH by London Weekend was thus more a question of simple economics. By 1980, with Britain in the grip of a recession and a growing awareness in ITV circles of a possible cash crisis due to a decline in advertising revenue, the commercial companies were keen to cut back on all possible 'extravagances'.[14] It seems that by the summer of that year, LWT had decided prestige film drama by PFH was one luxury it could no longer afford.

Just as at the BBC, PFH had found its bold ambitions to change the face of British TV thwarted by financial constraints beyond its control. It had also discovered that far from being the engine to break up existing TV monoliths, small 'independents' could all too easily be engulfed by them. At least in those pre-Channel Four days, if not later, partnerships with so-called 'independents' could never take place on a completely level playing field. 'Independents' were necessarily *dependent* on the vicissitudes of the dominant television order – not equal to or outside it.

By July 1980, Potter was bitter. Writing in the *Daily Mail*, he complained that British TV was 'going to the dogs'. It was Grade's assertion that the PFH deal demonstrated 'insurmountable difficulties' between 'independents' and the major broadcasters to which he took particular exception. This was, he retorted, a signal for ITV and the BBC to 'stand shoulder to shoulder … against intruders arrogant enough to claim the right and then the ability to make their programmes'. He shuddered to think of the future of native TV drama: 'All the doors are closing against it.'[15]

He, however, was not prepared to wait around for the answer, nor for that matter for the advent of Channel Four (which at that point he believed had 'been virtually handed over to the existing ITV companies'). Disgusted with British TV institutions, he was off to California to work 'on a big MGM movie that everyone here turned down flat'. Significantly, he added: 'I may even bump into Michael Grade in Hollywood. If his face is red, it won't be from the California sunshine.'[16]

What of the three completed films he left in his wake? As planned, they were transmitted by ITV over three consecutive Sundays from 19 October 1980 onwards. Alone of all Potter's single TV plays, these works were clearly tailored as a package to satisfy a pre-existing commercial deal – a fact signalled by the symmetry of the titles: *Blade on the Feather*; *Rain on the Roof*; *Cream in My Coffee*. Unlike his 1976 'trilogy', there is no real strong, developing thematic connection between each, though they do share important structural similarities.

The most significant of these is the memory of a father's death which haunts the three plays. In *Cream in My Coffee*, as the elderly Bernard Wilsher (played by Lionel Jeffries) visits the Grand Hotel in Eastbourne for the first time since the thirties, there are flashbacks to the time when he last visited, yet had to return home to attend the funeral of his father. In *Blade on the Feather*, Cartwright (Tom Conti), apparently an MI5 agent sent to kill an ageing British traitor, Cavendish (Donald Pleasance), remembers how his own father was murdered as a result of Cavendish's treachery. The key to understanding this motif lies in the third play, *Rain on the Roof*. Its central character is Billy (Ewan Stewart), a backward country youth who visits the house of a frustrated middle-class housewife, Janet (Cheryl Campbell), in order to receive tuition on how to read and write. Haunted by grief for his dead working-class father, he wants to learn to read so that he can find solace in the Bible. Potter uses this dramatic situation to contrast the working-class puritanism of Billy with the secular values of middle-class Janet. In so doing, he raises questions as to whether, despite his naivety, Billy's simple instinctive faith may ultimately have greater wisdom than the more 'sophisticated' yet somehow 'shallower' life Janet leads. In a key scene, Billy tells Janet:

BILLY: I've met Jesus … I been born again – all new. Like I've been washed all clean and shiny … Oh, you got no idea how low I was. Down in the dumps. Everything was like it was raining all the time … Raining on the slates …

JANET: Rain on the roof, yes.

BILLY: Rain on the blinkin' brain, I reckon. The Bible. That's the book I wanna read missus.[17]

Elsewhere, Potter has explained the 'Rain on the Roof' image of the title: 'The way rain glints on slate', he stated in a 1980 newspaper interview, 'has always seemed to be the colour of depression.'[18] As the play progresses, it becomes clear that Billy has been taking dangerous amounts of anti-depressants to assuage his grief over his father. At Janet's house, he suffers a blackout while attempting to decipher some words she has written for him on a page. The scenario recalls *Where the Buffalo Roam* fourteen years earlier. Again, there is the same concern for adult literacy, expressed through the figure of a backward youth ('Billy' instead of 'Willy') who is traumatised and inhibited from reading by the memory of his father.

The 1980 play ends in Grand Guignol fashion when, after a dinner party that ends in a blazing row between Janet and her husband John, the youth creeps back into the house and stabs Janet's womanising partner with a sliver of glass taken from his own greenhouse. As in previous 'outsider' plays like *Angels* and *Schmoedipus*, a frustrated middle-class housewife is thus liberated from her domestic prison by the intervention of a 'visitor' from outside . Billy, too, at last finds peace. As Janet stares down at her dead husband and trembles, the youth settles down to his reading and writing as if all were normal – his only comment being: 'Words. Funny things.'[19]

Leaving aside questions of its dramatic efficacy, underlying this violent dénouement is a clear symbolic subtext. Moving from inhibiting grief over his dead father to a new sense of peace and enthusiasm for words, Billy's progression mirrors Potter's own journey in the nineteen seventies towards a renewed spiritual optimism and instinctive religious faith expressed through writing. What is important to note is that *Rain on the Roof* links this progression with the death of a father.[20] Through the very extent of his distress, the death becomes a catalyst for Billy's discovery of faith and God. Out of sorrow and depression emerges an ultimate good, not only for him but for Janet as well. At the end of the play, her cynical adulterer of a husband is killed off and 'displaced' by someone of child-like simplicity and an instinctive faith. In terms of past Potter protagonists, the difference is that between a Jack Black or Daniel Miller and the later creation of Arthur Parker. It seems to be precisely this transformation in character which *Rain on the Roof* is symbolically charting.

If, of the three 1980 plays, *Rain* met with the most incomprehension on first transmission, *Cream in My Coffee* was undoubtedly the most successful and accessible. With two distinguished actors in the leading roles (Peggy Ashcroft and Lionel Jeffries), the play went on to win many awards, including the 1982 Prix Italia. Alternating between the life of a couple in their youth (during the thirties) and in old age, as they revisit the same hotel after a gap of forty years, the play is an exploration of memory and the passage of time. It occupies a similar territory to *Alice*, *Dreamchild* and *Late Call* – the events of youth are contrasted with old age and thereby the shape of an individual life is discerned. As Potter put it in his introduction to the published script, '*Cream in My Coffee* tries to show, among other things, how dangerous or corrosive it can be not to have some sense of the shape of your own life, and how damaging to seek what you are determined not to find.'[21]

In retrospect, perhaps the more interesting of the other plays is *Blade on the Feather*. Its title taken from an Eton boating song, this marked Potter's return, after many years of exploring spiritual themes, to an examination of the English class system. Like *Traitor*, *Blade* is a spy drama, dealing with treachery and guilt. It is also structured as an 'outsider' play.

In this case, the intruding visitor is one Daniel Young who pays an unexpected call at the home of retired Cambridge academic, Jason Cavendish – ostensibly because he is writing a thesis on Cavendish's Tolkien-like fantasy novel, *Cloud Cape*. In fact, no one is as they seem. Young is actually called Cartwright and has come to kill Cavendish because the latter was a former spy for the KGB who recruited Philby, Burgess and MacLean and who was also instrumental in the murder of Cartwright's father. Apparently the epitome of the reactionary upper-class gentleman, Cavendish and his butler Hill (Denholm Elliot) are both communists and traitors. They take great pleasure in acting out the class roles of master and servant in public, whilst in private remaining secret friends and confidantes. As the 'outsider', Cartwright succeeds in insinuating his way into this bizarre domestic situation, in a manner akin to Martin in *Brimstone*. In spite of the suspicion and hostility of Cavendish, he succeeds in charming the old man's daughter and wife – seducing one and later murdering the other. Then, it is the turn of the old man to die.

As Potter suggested around the time of transmission, *Blade* plays with the conventions of the English spy story. A sense of decline, however, permeates the play since the old rigid class order which legitimated that genre's narratives of betrayal and subterfuge is now shown to be hopelessly irrecoverable. The traitor Cavendish finds himself in a 'cosy, social democrat British Railways' post-war England from which he feels alienated and to which he cannot give his loyalty.[22] In this way, *Blade* clearly marks a development from Potter's previous explorations of social class. If, in *The Nigel Barton Plays*, the viewpoint on betrayal was firmly from the working class, in *Traitor*, Potter examined the question from the other side of the class divide, focusing on why someone from the upper class should choose to betray their own roots. Like Barton, Harris was portrayed very much as the exception rather than the rule – the outcast at school who forsakes his class in pursuit of the vision of a transcendent ideal.

With *Blade*, the traitor Cavendish lurks within the very bosom of English society. To all appearances, he is the image of the respectable English gentleman, yet in him categories of 'Left' and 'Right', 'patriotism' and 'treason' blur. He may have betrayed for the communists but paradoxically he is shown to have done so in the name of old England. All of this is brought into sharp relief by the play's ending. When Cartwright reveals to Cavendish he is here to kill him, he urges the traitor to 'play the game' and take his own life. Realising the impossibility of his situation, the old man relents. All, however, is still not quite what it seems. As shots ring out and Cavendish dies, Hill comes rushing over. Gradually, it becomes clear that, as in the best tradition of country house thrillers, it was the butler 'who done it' – he who was responsible for events all along. The closing dialogue between Hill and Cartwright reveals that the latter was no vengeful MI5 agent but a hit man from the KGB, contacted by Hill to kill the old man because in his dotage and guilt, Cavendish was in danger of confessing his secrets to his wife, an MI5 'sleeper'.

As Potter quite rightly suggested in 1980, *Blade on the Feather* is more than 'slightly gamey' as a play. It manipulates the conventions of the English spy story, finally turning them inside out. At the time, Potter hoped the play would communicate his sense of 'the decay of English life; of it being an over-ripe plum ready to fall – if not already rotting on the ground.'[23] His drama shows tired games of class warfare being played out in a 'social democrat' Britain in which the old social structures that once legitimated them have long since decayed. As a result, none of the main characters quite believes any longer in what they are doing and none are who they say they are. In spite of its illustration that the shell of the class system still pertains in British life, *Blade*'s message is that, ultimately, in terms of the attitudes which once ruled our country, we are all traitors now.

Tears Before Bedtime: Joseph Losey and the original *Track 29*

Originally, Potter and Trodd had intended to make the *Blade* script as a feature film, with James Mason and David Niven in the leading roles of the elderly traitors. That deal never came off, partly due to a long-standing feud between the two stars dating back to what each had done to help the British effort in wartime. As Kenith Trodd recalls, 'One stayed away. The other came back to fight.'[24]

The putative director of that project had been Joseph Losey who had long expressed a wish to work with Potter, in much the same way as he had collaborated with other British playwrights like Harold Pinter.[25] After meeting Potter to discuss *Blade* in December 1979, Losey kept in touch with him over the next few years, searching around for a suitable project on which they both could work. Now housed in the British Film Institute, Losey's personal files attest to his keenness to collaborate with Potter on a film aimed at audiences in his native America.

After a number of abortive suggestions (including an offer for Losey to direct Potter's first original stage play, *Sufficient Carbohydrate*), eventually, in January 1983, came a project on which they could both agree to collaborate. This was a new Potter film script, variously titled *Tears Before Bedtime* and *Track 29*. In fact, it was a reworking of *Schmoedipus*, with all of the action relocated from the London suburbs to Texas.[26] Behind the film was an attempt by Potter to reconcile his recent screenwriting activities with an older commitment to television and the BBC. The plan was that *Track 29* would mark the BBC's first real venture into feature film-making – that is, it would be a BBC film produced for TV transmission in Britain but also cinema release abroad. Following in the wake of the launch of Channel Four and its *Film on Four* initiative, the idea was, as Trodd puts it, 'to make the BBC recognise its place in the British film industry', whereby productions could have a 'double life' in the cinema as well as on television.[27]

After his recent experience (and relative lack of success) in Hollywood, such a model was also a chance for Potter to get back to the BBC on the terms he and Trodd had always wanted – as 'independents' operating in association with it. Whereas before, attempts to be equal partners with the established broadcasting institutions had always come unstuck because it was the latter who held the purse strings, the advent of Channel Four seemed to offer new opportunities. This time round, as it faced competition from the new channel, the BBC would be forced to recognise the 'independent' principle, particularly if the film were a co-production involving outside finance, in the manner of *Film on Four*.

In this spirit, two producers were attached to the project. Kenith Trodd was to act as the BBC's liaison in London, whilst Rick McCallum, the young executive producer of the MGM *Pennies*, was recruited by Potter to be his general representative in Hollywood, searching for American financial backing. By July 1983, all the elements of production seemed to be in place – ready to begin an August shoot in Texas. Not only had McCallum secured American co-production money, Losey had gathered an all-star cast for this feature film version of *Schmoedipus*: Vanessa Redgrave as the bored, frustrated housewife, Anthony Higgins as her long-lost 'son' and Lee Marvin as the model railway-enthusiast husband. With Potter's help, it seemed that for the first time the BBC had found a genuine way to compete with *Film on Four* – circumventing its own previous bureaucratic hesitations in working with 'independents' and, by so doing, successfully integrating itself with the wider world of international film production. For Losey, too, the project was also special as it provided him with his first opportunity to work in his native America since he fled to Europe from McCarthyism in the early fifties.

Sadly, it was never to be. While Losey was in Mexico, preparing for filming, news came through that the deal for *Track 29* had collapsed, only days before shooting was due to start. In his subsequent letters to the cast and crew, the director confessed his devastation at the collapse: 'I had begun to be too deeply involved', he wrote.[28] In all his thirty-two years of directing films, he had never known a project fold so late.[29]

According to Rick McCallum, the reason for the collapse was that the BBC, at the very last moment, reneged on its agreement to make the film on 35mm (the standard gauge for theatrical release). Instead, it insisted that the production would have to conform to the gauge used for its normal in-house filmed drama: 16mm. The decision proved incomprehensible to the film's American backers who promptly withdrew their support.[30]

The following year Losey died. Though he went on to complete one more film (*Steaming*, made in Britain, also with Vanessa Redgrave), he was never able to fulfil his wish of working in America again. His widow, Patricia Losey, has written of the *Track 29* episode:

> To make another film in the US … was something [Joe] really wanted to do and wanted to do for so long. If I put this first, before his desire to do a film with Dennis, it is only because the desire or need to make one more film in his own country preceded the unfulfilled collaboration with Dennis. If you were in your twenties or thirties and such a blow and such a humiliation fell upon you, I suppose it might make or break you, professionally and emotionally. Joe was already in his seventies and he survived in both ways. He made *Steaming*.[31]

According to Kenith Trodd, it needed that one casualty of *Track 29* in order for the BBC to get over its 'silliness' in not allowing some key prestige productions to be shot on 35mm for theatrical release abroad.[32] By 1984, he had become part of a working party within the BBC, convened to examine just this question and, more generally, the future of BBC Drama in the wake of *Film on Four* and the rise of independent film production. Its recommendation was the setting up of a separate film arm so that the BBC could be more flexible, taking advantage both of independents and the theatrical film market.[33]

Though through the eighties Trodd was to lament its slowness, change was coming to BBC Drama. By 1988, when Mark Shivas was appointed the new Head of Drama, the BBC's Plays department had been renamed BBC Films in consolidation of a trend away from studio to filmed drama which had been accelerating since the early eighties. Independent producers were now free to come and go. The American Rick McCallum was able to have his own office in the BBC, whilst Trodd, now on a free-lance rolling contract, encountered no more problems in reconciling his BBC activities with the outside world. By 1989 and the Trodd-produced film, *She's Been Away*, shooting and editing on 35mm for overseas theatrical release was being actively encouraged within the BBC.[34] Meanwhile, in 1987, *Track 29* finally did get produced – significantly, however, as an independent British film made *outside* the BBC (see Chapter 6).

Movies, radio, novels, theatre ... television?

One Potter screenplay which did get made in the early eighties was his adaptation of Martin Cruz Smith's best-selling novel about murder and corruption in the KGB, *Gorky Park*. Produced by Gene Kirkwood and Howard Koch Jr. for Orion Pictures in Hollywood, the film proved to be a disappointment for Potter – one that 'never looked or sounded right'.[35]

Part of the problem was a difficult shoot in Helsinki which (because the Cold War was still very much alive at this time) had to double as Moscow for the American film crew. This unsettled the film's British director, Michael Apted, who much prefers to shoot on actual locations. There was also disquiet about the film's casting of British comic actors (Michael Elphick, Alexei Sayle, Rikki Fulton) in Russian character roles, alongside the film's 'heavyweight' American stars: William Hurt, Brian Dennehy and Lee Marvin.

If Potter was right to suggest that all the elements ultimately do not gel, ironically, 1983's *Gorky Park* remains his one screenplay to have reached a mass international audience – despite or rather perhaps *because* of the fact that, as a conventionally plotted thriller adaptation tailored to the demands of Hollywood, it is his least 'authored'.[36] Behind the compromise lay his desire to channel money gained from Hollywood screenwriting back into indigenous British film production. Released in September 1982, the film version of *Brimstone and Treacle* marked the first fruit of his commitment to produce an annual British movie through PFH. Here too, however, compromise had begun to undermine the boldness of Potter's original dreams. Finance could not come from PFH alone but had to be raised jointly with American investors – an arrangement that ultimately led to the casting of a pop star, Sting, in the central role of Martin the 'demon'. Meanwhile, for different reasons, Potter had also been keen to inject a musical element into the film but found himself having to compromise for the sake of keeping his director, Richard Loncraine. As the movie's producer, Ken Trodd, recalls, the writer had wanted to 'radicalize' *Brimstone*, using the *Pennies* device of characters bursting into song. Loncraine would have none of this, fearing that his attempt to establish himself in feature films would be swamped by Potter trademarks. Eventually, for the sake of keeping the project on track, Potter backed down. This is why the film version of *Brimstone* remains faithful to the original TV play – a fact which drew fire from critics on the film's release, many of whom saw it as 'a bastard child' of the television studio which sat uneasily on the big screen.[37] Nor did the film do well at the British box office. Marketed brazenly on the notoriety of its source material, it was given an X-Certificate by the British Board of Film Censors, thus automatically precluding the bulk of the teen audience who might otherwise have gone to see it on the strength of Sting.

It would be another four years before Potter's next 'annual British movie' saw the light of day. *Dreamchild* was yet another illustration of the difficulties (and sometimes stormy feuds) that were beginning to cloud the PFH dream of being involved in feature film production. The original screenplay, based on *Alice*, had been completed as far back as April 1983 and had initially been offered by Rick McCallum to MGM. Perhaps understandably after the *Pennies* movie, the studio turned it down. By August of that year, however, following the collapse of Losey's *Track 29*, McCallum realised his next destination was England. Verity Lambert, then Head of Productions at Thorn EMI Films, had read the script and wanted to finance it as a British movie for the international market.

The resulting £2.8 million film began shooting for seven weeks in the summer of 1984, under *Cream in My Coffee*'s director, Gavin Millar, and with Coral Browne in the starring role of the elderly Alice Hargreaves. It was not until post-production, in the winter of 1984–85, that major problems began to emerge with the film, as Millar found his 'director's cut' being interfered with by others. According to him, it was those at Thorn EMI, led by Verity Lambert, who took the film away and re-edited it into the version finally released (in the process, leaving much on the cutting floor against his wishes).[38] This version of events is contradicted, however, by the film's two producers, Rick McCallum and Kenith Trodd, who both allege independently of each other that it was not Lambert or Thorn EMI but themselves and the film's executive producer, none other than Potter himself, who re-edited the film into a version much closer to the latter's original screenplay. The reason, according to McCallum, was that Millar had improvised a number of additional scenes which were not in the original script, making the pace of the director's version much too slow.[39] For Trodd, this was a difficult situation, as he felt it threatened a walk-out from the director. It was for this reason he often found himself, to the exasperation of others, 'tactically lining up' with Millar, urging patience so that the director could be allowed time to find 'his' film. Trodd well recalls Potter's response. To the writer, it was not Millar's but '*our*' film – a film by PFH which Millar had simply been hired by the company to direct.

Regardless of the rights and wrongs of this dispute (and there is clearly some bitterness involved), the episode illustrated the greater difficulties Potter would inevitably experience in trying to impose his personal authorial vision in cinema as opposed to television. Whilst in the writer's medium of television, Millar had been happy, with *Cream in My Coffee*, to function as Potter's *metteur en scène*, he was less pleased to be overruled in the world of feature films where directors normally liked to see themselves as the ultimate creative arbiters. Though the actual process of shooting films for TV may be essentially the same as for cinema, albeit on a different economic scale, perceptions of power and status can often be much altered. In the case of *Dreamchild*, Potter's decision to act as the movie's executive producer testified to his own keenness to exercise control over how the script was realised, even if that meant overruling the director and assuming direct responsibility for the editing of the film himself. As he commented to the *New York Times* on the film's release, the 'more control you have, the more likely something will come out somewhat as you hoped.'[40]

Battles for creative control also extended to the sharing of the production credit between McCallum and Trodd. As Trodd puts it, Potter thought that inviting McCallum to England would provide the perfect combination for his work – one producer (Trodd) for the 'creative rub of ideas', the other (McCallum) skilled in budgets, logistics and raising finances.[41] In the tough new world of independent film-making which Potter had entered, an American from Hollywood was a major asset in raising US finance for British films. Nevertheless, given that Trodd was Potter's long-standing producer and friend, associated in the public mind with the best of his television work, such an arrangement was always going to be an uneasy one. In 1988 relationships would finally blow apart during pre-production on *Blackeyes*, but the signs of major strain were already there as early as *Dreamchild* (see Chapter 6).

Principally, tension stemmed from both Potter's and McCallum's sense that Trodd was an absent producer on *Dreamchild*. As the writer put it in interview, 'There were two producers on *Dreamchild*: Rick doing all the work and Ken turning up for photo sessions.'[42] Naturally, Trodd's point of view is different. He claims that the allegations of neglect on *Dreamchild* arose from his attempts through the eighties to reconcile involvement in independent production with Potter, with his own continuing desire to produce films for the BBC. The inevitable division this caused could often foster the impression of a lack of interest in the day-to-day needs of a production. Moreover, Trodd suggests that lying behind the allegations of neglect was Potter's 'hurt' that the producer would never agree to work exclusively for the writer and PFH. Trodd recalls that Potter had once suggested this as an 'attractive financial proposition' but that he had refused.

Clearly, behind Trodd's determination to go his own way was a wish not to be seen as a simple functionary of Dennis Potter but instead to establish himself as a significant figure in his own right within British film and TV. Nevertheless, his insistence on combining Potter projects with other work inevitably created friction in the new three-way partnership that was being forged between himself, the writer and McCallum. Indeed, aside from those previously cited, one of the other reasons which may have induced Potter to invite McCallum over to England was simply a desire to get back at Trodd for the alleged 'hurt' caused by the latter's semi-detached role in PFH.

As if all of this were not enough, *Dreamchild* was to experience further troubles, even after editing had been completed. By March 1985, the film was ready for release but it would be another seven months before it gained a limited run in selected cities: first, in the USA from October 1985 and then in Britain from January 1986. The reason for this was that in the intervening period between its completion and release, Thorn EMI Films collapsed. No one consequently wanted to release *Dreamchild.* It was only Verity Lambert who supported the film and fought hard in the face of the crisis at EMI to let it be released. As a result of these troubles, any hopes the film had at the box office were effectively killed off. With no company actively behind it, seeking to recoup its investment, no one was much interested in publicising *Dreamchild.* Despite glowing reviews in both countries, the film had no coherent release pattern, but limped around a few major cities in Britain and the US before quickly closing – even, as the director puts it, 'while people were still queuing round the block to see it'.

By 1985, PFH Ltd's much-vaunted ideal of producing annual British movies was thus beginning to look considerably more threadbare than it had done in 1980, being increasingly hemmed in by economic pressures as well as by problems of artistic control. Potter's escape from British television had proved lucrative and exciting in terms of the deal-making possibilities of the 'independent,' but diversification away from the paternalist bureaucracy of the BBC had brought its own set of difficulties. It now took longer to nurse projects to fruition, and when they did get produced it could often be much more difficult to get them widely aired. Meanwhile, creative energies could be dissipated in the search for financial backing and the possible threat of artistic compromise that that entailed. Allied to these external pressures were internal ones: the battle for creative control which would inevitably result when a writer, accustomed to the privilege and protection of British television, attempted to impose his own strong authorial vision upon a medium which, by convention, had come to be regarded as the domain of the director. For all these reasons, the transformation of Potter from TV 'author' into cinema *auteur* was never going to be easy or painless.

In the early eighties, however, the writer had also diversified into other directions outside screenwriting. The desire for greater freedom and adventure which remission of illness had triggered not only led him away from television to feature films but also manifested itself in a new willingness to explore media he had previously shunned in favour of TV. An early example of this was his involvement in the launch of an independent local radio station in his home area of the Forest of Dean. With the help of fellow PFH partner, entrepreneur Clive Lindley, Potter helped put together a consortium which, in 1979, successfully bid for the first ILR franchise to be offered for the Gloucester and Cheltenham Area. The group won the franchise on the strength of its tender document, which Potter himself wrote. Amounting to a personal credo for broadcasting, it was much praised by the IBA as 'beautifully written, almost poetry.'[43] The launch of the new station, Severn Sound, took place in October 1980 and Potter remained a non-executive director on its Board until 1987.

Aside from cinema and radio, the early to mid eighties also saw Potter complete his second novel. Beginning with the image of a man breaking down on a train, *Ticket to Ride* would later become the inspiration for Potter's 1991 feature film, *Secret Friends* (see Conclusion). Published in September 1986, the novel itself received good reviews and was even called in by the judges of that year's Booker Prize.

Meanwhile, after several previous aborted commissions, Potter's first original stage play was premiered in 1983.[44] *Sufficient Carbohydrate* explored the battle of wills between two middle-aged executives, one American, one British, as they holidayed together with their wives on a Greek island. The play occupies similar territory to *The Bonegrinder* in as much as it tries to use dramatic conflict between the two men as a metaphor for the seedy post-war decline of Britain and the corresponding rise to world dominance of the US. This is thrown into sharp relief by the fact that both executives work for the same multinational food company – the homogenised processed food marketed by the company providing a concrete image for the play's view of the homogenising processed effects of US-inspired global capitalism.

Despite its status as a glittering, West End-style comedy of wills, a play written for theatre could never be the same, for the son of a coal-miner, as one written for television. It did not have the potential to reach a mass audience, composed of all social classes, in the way that television had. It could not give that 'feeling … when you know all kinds of and conditions of people are watching your work when you've got a play on screen.'[45]

By 1983, Potter was beginning to have serious doubts he would ever have that experience again. Writing in the preface to *Waiting for the Boat* (a published collection of three of his old TV scripts), he expressed his 'anger and frustration' that he 'may well have written his last 'original' … one-shot, one-slot play for television.'[46] It had been four years since his last, *Cream in My Coffee*: 'by far the longest such interval for nineteen years'.[47]

He had begun to realise that the desire for independence which he and other practitioners had expressed at the end of the seventies had helped put the final nail in the coffin of the single TV play. Long under pressure in the schedules from censorship and cost demands, the single play had finally been displaced by the greater consolidation of the film and TV industries – first through the independent film-making of *Film on Four* and then the feeling of the BBC (coupled with the genuine desire of leading drama producers like Trodd) that to compete it would have to make films. By 1984, the *Play for Today* slot had finished its final season and a new strand of films made by the BBC, *Screen Two*, was launched.[48] Though this change of title was in part cosmetic – the BBC had long made drama on film for *Play for Today*, side by side with recorded studio plays – Potter was not slow to realise that the move to all-film production marked a fundamental sea-change in the BBC's attitude towards writers of TV drama. As he had suggested as far back as 1976, British TV had only remained a 'writer's medium' through certain class anachronisms, chiefly revolving around TV drama's theatrical origins and the corresponding notion of a 'theatre of the airwaves'.[49]

If his desire to be independent of the broadcasting institutions and to make films both for the BBC and theatrical release meant Potter was partly complicit in the changes of the early eighties which he was subsequently to deplore, nevertheless by 1985, he had come to realise the move to filmed drama had succeeded in undermining the privileged position of the writer in British TV. As he put it in an interview in 1985, the move to all-film work was a sign that the director had begun to displace the writer as the key figure in British TV drama. The consequences of that, he suggested, were that

> in the end we'll get a director's television more than a writer's television, and everyone will say, 'Why is there nothing you can get your teeth into? Why is

it all so bland? Why are these issues all being skirted?' Mostly because directors are on the whole ... not so much interested in content as in that word which covers a great multitude of sins, 'style'.[50]

Inextricably bound up with this mid-eighties' pessimism was Potter's distaste for the Thatcherite market culture which had taken root in Britain during his absence from TV in the early eighties. What he disliked most about Thatcher's Britain was 'that sleaze in the air that corrupts' so that the whole of British life 'now seems to be taking place in a large hotel or supermarket. Everything is consumerist, including television.'[51]

After several years out 'in the cold', Potter had returned to the BBC in 1985 to adapt F. Scott Fitzgerald's *Tender Is the Night* into a six-part 'classic' serial for BBC-2. The economics of British TV had changed sufficiently to make this new work not a studio drama but an expensive filmed co-production in association with Twentieth Century Fox and the American cable network, Showtime, with one eye firmly fixed on programme sales abroad. Indeed with his screenwriting experience and his name now a familiar one to American backers, Potter was so keenly sought by the BBC for the project that he was able to win 'the kind of contract a writer dreams about'. The Corporation was not to ask how he was getting on with the writing, nor to see any scripts of the episodes until they were ready, nor to give him advice. As Potter put it in 1985, 'In other words, it was the kind of thing I'd always longed to have with the Americans, who continually say "Can we see some pages, sir?"'[52] If the ground on which he had based his writing career had irrevocably shifted by the mid eighties, Potter could at least return to television and be treated well on the basis both of his own past reputation and the BBC's need to have a 'name author' in order to deflect criticism from its output, whilst it continued its difficult transition away from recording drama in the TV studio towards producing films.

The resulting adaptation of *Tender Is the Night* won praise when the finished production was transmitted between September and October 1985. Most critics felt Potter had succeeded where Fitzgerald himself had twice failed in terms of adapting the novel in a manner that retained its fable-like quality. Some, however, wondered whether if, instead of an expensive American co-production, so much care and attention could not have been lavished on 'something closer to home' that was 'in more urgent need of such treatment.'[53]

The answer would come almost exactly a year later with Potter's first original six-part drama for BBC TV since *Pennies from Heaven*. By the time he was doing press interviews for *Tender Is the Night*, the scripts of this new work had already been written and Potter was very keen to talk about them. The new series was called *The Singing Detective* and he confidently assured journalists, it was going to 'make *Pennies from Heaven* look like a rehearsal'.[54]

The Singing Detective

Origins

The trouble with *Pennies*, Potter stated, was that it had really been 'a piece on one leg.' Once the novelty of characters bursting into song had worn off, there was nowhere for the drama to go except to keep on repeating the same device. *The Singing Detective* would be much more ambitious. The songs would have a revelatory, investigatory function, relating more to what the central character, Philip Marlow, '*doesn't* know about ... what he finds out gradually, which is what happened to him [as] a child.'[55]

Just as gradual was the process by which Potter was able to arrive at even this degree of clarity about his new TV project. According to its eventual director, Jon Amiel, the drama began life in a very round about way. In order to be commissioned by the BBC, Potter had gone direct to Jonathan Powell, Head of Series and Serials, with the idea for a new serial – working title, *The Singing Detective*. The project which Powell then commissioned, in co-operation with ABC Australia (who agreed to put in seed money with a view to a future co-production), was on the basis of a two- or three-line idea, revolving around an American serviceman who returns to London to search for a girl he met during World War II. According to Amiel, the fact that Potter's subsequent scripts bore little resemblance to this initial suggestion is typical of the writer's creative process: 'He'll allow the nature of the material to determine its own project.'[56]

The transformation of this simple detection idea in the act of writing into the highly complex work that eventually got produced – one embracing hospital scenes, flashback, fantasy as well as elements of *film noir* – was an equally circuitous process. According to Potter, 'the whole thing began to take shape several years [before] when I was feeling rather sad about the death of the studio play. It seemed to have gone forever.'[57] He began to write down some ideas he had for a play: a series of scenes set in a hospital ward. Dealing with the interaction of patients from all classes and walks of life, reluctantly thrown together through illness, it was really the 'idea for a sitcom'. Nevertheless, the writer kept on 'adding bits', with that growing 'sense of dread when you know you're digging out something'.[58]

What is striking is how closely the hospital scenes in the finished scripts resemble those from one of Potter's own 'lost' studio plays, written almost exactly twenty years before: *Emergency Ward 9* (see Chapter 1). This is not simply the case of a writer with experience of hospitals returning to familiar ground. Rather, certain characters and events from the 1966 play map directly on to the 1986 work, suggesting that the latter started life as a conscious reworking of *Emergency Ward 9* – an *hommage* to the studio drama upon which Potter and many of his contemporaries founded their careers yet which, by the mid-eighties, had itself become a patient, in terminal decline.[59]

Hence not only is it in name that Marlow, the central hospitalised protagonist of *The Singing Detective*, echoes the character called Padstow in *Emergency Ward 9*. Both are writers too. True to his Chandleresque moniker, the former is a writer of detective stories, while the latter, though ostensibly a teacher and lay preacher, bears all the hallmarks of an author surrogate. In the 1966 play, he is seen sitting up in bed, scribbling furiously: 'Still jotting it all down, Mr Padstow?' a nurse asks. 'Yes,' he replies. 'This is a good place to work' (p. 4).

Likewise, though twenty years separate the dramas, both protagonists find themselves beside recognisably similar patients in the ward. In Episode Two of the 1986 serial, Marlow's fellow patient in the next bed is George, an irascible old working-class Londoner. Like his equivalent, Flanders, in *Emergency Ward 9*, his relationship with the irritated writer is the source of much comedy. At the same time, the fact that his was the generation which helped win the war is also foregrounded. George tells Marlow how, as a soldier, he helped liberate Germany in 1945: 'They'd come out of holes, these krauts ... Holes in the grahnd' (p. 108).[60]

Also similar to *Emergency Ward 9* is the exploration of race relations in the hospital scenes. The equivalent to the black character, Adzola, of the 1966 play is Ali, a Pakistani occupying the bed next to Marlow's in Episode One (later to be occupied by George). In both works, Adzola and Ali are victims of racial abuse, yet in each case, expectations of how they will react are undercut. In *The Singing Detective*, when a junior doctor asks Ali whether Marlow has been making offensive remarks about his 'origins', the Pakistani gives a 'whoop of laughter', in mockery of the untried houseman and his high moral tone (p. 114).

The necessity of a tough-minded humour in hospital is underscored by the inclusion of very similar death scenes in both *Emergency Ward 9* and *The Singing Detective*. In the 1966 play, the death labours of an old man are counterpointed with Padstow's lofty theological speculation to Flanders that there is a heaven – a place of 'No money. No cares. Just perfect peace in God' (p. 267). In Episode 3 of *The Singing Detective*, it is the elderly George who dies. In a famous controversial scene, Potter returns to the same 'counterpoint' technique he used twenty years before in *Emergency Ward 9*. Here, however, it is sex and death which are contrasted: shots in 'the present' of doctors trying to save George's life are juxtaposed with flashbacks to the moment in Marlow's childhood when he witnessed his mother commit adultery with his father's best friend.

Sex and death become linked in Marlow's mind, as 'primal scenes' he has witnessed, connoting for him the unrelieved physicality and mortality of human life. As with the contrast between Padstow's belief and the reality of dying in *Emergency Ward 9*, the question *The Singing Detective* raises through the hospital scenes – a world of bed, bodies and death – is whether there is anything beyond what Potter labelled 'the suffocating materiality' of things.[61] To find that out and to attempt to uncover the roots of his own illness, Marlow confronts his own predicament by paradoxically escaping from it inside his head. Not only does he fantasise scenes from one of his old detective novels, he begins to delve into his own past – his remote rural upbringing in an 'English Forest' and the subsequent trauma he experienced when, as a boy, he was uprooted from this secure environment and taken by his mother in 1945 to the harsh, alien world of her native London (p. 29). In this way, it is possible to see the process by which Potter kept on 'adding bits' to his original hospital scenes, seeking to give his writer character a past, to explain through flashback the events that led to illness. What is significant is how closely the 'memories' given to Marlow resemble Potter's own.

As the writer himself suggested at the time, *The Singing Detective* was, in terms of his TV writing, his 'first official brush with the autobiographical form'.[62] This is not to say, however, that it was straightforward autobiography, as Potter was keen to stress in interview. He asserted the drama was definitely *not* his autobiography. Rather, exactly like *Hide and Seek*, it played 'with the autobiographical genre because that is a very powerful way of writing. One thinks, 'Oh this must be the truth.' And of course it isn't.' (See Chapter 3.)

Certainly, the use of surface detail from the writer's own life – the biographical 'facts' – is undeniable. Marlow is given the same crippling skin disease, psoriatic arthropathy, from which Potter himself suffered. Potter, too, was raised in an 'English Forest', from where in 1945, his mother took him to London for nine months (see Introduction). What, therefore, was the purpose of aligning Marlow's past to the writer's own so closely? As we have seen with *Hide and Seek*, Potter claimed very good artistic reasons: it lends the work a present tense immediacy so that 'it comes across as true … as characters you can't beat off … They're like somebody coming up to you and that's what I'm after.' Because, according to him, this use of his own autobiography was entirely selective and premeditated, *The Singing Detective* therefore *seems* to be more self-exposing than it actually is: 'I'm a reclusive character' was his assertion in interview. 'I don't expose myself. I appear to.' Manipulating one's own autobiography for fictional purposes was simply, for him, a very powerful convention – 'perhaps the most powerful one left in the hands of a writer.'

For someone with a dislike of self-exposure, this was surely, however, a very dangerous 'convention'. Regardless of the perceptions of the viewing audience as to the drama's autobiographical extent, was there not for the writer the ever-present danger that by endowing an imaginary character with so many of the 'facts' of his own life, that that character would somehow 'slip' off the page, moving from being the product of fantasy into something too close to reality? Clearly, to ask this is to return to the territory of *Hide and Seek*: the theme of characters escaping 'authors' and the progressive onion layer distinctions between surface 'fact', underlying 'fiction' and deeper 'truth' which that novel explored. As we shall see later, *The Singing Detective* owes much to Potter's first novel and indeed makes conscious allusion to it at certain points.

For the moment, however, it is worth noting that during the actual process of writing, Potter did feel an anxiety attendant upon reworking the pain of his own past experience for fictional purposes:

> When I sat down to write *The Singing Detective*, I was uneasy about the project. I continually tried to hold it away, thinking that it would be nauseous for the viewer. Then, I thought, write it. Get it out of the system. I couldn't write a horror story which is what it would have become so I used all the conventions I like – detective stories, musicals, situation comedy.[63]

Hence the *Pennies* 'distanciation' device of characters bursting into song became, here, a way for Potter to distance *himself* emotionally from too ready an identification with the 'horror story' of the ill central protagonist.

Likewise, it was from this standpoint that Potter was finally able to accommodate his 'sit com' hospital scenes with the forties' private eye narrative he was originally commissioned to write. Given that Marlow is in search of self-knowledge and a way out of illness, he is a kind of detective, casting his 'private eye' inwards. This persona is literally embodied in dramatised fantasy scenes (ostensibly from the old detective novel the main character is rewriting in his head) in which he is shown as the detective hero of his own fiction – 'The Singing Detective', solving, in 1945, the mystery of a drowned woman, at the behest of client (as well as prime suspect), Mark Binney.

As previously indicated, 1945 is not just the period setting of Marlow's novel but also the year of his childhood to which he keeps returning in memory. It was, of course, too, the year World War Two ended: a fact the drama registers through flashbacks to Marlow's sense as a child that, with the war rushing to an end, peace and harmony will prevail at last. As the boy tells himself, now the brave Allies have vanquished Nazi evil, 'Everything. It'll be alright' (p. 87).

This is contrasted with the adult's view of the same period in his detective fantasies. The 1945 thriller scenes of *The Singing Detective* are pure *film noir*: a world of suspicion and paranoia where nothing is as it seems. Gradually, as Marlow's thriller narrative unfolds intermittently over six episodes, it becomes clear that the case of Binney and the drowned woman is only part of a much wider conspiracy, involving British and American attempts to smuggle Nazi rocket scientists out from under the noses of the KGB in order to start a new Cold War against the USSR. The same 'moral murk' of *film noir* is visibly present in the thriller scenes of *The Singing Detective*: old wartime certainties of Good (the Allies) against Evil (the Nazis) have evaporated to be replaced by a new climate of confusion in which a former enemy has been co-opted in the fight against a previous ally. As suggested by the rocket conspiracy, hidden malevolent forces play under a public facade of propriety, with the result that no one is quite sure anymore who the true enemy is: the one in the East or someone much closer to home. This changed atmosphere suits the hard-boiled cynicism of a Chandler-like Singing Detective well.

It also, however, has clear links with both the 'real' Marlow's past and his hospital present. As dramatised by the thriller conspiracy, Britain's historical transition from Imperial moral crusader against the Nazis to a new Cold War role which is diminished and unclear alongside that of the United States, finds a parallel in Marlow's childhood and his sense of confusion and loss of integration – first on witnessing his mother's secret woodland adultery and then on being uprooted from 'The Forest' and taken to live in London. As the child sums it up on voice-over in Episode Three, 'Summat's wrong! ... This yunt never right. Where's our Dad then? Do him know about the woods? ... I thought everything was supposed to be alright when we ... beat them [Germans].' His thoughts are taken up on the soundtrack by the adult Marlow, reliving the confusion: 'Where we goo-ing? Mum? ... Round and round I reckon. Round and round' (p. 94).

'Round and round' describes the swirl of Marlow's memories and fantasies in hospital but, given the historical backdrop of 1945, it also hints at a wider view of Britain in spiralling decline since the war. As we have seen, this sense has emerged elsewhere in Potter's writing – in *The Bonegrinder*, *Blade on the Feather* but also, crucially, in *Emergency Ward 9* where the world of the hospital ward became a metaphor for Potter's view of post-war Britain, in seedy decline from its Imperial past and riven by class and racial strife. Given this play's links with the composition of *The Singing Detective*, something of the same symbolism seems to have carried over into the creation of the hospitalised Marlow: the image of the diseased patient, in mortal decline and self-inflicted exile from the rest of the world of the ward, coming to represent the ills of a wider body politic.

Written in 1985, *The Singing Detective* is thus, in one sense, Potter's personal assessment of the previous forty years of post-war history through which he had lived, from the high childhood hopes of VE Day to cynicism and diseased decline in the mid-eighties; in a changed world which, more and more within the drama, comes to parallel the paranoid, conspiratorial atmosphere of Marlow's *noir* detective thriller. The fact that the year in which *The Singing Detective* was written also marked Potter's fiftieth birthday seems no coincidence in this respect. The preoccupation with mortality and the concern to review the past right back to the year of 'that fateful age of ten' can both be related to this. At the same time, not only was 1985 the fortieth anniversary of that date, it also marked the twentieth of Potter's career as a television writer. As he himself suggested in pre-transmission interviews of the time, given that *The Singing Detective* marked his return to original TV writing after several years away, he had wanted to use it to play 'with the conventions – the musical convention, the situation comedy convention, the detective story convention – in order to see what TV drama can do.'[64]

The sentiment precisely echoes his evangelistic credo of the mid-sixties (embodied in such early plays as *Vote, Vote, Vote* and *Emergency Ward 9*) that the TV play should draw its vivacity from the other genres and programme styles around it (see Chapter 1). If the reworking of the *Emergency Ward 9* hospital scenes can be seen as part of Potter's general backward glance at his beginnings in TV drama, this is even more true of the inclusion within *The Singing Detective* of a scene almost identical to the Georgie Pringle classroom scene, featured in his first big success of 1965, *Stand Up, Nigel Barton*. As the writer put it in interview, one of the reasons for its inclusion was to show there *could* be continuity, even in what is commonly held to be the 'ephemeral medium' of television. It is in this light that his *hommage* to the studio play should also be seen – its terminal decline paralleling the mortal decline of the ill writer Marlow and by extension Potter's view of post-war Britain.

As suggested even by its very title, *The Singing Detective* is not, however, a pessimistic work. Rather, it evinces a resilient spiritual optimism in which reviewing the past becomes a means of self-renewal, a way in which to cope more successfully with a hostile present. In that sense, the work has to be seen in relation to the contemporaneous *Dreamchild* (itself a reworking of 1965 material, *Alice*) as well as to the *Late Call* serial of exactly ten years before. In each of these works, memory and fantasy become the means by which an ageing central protagonist gains a sense of the shape of his or her own life, re-establishing touch with the 'wonder' of a lost childhood. In so doing, each becomes rejuvenated – imbued once more with the sense of sovereignty and personal freedom that was felt in childhood. In *The Singing Detective*, the more the middle-aged Marlow succeeds, like a detective, in piecing together and understanding his own past, the more he is able to get well, until, finally, at the end of Episode 6, he is free to leave hospital, 'cured'.

If the works are similar, the difference between *The Singing Detective* and the other two lies in its ambition and scale. While in *Late Call* and *Dreamchild*, the review of the past was solely a function of the memories and imagination of an individual protagonist, in *The Singing Detective*, it is also, implicitly, a review of forty years of British post-war history, including Potter's twenty as a TV writer. Regardless of questions of its relationship to autobiographical 'fact', it is hence a work much closer to Potter himself. That is, in keeping with the modernist sensibility and self-reflexion of *Hide and Seek* and *Only Make Believe*, the decision to root a view of the past in the experiences and imagination of a writer protagonist, emphasises the fact that, far from being an objective assessment, any perspective on history can only ever be *subjective*. As Potter suggested prior to its transmission in 1986, all the events in *The Singing Detective* always return to 'one point of contact … [Marlow] in a hospital bed'.[65] The work can only ever be about itself and its writer. It is for this reason one must believe Potter when he also asserted that in writing *The Singing Detective*, he made 'the closest approach' yet to his own feelings: of 'why I am like I am'.[66]

Production

The script of *The Singing Detective* was filmed between January and July 1986. Post-production then began in August and lasted right through to the first transmission dates in November 1986 – a very tight timetable given the complexity of the £2 million drama and its subsequent edit. During filming, the director, Jon Amiel, had to shoot between four and five minutes of material a day just to keep on schedule (the average rate on a feature film, by comparison, is one and a half to two minutes per day).

That the seven-hour drama not only was completed on time but went on to earn great critical acclaim is thus a tribute to the efforts of the director, his cast and crew. This speed of assembly was not entirely a function, however, of the relatively modest BBC budget.[67] *The Singing Detective* had an initially troubled production which saw it acquire no fewer than three producers.

The first was John Harris, a BBC Series and Serials producer, assigned by Jonathan Powell as an appropriate liaison with his department. As suggested by his decision to be commissioned by Powell, Potter had been keen, after the wrangles over *Dreamchild,* to avoid the involvement of Trodd in the Plays Department. Harris, however, was a line producer with none of the experience of working on a *Pennies*-type 'drama with music' that Trodd had. Accordingly, the latter was drafted in as executive producer and music consultant: a job which required less hands-on involvement and still allowed him his wish to pursue his own film projects.

It was a measure of Potter's unease that he also specifically requested Rick McCallum to be brought in as co-executive producer. At that time, it was almost unheard of for an 'outside' producer (particularly an American with a Hollywood background) to be asked to help the Corporation on one of its home-grown drama projects. In interview, McCallum has no doubts why he was hired. He claims the production had 'languished' under Trodd who, far from being keen, was more interested in making Potter's *Christabel* script instead (see Chapter 6). McCallum states his task was to get the sets built, after which he departed, prior to the shooting of Episode 1 – lured away, in fact, by an offer to work on the Nic Roeg feature film, *Castaway*.

Hence, as the director Jon Amiel puts it, the whole production aspect of *The Singing Detective* was 'a curious hybrid' of three reluctant figures: McCallum, building the sets and promptly disappearing to the sunnier climes of *Castaway*; Harris, a line producer, allocating resources from his office; and finally Trodd, executive producer and music consultant, who, because of Harris' inexperience, begrudgingly found himself having to act as producer during shooting, with more appearances on set than was to his liking.

In turn, what this demonstrates is how much *The Singing Detective* was really the result of the effort of two individuals – Potter and his then relatively inexperienced director, Amiel. Rick McCallum admits this:

> In terms of society, I can live within the context that everybody thinks I did [*The Singing Detective*]. But in reality, those guys, the two of them, made that virtually almost by themselves ... And I mean it's one of the great, great collaborations of all time, between a director and a writer.

It was the first time that Potter had ever had such a relationship with a director. In the past, the writer had always been absent from the actual production process of his work. With the exception of perhaps one or two meetings with the director to discuss casting and possibly a visit to rehearsals or the actual set during shooting, his involvement with his scripts had always ended when he handed them over, complete, to be produced by the BBC or ITV. The task of the director was then to realise them technically, endeavouring at all times to stay close to the writer's intentions and 'meanings'. While this absence from production was partly due to Potter's poor health (and attendant reclusiveness), it also had much to do with the more general nature of TV play production during the sixties and seventies and in particular with the clear division of labour in this period between the writer's privileged 'creativity' and the director's less regarded 'technique' (see Introduction).

By 1985 and *The Singing Detective*, times had changed somewhat. As Potter had begun to register with trepidation, the rise of filmed drama was leading to a rise in the power and assertiveness of directors who were no longer quite so prepared to subordinate their contribution wholly to the demands of script and writer. Given Potter's fear that television would soon become inimical to his type of 'authored' drama, it is thus remarkable that Amiel managed to win the writer's trust and confidence on *The Singing Detective*, forging a relationship with him which the director describes as 'one of the most harmonious and exhilarating' he has ever had with a writer.

Essentially, the key to this was the absence of any producer intermediary. Amiel had not been the first choice to direct *The Singing Detective*: a number of other more well-known directors at the time, including Stephen Frears and *Dreamchild*'s Gavin Millar, had turned it down, on the grounds of not wishing to commit themselves 'merely' to television for six months. As one of the up and coming BBC-trained directors, Amiel had been offered the drama on the strength of his past television work. Because of the situation with the reluctant producers, however, he then found himself having to create his own relationship with Potter, without any of the normal support of a producer third party. In July 1985, having arranged for writer and director to meet for the first time, Kenith Trodd had opted to head for Italy (ostensibly to work on his own project, *The MacGuffin*) – a decision which so enraged Potter, he tried, unsuccessfully, to have Trodd sacked from *The Singing Detective*.[68]

In the long run, such a reduction of interest in the drama to two individuals paid dividends. In the short term, it produced what Amiel describes as two 'extremely difficult and confrontational' meetings with Potter. Having read the scripts, Amiel had felt he was in the presence of a rare television 'masterpiece'. As an ex-BBC story editor, however, he realised there were certain aspects of the original scripts that were 'not fully achieved'. These had to do with the relationship between Marlow and his wife, Nicola, the 1945 thriller strand (which Amiel felt needed to be brought out more strongly) and above all, the very end of the drama. The original dénouement, which differed considerably from that which finally made it on to the screen, seemed to the director to be neither emotionally strong enough nor satisfying.

Given these specific points, amidst his general admiration for the piece,

Amiel found himself in the difficult position of being the junior partner in a relationship with Britain's premier television writer and, worse, with no committed producer to back up his criticisms. Because of this, he expected Potter to be arrogant and unbending. Accordingly, he made up his own mind to be 'extremely arrogant and cocky' in the first meetings, spelling out all the things he thought were wrong with the scripts. As Amiel puts it, 'I was determined to prove I was not in awe of him – which I was.'

The result, predictably, was deadlock, with the writer's suspicions about the rise of directors merely fuelled. It was only once both sides opted to lay down their protective armour that real progress began to be made. The way this was done was precisely by breaking down the division of labour between creativity and technique that had always left Potter an 'outsider' in the production of his own work. As Amiel phrases it, just as he had to persuade Potter to allow a director for the first time to offer advice on the rewriting of scripts, so too had the director to make concessions, allowing the writer to become involved (again more or less for the first time) in the process of translating images on screen. Hence if, as occurred in one instance, Potter said he did not like the way a particular scene had been shot, the director would put aside his own 'bristling ego' and agree to do it again – though only if the writer would write it again. In this way, states Amiel, he and Potter forged a relationship through confrontation which eventually became a collaboration, with personal pride subordinated to the common interest of improving the work on screen.

In so doing, Amiel's crucial contribution to *The Singing Detective* was to readjust its whole emotional weight, making the plight of the central character much more sympathetic to an audience. In many ways, Potter resembled Brecht in as much as he always preferred to try and make his audience think, rather than simply feel.[69]. During the drafting of *The Singing Detective*, he also tried, as we have seen, to distance *himself* emotionally from too close an identification with the central protagonist. The result was what Amiel felt to be an 'extraordinary intellectual journey', though with little sense of an emotional release attendant on the process. This was particularly the case with the original ending which became almost a clinical 'pursuit of the writer' (who was finally revealed to be none other than 'Dennis Potter' himself).[70]

After initial hostility, Amiel's criticisms sent Potter back to the scripts but with one major proviso. As the writer told him seven weeks before shooting, if he was going to rewrite, then it would not just be certain bits. He would have to rewrite the lot, starting at page one. Understandably, this put a certain chill on proceedings. As a script editor, Amiel had seen 'the terrible tendency' of writers 'to throw dozens of babies out with the bathwater' on rewriting. This was not the case with Potter. While heavily under attack from psoriatic arthropathy, he rewrote seven hours of material of the utmost complexity from 'top to bottom' in time for shooting, working at the rate of effectively one episode per week. He also, according to Amiel, managed to rewrite 'with astounding editorial sense' – preserving what was good, excising what was weak. In this way, the plot of the 1945 thriller strand was strengthened but, more importantly, a greater emphasis came to be placed upon Marlow's vulnerability as a character. This is particularly the case in the rewritten final episode, where Marlow's love for his estranged wife, Nicola, is revealed through his fantasising of her death and his tearful realisation of how much he needs her. As Amiel puts it, finding that formula was important. Instead of simply tying up a series of parallel enigmas from the other five episodes (as before), the rewritten sixth episode took a giant leap sideways to solve them, in a manner designed both to satisfy 'the audience's needs for answers' *and* to give 'an emotionally coherent follow-through'. Marlow confronts his own feelings through fantasy for the first time and this sets the scene for the rewritten ending: a climactic shoot-out, in which he kills off his old sick self in order to achieve his own regeneration.

Amiel's emphasis on 'emotion' versus Potter's on 'intellect' continued into many other areas of production. In casting, the director even threatened to resign, unless he got his own way over the choice of lead. Potter's (and his producers') favourite for the part was the Shakespearian actor Nicol Williamson. The reasons were clear: Williamson was an actor of great stature, capable of capturing Marlow's inner rage. The director, however, would not have him, believing he was a performer of almost 'glacial coldness' who might incarnate Marlow's anger but not his vulnerability. Consequently, Michael Gambon was offered the part, as Amiel's 'only contender'.

Another area where Potter's views were challenged and overridden was on the question of film. Clinging to his preference for studio drama, the writer had originally wanted all of the hospital scenes to be recorded on tape in the multi-camera studio (in line with his *hommage* to the studio play). Not only was Trodd against it but by 1985, directors had grown used to working at the BBC on 16mm film, particularly on large projects such as this. As Amiel recalls, Potter did not need to be coaxed much into acquiescence. The logic of film had become unanswerable.

Once shooting began, this logic translated itself into a directorial concern to create an expressive *mise en scène*. Amiel worked closely with the designer (Jim Clay) and lighting cameraman (Ken Westbury) to give each of the main narrative strands of the drama its own distinctive look. In particular, there was a concern not to bathe the flashbacks of Marlow's childhood in sepia tones but to make the remembered world of the Forest more 'richly saturated with colour and intensely vivid' than the world of the present which would seem insipid by comparison. Accordingly, the rich greens and yellows of the Forest were contrasted by very soft, diffuse lighting for the hospital scenes in which design and costume were drained of all primary colours. Finally, for the thriller strand, low-key *film noir* lighting ('hard source lights with hard shadows') was Amiel's inevitable choice for evoking the paranoid Cold War atmosphere of 1945 London.[71]

Largely overlooked in reviews of the time, the director's contribution to *The Singing Detective* was thus a vital one. In key areas such as casting and *mise en scène*, he put his own stamp on the material, readjusting the whole emotional temperature. Moreover, in spite of his relatively junior status, he bravely did what no other director had ever done before with Potter – criticise his TV scripts and ask for rewrites. If, as Amiel maintains, Potter remains primogenitor and 'author' of the work (the director functioning as 'interpreter', refining and embellishing what was in the original scripts), nevertheless it seems clear that in the course of the actual production process of *The Singing Detective*, the writer came closest to his first real creative collaboration with a director.[72] This is particularly borne out by post-production where, true to their original bargain, Potter was, for the first time in his writing career, invited to be part of the process – joining Amiel in the cutting rooms for some of the editing of the six episodes. Together, they made a number of audacious changes (including greater 'associative' cross-cutting between the different narrative strands). Amiel quotes Potter as saying that in the editing, *The Singing Detective* received its 'last and most important rewrite of all'.[73]

Hence almost by accident, Potter's concern for intellectual rigour found a perfect complement in Amiel's directorial desire for greater viewer empathy. Arguably, it was just this blend of qualities that gave the drama its impact and made it such a success, not only amongst Potter's usual champions within the British press but to a large extent with the popular audience as well.

Interpretation

If Amiel's impact on the drama's emotional appeal was decisive, there can be no disguising how much of *The Singing Detective* is uniquely Potter's. True to its implicit status as a review of his twenty years in TV Drama, *The Singing Detective* distils all of his main themes and preoccupations as a writer, offering what is almost a television version of his first novel, *Hide and Seek*. Certainly, the links between the two works are palpable.

In each, a writer character probes his own work in search of autobiographical connections, or 'clues' to himself. In common with the 'Author' in *Hide and Seek*, Marlow realises he has revealed himself through fiction:

his attitude to women (as evinced by his constant drowning of female characters) and so clues to the roots of his own illness. Like the 'Author', he begins to 'rewrite' (replaying scenes in his own mind); a process that gradually brings him nearer and nearer to himself, as figures from his imagination start to converge on the 'real world' of the hospital ward. Throughout the fantasy thriller strand of the drama, two mysterious men in raincoats have dogged the Singing Detective's every effort to solve the case of the drowned woman. Ostensibly on the orders of 'Counter-Intelligence', it seemed to be their job to cover up the conspiracy by any means possible, including murder. Suddenly, at the end of Episode Six, it is this pair the writer finds by his hospital bedside. As they tell him, they are dissatisfied with their place in the story. Their roles are 'unclear': 'We're padding. Like a couple of bleed'n sofas' (p. 231).

Like Daniel Miller in *Hide and Seek*, these are self-aware characters who have decided to confront their malevolent 'Author'. Demanding to know who they are, they start to torture Marlow, yet as they do so, another of his fictions seems to cross into 'reality'. With guns blazing, The Singing Detective bursts into the ward. In the ensuing shoot-out, he kills one of the mysterious men but as he takes aim at the second, he is stopped by a shout from his 'other self': 'No! Wait! That's murder!' The detective turns to camera to address us, the audience: 'Murder, he says. I call it *pruning*. Only one of us is going to walk out of here. Sweeter than the roses' (p. 247). And suddenly he fires – though not at the mysterious man. Instead it is the 'real' Marlow, the ill figure in the bed, who receives a bullet in the skull. As the detective explains to camera: 'I suppose you could say we'd been partners him and me ... But, hell, this was one sick fellow from way back when. And I reckon I'm man enough to tie my own shoelaces now' (p. 248).

With that, the scene in the ward returns to apparent 'normality': busy, with all of the usual patients in place. Clear-cut distinctions between reality and fantasy nevertheless continue to be undermined as the curtains around Marlow's bed open to reveal him fully recovered, dressed and ready to leave hospital. As Nicola, his wife, arrives to take him home, Marlow mutters, 'I think I've cracked this case, folks.' He calls to her, 'Have you brought my hat?' Reaching into a hold-all, it is the Singing Detective's old trilby hat she hands to him. As Potter's script puts it, 'Marlow winks at her, veritably The Singing Detective and puts the hat on, jauntily' (p. 248).

Thus the writer cracks the case of his own recovery, symbolically 'pruning' his old weak, sick self and transforming himself into his own fictional ideal: the Singing Detective. The final confrontation with the mysterious men allowed the true villain of the drama to be unmasked. The 'Author' of the conspiracy – the arch-manipulator behind all the events in the thriller fantasy – was the writer himself. He was the 'Counter-Intelligence' behind the mysterious men, the patient who secretly did not want to get well.

The resurrection of the ill writer in the garb of the Singing Detective dramatises the psychological/spiritual renewal that has taken place *within* Marlow. It also echoes the ending of *Hide and Seek*, in which a troubled novelist achieved 'release' from his paranoid fiction by becoming his own fictional *alter ego*, Daniel Miller. In *Hide and Seek*, as the 'Author' got closer to himself through the Miller persona, he realised that his suspicions about his wife's infidelity were false. It was his own compulsive desire for prostitutes and corresponding inability to make love to her which had been the real problem in their marriage. In *The Singing Detective*, too, Marlow suspects Nicola of having an affair but as the drama progresses, it becomes clear this is simply a figment of his paranoid imagination. In a key flash-back scene in Episode 5, the truth is revealed: the writer is shown in bed with a prostitute, just as earlier, a fantasy scene from his 1945 thriller had portrayed his fictional 'villain', Mark Binney, sleeping with a glamorous Russian prostitute.[74] As with the 'Author' in *Hide and Seek*, Marlow's sexual angst is suggested as the cause of his estrangement with his wife. It was his attempts to submerge his sexuality which lay behind his drowning of female characters in fiction and his own furtive liaisons with prostitutes in 'reality'.

In both works, by confronting this guilt, the writer character at last achieves a position in which he can banish it. Facing up to his guilt over his adultery with prostitutes (and in the rewritten ending, his love for Nicola), Marlow is able, like his counterpart in *Hide and Seek*, to recog-nise himself as 'Author of his Fate'. Reshaping reality to become his own character, he escapes out into the 'open air' beyond the fiction (see Chap-ter 3). As Potter's script describes it, Marlow heads out of the ward with Nicola and 'along the corridor to freedom', his slow progress accompanied by 'the sound of Vera Lynn sweetly promising 'We'll Meet Again''; until, eventually, disappearing from view, 'the empty corridor is resonant with … birdsong and the sound of the wind in the leaves' (p. 249). In the best traditions of the romantic hero, Marlow 'the detective' 'gets the girl' in the end. Reunited with ('meeting again') his estranged wife, he heads off into the sunset – off the page, the screen – in order to live happily ever after.

Such a fictive fairy-tale quality is emphasised through the figure of Regi-nald, a fellow patient in Marlow's ward. Throughout the hospital scenes, he is shown engrossed in an old paperback thriller which, by dramatic coincidence, just happens to be the same novel Marlow is rewriting in his head. Even stranger, Reginald's progress through the book seems to keep pace with the writer's own mental review (and by extension, the audience's knowledge of events in the thriller strand). By Episode Five, Reginald has plucked up enough courage to ask the writer 'Oo killed 'er, then?', at the exact moment Marlow himself is ruminating on the mystery of the drowned woman in his novel. All he can mutter by way of reply is 'Christ. A reader' (p. 187).

In this way, Reginald the 'reader' assumes the role almost of viewer surrogate in the drama, confronting the 'Author' character with the audience's own unanswered questions. By having Reginald's progress through the novel mirror the progress of the TV audience through the drama, Potter draws attention to the 'manufacture' of *The Singing Detective* – of his TV text as a *process* unfolding to design. As viewer surrogate in the ward, it is highly appropriate that by the end of Episode 6, Reginald should reach the very last page of Marlow's 'Singing Detective' novel, just as we, the audience, have come to the end of Potter's drama. In the final scene, as Marlow heads out of the ward to freedom, Reginald reads aloud: 'And – her – soft – red – lips – clam – clamp – *clamped* – themselves – on – his. The – End–.' He looks up from his paperback and mutters: 'Lucky devil!' (pp. 248–9).

The story Reginald is reading – of a 'lucky devil' who cheats death and runs off with the girl at the end – is literally that of the writer, Marlow, unfolding before the TV audience's eyes. Not only does this self-reflexively gesture at Marlow's own fictionality (his status as a fictional Potter character), it also, within the drama, suggests he has *become* fiction. Like 'the Author' in *Hide and Seek*, he has transformed his life to become his own fictional character, the Singing Detective, in such a way that reality and fantasy have completely fused. Reality has *become* fantasy (Marlow a fiction) yet so too have Marlow's dreams and fantasies become reality within the ward.

Like *Double Dare*, *The Singing Detective* in this way sets up distinctions between reality and fantasy, in the form of separate narrative strands within the drama, only to collapse them at the end in order to show that all such boundaries are fluid and ultimately arbitrary. If at the beginning, external 'reality' seemed to reside in the hospital scenes, 'fantasy' in the 1945 thriller strand, by the end of *The Singing Detective*, these two realms have become thoroughly blurred. Characters from Marlow's imagination appear in the ward yet so too, through his slaying by the fictional Singing Detective, is the apparently 'real' writer shown to be a fiction. The diseased novelist is killed off at the end as a surface 'lie': a misanthropic public self behind which the real, inner 'private eye' was hiding from (self-) exposure.

The sense of this 'true' inner self re-emerging is emphasised right at the very end of the drama as the adult Marlow's progress out of the ward 'yields up fleeting images' from his past – flashback images of his home in the Forest; his dead father; 1945 London – before the figure of himself as a boy, perched on top of his favourite tree in the Forest, asserts itself on screen. The child stares out of the tree and straight to camera, as he delivers the last line of the drama: 'When I grow up I be going to be a detective.' Then, unexpectedly, he grins, 'as all the while', superimposed on screen, the adult Marlow 'struggles on, leaning on Nicola' (p. 249).

Not only is the 'We'll Meet Again' refrain suggestive of a reunion with Nicola, it also hints that the adult Marlow has regained touch ('met again') with his younger self, recapturing the 'wonder' of childhood, in the manner of Sylvia Calvert in *Late Call* or Alice Hargreaves in *Dreamchild.* Just as with these characters, memory and imagination are shown to be the tools by which the middle-aged Marlow re-achieves a sense of harmony and integration between himself and the wider world. Reality and fantasy, present and past, memory and imagination are fused in the final image of the 'long-lost' child from Forest days wishing he could grow up to be the fantasy *alter ego* of his adult self. The transformation of the adult Marlow into the Singing Detective symbolises the re-emergence of a vital, younger self which he had previously kept hidden away behind the diseased cynicism of a public adult exterior. When that surface persona is finally jettisoned at the end of Episode 6, the inner child is free to emerge at last.

With its common emphasis on 'getting back into the tree' by becoming the 'Author of one's Fate', *The Singing Detective* thus draws heavily from its sister work, *Hide and Seek*. Proof that this is no coincidence of theme but a conscious attempt to explore on TV ideas and obsessions which first surfaced in prose, is provided by the fact that Potter makes direct allusion to his first novel in Episode 2. In an initially hostile encounter with Dr Gibbon, a hospital psychotherapist, Marlow is forced to listen to the other man reading a 'purple passage' from his out-of-print detective novel; a disgusted account of sexual intercourse: 'Mouth sucking wet and slack at mouth, tongue chafing against tongue … skin … against skin … This is the sweaty farce out of which we are brought into being' (p. 58).

The 'purple passage' which Potter ascribes to Marlow is in fact taken from *Hide and Seek* where it forms part of the paranoid 'Author's' apologia in Section Two (see Chapter 3). It is thus possible to link Marlow's 'soiled paperback', the old out-of-print novel in which he too closely revealed himself, to *Hide and Seek*. By implication, *Hide and Seek* must have some bearing on *The Singing Detective*'s theme of a fictional work providing the road to recovery for its 'real' writer.

If *Hide and Seek* explains the significance of *The Singing Detective*'s final image – of Marlow 'getting back into the tree', re-achieving the sense of integration and 'wonder' he thought he had lost – it also begs the question of whether, in the drama, there is a Fall comparable to that which dislodged the child of the novel from the security of the oak and his sense of an 'Author-God' within as well as without. While there is no depiction of childhood assault in *The Singing Detective*, there is a direct structural equivalent embedded right at the very heart of the six-part serial – almost exactly at the drama's mid-point, near the end of the third episode. This is the famous controversial sex scene in which shots in 'the present' of the elderly George's death are counterpointed with Marlow's childhood memories of secretly witnessing his mother commit adultery with Raymond, his father's best friend. Moreover, through his handling of the lovers' dialogue prior to the adultery sequence, Potter implicates this as a Fall. From his tree top hide-out, the young Philip Marlow spies his mother walking down below with Raymond. Significantly 'descending' from the oak on to the forest floor to have a closer look, he overhears Mrs Marlow teasing Raymond as 'you dirty devil' (p. 112). After the pair unknowingly make love in full view of the boy, Raymond tells her he could 'bite' her. To him, she is as 'sweet as an apple' (p. 117).

This Fall imagery of the male as 'devil' and sex the fruit of temptation has been used before by Potter – for example, in *A Beast with Two Backs* which also contained a Forest adultery scene that seemed to stand for something else. As Chapter 1 noted, Michael Teague's encounter with the local 'whore', Rebecca, was sex that blurred into assault. It ended in her murder. Likewise, in *The Singing Detective*, sex and death are not only linked through juxtaposition of the Forest love-making with George's death labours in hospital. Within the adultery scene itself, sex is portrayed through the child's eyes as if it were an assault. Over point-of-view shots of the urgency of the lovers' struggle comes the troubled voice of the child on the soundtrack: 'Wos him a-doing? Wos him doing to our Mam? Mam!' (p. 115).[75]

If this suggests adultery as assault, also similar to *Hide and Seek* is the effect both have on the child's relationship to his world. In the novel, the shock of sexual assault changes even the boy's 'way of looking at' his beloved Forest Paradise, draining it of 'wonder'.[76] Even more explicitly in the drama, Philip's Fall – his premature discovery of the 'Forbidden Knowledge' of how he came to be – leads directly to his exile from 'Eden'. Immediately after the adultery sequence, the scene cuts to a train, inside which Philip is travelling with his mother away from the Forest to a much less certain destination (to the 'moral murk' of post-war London; the eventual setting for the adult's *noir* detective fantasies). The train journey functions as an objective correlative for the central protagonist's own emotional rite of passage: his journey away from the security and integration of childhood towards the strange, less morally stable, world of adults, in relation to which he feels anxious and separate.

Crucial to this growing disjunction the child perceives between himself and the world is his relationship to his parents. Metaphorically expelled from Eden, it is significant that he is accompanied by his mother. Ostensibly, they are heading to London without his father because the latter has to remain as a miner in 'the Forest'. As Philip has learned, however, the real reason is the irreparable state of the couple's marriage. Within the symbolic and narrative logic of the drama, Mrs Marlow thus functions as Eve, the 'fallen woman', to her son's Adam, exiled through Forbidden Knowledge. This is made clear through the adult Marlow's detective fantasies in the same episode (Episode 3) in which, juxtaposed with his childhood memories, are scenes depicting the Singing Detective's encounter with Lili, a prostitute cum Russian spy who haunts the street lamps directly outside Mark Binney's mews flat. As repeated shots show her peering up at Binney's window, it becomes clear that 'except for the colour of the hair and the luxury of the clothing', this mysterious *femme fatale* is 'Mrs Marlow.' In short, 'it is ... the same actress' (p. 99).[77]

The model for 'Lili' in Marlow's fiction is his own mother, as he remembers her *circa* 1945. She has become equated in his imagination with the 'fallen women' who haunt the London streets. The link becomes crucial at the end of the third episode, when Lili approaches the Singing Detective as he is leaving his client Binney's flat. Just as she is about to reveal vital details of an Allied plot to smuggle Nazi scientists out of Germany, shots ring out and two mysterious men in raincoats are glimpsed making their escape. With blood oozing from her mouth, the 'fallen' Lili dies, cradled in Marlow's arms, as his own suspicions of a conspiracy are confirmed.

Structurally, Lili's disclosure of secret knowledge to the detective Marlow at the climax of Episode 3 parallels the disclosure of forbidden knowledge which *the child* Marlow received earlier within the same episode from spying on her counterpart in the Forest. Within each narrative strand, the male protagonist's discovery, via a 'fallen' Eve figure, of a secret world behind the everyday world provides him with the crucial evidence he needs to unravel his 'case' – in the thriller fantasy, the mystery of the drowned woman; within the flashbacks, the possible roots of the adult's illness. Note, too, how such revelations are intimately connected to death: the slaying of Lili in Marlow's thriller; the death of George in hospital, against which the adultery flashback is juxtaposed.

Such a connection between Mrs Marlow and death is in turn explicitly developed in later episodes. In word association games with his psychotherapist Gibbon, the ill writer in Episode 5 suddenly finds himself having to confront his own attitudes to women, when he involuntarily blurts out the word-string: 'Woman. Fuck. Fuck. Dirt. Dirt. Death' (p. 77). Later, within that same episode, a flashback to 1945 provides the clearest answer yet as to why sex is so closely associated in his mind with death. Standing on a platform on the London Underground, waiting for a train to come, the young Philip Marlow reveals to his mother what he has seen in the Forest. Shocked by his knowledge, Mrs Marlow slaps him hard across the face, an action which only serves to worsen the boy's existing panic and fear. Taking off from her side, he runs along one of the many endless tunnels of the Underground. As Mrs Marlow makes to give chase, suddenly, an on-coming train emerges (p. 186).

The 'killer' of the 'fallen' Mrs Marlow/Lili is revealed in the penultimate episode to be Marlow himself. It was his revelation of sexual knowledge that directly contributed to her suicide and in turn it is his subsequent guilt which has outcropped in his detective novel, both in terms of the murdered Lili and in his penchant for drowning his fictional *femmes fatales*. Just as Episode 6 subsequently shows in relation to the wider 'conspiracy' of the mysterious men and the patient's resistance to recovery, all clues lead back to the writer himself. If, within *The Singing Detective*, the underground scene with Mrs Marlow provides the specific motivation for the drama's sex-death connection, it is significant to note how the relationship between the death of a mother and a child's acquisition of sexual knowledge echoes that of previous Potter works.[78]

Just as with *A Beast with Two Backs* and *Hide and Seek*, the effect of the revelation of forbidden knowledge is a loss of integration between the child protagonist and his world – a breach in the child's bond of absolute security and trust in his parents which comes to be expressed in terms of the 'death' of a mother yet also estrangement from a hitherto God-like father. In *The Singing Detective*, this estrangement is actually physical – after the Fall scene comes the boy's exile to London, far away from his father and the Forest Eden. On another level, it is also an emotional and spiritual separation.

This is well illustrated by comparison of flashback scenes between father and son prior to the Forest adultery in Episode 3 with those that follow after. In Episode 2, a scene in the local village working man's club conveys the depth of the son's affection and admiration for his father. Sitting in a corner of the club, listening to his 'dear old Dad' sing to a local audience, the young Philip stares 'wide-eyed across the smoke-filled room at his 'singing' father, glowing with pride' (p. 71). Such public admiration is in marked contrast to scenes after the Forest Fall when the son deliberately seeks to avoid contact with his father. In Episode 6, after Philip has returned home from London and his mother's death, Mr Marlow is seen searching deep within the Forest for his son. Perched on top of his favourite oak, Philip, however, refuses to answer even though, as Potter's script makes clear, 'he can clearly hear his father, and even see him through the bare branches, way below' (p. 232). The Biblical parallels are unmistakeable. Just as with Adam after he had eaten forbidden fruit from the Tree of Knowledge, Philip is too afraid and ashamed to answer when 'God his Father', the site of all his values and affections, comes looking for him in his Forest Eden. The boy's Fall from sexual innocence has fractured relations not only with his mother but with his father as well. The result is a sense of loss – a loss of integration between himself and the world which in turn breeds self-consciousness and an unwillingness to express emotion to his father.

This edgy self-conscious relationship between son and father is by no means unique to *The Singing Detective*. As we have seen, it is a key preoccupation of many Potter plays: *Stand Up, Nigel Barton*, *Lay Down Your Arms*, *Traitor*, *Son of Man* and so on. In each of these, the figure of the father (God the Father in *Son of Man*) functioned as the prime site of values for the 'torn' male protagonist, as he struggled against the world and himself in the name of 'conscience', like some latter-day Hamlet seeking revenge in the name of a ghostly patriarchal ideal. A similar sense of the father as the ghost of a lost past is strongly present in *The Singing Detective*. In another flashback to the village club in Episode 2, Mr Marlow is once more seen singing to an enraptured local audience. This time, however, things are not right. Instead of the young Philip glowing with pride at his father's performance, it is the hunched figure of the adult Marlow who is sitting in the corner – disfigured by disease and dressed in pyjamas, just as he has been seen in hospital. As the song on stage ends and Marlow tries to join in the applause for his father, he finds, to his horror, that he cannot clap his arthritically buckled amd crippled hands – not even for his 'dear old Dad'. The scene cuts to a wide shot, taking in the whole of the interior, as Marlow sees he is now alone in the long-abandoned club: 'But he was there – he was!' he cries out to no-one in particular. 'My lovely dear old Dad was there ... All the birds in the trees – all the love in the world – I heard him. I *saw* him.' It is only as this scene gives way to shots of the delirious patient in hospital that it becomes clear this eerie tableau has been Marlow's fevered nightmare. Through self-consciousness and the suppression of emotion, things the son had always wanted to say to his late father can now no longer be said. As Marlow cries out in the deserted club: 'There's so much I want to say – I need to talk to him very badly' (p. 78). It is too late, however. Like Hamlet's ghost, the 'airy' guilt spectre of the dead father haunts the living son.

The common 'Hamlet structure', noted with many Potter single plays, is thus readily visible in *The Singing Detective* (see Chapter 3). While previous Potter protagonists like Nigel Barton and Jesus in *Son of Man* were haunted by the patriarchal ideal of the father, Marlow's is incarnated as a ghost from the past. Also in common with Shakespeare's *Hamlet*, it is the specific knowledge of adultery between his mother and his 'uncle' (his father's best friend, Raymond) which is the cause of the ghostly displacement of the father within the moral universe of the young 'student Prince', Philip. From being the centre of his childhood affections, Mr Marlow evaporates to become the spectre of guilt that haunts the ramparts of the adult's imagination. In this light, Marlow's psychic quest for 'clues' to his own past becomes a search for atonement (a longing to be 'at one' again) with this spiritual ideal of the father. As with the tragic hero of Shakespeare's play, the motivation of the adult Marlow is 'revenge': a redressing of disorder (the psychic disorder caused by the adultery), in the hope of re-achieving the sense of integration he once felt in childhood between himself, 'God his Father' and the world. Like Hamlet, knowledge of his mother's adultery has tainted his view of the world, giving him a sense that all around 'something [is] rotten'.[79] As previously noted, the hospitalised Marlow is characterised by a deep misanthropy. This outcrops in his *noir* detective fantasies which are played out against a cynical post-war London backdrop of paranoia, suspicion and conspiracy. It is precisely this 'moral mess', within both the fiction and the wider 'reality' of the writer's life, which The Singing Detective is charged with clearing up. Hamlet-like, he pledges himself to the redress of all disorder. As he puts it on voice-over at the end of Episode 3, 'Something needed doing. I had to do it' (p. 126).

Nevertheless, like Hamlet, he, too, is haunted by doubt. As with many Potter protagonists, Marlow is a torn hero – almost literally so since there are two Marlows: the ill writer and his imaginary detective *alter ego*. Moreover, just as it has been shown that most of Potter's protagonists are torn between flesh and spirit, so too is this the case with Marlow. As noted previously, the world which the ill writer inhabits is one entirely 'of the flesh': a hospital landscape of bed, bodies and death. As Potter consistently makes clear throughout Episode 1, this is hell. 'A living Hell' is how Reginald's fellow patient, Mr Hall, complains of life within the ward, in the first few minutes of the drama (p. 9). This is echoed later by Marlow himself, as disease makes his body temperature spin out of control: 'Hot. Why is it so hot? Why am I so hot?' he mutters (pp. 23–4).

Marlow's 'hell', however, is as much spiritual as biological. This becomes clear in the penultimate scene of Episode 1, when he is confronted by a hospital registrar, who chides him for his despairing attitude to illness. Most patients, he is told, 'don't rail against the world and all that is in it.' When, Marlow is asked, is he 'going to find any equanimity?'

(pp. 39–40).

It is precisely this sense of finding equanimity – of restoring a balance that will allow him to recover from illness and so escape his hospital hell – which becomes Marlow's goal throughout the rest of *The Singing Detective*. His task is to heal the divisions in his personality: the flesh-spirit dichotomy which has torn him, ever since the Forest Fall of his boyhood. The fracture between the world and the self which childhood discovery of sex prompted has been internalised by him as a pull between inner and outer worlds – a tension between spiritual yearnings and fleshly desires; the strivings of the mind versus those of the body. In this way, Marlow's illness becomes symptomatic of a more profound mind-body schism: literally the eruption on to the body of feelings and desires which the mind has guiltily tried to repress. Healing this dichotomy is the only way for Marlow to heal himself from illness.

His imaginary *alter ego*, the Singing Detective, becomes the means of restoring psychic order. If, caught in a hospital hell of bodies and death, the figure of the diseased writer symbolises the 'flesh' side of the dichotomy that is tearing Marlow apart, the Singing Detective represents the 'spirit': an inner not an outer self. It is only by turning this 'private eye' inwards to probe the roots of his body-mind disjunction that Marlow will ever be able to achieve liberation from illness in the 'real' world outside. Moreover, the depth of this flesh-spirit dichotomy is indicated by a number of key flashback scenes in which the protagonist is seen as a child within the village school of the Forest, during the crucial year of his boyhood: 1945. As previously noted, these classroom scenes are a conscious reworking of the Georgie Pringle scenes in *Stand Up, Nigel Barton*. There are, however, a number of significant differences between the 1965 and the 1985 versions.

While Nigel Barton and the young Philip Marlow are both shown to be bullied by the other children of the village, on account of their scholastic abilities, their means of revenging their classroom ostracisation are markedly different.[80] While Nigel Barton steals a daffodil from the classroom windowsill, the extent of the moral 'mess' which the young Philip Marlow is in is graphically indicated by the fact that his rebellion is to sneak into the schoolroom after hours and defecate on the teacher's table. As with *Stand Up*, the teacher turns detective, interrogating the class in an attempt to uncover the culprit. Like Barton, the young Philip eventually cracks under this pressure and is hauled out to the front for further questioning. How this happens in *The Singing Detective* is significant since the drama links this 'unspeakable' classroom crime with that other 'crime of the flesh' for which the boy also feels guilty: the Fall in the Forest. This is first hinted in Episode Three as the village schoolteacher is seen in flashback giving her pupils a patriotic lesson on the Good Allies' routing of the Evil Nazis, together with a promise that come VE Day all their futures will be glorious. Over shots of rows and rows of her optimistic pupils, arms folded, 'eyes alive', intrudes a more cynical voice-over – the familiar side-of-the-mouth narration of the Singing Detective, the adult whose perspective on post-war Britain is much more jaundiced: 'I knew I was ankle-deep in the mess', it states. 'What I had to do now was to decide whether to let the ooze get up to my knee bones. Something needed doing. I had to do it' (pp. 98–9).

His voice carries over into the next scene, easing the visual transition from 1945 flashback to 1945 fantasy as Lili, Marlow's maternal *femme fatale* gazes up at the window of the mysterious Mark Binney's flat. The counterpoint is thus a stark one – the teacher's VE optimism displaced by post-war cynicism and disillusionment, her simple black and white view of a world of Good versus Evil undermined by a London landscape of shadows in which the moral 'mess' is too close to home and family. As the detective Marlow puts it, the 'ooze' is seeping up to his knee bones. He will have to do something about it. By Episode 4, it becomes clear what the disillusioned 'fallen' child of the Forest has decided to do. His defecation 'crime' in the classroom functions both as his reaction to the Forest adultery and as his rebellion against the moral authority of the teacher, with her too easy promises of a post-war heaven. Akin to his detective *alter ego*'s uncovering of conspiracies in the 1945 thriller, the child Marlow has unwittingly seen behind the rhetoric of adults, discovering in the Forest a gap between public postures and private deeds.

Moreover, through his handling of the dialogue in the classroom scene, Potter implies that what the young Marlow is ultimately rebelling against is patriarchy itself – the authority of traditional patriarchal structures. Hitherto the 'clever dick' amongst all the children, the young Philip, on being suspected by the teacher of complicity in the classroom crime, finds himself under threat of the 'Big Stick', precisely because of his superior knowledge over all the others (his knowledge of the 'flesh-crime').[81] If such phallic imagery, centring around observation and secret knowledge, again links the classroom scene with the Forest adultery, equally important is the sense of repression and punishment as essential for the continuation and maintenance of the phallocentric patriarchal order. Like Adam expelled by God from the Garden of Eden, Philip is to be humiliated in front of his peers because he has seen and knows too much of what that order likes to keep suppressed: namely (as suggested by the linkage of the classroom defecation with the Forest sex), anything connected with the body, 'the flesh'. Such a sense of patriarchal authority repressing as 'bestial' all bodily functions is explicitly invoked by the teacher, on first discovering the 'crime' on the school table: 'Cows do it in the field and know no better,' she cries. 'They are animals! ... But *we* are not animals ... *God* allowed us to tell the difference between the clean and the dirty' (p. 138).

As indicated earlier, it is precisely this flesh-spirit dichotomy ('flesh': of the animal; 'spirit': of Man made in the image of God) which lies at the heart of Marlow's illness. Thus what the classroom scenes seem to reveal, implicitly, through the dialogue, is its broader foundations within patriarchy itself. When the child defecates on the teacher's table, he rebels against a patriarchal authority structure that represses as 'bestial' anything connected with the body. Like Edmund in relation to his Old Testament patriarch of a father in *Where Adam Stood*, Philip rebels against a world-view that seeks to suppress knowledge of Man's 'animal' nature. Nevertheless, like Nigel Barton before him, when he is put under severe psychological pressure from the teacher to confess what he knows (and hence absolve his sins against the patriarchal order he has violated through acquisition of knowledge of 'the flesh'), he seizes upon a Georgie Pringle figure to blame – a backward child in the front row of the class who had earlier been pulling faces at him. He points to the supposed villain and utters his name to the teacher: 'Mark Binney, Miss. It was *Mark Binney*!' (p. 166).

At the climax of Episode 4, the identity of the mysterious shadowy client within Marlow's detective story is revealed to be, like 'Lili', a figure drawn from the writer's own past – a fictitious *noir* villain to rival the villain the child invented for the teacher in 1945. By the time of Episode 6 and the unmasking of Marlow himself as the true villain of the thriller strand, these connections have become even more pronounced. Just as Binney the child functioned as a convenient scapegoat for the young Marlow's 'flesh crime' in school, so, too, is the fictional Mark Binney finally shown to be a mere red herring in the novel's drowning of female characters: a cover for the adult writer's own sexual guilt.

Likewise, what the parallel flashback and fantasy strands draw attention to is the notion of the writer figure as liar. This is made explicit in a key scene in Episode 6 in which the ill Marlow relives his classroom guilt in the presence of his psychotherapist, Gibbon. Echoing the Georgie Pringle scene in *Stand Up*, Marlow recalls how the other children in the class, sensing blood, quickly seized on the chance to persecute an innocent, nailing the 'backward lad hands and feet to [his] story' (p. 212). As the crucifixion image suggests, the backward child 'dies', Christ-like, so that others may live – in this case, saving the clever child by washing away his sins, allowing him to remain blameless within the patriarchal authority structure so that he can carry on up its ladder of success.

Breaking down in front of Gibbon, as he recalls his guilt over the classroom betrayal, Marlow, by so doing, finds a way of excreting the pain of the past in order to achieve a kind of catharsis. This is indicated by Gibbon's call, immediately after he has wiped away his tears, for Marlow to stand up. For the first time in all six episodes of the drama, the protagonist finds he is able to struggle up from his wheelchair and take the first few faltering steps on his own previously crippled legs. His illness and attendant progress to health are thus inextricably linked with his attempts to overcome the repression and guilt which the authority structures of patriarchy, with their underpinning flesh-spirit dichotomy, have engendered in him.

While the classroom scene itself exposed the child Marlow as a villain, a liar, *recollection* of it gives the adult a sense of vocation and a shape to his chosen life as a writer. Under pressure in the classroom, the child in essence became a writer, learning that by 'telling stories', he could save himself. Likewise, this is precisely what the adult Marlow *re*-learns in a different way in hospital – that through fiction, he can save himself from illness and change his reality for the better. While originally the source of the 'fallen' child's guilt, recollection of the classroom scene points the way to the adult's liberation.

Hence behind the 'fallen' child's guilt and feelings of separation from his Forest roots lies the seeds of reintegration with that world: his seeming vocation as a writer which culminates at the end of the drama in his liberation through fiction. A clear example of such a movement to reintegration is Marlow's reunion in flashback with the 'ghost' of his dead father that comes near the end of Episode 6. In flashback, the boy Philip is seen, as before, in the Forest, hiding up a tree, while down below, 'God his Father' comes looking for him in 'Eden'. As the child silently observes, he witnesses a secret event on the forest floor, every bit as significant as his dead mother's adultery in Episode 3. Dejected that he cannot find his son, Mr Marlow walks slowly on through the Forest. Then, when it seems no one is looking, he stops dead, throws his head back and utters what Potter's script describes as 'one long and strange and almost animal-like cry of absolute grief and despair ... [a] terrible release of anguish.' The young Philip stares, eyes wide. The scene switches to the hospital 'present' and the figure of the ill Marlow in bed, as tense and motionless as the boy of memory. In the Forest, the young Philip suddenly breaks cover and runs up to be beside his father: 'Oh. There thou bist,' mutters Mr Marlow. 'Aye. Here I be,' answers the son. They walk on but now, 'almost slyly, certainly shyly, Philip reaches for and then curls his hand into his father's hand, as they walk' (p. 233).

As suggested by the juxtaposition of the remembering adult, this simple scene on the Forest path carries a much wider symbolic resonance within the drama as a whole – representing nothing less than the spiritual atonement of the middle-aged son and his reunion with the 'ghost' of his dead father, after years of emotional separation. The key to understanding this lies in Mr Marlow's cry of grief for his dead wife and 'lost' son which Potter's script directions describe as 'animal-like'. Coming in the same episode after the adult Marlow's own tears of grief over Mark Binney, middle-aged son and dead father are at last united through a common release of hitherto repressed feeling. Most importantly, it is this notion of repressing what is 'animal-like' which links them. Just as the young Marlow had to repress his guilt over the 'flesh crime' at school, so, too, does he discover that his father has 'animal' feelings and instincts that he also has bottled up. As with his mother's adultery, the child once more gains secret knowledge in the Forest of the 'flesh' side of Man which patriarchy and its authority structures (the village school) had taught to keep hidden.

The difference, here, is that it is the ultimate image of patriarchy – his own father, the living 'God' he so loved and admired, whom the child realises and comes to accept as 'animal' just like him. The feelings of inadequacy – of having 'fallen' from the grace of the Father – which prompted him to hide when 'God' came looking for him in Eden are thus banished. The child of memory is able to be reunited with his father on the Forest floor in an integration of equals. What is important to note is how, through the juxtaposition of scenes, this is achieved only by means of the ill Marlow's *recollection*. The disillusion and cynicism engendered by the 'fallen' youth's shock that all Mankind, including his own father, was an 'airy beast', gives way in middle-aged memory to a greater 'equanimity', a sense of reintegration with the father as equal, precisely because he, too, is recognised and accepted as 'animal', just like him. As suggested by Marlow's tearful release of guilt over Mark Binney, what is no longer accepted is the notion of a flesh-spirit dichotomy – the guilt structure of patriarchy which erected emotional barriers in the relationship between father and son. By the end of Episode 6 and the symbolic reunion scene with Marlow senior, the 'flesh' and 'spirit' sides of this dichotomy have blurred together. The ghost of 'God the Father' is shown in the Forest to be a Man with instincts of the 'flesh'.

The healing of the relationship between son and father therefore marks the healing of divisions within the protagonist between flesh and spirit – part of the 'We'll Meet Again' of the final song. The writer's imagination and his memories of the Forest blur to produce the symbolic reunion with his father on the Forest path. One of the most significant aspects of *The Singing Detective* is thus that it offers a critique of patriarchy from a male perspective. The flesh-spirit dichotomy which the drama implicitly postulates as underpinning patriarchy is shown to be destructive, particularly to relations between father and son. The Judaeo-Christian ideal of God the Father that traditional authority structures taught to worship and obey is shown to create a false or idealised image within the family, suppressing Man's 'animal' aspects while elevating the father, in the child's eyes, into a God beyond 'the flesh'. In turn, this leads to extreme guilt feelings in the child when he feels he has 'fallen' from the God-like standards of the Father or, alternatively, extreme cynicism and disillusion if either parent is seen to deviate from the standards they themselves embody. Far from the black and white view of the world taught by his village teacher, what Marlow's recollection of events reveals is a world not of 'either/or' but 'both and', in which events are not *either* good *or* bad but can have both positive and negative effects. What, to the child Marlow, seemed to be the nadir of his Fall from grace (his classroom lying and betrayal of Mark Binney) is recognised from the vantage-point of middle-age as the first step on his pathway to an eventual redemption through fiction. Similarly, as the child's secret observation of his father in the Forest attests, the same curiosity to see and to know which led to the Forest Fall also provides the means to an eventual reintegration with a world (and a father) from which he felt estranged and separate. The desire for knowledge that lies behind the drama's 'detective' metaphor functions as the source both of Marlow's Fall and ultimately that of his Redemption; a Redemption which allows him to see beyond what led him to the sense of a Fall in the first place: the flesh-spirit dichotomy of patriarchy. Jettisoning this, the protagonist is at last able to recognise the moral 'mess' or 'murk' that engendered cynicism and disillusion in his 'fallen' youth, as part of a movement away from the simple moral absolutes of an Old Testament upbringing, towards a 'deeper', more complex understanding of the world and his relationship to it.

It is this sense of a progression or journey from youthful cynicism to middle-aged 'equanimity' which seems to represent the ultimate narrative trajectory of *The Singing Detective*. The underlying structural dynamic is precisely that noted for Potter's 1976 'trilogy' of plays as well as for *Pennies from Heaven* – a movement away from the antinomies of 'Evil' versus 'Good', reality versus fantasy, 'flesh' versus 'spirit', towards a blurring and eventual collapse in distinctions between these categories (that is, a move from a simple 'either/or' view of the world to a more complex, even mystical one of 'both/and'). The difference with *The Singing Detective* is that whereas such a movement from despair to hope was previously traced across a series of consecutive works, here it is entirely *internal* to one work, dramatised over six episodes in the mental journey Marlow makes from misanthropy in Episode 1 to rejuvenation in Episode 6: from a Fall back to Redemption.

If this is Marlow's spiritual journey through the drama – from Paradise Lost to Paradise regained – it can be seen how closely it conforms to a Christian structure. Indeed, *The Singing Detective* is a veritable 'Pilgrim's Progress' in which the protagonist finally has to die in order to live again. Akin to the hanging and reappearance of Arthur Parker at the end of *Pennies*, Marlow's outwardly sick persona – his worldly or 'fleshly' self – has to be sacrificed ('crucified') at the end in order for his true inner self (his 'spirit') to be resurrected as the Singing Detective. Only in this way can he depart his hospital hell for the Heaven of freedom he knows lies just beyond the everyday *terra firma* of the ward.

In turn, this helps provide a context for understanding the relationship of *The Singing Detective* to Dennis Potter's own autobiography: the 'fact', 'fiction', 'truth' distinction which so complicates any assertion of this work as a simple factual account of the writer's 'life on screen'. As with *Hide and Seek*, Potter closely weaves the 'facts' of his own life into *The Singing Detective* (illness, career as a writer, Forest childhood and so on), wilfully blurring the distinctions between autobiography and fiction. At the same time, other events, such as the Forest adultery scene, are demonstrably pure fabrication.[82] In this way, the writer invents an authorial alter ego in his own image – a writer character with the same skin disease who also chooses to work in popular forms; in this case, detective stories. As this authorial *alter ego* embarks on his interior journey, the 'truths' he uncovers go beyond the literal facts of the 'real' writer's own past – his progression from crisis to recovery functions not as literal but something closer to emotional or spiritual autobiography.

That is, Marlow's journey in six episodes from cynicism and despair to equanimity mirrors the progress that previous chapters have noted across Potter's work of the previous twenty years – from the angry pessimism of his first *Wednesday Play*s to the sense of spiritual renewal detectable in such later scripts as *Pennies from Heaven* and *Dreamchild*. This seems ultimately to be the reason for *The Singing Detective*'s reworkings of scenes and themes from past Potter TV plays. The review of twenty years work is the story of Potter's own 'Pilgrim's Progress' as a writer: Marlow's journey to recovery over six episodes functioning not as a literal, factual account but as a metaphor for the writer's own journey over two decades. Though many of the themes of *The Singing Detective*, such as the exploration and resolution of a flesh-spirit dichotomy, had been explored in earlier TV plays, never before had Potter encapsulated so many of them in one work and through an authorial *alter ego* whose biographical 'facts' so closely resembled his own. Such a choice, in turn, helped emphasise how much the drama was a mirror of his own experience. As with *Hide and*

Seek, the similarity of surface 'facts' served as a guarantee of the authenticity of the deeper metaphorical or spiritual truths lying underneath. Delving down through layers of superficial fact, underlying fiction and deeper truth, the writer, like the Author character in the novel, succeeded in getting closer to himself than he had ever done before. It is in this way that *The Singing Detective* should be seen as nothing less than a synthesis and summation of Potter's entire writing career in television. Little wonder that after watching the transmission of the first episode in November 1986, Potter could comment to the *London Evening Standard*: 'I feel as if I've scraped out my own bone marrow with a spoon to offer viewers'.[83]

Reception

The question raised by subsequent reaction to *The Singing Detective* was whether Potter scraped away too much. Both the writer and the BBC combined forces to trail the drama heavily, prior to the transmission of the first episode on Sunday 16 November 1986. The writer embarked upon a lengthy round of interviews with the British press, whilst the BBC (perhaps mindful of the amount they had lavished on Potter to secure his return to the Corporation), heavily promoted the drama on-air, even using its own news programmes to carry items.[84] Thus, before the first episode had even been broadcast, the line between publicity and news had been successfully blurred with respect to *The Singing Detective*. An air of expectation was generated in which the drama came to be 'touted as this year's artistic biggie à la *Edge of Darkness*'.[85]

At least one reason why Potter's return was much heralded by the BBC was because of the very real difficulties the Corporation faced at the end of 1986. After an autumn in which the BBC, under Director-General Alasdair Milne, had been subject to almost constant external attack – from the Conservative Party over TV news coverage of the US bombings of Libya; from the Murdoch press (whose proprietor had his own ambitions in television); from assorted right-wing Conservative MPs and Clean-Up TV campaigners who harried it for 'unacceptable' levels of sex and violence – the return of Potter in the fiftieth anniversary year of BBC TV seemed to mark continuity with a happier public service past, at a moment when the very existence of the Corporation itself seemed to be under threat.[86] As Alasdair Milne adroitly phrases it in his memoirs, the transmission of *The Singing Detective* at the end of 1986 showed 'it was not all trouble [at the BBC] ... After a slight stumble, the Television Service was back in its stride again.'[87]

The BBC had an instinctive interest in promoting *The Singing Detective* as a television event at the end of 1986. As suggested by the drama's pre-publicity and its prime-time BBC-1 scheduling, in seeking to uphold public service broadcasting in the face of external attack, the BBC elevated the hitherto 'controversial' Potter into a brand-name of 'quality', marketing him as an example of all that was distinctive about the Corporation. *The Singing Detective* was sold almost as a *Pennies from Heaven* Mark II. As with the December 1978 repeat of *Pennies*, it was positioned in the schedules to maximum advantage – November to December, at the peak of the autumn drama season – in an attempt to catch the eye of jurors, as they made up their nominations for the British Academy television awards the following spring.

Just as the BBC promoted it as a symbol of the public service ethos, so too did Potter market *The Singing Detective* quite aggressively via dozens of pre-transmission interviews, using the press to try and maximise the audience for the drama. By selling the work in this way, he almost inevitably, however, became forced into selling himself. Such a Faustian bargain is evident in the way that all of the media coverage hinged on one factor: the links between *The Singing Detective* and his own illness. Two weeks before the transmission of the first episode, the *Mail on Sunday* described how *The Singing Detective* was the first work 'in which Dennis Potter has revealed his illness'.[88] Similarly, in an article published two days before the transmission of Episode 1, Adam Mars-Jones of the *Independent* dwelt almost exclusively upon Potter's relationship with his illness and how 'anyone who has an illness more than fleetingly must form a relationship with it'.[89]

This blurring between the writer selling the work and the writer selling himself affected the way in which *The Singing Detective* was subsequently reviewed by the British press. Given the extent of the pre-publicity, Episode 1 was widely reviewed and, almost without exception, the critics were kind. Noticeably, however, and somewhat to the chagrin of the director, neither Amiel nor the quality of the production itself received much of a mention. Instead the focus was almost exclusively upon the figure of Potter 'the author' and his courage in supposedly unpeeling himself and his illness for all the world to see. Thus, Martin Cropper in *The Times*, 17 November 1986, wrote: 'Laughing to keeping from crying is one way of coping with a chronic medical condition such as psoriasis'.[90] Likewise, Christopher Dunkley wrote in the *Financial Times*: 'It is impossible to avoid the feeling that the writer is at last portraying himself directly in his work.'[91]

By the time the Forest adultery scene was transmitted in Episode 3, general press construction of *The Singing Detective* as autobiography had shifted to consideration of the ethics of depicting sexual intercourse on television. Predictably, a gap in attitudes opened up between the mass market tabloids and the 'high-brow' broadsheets. Libby Purves in *The*

Times launched into an intense discussion of the scene in terms of the relationship between mothers and sons, even quoting a psychotherapist 'who had found the programme true to many of his male patient's nightmares: "one of the most appalling things is for a boy child to see his mother being dominated and transported like this. Even by his father." '[92] Inevitably, the tabloids took a less angst-ridden, more sensationalist line: 'Storm Over The TV Sex Scenes in Potter's *Singing Detective*', ran the *Daily Express*, complete with a still from the scene 'which shocked viewers last night'.[93] Relishing the opportunity to condemn Potter and the BBC for 'shocking' their readers, the tabloids simply served to further their cause by maximising public interest in the drama. Prurience masquerading as condemnation, the tabloids' emotive headlines and publication of stills helped transform *The Singing Detective* from a television into a *bona fide* news event.

The result was that Potter's drama quickly became yet another political football for those on the Right who had already spent much of that autumn attacking the BBC. In response to Potter's defence that the adultery scene was part of 'a very old tradition' depicting the 'relationship between sex and death', Mary Whitehouse fuelled the controversy by retorting that 'to link sex with death and violence is an insult to sex'.[94] Questions about the sex scene even came to be asked in the House: Conservative MP Gerald Howarth (a keen supporter of legislation to bring broadcasting under the terms of the Obscene Publications Act) complained to the Commons that even within the context of drama, 'it was no part of public service broadcasting ... to put on the television explicit scenes of sexual intercourse. Why is it suddenly in 1986 that it becomes acceptable?'[95]

According to the director Jon Amiel, the final decision to screen the adultery scene had in fact been reached only after lengthy debate between himself and Director of BBC TV Programmes, Michael Grade, as to whether it was indeed 'acceptable' to broadcast. Because of the tight production schedule, post-production on Episode 3 had only been finally completed on the Thursday before its scheduled Sunday transmission of 30 November. On Friday the 28th, Grade met Amiel and the producers Trodd and Harris to view the scene in advance. Almost two hours were spent debating the pros and cons of broadcasting it uncut. Was there anything prurient, pornographic or gratuitous about the content which could not be justified in terms of the dramatic context and the writer's and director's intention that the scene be deliberately shocking in order to convey the extent of the central protagonist's shock? Should perhaps one or two seconds be cut from the Forest love-making sequence, to spare the distress of anxious viewers? After two hours of what Amiel describes as 'very vigorous' debate, Grade finally accepted the argument of the production team that to lessen or mediate the impact of this pivotal scene would undermine the entire dramatic sense of *The Singing Detective*. Amiel says of Grade: 'I commend him for that. I commend the process by which it was argued and finally in which he allowed it to go out.' Tellingly, in his statement to the press on the night of Episode 3's transmission, Grade defended his decision by stating: 'There are very few people in television drama that you are prepared to trust with scenes like this. But Dennis Potter is one of them'. Significantly, he added that critics were already hailing *The Singing Detective* 'as the best television drama of 1986'.[96]

Hence, if Grade knew the scene would create a fuss in the tabloids and amongst Tory MPs, he was also secure in the knowledge that criticism of his decision would be effectively neutralised by others in the media who were already singing the drama's praises – a classic example of the BBC employing its cherished notion of 'balance' in order to justify its own position on an issue. The Corporation would be able to defend itself from those who opposed the drama by pointing to the equal numbers in favour, thus bolstering its claim to be a neutral reflector rather than an active participant in events. Certainly, this is what the aftermath of the Episode Three screening suggests. If, as Amiel claims, the controversy over the sex scene was sucked into a much wider, 'carefully orchestrated campaign' by the tabloids to undermine the BBC in the name of the television ambitions of their own proprietors, this was counter-balanced by the eulogies of the TV critics in the British press. Even in the case of journalists in the tabloid press, this was true. Whilst excoriating the BBC and Potter for 'explicit sex in our living-rooms', the *Daily Mirror* could simultaneously hail the drama as 'undoubtedly brilliant television'.[97]

Such a schizophrenic quality – of critical praise yet rejection of its controversial nature in equal measure – continued on into the TV awards ceremonies the following year. *The Singing Detective* was nominated for no less than eleven British Academy Awards – including Best Drama Serial, Best Actor (Michael Gambon), Best Actress (Alison Steadman) – and was widely expected to sweep the board.[98] In the event, at the main ceremony on 22 March 1987, it picked up only one major award, that of Best Actor. Asked about BAFTA's decision to give the best serial award not to *The Singing Detective* but to a BBC adaptation of the Fay Weldon novel, *The Life and Loves of a She-Devil*, Jon Amiel simply states: 'In the year *Pennies from Heaven* was produced, BAFTA in its infinite wisdom gave the best serial award to *Edward and Mrs Simpson*. That explains the history of BAFTA awards.'[99] Despite the BBC's best efforts to schedule the drama to maximum advantage for the awards, BAFTA jurors had once again gone their own way.

Meanwhile, what of the attitude of the general public to the work? As

Potter attested in interview, in terms of simple ratings, *The Singing Detective* 'held its audience', averaging eight million viewers for the first three episodes – a total which then crept up to ten million, in the wake of the controversy over the sex scenes. On the most basic of empirical evidence, audiences seemed to remain gripped by the work and were able to cope with its non-linear multi-narrative complexity. At least in the case of the 1986 serial, Potter's democratic faith in the ability of television drama to cut across socio-economic hierarchies of class and education seemed to find some justification.

Though it is beyond the scope of this study to offer any detailed sociological evidence on audience attitudes to the drama, viewer reaction, as gauged by the *Radio Times*, is worthy of note. *The Singing Detective* produced one of the magazine's biggest mailbags, with letters on the drama still coming in months after the original transmissions. Predictably, most of the correspondence polarised around the debate about sexual explicitness on TV – those violently against, followed up by letters seeking to defend the BBC and Potter from this kind of attack. Some viewers found the drama 'extraordinary and compelling' in the sense that all of the elements – flashback, fantasy, thriller – combined 'to give the clearest impression ... of the way in which thought itself works.' Others found it 'fidgety, sadistic [and] semi-pornographic.'[100]

Regardless of like or dislike, what the volume of correspondence reveals is the drama's *impact* upon the cultural landscape of the British television audience. Constructed in pre-publicity as a television event, transformed into a news event by the tabloid headlines following Episode 3 and hailed by key opinion-formers as a 'masterpiece', audiences tuned in to *The Singing Detective* literally to see for themselves what all the fuss was about.[101] In so doing, they collaborated in the final stage of the process by which Potter's drama moved from production to reception, transforming it into a social event.[102]

The drama's undoubted impact upon audiences brought almost instant accolades for Potter. Just over a month after the last episode was transmitted, he became the subject of a BBC-2 *Arena* documentary which interviewed him about his life and work. Later that summer, a BBC retrospective of some of his past television plays culminated in the first television screening of the hitherto banned *Brimstone and Treacle* – a fact which appeared to owe much not only to the self-vindicating precedent of Michael Grade's 'permissiveness' over *The Singing Detective* sex scene but also to the enforced departure from the BBC earlier that year of the play's original censor, the Director-General, Alasdair Milne.[103]

Even more was to follow as Potter rode this post-*Singing Detective* wave of canonisation as television *auteur*. Just as the original *Pennies from Heaven* had been bought and transmitted by American PBS in the late seventies, so, too, in 1987 did the BBC succeed in selling *The Singing Detective* to public broadcasting stations in the USA. In New York, it was first aired in early 1988, somewhat tentatively by Channel 13 in an 11pm Thursday night 'graveyard' slot. The following July, however, it gained a repeat in a more prominent slot – at 9p.m. across three consecutive evenings: a scheduling decision which suddenly got Potter noticed in a very dramatic way. Having seen the work on TV, the film critic, Vincent Canby, launched into thousands of words in praise of it in a *New York Times* article that asked 'Is The Year's Best Film on TV?' He even compared the work in favourable terms to Welles's *Citizen Kane*.[104] This, however, was only the start of Potter's rehabilitation in the USA, after the partial decline in interest which had accompanied the box-office flop of the MGM *Pennies from Heaven*. Spurred on by Canby's ecstatic praise, twenty-three TV stations had bought the drama by October 1988. By November, it was on the front cover of the *New York Times Magazine*, fortified by Canby's quote that the work was 'Better than anything I've seen this year in the theatre (live or dead).' At the same time, those very theatres were beginning to take notice. In December, the Joseph Papp Public Theatre in Manhattan (which had previously screened *Dreamchild* to large audiences) decided to première *The Singing Detective* on the big screen, running all six episodes together as if they comprised one seven-hour-long movie. These weekly marathon screenings were so successful that an initial six-week run was extended to twenty sell-out performances, lasting right through to 23 April 1989. As a consequence, the Public Theatre was honoured with a D. W. Griffiths Award from the National Board of Review for its efforts in bringing the work to the big screen.[105]

As all of this suggests, Potter's work was reclaimed and promoted by Canby and others as a cinematic 'discovery' – a pearl fished out from the general cess-pool of television. If much of this confusion had to do with US cultural privileging of cinema over television (the feeling that any work as complex as Potter's must by definition have its true place in a medium other than television), at the same time, the rapturous reception given to *The Singing Detective* in New York and elsewhere seemed to indicate a largely unfulfilled American appetite for more 'demanding' material on TV. If this was the view in fashionable New York, Hollywood, too, began to take interest. After completing his first theatrical feature film, *Queen of Hearts*, in Britain in 1988, Jon Amiel was invited to the USA to direct *Aunt Julia and the Scriptwriter* (released 1990) and subsequently *Sommersby*, with Richard Gere and Jodie Foster (released 1992). Meanwhile, similar to Potter's experience with *Pennies*, the possibility of turning *The Singing Detective* into a Hollywood movie was mooted. Potter wrote an American screenplay version in 1990, though, to date, this has not yet been produced.[106]

The Singing Detective thus rehabilitated Potter in the eyes of Hollywood, investing him with the ability to have projects and ideas considered seriously in LA. Likewise, in Britain, as the retrospectives and interviews attested, the social event of the transmission of *The Singing Detective* marked Potter's transformation within media discourses from 'distinguished television playwright' into genuine 'television *auteur*': a fine distinction but one, nevertheless, with significant material effects.

Despite all the adulation, Potter, by 1988, had grown worried. As he asked during a guest appearance that year on Terry Wogan's chat show, how was he going to get away from *The Singing Detective*? Because it had reached so close into his own experiences 'in terms of health and background and so on', it had become 'potentially very dangerous' to his continuation as a writer. 'It threatens me now', he claimed.

Potter had already felt the inhibiting effects of *The Singing Detective*, prior even to its first British transmission. As an *Observer* profile of 'the author' recorded in December 1986, all through that year he had been afflicted with a writer's block – ever since *The Singing Detective* had started shooting. He blamed this on having created Marlow too much in his own image: 'Without planning it, I have got too close to something', he said.[107]

As in the relationship between author and character in *Hide and Seek*, Marlow, having been endowed with so many of the 'facts' of the writer's own life, had apparently slipped from Potter's control, almost without him realising it. In trying to create a character in his own image who would come across as 'true', this particular creation had got too close for comfort. He had become too larger than life; too 'real'. The self-referential notion of showing to audiences how a work could only be about itself and its writer had impelled Potter to create characters and situations ever closer to himself and his own experiences. The question he faced at the end of 1986 with *The Singing Detective* was whether having got, like the 'Author' in *Hide and Seek*, 'nearer and nearer to himself', he had not exhausted himself as a writer; literally using himself up.

As he suggested at the time, there was one hope, however, of clearing this writer's block that seemed to get more and more threatening as he watched each transmission of *The Singing Detective* during autumn 1986. At the end of the sixth episode, there was a violent dénouement. Perhaps this might finally crack the block. He hoped for more: 'My disease is to some extent psychosomatic and in finally exorcising Marlow, I hope that somehow I may leave my illness behind', he told the *Observer*.'[108] Just as with *Hide and Seek* where the 'Author' changed his own reality through the 'release' of the fictional Daniel Miller, so, too, was Potter apparently hoping that Marlow's recovery from illness would free him from his own. The traffic of biographical 'fact' into fiction which had so worried him with the creation of Marlow might become two-way, as in *Hide and Seek* – the recovery at the end of the fiction might translate itself into physical 'fact'. Like Marlow at the end of *The Singing Detective*, he could kill off his old sick self.

In the event, if the biological reality of illness proved more resistant to change than Potter had hoped, equally problematic was press and public reaction to the drama.[109] As Potter put it in interview, too many reviewers and commentators made the 'crude and philistine assumption' with *The Singing Detective* that Marlow was literally him. Seeing only the surface level of the 'fact', 'fiction', 'truth' distinctions which he had been trying to demonstrate by fictionalising details of his own life, critics had equated Marlow too easily and threateningly with the writer himself. Having played the press game of satisfying curiosity about the life of the 'author' in order to maximise audiences for the work, Potter was now in danger of being framed by the very media discourses which he had attempted to manipulate to his own advantage, condemned to be ever more the 'author of the autobiographical *Singing Detective*', with all the attendant dangers of a writing block that that entailed. Little wonder, as he put it to Wogan in 1988, that the Canby eulogies in the *New York Times* had left him feeling 'like a dead man'.

By Christmas of 1986, Potter's immediate solution to the problems presented by the British reception of *The Singing Detective* was to turn to writing a novel: *Blackeyes*, begun on Boxing Day, 1986. If this produced the much needed freeing of his writer's block, nevertheless, as the plaudits from the USA showed in 1988, exorcising the ghost of Marlow and *The Singing Detective* would prove altogether more difficult, perhaps even impossible. As Potter put it on the *Wogan* show that year, this was why he hoped the public reaction to two of his forthcoming works would be favourable: 'I hope *Track 29* works now. I hope *Christabel*, which is on BBC next, works. In other words, I've got to get away from *The Singing Detective*.'

Conclusion

Thus although the eighties had been good to Potter, they brought with them their own sets of problems. Thatcherism had transformed Britain into a much more market-orientated environment in which, as Potter rightly suggested, everything had become 'consumerist, including television'. The rise and rise of a tabloid press culture (which Potter had foreshadowed as early as *Paper Roses* in 1971) placed new demands upon a writer's dream of a 'common culture'. To get space for his work, Potter, in common with many writers in the eighties, had to market himself much more aggressively, often until the lines between publicity and self-publicity, writer and celebrity, became hopelessly crossed.

Already in place by the time of *The Singing Detective*, these 'consumerist' tendencies were only heightened by the impact, in 1987, of a third Conservative election victory under Margaret Thatcher, with such manifesto promises as a shake-up in broadcasting and the imposition upon the BBC of a quota which would compel it to take 25 per cent of its programmes from independent producers. The resulting Government White Paper on Broadcasting the following year only further demonstrated that the Corporation had to change with the times, if it was to engage with seemingly imminent deregulation of the television environment and domination of market forces.

As the fast-talking American producer, Rick McCallum (himself symbolic of this new more competitive era), expressed it in 1990:

> It's a whole new world now ... [the BBC] have got to get their house in order ... It has to be able to compete now ... Ten years ago Channel Four didn't exist – all the rest of the world was a different place ... plus the BBC fiscally has to get its act together ... Agents don't want to send a script to the BBC when they can send it to Channel Four, to ITV – Anglia, Granada – and they'll respect them just as much, let them do it just as much, give them more money to make the film ... Times are not only tough but they're competitive now.

The appointment as Head of BBC TV Drama in 1988 of Mark Shivas – a former BBC producer who had also worked as an independent feature film producer in the world outside – was one more symptom of the BBC's feeling that it had to adjust to the prospect of new, more competitive times. Changing the name of BBC Plays to BBC Films ('because we make more films than plays'), Shivas, by 1990, had moved the Corporation into a far firmer engagement with the world of feature film production outside, than had ever been the case before.[110] Gone were the days of the single studio play, epitomised by *Play for Today*; in were the one-off single films of *Screen One* and *Screen Two*. As these were more costly products, this meant the BBC could produce only twenty a year, with up to half a dozen films on 35mm, the rest on 16mm. All, however, were financed with the help of co-production money. For Potter, whose whole aesthetic had originally been founded on the 'non-naturalistic' studio drama, the effects of this change were undoubtedly disorientating: 'You spend your life on building a structure and suddenly the ground on which it rests is taken away', he told me in 1990.

On the other hand, the success of *The Singing Detective* had left him in a better position than most to exploit the changes. He was marketable: an international commodity to barter with. Nowhere was this more clearly reflected than in the rival claims of his two producers at this time for his attention and his work: Rick McCallum eventually succeeding in turning Potter's old *Track 29* script into a feature film in 1988; Kenith Trodd producing a four-part BBC serial, *Christabel*, that same year.

What both these works had in common was, similar to *Dreamchild* and *Late Call*, the centrality of a female protagonist and a feminine (even fem*inist*) perspective. If, as Potter suggested, all his 'work is about what goes on inside people's heads', then something of a shift took place during this period. A focus on 'what goes on inside a man's head' was replaced for a time by 'what goes on inside a woman's': a shift that as the next chapter will show, culminated in Potter's 1989 television serial (adapted from his 1987 novel), *Blackeyes*.[111]

Behind the scenes, however, a very male battle was taking place as the always uneasy relationship between Potter's two producers, McCallum and Trodd, finally began to crack apart. The following final chapter will trace the circumstances of that split which eventually led to the break-up of the partnership between Potter and his oldest friend and colleague, Kenith Trodd. This is detailed through (sometimes wildly diverging) first-hand accounts from all those involved; accounts which in one sense are symptomatic of the wider uncertainties that were current within BBC TV Drama at that time. As a result, far more than any previous chapter, Chapter 6 records a plurality of opinions and statements which are intended to reflect the uncertainties (and possibilities) of a period when a hitherto public service institution attempted to adapt to a more market-orientated environment – when getting 'the deal' often became more important than making the programme.

6

Living dolls: from *Track 29* to *Blackeyes*

'Young at heart': Rick McCallum and *Track 29*

Track 29 opened at the Lumière Cinema, St Martin's Lane, London on 5 August 1988. As Chapter 5 outlined, it had had a long history of production, having originally been intended as a BBC film under director Joseph Losey, until financial complications caused the dramatic collapse of the project, only days before shooting was due to start in August 1983.

Four years later, Potter and his movie producer, Rick McCallum, decided to have another go at filming the 1982 screenplay – this time, as an independent feature outside the BBC. Losey had died in 1984 but it seems the choice of director for the new version was never in doubt. Immediately prior to returning to *Track 29*, McCallum had produced *Castaway* for the eminent British director, Nic Roeg, and found it one of the most delightful of collaborations. As McCallum puts it: 'That thing was such a great experience for me ... I wanted, desperately, for Dennis to get into part of that because he had made a first step with Jon [Amiel on *The Singing Detective*] that was unlike any other collaboration I've ever seen.'[1] In common with most of Potter's produced screenplays, the script which Roeg was then given to read was essentially a reworking of material originally written by Potter for television – in this case his 1974 TV play, *Schmoedipus*. Like the play, the film revolves around a female protagonist who is trapped in a childless suburban marriage and frustrated by her husband's obsessive toy train hobby. One day, while he is out at work, she is apparently visited by a strange young man who claims to be the child she had some twenty years ago when, as a schoolgirl, she was seduced in a near-rape by a youth at a fairground.

With a more international audience clearly in mind for the film, Potter's screenplay moves the action from London to the USA and transforms the central protagonist into an American called Linda: a more 'attractively late thirtyish' (p. 3) version of Elizabeth, the central character of the TV play.[2] In another change, Elizabeth's husband, Tom, becomes Henry Hendry, a doctor who is carrying on an affair with one of his nurses at the local clinic.

This culminates in an illicit trip he makes to a convention of toy train enthusiasts, at which he gives a comically evangelical address that ends with the entire gathering miming to Glenn Miller's 'Chattanooga Choo Choo'; its chorus providing the title of the film: 'Yes! Yes! Track Twenty-nine!' (p. 68). Meanwhile, Glen, the visitor from Canada in *Schmoedipus*, is transformed into Martin, an Englishman who tells Linda he has hitch-hiked 'across the pond in search of [his] mama' (p. 14). (In a clear borrowing from Martin 'the Devil' in *Brimstone*, he is described in the original script as 'demonic' and 'satanic', with a breath of 'sulferous [*sic*] hatred' (p. 5)).

While interior locations still predominate in *Track 29*, the domestic confines of the studio-bound television play are transcended through the use of American highway landscape exteriors, as well as flashbacks to Linda's fairground seduction/rape by a 'Martin look-alike' who sports a 'MOTHER' tattoo across his chest. Recurring at key moments throughout the film, these make *explicit* what was only *implicit* in Elizabeth Carter's climactic speech at the close of the TV play (see Chapter 2).

This is also true of the central relationship between Linda and her 'son' Martin, where the connotations of incest of the earlier play are heightened and made explicit in the film version. While Glen in *Schmoedipus* only asked breathlessly if Elizabeth ever breast-fed him as a baby ('Wow! I wish – I could remember'),[3] Martin in *Track 29* is far more daring. The script describes how, at one point, he pinions Linda with 'his knees, raunchily', while later, lying on top of her, 'he kisses her passionately' (p. 16).

Roeg read this film version and liked it, choosing to shoot from Potter's original 1982 screenplay rather than ask for a rewritten script. After a long period in which McCallum scoured the world for funds, finance for the project was finally secured from Handmade Films in Britain. The resulting $5 million movie began shooting on location in the USA in the summer of 1987, with a cast that included Gary Oldman as Martin, Christopher Lloyd as Henry plus Roeg's wife and regular lead in his films, Theresa Russell, in the central role of Linda Hendry.

To McCallum, out on location as both producer and production manager, it seemed full creative freedom was being enjoyed on the project in the absence of Handmade's two executive producers: George Harrison and Denis O'Brien. Despite his credit on the film, Harrison, the ex-Beatle, had no involvement at all in *Track 29*, McCallum claims. O'Brien, however, appeared more supportive, sending out many telexes to the cast and crew, indicating his love for the project.

When it came time to show him the final film, things became different. As McCallum explains, Handmade had concluded the deal for *Track 29* very quickly. On delivery of the film, it soon became clear that the company had not realised when it originally agreed financial backing that this was a movie with an 'incest' theme. McCallum has his own opinions on how such an apparently astonishing gaffe could have happened:

> Denis O'Brien ... is a businessman, he's a banker ... And he sees films as part of a portfolio – you know, the certain 'blue chip' films and the certain 'high risk' films ... But he was jet-lagged when he read the script ... He had literally come in on a Monday morning; had to have read it Monday because I was meeting with him on Tuesday to do the deal ... And you get into a lot of things with these guys and you think ... they control millions of dollars, they can't behave in such unprofessional ways. But they do, thank God they do!

McCallum's guerilla tactics had succeeded in getting backing for a very 'high risk' film but only finally to find himself locked into a battle with Handmade over its release. Despite the company's reputation for novelty and eccentricity, incest was apparently just too 'dangerous' a subject for Handmade to handle. O'Brien threatened not to release the movie unless cuts were made and it was only the intervention of Potter which finally saved the day. As McCallum recalls, Potter suggested that cuts be made but only certain cuts that would allow the incest theme to remain in the movie and perhaps even be heightened. In this way, the sequence described in the original screenplay where Martin pinions Linda in her bedroom 'with his knees raunchily' was edited out of the final film but the passionate on-screen kiss left in. As McCallum puts it, the process was like a 'negotiation' in which O'Brien thought he had won by getting the film-makers to acquiesce to cuts but where the film-makers themselves managed to retain the 'explosive' incest theme they had wanted all along.

After a delay, the picture finally opened in London in August and in Los Angeles in September 1988, mostly to good reviews. Some critics loved it. Margaret Walters of the *Listener* described it as having 'more zip and extravagant comic energy than any British film in years'.[4] At the box office, however, it did little business. As McCallum states, all his 'independent' film work with Potter had this one thing in common: while being relentlessly uncompromising in artistic terms and hence often a critical success, financially all the films were unsuccessful. He states: 'Between Dennis and I we've probably come close to losing $100 million. On one level I'm very proud of it in terms of guerilla independent film-making but as a lifestyle it's fucking appalling, I can tell you!'

In much the same way, when film critics have considered *Track 29*, they have tended to focus upon the uncompromising nature of its two acclaimed British *auteurs*, Roeg and Potter, and whether their conjunction on the same project was a collaboration or simply a collision of different *oeuvres*.[5] Adam Barker in *Monthly Film Bulletin* has argued the latter. Whereas Potter's is a dynamic, psychoanalytic kind of drama, he suggests the films of Nic Roeg create a world in which nothing makes sense except at the level of 'formal relations established within the film itself, which are abstract, objective relations between shapes, colours and incidents rather than subjectively motivated, psychological connections'.[6]

McCallum, who has worked with Roeg on three films to date, agrees: 'That's where Nic is brilliant', he states. 'Taking random events and putting them altogether.' He suggests that that is all Roeg ever looks for in his work: 'It may have no connective tissue immediately but he finds one in the film.' If the director's world is one where coincidence rules, then clearly this is why he would be attracted to the *Track 29* script, with its apparent coincidence of Martin the Englishman who bears an uncanny resemblance to Linda's fairground seducer of long ago.

What of Potter? Like *Schmoedipus* and much of his other work, *Track 29* makes 'subjectively motivated, psychological connections'. As with the earlier play, the film finally makes it clear that Martin is a projection of Linda's own tormented psyche. He is her 'dreamchild', returned to liberate her from an infantile childless marriage (as symbolised by her husband's obsession with toy trains). The difference from *Schmoedipus* is that while the earlier play ended as anxiously as it began with the return of husband Tom and a general retreat of the couple into a deluded infantilism, *Track 29* offers its female protagonist the possibility of liberation from this domestic prison.

In a substantial revision of the TV play, *Track 29* ends with the murder of Linda's husband who is stabbed by Martin, significantly with Linda's own kitchen knife. If Linda is freed by this, the film at its close makes clear that the murder has been not real but imaginary. After the audience has seen Martin stab Henry, the latter is still heard, apparently alive and well, calling to Linda from the room in which he has been playing with his toy trains. Meanwhile, immaculate for the first time in a white fifties style suit, Linda calmly packs her luggage into the back of her convertible and drives off, leaving Henry still calling, as Rosemary Clooney's version of 'Young At Heart' plays on the soundtrack.

The message is the same as *Dreamchild* and *The Singing Detective* and confirms the progression to optimism which previous chapters traced in Potter's writing from the mid seventies onwards. In contrast to the stalemate ending of *Schmoedipus*, *Track 29* suggests that psychological redemption from past trauma is possible but only, as the song says, if you become 'Young At Heart' and get 'in touch with your younger self' by confronting that past. Ironically, escape from the infantilism of grown-up life (as symbolised by Henry's toy trains) comes for Linda by recapturing the 'wonder' of being a child again, through the child-like development of a rich imaginative life. In *Track 29*, she fantasises a 'dreamchild' who will be a 'devil' and murder Henry. Akin to his namesake in *Brimstone*, Martin's apparently evil act brings a greater good. In the 1988 film, as opposed to the 1974 TV play, 'the outsider knocking on her door' functions as a dynamic agent of psychological healing for Linda who, like Philip Marlow in *The Singing Detective*, cures herself through her own imagination, freeing herself to become 'the Author of her own Fate' at last.

In terms of narrative coherence, the film leavens this moral with ambiguity, however, for under Nicolas Roeg's direction, the audience is teased right to the very end. As the 'Young At Heart' melody starts up, the camera begins a slow zoom to the ceiling of the ground floor lounge in the Hendry house. There, a blood stain is picked out, slowly spreading over a spot which the audience knows is directly below Henry's toy train room upstairs. Could it be that Martin is real, and if so did he really kill Henry? Or perhaps it was Linda? Is it all *really* her fantasy? If Potter's script emphasises imaginative liberation, Roeg's direction attempts to resist any definitive reading. As critic Richard Combs has put it, this is a common feature of Roeg's cinema:

> The theme of nothing is what it seems but also the way visual patterns and correspondences don't just reveal but stand in for psychological reality, creating a reality of their own (the slow zoom into the blood stain at the end has an autonomous force, independent of any question as to whether Martin has 'really' killed Linda's husband).[7]

With all of Potter's work revolving around 'what goes on inside people's heads' while Roeg's interest lay in the 'formal relations within the film itself', it is therefore possible to argue a 'collision' of *oeuvres*. Perhaps, however, for a film with such apparently 'explosive' subject matter as *Track 29*, that was no bad thing.

Casualties of War: Kenith Trodd and *Christabel*

While Rick McCallum was fighting battles in 1988 over the release of *Track 29*, Kenith Trodd was busily engaged on his own pet project, based upon a Potter script. Unusually for Potter, *Christabel* fictionalised the experiences of individuals still living. Based upon Christabel Bielenberg's 1968 autobiography *The Past Is Myself*, the drama tells the story of an upper class 'English rose' who married a German lawyer, Peter, in 1934, only to find herself living through the whole of the Second World War in Nazi Germany. This included her husband's arrest and detention in

Ravensbrück Concentration Camp as a result of his links with a failed German resistance plot to assassinate Hitler. Her subsequent bravery in securing his release culminated in an extraordinary episode in which she volunteered to be questioned by the Gestapo.

As we have consistently seen, Potter was always adept at drawing his material from any number of sources – real-life incident, historical detail, his own life and past work, even the Gospels – reworking it into a potent vehicle for personal expression and/or exploration. *Christabel*, too, can be seen in this light but it also has to be related to Potter's 'new entrepreneurism' period of the early eighties, when, flush with money from his lucrative Hollywood ventures, he bought an option on *The Past Is Myself* after reading a review of it in the *Economist*. The superlatives of that review give a clue to his interest in the material. The autobiography was praised as 'a magnificent contribution to international understanding and as a document of how the human spirit can triumph in the midst of evil and persecution'.[8]

Originally, Potter's plan had been to turn the book into a movie, under producer Rick McCallum. The financiers of *Dreamchild*, EMI Films, were offered the material but, as McCallum recalls, problems arose from the deal that Potter had got himself locked into with his real-life subjects which prevented much dramatic licence being taken with their story. The writer had been by no means the first to approach the Bielenbergs with the offer of a film deal. Various companies had tried in the past to buy the rights but had always been refused on account of their desire to 'sex' the book up – by having Christabel have an affair in the film and so on. Potter managed to persuade the Bielenbergs that he would do an honest, fairly literal job with the script and indeed granted them consultation rights on the project.[9] It was this which limited the story's box-office appeal to McCallum. When EMI Films collapsed, he lost interest in the *Christabel* project and the story went instead to the BBC and Kenith Trodd as a four-part serial for television.[10]

Hence, initially attracted by a powerful *Singing Detective*-like story of the triumph of the human spirit against all odds, Potter was unable, because of the agreement with his real subjects, to transform his fact-based material into a non-naturalistic 'Dennis Potter work' along the lines of a *Dreamchild* or *Casanova*. This is not to say that, unfettered by contractual obligations, he would have wished to write *Christabel* in such a way. He later maintained there was 'a deeper need for me to do a piece of naturalistic chronological narrative as an act of writerly hygiene, just as you might wash your brain under a tap.' Clearly, however, he was deprived of a rather important option, a familiar way of proceeding, as he himself conceded: 'I felt it hard to write, actually, because there was a real person out there who had the right to comment on the script … and because I didn't want to intrude in any way with my own box of tricks.' Instead, he endeavoured to make each scene 'a bit like a soap but full of reality and economy'.[11]

Nevertheless, while forsaking his familiar 'box of non-naturalistic tricks' in favour of dramatising the book into a series of pared-down episodes which are relayed naturalistically, Potter has still filtered the factual source material through his own imagination. Christabel's autobiography is reworked into a fictional form consistent with the mythic pattern of his own *The Singing Detective*: namely, the emotional journey of a central protagonist from darkness to light, despair to hope.

This is best illustrated by the climactic scenes in Episode 4 when Christabel is interrogated by the Gestapo. In her autobiography, she describes how, during her visit to Ravensbrück Concentration Camp where her husband was being held, she received a smuggled note from him, outlining the story he was sticking to under interrogation with regard to the failed plot against Hitler. Later, she wondered 'Why did he give me that note?', until it dawned on her – 'Of course … Peter had given me the message in case I should be interrogated – our evidence must tally.'[12] This is why she subsequently *volunteered* to be interrogated by the Gestapo, sensing a means to free her husband from suspicion by matching her testimony to his.

In Potter's version, however, Christabel is given no note by Peter. Indeed her encounter with the Gestapo immediately *precedes* the visit to her husband. In terms of narrative logic, the opportunity to see him comes as a reward for her confronting 'the heart of Gestapo darkness' single-handedly. Moreover, just as Philip Marlow overcame his particular 'darkness' in *The Singing Detective*, imagination is demonstrated to be the key to survival and eventual liberation. Unlike the original book, Potter has a female friend of Christabel's tell her, prior to the interrogation: 'Say anything! Promise anything! It's your only chance.'[13] As a result, she mentions to the Gestapo, in *faux-naïf* fashion, that Winston Churchill is a friend of her family, remembering her friend Lexi's advice that with German surrender imminent, 'some of the rats have enough sense to be frightened out of their filthy skins'.[14]

As with *The Singing Detective*, fiction (or 'lies') is therefore highlighted as the key to individual liberation. In contrast to the autobiography, it is also important to note that it is a liberation achieved wholly by female initiative and bravery (Christabel and Lexi) with no male help (no note from Peter). Like *Track 29* a year before, it may be no exaggeration to see *Christabel* as a quasi-feminist reworking of the narrative trajectory of *The Singing Detective*. This may explain, too, why, despite the apparent literalism of treatment, Potter's scripts were finally credited in the TV serial as not 'adapted from' but 'based on' *The Past Is Myself*.

Nevertheless, Potter was unhappy about the way *Christabel* eventually turned out, as many of those who worked on the production confirm. The drama's sound recordist Peter Edwards states: 'Dennis didn't like *Christabel*. He wanted nothing to do with it really towards the end ... His criticism was it wasn't flexibly shot.'[15] Similarly, its film editor, Clare Douglas, claims Potter's hatred of *Christabel* was one of the reasons he decided to direct *Blackeyes* the following year. It was shot very conventionally by director Adrian Shergold, and, Douglas asserts, very little of 'the feeling of menace in Nazi Germany' which Potter's scripts had evoked found its way on to film.[16]

As noted with regard to his involvement on *The Singing Detective*, Kenith Trodd, however, had been extremely keen to make *Christabel* and in pre-publicity, he was able to endorse it enthusiastically, hailing this 'faction' as a 'breakthrough' for Dennis Potter.[17] Certainly, in terms of pure ratings, it seemed to be Trodd's not Potter's view of *Christabel* which prevailed when the drama was transmitted on BBC-2 between 16 November and 7 December 1988. If many newspaper reviewers regarded it as deeply disappointing in terms of Potter's reputation for complex non-linear narratives ('Dennis Potter's War Drama Fails To Ignite' ran one headline), each of *Christabel*'s four episodes topped BBC-2's ratings with an average audience of seven and a half million – very high for a drama serial on BBC TV's minority channel.[18] With Potter, however, preparing for the first time to direct his next production and disdaining to engage in substantial pre-publicity for *Christabel*, a drama he would later deem a 'mistake', there can be no doubt, as Clare Douglas states, that Trodd 'knew Dennis hated *Christabel* and was very upset that he hated *Christabel*'.[19] There is no doubt either that these animosities spilled over into the production of what was Potter's own pet project: *Blackeyes*.

Blackeyes

'Too many producers ...'

As we have seen over many chapters, Kenith Trodd had always been the figure most associated with the production of Potter's work. In January 1989, however, this erstwhile friend was to find himself unceremoniously axed from the production of *Blackeyes*. In the course of a personal interview, Trodd provided a detailed account of this extraordinary, apparent end to what had hitherto seemed one of the most successful creative partnerships in British television.

On 14 December 1988, Michael Grade, the recently appointed Chief Executive of Channel Four, announced to the press that he had pulled off 'a major coup' by signing up two of Britain's top television writers, Alan Bleasdale and Dennis Potter. Potter, he indicated, was writing a six-part serial for Channel Four called *Lipstick on Your Collar*, which was going to be 'a partly autobiographical picture of post-war Britain from the 1950s onwards'.[20]

Trodd was furious since he claims this was a project which he and Potter had been developing, first as a movie and then as a six-part serial for the BBC. No one had told him about any Channel Four deal. He felt betrayed and impulsively decided to resign from the *Blackeyes* production, protesting that the arrangement between himself and Rick McCallum, whereby both were sharing production duties on Potter's work, was simply not working.

Despite the fact that, as he put it, 'all ... on the show' (bar Potter and McCallum) urged him not to go, Trodd then resigned from the production, though later over the Christmas period, he claims he and Potter made up their differences so that things were 'kind of going to be alright again'. In the New Year, however, on returning from Los Angeles where he had been promoting *Christabel*, he was subsequently to discover production on *Blackeyes* had been moved from his office at BBC Television Centre, McCallum having renegotiated his BBC contract in order to assume the role of sole producer.

As Trodd saw it, a 'coup' had been staged – one in relation to which he could find no support from the Head of BBC TV Drama, Mark Shivas. He also asserts that during the course of the next fortnight, following his return from Los Angeles, he had several phone conversations with Potter which were the worst he had ever had with anybody: 'They were just horrible and [so] that was that.'

As Trodd later discovered to his annoyance, the irony of the whole affair was that Grade's announcement which had sparked off the dispute had been distinctly premature since neither Potter nor McCallum had at that point signed any deal with Channel Four. Trodd states he should have known on the basis of his previous experience of Grade at LWT, that the *Lipstick* announcement was a characteristically self-publicising gesture on the part of the executive, as he tried to consolidate his presence at Channel Four. According to Trodd, Grade 'will do anything to get in tomorrow's papers'.

Both Potter and McCallum portray events in a somewhat different light to Trodd. For them, their negotiations with Channel Four were no betrayal of Trodd, simply good business and none of his. They also deny his claim that he 'made it up' with Potter over the Christmas period of 1988. According to Potter:

Michael Grade made this premature [announcement] ... and he resigned – I mean he's a resigner is Ken. He resigned ... and then Mark Shivas said don't resign, you know, and I said don't resign. He didn't talk to me *at all* so we had no row, nothing and then he finally withdrew his resignation and Mark wouldn't let him. It was as simple as that.[21]

For his part, Mark Shivas asserts he did not allow Trodd back on to *Blackeyes* because having two producers on it was proving 'unproductive'.[22] Clearly, behind the specifics of the *Lipstick* dispute lay a much deeper source of friction in Trodd and Potter's relationship, stemming from the latter's decision earlier in the decade to involve Rick McCallum in the production of his work. McCallum has no doubts why Potter hired him, claiming that while Trodd satisfied Potter's needs within the BBC, he was completely at sea in the outside world of independent production: a world of deals and the movement of money. Potter echoed this: 'The other thing about Ken is that he doesn't know anything about film, movies, money, structures, all those things a producer is – I mean he wouldn't exist outside the BBC.' A BBC producer, Potter stated, is basically 'a story editor'.[23]

Trodd would clearly deny he cannot function 'outside the BBC'. As Chapter 2 made clear, long before the advent of Channel Four, he helped form Kestrel in the late sixties – one of the first British independent production companies. Also, besides his credits on the Potter movies *Brimstone and Treacle* and *Dreamchild*, he produced the feature film *A Month in the Country* for Channel Four and PFH Limited in the mid eighties. Calling himself an 'independent' within the BBC, Trodd retorts that McCallum is a 'line producer' who is good at dealing with budgets and logistics: 'the end ... which I am not particularly interested in and which, if you've worked in institutional television, you haven't had to be'. Potter's original production ideal of having McCallum handle budgets whilst retaining Trodd for the 'creative rub of ideas' proved to be wrong, the latter states: 'It was like a writer writing a script ... It wasn't actually ... taking into account the inevitable rivalries, jealousies and conflicts that would ... arise between those two people.'

In addition to the arrival of McCallum on the scene, there was one other major source of strain on the Potter–Trodd relationship which had been building throughout the eighties and which finally came to a head on the *Blackeyes* production. This was Potter's growing desire to direct his own work – a desire which Trodd was clearly unhappy about and yet one which in many ways was a reaction to his own increasingly successful campaign of the seventies and eighties to have TV drama made on film as opposed to recorded in the electronic studio. In marked contrast to Trodd's rampant enthusiasm, Potter worried about the disappearance of studio drama and the rise of the BBC film, fearing television would become a director's medium with no place for the writer (see Chapter 5).

'A self-defensive structure' is therefore how Potter described his move from writer to writer-director on *Blackeyes*; an attempt to prevent the 'appropriation', as he saw it, of his work by directors.[24] Though the writer's reaction to *Christabel* undoubtedly contributed to the move, Trodd believes the idea of Potter as director had been on the cards for some time. As long ago as the writer's unusual casting suggestions for *Pennies from Heaven*, the producer knew directing would someday have to happen (see Chapter 4). It was not a prospect he relished. Despite his attempts to provide Potter with the best that was available in terms of production values and personnel, the writer, he felt, was still 'in a mean way' dissatisfied, believing there was something not being realised in his work. 'What it was that was missing', Trodd states, 'I don't know.'

It was during the mid-eighties, when the writer's fear of 'director power' had reached a peak, that Trodd first remembers Potter explicitly voicing a desire to direct his own work. This surfaced in the wake of the tensions surrounding the production of *Dreamchild* and soon became concretised around the notion of the writer directing the screen version of his own stage play, *Sufficient Carbohydrate*. According to Trodd:

> The ... idea was that Dennis would direct that because I had always envisaged that if we gave him the opportunity it would be in those rather limited, protective conditions: i.e. small cast, virtually one location, BBC-2, if it died it wouldn't matter that much and you know, there wouldn't be that much pressure on him.[25]

Potter, however, was later to claim that Trodd sacked him from the production which originally he was going to direct in the autumn of 1985 under the title *All of You*.[26] It was instead 'postponed', resurfacing a year later under Trodd, with a new title, *Visitors*, and a different director, Piers Haggard. Whilst agreeing that he and Potter fell out wildly over *Visitors* (tx. BBC-2 22.2.87), Trodd's version is that co-production money for the project simply fell through and so it could not be made. The following year, when funds became available, Potter was either 'ill again or writing ... or both' and so was not able to direct it. As a result, Trodd offered the material to Haggard and hence the 'opportunity had passed for Dennis to direct.' The next the producer knew was a year later when, out of very different circumstances, Potter suddenly decided he would direct the much bigger project of *Blackeyes*.

According to the producer, the different circumstances which pushed Potter into directing were simply that no other suitable director for *Blackeyes* could be found. Jon Amiel was offered the material but for straightforward career reasons turned it down, stating he did not want to work in television and direct another serial, even for Potter. Meanwhile, as Rick McCallum confirms, Nic Roeg, fresh from the *Track 29* collaboration, was offered the material but also turned it down, claiming it was not 'the way he looked at women'. Roeg replied that the vision in *Blackeyes* was so personal that only the writer should direct it. It was 'actually Nic's enthusiasm that pushed Dennis over into directing', McCallum asserts.

Thus one can see how far apart Trodd had grown from both Potter and McCallum on the issue of the writer directing *Blackeyes*: to Trodd, it was because no one else would do it; to McCallum, it was a matter of extending the individual artist's freedom of personal expression. What is also evident is that both Potter's desire to direct and the hiring of McCallum were reactions against an increasingly competitive environment outside, yet also within the BBC Drama Department in the age of the 'independent' producer, drama on film and the international co-production. As Potter affirmed in interview, production manoeuvres such as directing or becoming executive producer of his own work were simply attempts to 'take charge' in what he perceived to be 'an increasingly hostile environment' for his type of work. Ultimately, this was leading to a more intense search for 'the perfect deal' that would be both financially rewarding and provide the optimum production environment for his work.

In terms of TV, if that meant abandoning the BBC for a spell and Kenith Trodd, then so be it. By 1988 and the invitation to work for Channel Four, it seems Potter had to find a project quickly in order to negotiate a deal with Grade. The result was *Lipstick On Your Collar*, regardless of whose feathers it ruffled. As Rick McCallum crudely puts it, when 'a kind of window opens up, ... you've to got to make a deal before that window closes or you're fucked'. In this much more competitive environment, with its emphasis on the 'brand name' artist and the quick deal, the need for what Potter and McCallum term a 'story editor' producer had become increasingly redundant. When Trodd resigned from *Blackeyes*, he was perhaps only conceding a battle which, in the course of the previous decade, had long been lost.[27]

Sources

Blackeyes was transmitted as a four-part television serial on BBC-2 between 29 November and 20 December 1989.[28] The most immediate source of inspiration for Potter's scripts was his third novel of the same name, first published in Britain by Faber and Faber on 28 September 1987.

As the writer attested in interview, he had written *Blackeyes* as a novel as part of a deliberate attempt to escape from the enormous success of *The Singing Detective* which had begun to threaten him as a writer, since audiences were making 'the crude and philistine assumption' that the central protagonist, the misanthropic and misogynistic Philip Marlow, was in fact Potter himself. Written quickly during the winter of 1986–87 (from Boxing Day to St Valentine's Day) the *Blackeyes* novel can be seen as both a general exploration of man's inhumanity to women and an attempt by Potter to confront head-on the issue of his own treatment of women in previous work.

The plot itself is a demonstration of the not always straightforward connections between life and art. Maurice James Kingsley, an ageing half-forgotten literary roué, 'steals' his beautiful niece Jessica's account of her exploitation as a professional model, embroidering it into a sexy best-seller about the character of Blackeyes, a standard male fantasy figure who becomes a successful model, only to end up taking her own life by drowning herself in the Round Pond in Kensington Gardens: a passive victim of all the men who have used her. Thoroughly intertextual, Potter's novel mixes Kingsley's account of Blackeyes' rise and fall with description of Jessica's angry attempt to 'rewrite' Kingsley's book (*Sugar Bush*) and so reverse Blackeyes' fate and by implication her own and those of all women abused by men. Woven into this narrative tapestry are flashbacks to Jessica's childhood which gradually reveal that she was sexually molested by 'Uncle Maurice'. These are juxtaposed with a satiric account of an interview given by Kingsley to a self-professed New Journalist from *Kritz* magazine. As the narrative progresses, the reader is also gradually made aware that yet another man is trying to break into Jessica's narrative (and her life): someone who has been watching her from the mews flat opposite in a kind of Hitchcockian *Rear Window* scenario. By chapter 23 (of thirty-one in the novel), he feels able to step out from behind the narrative, with an omniscient 'I':

> It ill becomes the present writer to make snide remarks about his elderly colleague, for I have used the old fellow's narrative as the basis of my own account …
>
> Jessica, trying to do the same thing, was not up to it. (p. 135)

Although the novel never explicitly makes the connection, it becomes clear, through juxtaposition, that this 'other writer' is Jeff, the male hero of Kingsley's narrative: an advertising copywriter who has been trying to woo Blackeyes. Like the mysterious men in *The Singing Detective*, he functions as a kind of floating signifier in *Blackeyes*, having the apparent ability to cross over from Kingsley's prose into 'reality' as another would-be novelist who is also rewriting *Sugar Bush*. Though this writer appears to be a 'New Man' sensitive to women's needs, the last chapter of *Blackeyes* warns the reader of the gap between truth and illusion.

In this final chapter, Jessica, having invited her uncle to her flat for dinner, murders Kingsley by stabbing him with her stiletto heel. Then, in the dead of night, she drags him outside and buries him in her backyard. 'Rewriting was painful but now she had stepped forward into genuine first-order creation' (p. 183), the narrative states, as Jessica makes her way to the Round Pond of Kensington Gardens, just as Blackeyes had done at the end of Kingsley's novel. If, by this act, Jessica believes she has become the 'Author of her Fate' and escaped the clutches of men, the final paragraph reminds the reader that yet another male 'Author' is lurking in the narrative; one who, like Kingsley and all the others, is intent on appropriating both Jessica/Blackeyes and her story for his own ends. This is made clear in the very last sentence: 'As her lungs filled, she had the satisfaction of knowing that Blackeyes was free. Well, sort of free, anyway, for it is me that is waiting outside her door, ready to claim her' (p. 185).

Clearly, even before its transformation to screen, *Blackeyes* was a complex narrative. Akin to *The Singing Detective*, it conforms, however, to a basic *noir* narrative structure: a male investigation into disruptive female sexuality which is here focused around several male authors' attempts to 'know' the enigmatic Blackeyes. Jessica's rewrite of Kingsley's novel even deploys a stereotypical hard-boiled investigator: the cynical Inspector Blake who, suspecting there has been foul play in Blackeyes' death, goes hot on the trail of her male 'killers' and becomes obsessed by the dead girl.

Also like *The Singing Detective* is the way in which 'disruptive' female sexuality is eliminated within one of the narrative strands – through death by drowning. Kingsley's novel within the novel ends:

> The water came over her shining boots, swallowed up her knees and long thighs, and then made a line around the naked swell of her belly. In next to no time, there was nothing but her head to be seen and then a few strands of floating black hair and soon she was completely submerged, with no sign of fuss or struggle. Whatever traces she may have made on the lives of others, this girl, she had gone now without a ripple. The water smoothed itself flat and reflected back the sky. (p. 8)

Just as in the 'pulp thriller' strand of *The Singing Detective*, patriarchal order can only be restored in Kingsley's narrative by the complete submergence of the woman with no 'fuss or struggle'. As Christine Gledhill has observed, however, one of the delineating features of the *noir* style is 'the heroine's resistance to the male control of her story'. Feminist interest resides in the general 'proliferation of points of view and struggle within the text for one viewpoint to gain hegemony'.[29]

Potter, too, was clearly aware of these possibilities. In *Blackeyes*, Jessica attempts to rewrite Kingsley's male narrative, resisting his convenient portrayal of Blackeyes as a passive suicide victim by inventing Blake as an agent of retribution. The detective's task is to prove that someone else (some man) gave her 'a helping hand' (p. 15). As the investigation narrative proceeds, however, it becomes obvious that, as in *The Singing Detective*, the real culprit of the story is its own ageing misogynist author. Given that the narrative logic of thrillers always dictates the villain must be unmasked and eliminated for there to be any kind of resolution, the child abuser Kingsley therefore has to be killed at the end of the novel, just as the hospitalised Marlow had to be dispatched at the end of *The Singing Detective*. At the same time, Kingsley's death at the hands (or heel) of a woman, driven mad by jealousy and loathing, conforms to a typical *noir* stereotype: that of the 'unstable', 'treacherous' heroine whom it is the task of the male investigation narrative to bring under control.

The last paragraph of the *Blackeyes* novel achieves just this. Jessica goes to her death, believing she and Blackeyes have achieved 'autonomous identity' (p. 63). She has rewritten the second last paragraph of Kingsley's novel in order to ensure that by his murder both she and Blackeyes do not sink without a 'ripple' (p. 184). Achieving such negative, oppositional power to male control within the narrative does not, however, mean Jessica's viewpoint has gained hegemony, for to be true to the typical trajectory of the *noir* narrative (a narrative constructed by men), such a struggle of viewpoints must always end in a reaffirmation of patriarchal power and the inevitable male master 'waiting outside her door, ready to claim her'. Indeed the last sentence of Potter's novel hints that it can be no other way for Jessica/Blackeyes, whether in terms of art or even religion. If, as earlier works such as *Follow the Yellow Brick Road* and *Hide and Seek* sought to show, the 'God of Creation' is like a writer then, in dying, Jessica/Blackeyes has been 'claimed' by the ultimate male Author. Conversely, if, as those works also showed, a writer is like the 'God of Creation', then it is impossible for Jessica to escape the ultimate male 'Author' in *Blackeyes*: one who in the very last sentence both acknowledges his gender and foregrounds his anxieties that inevitably, too, he has 'stolen' like Kingsley and Jeff; appropriating feminist discourses for his own male ends.

Besides the general influence of the *roman noir*, other more specific sources suggest themselves for *Blackeyes*. The novel itself helpfully yields these, when Jessica is described at one point taking Kingsley's novel down 'from the shelf where it was sandwiched between a novel called *Laughter in the Dark* and another volume in fierce black and red covers called *The Myth of Women's Masochism* which she had only recently purchased' (p. 154).

The former is Vladimir Nabokov's first novel to be translated into English. Like his more famous *Lolita*, it concerns itself with a middle-aged man – a prosperous Berlin art dealer – and his obsession with a 'nymphet', in this case a 17-year-old cinema usherette called Margot Peters. First encountering her at a movie house, he embarks on a scandalous affair which brings him financial ruin, blindness and eventual death, when, at the close of the novel and after a grim struggle, Margot kills him with his own revolver.

Published fifty years after Nabokov's novel, *The Myth of Women's Masochism* by American feminist Paula J. Kaplan is an attempt to explode the myth that women are inherently masochistic. Kaplan asserts that on the contrary, the ' "Masochian" woman is the construct of a male imagination and acts in accordance with some men's fantasies; such men wish for women who would suffer for them.'[30] Examining the pervasiveness of this myth in various aspects of women's everyday lives, the book ends on a somewhat ominous note by suggesting that if women could understand how much of their behaviour has been misinterpreted as masochistic 'then we will be better able to search for the *real* sources of our suffering and begin to cleanse them from our lives.'[31]

The reference to these texts within Potter's own *Blackeyes* seems clear, for they both deal in contrasting ways with a related pair of male misogynist myths: the sadistic and the masochistic woman. Significantly, Kingsley's novel is 'sandwiched' between the two in Jessica's library, perhaps illustrating that both myths belong to the same lecherous male fantasy. In turn, the influence of these very different books provides Potter's novel with its general narrative dynamic. On the one hand, there is the influence of Nabokov's *roman noir* with its narrative playfulness, shadowy voyeurism and above all its focus upon a middle-aged man's sexual and metaphysical obsession with a 'dark lady' which leads, in a spiral of misogyny, to his murder at the hands of a heroine who defies patriarchal order. On the other, there is a recognition in *Blackeyes* of the contemporary feminist view of women as defined by the dominant patriarchal order and castigated as passive victims due to male fantasies of domination and control.

When it appeared in 1987, Potter's resulting novel gained wide, if not always favourable, reviews. Lorna Sage in the *Observer* called it 'a richly devious tale' (and was promptly quoted on the cover of subsequent imprints).[32] Writing in the *Listener*, however, Julian Symons pre-empted the critical furore which would erupt around the subsequent television version: 'This would-be moral tale', he wrote, 'surely finds its resonance and interest in the very material it deplores.'[33]

Production

Having 'felt that niggle that it wasn't done with', Potter then adapted

Blackeyes both as a screenplay and as a four-part TV serial.[34] The two sets of scripts are dated September 1988 and it seems Potter worked on them simultaneously 'with the various versions ... feeding off each other': the screenplay ending up as essentially an edited version of the longer TV material.[35] The original scripts also stuck closely to the novel. While Potter changed the order in which some appeared, almost every scene from the book was dramatised with a minimum of alteration and with little hint of the substantial alterations he would later make as director of the production.

As noted with regard to the Trodd dispute, pre-production on *Blackeyes* took place throughout the autumn and winter of 1988-89, with Potter preparing to sit in the director's chair for the first time. For BBC Head of Drama, Mark Shivas, this was surely an enormous gamble. Not only was he allowing a novice (in poor physical health) to direct an expensive addition to the BBC's 1989 autumn schedules, he had also given the go-ahead for *Blackeyes* to be shot simultaneously on 35mm as a feature film – as one of the first batch of such BBC films to be made for theatrical release abroad. According to Shivas, probably only the BBC would have agred to Potter's idea that he should direct for the first time. He recalls that *Blackeyes* was initially not going to be made on 35mm until the fact it could be done 'as a series and a movie came up as something [Potter] had wanted to do before but had never managed industrially'.[36]

While times had certainly changed since Potter's aborted 1983 attempt to give *Track 29* such a 'double life', as Kenith Trodd makes clear, the BBC still had to be made an offer it could not refuse. He states one of the reasons the Corporation was 'outmanoeuvred' when concluding the *Blackeyes* deal in late 1988 was that the novel had recently been published in the United States. Although the book was not terribly well received, this was at a time when Potter's reputation was sky-high in the USA in the wake of the tremendous success of *The Singing Detective*. As a result, various companies had made a number of early offers to turn *Blackeyes* into a movie. These were probably just 'straws in the wind', Trodd states but they were enough for Potter and his associates to go back to the BBC and say that unless they were given what they wanted, in terms of a production shot on 35mm with Potter as director, the Corporation could find itself with a competing feature film version of *Blackeyes* the following autumn. Trodd states: 'It was bullshit really but it was sharp, fair negotiating practice.'

As a result of this pressure, the BBC agreed to put up half the total £2.4 million budget of *Blackeyes*; the other half being made up of a variety of co-production monies. By Corporation standards, this was a sizeable budget for a 4 x 55-minute drama serial. Undoubtedly, it reflected a desire both to keep Potter working for the BBC and to share in the fruits of his now sizeable international reputation.

By the same token, Potter also succeeded in securing perhaps the most generous shooting schedule ever for any BBC drama production: six months in which to film four hours of material.[37] Filming began on 6 February 1989, with a cast that included Michael Gough as Kingsley, Carol Royle as Jessica, Nigel Planer as Jeff and a relative unknown, Gina Bellman, in the eponymous role of Blackeyes. In subsequent publicity for the serial, Potter consistently claimed that as director he had 'to fall in love with' Bellman as Blackeyes, if he was to make the production work on any emotional level.[38] The closeness of their working relationship is attested by *Blackeyes*' sound recordist, Peter Edwards (who also worked on *Christabel*). Edwards states Potter 'fell in love' with Gina Bellman: 'I'm not talking physically of course but he felt he had to.' He states the pair grew closer as the production went on.

The atmosphere on set, however, was often tense during shooting. According to Edwards, Potter was a very autocratic director who had definite ideas on what he wanted. There are many directors, he states, with whom members of the crew can collaborate in the form of suggesting ideas during shooting. This was definitely not the case with Potter – a fact Edwards puts down to his inexperience: 'Obviously the more experienced you are, the less worried you are about people saying "Well let me do this".'

Potter's carefully worked-out style of directing inevitably contributed to the lack of spontaneity on set since, as Edwards well remembers, it was very difficult to achieve technically. Much of *Blackeyes* consists of long single takes that often last five or six minutes and are broken up only by single flash edits or short montage sequences taken from other scenes in the drama. Within these long takes, Potter deploys a series of intricately designed camera movements which, circling around the actors in a kind of prowling ballet, resemble nothing more closely than the wanderings of a restless voyeur. In pre-publicity, Potter was happy to expound on the philosophy behind this style. In the *Listener* magazine, he asserted film was completely unaware of the techniques that had revolutionised literary fiction in the early twentieth century: 'We've got an infinite relativism of moral values, which only throws into question all the more urgently what is of value.'[39] Similarly, on Channel Four's *The Media Show*, he claimed the 'grammar' of film had been for too long taken for granted. In *Blackeyes*, he maintained, he was consciously striving against a certain form of shooting that imposed a certain rhythm: 'the two-shot, the one-shot, the medium shot, the long shot, the close shot [which] imposes itself upon everything you see'.[40]

Undoubtedly influenced by the experience of having written *Blackeyes* first as a novel, Potter clearly saw his aim as 'breaking up the grammar' of film in line with modernist innovations he knew from literature. Producer Rick McCallum is scathing, however, about this philosophy, claiming this was no more than 'bullshit' concocted for the media. He believes Potter's rationale was simply a cover for the fact that he 'was desperately intimidated and afraid about ... breaking up the action because it's much more technical, that process'. Potter, he asserts, was 'absolutely able to rationalise it' because the shooting schedule had been planned in such a way that the very first scene he had to direct was the relatively simple one of Kingsley waking up alone in his 'loft' apartment (which occurs in Episode 1 of the TV serial). McCallum alleges the scene had always been planned as a simple long take in order that Potter's transition from writer to director could be made as gentle as possible:

> That's why I planned it that way. I wanted him to start off in a room with one person, not have to worry about reverses and cut-aways and have to ... overlap dialogue, deal with movements that are based on total continuity ... But ... that was only going to be one section of the film because the loft is interspaced through all four episodes. And then once we got to the photographic studio [the next scene to be shot – between Blackeyes and a photographer: occurs Episode 2 of the serial] ... he started in it again. And we had a huge scene then. I said it's wrong, it's a mistake, you're not connecting, you're afraid ... We didn't speak for a couple of days. There was a bit of tension: major tension on the set and everything else.

McCallum believes Potter limited himself as a director due to this lack of 'coverage' – that is, his refusal to shoot additional footage which could then be utilised in post-production. For Potter, this was too much like 'playing safe' in terms of a capitulation to the conventional film grammar of continuity editing. For McCallum, it was a case of the writer/director depriving himself of one of his greatest gifts: his ability to manipulate images in post-production.

Sound recordist Peter Edwards provides further revealing insights into relationships between Potter, cast and crew during the rehearsing and shooting of *Blackeyes*. Because of the generous schedule won from the BBC, Potter had the film-maker's dream of copious amounts of time available for meticulous rehearsal. Unusually, both camera and sound man were invited. Edwards recalls that in rehearsals Potter would pace round and round the actors when they were rehearsing a scene, making jottings beside the script. Then, when it came time to shoot, the crew would be asked to repeat Potter's movements, using the camera equipment – with the grips pushing the camera around on tracks in exactly the same manner and direction in which Potter had moved around the actors during rehearsals. For Edwards, this made *Blackeyes* the most difficult film he had ever worked on. Despite stressing his admiration for Potter, he admits the writer/director 'did not understand or appreciate the difficulties that [he] as a sound mixer on location or Andrew Dunn the photographer were going through to get him what he wanted'. For the actors, the long ten-minute takes were also very difficult – rather like a return to the theatre in terms of having to act out long scenes but with the added pressure of negotiating a constantly moving camera. Edwards well remembers the tension: 'At one time I had sixteen pages of script taped together with all the actors ringed with different numbers on, according to which mikes and channels and you just went through the whole thing a bit like a live show. It was very, very nerve-racking.'

Potter, however, was impatient about too many technical rehearsals for the crew. Edwards states he would get bored with the whole business of film-making very quickly. The crew members were also aware that because of his ill-health, they could not wear him out by having rehearsal after rehearsal. This created the added pressure of getting these very intricate tracking shots right almost first time. Normally, Edwards states, one rehearses and rehearses at the BBC until the technical aspects are right but 'with Dennis you did it until Dennis was fed up and then you moved on and if Dennis was fed up on take one that was it, you never got anymore'.

Much of Blackeyes was shot at the BBC's Ealing Film Studios in order to provide Potter with a 'safe' environment. In addition, various sites in London and around Eastbourne were used for location shooting. A favourite Potter location, Hammersmith Bridge, features at the beginning of Episode 1, whilst the hotel used in *Cream In My Coffee* to such effect (the Grand at Eastbourne) was revisited for those scenes in which Blackeyes first encounters the copywriter Jeff. Surely these location shoots, featuring a great many extras, must have proved difficult for a first time director? According to Edwards, Potter rose to it all. His confidence curve as a director had grown with his learning curve and he was very confident by then.

Certainly, directing *Blackeyes* seems to have been something of an emotional journey for Potter; a shedding of reclusiveness. Rick McCallum asserts: 'Every day tapped into new emotions with him about how to deal with other people … all the unbelievable and difficult emotional context he's not had for twenty five years.' During pre-publicity for *Blackeyes*, Potter confirmed that since taking up directing he felt 'an utterly different person to the one who set out on the first day of rehearsals in the middle of January', having significantly made touch with his younger self.[41]

By August 1989, *Blackeyes* had gone into post-production under

Christabel's film editor, Clare Douglas. As we have seen, Potter had long been fascinated by the cutting room and on *The Singing Detective* he made considerable creative contributions. With *Blackeyes*, Douglas describes post-production as 'tightish', principally because of the complex soundtrack which, for the first time on a BBC production, was of feature film quality, having been recorded on Dolby SR. In fact, post-production on the TV serial went on almost up to the first transmission date: a temporal constraint which, in retrospect, Douglas regrets as 'there was no time to have debates on what was working and what wasn't'.

At the same time, Potter was constantly refining the material and testing new ideas in the cutting room, regarding the editing stage as the 'final rewrite'. In fact, all the way through *Blackeyes*, he had been making many changes to the original scripts, bringing in new ideas with a freedom he had never had before as a writer, when he had always been forced to hand his material over at a certain stage to another director.

For example, the television serial opens with a highly stylised sequence in which Blackeyes, surrounded by mannequins in an otherwise empty set, is hounded by Potter's voyeuristic camera to the strains of 'I'm Getting Sentimental Over You'. This appears nowhere in the original scripts and, according to Peter Edwards, was in fact the very last scene to be shot. Similarly, an explicit sex scene between Blackeyes and her employer, Jamieson, is included in the serial whereas merely portrayed 'post-coitus' in both the novel and original scripts. The frequency and haste of many of these changes is perhaps best exemplified by one of the serial's most pervasive features – Potter's addition of a voice-over (read by himself) which both narrates and makes ironic comment upon the action unfolding on screen. How this works aesthetically will be examined in detail later but it is important to note that nowhere is it mentioned in the original scripts. Indeed, according to Edwards, its inclusion in the final version was a big surprise to many in the crew since at no time during the shooting had it been it mentioned. Clare Douglas confirms that the decision to add a voice-over was made 'during the editing'.

According to the editor, Potter was trying to be a little bit Brechtian with this device: 'He was trying to distance you from those characters', she states. 'He didn't want you to like any of them. He didn't want you to like Kingsley because Kingsley was a child-molester ... even though he was a very attractive character.'

Could there perhaps have been a more mundane reason, however? We have seen how much of *Blackeyes* consists of long tracking shots designed to mimic the restless gaze of a voyeur and how, during shooting, Potter was much criticised by Rick McCallum for his lack of 'coverage'. Is it conceivable that a voice-over was added in post-production in an attempt to paper over the visual tedium of these long single takes? After all, none of the scenes with long tracking shots could be broken up visually without a loss of continuity since Potter had shot them in a way that precluded the possibility of shortening. Peter Edwards states: 'That's what we said all along. We said if you do this all in one long track, great! But how are you going to cut it? 'Don't worry about that', he would say.'

Because of Potter's shooting style, the way in which *Blackeyes* was finally broken up visually through editing is therefore the only way it could have been broken up by the post-production stage: namely, through elaborate montage sequences using images taken from other scenes in the drama. With Potter directing long scenes with long tracking shots and long pauses between actors, perhaps the only option available by post-production to lend the resulting collection of long single takes and jump cuts any coherence within the framework of a television narrative was the use of a voice-over to bind it all together. When pressed, the editor Clare Douglas concedes just this. She admits that the producer Rick McCallum thought 'the whole thing was totally incomprehensible and it needed someone to explain it'.

Interpretation

Given the many changes which Potter made during both shooting and production, is it, then, even possible to 'explain' the finished TV version of *Blackeyes*? On one level, it might seem an impossible job but on another, it *is* important to note that the inclusion of explicit sex scenes; the stylised opening; the use of a voyeuristic camera ballet and the addition of a voice-over provided by the 'author' himself, all perform a similar function within the narrative. They all foreground issues of spectatorship and authorship and, by this, signal the manufacture of the drama.

In terms of spectatorship, *Blackeyes* attempts to position its viewer as self-aware voyeur by forbidding a perspective of detached or passive omniscience with regard to events taking place on screen. Employing few reverses or cut-aways, Potter's long tracking shots only ever provide the audience with a single means of viewing each scene, through the eye of a moving camera as it circles and prowls around the protagonists in a voyeuristic sweep. The eye of the camera is thus made synonymous with the eye/I of the audience: its movements around the characters becoming the viewer's movements. With its shifting point of view on events, the single moving camera also draws attention to the subjectivity of that view; to the directorial artifice of it and to the audience's own position at the heart of events as an active, not a passive producer of meaning. By presenting the sexual exploitation of the model Blackeyes as if through the eye of a restless voyeur, Potter's aim is clearly to produce an ambivalent spectator; forcing the audience into the uneasy position of recognising and confronting its own complicity with that exploitation.

All of this seems to be what Potter had in mind when he asserted he was 'breaking up the grammar of film' in line with modernist innovations in literature. His emphasis on subjective, as opposed to omniscient, viewing positions closely parallels the displacement in the early twentieth-century literary novel of omniscient modes of narration with a variety of fractured, modernist perspectives. For Potter, as we have seen, most television is still 'pre-modernist' insofar as it conceals its own manufacture and the inherent subjectivity of the 'truths' it offers. *Blackeyes*, by contrast, signals that manufacture and subjectivity not only by foregrounding the act of spectatorship but to a considerable extent by highlighting its own authorship as well, as the stylised opening of the serial and the addition of a voice-over both confirm. Just as the audience is forced to confront the ambivalence of its own viewing position with regard to the serial, the identity and attitudes of this 'author' who inserts himself into the drama by means of voice-over are also rendered deeply ambiguous. Is he exposing sexploitation or merely revelling in it? Does this authorial character wish to liberate Blackeyes or capture her for his own male ends? These questions come into sharp focus at the very end of the serial, which differs markedly from that of both the novel and the original scripts.

After Jessica has drowned herself, Blackeyes is shown in Jeff's clutches at his manor in the country. He looks directly to camera and informs the viewer that Blackeyes 'is free. Well sort of free, anyway'. He kisses her: 'Because now she's mine.'[42] Whereas the novel and the original scripts both end here on this pessimistic note, in the finished television version, the authorial voice-over intervenes:

> But pardon me, Mr Smug. There's just one thing. You're in front of this camera, right? And if she's a character, a piece of make-believe then so are you. Lights, music, speech, it's beyond your control ... Watch what I can do. Yes, me, because of course I'm the man who's made all this up.

The voice-over announces to Blackeyes: 'I have plans for you, my angel. Feminism is all very well but in this business someone always gets the girl. It's known as a happy ending.' Stated authorial intention is contradicted, however, by the *mise en scène* – Blackeyes shakes her head in refusal at Jeff, yet significantly at the camera as well. She runs out of Jeff's house and into his garden, making to escape from all these male authors through a gate at the far side. Meanwhile, the now seemingly helpless authorial voice-over is left pleading: 'Hey Blackeyes! Come back! ... Don't you start rewriting!'; his increasingly desperate calls finally petering out into an ambiguous sigh: 'Oh, Blackeyes. Thank you for breaking my heart.'

On one level, the addition of the voice-over is simply an extension of the ending of the original novel but with another male author taking over from Jeff. At the same time, however, in marked contrast to both novel and scripts, the heroine does appear to succeed in resisting the male narrative. She escapes its pressure for recuperation of feminine disruption within patriarchal order – in other words, the traditional device of the 'happy ending' in which the male hero always 'gets the girl'. The female protagonists of *Blackeyes* at last seem to succeed in their aim of 'rewriting the book'.

What made Potter change his mind about the chances of a successful female challenge to male control? In interview, he stated it was simply that since writing the novel, he had 'learned' a little bit more: 'The man took possession of her at the end [of the novel] and [in the serial] I just allowed her to say "No".'[43] Rick McCallum confirms it was the experience of directing *Blackeyes* and of working with actress Gina Bellman which prompted the change of heart: '[It] had to do with Dennis' feelings about Gina when he was making it ... She's playing victim and it's very hard to be with somebody who's not a victim ... You have no control over them.'

As the final ambiguous words of the authorial voice-over demonstrate, however, the serial's continual oscillation between the possibilities of male authorial possession and female liberation is sustained right to the very end of the narrative. Can a character really escape its creator or is it all simply a cruel trick on the part of a malevolent male 'author'? As film editor Clare Douglas confirms, Potter wished to keep his audience guessing even to the final frame and beyond. She states that at the point where Blackeyes is seen making her escape through the garden gate at the end of the serial, Potter, in the cutting room, deliberately insisted on freezing the image before she could make it through the door – in this way sustaining the ambiguity right to the very end.[44]

The reasons for this were clearly spelled out by the director himself during his extensive pre-publicity for the serial. They also explain his positioning of the audience as ambivalent voyeurs. As Potter suggested:

> No matter how 'feminist' some of the aspirations might be, the basic fact remains that I am a man writing it. So I wanted to bring that ambivalence right into the centre ... The narration aches with that ambivalence. In fact it is very much the dramatic tension of the piece: are you complicit with what you are allegedly exposing? ... At the end of *Blackeyes* it is clear for all to see that there is complicity but the complicity itself is shown for what it is.[45]

At the same time, *Blackeyes*' central conceit of a character attempting to escape its malevolent 'Author' is one which Potter has clearly borrowed from his own first novel, *Hide and Seek* (see Chapter 3). Moreover, just as was shown in relation to *The Singing Detective*, *Hide and Seek* can be demonstrated as a major influence, too, on *Blackeyes*.

For example, both works foreground the creative process (of writing a novel) and both significantly adopt a recursive narrative strategy. In *Hide and Seek*, Daniel Miller was a character attempting to escape from a malevolent God-like 'Author' but the question which the novel raised was whether this 'Author' himself was merely a character in someone else's book. As Chapter Three noted, that was both an aesthetic and a religious question, for ultimately what was being examined was not only the relationship of character to author but of Man to God.

Similarly, in Episode 1 of the TV version of *Blackeyes*, the authorial voice-over asks: 'I wonder. Do we invent ourselves? Or have others already done it for us? Do we think? Or are we thought?'[46] As noted earlier, *Blackeyes* the novel was about a character (Blackeyes), written by a male author (Kingsley) and rewritten by his niece (Jessica); all of whom were in turn being written by a male author (Jeff). Just as with *Hide and Seek*, the television serial takes that recursion one step further in order that the identity of the ultimate male Author (and exploiter) of the narrative may be revealed.

In the serial, the 'real' author of *Blackeyes* is exalted into the 'God of Creation', as he delights in his new power as director to manipulate reality and create new versions of it. As he tells Jeff at the end, 'Lights, music, speech, it's beyond your control ... Watch what I can do.' Moreover, just as Daniel Miller in *Hide and Seek* felt himself to be 'written about, pinned down' by 'an inescapable Author with evil designs and total power',[47] so too is Blackeyes – for example, in the stylised opening of the TV serial where she finds herself hounded by a voyeuristic camera and the attendant male voice-over, with its snide observation: 'My own yearning sneaked up on me as I hunted her down ... I'll have to hide my face but she can't hide, not here in this inky nowhere.' In *Hide and Seek*, it was shown that the way to escape this manipulative Author was to become one yourself: 'the narrator. The Author. Creator of all!'[48] Similarly, in *Blackeyes*, the eponymous heroine can only become the 'Author of her own Fate' by confronting and rejecting the ultimate male exploiter of her narrative: its malevolent God-like Author.

All of this is not to say, of course, that the manipulative male oppressor whom she ultimately rejects is the 'real' Dennis Potter simply because he provides the authorial voice-over. As noted with both *Hide and Seek* and *The Singing Detective*, Potter liked to play with autobiographical conventions in order to lend his work extra potency by giving it a much more 'personal feel' (see Chapters 3 and 5). At the same time, the TV serial's recasting of the novel's original *noir* ending does serve to place greater emphasis on the exploration of the relationship between Blackeyes and the 'Dennis Potter' voice-over: that is, between a beautiful young woman and a (middle-aged) male 'author'. In turn, this recalls the theme of another earlier Potter work, *Double Dare*. Indeed the TV *Blackeyes* makes explicit reference to the 1976 play when, in one scene in Episode 2, a poster of Blackeyes advertising a chocolate 'Fraggie Bar' is made clearly visible within the *mise-en-scène*.

As Chapter 2 noted, *Double Dare* dealt with the often blurred relationship between life and art, as symbolised by a writer's relationship with a young actress. One of the questions it raised was: to what extent one can separate role-playing from 'reality' – is it possible to distinguish? Does the acting out of a role not hint at a deeper 'truth' behind the surface illusion? Likewise in *Blackeyes*, at the end of an explicit sex scene between Blackeyes and her advertising employer Jamieson, the authorial voice-over intervenes: "Fiction. How strange a thing it is. Was that a real orgasm, do you think? No. All a fake, of course. But what happens to her, to me, if made to pretend, we pretend too often? When do you collect the bill and how pay it?'[49]

By raising questions about the relationship between role-playing and reality, Potter is clearly seeking to demonstrate the fragility of conventional lines between 'truth' and 'fiction', in much the same way as *Double Dare* sought to do. At the same time, however, he has also *extended* the theme of the earlier play, moving it beyond its limits within a clearly delineated work of fiction and literally putting it into practice as writer-director of *Blackeyes*. Is it not the case that by portraying a character in a drama who is exploited by a male God-like Author, the actress who played Blackeyes has in some way 'really' been exploited? If so, what does that make the writer-director playing the exploiter? The answer, as we have seen, comes at the end of the serial. Just as with other writer characters, like Martin in *Double Dare* and the diseased Marlow in *The Singing Detective*, the 'Author' finds himself to be guilty of a crime against women, with the result that punishment and relief from guilt can only come through self-recognition and public atonement – in the case of *Blackeyes*, by the 'Author' undergoing the public humiliation of the heroine's rejection of him in front of the watching TV audience.

Also echoing other Potter works is the use of fairy tales in *Blackeyes* as bedrocks of narrative structure. If Kingsley is Jessica's 'wicked old uncle', appropriating his niece's life for his own ends, he is also the evil hobgoblin, Rumplestiltskin, locked in his 'wintry attic', spinning the straw of Jessica's life into literary gold.[50] Meanwhile, first encountering Jeff in a ballroom inside a 'Grand Hotel', Blackeyes is *Almost Cinderella*.[51] As the morgue pathologist makes clear to the vengeful *noir* investigator Blake, in looking for a suicide note to explain her subsequent drowning: 'We're playing Hunt The Slipper, Mr Blake.'[52] In appearance, however, she is most definitely Snow White, as Kingsley makes clear to Jessica at the very beginning of the TV serial, when he tells her that out of her experiences as a model, he proposes to create an enchanted fairy-tale creature: 'Her skin … as white as snow, her hair as black as ebony and her lips as red as the blood that had not yet been spilt.'[53]

Given her shifting identities within the narrative, who, then, is the mysterious Blackeyes? Or rather, perhaps the question should be who is the 'dark lady' that haunts much of Potter's work?

In *Casanova*, for example, the central protagonist is haunted by perhaps the only woman he has loved amongst all those he has known: a dark-haired country girl called Cristina. Casanova enthuses to a friend: 'Her big black eyes look right into your soul, deep into your heart.'[54] Similarly, in *Hide and Seek*, the troubled 'Author' of the Daniel Miller narrative describes another 'inaccessible lady': one he has spied in a tawdry coffee bar. As with Casanova's Cristina, the sight of this woman is like an epiphany to him. She is described as an 'entrancing creature, pale and dark-haired' and wearing long, red, shiny boots.[55] To him, she resembles 'Snow White in the glass case, the Princess at the ball.'[56]

There are many other such 'dark ladies' in Potter's work: creatures of male desire, of overpowering, almost disruptive sexuality; usually prostitutes. For example, in Potter's 1986 novel *Ticket To Ride* (remade in 1991 as a feature film, *Secret Friends*), the main character, John Buck, is both fascinated and repelled by prostitutes. From the window of his tiny Paddington mews flat, he regularly watches one patrol the street below. She has 'long black hair, small white boots, long legs and a slender figure'.[57] Likewise, in the forties' *noir* thriller strand of *The Singing Detective*, Sonia, the Russian agent cum prostitute whom Mark Binney takes back to his mews flat, is described in the original scripts as 'a sad-eyed beautiful girl with long black hair'.[58] She is later found drowned near Hammersmith Bridge (see Chapter 5).

On being questioned about the similarity of these figures, Potter, in interview, comically refused to be drawn: 'Is there? Yeh. I don't know … Well there you are! God only knows!'[59] With the writer amused but giving no clues as to the inspiration for his 'dark lady', perhaps *Blackeyes* itself can furnish some more evidence. One of the pieces of music used to great effect in the serial first occurs towards the end of Episode 1 when Blackeyes auditions for a television commercial in front of a group of leering advertising men. The scene is a long set piece and in both the novel and TV serial, Potter specifies that the music to which Blackeyes should provocatively audition is Eric Coates' 'Sleepy Lagoon' (its title carrying obvious resonances with the model's ultimate watery fate).[60] To the British audience, this piece of music is instantly recognisable as the theme tune to the long-running BBC radio programme, *Desert Island Discs*. Curiously, however, when it recurs in Episode 4, just as Jeff is about to 'claim' *Blackeyes*, Potter's authorial voice-over intones: 'The song is stolen. The sweet sweet song. *My* song.'

Perhaps it is merely a coincidence but in December 1977, Potter himself appeared on *Desert Island Discs*, selecting the eight records he would most wish to have with him if stranded on a desert island. He explained his fourth choice by means of a strong adolescent image of liberated female sexuality; an image which just perhaps became the basis of an entire television serial twelve years later:

> Well the next one I've chosen is 'Twelfth Street Rag' … especially because I had this particularly strong image of Form 2A at Bells Grammar School in Coleford. When the teacher left the room for a rather prolonged period and seeing this thirteen year old startlingly attractive black-haired girl, cheekily going to the front and to the desk and picking up a twelve inch ruler and beating out with enormous vigour 'Twelfth Street Rag' at the top of her voice and … all the signals, the sort of adolescent sex … flaring up at the sight of this pretty girl doing 'Twelfth Street Rag'. I can never hear 'Twelfth Street Rag' without being reminded of some of the great joys of life. And I think on my island I would need to think about; not just about that thirteen year old but of all the women of the world.[61]

Reception

By the time its last episode was transmitted by the BBC on 20 December 1989, the TV version of *Blackeyes* had been written off as an abject failure by almost all the reviewers of the British press. Richard Last of the *Daily Telegraph* summed up the critical mood:

> All freedom corrupts and absolute freedom corrupts absolutely … If you remove time, place and reality, as the four episodes of *Blackeyes* successively did, there's not much left except incomprehension … And Dennis, as author, confessed what had been apparent to the least sophisticated all along, namely that he had been writing out his own sick fantasies at inordinate length and huge cost.[62]

In terms of its ratings, Episode 4 of the serial was watched by 3.87 million British viewers. This compares with 5.32 million for Episode 3; 5.73 million for Episode 2 and a record 7.15 million for Episode 1: the highest BBC-2 audience that year for a single screening, aside from sporting events. Unlike *The Singing Detective* or *Christabel*, *Blackeyes* failed to hold its audience, though it is fair to point out that to maintain nearly four million viewers is a very respectable achievement for a drama on BBC TV's minority channel.[63] Nevertheless, *Blackeyes*' 'audience appreciation' ratings were not good. As the drama's chief 'patron', Mark Shivas, confirms, BBC audience research showed that while viewers did not switch over to anything else, they did not like what they saw. Hence although Potter maintained that *Blackeyes* 'defied its slot'[64] in terms of ratings, there can be no doubt much of its audience hated it.

Why, then, did the serial fail in Britain? What made it different from Potter's other work – most of which had been judged a critical and often a popular success in the past? Although it is beyond the scope of this study to offer detailed empirical evidence on audience attitudes, nevertheless several reasons for the drama's failure can be adduced from its ratings, the pre-publicity and not least the actual production itself.

One reason was that the drama was massively 'overhyped'. To some extent, it was inevitable that the British tabloids would have a field day with *Blackeyes*, given the drama's apparent concern with that great newspaper selling point: sex. This was doubly true in the light of the previous controversies the press had whipped up surrounding this subject in Potter's work, particularly with regard to *The Singing Detective*. True to form, the *Sun* newspaper crowned Potter 'telly's Dirty Drama King' for his work on *Blackeyes* whilst the *News of the World* branded him 'Television's Mr Filth'.[65]

If one can sympathise with Potter as a victim of the animus of the British tabloids, at the same time it is clear that all the press was doing was reacting, in its own predictable way, against premeditated construction of *Blackeyes* as a media event. Potter did an enormous amount of pre-publicity for the drama prior to its British transmission – much of it, whether intentionally or not, selling the work on the basis of its sexual content. A clear example of this was an interview he gave to host Sue Lawley on her BBC TV chat show, *Saturday Matters*, two weeks before the transmission of the first episode. In the course of the interview, a short illustrative clip from Episode 1 was shown – namely, the scene in which Blackeyes strips at an audition in front of leering advertising men. Taken out of context in this manner, such an extract could only help foster the misleading impression in the public and press mind that *Blackeyes* was synonymous with sexual titillation. If this was a strategy to lure a mass audience to a work with 'feminist aspirations', it was, as subsequent reviews would prove with their accusations of 'sick fantasies', a grave miscalculation.

As one previewer from the *Independent* observed, the combined effect of all this pre-transmission hype was that when the serial finally hit the screens, one had 'the impression of [it] having been around for some time already'.[66] Four days before Episode 1 was even transmitted, he could make the following self-fulfilling prophecy as much to his journalistic colleagues as to his readers: 'Any takers for the Potter backlash?'[67]

Who was responsible for all this publicity? Clare Douglas states: 'Potter connived in it but it was set up by Rick'. She claims that every other day during post-production, Rick McCallum would send along journalists and film crews to interview Potter, until finally the writer refused to do any more. The final straw came, she states, when Potter discovered his producer had sent him someone who turned out to be writing a house magazine for a bank! McCallum, for his part, admits his desire was for a 'popular' as opposed to 'critical' success but denies the charge of too much publicity, stating he set the 'platform' right but 'then this juggernaut took over … It was tabloid-driven.'

Having secured, by a variety of means, a record 7.1 million viewers for the first episode of a BBC-2 drama, what went subsequently wrong? Those involved with the production have their own theories. Clare Douglas believes the drama's main problem was its complexity: 'It had just one level too many for most people.' She adds that, as a woman, she felt the character of Blackeyes was not properly focused, being half 'real', half fantasy. Because of the tight post-production schedule, she claims, however, there was no time during editing to discuss these matters.[68] Meanwhile, Potter in interview stood by the work but stated the thing that most upset him about *Blackeyes* was how personal the reviews were. 'Instead of dealing with the work … they were dealing with me and the work', he stated.[69]

All these points – its complexity; the characterisation of Blackeyes; the press reception – are valid reasons for the dwindling of the drama's audience. One other explanation suggests itself, however, both from the ratings and the comparative success of past Potter works like *The Singing Detective*. As Potter demonstrated decisively with *The Singing Detective*, a mass television audience could enthusiastically embrace a multi-narrative serial drama structured in a non-linear fashion. What the evidence of *Blackeyes* suggests is that many of those same viewers found themselves lost by the lack of a consistent narrative strand denoting 'external reality', by means of which they could orientate themselves in the work from week to week. Although, as we have seen, Potter wilfully blurred distinctions between external and internal 'reality' at the climax of *The Singing Detective*, for most of that drama, the hospital scenes fulfilled such a function for viewers (see Chapter 5). They served as the anchor-point of external reality around which Marlow's memories and fantasies could swirl. In *Blackeyes*, all such notions of external reality are constantly undermined. Kingsley may, like Marlow, be revealed as the 'real' writer of one of the fantasy narrative strands but then he is subsequently revealed to be a fictional creation of Jeff who in turn is revealed to be a fictional creation of the 'Dennis Potter' voice-over and so on in the recursive manner of *Hide and Seek*. As with many of his 'non-naturalistic' techniques, Potter was clearly trying to suggest the existence of deeper 'truths' behind normal assumptions of 'reality' but for most of his viewers, it seems, the drama lacked a 'point' precisely because it was not founded upon *any* consistent representation of material reality.[70]

Certainly, analysis of the viewing figures provides circumstantial evidence that in 1989 Britain the television audience was extremely unwilling to have its assumptions of what is 'real' unpicked in such a manner. If, between Episodes 1 and 2, as might have been predicted, the serial failed to hold the high audience lured to BBC-2 as a result of media hype, the equally large fall between the third and final episodes (from 5.32 million to 3.87 million) seems to suggest that many of those who stayed with it finally lost patience by the end of Episode 3. It may be no coincidence that this episode concludes with the revelation that Jeff is not only a character in the unfolding narrative but an 'author' as well.

At the same time, there can be no doubt that the drama's production of an ambiguous viewer-voyeur made the audience uneasy, splitting it along clear gender lines. As one viewer commented in a letter to the *Observer* newspaper: 'Most of my female friends angrily switch[ed] off, while I felt seriously challenged by having my private fantasies so roundly exposed. I can't be the only male to have winced, can I?'[71]

If clearly not the way to boost TV ratings, what do such sharp gender divisions reveal about Potter's treatment of women? Writing in the *New Statesman* just prior to the transmission of *Blackeyes*, John Wyver voiced concerns about representations of women in Potter's writing as a whole. Women, he wrote, were invariably cast 'in the conventional stereotypes of angel and whore'. Potter's male protagonists were 'afraid of women's sexuality and disgusted by it' while sexuality was also frequently connected to death: 'often to the violent death of a woman'.[72]

On a superficial level, many of the works which this book has examined provide an abundance of evidence to support Wyver's assertion. Rather than fully rounded characters, women are often portrayed in Potter's work as whores and 'dark ladies', seeking to tempt the male hero from the purity of his ideals. Alternatively, they can be angels: 'unattainable ladies' like Cristina in *Casanova* or Eileen in *Pennies from Heaven* who are capable of being idolised by the male protagonist because they seem to offer the keys to that elusive 'Eden' for which he is constantly searching.

Nevertheless, it is important to note that such a dichotomy is simply a function of the much wider schism between 'flesh' and 'spirit' which, as successive chapters have shown, runs right through Potter's work and which 'tears' at many of his male protagonists. Moreover, as Wyver correctly states, notions of 'whore' versus 'angel' are also simply 'conventional stereotypes', embedded deep within our culture. They are, in fact, Western society's traditional way of looking at women.[73]

Thus, in sharp contrast to the view that Potter's representation of women is peculiarly problematic, it can be argued that what his work is actually trying to do is to explore and expose this as a problematic at the very heart of patriarchy itself. The dichotomy between 'flesh' and 'spirit', embodied in the disjunction between woman as 'angel' and woman as 'whore', is precisely the dichotomy which his work as a whole is seeking to *overcome*. As Chapter 5 suggested with *The Singing Detective*, when Philip Marlow succeeds in coming to terms with patriarchal guilt over his 'animal' nature, he does so in order to progress beyond the 'disgust' with sexuality and the images of 'violent female death' which Wyver sees as so disturbing in Potter's writing as a whole. Dramatising what goes on inside his male characters' heads, Potter is ultimately investigating the nature of patriarchy itself and how men have traditionally been taught by their culture to view women. As with many of his other 'non-naturalistic' techniques, he foregrounds this as a problem in very bold terms, through the use of traditional patriarchal imagery of 'angel' versus 'whore'. It is this very dichotomy which his work is struggling against.

Moreover, as this chapter has outlined, in the late eighties, the writer increasingly began to explore the implications of that dichotomy from a female, as opposed to male angle – moving on from dramatising what goes on inside a man's head to investigating what goes on inside a woman's as various female protagonists, like Marlow before them, tried to 'rewrite the book' and overcome patriarchal repression, albeit from a very different perspective. In works like *Track 29* and *Blackeyes*, it is the female not the male characters who are emphasised as the 'suffering martyrs' of patriarchy. The male protagonists are portrayed as abusers and manipulators from whose control figures like Linda Hendry and Blackeyes must extricate themselves if they are ever to overturn oppressive patriarchal structures and transform themselves, God-like, into 'Authors of their Fate'. As Blackeyes cries to heaven towards the end of Episode 2 of the serial: 'Jesus, why weren't you a woman?'

It is in just such terms that Potter himself regarded the shift of emphasis that took place in his work of the later eighties. In interview, he rejected the charge of misogyny, claiming that many commentators seemed to have lost sight of what fiction is. At root, he thought there was a confusion between his explorations in drama of traditional male attitudes to women and assumptions about his own views. He himself neatly sums up the counter-argument to this position:

I believe that men treat women badly. I know they do … I take it for granted that men exploit women as a fact to deal with and show. That doesn't mean that a) I do (because I don't believe I do as a person) but b) that I approve of it … I'm at a loss when given that as an attribute of my work.

Conclusion

End of the road

Potter was speaking in 1990, when the wounds caused by the British reception of *Blackeyes* were still very fresh: 'the pain' of the personal attacks 'still bumping within'.[1] In interview, he was always very generous, co-operative and above all highly skilled and articulate in fielding questions about his work. Ultimately, he asserted that his life as a television writer had been an attempt to build, over more than a quarter of a century,

> a body of work that is consistent with itself, that *does* send out tentacles and relationships and nudges and hints to other work within the sequence of work and will unashamedly repeat themes, motifs because ... that would be acceptable in a novel, it would be acceptable in the theatre, it would be acceptable in any other ... form. But because television is so unregarded and treated normally with such intellectual contempt, it became all the more imperative, having thought about it and thought about it and thought about it that I tried to do what other television writers had not tried to do ... because they usually then wanted to go on and write for something else.[2]

The aim of this book has been precisely to unravel over six chapters those many 'tentacles and relationships'; to 'follow the yellow brick road' of Potter's artistic life on screen, with a view to showing a consistency and progression of 'authorial' themes. Now, having examined the works in turn, it is possible to fit them together, like pieces in a mosaic, in order to offer an overall view of the shape of this 'road' which Potter both followed *and* built throughout his career.

The first and perhaps even the most important stepping stone in Potter's writing career strictly speaking predated it. The 1958 *Does Class Matter?* interview, together with his subsequent *Between Two Rivers* documentary and experiences as a political candidate, were all crucial to the early work insofar as they were what it was implicitly reacting against. Through his experiences of TV current affairs and the actuality of political campaigning, Potter learned how 'facts' could be 'lies' because they so often served to obscure the underlying truth of a situation: 'what was on either side of the camera'.[3] Turning away from the world of facts towards writing dramatic fiction, Potter, in *The Nigel Barton Plays*, was able to say all he had wanted to say about social class in his TV documentary and political campaign but in a more effective way, with less risk of engendering a personal sense of betrayal or incurring the wrath of his local village. Plays, by definition, were not as 'real' as current affairs. They could not harm anyone in quite the same way. What they could do, however, was present a more 'truthful', rounded picture of the effects of class upon an individual – its emotional pressures, tensions and ambiguities – than any number of interviews or documentary voice-overs.

This seems to be where Potter's 'non-naturalism' fits in – the distinctive dramatic style which was clearly present even in his very first plays. 'Non-naturalistic' techniques, such as use of flashbacks, characters' direct address to camera and adult actors as children, were all important to Potter because unlike current affairs, they were a means of showing 'what was on either side of the camera': the 'frame in the picture' rather than 'the picture in the frame', as he subsequently was to put it in his 1977 'Realism and Non-Naturalism' paper.[4] Where current affairs presented, uncontextualised and in its immediacy, the 'picture in the frame' of an individual addressing the issue of social class, with drama there was the possibility of getting behind the picture – of sketching in and *explaining* all the pressures, motivations and tensions which underlay a particular individual's need to grapple with the issue of class at a particular moment. If this is precisely the trajectory of *Stand Up, Nigel Barton* – the tracing of a personal history of class tension, stretching back to schooldays, which finally leads the central protagonist to a 'present' moment of public confession – it can be seen how much this owes to Potter's sense of the underlying 'truth' of his own experience: his need to retrace old ground becoming a need to explain the circumstances and motives which led him (twice) to discuss class in personal terms on television.

Stand Up is also important to Potter's writing in terms of the link it forges between the clever child (the 'liar' or embryo 'storyteller') and the backward child (the village 'idiot') as the same type of persecuted outcast from the community. This clever child-backward child symbiosis is traceable across many plays. It is present, for example, in the figure of Willy Turner in *Where the Buffalo Roam*. His plight is the flip side of Nigel Barton's for, unlike Barton, he is the 'outlaw' from the working-class community who cannot get away. It is also there in the relationship between 'looney' outcast and artful traitor that links Jesus and Judas in *Son of Man*; the Accordion Man and Arthur Parker in *Pennies*; Mark Binney and Philip Marlow in *The Singing Detective* and (implicitly) Donald Duck and Wallace Wilson in *Blue Remembered Hills*. Lying behind this symbiosis between 'outcast' and 'hero', 'victim' and 'villain' is a relativism of perspective in which characters are made ambiguous and 'rounded'. Potter endows his central protagonists with a series of shifting identities: hero-outcast, villain-victim, 'looney'-dreamer, writer-detective and so on; a feature which is at least partially due to the fact that as the writer acknowledged about himself, 'ambiguity haunts one's mind'.[5]

Particularly in the early work, his protagonists are 'torn'. Not only does ambiguity haunt their creator's mind, they themselves are unsure of whether they are heroes or villains. The trajectory of many of the plays is precisely a psychological quest by the protagonist to answer this very question of his own identity. This is what links disparate works such as *Stand Up, Traitor* and *Son of Man*, each of which portrays a character on the rack, haunted by doubt – in the case of Christ in *Son of Man*, doubt, even, as to whether or not he is the Messiah. As many of the chapters have noted, this 'torn' quality in characterisation resolves itself into one central dichotomy that runs through all the work: a schism between material and non-material desires; between flesh and spirit.

The key recurring theme in Potter's writing, the problem posed by each of the plays is precisely the problem of how to overcome this felt dichotomy. Moreover, in many works, the protagonist is not simply caught between the rival claims of the material and spiritual. Rather, as in *The Nigel Barton Plays*, *Traitor* and *Son of Man*, there is a conscious attempt to *oppose* one over the other – a battle of the 'spirit' over the 'flesh'. What feeds the 'torn' nature of protagonists like Barton, Adrian Harris and Potter's Christ is not so much indecision or hesitation as to which 'yellow brick road' (material or spiritual) to follow but rather the doubts, fears of failure and rival temptations attendant upon doggedly choosing to pursue a transcendent spiritual ideal in the face of what are seen to be the vagaries and hostilities of an external, wholly material world. As with *Son of Man* where the metaphor is made literal, crucial to this is the sense of a father, in whose name the protagonist struggles, as being perceived almost as God. The quest of the male protagonist becomes that of atoning (being 'at one') with this God-like patriarchal authority. What haunts and tears at him is the doubt that this ideal of the father to which he aspires is just too high; that the mortal frailties of the material world (the 'flesh') to which he is heir will always in the end defeat and punish him.

As Chapter 5 noted with reference to *The Singing Detective*, this elision of the father with God can be related to the traditional authority structures of patriarchy itself. Judaeo-Christian worship of a male 'God the Father' traditionally mirrored and helped legitimate the authority of the father within the patriarchal family group. In this way, it became easy for the child to elide the identity of his father with that of God as 'the progenitor of all things'.

The 'spirit' in the name of which many male Potter protagonists struggle against the material world is ultimately a patriarchal ideal. If this is so in *Traitor*, in terms of Adrian Harris' search for his father's Camelot, it is also true for *The Nigel Barton Plays*. In his climactic speeches at the close of both *Stand Up* and *Vote, Vote, Vote*, Barton's detailed references to the life of his coal-miner father make it clear how much the latter functions as the site of all his values and is the reason for the various 'stands' he adopts in each play. Similarly, in the tellingly named *Son of Man*, Christ the Son's struggle to oppose his 'spirit' over his own physical suffering and instinctual fears is explicitly undertaken in the name of his Father – God the Father. In each instance, a relationship with a father plays the crucial role in fostering 'conscience' within the central character. The quest of the son is to follow that patriarchal ideal of conscience: indeed to *be* it. As with Christ's crucifixion in *Son of Man*, the son longs to join his father; to be 'at one' with him. To do so is to be in 'heaven'.

To reach this idyllic state, the son must go through agonies, however, repressing the 'flesh'; forsaking the pleasures and temptations of the material world. If, as in the case of Potter's Christ, that struggle against the world and the body is an apparent success, sustained to the last, in other works like *Stand Up* and *Traitor*, failure fully to live up to the demands of conscience leads to a sense of guilt or self-questioning. To understand why, it is necessary to examine one of the key recurring motifs in Potter's work; one which many of the plays posit as the root of the flesh-spirit dichotomy that 'tears' at their male characters: namely, the notion of a Fall from a childhood Eden of innocence, wonder and above all, integration.

In various graphic ways, a number of works portray a traumatic Fall experienced by the central protagonist which results in a shock that 'change[s] even the [very] way of looking' at things.[6] In *Angels Are So Few*, Biddle the 'angel' loses his wings and his child-like wonder in Creation as a result of seduction by a serpentine suburban housewife. In *Hide and Seek*, the traumatic event is childhood sexual assault by a man with 'spiky hair … and eyes … the colour of phlegm', just as with Potter's 1969 play, *Moonlight on the Highway*.[7] For the female protagonists of *Schmoedipus* and the reworked *Track 29*, it is forced teenage seduction/rape. In *Brimstone and Treacle*, meanwhile, a teenage daughter's shock of sexual discovery in relation to her father literally, within the play's dramatic logic, strikes her dumb. Finally, in *A Beast with Two Backs* and *The Singing Detective* the trauma is assault/adultery in the Forest, witnessed by a child protagonist, in which sex and death become intimately connected and blurred.

As both *Hide and Seek* and *The Singing Detective* particularly illustrate, the aftermath of such a Fall is the sense of a loss of wonder. Through flashback, both works portray their central character as a child, perched on top of his favourite oak, from which he views his Forest Eden from all sides, with a sense of security and integration that later comes to be lost through his Fall. Far from being a 'torn' hero, striving to be at one with a patriarchal God, the central character, as a child on top of his oak, feels in perfect peace and union with the external world and 'God the Father'. At that moment, God is seen not as a goal, an authority without to be striven for but something within him: 'a protective grace moving above … and yet within itself … in and of things … breathing through them, breathing out of them'.[8]

It is this sense of a God within which the subsequent Fall comes to shatter. Most important in this respect is the sense of the Fall fracturing the child's relations with his parents, particularly his father. In *The Singing Detective*, the 'shock' of the child's sexual discovery through witnessing the Forest adultery leads not only to the death of his mother but to an estrangement from the warmth and intimacy of his coal-miner father. A similar fracture in the child's relations with a parent is portrayed in *A Beast with Two Backs*. Significantly, however, it arises not through a son's feelings of unworthiness but quite the opposite: an undermining of the moral authority of the father, in the eyes of a child. As the Old Testament-like patriarch within the village, Ebenezer's murder of Rebecca – his repression of a sex-crime before Rufus' very eyes – destroys his moral authority within the play, reducing him, as he himself later confesses in the pulpit, to an 'airy beast'. Far from being God-like, the patriarch is revealed to be only too human, consumed with a guilt that leads eventually to his suicide. Through a dead 'mother' and a guilty father, Rufus' separation from and loss of integration with the Forest around him is thus complete. The horror from which he flees at the end of the play is the realisation that far from being God-like, Man (indeed his own father, not the bear) is the real 'beast'. Faith in a father-God and a set of patriarchal moral absolutes is destroyed, seemingly forever.

As with Philip Marlow in *The Singing Detective*, the result of this changed way of looking at the world and at 'God the Father' is cynicism, misanthropy and despair. In turn, as illustrated by Barton's stealing of the daffodil and Marlow's classroom defecation, this seems to be what lies behind the rebellion of the child protagonist against patriarchal authority at school. It is important to note that while secretly in rebellion against it, the protagonists in both *Stand Up* and *The Singing Detective* publicly submit, via their betrayals of the class 'looney', to the dictates of that patriarchal authority. The key to understanding this lies in the Hamlet structure which, as Chapter 3 noted, is common to many Potter plays. Haunted by doubt and 'torn' between flesh and spirit, protagonists like Nigel Barton nevertheless make their 'stands', fighting for truth and honesty in the name of a ghostly patriarchal ideal. As demonstrated by the portrayal of incessant conflict between father and son in *Stand Up* and also *Lay Down Your Arms*, though the protagonists' relations in adulthood with their real fathers may be fractured and 'fallen', nevertheless what they are striving for is a *lost* childhood ideal of atonement and integration. By submitting to patriarchal authority and climbing its ladders of success, protagonists like Barton and Private Hawk get on in the world in order to try to change it in the name of that ideal. Theirs is the revenge quest of Hamlet for a lost, ghostly ideal of the father: an attempt to resolve the loss of integration they feel between their adult selves and the wider world.

As all of this shows, the general terrain of Potter plays is that of anxiety, persecution and separation from class, home roots and ultimately family. Characters like Barton and Harris the traitor are failed idealists: persecuted outcasts of a world that does not want to know their visions of the truth. Gloomy about the prospects of political change, many of the works take an equally gloomy view of humanity which is by turns depicted as 'bestial' and narrowly conformist in terms of its capacity to transform any lie into a truth for the sake of persecuting an innocent who is 'different'. Underlying all this is the sense of a Fall from a childhood characterised as a bright 'lost land', via a traumatic childhood event that is implicitly related to the shock of sexual discovery. As a result, many Potter protagonists find themselves prematurely forced into adulthood, 'torn' between flesh and spirit. Doubting yet driven, they comply with patriarchy and its authority structures only in order to try to get on and change them. Like Harris the double-agent in *Traitor* or the left-wing Hawk ensconced within the War Office in *Lay Down Your Arms*, they are moles within the system, impelled by their need to struggle for a lost ideal which they once thought they knew in childhood. Their goal is a re-integration with the world in relation to which, as adults, they feel anxious and separate. Their sense is that that goal is an impossible dream, destined always to defeat and failure.

This, however, is only half way along 'the yellow brick road' of Potter's life on screen. As Chapters 2, 4 and 5 suggested, there is another half to the journey: exactly akin to the structure of *The Singing Detective*, an upward progression in the work; a movement from a sense of Paradise lost to Paradise regained. It starts at the very nadir of despair in Potter's work, the period he himself labelled as one of 'in-turned spiritual nihilism': around the time of his 1972 play, *Follow the Yellow Brick Road*.[9] As Chapter 2 argued, *Son of Man* in many ways led Potter into consideration of the 'deeper' spiritual questions which had underlain the broadly political concerns of his sixties' plays. By 1972, with *Follow the Yellow Brick Road* and the *Hide and Seek* novel, his own previously attested position of atheism had been replaced (in the work at least) by characters who felt themselves hounded by a malign God-like 'Author' – not an oak-top integration with a God within but a wrathful Old Testament authority from without, in relation to which central protagonists felt themselves entirely separate and pushed around as innocent victims.

If atheism had evaporated, only to be replaced by spiritual disgust with a malign external deity, *Follow the Yellow Brick Road* touched on a theme that would form a crucial part of the upward progression in Potter's writing. In the world of the commercials, the central character, Jack Black, found a perfect world of happy families that appeared to him like a dream of perfection: a religious radiance. As Potter was later to put it, with *Follow the Yellow Brick Road*, he himself had begun to come to an understanding that 'the human dream for *some* concept of 'perfection', some Zion or Eden or Golden City, will surface and take hold of whatever circumstances are at hand – no matter how ludicrous.'[10] Even in the dead, material world of money and commercials, the 'spirit' would always outcrop.

Meanwhile, in the conclusion of *Hide and Seek*, there was also a similar optimistic qualification to the general sense of disgust with a malevolent Creation. Persecuted protagonist and God-like 'Author' were shown to be one and the same at the close of the novel. By recognising that every character was their own 'Author' and vice versa, both as one realised they had the power to reshape reality as their own God, thus re-gaining the sense of a God within which they had felt as children. By 1976, these optimistic strands within the work had become more fully developed in terms of a loose 'trilogy' of television plays in which there was a detectible movement away from antinomies of Good versus Evil; reality versus fantasy; flesh versus spirit, towards a blurring and coalescence of each of these categories. Instead of characters 'torn' between *either* flesh *or* spirit, there was a more complex sense of *both and.* The sense of a Fall and an attendant loss of faith which had marked much of Potter's earlier writing was replaced with a more 'holistic' awareness of a world of blurred categories in which instinctive faith in an ultimate Good (God) was posited as an alternative response to despair and disgust with the world. In many ways, the key to understanding this was the third play in the 1976 'trilogy', *Where Adam Stood.* As symbolised by young Edmund Gosse's rejection of an Old Testament-like father who threatened his very survival, literal Old Testament notions of Man suffering a Fall from grace were thrown off in favour of a more complex religious world-view. When Edmund rejected his father, he was, in effect, overthrowing patriarchy itself: traditional patriarchal suppression of Man's 'animal' nature which Darwin's theories also challenged in the play. Notions of somehow having undergone a Fall from God could thus be jettisoned. 'Where Adam Stood' once in terms of childhood belief in moral absolutes, there was now a sense in Potter's work of Man and God equal again; of Man having a God within that allowed him to shape his own destiny. This jettisoning of the concept of a Fall from innocence in turn had important repercussions for work that followed the 1976 'trilogy'. It allowed childhood in *Blue Remembered Hills*, for example, to be characterised not as a pre-lapsarian state of innocence but one in which the children were already 'fallen' and in possession of 'original sin'. Just as with the 1976 plays, simple moral antinomies of Good versus Evil, spirit versus flesh were jettisoned. The children were shown to be both innocent in their unknowingness *and* guilty in their sins.

A similar *both and* treatment of the central character can be found in 1978's *Pennies from Heaven*, in which Arthur Parker was shown to be simultaneously innocent and guilty of the murder of the blind girl for which he was eventually hanged. Moreover, in *Pennies*, Arthur's 'spirit' outcropped in his material dreams to such an extent that it was impossible to separate the flesh from the spirit in his character. Just as Potter first began to sense with *Follow the Yellow Brick Road*, so Arthur's 'Zion or Eden or Golden City' expressed itself in material terms: through his dreams of wealth, his compulsive womanising and above all in the cheap commercial songs of the day he peddled. By the time of *Pennies*, the flesh-spirit dichotomy in Potter's writing had blurred irrevocably. In stark contrast to earlier Potter protagonists, Arthur was not an agonised figure, 'torn' between flesh *or* spirit and haunted by doubt as to whether he was a villain *or* a victim. Rather, he was *both and*: an unrepressed *integrated* personality whose battle was entirely with the repressions of patriarchal society outside.

The upward journey of Potter's work from 1972 on was thus a journey towards an integration of the flesh-spirit dichotomy, together with a jettisoning of the simple antinomies and traditional moral absolutes of patriarchal social structures. As Chapter 5 argued, one of the most significant aspects of Potter's work was that it offered a critique of patriarchy from a male perspective. If this was what made Potter seek common cause with feminist critiques in *Blackeyes*, perhaps the clearest example of his jettisoning of the traditional values of patriarchy was the work that most definitively summed up this upward curve from despair to hope in his writing: *The Singing Detective*. As Chapter 5 noted, the central protagonist Philip Marlow was able in middle age to achieve psychological atonement with his dead father, not by striving to impose his spirit over the desires of the flesh (as earlier Potter protagonists had tried to do) but by jettisoning altogether this notion of a flesh-spirit dichotomy – the traditional guilt structure of repression of the flesh and elevation of the spirit, which underpins patriarchy. By recalling his father's 'animal-like' cry of grief, Marlow was able to be 'at one' with him again on equal terms; no longer with the awe of the God-like patriarch which had resulted in his original emotional separation and feelings of unworthiness after the Fall.

If, in the later work, notions of a Fall were thrown off, it was in the name of this striving for reintegration with the lost father that was also more generally a striving for re-integration between the self and the world: the 'oak-top' integration which the child in *Hide and Seek* had once felt in the Forest. Moreover, this suggests deeper roots behind Potter's early socialist idealism and the later commitment he made to write for television. The striving to communicate with a working-class audience, to create a 'common culture', can be related to the striving for community and integration with working-class childhood roots which was felt to have been lost at an early age. As Potter himself once expressed it, the desire to write for TV was like 'being [back] in the primary school again and making everything alright'.[11] It provided a means of overcoming feelings of separation from others of the same class as a result of knowledge of and guilt over a 'crime' which, as the various false scapegoats in the work attest (Georgie Pringle; Mark Binney; the Italian intruder unfairly persecuted by the villagers in *A Beast*), the child of the Forest subsequently tried to pin on others.

If such a search for a lost integration between the self and the wider world is ultimately what lies at the end of Potter's yellow brick road, as the writer acknowledged in interview, the 'seeking' was always the engine which drove his work. His weaving of threads and connections between disparate works was not, he asserted, a deliberate game of 'hide and seek' for its own sake. At the same time, it was not *unconscious* either. As Chapter 3 noted, his view was that:

> The closer writing approaches to therapy, the worse it becomes. I believe that passionately. So you've got to have that ruthless discipline about whether you're doing this to ease and soothe or as a balm to your soul or not – I mean I've destroyed lots of things where I felt that was happening ... So there's always that monitoring eye.[12]

As this suggests, his work was not simply the unconscious 'disembowelling of his own psychological condition'.[13] Akin to the progression in his writing away from simple antinomies of flesh versus spirit, the question of how consciously or unconsciously the connections between works were forged, was ultimately not one of 'either or' but of *both and*. Potter was conscious of building a body of work and of making connections between works but not so explicitly during the act of writing that it became mere manipulation or games-playing. Conversely, there were 'personal connections' buried in the writing of which the writer may have remained only half aware, yet not to such an extent that the work could be labelled therapy. As he put it, "just letting it out' is one of the definitions of bad art.'[14] His work was much more disciplined and self-conscious than that – equipped as it always was with a protective 'monitoring eye', vigilant against too much self-revelation.

In turn, this conscious–unconscious, *both and* synthesis helps provide a final answer to the question of the relationship of Potter's work to autobiography. In interview, he himself quoted H. G. Wells: 'Who would write novels if they could write autobiography flat out?' He also referred to Nabokov's comment about the links between life and fiction: 'Of course it's not me but if what I was writing was not in some sense true other than my imagination, it wouldn't come across as true' (see Chapter 3). As with the fact–fiction–truth distinction of *Hide and Seek*, imaginative writing functioned as an indirect means of truth-telling about the writer. The works were deliberate artifice but through their very indirectness as fiction, the writer could be more freely and deeply truthful about himself than he would have ever allowed himself to be by means of direct autobiographical confession.

Potter's work was thus a much more ambiguous fragile structure than that covered by the simple categories: 'autobiography', 'dramatic fiction', 'personal therapy'. It was both him *and* not him: clear fictions yet also the 'truth' about himself. As he put it, this 'both and' status meant his was a very fragile enterprise because of 'the delicate danger of both dealing and not dealing' in works like *Hide and Seek* and *The Singing Detective* with obsessed and tormented characters whose lives 'certainly medically, geographically, age terms, socially' mirrored his own.[15] Though in a sense, this blurred relationship between life and art is true of every writer (an inevitability of all writers that their own closest experiences or emotions will sooner or later outcrop in the work), the difference with Potter was that he *chose* to foreground this interplay between the life and the work in a much more explicit way, endowing characters like Philip Marlow or the 'Author' in *Hide and Seek* with many of the well-known 'facts' of his own life. Sprinkled upon the surface of the fiction, the use of his own biographical 'facts' was a means of hinting that underlying the artifice were emotional or 'spiritual' truths within the work; that the plays and the novel were in a sense works of personal spiritual exploration, with hidden depths.

The work was therefore the life – not in the straightforward sense of factual autobiography but in terms of the deeper emotional or spiritual concerns to which it gave expression. Certainly, it was in these religious terms that Potter saw his own writing. He talked in interview of having a 'longer *purpose*' and vocation as a writer, believing that because of his religious temperament, he was 'cursed with the desire to have a vocation of one kind or another'.[16] As with the 'Author' in *Hide and Seek* who got closer and closer to himself through fiction, Potter's creation of work so close to himself (through, for example, manufacturing writer characters in his own image) was one way of emphasising his religious sense of the work as a product of the 'spirit'. Because of this feeling of vocation, Potter made his work run alongside his life and vice versa. Just as with Philip Marlow's transformation into his fantasy hero at the end of *The Singing Detective*, there was an interplay between the two: the writer made the text but so too could the text (re-)make the writer. A veritable 'Pilgrim's Progress', Potter's own life followed the clear curve from pessimism to optimism of his work – moving from despair to redemption, precisely through a developing recognition of the work itself as the product and reflection of the power of an active, shaping 'spirit'.

Given such a view of a life in tandem with the work, it can be seen how much both fed off each other. Echoing his father's background as a coal-miner in the Forest of Dean, Potter literally mined himself, returning to the same themes and key events, as if to a particularly rich seam. In interview, he finally summed himself up this way:

> At the end of the day … I remain somehow or other against all the odds a Christian. It's what I actually in the end believe in, even though intellectually, I am appalled by the very baldness of such a statement. I know that at root somewhere, somehow that is what I turn and respond to. That is what tortures or torments me. And that whatever travails, mental or physical or social or sexual or whatever that I go through, I end up somehow or another getting my life into order. And in the getting my life into order, my work improves or broadens or widens the more surely I tame myself and put it all on to the page.[17]

The *value* of Potter's work is thus that he demonstrates to audiences that far from simply being determined by a set of external events and imperatives beyond their control – the social, cultural, sexual, health 'facts' of their background – they have the active power to take control; to get their own 'lives in order', shaping them in any way they choose. Just as with *The Singing Detective* in which the central protagonist, Philip Marlow, overcame the dislocations in his life caused by the trauma of past events and in so doing literally transformed himself into a new person, Potter's work was concerned with reminding audiences of their own sovereignty and agency; that not only were they 'made' but 'making'.

In one sense, this individualistic emphasis is but another version of the familiar 'American Dream' of (material) self-improvement sold by consumer capitalism. In works like *Follow the Yellow Brick Road* and *Pennies from Heaven*, Potter's achievement was to show that while such dreams may appear false and debased (from a Leftist standpoint such as his own), they nevertheless derive their hold and their power over large sections of the population precisely from the fact that they speak in terms directly addressed to the individual of the old 'human dream for some concept of perfection, some Zion or Eden or Golden City' – that 'somewhere, somehow, I can get better than this'.[18] The material dream, as Arthur Parker showed in *Pennies*, is inseparable from the spiritual yearning.

Potter's emphasis on agency and a sense of the world available to be remade not only unites religion with capitalism but paradoxically his broadly Christian outlook with Marxist perspectives. Potter's work shared much with the latter in terms of its emphasis on the *empowerment* of audiences. Like Brecht's, for example, his drama strove for an active spectator, eschewing empathy for its own sake, encouraging audiences to think not feel.[19] There, however, all similarity ends. While both Brecht and Potter shared a dislike of 'naturalism', the latter's stemmed not from any need to find new more effective forms of conveying a political message. In his view, all political drama ultimately did was 'to buck up and cheer up those who who support your side' so that its message would 'not drop an ounce' with those who were unsympathetic to it.[20]

Potter's terrain was instead an intimate 'interior drama' – his TV 'non-naturalism' an attempt to get under the skin of *all* viewers, Right or Left, in an attempt to draw their attention to their own individual agency or sovereignty. Ultimately a religious not a politically didactic writer, his achievement was to redefine conventional notions of Christianity – throwing off the patriarchal structures of authority and guilt in which they had become embedded. Spirituality was instead redefined in terms of individual agency, almost to the extent where Man was no longer seen as the Creation of God but God the function of Man: an expression of the latter's spiritual dreams of perfection and community with the wider world. In this way, his writing probed the roots of romantic and political idealism. His television work was an attempt to make audiences look afresh with new 'wonder' not only at what *is* but at what can be. A Christian optimist, he can, in the final analysis, quite accurately be labelled a television idealist too.

'The Golden City'

> Let the hard oak bring forth golden apples,
> Let narcissus bloom in the elder ...
> Ah! If the last days of my life could only be prolonged,
> To see the whole of creation rejoice
> In the age that is yet to come.
> (Virgil, quoted in *Casanova* by Dennis Potter, 1971)[21]

> Below my window in Ross, the blossom is out in full. It's a plum tree [but] it looks like apple blossom ... Looking at it through the window when I'm writing, it is the whitest, frothiest, blossomiest blossom that there ever could be ... And if people could see that – there's no way of telling you, you have to experience it ... The fact is that if you see the present tense, boy do you see it, and boy can you celebrate it!
> (Dennis Potter, interview, March 1994)[22]

If Potter was television's greatest idealist, nowhere was this more evident than in the final weeks and days leading up to his death from cancer in June 1994. Though terrible on one level, on another the demise of Potter represented almost a kind of triumph of everything he had striven for in his working life; a belated vindication of all his 'golden' ideals. To understand the full shape and significance, however, of this, the final coda of Potter's life on screen, one must go back to the early nineties and the immediate aftermath of the *Blackeyes* debacle.

In retrospect, the production and reception of *Blackeyes* which the previous chapter analysed can be seen to have had a decisive effect upon the two final works which gained a public airing during Potter's lifetime: *Secret Friends* and *Lipstick on Your Collar*. Each in their own way was a reaction against the pain caused by *Blackeyes*' British reception. Released in September 1992, the feature film, *Secret Friends*, was a cussed attempt by Potter to make no compromises with the critics. Journalist Simon Hattenstone detected this feeling when he visited Potter on the set, during shooting in 1991: 'So they say I can't direct? Good. *Secret Friends* will be the first full-length feature I direct. So they can't handle my sexual fantasies peppered with puritanical revulsion? Well, tough, because that's what I'm about.'[23]

Reviews of this adaptation of Potter's 1986 novel, *Ticket to Ride*, were scathing. As with *Blackeyes*, the writer-director had worked in the editing suite to collapse distinctions between reality and fantasy, as he attempted to portray the psychic disorientation of the film's central character, John Buck. Once more, however, his refusal to give any fixed perspective of external reality from which the various fantasy strands of the narrative could be ordered, had only served to alienate his British audience. *Empire* magazine dubbed the film a meaningless 'pile of psycho-twaddle', whilst *Sight and Sound* suggested 'it was time ... Potter pulled the communication cord on this particular train of thought.'[24] Significantly, Potter himself agreed. By September 1992, he had disowned *Secret Friends*. Asked by a journalist if he would be going to the cinema to see it, he replied: 'Oh, I might ... I might walk up and down for ten minutes. Until I see people walking out. Then I'll join them.'[25]

Potter was speaking on the set of *Lipstick on Your Collar*, his final six-part television 'serial with music' which was then currently in production. If *Secret Friends* represented a sour turning away from television towards an 'art cinema' experimentation, *Lipstick* was a deliberate attempt by Potter to restore his reputation to the levels he had enjoyed with *The Singing Detective*, by embracing a simplicity of form. Drawing upon his experiences of National Service in the War Office, the drama was essentially a reworking of *Lay Down Your Arms* of twenty years before. In contrast to *Blackeyes*, however, it deliberately opted for a simple linear plot. As the writer himself put it, the serial had 'no narrative complications ... It [did] not make *those* sort of demands on you.'[26] Its only 'non-naturalistic' turn was the use of Potter's by now thoroughly familiar device of characters miming to popular music – in this case, the rock n' roll songs of the fifties which became in the drama symbols of youthful rebellion against the rigid class order of Britain at the time of Suez.

It was this very attempt at familiarity for an audience that could not understand *Blackeyes* which ironically proved to be the drama's partial undoing when it was transmitted on Channel Four between 21 February and 28 March 1993. Whilst it certainly did not generate the critical opprobrium of *Blackeyes*, there was a sense amongst reviewers that *Lipstick* did not take its audience anywhere; that it said nothing new. The device of characters miming to popular music, once so radical and innovative, seemed to have become, by 1993, nothing more than a tired Potter trademark.[27]

Certainly, there was a sense with *Lipstick* of the writer having reached exhaustion point; of the old ideal of striving for a 'common culture' through television having finally lost all residue of meaning after *Blackeyes*. Underlying the apparent superficiality of *Lipstick*, there was, however, a complexity of theme. The main characters of Mick Hopper and Francis Francis, the two young squaddies thrown together as Russian language clerks in the War Office, demonstrably represent alternate sides of the flesh-spirit dichotomy that so tore at their predecessor: the single central protagonist, Hawk, of *Lay Down Your Arms*. With his love of poetry and acceptance into Oxford after National Service, the Welsh scholarship boy,

Francis, stands for all things of the spirit. Meanwhile, Hopper, the working-class Londoner whose sex-fuelled fantasies of becoming a rock n' roll star motivate the many musical interludes in the drama, is clearly possessed of more material aspirations. As the drama progresses, these opposite poles of flesh and spirit nevertheless begin to mingle and blur. The love-lives of the two young soldiers become hopelessly entangled, as each finds himself attracted to the girl with which the other eventually ends up at the close of the serial. In this way, Francis' romantic idealism of the 'spirit' is shown to be inextricably bound up with an 'animal' carnality.[28] Similarly, while Hopper's desires may appear to be entirely of the 'flesh', his material aspirations are ultimately shown to spring from the same source as his spiritual yearnings. As expressed through popular music, his wishes for a better life beyond the War Office represent exactly that dream of '*some* concept of perfection, some Zion or Eden or Golden City' which Arthur Parker shared, too, in *Pennies from Heaven*. In keeping with the progression noted in Potter's writing from the mid-seventies onwards, the battle-lines of flesh and spirit which Hawk found himself torn between in *Lay Down Your Arms* have blurred irrevocably by the time of *Lipstick on Your Collar*.

If this is the underlying structure of the drama, as the Arthur Parker comparison makes clear, Potter had said exactly the same thing, using the same miming device, in *Pennies from Heaven* fifteen years before. Something of this sense of going over old ground, of not knowing how to move his writing on, is tellingly revealed in a comment he made at the time of the drama's transmission: namely, that he had suffered from a block after he had written Episode 1 of *Lipstick*. For a while, he did not know what to do with the characters he had created nor how to take the narrative further.[29]

All of this seems to hint at deeper problems in Potter's writing of the late eighties and early nineties: problems which manifested themselves in the dip his reputation undoubtedly took after *Blackeyes*. In many ways, the roots of it can be traced back to *The Singing Detective*. As Chapter 5 described, Potter had been very worried about the success of *The Singing Detective*, fearing he would never get away from the character of Philip Marlow. Without planning it, he felt he had got too close to something, creating a character too near to himself.

Moreover, in that 1986 work, he had written out in one drama the story of the progression of his writing of the previous twenty years – from the guilt and anxiety expressed in the early plays to the resolution of the flesh-spirit dichotomy evident in the later works. The very tension which had provided the dynamic of the early plays' explorations had been resolved by the nineteen eighties. In writing out that journey from anxiety to optimism in *The Singing Detective*, Potter had both commented upon and drawn a line under his work of the previous twenty years. Thus what was left for the future? If, as Chapter 6 outlined, he initially moved to consideration of the impact on women of the male flesh-spirit dichotomy, by the early nineties there did not seem too many new angles left for him to explore. The rich seam he had mined for twenty-five years seemed on the point of exhaustion. Potter himself appeared to hint at this in 1993 when, asked whether he would always wish to write until he could not write anymore, he replied: 'I think I'm already at that stage, don't you? I'm about there.'[30]

This, in turn, may explain why, in the final year of his life, Potter increasingly moved away from his writer's study in order to voice more stridently his opinions on the state of Britain in the nineties. Under the patronage of Michael Grade at Channel Four, he launched a highly personal attack on the Murdoch press for the channel's *Opinions* slot – undoubtedly as an act of revenge for his treatment at the hands of the tabloids in recent years.[31] Then, in August 1993, he delivered the annual James MacTaggart Lecture at the Edinburgh International Television Festival. In a speech that was widely reported in the press and news media, Potter intervened in the debate about the future of public service broadcasting, attacking BBC Director-General John Birt and Chairman Marmaduke Hussey, after seeing the effects of their new 'internal market' at first hand, whilst working with the Corporation on the production of his feature film script, *Midnight Movie*.[32] Memorably, Potter lambasted Birt as a 'croak-voiced dalek ... in an Armani suit' and suggested that if public service broadcasting was not safe at the BBC, then the Corporation should be broken up to make way for other, smaller trustees of its heritage.[33] Significantly, he even offered to replace Hussey as BBC Chairman and while this was mainly taken as a joke by his audience, it may have hinted at Potter's own desire to seek a new public role for himself, in the face of the apparent decline of his writing.

Events the following year would not only reverse that decline but simultaneously enhance his stature as a public figure. At the same time, they would be inextricably bound up with personal tragedy. As was widely reported, Potter, having successfully nursed his wife through breast cancer in 1992, suddenly found himself stricken in early 1994 with an inoperable, terminal cancer of the pancreas (with secondary cancers in the liver). His condition was diagnosed on St Valentine's Day, and he was given three months to live. In March, having been approached by Melvyn Bragg, he characteristically decided to bid a very public farewell, through one final interview for his beloved, 'people's medium' of television.

Transmitted by Channel Four on 5 April 1994, that interview had a massive cultural impact. The very dramatic context of an individual staring death in the face – talking with humour and courage about his own illness, as well as his fears for the future of television and society – touched off something in the minds of both press and public. Undoubtedly, it had to do with growing disaffection about the way society and culture were going, after fifteen years of unbroken Conservative rule. In his Channel Four interview, Potter said many of the things he had said before but now it was the context, the audience's knowledge that death for this man was only weeks away, which made him become almost the embodiment for many of that wider dream of community – of '*some concept* of perfection' in society – which had also seemed to be dying in British life, as a result of the changes of the previous decade. Reaction to Potter's interview was like a lament for the passing of that old dream, with the writer himself elevated into a kind of symbol for a society waking up to the direction in which it was travelling and deciding it wanted to turn back.[34]

The *Without Walls* interview had other significant aspects too. As compensation for the fact of cancer, Potter talked of how knowledge of death had made him aware of the 'nowness' of everything which, he stated, was 'absolutely wondrous'. The idea of living for the moment – of recapturing the 'wonder' of the present tense that children felt – was something he had often talked and written about. Now, the imminence of death made it a felt reality. Likewise, the prospect of death had put new energy into his old ideal of striving for a 'common culture' through television. By the time of his cancer diagnosis, Potter had almost completed a new, original four-part serial for the BBC called *Karaoke*. Now, he said, he wanted to complete one final television work in order that he could provide his own posthumous 'memorial'. Even after death, he said, he 'wanted to continue to speak'.[35]

If the theatricality of this can partly be ascribed to a certain kind of writer's arrogance (a desire almost to make things happen in reality as if they were from the pages of one of his own scripts), the conception had deeper roots in Potter's old dream of a 'common culture'. By way of his Channel Four interview, the writer craftily used the tactic of emotional blackmail on the Controller of BBC-1 and the Chief Executive of Channel Four, Alan Yentob and Michael Grade respectively. By announcing publicly that his dying wish was for the BBC and Channel Four jointly to produce and screen his two last TV dramas, *Karaoke* and his new script, *Cold Lazarus*, Potter made sure that TV executives would have no choice but to comply with his will, for fear of incurring public wrath of having gone against the wishes of a dying man. Moreover, that wish can be seen as precisely Potter's attempt to create, for one final time, the possibility of a 'common culture' through television. Joint transmission of the two dramas would cut across the fragmentation of the multi-channel television environment of the nineties, producing the kind of public event television used to be able to offer the writer when he first started out as a dramatist in the mid-sixties. His final works, *Karaoke* and *Cold Lazarus*, would be his 'memorial' because, however temporarily, they would bring people together to participate in a television event, so that just for a moment Potter's old dream of a 'common culture' would live again.

It is in this way that the very public event which the writer made of his death can be seen to represent some kind of triumph of all he strove for in his working life. Though terrible on the level of individual loss and personal tragedy, the events culminating in his death seemed to signal the achievement of what all his life had been a struggle to reach. Akin to the double-edged ambiguous nature of some of his dramas like *Joe's Ark* and *Pennies from Heaven*, assessment of the significance of Potter's death finally becomes all a matter of from which perspective one chooses to look. Certainly, in the final weeks after the transmission of the *Without Walls* interview, the writer was buoyed up by the wave of public sympathy and affection which came his way, as evidenced by the avalanche of mail he received at his home. Fighting against and finally defeating the numbing pain of cancer, he succeeded in completing his final work, *Cold Lazarus*, against all the odds. Moreover, in the course of repeated trips to London, he busily set about tending to his affairs, with a compassion and panache which, according to Kenith Trodd, left others 'gawping in the face of his tenacity, the old sustained abrasiveness and now a courteous wariness of death, with rarely a hint of fear'.[36]

As this suggests, the prospect of death also brought about a reconciliation between Potter and his old friend and colleague, Trodd. For sentimental reasons, the latter was appointed producer of Potter's two final works, with a brief to make sure they were realised according to his wishes. Meanwhile, the writer himself helped advise the BBC and Channel Four on how they could jointly finance and produce *Karaoke* and *Cold Lazarus*, extracting promises from both that the works would be produced in 1995 for planned transmission in 1996.

Potter finally died on 7 June 1994, only nine days after cancer had also claimed his wife Margaret.[37] The media coverage accorded to his death was on a scale normally reserved for the passing of a major national figure: items on all the main TV news broadcasts; a full-length television tribute broadcast on the night of his death; full-page obituaries in the national press; even a tribute from the then Heritage Secretary Peter Brooke MP.[38] It was final proof and vindication that Potter as television writer had been successful in his aim of trying to cut across the lines in British society. Through television, his writing and ideas had reached out to a far greater range of people, communicating with them and touching their lives to a far greater extent than if he had been a figure predominantly of the theatre or of literature.

In managing to complete his final works, Potter thus achieved success on many levels. There was the personal triumph of having completed them at all in the face of extreme illness. There was also the achievement that his final interview and his own passing managed to cut across cultural hierarchies, prompting many to examine the direction in which television and the country in general were heading. Particularly through his final television 'memorial', he achieved, too, a kind of artistic immortality, producing original work that will continue to 'speak' long after he is gone. In this way, Potter not only reached his 'golden city' at the end, he himself engineered it, ensuring that his words and presence would survive even beyond his death. Perhaps, once more, it is his old friend and sparring partner, Kenith Trodd, who provides the most concise final summary of the remarkable achievements in death of this undoubtedly remarkable writer. Writing in a newspaper obituary, the producer stated that for him, the last weeks of Potter's life were: 'a glorious revitalisation of the cliché about nothing in life becoming one like the leaving of it. In those three and a half months alone, [Potter] brought off more than most of us achieve in our whole life.' Significantly, he concluded: 'Dennis' work will go on speaking for itself for a long time but I return to cliché to say that great writer he obviously is, ... I now think of him also as rather a Great Man.'[39]

Plate 7 'Let's Face the Music and Dance...': Steve Martin and Bernadette Peters in the MGM movie version of *Pennies from Heaven*

Plate 8 ‘‘The Devil’s Prayer’: Sting in the 1982 film version of *Brimstone and Treacle*

Plate 9 'The Best Things in Life Are Absolutely Free…': Albert Finney as the dying Daniel Feeld sings what people 'ought to know' in *Karaoke*

Plate 10 "No biography?': Steven Macintosh does a double-take with Dennis Potter lookalike, Ian MacDiarmid, in *Karaoke*

'Stars in My Crown ...?' A personal afterword (1998)

In July 1994, when the words over the page were written (barely one month after Potter's death), expectations were high that *Karaoke* and *Cold Lazarus* would prove decisive in restoring the writer to the levels of success he had enjoyed in the past. The omens seemed good: after all, *that* final TV interview had produced such a remarkable outpouring of public goodwill and sympathy. Meanwhile, Kenith Trodd was extolling the finished scripts to the press as amongst the best, if not *the* best, of Potter's writing.

Four years on and two years after the UK transmission of the finished productions, things have not turned out quite as rosy as everyone expected. On the whole, British press reviews of *Karaoke* and *Lazarus* were either hostile or indifferent while, in spite of unprecedented collaboration between the BBC and Channel Four in cross-scheduling the dramas to maximum advantage, audience ratings were poor.[1] As a surprised Ken Trodd put it in July 1996:

> I had assumed that the goodwill that Dennis had created when he did the Bragg interview would carry over, and that those pieces would be seen, not in any particularly indulgent light, but would be received as important new works and then would sink or swim on their merits. But I don't think that's what happened ...[2]

The reasons why are interesting and they tell us much about the present state of media culture in Britain and the direction in which it is heading for, despite press attacks on the alleged 'self-indulgence' of the scripts as well as internal production wrangles over the quality of the direction, favourable critical reaction overseas shows the works were by no means as bad as painted at home.[3] Certainly, when I first read the original scripts I rated them Potter's 'best' since *The Singing Detective* and I would still stick to that opinion.

In interview with me in 1990, Potter acknowledged the many themes and deliberate connections between works which this book has tried to map out and trace but he also added:

> There is a sense in which I could abandon all my previous work as inadequate and incomplete versions of the work that one day I will write … Somehow all these threads will come together. One piece of work will finally do what I'm at, maybe. And then I'll kill myself !

If not quite that big *meisterwerk*, the posthumous *Karaoke* and *Cold Lazarus* bravely draw many of those threads together in order to offer one final statement. For the dying Potter (writing in the introduction to a published edition of his scripts he knew he would never live to see) they were 'as fitting a summation as they are a testament both to my character and to my career as I should ever want' (p.xv).[4]

Both works are really one. In *Karaoke*, we meet Daniel Feeld (played by Albert Finney) – a cantankerous middle-aged screenwriter, beset by the usual writer's problems, including an arrogant, adulterous director, Nick Balmer (Richard E. Grant) who insists on altering his latest script during production (for example, substituting Daniel's song 'Why Must I Be A Teenager in Love ?' for his own highly appropriate soundtrack choice, 'Your Cheatin' Heart'). Though he does not yet know it, Daniel is also dying from cancer and the increasingly sharp jabs of stomach pain he feels as he wanders around the Soho cutting rooms and wine bars of rain-splashed London, somehow or other seem to be mixed up with another equally painful feeling: that incredibly, his script is coming alive. People around him keep repeating his dialogue and when he overhears in a brasserie, a young woman, Sandra (Saffron Burrows), say lines he is convinced will lead inexorably to her death, he drunkenly decides to follow her to the sleazy Karaoke club where she works as a hostess in order to try and warn or rescue her. But in the rewritten *Karaoke* (Potter, once he learned he was dying, rewrote his original version to save it from 'the muddle' he thought it had become), is Daniel's script really coming alive or has it been all in his head?[5] In a crucial scene in Episode Four, the writer is told by his hospital consultant that he has only weeks to live. Suddenly, however, he is *laughing*:

> DANIEL (*laughs*): … When all these dreadful pains began … I thought that a story I had written had somehow *got out* into the world … wandering about out there … But no … there's been another story going on all the time. *This* one. The one I didn't know about …

Smiling, he tells the consultant that when he was a child:

> DANIEL: I always used to … make believe I was in the middle of a book – the one bright book! – in which there was a shape, a meaning, and a good ending. … Where I can tidy up all the loose bits and bobs, tie up all the

> loose ends, find the *shape* of it – Yes. That's what I'll do … I'm back in charge of my own story. I can take control of it now … I know what to do …
>
> CONSULTANT (*quietly*): Good man. (pp. 171–2)

The tone is wry and tender. It is clearly what Dennis Potter himself was doing in his final days – 'taking control' of his own story, finding a meaning to his death by using the time left to write his own TV memorial; to make a 'good ending'. As with much of the later work looked at in this book, the emphasis in the drama is on finding a shape to one's life, even if that means creating one yourself. There may be no meaning beyond ourselves but it is we who make things special: as Arthur Parker once expressed it in *Pennies*, it is us that 'puts the real meaning into them songs' (see Chapter 4).

Then again, as Daniel discovers at the end of *Karaoke*, though we often may think we are all alone in making up the story of our own lives, it can be a great shock when we suddenly find we have been characters all along in a much larger drama we knew nothing about. This is the metaphor behind the serial's use of the karaoke machine. As Daniel tells Sandra, it is that dizzying feeling that 'the song or the story of our lives is already made up for us' (p. 95). Or as Potter described karaoke in his *Without Walls* interview: 'you have your little line. You can sing it, and everything is written for you and that is the way life feels to a lot of people. For some, you haven't much space and even the space you've got, although you use your own voice, the words are written for you'. In the seventies, Potter's characters expressed their freedom of 'spirit' through miming to popular song. The nineties equivalent, he suggests, is a pale imitation in which free citizens have been downloaded into passive consumers.

We may all ultimately be characters in someone else's script but *Karaoke* is also defiantly optimistic. It suggests we do have the awesome power to break free. Like all his later work, the drama is deeply concerned with issues of personal 'sovereignty' and freedom: that not only are we 'made' but 'making'. Daniel Feeld may be facing his irrevocable end but at the same time he realises he has the power to shape it. He can rewrite the script and in so doing (the two are synonymous for Potter) 'reright' past wrongs, leaving the world better than he found it. The serial illustrates this through both its symbolically linked main characters: the director, Nick Balmer, finally repents of his adultery with his leading actress, Linda Langer and reconciles with his wife at the close. Meanwhile, in a deliberate echo of Shaw's *Pygmalion*, Daniel Feeld takes the cockney Sandra under his wing, bequeathing his fortune to her on condition she does not return to the karaoke club where she was effectively a prostitute. Just to make sure, the dying patient takes up his bed for one final time and with nothing to lose, shoots the club's owner, the villainous 'Pig' Mailion (Hywel Bennett), thereby guaranteeing that an old life is killed forever.

The deeply Christian structure of repentance and redemption is unmistakable as are all the links with past works. There is the self-reflexion (a drama about a writer writing a drama) familiar from *Only Make Believe* and *Double Dare* and the same two-way traffic between reality and fantasy: like an alchemist with base metal, the writer may transform his reality into fiction but so too, the drama shows, can that fictional 'gold' become reality. There is also the deliberate playing with teasing autobiographical connections which reached its apotheosis with *The Singing Detective*: 'I remember when I could make a whole ward *sing*,' says Daniel ruefully at one point (p. 81). Subsuming all of these links, however, is the serial's acknowledgement of its debt to what this book has argued was the pivot in Potter's own upward journey as a writer; the work that was 'loved heart and soul' and which provided the blueprint for all those others mentioned: Potter's 1973 novel, *Hide and Seek*.[6] Not only does *Karaoke* echo that novel's characters, Daniel Miller the writer and Sandra, the prostitute whom an awe-struck Miller once spied in a cafe (as opposed to Feeld's brasserie). Its central theme is also, ultimately, the relation between God and Man – of believing at first you are helpless to control the dark drama unfolding in front of you until, suddenly, the realisation comes that you *do* have the power within to be 'Author of your Fate' and so make things brighter. In that recognition comes redemption and an optimism which, even in death, by laying down one's life and 'rescuing' another from a tawdry script, means you will be born anew.

In *Cold Lazarus*, Daniel Feeld achieves that resurrection but, as the title implies, the world he wakes up to is far from heavenly. It is 2368 and scientists of the future are trying to stimulate Daniel's four hundred year old, cryogenically preserved severed head, in an experiment to see if they can actually succeed in tapping into the memories of a human being. If *Karaoke* ploughed Potter's familiar 'feeld', offering in the process a 'glancing valediction' to all the works that had gone before, *Cold Lazarus* plunges us into what seems entirely new territory: science fiction.[7] Amazingly, Potter, at his end, projects forward, beyond his own destruction, envisioning with very great detail in his scripts an entire future landscape of automatic bubble cars, strange linguistic evolutions ('Godolo'; 'manolo') and (importantly for the plot), virtual reality helmets and data gloves, in a Britain that has long ago ceased to exist as a political entity but is instead ruled ruthlessly by giant, multi-national corporations. It is meant to be a stunning *coup de theatre* on the part of the dying writer, an audacious voyage into the unknown beyond his usual concerns, though like all the best science fiction, its vision of the future can really be seen as a comment on the present.

In his 1993 MacTaggart tirade against the BBC 'internal market', Potter announced he was grappling with what it feels like to 'be a citizen (or do I mean a consumer?) in the United Kingdom plc', demanding 'what is at the heart of such a distorted society?'[8] In *Cold Lazarus*, we are given his answer: 'Oh it's this precious internal market of the Masdon Group', cries the chief scientist, Emma Porlock (played by Francis de la Tour), in despair. 'They'll charge a fee for anything that could be argued as outside our remit' (p. 228). As this suggests, there is more than a hint of satire against the modern BBC in Potter's future vision. The scientists, on the threshhold of a new discovery, are pursuing knowledge for its own sake but rather like Potter's view of creative people at the BBC, the quality of their work is constantly undermined by 'management' breathing down their neck, with values that measure worth only in relation to short-term commercial gain. Through a complicated system of departmental spies and virtual reality monitoring, the witch-like boss of the cryogenic labs, Martina Matilda Masdon (Diane Ladd), hovers like God over her terrified employees, her bony fingers into every pie, in a manner that seems to make her a cross between Potter's 'croak-voiced' Director-General, John Birt and former BBC Chairman Marmaduke Hussey (note the linguistic echo between 'Martina' and 'Marmaduke').

The supreme irony, however, is that in so relishing her reign of terror, Masdon's emphasis on short-term profit blinds her to the fact that what her employees have actually stumbled upon is pure gold-dust. It is up to another, far more shrewd, entrepreneur, media mogul, Dave Siltz (Henry Goodman), to realise that the memories of the twentieth century spilling out of the dead man's head are financial dynamite: literally, pennies from heaven. Accordingly, he resolves to steal Masdon's 'golden apple' right from under her nose, guilefully capitalising on the sleeping assets of another in a manner that makes him directly akin to Potter's *bete noir*, Rupert Murdoch, driving 'a golden coach and team of wild-eyed horses straight through the gap' of the blinkered, insecure giant, the BBC.[9]

The world of *Cold Lazarus*, then, is a veritable dystopia, entirely the antithesis of everything Potter believed and wanted to see in his life: a world that is wholly material, where science and commerce rule like gods in an unholy alliance and more 'spiritual' values of art and culture have been forced underground, to be cherished like forbidden fruit only by a dissident network of 'R.O.N' ('Reality or Nothing') terrorists, pledged to the overthrow of the present and restoration of more 'real' values such as 'freedom' and 'community' – values ironically which they think they have spied in the twentieth century. In this way, everyone is interested in plundering Daniel Feeld's mind: Siltz for the profit of beaming its content into the world's virtual reality head-sets; the terrorists because they believe Siltz may have been too clever for his own good. As R.O.N. agent amongst the scientists, Fyodor Glazunov (Ciaran Hinds), puts it, Feeld's memories will show the present that 'there were other ways to live ... Let the past speak ! Let it *accuse*!' (p. 308).

In this future that is like the present, everyone is running around making a great fuss about the 'facts' that lie hidden in the writer's mind but as his memories begin to tumble out on to the video wonderwall of the scientists' lab, it becomes clear that so much profit and expectation are riding on recollections that are, in truth, very simple and very poignant. As Potter suggested in his *Without Walls* interview, in making his final farewell to television drama, Feeld's memories are his own memories or, as he very importantly qualified it, 'what I choose to make my memories'. From the vantage point of a harsh and distorted future, the scientists (and we) watch, fascinated, as recollections of a distant childhood spent in the far gentler world of the tellingly named 'Forest of Nead', begin to unspool. We also witness a nervous mid-twentieth century courtship between Daniel and a girl from the Forest, the 'green-eyed dazzler', Beth, whose subsequent death the writer cannot help feeling guilty for.[10] It soon becomes clear that his later attachment to Sandra was out of yearning for this lost love. Right in the very heart of the Paradise, however, a darker shadow also stalks the Forest, as the writer's memories conjure up a horrific sexual assault which, in this version (as opposed to, say, the Italian P.O.W of *Hide and Seek*), the child suffers at the hands of a half-mad cockney tramp.

Yet as the scientists, like the TV audience that followed Potter's career, view it all bit by bit and try to piece together this 'life on screen', can they really be sure that what they are watching *actually* happened? The dead writer's audience of the future is shown to be utterly literal-minded, only interested in draining the objective 'facts' as it sees them, but as the scientists keep watching, they begin to reach the unsettling conclusion that what they are seeing cannot possibly be real for, there, wandering around within his own memories of childhood, is the presence of the *adult* Daniel Feeld – the middle-aged writer of *Karaoke*. If the device is a last nod back to Potter's celebrated adults-as-children device, the reasons for using it are the same as before since, as one of the scientists, Luanda, comes to realise: 'don't we sometimes place ourselves as we are now back into the unravelling of an old recollection? ... I can be as I am now when I dream of my childhood'. Memory and dream, she comes to see, are first cousins: 'My dreams are built from the things that happen to me in the waking world. And my memories can also adapt and shape the past ... Memory ... is also a tool, an editor, a judge, a jury!' (pp. 252–3) Just as *Karaoke* showed, the traffic between reality and fantasy is two-way: one's dreams are built from real events but so too can those dreams in turn shape 'the real'. It is Potter's artistic philosophy summed up in a nutshell and a warning to anyone 'crude and philistine' enough to confuse drama with autobiography.[11] As Emma Porlock admits simply at one point in *Cold Lazarus*, writers 'tell *tales*. They make things up' (p. 285) – what we may be actually seeing is the 'infinitely cunning operations of an infinitely complex mind ... at work!' (p. 253) The fact-fiction-'truth' distinctions argued in this book apply: beneath the judicious sprinkling of a few autobiographical 'facts' as signposts on top lies a dramatic fiction but underneath that is the guarantee of spiritual or emotional 'truth'. As Luanda states in *Lazarus*, 'At base, it's real. It's true!' Potter's point is that one's recollections of the past are constantly interpenetrated by one's feelings in the present. For him, there is no such thing as objective memory.

As all this shows, much of *Cold Lazarus* is actually a metaphorical treatise (informed by considerable reading, on Potter's part, of the latest neuro-science) on the workings of the mind. It fascinates the writer because it is precisely the area where science intrudes upon religion; not to mention the terrain of his own drama, with its emphasis on quasi-religious or artistic notions of the 'spirit'. The urgent question which the serial poses is, are we free or simply machines: the Pavlovian product of a random series of electro-chemical stimuli within the brain? At first, it seems to be the latter as the scientists succeed in summoning up almost at will certain kind of memories from Feeld by stimulating the requisite areas of the brain. Yet as they research further, they come to the disquieting conclusion that there is volition; that the brain is somehow 'alive' and aware of its own condition. When the scientists finally discover that the head has been transmitting memories which they did not stimulate, they realise it is time to stop. As Professor Porlock tells her 'sugar-daddy' Siltz, who has been funding her research in the hope that Daniel's sexual memories can be raided for pornographic profit, it would be 'a moral outrage for us to proceed further' (p. 387). Fyodor Glazunov puts it another way: in plundering the story of the writer's private life, 'we are his torturers' (p. 377).

The drama ends with Fyodor making it to the cryogenics lab before Siltz's private militia can catch him, barricading himself in and smashing up all the contents. When Siltz appears outside and tries to tempt him with riches to stop, Fyodor shoots him through the throat (as Potter said of Rupert Murdoch in his final TV interview, 'if I had the time ... I would shoot the bugger'.) Looking to the video wall, Fyodor sees an image of Daniel Feeld holding up a pad in which the legend 'LET ME GO !' is written and with this definitive proof of the head's volition and deep desire for freedom, Glazunov shoots the box which contains it, uttering the words, 'Personal guarantee, Daniel' (p. 390). We watch the destruction as the head, encased in liquid nitrogen, explodes and with fire sweeping through the whole lab, killing Fyodor instantly, we are aware that we are watching not only the controlled self-destruction of Daniel Feeld but in a sense that of Potter himself. The video wall lights up as we review and recall the legacy for one final time: a series of swirling memories and images from the past, as Daniel's 'spirit' disappears down a white vortex which may be leading to heaven, accompanied by the hymn 'Will There Be Any Stars in My Crown ?' and with the triumphant cry of blessed release: 'Ye – e – e – e – s!' (p. 392)

For a writer, at that point, so near to death himself, it is an amazing affirmation from Potter; of a sense of optimism and personal freedom found precisely at the end through the quality of his own 'art'. As such, the completion of *Cold Lazarus* and its sister *Karaoke* against all the odds, stands as a personal vindication of everything he stood for in his working life. The Christian structure and links with *Karaoke* are evident too: just as Daniel effectively laid down his life for Sandra at the end of the first drama, rescuing her from the tawdry script that was her fate, so Fyodor at the close of *Lazarus* does the same for Daniel, saving him from the commercial degradation of Siltz: a 'personal guarantee' that repays the promise Daniel made to Sandra and in so doing, finally allows him to receive his reward of 'heaven'. From its avowedly Christian perspective, defending the trapped and the helpless is shown to be the only possible salvation within the world the drama presents. If, through its cryogenics plot, *Lazarus* plays with the idea of how tempting it might be to survive in some physical form beyond death, the final conclusion is that such a thing would be grotesque and unnatural. We have an allotted life-span and within that span, freedom of 'spirit' and scientists meddle with both these areas at their peril. Its title catching at the tensions between life and death, *Cold Lazarus* shows the only possible immortality is in 'art' where, plugged into the 'video walls' of a million TV homes, the writer's memories, emotions and fantasies may 'continue to speak' through an endless play of dramatic simulations.[12]

The themes of the two dramas and their many links with other work are seamlessly woven together with (given the circumstances of extreme duress in which they were produced) an amazing degree of control. And yet as noted earlier, these final works were not at all well received on transmission – in Britain at any rate. There seem to be a number of different explanations for this. One is simply the gap between script page and screen. There was, it is true, some 'flatness' in the direction of the actual productions; a literalism of approach that saw Potter's scripts perhaps treated more as solemn stone memorials rather than living, breathing dramas – though this is a facet that can be over-exaggerated. It does not account for the degree of scorn which the productions received in some quarters of the British press. An alternative explanation lies in another gap: the two years between Potter's last TV interview, announcing the works, and their actual transmission. Producer Ken Trodd is a shrewd commentator on this when he states: '... the awe with which Dennis laid waste his own death in the Bragg programme, silenced virtually every critic, and this meant that in some unconscious way they waited two years [at which point] they felt they could go for him and accuse him of power tripping and so on'.[13]

Reviewers somehow felt they could have a 'go' at Potter now he was dead: after all, it is difficult to knock very easily the pronouncements of a dying man but it is surely fair game to criticise the quality of his posthumous writing. This touches on one of the sad ironies of Potter's career. As this book has shown, Potter decisively turned away from the public world of current affairs and politics towards the private 'truths' of writing because he saw 'facts' as 'lies' that served to conceal underlying emotional realities (see Introduction). The irony is that towards the end of his life, he actually came to be more valued in British culture for his public interventions (MacTaggart lecture; Bragg interview) than for his drama. In what he labelled our 'over-manipulated and news-stuffed world' of the nineties, many people could respond to and agree with the 'factual' value of his public personality but they could not understand so readily the metaphorical 'truths' he embedded in his plays.[14]

If the reason for that was partly Potter's own refusal to write simple or politically explicit drama (as he put it to me, 'all political drama does is buck up and cheer up those who support your side': see conclusion), it also has much to do with changing attitudes and values in British media culture of the nineties. Again, Ken Trodd is shrewd on this. He describes how a *Guardian* review by high-profile journalist Mark Lawson appeared a full two weeks before *Karaoke* and *Cold Lazarus* had even begun transmission. Having read the scripts and watched a video only of the first episode of *Karaoke*, Lawson nevertheless felt confident enough to write off the finished productions as not of the standard of earlier Potter works. As Trodd puts it: 'that was all about that awful business of everyone wanting to get in first'. He adds: 'What you're dealing with here is much more the jungle of columnists competing with each other in some dreadful deadline-driven purgatory than any concerted agenda against Dennis Potter. But certainly that piece set a tone ... [and] it gave other people an excuse to be shits in their own turn'.[15]

If Trodd's feelings about the uncharitableness of much of the comment surrounding the posthumous Potters is evident here, he also puts his finger on the much harsher competitiveness of the new, deregulated British media environment, where, increasingly, the only rules of the game appear to be 'first, fastest and loudest'. Because there was so much expectation that his last works would be *formidable* (partly as a result of Potter's own hyping of them in his final interview in an effort to make sure they would be produced), it was almost inevitable they would produce their detractors. After all, what better way to get a headline and make a splash than to say the works are not as good as they were hyped up to be? As Trodd is acutely aware, the media climate today is much 'draughtier for somebody like Dennis Potter'.[16] In the aggressively commercial, ratings-driven world, epitomised by the likes of Murdoch's British Sky Broadcasting or the new terrestrial Channel Five, the values that produced a Dennis Potter seem a million miles away. A new generation of press reviewers has emerged in the last decade which, like the new, younger generation of British TV viewers whose opinions it reflects, does not regard television as a unique cultural resource 'that made [the] heart *pound*' but as simply a mundane multi-channel utility of invariable low quality and inevitable, accepted commercialism.[17]

In this new world, a Dennis Potter sits very awkwardly, largely because, despite its often beguiling surfaces, his drama is 'serious' and 'difficult'. While U.S. viewers, long accustomed to deriding their TV (rightly or wrongly) as commercial 'trash', welcome Potter as a challenging, exotic voice, British TV seems to be heading in precisely the opposite direction, jettisoning its public service roots as no longer 'relevant'. The single play, for example, which nurtured Potter, has been gone from the British prime-time TV schedules for almost a generation. This fact, in turn, perhaps explains the very low audiences for *Karaoke* and *Cold Lazarus*: viewers have simply got out of the habit of watching the kind of 'difficult' metaphorical drama Potter wrote. They are no longer quite so willing to give his type of 'art' television a fair hearing.[18] By a vicious if inevitable cycle, what audiences and critics cannot tolerate or understand, they then condemn as 'self-indulgent' or 'in need of rewrites' or (in the case of the Daniel Feeld–Sandra bond in *Karaoke*), the 'fantasies of a dirty old man'. Certainly, there was a feeling with much of the British press comment that Potter was regarded as part of an old, indulged broadcasting culture: that he had been over-rated in the past and over-cossetted by the TV Establishment; his fantasies about 'writers writing scripts' now recognised as of no 'relevance' to audiences whatsoever.[19] Many of the reviews, such as Lawson's, seemed determined to consign him to history, asserting that the writer's monuments were *Pennies*, *The Singing Detective* and *Blue Remembered Hills* while the rest showed evidence of a sad decline, particularly post-*Blackeyes*. In Chapter Six of this book, I tried to analyse reasons for *Blackeyes*' poor British reception, asking what was it in that drama that made it so different from Potter's previous successes? In retrospect, part of the answer may lie not so much with Potter himself but the fact that what we were seeing at that time was the beginning of a change in British media culture which has been so much more evident since: a move away from the earlier, cosier world in which *Pennies* and *The Singing Detective* had been given a respectful chance to become monuments; one that may say just as much about a change in attitude amongst reviewers of the British press as the actual quality of the work reviewed.[20]

This much more ferocious media bear garden has had other unwelcome effects on the Potter 'legacy' too. In April 1997, the (Rupert Murdoch-owned) *Sunday Times* newspaper ran the following 'exclusive':

> **Potter's life of vice girls is revealed**
> Dennis Potter, whose television plays scandalised viewers ... was tortured by a secret in his private life. [His] official biographer ... will reveal that he was racked by guilt for his regular encounters with ... as many as 136 prostitutes ... The allegations will cast fresh light on the guilt-ridden attitude to sex in Potter's masterpieces such as *Pennies from Heaven* and *The Singing Detective* ...[21]

For the seasoned Potter-watcher, the links with *Cold Lazarus* are all just a little too delirious: the helpless writer drained of a 'salacious' sexual memory that is used on behalf of a powerful media mogul for public titillation and private profit. But who is the author ruthlessly plundering the most intimate parts of Potter's past for present-day gain? His name is Humphrey Carpenter – and not only is he a regular book reviewer for Murdoch's *Sunday Times* but a biographer who has been appointed by Potter's very own estate.[22]

How can this be? As this book has traced, the whole thrust of Potter's work was to view 'facts' as lies that obscured the emotional 'truth' and he always argued that his work should not be reduced to the level of simple biography. How could his own estate do this to him? Two years on from first claiming that he 'did not know Potter's views on biography', Carpenter and presumably the estate's current position is that the dying Potter 'accepted' at the very end that a biography would be written and that both his family and literary executor, Judy Daish, were actively looking for a biographer. Potter himself, it is alleged, even expressed a wish to meet his biographer.[23] But how does this square with the final terrified cry Potter puts into the lips of his writer alter ego, Daniel Feeld as, surrounded on his death-bed by his agent and entourage, he dies, while the scientists in

Cold Lazarus look on via their video wall ? The dying Potter's script directions render the sheer horror of this with all the force he can muster:

> More and more discernible and hideously upsetting, a head seems to float in liquid nitrogen, all wired-up with antennae, neurotransmitters and hair-thin coils of tubes. But the eyes are open, full of terror, and the mouth seems to be trying to make word-shapes ...
> ... DANIEL: (*Off, near scream*): No biography! (p. 245)

What is the dramatist trying to emphasise here ? Why put such a death scream into the lips of Daniel Feeld ? Is this a desperate cry from the past to the future; from a writer, like Feeld, so weak and vulnerable yet helplessly trying to protest ? Ironically, the biographer, Carpenter, shrugs off any such connections between the work and the life in *this* particular case. The deathbed cry, he claims, is one of the great literary jokes from 'a very manipulative subject': 'it's a joke. [Potter] accepted that a biography would be written ... Besides, he spent a lot of time talking about himself to interviewers'.[24]

He certainly did. In interview with me in 1990, he stated: 'I despise biographies. They're hidden novels ... And I do think that biographical criticism is such an easy way of assuming you get ... the key to a body of work. I just know that that is not the case'. Ironically, much of our interview had actually been *about* discussing to what extent his work was simply a product of the 'facts' of his life. Potter described such a view as 'reductionist criticism in the extreme' and as we have seen, while acknowledging that like any writer, certain real events were in there, asserted his work was much more than the simple product of his own biography (see Chapters 3 and 5). He suggested that he self-consciously used the 'conventions of autobiography' as his deliberate means of making connections with the audience and he also ventured that this was his way of gaining attention: 'people are infinitely curious ... and the point is that that curiosity is exactly what I'm trying to use'. He added that if he went through each of his works saying: 'Oh well, that was partly true, that was totally untrue, I would destroy the very machine that I'm building – the engine. I would be draining the fuel out of it'. It was for this reason, he stated, he had actively stopped people from trying to write his biography in the past. In 1989, he personally went to see a woman journalist to stop her (a fact, incidentally, which I cannot believe his agent and entourage would be unaware of).[25] He said that in looking at his work purely in terms of biography, people were actively misunderstanding the nature of it. He told me he was concerned about all the probing into his life, which he himself had partially elicited by stoking public curiosity about his life in order to get an audience for his work: 'I'm concerned', he said, 'Not in any defensive way but as a writer' that everyone is 'on the wrong tack'.

How could a man with such strong opinions against biography undergo such a sudden death-bed conversion at the end? Does this mean he was lying in all those interviews he gave throughout his life, in an effort to conceal the secret autobiographical 'truth' from prying eyes? After all, it is certainly true he was a shy and reclusive man and like most people, there may well have been private aspects of his past that he did not want publicly aired. Once he was dying, did that not matter anymore? Or does this posthumous view of the *wholly* 'manipulative subject' rather too neatly elevate the importance of the biographer as uncoverer of the 'real' secret truth, providing an ethical justification for the raking into the late writer's private life that is now underway? And if we are to take the story of his last-minute acceptance of an 'official' biography at face value, at what point does 'accept' mean 'wholeheartedly agree'? Does the evidence of *Cold Lazarus*, as well as my own interview with him, not put the lie to such posthumous claims ?

What is clear is that as Potter stated about his work in my 1990 interview, people 'want to know 'is this true?' which is a very curious question to ask about a play or novel'. He himself was acutely aware that in what he regarded as our 'news-stuffed' journalistic media culture, the only kind of 'truth' many people would accept today was 'facts' – in terms of 'art' and criticism, the only kind of meaning, biographical meaning. This was why he recognised the ''autobiographical' convention ... as perhaps the most powerful one left in the hands of a writer'. In 1992, he also told Graham Fuller: 'autobiography is the cheapest, nastiest literary form; I think only biography beats it. It's very interesting that they are the two most popular forms at the moment'.[26] Potter knew that biographies are the tabloids of the chattering classes; that they sell: looking at writers' lives is far more of a commercial proposition, say, than critical studies looking at their work (could this possibly be the reason why Potter's publisher has done a deal with his estate to produce an 'official' biography after his death?)[27] In his lifetime, Potter had a shrewd understanding of these trends yet he also saw the limitations of the biographical 'method' in failing to deal with what, for him, was the inner emotional 'truth' of a writer's work that could so often be obscured by a preoccupation with the external material 'facts' of the life (see Conclusion). His artistic achievement, in many ways, was to turn today's insatiable biographical curiosity in and against itself – self-consciously using it to lure a mass audience to attend to what he saw as the deeper 'spiritual' themes of his work. The problem is that after his death it makes it very easy for others to come along in his wake and read the work in straightforward autobiographical ways, reducing it to the level of simple public confession or unconscious personal therapy and thereby in a sense dismissing it. In our 'fact'-obsessed media culture, the biography will then be held up as having revealed the 'truth' and people will inevitably turn away from the work. In a very real way (particularly if it is remembered how much of Potter's work is locked up in the vaults of TV companies), the biography will replace the fiction.

All of this is why the death-cry in *Cold Lazarus* seems no 'joke' for it appears the dying Potter was well aware at the end that his very reputation was at stake. The 'No biography! ' shout seems absolutely central to the plot of his final drama. It is through the constant replaying of this cry without their specific chemical stimulation, that the scientists come to realise the brain of their 'manipulative subject' does indeed have volition. The head is aware of its condition and resisting: it does not want its life story to be replayed for public consumption and besides, as the scientists come to realise, the memories they are seeing are not wholly factual anyway but inherently subjective: they really are 'no biography'. Deeply concerned with issues of personal 'sovereignty' and an individual's right to privacy even after death, there is powerful evidence that Potter, in his final work, was determined to tell 'what the world ought to know'.[28] His 'message for posterity' was that like the head, he, too, was aware of his condition at the end and resisting; that there had indeed been volition in his work all along and that above all, like his alter ego Feeld, he did not want to end up as a character in someone else's story, diminished and exploited for profit.

In the introduction to the published scripts of *Lazarus*, Potter wrote: 'the way I live, work and feel ... is the way I *write*' (p. vii). If this accounts for the inner emotional 'truth' buried in his final work, it also shows that of course, there *were* connections at this much deeper level between Potter's life and his writing. Because writing, for him, was such a personal act, Potter in many ways *used up* his life in his work, intruding into very intimate and tender aspects of himself which others might not have chosen to reveal.[29] As anyone who looks at his work quickly realises, there is a darkness, caused by sexual damage, upon which he drew for his writing. It is tracing this that (perhaps literally) feeds the biographer, even though it was Potter himself who long ago bravely chose to reveal the overall contours in his work – as an earlier putative biographer came to realise, he 'wrote his life his own way'.[30] Hence apart from the obvious commercial gains, what is the need for an 'official' biography? Because of the writer's very 'personal' artistic style, Potter's audience already feel they 'know' him through his work. While no doubt providing much of historical interest and diversion, all such a volume can do is sketch in more factual detail about what we broadly know already. In this way, there is something narcissistic about the approach of literary biography: it can only ever see a writer's work as the (self-) reflection of certain secret 'facts' which the biographer takes it upon himself (to claim) to discover, rather than a writer's moving beyond the self towards an attempt at a genuine communication of ideas and concerns with an audience. 'Only connect', said Potter, quoting E. M. Forster in his 1993 MacTaggart lecture as he described his kind of public service broadcasting: the discovery of 'something you didn't know that you knew'. If Potter dramatised aspects of himself in his work, he did so deliberately to illuminate the drama that is all our lives.

The underlying assumption of this 'non-biographical' critical study has been that mere source-hunting will never provide the 'key' to Potter: as I quickly discovered in my research, because he was someone who almost literally lived to write and *communicate*, the truth about the man is not in his life but there right in front of us, in his work, if we only care to look.[31] The evidence this book has uncovered (from directly talking to Potter, plus from many other sources) was that rather than easy autobiographical connections, there was a self-conscious *interplay* between the work and the life: it was the work that provided the battleground for the spiritual struggles which fed the 'facts' of Potter's life and it was the work that finally provided the writer with the joyful realisation that he could transcend the dark forces of his past and so change his life for the better. In many ways, because of the restrictions of his illness, his work *was* his life and his life really just was 'on screen'. As the book has also argued, his over-riding dramatic imperative was the primacy of personal freedom and agency and it is perhaps a crime that in the wake of his death and the inevitable competitive flurry to sweep into print and profit, simple mechanistic models of the writer are emerging at an ever rapid rate, all of which cannot help but serve to reduce and so dismiss the writer and what he was trying to communicate: Potter as secret autobiographer; as wild-eyed Puritan; as misogynist; as simple product of the 1950s and Richard Hoggart's *The Uses of Literacy*; as 'manipulative' games-player and so on.[32] As *Cold Lazarus* proves, it is a deterministic future which Potter himself predicted.

Because the researching and writing of this book largely predates all of that, I have had a unique ring-side seat watching the processes by which a posthumous reputation has been shaped in our competitive media culture – and threatened. And at such a crucial time for Potter's standing, I am delighted that the publisher of this book has decided to offer it a second life by reissuing the volume in a glossy new imprint. As I finally leave the late playwright behind, after quite a number of years involved with his work and his legacy, I cannot help wondering whether Potter's writing will ever receive a similar privilege. Having met and helped Humphrey Carpenter, in a perhaps vain attempt to influence his biography from 'the inside' as it were (given its publication is now a commercial inevitability), my conclusion is that I only hope the darker patches of Potter's early life of illness and psychological pain will not end up as sensationalist fodder for newspapers with interlocking interests in commercial TV, that almost seem determined to kick away the traces of the kind of values of public service and personal communication which the more spiritually self-tamed writer would later come to represent. Because, towards the end of his life, Potter became the embodiment of (perhaps too) many of these values for great numbers of people, this is why the issue of his posthumous reputation is of wider relevance because to trash him will inevitably mean to trash many of the central planks of the argument for 'quality' public service broadcasting as the debate is currently conducted within our media culture. It would also be deeply unfair to Potter and his personal artistic achievements, my admiration for which deepened as a result of my original research.

Hopefully, Humphrey Carpenter will make the best of a bad publishing commission which, in putting the 'official' stamp (for apparently commercial reasons) on a way of looking at his work as simply the product of the 'facts' of his life, is against the spirit, if not the letter, of Dennis Potter: the very antithesis of everything he believed and asserted when he was alive. Because the very *raison d'etre* of literary biography is to prove that however tenuously, the fiction all came out of the life, an 'official' biography seems emphatically the wrong way to honour the memory of this most autobiographically self-conscious and reflexive of writers. Slipping adroitly under the commercial net which the estate has tried to impose on anyone other than the 'official' biographer writing about him after his death, perhaps the walk-on role of this book in the larger unfolding script has been to offer an alternative view – to offer powerful evidence that the 'truth' about Dennis Potter is much more complex than the beguiling, media-friendly simplicities of the 'facts' of his life. Ultimately, however, it is up to readers and viewers to decide which version they prefer; what kind of view of Potter they want to believe. At the end of *Cold Lazarus*, the very last 'song' ever to be sung in a Dennis Potter drama was 'Will There Be Any Stars, Any Stars in My Crown?' Clearly looking to the future beyond his own death, the late writer was wondering at the end how he and his work would be remembered. The answer, of course, to that question is that it is now in our own hands. As Fyodor Glazunov realised in *Lazarus*, 'we are his torturers'.

John Cook
August 1998

Notes

Introduction

1 Madeleine Pallas, 'The Pain that Drives Potter Potty', *Sun*, 30 Nov. 1989, p. 12. 'Television's Mr. Filth' was what the *News of the World* dubbed Potter. Qtd in Dennis Potter, 'Black Cloud Lifts at Last for Potter', interview by Martina Devlin, *Edinburgh Evening News*, 10 Feb. 1990, Weekend sec., p. 7.

2 Two book-length publications did appear in the last year of Potter's life but though both useful, neither could truly be said to offer a 'substantial critical assessment'. The first was *Potter on Potter* edited by Graham Fuller and published by Faber and Faber in March 1993: a series of interviews with Potter. The second was a short critical appreciation of Potter: *Dennis Potter*, written by Peter Stead and published by small Welsh publisher, Seren books in October 1993. Since the playwright's death, however, there has been the predictable commercial scramble to produce 'the Potter biography'; first there was W. Stephen Gilbert's 'unauthorised' critical biography, *Fight and Kick and Bite*, published by Hodder and Stoughton in late 1995, quickly followed by the announcement of Humphrey Carpenter's 'official' biography, now expected in 1998. More may also be on the way. For discussion of the ethics of all this, see Afterword (1998).

3 Rosalind Coward, 'Dennis Potter and the Question of the Television Author', *Critical Quarterly*, 29: 4, 1987, p. 87.

4 Coward, 'Potter and the Question', p. 82.

5 John Caughie, 'Progressive Television and Documentary Drama', *Popular Television and Film*, eds. Tony Bennett, Susan Boyd-Bowman, Colin Mercer and Janet Woollacott (London: British Film Institute, 1981), p. 335.

6 *Ibid.*, p. 328.

7 Dennis Potter, 'The Artist', *The Dane*, magazine of St Clement Dane's Grammar School, 35: 13, July 1953, p. 441. Hammersmith Public Library, West London.

8 Dennis Potter, 'The Values of a Playwright', interview by Robert Cushman, *Radio Times*, 3–9 Apr. 1976, p. 62.

9 Philip Purser, 'Dennis Potter', *British Television Drama*, ed. George W. Brandt (Cambridge: Cambridge University Press, 1981), p. 169.

10 Dennis Potter, 'Some Sort of Preface ...', *Waiting for the Boat, On Television* (London: Faber and Faber, 1984), p. 33.

11 Unless otherwise stated, this and all subsequent comments attributed to Dennis Potter are taken from a personal interview, recorded at Eastbourne Mews, London, 10 May 1990.

12 Potter, 'Some Sort of Preface ...', p. 33.

13 Roger Smith, personal interview, recorded in Peckham, South London, 16 Mar. 1990.

14 Dennis Potter, qtd in Simon Hattenstone, 'The Shooting Party', *Guardian*, 11 Oct. 1991, sec. 2, p. 34.

15 Smith, personal interview. In 1957, British Prime Minister Harold Macmillan's claim was that 'most of our people have never had it so good. Go round the country, go to the industrial towns, and you will see a state of prosperity such as we have never had in my lifetime – nor indeed ever in the history of this country' (qtd in John Hill, *Sex, Class and Realism* (London: British Film Institute, 1986), p. 5).

16 Dennis Potter, 'Base Ingratitude', *New Statesman*, 3 May 1958, p. 562.

17 Dennis Potter, radio talk, 'A View of Oxford from the Editor of Isis', *Town and Country*, (tx. BBC Home Service, 29 May 1958).

18 Dennis Potter, interview, *Does Class Matter?*, Programme Two: 'Class in Private Life' (tx. BBC TV, 25 Aug. 1958). Transcript, BBC Written Archives, Caversham.

19 This and all subsequent quotations from *Stand Up, Nigel Barton*, are from Dennis Potter, *The Nigel Barton Plays* (Harmondsworth: Penguin, 1967).

20 Dennis Potter, *The Glittering Coffin* (London: Gollancz, 1960), p. 79.

21 Qtd in *ibid.*, p. 71. Potter later received an apology from the newspaper, after he threatened legal action against it.

22 Dennis Potter, letter to Christopher Mayhew, 1 Sept. 1958. Access to this correspondence granted by kind permission of Lord Mayhew.

23 Christopher Mayhew, letter to Dennis Potter, 14 Oct. 1958.

24 Denis Mitchell, letter to the author, 13 July 1990.

25 Dennis Potter, interview, *Arena* (tx. BBC-2 30 Jan. 1987).

26 Dennis Potter, 'The Spectre at the Harvest Feast', review of *Never and Always* (dir:. Denis Mitchell), *Sunday Times*, 19 June 1977, p. 22.

27 Mitchell, letter to the author.

28 Richard Hoggart's pioneering study of the decline of traditional working-class culture, *The Uses of Literacy* (1957; Harmondsworth: Penguin, 1959), was a seminal text for Potter and many of his generation. In *The Glittering Coffin*, the student ranks it highly – on a par with the work of Raymond Williams (p. 8). Hoggart, indeed, was one of the contributors to Mayhew's *Does Class Matter?* programme of 1958. In the course of a studio discussion, he praised Potter's interview on class at Oxford as 'most moving'.

29 Soundtrack, *Between Two Rivers* (wr. and narr. Dennis Potter; ph. A. A. Englander; dir. and prod. Anthony de Lotbinière; tx. BBC TV, 3 June 1960). National Film Archive Viewing Print.

30 Dennis Potter, 'A Playwright Comes of Age', interview by Philip Purser, *Sunday Telegraph Magazine*, 2 Apr. 1969, p. 10.

31 In 1959, Potter had married Margaret Morgan, a local girl from the Forest of Dean whom he had met at a barn dance. Roger Smith was their best man. The devoted couple had two daughters, Jane and Sarah, and later a son, Robert. Tragically, Potter's wife died of cancer in 1994, just nine days before her husband.

32 Hoggart, *Uses of Literacy*, p. 203.

33 Smith, personal interview.

34 Dennis Potter, interview, *Complete Programme Notes for a Season of British Television Drama 1959-73, Held at the National Film Theatre 11–24 Oct. 1976*, ed. Paul Madden, (London: British Film Institute, 1976), p. 34. Examples of Nathan's and Potter's contributions to the series have been preserved for posterity in a published collection of *TW3* sketches: *That Was the Week That Was*, ed. David Frost and Ned Sherrin (London: W. H. Allen, 1963). As these illustrate, Nathan's and Potter's contributions to the show were less about humour and more about motivated political comment on the issues of the day, based upon their research as journalists.

35 Dennis Potter, *The Changing Forest: Life in the Forest of Dean Today*, Britain Alive series (London: Secker and Warburg, 1962). In 1996, the book was reprinted by Minerva and extracts also serialised on BBC Radio 4.

36 Dennis Potter, interview, *Wogan* (tx. BBC-1, 25 Sept. 1987).

37 See, for example, interviews with *Wogan* (1987); with Joan Bakewell, 'Wrestling with a Vision', *Sunday Times Magazine*, 14 Nov. 1976, p. 66 and comments quoted in 'Singing for Your Fiction Takes the Sting Out of Life', Profile, *Sunday Times*, 23 Nov. 1986, p. 27.

38 See Bakewell, 'Wrestling with a Vision', p. 66.

39 Dennis Potter, 'Diamonds in the Dustbin', interview by Tim Lott, *New Musical Express*, 15 Nov. 1986, pp. 30–1.

40 Madden (ed.), *Complete Programme Notes*, p. 35.

41 Potter, Introduction, *The Nigel Barton Plays*, p. 8.

42 *Ibid.*, p. 11.

43 Dennis Potter, 'Reaction', *Encore*, 11:3, May–June 1964, p. 39.

Chapter 1

1 This and all subsequent quotations from *The Confidence Course*, are from the camera script, Feb. 1965. BBC Television Script Unit.

2 For published histories of *The Wednesday Play*, see, for example, Irene Shubik, *'Play for Today': The Evolution of Television Drama* (London: Davis-

Poynter, 1975) and Paul Madden's *Complete Programme Notes for a Season of British Television Drama 1959–1973* (BFI, 1976) which contains interviews with key *Wednesday Play* practitioners, including Potter, Ken Loach and David Mercer.

3 See Chap. 2 for discussion of *Angels Are so Few* – a 1970 play which Potter wrote for Smith. This deals with an apparent 'angel' who transforms the life of a trapped, repressed housewife.

4 Madden (ed.), *Complete Programme Notes*, p. 35.

5 Smith, personal interview.

6 Hazlitt was undoubtedly a key influence on the formation of Potter's attitudes. In a 1976 radio broadcast, *With Great Pleasure*, Potter commented that Hazlitt was the writer he revered 'above all others for the trenchant pertinence of his opinions, for his wit and style and honesty and for his brave, uncompromising spirit and insights' (Dennis Potter, Interview, *With Great Pleasure* (tx. BBC Radio 4, 5 Sept. 1976). Transcript, BBC Written Archives, Caversham).

7 Compare the 'shadow-with-eyes' with the later demon outsiders of Sam in *The Bonegrinder* and Martin in *Brimstone and Treacle* (see Chap. 2).

8 Raymond Williams, 'Realism and Non-Naturalism 1', *The Official Programme of The Edinburgh International Television Festival 1977*, Aug. 1977, p. 30.

9 *Ibid.*, p. 32. Williams associates this 'counter-sense' with the rise of Marxism.

10 Troy Kennedy Martin, ' "Nats Go Home": First Statement of a New Drama for Television', *Encore*, 11:2, Mar.–Apr. 1964, p. 24.

11 *Ibid.*, pp. 31–2.

12 *Ibid.*, pp. 26–7.

13 '*Studio 4*', preview, *Radio Times*, 18 Jan. 1962, p. 19.

14 Smith, personal interview. Formed in 1959 and continuing until 1963, the aim of the Langham Group, as enunciated by its leader Anthony Pélissier, was 'to break away from the inheritance of the theatre and the cinema … and evolve something that is exclusive to the medium'. (*Radio Times*, 11 Dec. 1959, p. 4) Though tending to be more 'high-brow' in approach, some of the methods the Group used were similar to the later 'Nats Go Home' experimenters: for example, use of unrelated images and the divorcing of picture from sound.

15 Kennedy Martin, '"Nats Go Home"', p. 32.

16 Roger Smith, for example, recalls writing a studio play for the later *Teletale* called *Catherine*, which consisted almost entirely of voice-over narration married to images. The play was the first television work to be directed by Ken Loach.

17 Troy Kennedy Martin, 'Reaction', *Encore*, 11:3, May–June 1964, p. 48.

18 Raymond Williams, 'A Lecture on Realism' *Screen*, 18:1, Spring 1977, p. 72. Williams argues that *The Wednesday Play* work of Ken Loach and his producer Tony Garnett should be described less as naturalism than realism, insofar as an attempt was frequently made to introduce 'a consciousness, classically defined as realism in contrast with naturalism, of the movements of history which underlie the apparent reality that is occurring'.

19 This distinction between naturalism as 'descriptive' and realism as 'narrative' was first formulated by Georg Lukács in his discussion of the difference between realism and naturalism in the nineteenth-century novel as being that between 'narrate' and 'describe'. See Georg Lukács, 'Narrate or Describe?', *Writer and Critic*, (London: Merlin Press, 1970).

20 Troy Kennedy Martin, '*Up the Junction* and After', *Contrast*, 4:5–6, Winter 1965–Spring 1966, p. 137.

21 In contrast to the engagement with 'reality' of Loach and Garnett, Potter's work, for example, has been referred to as 'the approval and celebration of the mere appearance of style and stylisation' (Caughie, 'Progressive Television', p. 339).

22 Williams, 'Realism and Non-Naturalism 1', p. 30.

23 Potter claimed 'All my plays are about the same thing ... They are about what goes on inside people's heads'. Dennis Potter, qtd in 'Singing for Your Fiction Takes the Sting Out of Life', Profile, *Sunday Times*, 23 Nov. 1986, p. 27.

24 Raymond Williams, *Drama From Ibsen to Brecht* (1968; London: Pelican, 1973), p. 393. Williams goes on to make a further distinction between 'psychological expressionism' and what he calls the 'social expressionism' of Brecht.

25 Smith, personal interview.

26 Barry Norman, 'What The Class Barrier Did For Dennis Potter', *Daily Mail*, 13 Dec. 1965, p. 9.

27 *Vote, Vote, Vote* won an SFTA award in 1966. That same year, the Screenwriter's Guild judged it Best Play of the Year and in an unprecedented move, gave the Runners-Up Award to *Stand Up*. Source: Kenith Trodd, Preview, '*Emergency Ward 9*', *Radio Times*, 7 Apr. 1966, p. 20.

28 As implemented by the 1945 British Labour Government, the 1944 Butler Education Act had abolished tuition fees at state-maintained schools, raised the school-leaving age to fifteen and established a tri-partite system of secondary schools (grammar, modern and secondary modern). In this way, it was hoped the brightest working-class children would progress to grammar school and later university via 'scholarships' won as a result of passing the 11-plus examination. One of the unforeseen social consequences of this, however, was the creation of a new class of 'scholarship boy' who, like Potter and his dramatic *alter ego*, Nigel Barton, felt separated from their origins. As Richard Hoggart outlined in *The Uses of Literacy*, 'scholarship boys' were the 'uprooted and anxious', belonging neither at home nor in their new university environment (p. 292)

29 This and all subsequent quotations from *Vote, Vote, Vote for Nigel Barton*, are from *The Nigel Barton Plays* (Harmondsworth: Penguin, 1967). This fear of Wilson's Government 'selling out' is explicitly referred to at one point by Nigel's wife, Ann, when she condemns 'Labour Colonial Secretaries hobnobbing with corrupt old sheikhs. Labour Defence Ministers paying for Polaris on the never-never. Harold being buddy-buddy with Lyndon [Johnson]' (p. 90).

30 Norman, 'What the Class Barrier Did', p. 9; 'passion and narrative power' qtd in Trodd, Preview, '*Emergency Ward 9*', p. 20: 'Rarely have the critics greeted the work of a newcomer with such unanimous enthusiasm – welcoming 'a writer of relentless wit, passion and narrative power''.

31 *The Generations* was the collective title for three David Mercer plays, transmitted by BBC TV between 1961 and 1963: *Where The Difference Begins, A Climate of Fear* and *Birth of a Private Man*. In these, Mercer sought to explore themes of class, politics and generational conflict as they affected different generations of the same family. *Lena, Oh My Lena* (wr. Alun Owen; dir. William T. Kotcheff; prod. Sydney Newman) was an ITV *Armchair Theatre* production, first transmitted on 25 Sept. 1960. Like *Stand Up*, it dealt with the problems of a 'scholarship boy', separated from his working-class background through education. Tom (played by Peter McEnery) takes on a summer job in a warehouse in a vain attempt to return to his class roots but runs into conflict with the other workers. See Alun Owen, *Three TV Plays* (London: Jonathan Cape, 1961) for the published script.

32 See Introduction for comparison of Nigel's fictional interview with Potter's *real* interview as a student on the 1958 TV series, *Does Class Matter?*.

33 Aneurin Bevan (1897–1960) was the famous politician of the Labour Left who, as Minister of Health in Atlee's Government, was widely credited as instrumental in the formation of the National Health Service in 1948. According to Roger Smith, Bevan was a key influence in the formation of the young Potter's political and moral outlook: 'Bevan's sense of rhetoric, of wit and also being Welsh – Potter had an enormous amount of respect for him' (Smith, personal interview)

34 *Where the Buffalo Roam* (wr. Dennis Potter; dir. Gareth Davies; prod. Lionel Harris, tx. BBC-1 *The Wednesday Play*, 2 Nov. 1966). National Film Archive Viewing Print. This and subsequent quotations are from the soundtrack.

35 Philip Purser, review of *Message for Posterity*, *Sunday Telegraph*, 7 May 1967, p. 21.

36 Potter, Introduction, *The Nigel Barton Plays*, p. 17.

37 Smith, personal interview. Though Smith now admits that tired of institutional life, he had been keen to leave the BBC in any case. The *Vote, Vote, Vote* controversy provided him with an excuse.

38 Sydney Newman, personal interview recorded in North London, 28 Feb. 1990.

39 Potter, Introduction, *The Nigel Barton Plays*, p. 18.

40 Potter in Madden (ed.), *Complete Programme Notes*, p. 35. Potter told Paul Madden in 1976: 'The original ending had the candidate saying, 'If you object, write to your M.P. and the Best of British!' ... [The BBC] were really objecting to the general tone of the piece, the lack of conventional respect for politics. They had to focus upon something in the play to which they could point at, and say 'We object to that' so they objected to the ending which summed it all up'. Speaking on the BBC *Late Show* tribute to Potter, broadcast on the night of the writer's death, the actor who played Nigel Barton, Keith Barron, asserted that Barton's closing gesture in the original ending was to have been another 'two-fingered salute' (Keith Barron, interview, *Dennis Potter: A Life in Television* (tx. BBC-2, 7 June 1994)).

41 Potter, Introduction, *The Nigel Barton Plays*, p. 13.

42 Potter, Introduction, *The Nigel Barton Plays*, p. 11.

43 Potter, Introduction, *The Nigel Barton Plays*, pp. 13-14.

44 Confirmation of this comes from Potter's 1976 interview with Paul Madden: 'I suspect *Stand Up, Nigel Barton* is a better play than *Vote, Vote, Vote for Nigel Barton* because I used television techniques with more ease. Up to *Vote, Vote, Vote*, I was obtrusively thinking, 'How do I use television, how do I go from that scene to that scene, using television in the best way?' After that, it became second nature. I've never since had to think about the grammar of television' (*Complete Programme Notes*, p. 36). Potter found his natural 'television grammar', once he linked scenes associatively as memories taking place inside the head of his central protagonist.

45 For further discussion of the use of this scene as a structuring device, see Chap. 3.

46 Potter, personal interview. The adults as children device would later be famously returned to in *Blue Remembered Hills* (see Chap. 3).

47 Potter in Madden (ed.), *Complete Programme Notes*, p. 37.

48 Dennis Potter, 'Cue Telecinè – Put On The Kettle', *New Society*, 22 Sept. 1966, pp. 456–7. Potter later reworked substantial portions of this article for his Introduction to the published *Nigel Barton Plays*.

49 Potter, 'Cue Telecinè', p. 457. It is significant to note that here, Potter formulates the idea of television 'flow' eight years before Raymond Williams in *Television: Technology and Cultural Form* (London: Fontana, 1974; repr. London: Routledge, 1990).

50 Potter, 'Cue Telecinè', p. 457.

51 *Ibid.*

52 *Ibid.*

53 *Ibid.*

54 This and subsequent quotations are from *Emergency Ward 9*, BBC camera script, Apr. 1966. BBC Television Script Unit. Note the striking similarities between the setting of this 'lost' little play and that of the much more famous *The Singing Detective* (see Chap. 5).

55 *Emergency – Ward Ten* was Britain's first twice-weekly 'soap': a hospital drama, produced by ATV, that ran from 1957 to 1967. The reference to *Britannia Hospital* is in relation to the 1982 film of the same name, directed by Lindsay Anderson. This also played satirically with the idea of hospital as microcosm of the 'state of the nation'.

56 Though *Message for Posterity* is not quite so 'lost' as it once was. Remarkably, in 1994, Potter's script was resurrected from the archives and given a new production for BBC-TV's *Performance* season of plays by major dramatists. Transmitted on 29 Oct. 1994 on BBC-2, this new production starred John Neville as Sir David Browning and Eric Porter as James Player.

57 This and subsequent quotations are from *Message for Posterity*, BBC Camera Script, Apr. 1967. BBC Television Script Unit.

58 James Green, 'Talking TV', *London Evening News*, 7 Sept. 1966, p. 7.

59 Significantly, however, the play had not been intended as a *Wednesday Play* at all but had been commissioned as a drama for the BBC-2 play slot, *Theatre 625* in June 1965 and delivered by Potter in January 1966. Its original recording had been postponed because of what the *London Evening News* euphemistically deemed 'administrative reasons' (Green, 'Talking TV', p. 7). Instead, it was eventually decided to produce the play under the more suitable umbrella of the 'controversial' *Wednesday Play* and some dialogue changes were made to try and dissociate the Browning character from the (very obvious) implication that it was Churchill. This was done by having Browning refer to Churchill at one point within the play itself. The play was finally recorded between 13 and 15 Apr. 1967 for transmission a fortnight later.

60 Hence here, art is indicated as transcending politics. Player achieves dominance in art over a member of the class that had dominated him in life.

61 This and the following quotations are from *Shaggy Dog*, LWT rehearsal script, Apr.-May 1968. BFI Script Library.

62 *The Inheritors* is set in pre-history and postulates that the emergence of *homo sapiens* was at the expense of the genocide of a gentler, more imaginative primate: Neanderthal man. Hence the similarity to Potter's 'Rarys'. See William Golding, *The Inheritors* (London: Faber and Faber, 1955).

63 This and subsequent quotations are from the soundtrack of *A Beast with Two Backs* (wr. Dennis Potter; dir. Lionel Harris; prod. Graeme McDonald; tx. BBC-1 *Wednesday Play*, 20 Nov. 1968). Repeat transmission BBC-1, 4 Aug. 1987.

64 Philip Purser, review of *A Beast with Two Backs*, *Sunday Telegraph*, 24 Nov. 1968, p. 23.

65 *Lord of the Flies* portrays the descent of a group of boys into savagery, after they become marooned on a desert island. The Lord of the title (in fact, the head of a dead pig on a stick) becomes a metaphor for the 'beast within' the boys.

66 Henry Raynor, review of *A Beast with Two Backs*, *The Times*, 21 Nov. 1968, p. 12.

67 Stanley Reynolds, 'Beastiness', review of *A Beast with Two Backs*, *Guardian*, 21 Nov. 1968, p. 7.

68 Potter, personal interview. Immigration had grown through the sixties as a political issue. It had reached a critical point by 1968, with Enoch Powell's famous speech in which he prophesied 'Rivers of Blood' as a consequence of the large numbers of 'coloured' immigrants who had come to settle in Britain after the British Nationality Act of 1948 had granted them UK citizenship.

69 William Shakespeare, *Othello*, I, I, 117–19, *The Complete Works of William Shakespeare*, eds. Stanley Wells and Gary Taylor (Oxford: Clarendon Press, 1988), p. 822.

70 Dennis Potter, *Hide and Seek*, (London: André Deutsch\Quartet Books, 1973; repr. London: Faber and Faber, 1990) p. 113. (page reference is to the reprint edition).

71 Potter, personal interview.

72 *The Ross Gazette*, 17 May 1945, p. 2. More evidence confirming this interpretive link between the bear and sexual assault has recently come to light. According to Gareth Davies, director of many of the early plays, the original spark for *A Beast* came from something Potter had seen on television: 'Someone who had attacked and sexually assaulted a child was hurried into a magistrates' court ... and there was a lot of screaming people ... hurling abuse ... Dennis was shocked by that and interested in the duality of people attacking the man as violent and being violent themselves' (qtd in W. S. Gilbert, *Fight and Kick and Bite: The Life and Work of Dennis Potter*, London: Hodder and Stoughton, 1995), p. 169. Potter, it appears, then thought back to 'the bear story' he had heard as a child.

73 This and subsequent quotations are from the soundtrack of *Son of Man* (wr. Dennis Potter; dir. Gareth Davies; prod. Graeme McDonald; tx. BBC-1 *Wednesday Play*, 16 Apr. 1969). Repeat transmission, BBC-1, 28 July 1987.

74 Dennis Potter, *Son of Man: A Play* (London: Samuel French, 1970), p. 35. In common with *Vote, Vote, Vote for Nigel Barton* (staged at the Bristol Old Vic, 1968), *Son of Man* was subsequently produced for the stage. Its first performance was at the Phoenix Theatre, Leicester, on 22 Oct. 1969, with Frank Finlay (who would later play Potter's Casanova on TV) in the central role of Christ. Potter rewrote the play for staging and this script was later published in the form indicated above.

75 Potter, *Son of Man: A Play*, p. 51.

76 Potter, *Radio Times* p. 33.

77 Michael Williams, '*Son of Man*', *Radio Times*, 29 May 1969, p. 31. Because of reaction to its first showing, *Son of Man* received an exceptionally early repeat on 4 June 1969.

78 Potter, *Son of Man: A Play*, p. 51.

79 Philip Purser, review of *Son of Man*, *Sunday Telegraph*, 20 Apr. 1969, p. 30.

80 Dennis Potter, 'A Playwright Comes Of Age', interview by Philip Purser, *Sunday Telegraph Magazine*, 2 Apr. 1969, p. 37.

81 Brian Dean, 'Storm Over TV Christ', *Daily Mail*, 17 Apr. 1969, p. 1.; Ken Irwin, 'Tough Guy Christ Shocks Viewers', *Daily Mirror*, 17 Apr. 1969, p. 2.; 'A Quiet Reception for New *Son of Man*', *Guardian*, 18 Apr. 1969, p. 1.

82 Graeme McDonald, personal interview recorded at Anglia Films, Central London, 1 Mar. 1990.

83 Qtd in 'A Quiet Reception', p. 1. The comments were from members of the Church of England and The Jesuits respectively.

84 Julian Critchley, 'Considerable Achievement', review of *Son of Man*, *The Times*, 17 Apr. 1969, p. 14; James Thomas, 'Jesus the Agitator', review of *Son of Man*, *Daily Express*, 17 Apr. 1969, p. 4; Robert Ottaway, 'This Gospel of Our Times', review of *Son of Man*, *Daily Sketch*, 17 Apr. 1969, p. 20.

85 These insults of 'madman' and 'looney' echo the theories of Scottish psychiatrist, R. D. Laing, whose famous formulation was that the 'mad were the only sane ones' in society. Laing's ideas on madness and schizophrenia gained currency in the sixties and influenced many of the counter-culture generation of writers and artists. His shift of the problem of sanity away from the individual and on to the wider society meshed perfectly with the attack of the sixties' counter-culture on dominant 'bourgeois' values. Now, the madness lay not so much with the individual but society as a whole so that to become one of society's drop-outs was seen almost as an act of mental hygiene. If Potter's use of 'mad' outsider heroes who expose the madness of the *status quo* they challenge echo Laing's ideas, it is *Son of Man*, with its drop-out Christ branded a looney for his opposition to the 'madness' of the Roman Occupation, which seems most directly to parallel the ideas of Laing.

86 Potter, 'A Playwright Comes of Age', p. 37. 'Danny le Rouge' was student leader of the May 1968 Paris protests, Daniel Cohn-Bendit. Potter admired him, in contrast to his English public school counterparts. See, for example, Potter, 'Teabag Rebels', *Sun*, 17 June 1968, p. 12: 'I listened to him talk, stocky, voluble, undogmatic ... A bringer of hope, a dismantler of prisons'. Inspiration for Potter's own 'stocky, undogmatic' Christ, perhaps?

87 See Maurice Wiggin, 'Potter's Progress', review of *Son of Man*, *Sunday Times* 20 Apr. 1969, p. 23: Judas 'emerged not as a mercenary traitor but as a sympathetic liberal figure, anxious to mediate and ultimately rejected by both sides'.

88 Potter, *Son of Man: A Play*, p. 34.

89 Nancy Banks-Smith, 'Violent Christ According to Potter's Gospel', review of *Son of Man*, *Sun*, 17 Apr. 1969, p. 14.

90 Ian Hamilton, 'Speeches in Palestine', review of *Son of Man*, *The Listener*, 24 Apr. 1969, p. 17.

91 Dennis Potter, qtd in 'The Son of Man – But Will You Agree?', preview, *Daily Mirror*, 16 Apr. 1969, p. 20; '*Son of Man* Reviewed', *Sun*, 21 Apr. 1969, p. 12.

92 Dennis Potter, qtd in Richard Tydeman, '*Son of Man*: Improbable Attempt at the Impossible', *Church of England Newspaper*, 25 Apr. 1969, p. 13.

93 Potter, 'A Playwright Comes of Age', p. 37.

Chapter 2

1 Kenith Trodd, 'In at the Birth and Death of Kestrel Productions', interview by Ann Purser, *Stage & Television Today*, 25 June 1970, p. 15.

2 *Ibid.*

3 Though Garnett's and Trodd's ambitions went much further than this. Kestrel was conceived as a collective that would also produce feature films. Amongst the films which gained a cinema release during Kestrel's two-year association with LWT were *Kes* (dir. Ken Loach, 1969) and *The Body* (dir. Roy Battersby, 1970).

4 T. C. Worsley, 'Special Cases', *Financial Times*, 16 Apr. 1969, p. 14.

5 The play was called *The Franchise Trail* (wr. Nemone Lethbridge; tx. 24 Aug. 1968). It split the LWT Board of Management at its preview because it implied that commercial TV was a licence to print money.

6 Kenith Trodd, interview, *The Media Show* (tx. Channel Four, 3 Feb. 1991).

7 Trodd, 'In at the Birth and Death', p. 15. Twenty years on, Trodd has grown less sure. Realising with hindsight that Kestrel was Britain's first truly 'independent' TV drama production company, he now thinks Garnett and he should have stayed with LWT and not sold their shares.

8 This and subsequent quotations are from the soundtrack of *Moonlight on the Highway* (wr. Dennis Potter; dir. James MacTaggart; prod. Kenith Trodd; tx. ITV *Saturday Night Theatre*, 12 Apr. 1969). National Film Archive Viewing Print. Al Bowlly was perhaps the most famous British dance band crooner of the thirties: his name forever associated with the 'legendary' Lew Stone Band. See, for example, Kenith Trodd, *Lew Stone: A Career in Music* (London: Joyce Stone, 1971). Trodd is an acknowledged expert on the popular music of the thirties and forties and in 1968, he began recording interviews with Lew Stone for a planned biography of the musician. Stone, however, died in Feb. 1969 before this research could be completed and so Trodd turned his book into a detailed discography and review of Stone's career, using old newspaper clippings. Given this context, it is not difficult to see how Potter's central plot idea of a young man, obsessed with the popular culture of another era, was arrived at. This idea of Bowlly was added to the play after the original draft of *Moonlight*, called *By The Rivers of Babylon*, was rejected by Trodd at the BBC in 1967 as too 'raw'. Tellingly, it concerned a married man's liaisons with prostitutes.

9 Also like *A Beast* is the figure of an 'airy' ghostly father. Peters' father was killed by a V-2 rocket in 1945, thus linking him with Bowlly too.

10 *Paper Roses* was the only Potter play produced by Trodd during his two-year spell working for the Drama Department at Granada: the ITV company to which he departed in 1970 after the break-up of Kestrel.

11 This and subsequent quotations are from *Paper Roses*, rehearsal script. BFI Script Library.

12 William Shakespeare, *King Lear*, I, IV, 131, *The Complete Works of William Shakespeare*, ed. Stanley Wells and Gary Taylor (Oxford: Clarendon Press, 1988) p. 932.

13 Kenith Trodd, personal interview recorded at BBC Television Centre,

London, 8 Nov. 1989. Potter's portrayal of an old man also seems partly based on veteran reporter Maurice Fagence whom he knew at the *Daily Herald*.

14 This and subsequent quotations are from the soundtrack of *Lay Down Your Arms* (wr. Dennis Potter; dir. Christopher Morahan; prod. Kenith Trodd; tx. ITV *Saturday Night Theatre*, 23 May 1970). National Film Archive Viewing Print.

15 This and subsequent quotations are from the soundtrack of *Traitor* (wr. Dennis Potter; dir. Alan Bridges; prod. Graeme MacDonald; tx. BBC-1 *Play for Today* 14 Oct. 1971). Repeat Transmission BBC-1, 21 July 1987. In an interview for BBC-2's *Late Night Line-Up*, transmitted on the same evening as *Traitor*, Potter stated: 'You know ... I suggested enough reasons why there are psychological motivations pushing such a man this way. But also allowing him to say – "I did what I did because of what I believed". And we must always accept this about a man.' (Dennis Potter, interview, *Late Night Line-Up* (tx. BBC-2 14 Oct. 1971). Transcript BBC Written Archives, Caversham).

16 Potter, Interview, *Late Night Line-Up*.

17 Dennis Potter, interview by Graham Fuller, *American Film*, Mar. 1989, p. 33.

18 Following its transmission, Potter summarised the critical reaction in his weekly column for the pre-Murdoch *Sun*: 'Sour. Malicious. Full of Hatred. Bilious. Venomous. Crude. Spiteful. That's me apparently.' (Dennis Potter, 'Writer Exposed', *Sun*, 20 May 1968, p. 13)

19 This and the following quotations are from the soundtrack of *The Bonegrinder* (wr. Dennis Potter; dir. Joan Kemp-Welch; exec prod. Peter Willes; tx. ITV *Playhouse* 13 May 1968). National Film Archive Viewing Print.

20 Dennis Potter, interview by Stanley Reynolds, *Guardian*, 16 Feb. 1973, p. 11.

21 *The Wednesday Play* mutated into *Play for Today* in Oct. 1970, when it gained a new Thursday time-slot.

22 This and subsequent quotations are from *Angels Are So Few*, camera script. BBC Television Script Unit.

23 Dennis Potter, '*Son of Man*', interview by Russell Twisk, *Radio Times*, Apr. 10 1969, p. 33.

24 Dennis Potter, qtd in Richard Tydeman, '*Son of Man*: Improbable Attempt at the Impossible', *Church of England Newspaper*, 25 Apr. 1969, p. 13.

25 In Potter's first novel, *Hide and Seek*, this same image of a child in peril of 'falling' recurs (see Chap. 3). The innocent 'rary' in *Shaggy Dog*, which jumps from a cliff before it is pushed, also echoes this (see Chap. 1).

26 The play is listed as a 'Fable for Television' in Gordon Burn, 'Television Is the Only Medium that Counts', interview with Dennis Potter, *Radio Times*, 8 Oct. 1970, p. 66.

27 Dennis Potter, 'Television Is the Only Medium ', interview, p. 67.

28 This and subsequent quotations are from *Schmoedipus*, camera script. BBC

Television Script Unit.

29 Dennis Potter, Introduction to *Joe's Ark, Waiting for the Boat, On Television* (London: Faber and Faber, 1984), p. 89.

30 Potter, 'Some Sort of Preface', *Waiting for the Boat*, p. 20.

31 Dennis Potter, Introduction, *Brimstone and Treacle* (London: Eyre Methuen, 1978), p. 3.

32 This and subsequent quotations are from *Joe's Ark, Waiting for the Boat*.

33 For example, Lucy, earlier in the play, told the student John: 'His Christianity survived the death of my mother and the defection of my brother, but not *this*, I think' (p. 104).

34 Potter, 'Some Sort of Preface', *Waiting for the Boat*, p. 20. As an illustration of the conflicting readings which the play purposively sustains, it is worth comparing this optimistic slant with comments Potter made on the play several years earlier (in 1978), in which he stated that when Lucy dies, 'her father capitulates again to the old hope ... not as a triumph of faith, nor as a sudden widening of his moral and intellectual capacities, but simply as a banal regression to 'comfort' that lies too shallow for thought' (Introduction, *Brimstone*, p. 3).

35 Potter, Introduction, *Brimstone*, p. 3.

36 *Ibid.*, p. 2.

37 Published in 1907, *Father and Son* is a classic statement of the rebellion of twentieth-century sons against Victorian fathers. Its author, Edmund Gosse, was a literary critic who became associated with the modernist movement. In his memoir, he charts his growing estrangement from the religious fundamentalism of his father: a rebellion which, ultimately, can be read as that of the twentieth century against the nineteenth; of a new secular relativism overthrowing the authoritarianism of Victorian values. One can see the memoir's many points of interest to Potter: childhood; the nature of autobiography; the legacy of literary modernism; the relationship between a son and a father. Above all, there is the question of how to redefine spirituality in a modern age, in terms of overthrowing religious literalism in favour of a new emphasis on the centrality of literature and metaphor.

38 For Gosse senior, the key to the problem lies in Adam's navel. As he tells one of his fellow naturalists, 'Adam had a navel though he came from no womb' because God intended him to serve as a model for the human race. Life is a reproductive cycle. Genesis, however, was a breaking into that circle in which God made it *appear* that all living things had a history: 'This means that where Adam stood he would see all around him the stigmata, so to speak, of a pre-existent existence. On the trunk of a tree. From his own stomach. From the fossils on the rocks that make them seem so very, very old even to Adam himself' (Phillip Gosse on the soundtrack of *Where Adam Stood* wr. Dennis Potter; dir. Brian Gibson; prod. Kenith Trodd, tx. BBC-2 21 Apr. 1976). Repeat transmission, 30 June 1987. Subsequent quotations in this Chapter are from the same soundtrack.

39 It is important to note how, in line with his own interests, Potter has completely transformed this incident from one mentioned in passing by Edmund Gosse in *Father and Son*. In the book, Gosse recalls how, as a child, he was momentarily abducted by a mad woman called Mary Flaw – a member of his father's religious sect who seized him one Sunday in Church. A few minutes later, the boy was found sitting on the doorstep of the village butcher, unharmed (Edmund Gosse, *Father and Son* London: J. M. Dent, 1907, p. 83).

40 Potter, personal interview.

41 The *Oxford English Dictionary* defines 'Brimstone and Treacle' as an 'old fashioned prescription consisting of sulphur and treacle; a medical compound composed of many ingredients and an antidote to venomous bites, poisons generally and malignant disease'.

42 This and subsequent quotations are from the soundtrack of *Brimstone and Treacle* (wr. Dennis Potter; dir. Barry Davis; prod. Kenith Trodd; BBC TV *Play for Today* tx. BBC-1, 25 Aug. 1987).

43 Potter, Introduction, *Brimstone* (1978), p. 4.

44 Potter, personal interview.

45 *Ibid.*

46 *Ibid.*

47 This and subsequent quotations are from the soundtrack of *Double Dare* (wr. Dennis Potter; dir. John McKenzie; prod. Kenith Trodd; tx. BBC-1 *Play for Today* 6 Apr. 1976). National Film Archive Viewing Print. Prior to writing *Double Dare*, Potter himself had been suffering from a writer's block and had asked Ken Trodd to set up a meeting with Kika Markham (Helen in the play). This then allowed him to get that dizzying feel in his script of the *interplay* between reality and fantasy which he needed to evoke in order to make the play work.

48 The advert which the play parodies is the famous Cadbury's 'Milk Flake' campaign, dating from the 1970s, in which a woman would invariably be seen in a seductive pose, biting into a 'Milk Flake'.

49 As this shows, the 'proto-feminist' concerns around the sexual exploitation and commodification of women which Potter would later articulate in *Blackeyes*, were already visible at the time of *Double Dare*. This helps explain the references to *Double Dare* in *Blackeyes* (see Chap. 6).

50 Dennis Potter, qtd in Peter Fiddick, 'Writ Sought Against the BBC', *Guardian*, 24 Mar. 1976, p. 2.

51 Barry Davis, personal interview recorded at BBC Scotland, Glasgow, 1 May 1990.

52 Alasdair Milne, personal interview recorded at Holland Park, London, 5 Mar, 1990.

53 Kenith Trodd, qtd in Barry Powell, 'Rape Row Threat to £300,000 TV Plays', *News of the World*, 28 Mar. 1976, p. 8.

54 Milne, personal interview. The article was by Robert Cushman: 'Dennis Potter: The Values of a Playwright', *Radio Times*, 3–9 Apr. 1976, pp. 61–5.

55 Milne, personal interview.

56 Alasdair Milne, qtd in Dennis Potter, 'A Note from Mr. Milne', *New Statesman*, 23 Apr. 1976, p. 648. Potter used his TV column for the *New Statesman* that week to quote the letter in full and to give his own riposte to the banning of *Brimstone*.

57 Davis, personal interview.

58 Dennis Potter, qtd in 'Potter Will Try to Stop', p. 17.

59 Potter, 'A Note from Mr. Milne', p. 548.

60 Caughie, 'Progressive Television and Documentary Drama', p. 328.

61 *Ibid.*, p. 333.

62 Milne, personal interview.

63 Trodd, personal interview.

64 Indeed as the London listings magazine *Time Out* asked at the time, with *Brimstone*, it is really a case of 'What rape scene?' ('Television: Selections – Cowgill Beefs', *Time Out*, 26 Mar.–1 Apr. 1976, p. 17) The two instances of sexual assault are both implied in the TV play, never depicted: the director always moving into a tight close-up of Martin's face. Potter even provides his own warning within the play itself, by having his demon directly address viewers, prior to the first rape of Pattie: 'If you are a nervous type out there / Switch over or off for some calmer air / But you'd have to be smug or very frail, / To believe that no man has a horn or tail.' (soundtrack, *Brimstone*).

65 Caughie, 'Progressive Television and Documentary Drama', p. 329.

66 *Ibid.*, p. 332.

67 *Ibid.*, p. 330.

68 Davis, personal interview.

69 In the years immediately following the ban, Potter and Trodd did everything in their power to bring *Brimstone* to as wide an audience as possible by reworking the TV script into a number of different versions for other media. A stage version was premiered at the Sheffield Crucible Theatre in Oct. 1977 and a run in the London West End followed in 1978. Three years later, Potter reworked the material into a feature film script. Released the following year, this was produced by Trodd and starred the rock star Sting as Martin Taylor. Finally, in 1987, the BBC 'unbanned' *Brimstone* and transmitted it as part of a summer retrospective season of Potter work (see Chap. 5).

70 Trodd, personal interview.

71 Ian Trethowan, qtd in Mike Hollingsworth and Richard Norton-Taylor, *Blacklist*, (Basingstoke: Macmillan, 1988), p. 116.

72 Hollingsworth and Norton-Taylor, *Blacklist*, p. 98.

73 Milne, personal interview.

74 *Ibid.*

75 Potter, 'A Note from Mr. Milne', p. 549.

76 Qtd in 'Banned by the BBC – Then the Show Wins a Top Award for Their

Rivals', *Daily Mail*, 27 Mar. 1976, p. 6.

77 Trodd, personal interview.

78 Dennis Potter, qtd in 'Banned by the BBC', p. 6.

79 Dennis Potter, 'The Values of a Playwright', interview by Robert Cushman, p. 62.

80 Dennis Potter, 'God Does Not Let Us See Him Because There's a Grin on His Face as He Looks Down on Our Antics', interview by James Murray, *Daily Express*, 22 May 1976, p. 14.

81 Dennis Potter, qtd in Day-Lewis, 'Will the Devil Get His Due?', p. 12.

82 This formed part of a series of six Hardy short stories adapted by different TV playwrights and transmitted under the umbrella title, *Wessex Tales*. *A Tragedy* was undoubtedly given to Potter because its themes are essentially those of *The Nigel Barton Plays*. As Potter summarised them in the *Radio Times*: 'the contradiction between ambition and conscience, the theme of class and the theme of filial shame which is universal to all ages and all times' (Dennis Potter, interview, 'The Kind of Stories that Countrymen Tell', *Radio Times*, 1 Nov. 1973, p. 83). The 'tragedy' is of a 'torn' hero, or in this case two: Joshua and Cornelius Halborough, a pair of ambitious sons who decide to kill their drunken artisan father in order to preserve their reputations as men of the cloth.

83 Betty Willingale, letter to the author, 4 July 1990.

84 Potter exploited the connection in 1991 when he cast the leading actor of *Mayor*, Alan Bates, in *Secret Friends*: the film version of his novel, *Ticket to Ride*. This concerns a man who begins to confuse his wife with a prostitute (see Conclusion).

85 Dennis Potter, 'Wrestling with a Vision', interview with Joan Bakewell, *Sunday Times Magazine*, 14 Nov. 1976, p. 70.

86 Angus Wilson, interview by D. A. N. Jones, *Radio Times*, 27 Feb. 1975, p. 3.

87 Potter, 'The Kind of Stories', p. 83. Though twenty years later, Potter would claim that what is more interesting about adaptations is 'if that other ground that someone has occupied happens here and there to nudge something in the top right-hand or left-hand corner of yourself. Then it's more likely a so-called adaptation will work.' (Graham Fuller, (ed.), *Potter on Potter* (London: Faber and Faber, 1993), p. 68). This is certainly the case with *Late Call* (see Chap. 3).

88 Milne, personal interview.

89 Dennis Potter, qtd in 'PFH Will Now Produce Six Potter Plays with LWT', *The Stage and Television Today*, 24 May 1979, p. 18. See Chap. 5 for extended discussion of Potter's 'defection' to LWT.

90 Milne, personal interview.

91 Dennis Potter, interview, *Anno Domini* (tx. BBC-1, 13 Feb. 1977). Transcript, BBC Written Archives, Caversham.

92 Potter, Introduction, *Brimstone* (1978), p. 4.

93 Potter, *Anno Domini.*

94 Potter, *Brimstone* (1978), p. 4.

95 Dennis Potter, radio talk, *And with No Language but a Cry* (tx. BBC Radio 4, 27 Dec. 1976). Transcript, BBC Written Archives, Caversham.

96 Potter, *Anno Domini.*

97 Potter, *And with No Language.*

98 Dennis Potter, interview, *Tonight* (tx. BBC-1, 7 Nov. 1977). Transcript, BBC Written Archives, Caversham.

99 Potter, *Anno Domini.*

Chapter 3

1 Dennis Potter, radio talk, *A Christmas Forest* (tx. BBC Radio 4, 26 Dec. 1977).

2 Angus Wilson, *Late Call*, (London: Secker and Warburg, 1964), p. 12.

3 Soundtrack, Episode 3, *Late Call* (ad. Dennis Potter (from the novel by Angus Wilson); dir. Philip Dudley; prod.: Ken Riddington; tx. BBC-2, 15 Mar. 1975). Videocassette Recording, National Film Archive.

4 See Chap. 6 for discussion of the influence of Nabokov on Potter. At one point in a flashback scene in the original scripts for *Blackeyes*, Jessica is described as a child, asleep in her uncle Kingsley's car: 'her dress reeved up like a little Lolita' (*Blackeyes*, Episode 4, Television Scripts, Sept. 1988, p. 34; courtesy, Rick McCallum).

5 This and subsequent quotations are from the soundtrack of *Alice* (wr. Dennis Potter; dir. Gareth Davies; prod. James MacTaggart; tx. BBC-1 *The Wednesday Play*, 13 Oct. 1965). National Film Archive Viewing Print.

6 This is based on historical fact. The 'golden afternoon' was 4 July 1862 and it became the influence for the *Alice* books. In *Alice in Wonderland*, Carroll/Dodgson appends some prefatory verses to the text which make this clear: 'All in the golden afternoon / Full leisurely we glide, / For both our oars, with little skill, / By little arms are plied' (Lewis Carroll, *Alice in Wonderland and Through the Looking Glass*, 1865; London: J. M. Dent, 1965, p. 81).

7 The coinage 'dream-child' comes from Dodgson / Carroll's prefatory poem in *Alice in Wonderland.* He uses it to describe his fictional version of Alice Liddell, as the children in the rowing boat that 'golden afternoon' listen to the story of her adventures: 'Anon, to sudden silence won, / In fancy they pursue, / The dream-child moving through a land, / Of wonders wild and new.' (Carroll, *Alice in Wonderland*, p. 81). The elderly Alice Hargreaves' 'Recollections of Carrollian Days' were published in Columbia University's *The Cornhill Review*, July 1932.

8 This and subsequent quotations are from *Dreamchild*, original screenplay, 26 Apr. 1983, p. 35, courtesy, Gavin Millar.

9 The story-book characters of *Alice in Wonderland* were portrayed in the film by life-size puppets, provided by Jim Henson's Creatures Workshop.

10 A. E. Housman, 'Into my heart an air that kills', qtd in Dennis Potter, *Blue Remembered Hills, Waiting for the Boat, On Television*, (London: Faber and Faber, 1984), p. 85. Housman's untitled two verse poem comes from his collection, *A Shropshire Lad* (London: Harrap, 1940).

11 Potter, Introduction, *Blue Remembered Hills*, p. 39.

12 Dennis Potter, 'Innocence and Experience', interview by Lesley Thornton, *Radio Times*, 27 Jan.–2 Feb. 1979, p. 7.

13 This and subsequent quotations from *Blue Remembered Hills* are from the published script in *Waiting for the Boat*, see note 10.

14 Potter, 'Innocence and Experience', p. 7.

15 Potter, personal interview. For Potter, *Blue Remembered Hills* itself becomes that act of 'remembering'. Having thrown off notions of an irredeemable Fall from Eden, childhood can be freely returned to and re-experienced through the power of memory and imagination.

16 Dennis Potter, radio talk, *The Other Side of the Dark* (tx. BBC Radio 4, 23 Feb. 1978). Transcript, BBC Written Archives, Caversham.

17 *Ibid.*

18 Potter, personal interview.

19 Dennis Potter, Introduction, *Brimstone and Treacle* (London: Eyre Methuen, 1978), p. 2.

20 Dennis Potter, *Hide and Seek* (London: André Deutsch / Quartet Books, 1973; reprint, London: Faber and Faber, 1990), p. 3. (This and all subsequent page references are to the reprint edition.)

21 In *The Singing Detective*, Potter reproduces this passage in order to indicate the extreme sexual disgust of his central character, Philip Marlow (see Chap. 5). See Chap. 6 for further discussion of the significance of the beautiful black-haired girl in 'The Lollipop'.

22 At the same time, the third person narrative of Part Four also renders the thoughts of the beautiful black-haired girl. From this, the reader learns that the woman, Sandra, is indeed a prostitute and although the 'Author' does not know it, she, too, comes from the Forest of Dean where she was sexually abused by her stepfather. Both prostitute and client in *Hide and Seek* are therefore victims, linked by sexual abuse.

23 See Chap. 1.

24 Potter, *A Christmas Forest.*

25 This equally applies in the case of Potter himself. As he *appeared* to attest in interview with me, 'I won't hesitate to use journalism and all those things [which] I don't believe have the same constraints, the same necessity for truth as the plays do. What I say about them and what they are are not necessarily the same thing.' The writer may hint at some of the hidden depths in his work but he certainly will not expose them. The idea is that one must look first to the plays and serials for the 'truth' about the work – assessing the veracity of the writer's statements on the basis of how much certain points seem to be confirmed by one's own reading of the work. Particularly with Potter, one needs, always, to sift sources.

26 Potter, personal interview.

27 Potter, personal interview.

28 *Double Dare* also carries clear tracemarks (see Chap. 2). Like *Hide and Seek*, it is in part an enquiry into the creative process itself, with a writer, producer and actress assembling in a hotel to discuss their craft: television drama. Martin is another blocked 'Author', seeking 'healing release' (both sexually and creatively) from a figure he fantasises into a prostitute.

29 This and subsequent quotations are from Dennis Potter, *Follow the Yellow Brick Road*, in *The Television Dramatist*, ed. Robert Muller (London: Elek, 1973). In 1973, Potter's script of *Follow the Yellow Brick Road* was published in an anthology of television plays, edited and with an introduction by the TV writer Robert Muller. The writer of each play also appended a short introduction to their published script.

30 Potter, 'Some Sort of Preface', *Waiting for the Boat*, p. 19.

31 Potter, Introduction, *Brimstone and Treacle*, p. 3.

32 Potter, Introduction, *Follow the Yellow Brick Road*, *The Television Dramatist*, p. 303.

33 This and subsequent quotations are from the soundtrack of *Only Make Believe* (wr. Dennis Potter; dir. Robert Knights; prod. Graeme McDonald; tx. BBC-1 *Play for Today*, 12 Feb. 1973). Videocassette recording, National Film Archive.

34 Bruno Bettelheim, *The Uses of Enchantment: The Meaning and Importance of Fairy Tales* (London: Thames and Hudson, 1976), pp. 3–5.

35 Potter, personal interview.

36 Bettelheim, *Useful Enchantment*, p. 9.

37 Bettelheim traces the origins of the 'Sleeping Beauty' story back to the 'Sun Moon and Talia', a tale contained in *The Pentamerone* (1636). This older story told of Talia, the daughter of a king, who one day fell to the ground, lifeless, after a splinter of hemp got under her fingernail. Leaving his inert daughter seated on a velvet chair in a room in his palace, her father, the king, locked the door and departed forever, determined to obliterate the memory of his sorrow. Some time after, another king wandered into the palace and found Talia asleep. As Bettelheim puts it, this king, falling in love with her beauty, 'cohabited with her, then he left and forgot the whole affair' (p. 228). Nine months later, the still sleeping Talia gave birth to two children. One of the babies drew out the splinter and Talia was raised from her deep sleep. Hence the 'kiss' in the Brothers Grimm tale is but a sanitised version of the rape of a lifeless human 'vegetable' – just as with Potter's *Brimstone and Treacle*.

38 As told by the Brothers Grimm, the 'Rumplestiltskin' tale deals with the daughter of a poor miller who is locked overnight in a castle, having been ordered by the king to spin straw into gold. Unable to do so, she turns in despair to a demon helper, 'a funny little man', who offers his services for a price. After she apparently spins straw into gold, the king marries the girl. When, however, their first child is born, the little demon returns to claim his side of the bargain. Only if the queen can name him, he states, will she able to keep her baby. Searching high and low throughout the kingdom, one of her messengers spots the little man in a forest clearing. Dancing around on one foot, he is shouting: 'Tee hee ha ha isn't it a shame / That none of them can guess Rumplestiltskin's name'. When the queen hears this, she is able to name the little goblin and so destroy his hold on her forever. See *Selected Tales*, comp. Jacob and Wilhelm Grimm, trans. David Luke (Harmondsworth: Penguin, 1965), pp. 53–5. Potter once wrote his own script, based around his favourite fairy tale but it was never produced (see bibliography).

39 Potter, *Hide and Seek*, p. 29.

40 William Shakespeare, *Hamlet*, III, I, 58, *The Complete Works of William Shakespeare* ed. Stanley Wells and Gary Taylor (Oxford: Clarendon Press, 1988), p. 668. Hamlet's questioning of whether to take up arms is, of course, a contemplation of his own suicide. This connects with the suicidal nature of Willy's rampage in *Where The Buffalo Roam*.

41 This is illustrated by a flashback scene in which Harris' mother expresses her worries to her husband about their 'strange' and 'withdrawn' child. While Harris senior is unconcerned, she urges a more 'normal' relationship between father and son: 'He's fascinated by you … He hears you talking about King Arthur and – well, you should talk to him more' (soundtrack, *Traitor*).

42 Besides those mentioned in the text, one can see the use of character trios in plays such as *Vote, Vote, Vote for Nigel Barton* (where Barton is 'torn' between the ideological 'purity' of his wife versus the cynicism of his political agent); *A Beast with Two Backs* (Rufus 'torn' from the Forest by the sight of a 'dead' mother and 'airy' father), as well as the 'outsider' cycle of plays which all involve a young man disrupting the lives of an older suburban husband and wife. In this way, the inner tensions and conflicts of central protagonists are embodied externally through appropriate representative figures within the drama.

43 Laurence Olivier, voice introduction, *Hamlet* (dir. Laurence Olivier), 1948.

44 Potter, personal interview.

45 The idea of this private, 'secret self' living within was most fully explored by Potter in his second novel, *Ticket to Ride*, which was written in 1985, between drafts of *The Singing Detective* and published a year later. It also formed the basis of a screenplay, the tellingly named *Secret Friends*, which Potter himself directed as a feature film in 1991 (see Conclusion). In both novel and film, the main character, John Buck, is portrayed as a man racked by warring aspects of his own personality: his 'surface' public persona versus a rebellious 'imaginary friend' whom he invented as a child in secret protest against the moral piety of his preacher father.

46 Potter, *Radio Times*, 27 Jan.–2 Feb. 1979, p. 7.

47 Raymond Williams, 'Realism and Non-Naturalism 1', p. 30.

48 'Agitational contemporaneity' was a phrase coined by Sydney Newman to sum up the spirit behind *The Wednesday Play* – the drive of many of its key practitioners not only to reflect 'contemporary' society but to try to 'agitate' for change.

49 Williams, 'Realism and Non-Naturalism 1', p. 30.

50 Dennis Potter, 'Realism and Non-Naturalism 2', *The Official Programme of The Edinburgh International Television Festival 1977*, Aug. 1977, p. 35.

51 *Ibid.*, p. 36.

52 *Ibid.*

53 *Ibid.*

54 *Ibid.*

55 Williams, 'Realism and Non-Naturalism 1', p. 30.

56 Dennis Potter, interview, *Tonight* (tx. BBC-1, 7 Nov. 1977). Transcript, BBC Written Archives, Caversham.

57 Potter, Introduction, *Follow the Yellow Brick Road*, p. 305.

Chapter 4

1 Dennis Potter, 'Potter's Path', interview by Philip Oakes, *Sunday Times*, 7 Nov. 1971, p. 24. *Casanova* consisted of six fifty-minute plays.

2 Potter, Introduction, *Follow the Yellow Brick Road*, p. 305.

3 Mercer's *Generations* trilogy – *Where the Difference Begins* (tx. 15.12.61), *A Climate of Fear* (tx. 22.2.62) and *The Birth of a Private Man* (tx. 8.3.63) – was marked by both continuity of character and theme, as the future of socialism was explored through representative figures from different generations of the same family. John Hopkins' quartet of plays, *Talking to a Stranger* (tx. 2–23 Oct. 1966, in BBC-2's single play slot, *Theatre 625*) was marked by the same willingness to engage in 'modernist' experimentation with television form, as Potter was also pioneering in his single play work at this time. The breakdown of a suburban family was examined from the differing perspectives of each of the family members; the drama often taking the audience inside the characters' heads to portray the same events from differing points of view.

4 By 'unauthored', it is meant that series and serial production did not normally encourage the expression of a single authorial point of view, as with the single play.

5 This and subsequent comments by Mark Shivas are based on an interview recorded at BBC Television Centre, London, 19 Mar. 1990.

6 'Henry and His Wives – Seven Reasons for a Triumph', *Radio Times*, 7 Jan. 1971, p. 58.

7 'The Greatest Lover', front cover, *Radio Times*, 11 Nov. 1971.

8 Yvonne Thomas, 'Frank Finlay About to Lose His Anonymity to Casanova', *Radio Times*, 11 Nov. 1971, p. 17; Potter, 'Potter's Path', p. 24.

9 Potter, 'Potter's Path', p. 24. The six volumes of Casanova's memoirs were first published in Britain, in full, unexpurgated form, towards the end of the sixties. If this publishing event provided Potter with the inspiration for his drama, as the writer made clear many years later, he never really read the memoirs: 'I had a list of his dates, when he was in prison, when he escaped, how he ended, and the details of some of the women, but that was about it. Most memoirs are self-serving and adorned with lies and I thought his were probably the same'. (Graham Fuller (ed.), *Potter on Potter* (London: Faber and Faber, 1993), pp. 69–70) As this shows, far from being an 'historically accurate' adaptation, *Casanova* was just as much a personal, authorial work, as any of Potter's single plays. For comparison with the memoirs, see Giacomo Casanova, *The History of My Life*, 6 vols., trans. Willard Trask (London: Longmans, 1967, 1968, 1969).

10 Kenith Trodd, 'In at the Birth and Death of Kestrel Productions', p. 15. Trodd's reference to 'three girls in a flat' seems to be to the popular BBC series of the time, *Take Three Girls*.

11 This and subsequent quotations are from *Casanova* camera scripts for Eps. 1–6, BBC TV script unit.

12 Potter, 'Potter's Path', p. 24. This seems to be a reference to Mary Whitehouse.

13 Mark Shivas, 'Henry and His Wives', interview, *Radio Times*, 7 Jan. 1971, p. 58. The producer claimed that 'different facets of Henry's character were polished each week and almost for the first time, we were able to understand this extraordinarily complex man'.

14 Dennis Potter, interview, *Scan*, tx. BBC Radio 4, 25 Nov. 1971. Transcript, BBC Written Archives, Caversham.

15 Other links with *The Singing Detective* are the use of flashbacks and the juxtaposition of competing narrative strands by means of which the audience are invited to piece together, as in a detective story, clues to the central protagonist's life.

16 Potter, personal interview. In fact, Potter did receive some good reviews for the work. Nancy Banks-Smith declared in the *Guardian* after Episode 1 that she liked *Casanova*'s 'night-day, waking-dreaming swing' between freedom and imprisonment, while Barry Norman in *The Times* expressed his satisfaction that Potter's Casanova was 'obviously not going to resemble the jolly laughing seducer of myth and legend' (Nancy Banks-Smith, review, *Guardian*, 17 Nov. 1971, p. 10; Barry Norman, review, *The Times*, 17 Nov. 1971, p. 14.).

17 Qtd in 'TV Play 'Lewd' Complaint', *The Times*, 2 Dec., 1971, p. 5. Mary Whitehouse's view was that the BBC was 'now well-launched into the *Oh Calcutta! – Playboy* scene' with *Casanova*.

18 This is a state of affairs which Potter would later become adept at milking as a means of securing a large popular audience for his work – for example, with *Blackeyes* (see Chap. 6).

19 Christopher Dunkley, 'Tuesdays Will Seem Dull for a While', review of Episode 6, *Casanova*, *The Times*, 22 Dec., 1971, p. 10. By a lack of narrative 'sign-posting', it is meant that the viewer has little guidance between the different narrative strands: Casanova's time in prison and his life as a libertine are constantly juxtaposed, each functioning as a metaphor for the other. The drama does not privilege one narrative strand over the other nor explicitly foreground which is 'flash-back' and which present-day 'reality'.

20 The re-edited *Casanova* was screened over two episodes on 9 and 10 Sept. 1974, on BBC-2.

21 Note that Potter later used the crooner as seducer figure in *Cream in My Coffee* (see Chap. 5).

22 Kenith Trodd, sleeve notes, *Pennies from Heaven. 48 Recordings Featured in the BBC TV Serial*. BBC Records, REF 768, 1990. The song was 'The Clouds Will Soon Roll By', sung by Elsie Carlisle.

23 This and subsequent quotations from *Pennies from Heaven* are from BBC scripts.

24 Potter, personal interview.

25 Margaret Potter, 'Man on the Moon', interview by Anne Batt, *Daily Mail*, 5 Apr. 1977, p. 16. The 'new play' Mrs Potter was referring to appears, from the evidence, to be the second episode of *Pennies*.

26 This and subsequent comments by Piers Haggard are based on an interview recorded in North London, 13 Mar. 1990. Unusually for Potter, the director of *Pennies* was approached in the winter of 1976 before the drama was even written and while Potter was still pondering what to do next.

27 Potter, personal interview. *Chicago Joe and the Showgirl* (dir. Bernard Rose) was released in 1990, though the script by David Yallop had been nearly twenty years in gestation. For the published novelisation of the script, together with an epilogue giving details of the real 'Chicago Joe' case, see M. Gaynor, *Chicago Joe and the Showgirl* (London: New English Library, 1990). Producer Kenith Trodd claims he also fed Potter with press clippings from the thirties during the writing of *Pennies*, including one about a salesman and murder, though in interview, when asked about this, 'Chicago Joe' was the main inspiration Potter volunteered.

28 Details of the Hulten and Jones case are taken from Gaynor, *Chicago Joe*, pp. 138–54.

29 Potter, of course, was a boy in Hammersmith in 1945. Hulten's and Jones' rampage as a result of the power of popular culture recalls Willy Turner's in *Where the Buffalo Roam*. See Chap. 5.

30 *The Chester Mystery Plays* were first transmitted by BBC-1 on Easter Day, 18 Apr. 1976. They won strong praise from viewers. Letters to the *Radio Times* hailed the BBC's production as 'miraculous', in terms of the 'clear and gem-like quality of colour [which] the CSO technique so magically produced'. ('Letters', *Radio Times*, 8–14 May 1976, p. 60) As Piers Haggard described it in the *Radio Times*, shooting actors against painted backgrounds, using colour separation overlay, meant you could make 'magic' in the studio, recapturing 'the fantasy fairy-tale quality of the plays' with 'the graphic clarity and speed of a cartoon' ('The Word Made Flesh', interview by Julian Mitchell, *Radio Times*, 17–23 Apr. 1976, p. 5). Such conceptions of lending television drama a 'fantasy, fairy-tale quality' undoubtedly fed into *Pennies*.

31 At the same time, graphic sequences are used to illustrate several of the songs. At one point in Episode 1, when Arthur begins to mime 'Roll Along Prairie Moon', he is slowly transformed into a painted 'cowboy below the moon on a romantically drawn song-sheet'. (Ep. 1 p. 97).

32 Potter's wish for Hudd was belatedly fulfilled, when the comic was cast in the role of Harold Atterbow, the mad organist, in *Lipstick on Your Collar* (see Conclusion).

33 Michael Elphick went on to play the part of Peter in *Blue Remembered Hills* (see Chap. 3). The consideration of Hywel Bennett for the role of Arthur clearly links in with *Pennies*' and *Where the Buffalo Roam*'s shared theme of living out one's fantasies through popular culture.

34 *On the Move* was first transmitted in Oct. 1975 and won much praise from Potter who, as TV critic, labelled it 'just the most successful and elegant and inspiring series now running on TV' (qtd in Barry Took, 'Voice-Over', *Radio Times*, 7–13 Oct. 1989, p. 95).

35 Though 'aesthetically a dog's dinner', according to Haggard, this combination of recording on tape and shooting on film stemmed from the BBC's investment in studio space in the late fifties and early sixties. It would later be superseded in the eighties by a move to all-film production: a move which Haggard laments since he believes the method of shooting television drama today means most of it is underrehearsed.

36 In the 'Blue Moon' number, the idealised vision of home-life dreamed of by Arthur's wife, Joan, is indicated by her miming to the song, whilst bathed in a wistful blue light.

37 This is confirmed by *Pennies*' film cameraman, Ken Westbury, who recalls that at least one prominent cast member was 'more than a little concerned' as to the effect this 'drama with music' would have on her subsequent career (Ken Westbury, personal interview recorded in Whitton, Twickenham, London, 15 Mar., 1990).

38 Peter Buckman, review of Episode 6, *Pennies from Heaven*, the *Listener*, 20 Apr. 1978, p. 519.

39 Michael Radcliffe, review of Episode 1, *Pennies from Heaven*, *The Times*, 8 Mar. 1978, p. 9.

40 James Murray, 'Brave New World for Dennis', preview of *Pennies from Heaven*, *Daily Express*, 10 Feb. 1978, p. 12.

41 *Pennies* was repeated on BBC-2 for three consecutive weeks, beginning 1 Dec. 1978. Two episodes were shown per evening.

42 Karen Moline, *Bob Hoskins: An Unlikely Hero* (London: Sidgwick and Jackson, 1988), p. 79.

43 Trodd, personal interview. Trodd attested that Potter was worried that the drama 'would not stand up today', whereas the producer was sure that it would. The drama was repeated between 7 Feb. and 14 Mar. 1990 on BBC-2 and was generally well received.

44 Ian Colley and Gill Davies, '*Pennies from Heaven*: Music, Image, Text', *Screen Education*, 35, Summer 1980, p. 65.

45 The year 1977 was not simply the Queen's Silver Jubilee but a time widely believed by many in Britain to be one of political and economic turmoil. Echoing Arthur's fellow salesmen in *Pennies*, there was a general feeling of the 'country going to the dogs' – of inflation roaring out of control; of enterprise stifled by excessive bureaucracy and nationalisation; of the trades unions being too strong (thus making Britain the 'sick man of Europe' on account of the number of working days lost through strikes). Such a view was enthusiastically promulgated by popular newspapers like the *Sun* and the *Daily Mail* against the Labour administration of James Callaghan, while the Right regrouped under its new Conservative leader, Margaret Thatcher. In *Pennies*, Potter is therefore echoing and parodying a popular feeling of the time through his grumpy salesmen: figures whom, it is implied, are blind to the spiritual optimism which Arthur feels through the songs.

46 Arthur's colleagues want to emigrate to the USA where 'salesmanship' is not 'a four letter word'.

47 As with *Brimstone and Treacle*, sexual assault (Arthur's forced seduction of Eileen) thus becomes a transformative act. It coarsens Eileen but it also makes her stronger – a particular evil brings an ultimate good (see Chap. 2).

48 Potter, Introduction, *Brimstone and Treacle*, p. 3.

49 Dennis Potter, *The Singing Detective* (London: Faber and Faber, 1986), p. 220. This is what Potter has his main protagonist, Philip Marlow, tell Nurse Mills in his 1986 drama (see Chap. 5). Hence 'the songs' are indelibly lodged in the memory as one of the first things heard in childhood. In that sense, they provide access to that lost childhood of 'long ago'.

50 Dennis Potter, 'When the Penny Dropped', interview by Ray Connolly, *London Evening Standard*, 21 Mar. 1978, p. 8.

51 Far from being a location choice of the director, Piers Haggard, Potter specifies in his original script that it should be Hammersmith Bridge. In interview, he explained the reason for the recurrence of the motif of Hammersmith Bridge in his work. When, in 1945, he came to London as a child of 10 and stayed in Hammersmith for nine months, he and his sister used to walk along Hammersmith

Bridge. Half way along, there was a little plaque which indicated that a Captain had jumped off the bridge and drowned (just like the Accordion Man in *Pennies*). Potter stated that that image used to haunt him as a 10-year-old because the bridge trembled in high wind. For the writer, it became an 'emblematic symbol of childhood terror' (Potter, personal interview). See Chaps 5 and 6 for discussion of the use of 'Hammersmith Bridge' in *The Singing Detective* and *Blackeyes*.

52 Though only implicit here, Potter would explore this transformation more *ex*plicitly in *The Singing Detective*.

53 Dennis Potter, 'Paradise, Perhaps', interview by John Wyver, *Time Out*, 3–9 Mar. 1978, p. 13.

54 Dennis Potter, 'Flavour of Decay', interview by John Cunningham, *Guardian*, 6 Dec. 1983, p. 11.

55 Dennis Potter, 'Potter to the Rescue', interview by P. J. Kavanagh, *Sunday Telegraph Magazine*, 4 June 1982, p. 44.

56 Clare Downs, 'Producers Profile: AIP Chairman Kenith Trodd', *AIP & Co.*, 27, July–Aug. 1980, p. 19.

57 Dennis Potter, 'Potter Rights', letter to the editor, *Broadcast*, 6 Oct., 1980, p. 9. For viewers of the original drama, the relocation of Arthur to Chicago has a clear symbolic significance. Arthur finally reaches his 'holy city' (though only to be caught up in the American Depression).

58 *Ibid.*

59 Potter, 'Potter to the Rescue', p. 44. Set both in London and New York, *The Turning Point* sequel was to have revolved around a 'torn' heroine: a ballet dancer caught between her career and motherhood ('Potter's Next Stop – Dollars from Heaven', *London Evening Standard*, 1 Mar., 1979, p. 6) Though Potter did write the screenplay, the film, called *Unexpected Valleys*, never got made. By this time, however, Ross, a former dancer and choreographer, had established himself as one of the premier directors in Hollywood; his last two films, *The Turning Point* and *The Goodbye Girl* (1978), having been both popular successes and Academy Award winners. Together with his producer wife, the late Nora Kaye (a former ballerina), he was thus in a position to pick and choose more personal 'artistic' projects like *Nijinsky* and then the *Pennies* movie.

60 This information on the pre-production of the *Pennies* movie comes from a personal interview with Rick McCallum recorded at BBC Television Centre, London, 9 Mar. 1990. In 1980, McCallum was a 27-year-old ex-Columbia business school graduate, then resident in Hollywood, who had been hired by Ross to act as the movie's executive producer. More recently, McCallum has gone on to work with George Lucas on the much-hyped *Star Wars* re-releases and 'prequels'.

61 Piers Haggard, in interview, remembers feeling 'pretty cheesed' at the suppression of the TV *Pennies*, as did most of the cast and crew. It was only in 1990 that the BBC were again able to show the original *Pennies*, when its overseas enterprise arm, Lionheart, bought the rights back from media mogul Ted Turner (the

new owner of MGM).

62 Clive Hodgson, review of MGM *Pennies from Heaven*, *Films and Filming*, Apr. 1982, p. 25.

63 Potter, 'Potter to the Rescue', p. 44.

64 Dennis Potter, 'Dollars from Hollywood', interview by Robert Brown, BFI *Monthly Film Bulletin*, 49:582, July 1982, p. 129.

65 *Pennies from Heaven*, screenplay, MGM final draft, 18 Aug. 1980 (with revised pages, 1981), p. 119. BFI Script Library.

66 Potter, 'Dollars from Hollywood', p. 129.

67 *Ibid.*

68 Rick McCallum, interview, *The Late Show* (tx. BBC-2, 12 Apr. 1990). Focusing on the preview process of new feature films, this programme included a brief examination of *Pennies*' disastrous preview.

69 'A bowdlerised comic strip version of the original, in which cheap music has once again been rendered impotent', was how Clive Hodgson described the film p. 24.

70 Pauline Kael, 'Dreamers', review of MGM *Pennies from Heaven*, first published in *The New Yorker*, 14 Dec. 1981. Reprinted in *Taking It All In* (London/New York: Marion Boyars, 1982), p. 277.

71 Indeed several years later, the studio was bought out by the Turner Entertainment Company.

72 Dennis Potter, 'Potter's Art', interview by Steve Grant, *Time Out*, 8–15 Oct. 1986, p. 25.

73 Potter, 'Potter Rights', p. 9.

74 Potter, 'Dollars from Hollywood', p. 129.

75 Dennis Potter, 'Return of the Prodigal Potter', interview by Sue Summers, *Sunday Times*, 15 Sept. 1985, p. 17.

76 Sean Day-Lewis, 'Potter Switches Screens', *Daily Telegraph*, 20 Oct. 1980, p. 10.

Chapter 5

1 The formation of an 'open' fourth TV channel having been recommended by The Annan Committee three years earlier, this became law, under the first Conservative Government of Margaret Thatcher in Nov. 1980, when a new Broadcasting Bill bringing Channel Four into existence received its Royal Assent. The Channel was launched exactly two years later, in Nov. 1982, with a remit to act as 'publisher' for the work of independent TV producers.

2 Dennis Potter, 'For 17 Years I've Been Fantasizing About How to Improve TV', interview by Richard Grant, *London Evening News*, 21 May 1979, p. 10.

3 Dennis Potter, qtd in 'PFH Will Now Produce Six Potter Plays with LWT', *The Stage & Television Today*, 24 May 1979, p. 18. Powell's *A Dance to* *the Music of Time* clearly connected with some of Potter's own interests as a writer: the relationship between a writer's fiction and his autobiography; the interplay between past and present; the shape of history and of character's lives within history.

4 Potter, 'For 17 Years', p. 10.

5 Clare Downs, 'Producers Profile: AIP Chairman Kenith Trodd', *AIP & Co.*, 27, July–Aug. 1980, p. 18. Besides the Potter scripts, *Blade on the Feather*, *Rain on the Roof* and *Cream in My Coffee*, which did eventually get produced, the other three Potter projects cited in the original deal included a rough idea for a drama revolving around the singer Sam Browne. There was also a sketchy outline for a Potter drama based on a meeting between Charles Dickens and Hans Christian Andersen, as well as an idea for a play about Hitler's last days in the Bunker in 1945. These notions were never developed into scripts. They were really just ideas quickly sketched out in order to conclude the deal with LWT.

6 Potter, 'For 17 Years', p. 10.

7 Downs, 'Producers Profile', p. 18. In interview, Trodd asserts his belief that the reason Grade presented the LWT Board with seriously underestimated costs for the first three Potter plays was because he had simply compared the budgets of Trodd's BBC work and thought the producer could deliver the equivalent for the same costs at LWT. What he had failed to realise was that (at least before the days of 'Producer Choice'), all costings at the BBC had to be treated with extreme caution because there was an 'above the line' and a 'below the line' budget. 'Above the line' was the budget individually given to Trodd by the BBC to produce a particular play but underneath this was a whole raft of hidden costs that were met elsewhere within the Corporation. These had to do with the employment and maintenance of a fixed staff which worked across a range of BBC productions. Before the days of 'Producer Choice' and the extensive use of free-lance crews at the BBC, every production was thus cushioned by hidden subsidies that were beyond the accounting of the individual producer. It was this fact which Grade seems to have overlooked in his 'purchase' of Potter and Trodd and which led to trouble over budgets.

8 Peter Fiddick, 'Counting the Pennies', *Guardian*, 29 July 1980, p. 9.

9 Downs, "Producers Profile', p. 19. After its rejection by LWT, Trodd took the two-part *The Commune* back to the BBC where it became a single film, *United Kingdom* (wr. Jim Allen; dir. Roland Joffé; tx. BBC-1 *Play for Today*, 11 Dec. 1981).

10 Downs, "Producers Profile', p. 19.

11 Michael Grade qtd in Robin Stringer, 'LWT Drops Potter Films', *Daily Telegraph*, 29 July 1980, p. 1.

12 Fiddick, "Counting the Pennies', p. 9.

13 John Wyver, 'For a Few Pennies More', *Time Out*, 8–14 Aug. 1980, p. 24.

14 Wyver, 'For a Few Pennies More', p. 24.

15 Dennis Potter, 'Why British TV Is Going to the Dogs', *Daily Mail*, 30 July 1980, p. 12.

16 *Ibid.*, p. 12. The irony, of course, is that Grade – the enemy of the 'independent' producer in 1980 – would, later in the decade, take over from Jeremy Isaacs as Chief Executive of Channel Four (in 1988). Potter and Grade would also become firm allies and friends again – indeed to such an extent that the writer, in his final interview, would cite his fondness for Grade and entrust him (along with BBC-1 Controller Alan Yentob) with the task of making sure his final works, *Karaoke* and *Cold Lazarus*, were produced in accordance with his last wishes (see Conclusion).

17 Soundtrack, *Rain on the Roof* (wr. Dennis Potter; dir. Alan Bridges; prod.: Kenith Trodd; tx. ITV, 26 Oct. 1980).

18 Dennis Potter, 'My Heritage is Chips Says Dennis Potter', interview by Anne de Courcey, *London Evening News*, 17 Oct. 1980, p. 9.

19 The names of the husband and wife in the play, Janet and John, echo the adult literacy theme.

20 Note that Potter's father died in Nov. 1975, at a time which coincided with a move to a greater faith and spiritual optimism in the writer's own work (see Chap. 2).

21 Dennis Potter, 'Some Sort of Preface', *Waiting for the Boat, On Television* (London: Faber and Faber, 1984), p. 34.

22 Dennis Potter, 'The Long Non-Revolution of Dennis Potter', interview by John Wyver, *Time Out*, 17–23 Oct. 1980, p. 18.

23 Fiddick, 'Counting The Pennies', p. 9.

24 Niven went to Hollywood. Mason stayed in Britain during the war.

25 Losey, an American exile from McCarthyism, had based himself in England for many years, before taking up residence in France in the seventies and early eighties. He famously collaborated with Pinter on *The Servant* (1963), as well as *Accident* (1967) and *The Go-Between* (1971).

26 In keeping with his 'new entrepreneurism' of the early eighties, Potter used his money from scriptwriting in Hollywood to buy up the rights to some of his old television plays – for example, *Alice* and *Double Dare* – with a view to turning them into feature film scripts. *Schmoedipus* was one of those.

27 Under producer David Rose, Channel Four's *Film on Four* initiative had funded feature films for theatrical release and subsequent television transmission. By 1982, with producers like Trodd campaigning for all-film drama, the BBC had begun to realise it would have to respond to this new competition which was in danger of sucking away its dramatic talent.

28 Joseph Losey, letter to Ann Duffey, 17 Aug. 1983. Losey Archive, British Film Institute.

29 Joseph Losey, letter to Anthony Higgins, 17 Aug. 1983. Losey Archive.

30 This and subsequent comments by Rick McCallum are based on a personal interview recorded at BBC Television Centre, 9 Mar. 1990. The BBC's decision was undoubtedly for budgetary reasons. It clearly felt that with no in-house facilities of its own in this area, the costs of production and post-production on 35mm were going to be too expensive for a single film.

31 Patricia Losey, Afterword, *Conversations with Losey*, ed. Michel Ciment (London: Methuen, 1985), p. 385.

32 Kenith Trodd, 'Trodd on the Road to Success', interview by Roma Felstein, *Broadcast*, 3 Aug. 1984, p. 23.

33 Kenith Trodd, 'Infiltrating Aunty', *AIP & Co.*, 68, Oct. 1985, p. 8.

34 Such a trend towards film-making has continued in BBC TV drama into the nineties, though it has seemed to be undergoing something of a retrenchment under the Director-Generalship of John Birt. With the appointment of Charles Denton as Head of the Drama Group in 1993, Mark Shivas was moved sideways and, at the time of writing, heads only the Corporation's film arm (BBC Films). There has been talk of the single television studio play making a comeback (a move which may be as much for reasons of production cost, as any desire to see a flowering of new writing and directing talent).

35 Dennis Potter, 'A Suitable Sleuth for Treatment', interview by Philip Oakes, *Radio Times*, 1–21 Nov. 1986, p. 100.

36 This is in accord with Potter's adaptations for TV where he seldom sought to impose his own authorial point of view (see Chap. 2).

37 For example, see Robert Brown, review of *Brimstone and Treacle* feature film, BFI *Monthly Film Bulletin*, 49:584, Sept. 1982, pp. 195–6.

38 Gavin Millar, personal interview, recorded in Central London, 14 Mar. 1990.

39 The scenes improvised by the director that ended up on the cutting room floor included those of Dodgson as a 'good uncle' figure, playing with Alice and her friends. Also, one whole character was cut out of the film: Nigel Hawthorne was cast in the role of Alice's father, the Dean of Oxford, only to find himself completely edited out of the released version of the movie.

40 Dennis Potter, interview by Aljean Harmetz, *New York Times*, 4 Oct. 1985, p. 20.

41 Though Potter in interview denied that Trodd ever had much to do with the creation of his work: 'I always self-generate [projects] and then go to somebody with them and it was always to him until suddenly with the new drugs and what have you, I started going out a little bit more into the world' (Dennis Potter, personal interview, recorded at Eastbourne Mews, London, 10 May 1990). For further discussion of Potter's disputes with Trodd in the eighties, see Chap. 6.

42 Potter, personal interview. Potter's opinion may seem biased but his view is confirmed independently by *Dreamchild*'s director, Gavin Millar. Millar states it would be wrong to think Trodd played no part in the making of the film but it is true to say the producer was less in evidence than during the shooting of *Cream in*

My Coffee. To all intents and purposes, in terms of servicing the director's day-to-day needs, Millar states McCallum 'was the producer of *Dreamchild*'.

43 Qtd in Aurthur Osman, 'Potter's Right Royalty Gesture', *The Times*, Midland Diary, 23 Sept. 1980, p. 3.

44 *Sufficient Carbohydrate* was premiered at the Hampstead Theatre in Dec. 1983. The play subsequently transferred to the West End in Feb. 1984 where it enjoyed a successful run at the Albery Theatre. Potter later adapted it into a film, *Visitors* (dir. Piers Haggard; tx. BBC-2 *Screen Two*, 22 Feb. 1987). The writer had been approached before by various parties to write for the stage. In 1968 the National Theatre had commissioned a work from him and in 1976 the Oxford Playhouse but until his diversification away from television in the early eighties nothing had ever appeared. A number of his television plays had, however, been adapted for the stage: not only the banned *Brimstone and Treacle* but also *Son of Man*, *Only Make Believe* and *Vote, Vote, Vote for Nigel Barton* (in which additional material from *Stand Up* was incorporated). More recently, *Blue Remembered Hills* has been staged by a number of theatre companies. These theatre runs were only ever after the television event and always secondary to it. In contrast to his vision of the more democratic space of television, Potter's consistent view of theatre was that it was a minority pursuit for the middle classes.

45 Dennis Potter, 'God Does Not Let Us See Him Because There's a Smile on His Face as He Looks Down on Our Antics', interview by James Murray, *Daily Express*, 22 May 1976, p. 14.

46 Potter, 'Some Sort of Preface', p. 32. If one ignores the 1987 *Screen Two* film, *Visitors*, this thought proved correct.

47 *Ibid.*, p. 33.

48 Trodd was instrumental in these changes. Along with Graham Benson, he became one of the two producers appointed to oversee the first run of *Screen Two* films, launched in Jan. 1986.

49 Potter, 'The Values of a Playwright, p. 61.

50 Dennis Potter, 'Dennis in Wonderland', interview by James Saynor, *Stills*, 21, Oct. 1985, p. 13.

51 Dennis Potter, qtd in 'Redemption from Under the Skin', profile, *Observer*, 7 Dec. 1986, p. 9.

52 Dennis Potter, 'Return of the Prodigal Potter', interview by Sue Summers, *Sunday Times*, 15 Sept. 1985, p. 17.

53 Philip Purser, *Halliwell's Television Companion*, ed. Leslie Halliwell with Philip Purser (London: Grafton Books, 1986), p. 813.

54 Potter, 'Return of the Prodigal Potter', p. 17.

55 Dennis Potter, 'Potter's Art', interview by Steve Grant, *Time Out*, 8 Oct. 1986, p. 25.

56 This and subsequent comments by Jon Amiel are based on a personal interview recorded in Highgate, London, 27 Feb. 1990.

57 Potter, 'A Suitable Sleuth', p. 98. In 1981, Potter wrote an unproduced script treatment for LWT called *Under My Skin* which also bears striking hallmarks to the hospital scenes of *The Singing Detective*. One draft title for *The Singing Detective* was going to be *Smoke Rings* (later reused as a title for 'the script within a script' of *Midnight Movie*).

58 Potter, 'Potter's Art', p. 25.

59 *Emergency Ward 9* had the thirty minute format of the sit-com. As Chap. 1 noted, it was a social comedy about the misunderstanding and resentment between different social classes in a hospital ward. Like the whole era of the studio play itself, it too had long been 'lost'.

60 This and subsequent quotations are from Dennis Potter, *The Singing Detective* (London: Faber and Faber, 1986).

61 Potter, 'Some Sort of Preface', p. 19.

62 Potter, 'Potter's Art', p. 23.

63 Dennis Potter, 'Philip Marlow, Spotted Dick', interview by David Lewin, *You Magazine*, *Mail on Sunday*, 2 Nov. 1986, p. 11.

64 Potter, 'Return of the Prodigal Potter', p. 17.

65 Potter, 'A Suitable Sleuth', p. 99.

66 Dennis Potter, 'Potter Bears All', interview, *London Evening Standard*, 17 Nov. 1986, p. 6.

67 This information on the schedule and budget of the production was provided by the journalist James Saynor who visited the set during shooting, in a personal interview recorded in Marylebone, London, 10 Nov. 1989. BBC costings always have to be treated with caution, however: see note 7.

68 The choice of Amiel to direct *The Singing Detective* was something which, Trodd states, he had an 'instinct about'. Amiel was a former RSC and BBC script editor whose ability to handle writers would stand him in good stead when dealing with Potter. He had made the transition to directing through a number of BBC productions, though it was two of his pieces in particular, *Busted* and *Gates of Gold*, which, the director states, convinced Potter that he had the necessary directorial range to work on *The Singing Detective*. In the wake of the success of working on Potter's drama, Amiel has since graduated to making Hollywood feature films.

69 In interview, Potter stated there was only really one aspect of Brecht he shared and valued and that was the idea of avoiding emotional empathy – in other words, that it is easy to generate emotions in audiences but more difficult to make them think. See Conclusion for further discussion of Potter in relation to Brecht.

70 This ending is of some interest. As both Potter and Amiel describe it in interview, the drama was originally to have ended with a revelation about who the real arch-manipulator of all the narrative strands has been. In a comic twist, the name of one of Marlow's fellow patients, a senile old man whom Marlow had christened 'Noddy' (on account of his inability to stop nodding his head), was to have been revealed at the end as none other than 'Dennis Potter' himself. As Potter put it in interview, it was an ending which Jon Amiel did not find satisfying: 'It was a joke Jon couldn't live with. And I thought maybe [he's] right.' Amiel, for his part, states that after the big emotions which the previous five episodes had explored, this ending for the drama was too much like a writer games-playing: 'Like a solution to a cross-word puzzle'. Notwithstanding this observation, such an ending, in which all layers of the drama are peeled away to reveal the 'real' writer, echoes the gradual stripping away of layers of 'fact' and 'fiction' which similarly revealed the 'Author' in *Hide and Seek* (see Chap. 3). Note that the special relationship which develops between Marlow and 'Noddy' in the 1986 drama is the remnant of this original plot idea of 'Noddy' as creative progenitor of Marlow.

71 For the *film noir* scenes, Amiel states he deliberately drew upon the image from the famous fifties advertisement, 'You're Never Alone With A Strand', when framing shots of Marlow the detective, standing on Hammersmith Bridge alone, smoking a cigarette.

72 In an essay titled 'Who Done it?', which appeared in *British Television Drama in the Eighties*, Joost Hunningher gave an outline of some of the production details from *The Singing Detective* and in so emphasising the contributions of the director and other personnel, almost gave the impression that it was Amiel 'who done it' rather than Potter. ('*The Singing Detective* (Dennis Potter): Who Done It?', *British Television Drama in the Eighties*, ed. George Brandt (Cambridge: Cambridge University Press, 1993), pp. 234–57). This seems to be going too far. As the director made clear in interview, *The Singing Detective* had changes made to it in terms of its ending and overall tone but this was only ever 'in terms of what was already there'. The production was realised in terms that stuck very closely to Potter's original blueprint. Amiel's chief contribution to the creative conception of *The Singing Detective* was in terms of his ability to act as story editor, urging Potter to rewrite and dig into himself more in order to bring out the emotions from which, because the material was so personally close to him, the writer had initially distanced himself. Amiel was thus the writer's catalyst rather than the sole progenitor of *The Singing Detective*. Given the drama's strong structural and thematic links with his other writing, to play down Potter's creative contribution to the work that ultimately reaches so closely into himself, seems somewhat perverse.

73 Examples of 'rewrites' that Amiel and Potter undertook at the editing stage principally revolve around flash-edits or short montage sequences consisting of shots taken from different episodes. The most memorable example of this is at the very end of the drama where a variety of images taken from all six episodes are juxtaposed associatively, as Vera Lynn's 'We'll Meet Again' plays on the soundtrack.

74 To emphasise the parallel, the parts of both the Russian, 'Sonia', and the 'real' prostitute (upon whom Marlow has clearly based his thriller *femme fatale*) are played by the same actress (Kate McKenzie) in the finished production.

75 Potter's script directions make clear that 'from the boy's incredulous point-

of-view, the love-making seems akin to violence, or physical attack' (p. 113).

76 Dennis Potter, *Hide and Seek* (London: André Deutsch/Quartet Books, 1973; reprint, London: Faber and Faber, 1990), p. 115. (Page reference is to the reprint edition.)

77 The characters of 'Lili' and Mrs Marlow were both played by Alison Steadman in the production.

78 Thus in *Hide and Seek*, the infant Miller's awareness of 'red marks' on his mother's neck 'turning purple', becomes associated in the adult's mind with touching her cold, dead cheek (p. 33). Similarly, one sees sexual assault associatively linked with the death of a 'mother' in *A Beast with Two Backs*, *Moonlight on the Highway* and also in terms of the 'dead' mother-child bond in *Schmoedipus/Track 29*.

79 William Shakespeare, *Hamlet*, I, IV, 67, *The Complete Works of William Shakespeare*, eds. Stanley Wells and Gary Taylor (Oxford: Clarendon Press, 1988), p. 661.

80 'Clever dick! Clever dick! Makes me sick!' are the taunts which the young Philip Marlow receives from his fellow pupils in Episode 2 of the drama (p. 76).

81 The teacher's diction here is significant – if the young Philip does not own up to what he knows, to what he has *seen*, regarding the 'mess' on her table, then he will have to have 'the Big Stick': 'You *do* know this', she warns him. 'You *do* know that you will have to have the Big Stick … in front of the whole school.'

82 This has been legally proven. In 1990, Potter's elderly mother won substantial damages from the BBC and the *Listener* magazine in relation to comments which Mary Whitehouse made on the BBC Radio Four programme, *In the Psychiatrist's Chair* about *The Singing Detective* revolving around Potter having witnessed his mother commit adultery. The *Listener*, which printed the interview, subsequently had to carry an apology, making it clear that Mrs Potter had always been faithful to her late husband.

83 Potter, 'Potter Bears All', p. 6: 'Thus the playwright described … his first thoughts the morning after watching the first episode of … his new BBC television play'.

84 For example, an item on *The Singing Detective* appeared on the BBC's *Breakfast Time* news programme (tx. BBC-1, 14 Nov. 1986). Also the BBC trailed the drama heavily prior to transmission, using clips from the drama with extracts from an interview featuring Potter talking about his new work.

85 John Lyttle, 'Sing as You Go …', *City Limits*, 6–13 Nov. 1986, p. 21. First transmitted in Nov. 1985, the Troy Kennedy Martin scripted thriller, *Edge of Darkness*, was an 'authored' serial, the success of which with audiences and critics had largely been greater than its original BBC-2 scheduling had anticipated. The drama subsequently went on to win many awards for the BBC.

86 The media mogul Rupert Murdoch, who owned many British newspaper titles, including the popular *Sun* tabloid, eventually gained his wish to move into television, when his Sky satellite channel was launched in Feb. 1989.

87 Alasdair Milne, *D.G.: The Memoirs of a British Broadcaster* (London: Hodder and Stoughton, 1988), pp. 181–2.

88 David Lewin, 'Philip Marlow, Spotted Dick', p. 33.

89 Adam Mars-Jones, 'The Art of Illness', *Independent*, 14 Nov. 1986, p. 11.

90 Martin Cropper, 'Arch-Manipulator in Promising Form', review of Episode 1, *The Singing Detective*, *The Times*, 17 Nov. 1986, p. 13.

91 Christopher Dunkley, 'Every Sunday for Six Weeks: Drama from Heaven', review of Episode 1, *The Singing Detective*, *Financial Times*, 17 Nov. 1986, p. 23.

92 Libby Purves, 'Sons and Stinging Invective', *The Times*, 3 Dec. 1986, p. 15.

93 Maureen Paton, 'Is There Real Menace in Dennis?', *Daily Express*, 2 Dec. 1986, p. 5.

94 Qtd in Louise Court, 'Writer Defends BBC Sex Scenes', *Daily Express*, 1 Dec. 1986, p. 3.

95 Gerald Howarth MP qtd in *Signals: Sex on Television* (tx. Channel Four, 2 Nov. 1988).

96 Michael Grade qtd in 'Writer Defends BBC Sex Scenes', *Daily Express*, 1 Dec. 1986, p. 3. Grade was later to deploy a similar argument, based on Potter's reputation and the BBC's paternalist 'trust' of him, when he unbanned *Brimstone and Treacle* in 1987.

97 Tony Purnell, 'TV Comment', *Daily Mirror*, 2 Dec. 1986, p. 13.

98 See for example, Patrick Stoddart, 'The Winning Detective?', *Radio Times*, 21–27 Mar. 1987, p. 3.

99 Nevertheless, there was a consolation prize. Two weeks later, on 3 Apr. 1987, Potter was honoured twice by the Broadcasting Press Guild. As its Chairman, Martin Jackson, put it, when he gave the award of best TV serial to *The Singing Detective*, 'this is the 'to hell with BAFTA' award'. (qtd in 'And to Hell with BAFTA, Mr. Potter', *Daily Mirror*, 4 Apr. 1987, p. 4).

100 Qtd in 'Letters', *Radio Times*, 17–23 Jan. 1987, p. 80. The magazine reported that *The Singing Detective* 'had produced [its] biggest postbag' and that the balance of opinion was tipped by letters (652 in all) expressing hostility towards depiction of Marlow's psoriasis and particularly, the sex scenes in Episode 3. On the other hand, it reported that the view of correspondents who stuck with the serial beyond the half-way point was '3 to 2 favourable'.

101 Evidence for this comes from the correspondent who found the drama 'sadistic and semi-pornographic'. The only reason, she claimed, that she and her husband had bothered to watch the drama right to the end was 'because it had such unanimous acclaim by the critics we felt we were missing something' ('Letters', p. 80).

102 This concept of television drama as 'social event' has been raised and discussed by, amongst others, John Caughie and John Tulloch. See Caughie, 'Progressive Television and Documentary Drama', *Popular Television and Film*, eds. Tony Bennett, Susan Boyd-Bowman, Colin Mercer and Janet Woollacott (London: British Film Institute, 1981). Also, Tulloch, *Television Drama: Agency, Audience and Myth* (London: Routledge, 1990).

103 *Brimstone and Treacle* was finally transmitted by BBC-1 on 25 Aug. 1987. It was followed by a special *Did You See?* programme, reviewing the play and discussing the reasons for its original ban.

104 Dennis Potter, interview, *Wogan* (tx. BBC-1, 15 July 1988). Appearing on the chat show, Potter described these events with some astonishment.

105 Graham Fuller, 'Dollars from Heaven', *Listener*, 4 May 1989, p. 31. This article reported on the success in America of both Potter and Mike Leigh.

106 The feature film script of *The Singing Detective* makes interesting reading. Potter changes the name of his main character, Philip Marlow, to Dan Dark (his Christian name an echo of Potter's afflicted 'Daniel' in *Hide and Seek*). As with the Hollywood *Pennies* script, events are relocated to Chicago but unlike the TV version of *The Singing Detective*, the period setting of the thriller strand is not the forties but the fifties. This allows Potter to have his characters mime to rock n'roll songs from the fifties, such as 'Heartbreak Hotel', in a similar fashion to his use of music in *Lipstick on Your Collar* (see Conclusion).

107 Dennis Potter, qtd in 'Redemption from under the Skin', Profile, *Observer*, 7 Dec. 1986, p. 9.

108 *Ibid.*

109 As Potter told Terry Wogan in an appearance on his chat show in 1987, 'I thought I'd hit on the secret! All I have to do is write about [the illness] in a particularly graphic way and it won't come. It'll stay there like a distant curse. Then – bang! Out of the sky ... if you ever assume too much, you see – bang!'

110 Shivas, personal interview. Though, as noted previously, the pendulum may now be swinging away from expensive film production back to a revival of the single studio play.

111 Dennis Potter, qtd in 'Singing for Your Fiction Takes the Sting Out of Life', Profile, *Sunday Times*, 22 Nov. 1986, p. 27.

Chapter 6

1 This and all subsequent comments by Rick McCallum are based on a personal interview recorded at BBC Television Centre, London, 16 Mar. 1990.

2 This and subsequent quotations are from the original screenplay of *Track 29*, 16 Oct. 1982. Joseph Losey Archive, British Film Institute.

3 *Schmoedipus*, BBC camera script, p. 23. BBC Television Script Unit.

4 Margaret Walters, 'Railway Children', review of *Track 29*, *Listener* 4 Aug. 1988, p. 32.

5 'Collaboration or Collision?' was the title of a Glasgow Film Theatre season in Oct. 1988 which featured the work of Nicolas Roeg and Dennis Potter.

6 Adam Barker, 'What the Detective Saw or A Case of Mistaken Identity', BFI *Monthly Film Bulletin*, 55:654, July 1988, p. 194.

7 Richard Combs, review of *Track 29*, BFI *Monthly Film Bulletin*, 55:654, July 1988, p. 192.

8 'Not Guilty', review of *The Past Is Myself* by Christabel Bielenberg, *Economist*, 13 Nov. 1982, p. 116.

9 These details are taken from a personal interview, taped in Marylebone, London, on 10 Nov. 1989, with the journalist James Saynor who researched the production background of *Christabel* for an article that appeared in the *Listener* magazine in 1988 ('One Girl's War', *Listener*, 28 July 1988, pp. 3–5).

10 According to McCallum, the then Head of BBC TV Drama, Peter Goodchild, loved the book and put intense pressure upon Trodd to bring it to the BBC.

11 Dennis Potter, interview by Graham Fuller, *American Film*, 14:5, 1989, p. 33.

12 Christabel Bielenberg, *The Past Is Myself* (1970; London: Corgi, 1988), p. 225.

13 Dennis Potter, *Christabel*, published script (London: Faber and Faber, 1988), p. 90.

14 *Ibid.*, p. 89.

15 This and all subsequent comments by Peter Edwards are based on a personal interview recorded at BBC Television Centre, London, 19 Mar. 1990.

16 This and all subsequent comments by Clare Douglas are based on a personal interview recorded at Central London, 28 Feb. 1990.

17 Kenith Trodd, interview, *Kaleidoscope* (tx. BBC Radio 4, 24 Nov. 1988).

18 Peter Tory, review of *Christabel*, *Daily Express*, 10 Dec. 1988, p. 32.

19 Potter later claimed '*Christabel* was a mistake … in that I stood aside from the source of my feelings' (Dennis Potter, 'Arrows of Desire', interview by John Wyver, *New Statesman and Society*, 24 Nov. 1989, p. 18).

20 Michael Grade, qtd in 'Grade Dramas', *Daily Express*, 15 Dec. 1988, p. 9.

21 Potter, personal interview.

22 Mark Shivas, personal interview recorded at BBC Television Centre, London, 19 Mar. 1990.

23 Potter, personal interview.

24 Potter, personal interview.

25 Trodd, personal interview.

26 Dennis Potter, 'Dennis in Wonderland', interview by James Saynor, *Stills*, Oct. 1985, p. 13.

27 Though in 1994, Potter and Trodd's love-hate 'marriage' as long-time friends and colleagues, would very much harmonise again, for sentimental reasons, as a result of events surrounding the diagnosis of Potter's terminal cancer. Trodd would be entrusted to produce Potter's final television plays, *Karaoke* and *Cold Lazarus* (see Conclusion).

28 In early 1990, the material was then re-edited as a feature film for theatrical release abroad, though, in the wake of British critical reaction to the TV version, it never achieved international distribution as a film.

29 Christine Gledhill, '*Klute* 1: Contemporary *Film Noir* and Feminist Criticism', *Women in Film Noir*, ed. E. Ann Kaplan (1978; London: BFI, 1980) p. 17.

30 Paula J. Kaplan, *The Myth of Women's Masochism* (London: Methuen, 1986), p. 19.

31 *Ibid.*, p. 228.

32 Lorna Sage, 'Old Man's Dream', review of *Blackeyes* novel, *Observer*, 4 Oct. 1987, review sec., p. 27.

33 Julian Symons, 'Literary Cartwheels', review of *Blackeyes*, *Listener*, 1 Oct. 1987, p. 22.

34 Potter, 'Arrows of Desire', p. 17.

35 Dennis Potter, 'Dark Angel', interview by Nigel Andrew, *Radio Times*, 25 Nov.–1 Dec. 1989, p. 4.

36 Shivas, personal interview. Though, as noted above, *Blackeyes* in the end did not receive international distribution as a film.

37 The main reason for this was to protect Potter's health. In his desire to direct, he had deliberately put himself at physical risk by returning in Oct. 1988 to an old 'cytotoxic' drug, methotrexate, which, though guaranteeing he would not suffer a severe attack of psoriatic arthropathy whilst working on *Blackeyes*, also entailed some unpleasant side-effects. Weekends, for example, were ruled out for shooting, being set aside for what Potter termed 'upchuck time'.

38 Dennis Potter, interview, *Saturday Matters with Sue Lawley* (tx. BBC 1, 11 Nov. 1989).

39 Dennis Potter, 'Black and Blue', interview by James Saynor, *Listener*, 1 June 1989, p. 7.

40 Dennis Potter, interview, *The Media Show* (tx. Channel Four, 16 Apr. 1989). This interview formed part of a feature on *Blackeyes* 'in production'.

41 Potter, 'Arrows of Desire', p. 17.

42 This and subsequent quotations from Episode 4 are from the soundtrack of *Blackeyes* (tx. BBC-2, 20 Dec. 1989).

43 Potter, personal interview.

44 Douglas states: 'You probably don't see it on the television screen because it's in too much of a long shot but the picture freezes as she opens the door, the gate in the wall.'

45 Potter, 'Arrows of Desire', p. 17.

46 Soundtrack, *Blackeyes*, Ep. 1 (tx. BBC-2, 29 Nov. 1989).

47 Dennis Potter, *Hide and Seek*, (London: André Deutsch/Quartet Books, 1973; repr. London: Faber and Faber, 1990), p. 11. (Page references are to the reprint edition.)

48 *Ibid.*, p. 163.

49 Soundtrack, *Blackeyes*, Ep. 2 (tx. BBC-2, 6 Dec. 1989).

50 Potter, *Blackeyes*, p. 79.

51 The reference is to the title of an early Potter single play script which never got produced. In 1966, Potter was commissioned by the BBC to write a 'Christmas play'. The result was *Almost Cinderella* – a play that inverted the Cinderella tale and which in so doing, so upset the then Head of BBC Plays, Gerald Savory, that he never let get it beyond the script stage. As Kenith Trodd recalls, Prince Charming was to have had a club foot and a hare-lip, while Cinderella was to be 'the character of the Snow Queen – [the] idea of the unattainable, upper-class girl.' (Trodd, personal interview) The 'Cinderella' motif in *Blackeyes* may, similarly, be an echo of that early, fierce exploration of male sexual angst and longing which so ruffled feathers at the BBC.

52 *Blackeyes*, original screenplay, Sept. 1988, p. 16. Courtesy, Rick McCallum.

53 Note that this is a direct quotation from the Brothers' Grimm fairy tale. See Jacob and Wilhelm Grimm, *Selected Fairy Tales*, trans. David Luke (Harmondsworth: Penguin, 1982), p. 74.

54 *Casanova*, Ep. 1, BBC camera script, June 1971, p. 73.

55 Potter, *Hide and Seek*, p. 77.

56 *Ibid.*, p. 82.

57 Dennis Potter, *Ticket To Ride* (London: Faber and Faber, 1986), p. 188.

58 Dennis Potter, *The Singing Detective*, published script, (London: Faber and Faber, 1986), p. 23.

59 Potter, personal interview.

60 Dennis Potter, *Blackeyes*, Ep. 1, television script, Sept. 1988, p. 50. Courtesy, Rick McCallum.

61 Dennis Potter, interview, *Desert Island Discs* (tx. BBC Radio 4, 17 Dec. 1977). Transcript, BBC Written Archives, Caversham.

62 Richard Last, 'The Emptiness of Potter's *Blackeyes*', review of Ep. 4, *Blackeyes*, *Daily Telegraph*, 21 Dec. 1989, p. 13.

63 BARB ratings as published in *Broadcast*, 15 and 22 Dec. 1989, p. 32 and p. 21 respectively (Eps. 1 and 2); *The Stage & Television Today*, 4 and 11 Jan. 1990, p. 17 and p. 19 respectively (Eps. 3 and 4).

64 Potter, personal interview.

65 'Telly's Dirty Drama King' in Madeleine Pallas, 'The Pain that Drives Potter Potty', *Sun*, 30 Nov. 1989, p. 12; 'Television's Mr Filth' qtd in Dennis Potter, 'Black Cloud Lifts At Last for Potter', interview by Martina Devlin, *Edinburgh Evening News*, 10 Feb. 1990, weekend sec., p. 7.

66 Stephen Pope, 'Model Dennis Potter', preview *Blackeyes*, *Independent*, 29 Nov. 1989, p. 9.

67 Stephen Pope, 'Next Week's Television', preview *Blackeyes*, *Independent*, 25

Nov. 1989, p. 55.

68 Douglas stated Potter 'does listen and he especially listens if different people make the same point ... but we didn't have the time in the editing.'

69 Potter, personal interview.

70 This seems to be what lay behind Richard Last's comments in the *Telegraph* about *Blackeyes*' 'emptiness'. All he could feel was 'incomprehension', precisely because Potter had undermined 'time, place and reality'. Without those, the drama, to him, had no point.

71 'Letters', *Observer* 31 Dec. 1989, p. 26.

72 John Wyver, 'Arrows of Desire', *New Statesman and Society*, 24 Nov. 1989, p. 18.

73 For an interesting historical analysis of this, see, for example, the work of the religious scholar, Elaine Pagels. She has convincingly related women's traditional subordination within Western culture to the development of early thinking in the Christian Church around sexual matters and the Old Testament myth of the Fall. The links here with Potter's own attempts to deal with and overcome notions of a Fall are palpable. See Elaine Pagels, *Adam, Eve and The Serpent* (Harmondsworth: Penguin, 1988).

Conclusion

1 Potter, personal interview.

2 Potter, personal interview.

3 Dennis Potter, interview, *Arena* (tx. BBC-2, 30 Jan. 1987).

4 Dennis Potter, 'Realism and Non-Naturalism 2', *The Official Programme of The Edinburgh International Television Festival 1977*, Aug. 1977, p. 36.

5 Potter, personal interview.

6 Dennis Potter, *Hide and Seek*, (London: André Deutsch/Quartet Books, 1973; repr. London: Faber and Faber, 1990), p. 115. (Page references are to the reprint edition.)

7 *Ibid.*, p. 113.

8 *Ibid.*, pp. 109–10.

9 Dennis Potter, Introduction, *Brimstone and Treacle* (London: Eyre Methuen, 1978), p. 2.

10 *Ibid.*, p. 3.

11 Dennis Potter, interview, *Wogan* (tx. BBC-1 25 Sept. 1987).

12 Potter, personal interview.

13 Lynne Truss, 'Margins', *Listener*, 15 Mar. 1990, p. 48. Truss accused Potter of this in 1990. This prompted the latter to write a stinging letter to the *Listener*, denying the accusation. See 'Letters', the *Listener*, 29 Mar. 1990, p. 22.

14 Potter, personal interview.

15 *Ibid.*

16 *Ibid.*

17 *Ibid.*

18 Dennis Potter, 'Dollars from Hollywood', interview by Robert Brown, BFI *Monthly Film Bulletin*, 49:582, July 1982, p. 127.

19 In interview, Potter stated that the one belief he shared with Brecht was that in drama 'it is easy to play on emotions … easy to make people laugh; easy to make them cry.'

20 Potter, personal interview.

21 *Casanova*, Ep. 6, camera script, p. 2. BBC Television Script Unit.

22 Dennis Potter, interview, *Without Walls Special* (tx. Channel Four, 5 Apr. 1994).

23 Simon Hattenstone, 'The Shooting Party', *Guardian*, 1 Oct. 1991, sec. 2, p. 34. *Secret Friends* was co-funded by Channel Four as a *Film on Four*. The plan for the film was that it would gain a theatrical release, prior to its television transmission on Channel Four. By Nov. 1991, however, it had become clear that no distributor was willing to pick it up. It would take another ten months before it gained a limited theatrical release, limping around the art-house circuit.

24 Phillipa Bloom, review of *Secret Friends*, *Empire*, 40, Oct. 1992, p. 38; Jonathan Romney, review, *Sight and Sound*, 2:6, Oct. 1992, p. 55.

25 Dennis Potter, interview by Tom Hibbert, *Empire*, 40, Oct. 1992, p. 49.

26 Dennis Potter, interview by Graham Fuller in Fuller (ed.), *Potter on Potter* (London: Faber and Faber, 1993), p. 98.

27 For example, such sentiments were certainly the opinion of the *Daily Telegraph*'s reviewer who declared, after seeing Episode 1, that whilst making for excellent entertainment, the miming device was beginning to look threadbare: 'One was left with the suspicion that what had started out as a useful shorthand for the discrepancy between people's interior and exterior lives had become simply a way of giving the story a bit of variety' (Max Davidson, 'Privates on Parade', review of *Lipstick on Your Collar*, *Daily Telegraph*, 22 Feb. 1993, p. 17).

28 Potter makes this clear at the very end of the drama, when Francis is temporarily in hospital with a broken leg. He receives a visit from Lisa, the niece of an American colonel and the resulting scene between them clearly shows that the pair are highly compatible with each other since both share the same bookish interests. After the couple talk for a while, excitedly sharing their love of Proust and Nietzsche, Francis asks what her father does for a living. She lowers her eyes and embarrassed, confesses that he is simply a 'Philistine' who owns a lot of oilwells in Texas. With that, Potter's script directions state the scene should cut from 'one brief swoop at Francis' incredulous face and explode into an oil gusher. Dramatic, almost violent – black gold going whoosh!' (Dennis Potter, *Lipstick on Your Collar*, published script, London: Faber and Faber, 1993, p. 201) As the ejaculatory force of the image suggests, Francis' 'love of the mind' for Lisa is finally cemented by more 'material' desires and ambitions – sexual attraction, mixed in with his realisation that if he sticks beside her, he can get rich.

29 Steve Clarke, 'Potter's Cold Feet at Lipstick on the Collar', *Daily Telegraph*, Television and Radio Section, 20 Feb. 1993, p. 19. The article reported that after completing Episode 1, Potter had run out of ideas and wanted to call the whole thing off. He actually returned his fee to Channel Four but the channel refused to accept the cheque.

30 Potter, *Potter on Potter*, p. 140.

31 Potter's attack on Rupert Murdoch came in *Opinions: Britain 1993* (tx. Channel Four, 21 Mar. 1993).

32 *Midnight Movie* was an old feature film screenplay, dealing with the arrival of an American film producer and his wife in England, which Potter wrote for Herbert Ross in the early eighties but which after the flop of the MGM *Pennies*, never got made. Having formed a new independent production company in 1990 (Whistling Gypsy Productions), Potter reworked the script as a film for the BBC in 1993 and co-financed it with his own money. No distributor, however, would pick it up and the film, directed by Renny Rye, was only shown on BBC TV after Potter's death (tx. BBC-2, 26 December 1994). This trend continued with *Mesmer*, a screenplay Potter had originally written in 1984 (developed from earlier material by American writer Jonathan Sarno) about the eighteenth-century hypnotist and Casanova-type fraudster, Anton Mesmer. Potter's script deals with a very personal theme of the 'awesome' spiritual powers of the mind triumphing over illness and in 1993, it was finally produced, under the direction of Roger Spottiswoode and starring Alan Rickman. The finished film, however, was remarkably never released due to a dispute with the distributor revolving around uncontractual changes made to the agreed shooting script during production.

33 Dennis Potter, 'Occupying Powers', 1993 James MacTaggart Lecture, repr. the *Guardian*, 28 Aug. 1993, sec. 2, p. 21.

34 This is suggested by the rapturous way in which the interview was received by reviewers in the British press – all of whom in various ways viewed Potter as symbol of an old idealism which had now largely vanished from British television and British society in general. Thus Allison Pearson claimed that with the death of Potter, 'we may be saying goodbye to the hope of a civilised intelligence to proclaim the truth of things' (Allison Pearson, 'Under Our Skin to the Last', review of *Without Walls Special*, *Independent on Sunday*, 10 Apr. 1994, review sec., p. 24).

35 Potter, *Without Walls Special.*

36 Kenith Trodd, 'Giant of the Small Screen', *Daily Telegraph*, 8 June 1994, p. 21.

37 His wife, Margaret, had suffered a relapse of breast cancer after Potter's diagnosis and died very quickly. From this it is not unreasonable to speculate that since she and Potter had always been a devoted couple, she lost all will to live once it became clear her husband was dying.

38 The television broadcast was a special *Late Show* tribute, featuring archive clips of Potter plays, together with interviews with some of his television colleagues: *Dennis Potter: A Life in Television* (tx. BBC-2, 7 June 1994). Heritage Secretary Peter Brooke had been a contemporary of Potter's at Oxford. He told the press on the day of the writer's death: 'He was one of the greatest writers for television that the country has produced and a man who endured illness with fortitude and humour. His death robs us of a great talent' (Peter Brooke MP, qtd in Susannah Herbert, 'Dennis Potter Dies of Cancer Nine Days After His Wife', *Daily Telegraph*, 8 June 1994, p. 1).

39 Kenith Trodd, 'Potter Tributes', *Guardian*, 8 June 1994, sec. 2, p. 3.

Afterword (1998)

1 *Karaoke* and *Cold Lazarus* received their British TV premieres between 28 April and 17 June 1996. Each episode was shown twice weekly – once on BBC TV, once on Channel Four. Despite this unprecedented promotion, the prime-time audience remained very low (2–3 million). In keeping with Potter's wishes, the dramas' producers were Kenith Trodd and Rosemarie Whitman; the director was Renny Rye.

2 Kenith Trodd, 'Interview ... for *Vertigo*, July 1996', *Vertigo* magazine, Autumn 1996, p. 48. An earlier version of this analysis was given at a guest lecture at De Montfort University, Leicester on 21 May 1996 (as part of my own Dennis Potter course), at which the producer also premiered extracts from *Cold Lazarus*, prior to its first transmission on 26 May.

3 For one example amongst many, see David Bianculli's reaction to the dramas in the *New York Daily News*: 'They are remarkable works ... because [Potter] crafted a fitting final TV opus that while wholly successful as an independent entity, illuminates and embraces so much of his previous work' (June 19 1996). In June and July 1997, *Karaoke* and *Cold Lazarus* were screened to a wide audience throughout the United States and Canada on the 'Bravo' cable channel, winning yet more critical acclaim.

4 This and all subsequent page references in the text are from the published edition of the scripts: Dennis Potter, *Karaoke* and *Cold Lazarus* (Faber and Faber, 1996).

5 Potter, Introduction, *Karaoke* and *Cold Lazarus*, p. x.

6 The reference is to the very last line of what Potter called his 'first and last' short story, published just three days before his death. In May 1994, Potter was commissioned by the *Daily Telegraph* to write one very last work. The result was called 'Last Pearls' and like *Karaoke*, it is about a writer, Jack, who is dying of cancer and who wants to rewrite a tawdry narrative he has let out into the world: his last published work, called *Black Pearls*. While mirroring aspects of Potter's own 'controversial' *Blackeyes*, the story has lots of echoes with *Hide and Seek*: there is the same idea of the rewriting of a piece of work by an 'Author' character made in the writer's image; a process that only leads Jack back to 'the beginning' (see Chapter 3). The story closes with Jack realising as he dies that far from changing it, he has simply 'rewritten *Black Pearls* word for word'. The last line is: 'He must have loved that book heart and soul, they said'. The fact these were the very last words Potter himself ever wrote as a creative writer seems a significant acknowledgement of an underlying consistency in his writing, in which he kept returning to mine ideas and themes this first novel had uncovered, searching for even more literary 'pearls'. See 'Last Pearls', *Daily Telegraph*, 4 June 1994, arts sec., p. 2.

7 Potter, Introduction, *Karaoke* and *Cold Lazarus*, p. vii. Science fiction may have seemed new for Potter at the end but it was well contemplated. When, in January 1992, the Museum of Television and Radio in New York (an American champion of the writer) held a major retrospective of his work, Potter was asked to pen an essay for the official programme, prior to his own visit there. The result was called 'Downloading' in which he wryly dissected the ironies of his own past work being viewed many years hence in an utterly 'alien' culture to that in which it was first produced. 'Part of me is flattered', Potter said, ' ... that someone is trying to reanimate the long-stored molecules of my former passions' but he added, 'downloading old pictures from dead brain cells ought better to take place in the cephalarium of a cryonic chamber'. (Potter, 'Downloading', *The Television of Dennis Potter*, Official Programme of a Complete Retrospective, 23 January–31 May 1992, Museum of Television and Radio, New York, p. 55) If this looks ahead to *Cold Lazarus*, it also shows how much the symbolism of that drama is concerned with the way in which Potter's own work will be regarded retrospectively by future audiences. Science fiction becomes an appropriate metaphorical vehicle for exploring these themes – its 'way of pushing the world back into an utterly otherly place' dovetailing perfectly with the concerns of the writer's own 'non-naturalism' (Introduction, *Karaoke* and *Cold Lazarus*, p. xiv).

8 This and subsequent quotations in the text attributed to Potter's 1993 James MacTaggart Lecture are taken from *Dennis Potter in Edinburgh* tx. Channel Four, 23 August 1994 – a recording in full of Potter's James MacTaggart Memorial Lecture, 'Occupying Powers', which he delivered at the Edinburgh International Television Festival on 27 August 1993.

9 Potter, MacTaggart Lecture.

10 Potter often talked of his own late wife, Margaret, as a 'green-eyed dazzler' whom he first met at a dance in the Forest of Dean (see, for example, his Introduction to *Karaoke* and *Cold Lazarus* where he knowingly refers to her as 'the steadfast green-eyed one ever': p. xv) She, too, was dying of cancer by the time he wrote *Cold Lazarus* and it is clear that in Daniel's nervous courtship of Beth, we find 'subjective' memories of Potter's own wife deliberately and movingly mixed into the fiction as perhaps an attempt to lend her a kind of immortality. In the drama, Daniel Feeld experiences guilt over Beth's death since she was knocked down and killed by a car driven by his own 'mad' twin brother, Chris. The underlying emotional 'truth' seems to be the acknowledgement and exorcism of a kind of writer's irrational guilt that somehow or other he is to blame (either through past wrong or past neglect) for the death of the 'green-eyed one'.

11 Potter, personal interview.

12 In his final TV interview, Potter explicitly signalled that through his last works, he wanted 'to continue to speak' to audiences even after his death.

13 Trodd, interview, *Vertigo*, p. 49.

14 Potter, MacTaggart Lecture. The writer's assertion was that 'drama or fiction is one of the last few remaining acres of possible truth-telling left to us in our over-manipulated and news-stuffed world'.

15 Trodd, *Vertigo*, p. 49. Lawson's article appeared in the 'Comment and Analysis' section of the *Guardian*, 15 April 1996, p. 17.

16 Trodd, *Vertigo*, p. 48.

17 Potter, MacTaggart Lecture: 'I first saw television when I was in my late teens. It made my heart *pound*'.

18 Here, it is worth comparing reaction to Potter's 'authored' drama with the acclaim writer Peter Flannery received for *Our Friends in the North* – a political serial, following the lives of four Newcastle friends from the sixties to the present-day. First transmitted in nine parts from January to March 1996, it won, in contrast to Potter, rave reviews from the British press and hence almost inevitably many British Academy Awards in the following year's ceremony (including the Best Writer's Award for Flannery), while Potter's works went away empty-handed. One reason may be its realism: it conformed to the conventional style of the vast bulk of British TV drama and indeed as it followed the lives of four friends over time, employed elements of popular soap opera. Its themes were also easier to 'relate to': its portrayal of the impact of politics on ordinary lives could be seen as instantly relevant in 'news' terms to a journalistic media culture, in a way that Potter's far more non-naturalistic, 'spiritual' drama was perhaps not (this is by no means to devalue the quality of the Flannery work, simply to point out the interesting differences in press reaction). Potter's works also perhaps suffered in following Flannery's that year: the latter was 'discovered' by the press as a fine writer in a way that the long-established and much-hyped Potter could not be. His works were expected to be 'great' and the fanfare preceding them (which the press itself had a large part in creating) helped contribute to the reaction against.

19 See, for example, reviews of Thom Sutcliffe in the *Independent*; Roy Hattersley in the *Daily Express* and Lynne Truss in *The Times* during the period of the transmissions, a good instance being on 29 April 1996, following the premiere transmission of Episode One of *Karaoke* the previous evening.

20 One 'political' reason for that change in attitude may be that as Ken Trodd has stated, 'all of the newspapers, including the *Guardian*, now have their own TV interests. The press and the screen media always were competitive, but not in the interlocking way that they are now' (interview, *Vertigo*, p. 49). In interview with me in 1990, Potter thought he was 'in for it' from the British press, after *Blackeyes*: 'About time, you know. Good job. Good for my soul. But painful'. So it largely proved – on all counts.

21 Nicholas Hellen, 'Potter's Life of Vice Girls is Revealed', *Sunday Times*, 13 April 1997, p. 3.

22 Humphrey Carpenter is the author of previous biographies on J. R. R. Tolkien, W. H. Auden, Benjamin Britten and perhaps most recently and controversially, the former Archbishop of Canterbury, Robert Runcie. Interviewing him in the *Guardian*, journalist Clare Longrigg commented: 'Carpenter ... is gaining a reputation as a muckraker. Runcie was said to be very distressed by the book, which reported his candid views on gay priests and the parlous state of the Wales's marriage ... In his biography of Britten, he got to grips with "one huge central issue". Don't tell me. "His sexuality. His relations with young boys"' (Clare Longrigg, 'Blue Remembered Thrills', *Guardian*, 16 April 1997, pp. 2–3). It is expected that Carpenter's 'official' biography of Potter will be published by (the late playwright's own publisher), Faber and Faber in October 1998.

23 Humphrey Carpenter, qtd. in Richard Brooks, 'A Matter of Life and Death', the *Observer Review*, 4 June 1995, p. 2. This article reprinted extracts from my interview with Potter and asked Carpenter and others to justify themselves in the light of the late writer's opinions against biography. Potter's literary executor, Judy Daish, was previously what the writer himself had described as his 'redoubtable' literary agent (Introduction, *Karaoke* and *Cold Lazarus*, p. xi). Potter's *Without Walls* interviewer, Melvyn Bragg, had originally been the estate's first choice as biographer but (perhaps wisely) turned the commission down to concentrate on fiction. Carpenter, however, had already written to the estate volunteering his services (Source: Conversation with Humphrey Carpenter [unrecorded], 7 May 1997, London). To what end Potter wanted to 'meet' his biographer, as is alleged, is not clear (to congratulate or protest?). The only reference *in the work* to possible interest in a future biography is in 1973's *Hide and Seek* when 'the Author' comments at one point, 'my biographers will discern a significant shift in sensibility here ...' (Potter, *Hide and Seek*, London: Andre Deutsch, 1973; repr. Faber and Faber, 1990, p. 139) But as previously shown, this 'Author' character is deliberately portrayed as arrogant, vain and paranoid – an 'unreliable narrator'. Hence the mention of biography (see Chap. 3).

24 Humphrey Carpenter, qtd in Longrigg, 'Blue Remembered Thrills', p. 2.

25 The journalist was *Independent* columnist, Angela Lambert. On the day after Potter's death, she wrote a reminiscence of her meetings with him, giving her reactions to his demise and hoping that his wish not to have a biography would be adhered to since 'he wrote his life his own way' (Angela Lambert, 'He Wrote His Life His Own Way', *Independent*, 8 June 1994).

26 Dennis Potter, interview by Graham Fuller in Fuller (ed.), *Potter on Potter*

(London: Faber and Faber, 1993), p. 10.

27 Because they sell (as opposed to its traditional territory of poetry and new fiction), Faber and Faber have increasingly moved into publishing biography and books about 'film'. The Potter biography follows a trend of turning Faber authors into subjects for 'controversial' biographies e.g. Andrew Motion on Philip Larkin (1993) (a book which painted such an unpleasant portrait of its subject, Larkin was taken off some university reading lists) and Michael Billington on Harold Pinter (1997) in which Billington 'revealed' an old affair between Pinter and Joan Bakewell in the sixties. Is Potter in for the same kind of treatment? Because of their joint 'investment', in Autumn 1994, Faber and the Potter estate acted quickly to try to stop journalist and critic W. Stephen Gilbert from writing an 'unauthorised' critical biography of Potter, by withholding copyright permission from him to quote large chunks from Potter's works. Faber Chairman, Matthew Evans, was upfront about the reasons – 'we have got to protect our own interests', he said (qtd in 'Media Diary', *Guardian*, 14 November 1994). Complaining of a censorship that Potter always set his face against, Gilbert nevertheless rushed through his book, *Fight and Kick and Bite: The Life and Work of Dennis Potter* in a mere eight months, under pressure from his aggressively commercial publisher, Hodder and Stoughton (owned by Rupert Murdoch) and borrowing an unpublished manuscript from fellow journalist John Wyver. Though offering some interesting research from internal BBC archives on the early plays, plus a useful bibliography, Gilbert's book suffers considerably from the panic-like haste in which it was thrown together. Published in time to catch the Christmas markets 1995, several months after the first edition of this volume, the two books found themselves reviewed together in the British press in ways, I guess, that got both wide coverage and did neither much harm.

28 Potter, *Without Walls* interview.

29 In 1968, Potter wrote in his column for the pre-Murdoch *Sun*: 'I find that in my writing I can only use myself, use up myself. So when I die I want to be completely emptied and completely exhausted' (Dennis Potter, 'Dennis Potter Exposed', *Sun*, 20 May 1968, p. 4). His character, Philip Marlow, puts it another way in *The Singing Detective* – in the constant, ruthless search for new material: '... writers ... They'll use anything and anybody. They'll eat their own young' (Dennis Potter, *The Singing Detective*, Published Script, Faber and Faber, 1986, pp. 210–11.)

30 Lambert, 'He Wrote His Life His Own Way', *Independent*, 8 June 1994. According to Carpenter, the sexual aspects his 'official' biography will uncover include details of old affairs, sexual obsessions, the childhood sexual assault (an unmarried maternal uncle when Potter was a ten year old living in Rednall Terrace, Hammersmith, London) as well as the anguished confessions Potter allegedly made to friends such as Roger Smith in 1963, prior to his career as a writer, concerning the '136 prostitutes' mentioned in the *Sunday Times*. The biography has also dug up case notes from the psychotherapist Potter confidentially spoke to in hospital in 1962–63, at a time when the latter told me in interview he was 'first ... ill beyond any measure I could possibly tell you' and felt he needed 'to talk to someone' (Source: Carpenter, Conversation [Unrecorded], 7 May 1997). This will be what is used to sell the biography. If, on one level, it is all rather distasteful digging up details of what was clearly a personal crisis Potter underwent in 1962–63, as a result of having contracted a terrible skin disease, on another, the sharp-eyed reader of this volume will spot that the number 136 is what the *fictional* David Peters publicly confessed to in *Moonlight on the Highway* (see Chap. 2). The main source for the *Sunday Times* story was Roger Smith, Potter's best friend until they had a major row in the mid-seventies. Did Potter confess that actual number to him? According to Smith, 'He did say there were rather a lot of them without giving a precise number' (qtd *Sunday Times*, 13 April 1997, p. 3). Hence the apparently authoritative number in the article is a fiction: a hypothesis made from a *play*. What this proves is that Potter was serving up fictions about a fascination for 'a life of vice girls' long before Humphrey Carpenter and the *Sunday Times*. In *Moonlight*, the 'patient', Peters, rebels against the too easy assumptions of the psychiatrist, yet in life, the case notes of the latter's real counterpart will be used by the biographer to present an 'external' picture of Potter which the writer himself clearly found inaccurate – not emotionally 'true' enough, as demonstrated by the central theme of his play (see Chap. 2). The unofficial word is that Carpenter is actually struggling to fill out his biography with such material since Potter spent most of his life either ill or writing and did not keep detailed records of such experiences as he had.

31 Ironically, in a new academic monograph on Potter, Glen Creeber has mounted an attack on the first edition of this book, alleging (somewhat offensively) that it, too, is 'biographical interpretation ... disguised as critical analysis' (Creeber, *Dennis Potter – Between Two Worlds: A Critical Reassessment* (Basingstoke: Macmillan, 1998), p. 16). This despite the book's extensive problematising of any simple link between the life and the work (e.g. see Chaps 3 and 5), even before the new Afterword (written prior to knowledge of Creeber's work)! Yet despite the loud protests that his is different, closer scrutiny of Creeber's book in fact shows it to be heavily influenced by this one; something, of course, which it cannot acknowledge since (as spelled out in the main text), the 'posthumous Potter' publication wars are getting ever more fierce, while in tandem, the late playwright's reputation sinks further and further in the eyes of the British press and wider media.

32 In order for a biography to work, Potter must be portrayed as simply a 'manipulative games-player': one whose pronouncements against the biographical 'method' concealed a secret autobiographical game of 'hide and seek' which the biographer can then uncover. Yet when I put precisely that early theory of mine to Potter in 1990, he said: 'Alright, you're attracted by this game of hide and seek

… That's fair enough for a little way. It has some relevance but to love it too much is to obscure and not see what is there … That's probably why I'm bristling. I don't like playing games in that sense …' (Potter, personal interview). Potter hinted here there was something more. The danger is that it is this which will be dismissed now that he is gone.

Bibliography

Works by Dennis Potter

Television drama

Note: Dates given are original transmission dates for British television.

24.2.65 *The Confidence Course*, BBC-1 *The Wednesday Play*.

13.10.65 *Alice*, BBC-1 *The Wednesday Play*.

8.12.65 *Stand Up, Nigel Barton*, BBC-1 *The Wednesday Play*.

15.12.65 *Vote, Vote, Vote for Nigel Barton*, BBC-1 *The Wednesday Play*.

11.4.66 *Emergency Ward 9*, BBC-2 *Thirty-Minute Theatre*.

2.11.66 *Where the Buffalo Roam*, BBC-1 *The Wednesday Play*.

3.5.67 *Message for Posterity*, BBC-1 *The Wednesday Play*. Note: new production 29.10.94 BBC-2 *Performance*.

13.5.68 *The Bonegrinder*, Rediffusion *Playhouse*.

10.11.68 *Shaggy Dog*, LWT *Company of Five*.

20.11.68 *A Beast with Two Backs*, BBC-1 *The Wednesday Play*.

12.4.69 *Moonlight on the Highway*, Kestrel/LWT *Saturday Night Theatre*.

16.4.69 *Son of Man*, BBC-1 *The Wednesday Play*.

23.5.70 *Lay Down Your Arms*, Kestrel/LWT *Saturday Night Theatre*.

5.11.70 *Angels Are So Few*, BBC-1 *Play for Today*.

13.6.71 *Paper Roses*, Granada *Sunday Night Theatre*.

14.10.71 *Traitor*, BBC-1 *Play for Today*.

16.11.71–21.12.71 *Casanova*, BBC-2, 6 episodes.

4.7.72 *Follow the Yellow Brick Road* BBC-2 *The Sextet*.

12.2.73 *Only Make Believe*. BBC-1 *Play for Today*.

21.11.73 *A Tragedy of Two Ambitions*, BBC-2 *Wessex Tales* (adapted from the short story by Thomas Hardy).

14.2.74 *Joe's Ark*, BBC-1 *Play for Today*.

20.6.74 *Schmoedipus*, BBC-1 *Play for Today*.

1.3.75–22.3.75 *Late Call*, BBC-2, 4 episodes (adapted from the novel by Angus Wilson).

1976 (banned) *Brimstone and Treacle*, BBC-1 *Play for Today*. Original planned transmission date: 6.4.76.
Unbanned: 25.8.87 BBC-1 Potter Retrospective Season.

6.4.76 *Double Dare*, BBC-1 *Play for Today*.

21.4.76 *Where Adam Stood*, BBC-2 *Playhouse* ('based on incidents from' *Father and Son* by Edmund Gosse).

22.1.78–5.3.78 *The Mayor of Casterbridge*, BBC-2, 7 episodes (adapted from the novel by Thomas Hardy)

7.3.78–11.4.78 *Pennies from Heaven*, BBC-1, 6 episodes.

30.1.79 *Blue Remembered Hills*, BBC-1 *Play for Today*.

19.10.80 *Blade on the Feather*, PFH/LWT.

26.10.80 *Rain on the Roof*, PFH/LWT.

2.11.80 *Cream in My Coffee*, PFH/LWT.

23.9.85–28.10.85 *Tender Is the Night*, BBC-2, 6 episodes (adapted from the novel by F. Scott Fitzgerald).

16.11.86–21.12.86 *The Singing Detective*, BBC-1, 6 episodes.

22.2.87 *Visitors*, BBC-2 *Screen Two* (based on Potter's 1983 stage play, *Sufficient Carbohydrate*).

16.11.88–7.12.88 *Christabel*, BBC-2, 4 episodes (based on *The Past is Myself* by Christabel Bielenberg).

29.11.89–20.12.89 *Blackeyes*, BBC-2, 4 episodes (based on Potter's 1987 novel *Blackeyes*).

21.2.93–28.3.93 *Lipstick on Your Collar*, Channel Four, 6 episodes.

26.12.94 *Midnight Movie* BBC-2 *Screen Two*.

28.4.96–20.5.96 *Karaoke* BBC-1 and Channel Four.

26.5.96–17.6.96 *Cold Lazarus* Channel Four and BBC-1.

Unproduced television scripts (known)

Note: The following list excludes titles of commissions and treatments which were never developed into full scripts.

Almost Cinderella (commissioned BBC TV 1966).

By the Rivers of Babylon (original draft for the BBC of what became *Moonlight on the Highway* – rejected, 1967).

A Dance to the Music of Time (adaptation of Anthony Powell's sequence of novels. Aborted when Potter and Trodd quit the BBC for LWT in 1979).

Mushrooms on Toast (rejected by the BBC in 1972).

Rumplestiltskin (Potter's version of his favourite fairy tale, found amongst his files after his death).

See You in My Dreams (delivered to the BBC June 1966 but never produced).

Feature films (in order of production)

1981 USA. *Pennies from Heaven*, dir. Herbert Ross.

1982 UK. *Brimstone and Treacle*, dir. Richard Loncraine.

1983 USA. *Gorky Park* dir. Michael Apted.

1985 UK. *Dreamchild*, dir. Gavin Millar.

1987 UK. *Track 29*, dir. Nicolas Roeg.

1991 UK. *Secret Friends*, dir. Dennis Potter.

1993 UK/Aus. *Mesmer*, dir. Roger Spottiswoode. (*Note*: This film has never been released due to legal problems with the distributor relating to directorial deviations from the agreed shooting script.)

Unproduced screenplays (known)

Note: The following is a list of titles of screenplays which are known to have been written by Potter at various stages of his career, yet which to date remain unproduced. In most cases, the actual scripts are unavailable because they remain the exclusive property of the commissioning film companies. The titles have been culled from a variety of sources, including personal interviews with practitioners, as well as from passing references to them in various published articles. Details collected in this fashion are necessarily vague and so the list has been compiled in alphabetical order by title rather than chronological sequence. Estimates of approximate periods of composition are, however, provided in parentheses.

Double Dare (early eighties American screen version of Potter's 1976 television play).

The Flipsider (written for Paramount).

The French Lieutenant's Woman (In autumn 1975, Potter wrote a screenplay draft of John Fowles' novel. The eventual 1981 film version was directed by Karel Reisz from a script by Harold Pinter.)

Ghost Writer (treatment of a proposed film, originally to have been directed by Piers Haggard, which was submitted to the National Film Development Fund in 1978).

James and the Giant Peach (Potter was hired by Disney to write the original screenplay version of Roald Dahl's book but his script was seen as too 'personal' and the 1995 film was shot using another script).

The Next Step/ Unexpected Valleys (unproduced sequel to Herbert Ross' 1977 ballet film, *The Turning Point*. Written for Ross *c.* 1979–80).

Opium Blue (Potter completed Dickens' last unfinished novel, *The Mystery of Edwin Drood*, in screenplay form during the late eighties).

The Phantom of the Opera (updating of the famous story to Paris during the Nazi Occupation. Written for Lorimar but rejected in 1988 by the company's assigned director, Wolfgang Petersen).

Pushkin (based on the life of the Russian poet, Aleksandr Pushkin. Written in late eighties for Quincey Jones at Warner Bros. but shelved).

The Singing Detective (unproduced American screen version of Potter's 1986 TV serial. First draft of screenplay dated October 1990).

Under the Volcano (adaptation of Malcolm Lowry's novel, written in the early to mid-seventies for director Alan Bridges).

White Clouds (Potter wrote an adaptation of Tim Parks' novel *Cara Massimina* in late 1993 for BBC Films. Though still in production, the script has since been extensively revised and rewritten by other hands).

The White Hotel (adaptation of D. M Thomas' novel, written in 1990, originally for director David Lynch).

Television and film scripts

a. Published television scripts

Blue Remembered Hills in *Waiting for the Boat, On Television* (London: Faber and Faber, 1984).

Christabel (London: Faber and Faber, 1988).

Cream in My Coffee in *Waiting for the Boat, On Television* (London: Faber and Faber, 1984).

Follow the Yellow Brick Road in *The Television Dramatist*, ed. Robert Muller (London: Elek, 1973).

Joe's Ark in *Waiting for the Boat, On Television* (London: Faber and Faber, 1984).

Karaoke and *Cold Lazarus* (London: Faber and Faber, 1996)

Lipstick on Your Collar (London: Faber and Faber, 1993).

Pennies from Heaven (London: Faber and Faber, 1996).

The Singing Detective (London: Faber and Faber, 1986).

Stand Up, Nigel Barton in *The Nigel Barton Plays: Two Television Plays* (Harmondsworth: Penguin, 1967).

Vote, Vote, Vote for Nigel Barton in *The Nigel Barton Plays: Two Television Plays* (Harmondsworth: Penguin, 1967).

b. Unpublished scripts

Note: The following is a list of unpublished television and film scripts by Potter which were consulted during the researching and writing of this project. Details of archive sources are given.

i) Television

Angels Are So Few, BBC camera script, April 1970. BBC Television Script Unit.

Blackeyes, TV version, Episodes 1–4, September 1988. Rick McCallum.

Blade on the Feather, pre-production script, May 1980. BFI Script Library.

The Bonegrinder, camera script, Associated Rediffusion, November 1967. BFI Script Library.

Casanova, BBC camera scripts, Episodes 1–6, June–October 1971. BBC Television Script Unit.

Casanova, draft scripts, Episodes 1–6. Mark Shivas Collection, BFI.

The Confidence Course, BBC camera script, February 1965. BBC Television Script Unit.

Cream in My Coffee, pre-production script; shooting script; rehearsal script, March 1980. BFI Script Library.

Emergency Ward 9, BBC camera script, April 1966. BBC Television Script Unit.

Message for Posterity, BBC camera script, April 1967. BBC Television Script Unit.

Paper Roses, Granada rehearsal script, November 1970. BFI Script Library.

Pennies from Heaven, BBC rehearsal scripts, Episodes 1–6, August 1977. BBC Television Script Unit.

Rain on the Roof, LWT rehearsal script, January 1980. BFI Script Library.

Schmoedipus, BBC camera script, December 1973. BBC Television Script Unit.

Shaggy Dog, LWT rehearsal script, April 1968. BFI Script Library.
The Singing Detective, rehearsal script, Episodes 1–6. Jon Amiel.

ii) Screenplays (unpublished)

Blackeyes, feature film version, September 1988. Rick McCallum.
Brimstone and Treacle, final draft, 23 August 1981. BFI Script Library.
Dreamchild, original draft, 26 April 1983. Gavin Millar.
Gorky Park, revised third draft, 20 December 1982. BFI Script Library.
Mesmer, final draft, 5 April 1993. Hollywood Scripts Ltd.
Pennies from Heaven, final draft (MGM), 18 August 1980, with revised pages, 1981. BFI Script Library.
Pennies from Heaven, original draft (Greg Smith, Norfolk International Productions), 28 December 1978. BFI Script Library.
The Singing Detective, first draft, October 1990. Hollywood Scripts Ltd.
Track 29, original draft, 16 October 1982. Joseph Losey Archive, BFI.
Track 29, combined dialogue and continuity, post-production release script, 10 March 1988. BFI Script Library.

Published theatre scripts

a. Original stage play

Sufficient Carbohydrate (London: Faber and Faber, 1983).

b. Stage plays adapted from original television material

Brimstone and Treacle (London: Eyre Methuen, 1978; repr. London: Samuel French, 1979).
Son of Man: A Play (London: André Deutsch/Samuel French, 1970).

Radio drama

Note: In the late seventies and early eighties, two of Potter's old television plays were adapted for BBC radio by Derek Hoddinott. Transmission details are as listed in the Programme Indices, BBC Written Archives Centre, Caversham.

28.11.79 *Alice* BBC Radio 4.
20.5.81 *Traitor* BBC Radio 4.

Published fiction

a. Novels

Blackeyes (London: Faber and Faber, 1987; rev. edn., 1989).
Brimstone and Treacle (London: Quartet Books, 1982). (*Note*: novelisation of Potter's 1981 screenplay, adapted by his daughter, Sarah Potter.)
Hide and Seek (London: André Deutsch/Quartet Books, 1973; repr. London: Faber and Faber, 1990).

Pennies from Heaven (London: Quartet Books, 1981). (*Note*: novelisation by Potter of his own *Pennies* screenplay.)
Ticket to Ride, (London: Faber and Faber, 1986).

b. Short stories

'Excalibur'. Posthumous reading tx. BBC Radio 4, 8 June 1998.
'Last Pearls', *Daily Telegraph*, 4 June 1994, arts sec., p.2. Also tx. BBC Radio 4, 9 June 1998.

Published poetry

'The Artist', *Verse and Prose*, ed. Dennis Potter, *The Dane*, magazine of St Clement Dane's Grammar School, 35:13, July 1953, p.441. Hammersmith Public Library, West London.

Published non-fiction

a. Monographs

The Changing Forest: Life in the Forest of Dean Today, Britain Alive series, (London: Secker and Warburg, 1962; repr. London: Minerva, 1996).
The Glittering Coffin (London: Gollancz, 1960).

b. Collected interviews

Potter on Potter, ed. Graham Fuller (London: Faber and Faber, 1993).
Seeing the Blossom (London: Faber and Faber, 1994), comprising transcripts of Potter's 1994 *Without Walls* interview; 1993 James MacTaggart Lecture; 1987 *Arena* interview.

c. Introductions and prefaces

'Downloading', Official Programme Guide to Complete Retrospective Season, *The Television of Dennis Potter*, The Museum of Television & Radio, New York, USA, 23 January–31 May 1992, p. 55–8.
Introduction, *Brimstone and Treacle* (London: Eyre Methuen, 1978), pp. 1–4.
Introduction, *Follow the Yellow Brick Road*, in *The Television Dramatist*, ed. Robert Muller (London: Elek, 1973), pp. 303–5.
Introduction, *Karaoke* and *Cold Lazarus*, (London: Faber and Faber, 1996), pp. vii–xvi.
Introduction, *The Mayor of Casterbridge* by Thomas Hardy (London: Pan Books, 1978), pp. vii–ix.
Introduction, *The Nigel Barton Plays: Two Television Plays*, (Harmondsworth: Penguin, 1967), pp. 7–22.
Introduction by Kenith Trodd, *Pennies from Heaven*, (London: Faber and Faber 1996), pp. vii–xvi.

'Some Sort of Preface …' and Introductions to *Blue Remembered Hills*, *Joe's Ark* and *Cream in My Coffee* in *Waiting for the Boat, On Television* (London: Faber and Faber, 1984), pp. 11–35; 39–40; 89–90; 135–7 respectively.
'Strike Up the Band', Introduction to *Pennies From Heaven*, *Radio Times*, 4–10 March 1978, p. 72.

d. Scripts

'Atlee', 'Budget Day', 'Canon Collins', 'Entitled to Know', 'Filth', and 'Mother's Day' (sketches co-written with David Nathan) in *That Was The Week That Was*, ed. David Frost and Ned Sherrin (London: W. H. Allen, 1963), pp. 98–9; 53; 108–9; 44–5; 24–5; 90–1 respectively.

e. Lectures and speeches

'Occupying Powers', 1993 James MacTaggart Lecture, Edinburgh International Television Festival, published in *Seeing the Blossom* (London: Faber and Faber, 1994).
'Realism and Non-Naturalism 2', Paper, 1977 Edinburgh International Television Festival, published in *The Official Programme of The Edinburgh International Television Festival 1977*, August 1977, pp. 34–7.

f. Key articles

Note: Potter's journalistic output was prodigious in his early career and hence far too extensive to list. The following is a selection of some key articles which are either cited in the text or which seem germane to his work as a creative writer and dramatist. Potter's journalism included not only feature-writing and TV criticism for the *Daily Herald* (between 1961 and 1964) but also a weekly personal column in the pre-Murdoch *Sun* (1968), as well as television and book reviewing for the *New Statesman*, *New Society*, *The Times* and the *Sunday Times*, throughout the nineteen sixties and seventies. After he resigned from the *Sunday Times* in November 1978, his journalistic output became far more sporadic. Articles listed here are given alphabetically by title.

'Base Ingratitude', *New Statesman*, 3 May 1958, p. 562.
'*Blackeyes* and Bruises' (on directing *Blackeyes*), *Sunday Telegraph*, 26 November 1989, TV and radio sec., pp. 24–5.
'A Boswell in the Bicarbonate', review of *Churchill: The Struggle for Survival* by Lord Moran, *New Society*, 26 May 1966, p. 26.
'Cue Teleciné – Put on the Kettle', *New Society*, 22 September 1966, pp. 456–7.
'George Orwell', *New Society*, 1 February 1968, pp. 107–8.
Review of *Holocaust*, *Sunday Times*, 10 September 1978; repr. *Encounter*, December 1978, pp. 16–17.
'How I'm Shaking Up the Mush Machine', *Daily Mail*, 25 May 1979, p. 9.
'I Really Must Tell You I'm So Very Happy', *Sun*, 13 May 1968, p. 3.
'Metaphysics of a Chocolate Maker', review of *Despair* by Vladimir Nabokov, *New*

Society, 28 July 1966, pp. 167–8.

'A Note from Mr. Milne', *New Statesman*, 23 April 1976, p. 648.

'Painted Ocean', review of Sir Francis Chichester's televised knighthood, *New Statesman*, 2 June 1967, p. 773.

'Reaction', *Encore*, 11:3, May–June 1964, p. 39.

'Small Victim', *New Statesman*, 21 June 1958, p. 800.

'The Spectre at the Harvest Feast', review of *Never and Always* (dir. Denis Mitchell), *Sunday Times*, 19 June 1977, p. 22.

'Sting in the Brain', review of *In Two Minds* (wr. David Mercer), *New Statesman*, 10 March 1967, p. 338.

'Switch On, Switch Back', *The Times*, 5 July, 1969, pp. 17; 22.

'Switch On, Switch Over, Switch Off', *The Times*, 15 March 1973, p. 10.

'TV Drama – Last Refuge of the Individual', *TV Times*, 18–24 October 1980, pp. 127; 130.

'Why British TV Is Going to the Dogs', *Daily Mail*, 30 July 1980, p. 12.

'Writer Exposed', *Sun*, 20 May 1968, p. 13.

'Writers Are Kings without Riches', *Daily Herald*, 25 January 1964, p. 12.

g. Published letters

Letter. *Listener*, 29 March 1990, p. 22.

'Potter Rights', *Broadcast*, 6 October 1980, p. 9.

'Writers' Attitudes to Wealth Creation', *Independent*, 17 June 1987, p. 17.

h. Documents

Severn Sound, ILR Franchise Application (Gloucester: Gloucestershire Broadcasting Company, 1979). IBA Archive.

i. Records

Sleeve Notes. *The Singing Detective*. Music from the BBC TV Serial. BBC Records, REN 608. 1986.

Non-fiction broadcasts

a. Television

3.6.60 *Between Two Rivers* BBC TV Documentary

16.10.60–25.6.61 *Bookstand* BBC TV Book Programme

5.1.63–28.12.63 *That Was the Week That Was* BBC TV

13.6.67 *Bravo and Ballyhoo* BBC-1 Documentary. Commentary written and narrated by Dennis Potter.

9.7.83 *Shakespeare in Perspective: 'Cymbeline'* BBC-2. Introduction by Potter to BBC Television Shakespeare Production of *Cymbeline*.

21.3.93 *Opinions: Britain 1993 – Dennis Potter* Channel Four

23.8.94 *Dennis Potter in Edinburgh* Channel Four. 1993 MacTaggart Lecture transmitted in full.

b. Radio

29.5.58 *Town and Country* BBC Home Service 'A View of Oxford from the editor of *Isis*'.

5.9.76 *With Great Pleasure* ... BBC Radio 4. 'Dennis Potter presents his personal choice of poetry and prose'.

27.12.76 *And with No Language but a Cry* BBC Radio 4.

26.12.77 *A Christmas Forest* BBC Radio 4

2.1.78 *Serendipity* BBC Radio 4. 'Dennis Potter goes to the archive auction'.

23.2.78 *The Other Side of the Dark* BBC Radio 4.

Major broadcast interviews and appearances

Television

25.8.58 *Does Class Matter?* 2: 'Class in Private Life' BBC TV.

8.2.60 *Tonight* BBC TV. On *The Glittering Coffin*.

7.12.65 *Late Night Line-up* BBC-2. On *The Wednesday Play*.

1.1.67 *The Look of the Year* BBC-1.

20.4.69 *Son of Man Reviewed* BBC-1.

1.3.70 *Heroes and Hero Worship – What I Believe* BBC-1.

23.5.71 *Myth and Truth: Death and Resurrection Stories* BBC-1.

14.10.71 *Late Night Line-up* BBC-2. On *Traitor*.

15.2.73 *Real Time* BBC-2.

14.8.73 *The Hart Interview: Dennis Potter*. BBC-1.

1.10.76 *Russell Harty* LWT.

13.2.77 *The Anno Domini Interview* BBC-1. On religious beliefs.

7.11.77 *Tonight* BBC-1.

11.2.78 *The South Bank Show: Man of Television* LWT. Profile and interview by Melvyn Bragg.

17.5.80 *The Levin Interviews* BBC-2.

16.5.82 *Omnibus* BBC-1. On MGM *Pennies*.

9.3.84 *Whicker!* BBC-2. Chat show guest.

24.1.86 *Saturday Review* BBC-2. Interview.

22.1.87 *Question Time* BBC-1. Panelist.

30.1.87 *Arena* BBC-2. Profile and interview by Alan Yentob.

25.8.87 *Did You See ...? Special: Brimstone and Treacle* BBC-1.

25.9.87 *Wogan* BBC-1. Chat show guest.

15.7.88 *Wogan* BBC-1. Chat show guest.

16.4.89 *The Media Show* Channel Four. On *Blackeyes*.

11.11.89 *Saturday Matters with Sue Lawley* BBC-1. Chat show guest.

27.11.91 *Channel Four News*, Channel Four. On *Secret Friends*.

7.12.92 *The Late Show* BBC-2. Tribute to Denholm Elliott by Potter.

30.8.93 *Right to Reply Special: Dennis Potter in Edinburgh* Channel Four. Excerpts of Potter's 1993 MacTaggart Lecture, plus subsequent discussion with Potter.

5.4.94	*Without Walls Special: An interview with Dennis Potter* Channel Four. Potter's last television interview.
7.6.94	*Dennis Potter: A life in Television* BBC-2. *Late Show* tribute, including interviews with Potter colleagues; archive clips from past Potter plays and Potter interviews.

Radio

13.2.60	*The World of Books* BBC Home Service. *The Glittering Coffin*. Recorded Speaker.
6.10.61	*Ten O'Clock News and Comment* BBC Home Service. 'The Establishment'. Recorded Speaker.
31.5.62	*Books and Authors* BBC Third Programme. *The Changing Forest*.
16.4.63	*Woman's Hour* BBC Light Programme. 'Aspects of University Life: The Pull Between Home Roots and College'. Recorded Speaker.
3.5.67	*The World at One* BBC Home Service. On *Message for Posterity*.
25.11.71	*Scan* BBC Radio 4. On *Casanova*.
25.4.76	*Sunday* BBC Radio 4.
30.4.76	*Thought for the Day* BBC Radio 4. Interview.
17.12.77	*Desert Island Discs* BBC Radio 4. Guest.
13.3.78	*Start the Week* BBC Radio 4. On *Pennies from Heaven*.
15.3.78	*Kaleidoscope* BBC Radio 4. On *Pennies*.
31.1.79	*Kaleidoscope* BBC Radio 4. On *Blue Remembered Hills*.
5.5.86	*Kaleidoscope Special: Making Television Sing* BBC Radio 4.
17.11.86	*Start the Week* BBC Radio 4. Guest.
20.11.89	*Third Ear* BBC Radio 3. On *Blackeyes*.
4.12.89	*Start the Week* BBC Radio 4. Guest.
29.6.91	*Writers Revealed* BBC Radio 4. On religious beliefs.

Selected published interviews

Appleyard, Bryan, 'A Risky Stand Against the Ironic Mode', *The Times*, 14 March 1984, p. 12.

Appleyard, Bryan, 'Dennis Potter, Making a Drama out of a Crisis', *The Times*, 9 September 1986, p. 12.

Bakewell, Joan, 'Wrestling with a Vision', *Sunday Times Magazine*, 14 November 1976, pp. 64–70.

Bakewell, Joan, and Nicholas Garnham, interview in Bakewell and Garnham, *The New Priesthood*, (London: Allen Lane, Penguin Press, 1970), pp. 82–4.

Brooks, Richard, 'All in the Eye of the Beholder', *Observer*, 19 November 1989, review sec., p. 35.

Brooks, Richard, 'A Matter of Life and Death', *Observer*, review sec., 4 June 1995, pp. 2–3.

Brooks, Richard, 'Return of Politically Incorrect Den', *Observer*, 14 February 1993, review sec., p. 63.

Brown, Robert, 'Dollars from Hollywood', BFI *Monthly Film Bulletin*, 49:582, July 1982, p. 129.

Burn, Gordon, 'Television Is the Only Medium that Counts', *Radio Times*, 8 October 1970, p. 66.

Connolly, Ray, 'When the Penny Dropped', *London Evening Standard*, 21 March 1978, p. 8.

de Courcey, Anne, 'My Heritage Is Chips Says Dennis Potter', *London Evening News*, 17 October 1980, p. 9.

Craig, Mary, 'Grounds for Religion: Dennis Potter on "A Protective Institution"', *Listener*, 13 May 1976, p. 613.

Cunningham, John, 'Flavour of Decay', *Guardian*, 6 December 1983, p. 11.

Cushman, Robert, 'Dennis Potter: The Values of a Playwright', *Radio Times*, 3–9 April 1976, pp. 61–5.

Devlin, Martina, 'Black Cloud Lifts at Last for Potter', *Edinburgh Evening News*, 10 February 1990, weekend sec., pp. 6–7.

Dougary, Ginny, 'Potter's Weal', *The Times*, 26 September 1992, review sec., pp. 4–10.

Fuller, Graham, 'Dennis Potter', *American Film*, 14:5, March 1989, pp. 31–3; 54–5.

Grant, Richard, 'For 17 Years I've Been Fantasising About How to Improve TV', *London Evening News*, 21 May 1979, p. 10.

Grant, Steve, 'Potter's Art', *Time Out*, 8–15 October 1986, pp. 22–5.

Grant, Steve, 'Potter's Gold', *Time Out*, 10–17 February 1993, pp. 30–1.

Harmetz, Aljean, Interview, *New York Times*, 4 October 1985, p. 20.

Hattenstone, Simon, 'The Shooting Party', *Guardian*, 1 October 1991, sec. 2, p. 34.

Hibbert, Tom, 'Dennis Potter: Controversial Genius', *Empire*, 40, October 1992, pp. 48–9.

Hibbert, Tom, 'Who the Hell Does Dennis Potter Think He Is?', *Q*, 80, May 1993, pp. 7–9.

Kavanagh, P. J., 'Potter to the Rescue', *Sunday Telegraph Magazine*, 4 June 1982, pp. 43–4.

'The Kind of Stories that Countrymen Tell', *Radio Times*, 1 November 1973, p. 83.

Koenig, Rhoda, 'The Pain of a Black Eye from the Critics', *Independent*, 18 December 1989, p. 12.

Lawson, Mark, 'Skin Flicks', *Independent Magazine*, 13 February 1993, pp. 28–32.

Lennon, Peter, 'A Man with a Lash', *Listener*, 20 November 1986, pp. 14–15.

Lewin, David, 'Philip Marlow, Spotted Dick', *You Magazine*, *Mail on Sunday*, 2 November 1986, pp. 32–4.

Lott, Tim, 'Diamonds in the Dustbin', *New Musical Express*, 15 November 1986, pp. 30–1.

Lyttle, John, 'Sing as You Go ...', *City Limits*, 266, 6–13 November 1986, p. 21.

Madden, Paul, interview in Madden (ed.), *Complete Programme Notes for a Season of British Television Drama 1959–1973, held at the National Film Theatre 11–24 October 1976* (London: British Film Institute, 1976), pp. 35–7.

Mars-Jones, Adam, 'The Art of Illness', *Independent*, 14 November 1986, p. 11.
Murray, James, 'God Does Not Let Us See Him Because There's a Grin on His Face as He Looks Down on Our Antics', *Daily Express*, 22 May 1976, p. 14.
Norman, Barry, 'What the Class Barrier Did for Dennis Potter', *Daily Mail*, 13 December 1965, p. 9.
Oakes, Philip, 'Potter's Path', *Sunday Times*, 7 November 1971, p. 24.
Oakes, Philip, 'A Suitable Sleuth for Treatment', *Radio Times*, 15–21 November 1986, pp. 98–100.
'Potter Bears All', *London Evening Standard*, 17 November 1986, p. 6.
Purser, Philip, 'A Playwright Comes of Age', *Daily Telegraph Magazine*, 2 April 1969, pp. 10–11.
Reynolds, Stanley, interview, *Guardian*, 16 February 1973, p. 11.
Saynor, James, 'Black and Blue', *Listener*, 1 June 1989, pp. 4–7.
Saynor, James, 'Dennis in Wonderland', *Stills*, 21, October, 1985, pp. 122–13.
Summers, Sue, 'Return of the Prodigal Potter', *Sunday Times*, 15 September 1985, p. 17.
Thornton, Lesley, 'Innocence and Experience', *Radio Times*, 27 January–2 February 1979, pp. 7–8.
Twisk, Russell, '*Son of Man*', *Radio Times*, 10 April 1969, p. 33.
Wright, Patrick, 'The Last Acre of Truth', *Guardian*, 15 February 1993, sec. 2, p. 2.
Wyver, John, 'Arrows of Desire', *New Statesman and Society*, 24 November 1989, pp. 16–19.
Wyver, John, 'The Long Non-Revolution of Dennis Potter', *Time Out*, 17–23 October 1980, pp. 18–19.
Wyver, John, 'Paradise, Perhaps', *Time Out*, 3–9 March 1978, pp. 12–13.

Personal interviews

Note: The following is a complete list of interviews personally conducted and recorded by the author for this project. Interviewees are listed alphabetically by surname, with details, where appropriate, of location, as well as date of interview. Also provided in parentheses is description of the status of the interviewee in relation to this study.

Amiel, Jon. Highgate, North London, 27 February 1990 (director: *The Singing Detective*).
Bridges, Alan. Richmond, Surrey, 6 March 1990 (director: *Studio 4* plays; *Traitor*, *Follow the Yellow Brick Road*, *Joe's Ark* and *Rain on the Roof*).
Calder, Gilchrist. Central London, 12 March 1990 (director: *The Confidence Course*).
Daish, Judy. Eastbourne Mews, London, 10 May 1990 (literary agent: Potter's agent from the mid seventies until his death).
Davis, Barry. BBC Scotland, Glasgow, 1 May 1990 (director: *Paper Roses*, *Schmoedipus* and the banned *Brimstone and Treacle* (died Sept. 1990)).
Douglas, Clare. Central London, 28 February 1990 (film editor: *Christabel*, *Black-*

eyes and later, *Secret Friends* and *Lipstick on Your Collar*).

Edwards, Peter. BBC Television Centre, London, 19 March 1990 (sound recordist: *Where Adam Stood*, *Visitors*, *Christabel* and *Blackeyes*).

Haggard, Piers. North London, 13 March 1990 (director: BBC TV *Pennies from Heaven* and *Visitors*).

Losey, Patricia. Telephone interviews, 4 and 5 June 1990 (widow, film director, Joseph Losey).

McCallum, Rick. BBC Television Centre, London, 9 and 16 March 1990 (film and television producer: MGM *Pennies from Heaven*, *Dreamchild, Track 29* and *Blackeyes*).

McDonald, Graeme. Anglia Films, Central London, 1 March 1990 (former BBC plays producer; former Head of BBC-2, 1983–8; producer of *A Beast with Two Backs*, *Son of Man*, *Angels Are So Few*, *Traitor*, *Only Make Believe* and *Joe's Ark*).

Millar, Gavin. Central London, 14 March 1990 (director: *Cream in My Coffee* and *Dreamchild*).

Milne, Alasdair. Holland Park, London, 5 March 1990 (former Director BBC TV Programmes, 1973–77; former BBC Director-General, 1982–87; the banner of *Brimstone and Treacle*).

Newman, Sydney. Central London, 28 February 1990 (former Head of BBC TV Drama Group, 1963–68; original architect of *The Wednesday Play*; 'censor' of *Vote, Vote, Vote for Nigel Barton* (died Nov. 1997)).

Potter, Dennis. Eastbourne Mews, London, 10 May 1990 (TV playwright and novelist (died June 1994)).

Purser, Philip. Central London, 1 March 1990 (retired television critic, *The Sunday Telegraph*: reviewer of original broadcasts of Potter plays).

Saynor, James. Marylebone, London, 10 November 1989 (journalist: visited the sets and researched the productions of *The Singing Detective*, *Christabel* and *Blackeyes*).

Shivas, Mark. BBC Television Centre, London, 19 March 1990 (former TV producer and Head of BBC TV Drama Group, 1988–93; producer of *Casanova* and commissioner of *Blackeyes* in 1988).

Smith, Roger. Peckham, South London, 16 March 1990 (first story editor of *The Wednesday Play*; Potter's best friend from university days until the early seventies).

Trodd, Kenith. BBC Television Centre, London, 8 November 1989 (television and film producer: long-standing Potter friend and colleague, the producer most associated with Potter's work).

Westbury, Ken. Whitton, Twickenham, 15 March 1990 (film cameraman: *Casanova*, *Pennies from Heaven, Tender Is the Night* and *The Singing Detective*).

Correspondence

Mitchell, Denis, letter to the author, 13 July 1990.

Willingale, Betty (former BBC script editor), letter to the author, 4 July 1990.

Unpublished Potter correspondence

Note: the following is an itemisation of private correspondence that took place between Christopher Mayhew and Potter, in the aftermath of the latter's *Does Class Matter?* interview in 1958. This was made available for research purposes by kind permission of Lord Mayhew.

Mayhew, Christopher, letter to Dennis Potter, 14 October 1958.
Potter, Dennis, letter to Christopher Mayhew, 24 June 1958.
Potter, Dennis, letter to Christopher Mayhew, 1 September 1958.
Potter, Dennis, letter to Christopher Mayhew, 14 November 1959.

Potter-related criticism and biography

Criticism

Ansorge, Peter, Sections on Potter in *From Liverpool to Los Angeles: Writing for Theatre, TV and Film* (London: Faber and Faber, 1996).

Barker, Adam, 'What the Detective Saw or a Case of Mistaken Identity', BFI *Monthly Film Bulletin*, 55:654, July 1988, pp. 193–5.

Bondebjerg, Ib. 'Intertextuality and Metafiction: Genre and Narration in the Television Fiction of Dennis Potter', *Media Cultures: Reappraising Transnational Media*, ed. M. Skormand and K. C. Schrøder (London: Routledge, 1992), pp. 161–79.

Colley, Ian, and Gill Davies, '*Pennies from Heaven*: Music, Image, Text', *Screen Education*, 25, Summer 1980, pp. 63–78.

Cook, John, Entries on 'Dennis Potter', 'Kenith Trodd' and '*The Wednesday Play*' in *International Encyclopedia of Television* (ed.) Horace Newcomb, (US: Fitzroy Dearborn, 1997).

Cooper, Howard, 'The Angel in Us', *The Month*, September–October 1995, p. 345–49.

Corrigan, Timothy, 'Music from Heaven, Bodies in Hell: *The Singing Detective*', *A Cinema Without Walls: Movies and Culture after Vietnam* (London: Routledge, pp. 179–93.

Coward, Rosalind, 'Dennis Potter and the Question of the Television Author', *Critical Quarterly*, 29:4, 1987, pp. 79–87.

Creeber, Glen, *Dennis Potter – Between Two Worlds: A Critical Reassessment* (Basingstoke: Macmillan, 1998).

Day-Lewis, Sean, 'Switch on, Tune in and Grow' (on *Karaoke* and *Cold Lazarus*) in *Talk of Drama: Views of the Television Dramatist Now and Then* (Luton: University of Luton Press, 1998).

Delaney, Paul, 'Potterland', *Dalhousie Review*, Vol. 68, part 4, 1988, pp. 511–21.

Hunningher, Joost, '*The Singing Detective* (Dennis Potter): Who Done It?', *British Television Drama in the 1980s* (Cambridge: Cambridge University Press, 1993), pp. 234–57.

Hunt, Albert, 'Plays Portentous' (on the three LWT Potter plays), *New Society*, 6 Nov. 1980, pp. 18–19.

Lichtenstein, Therese, 'Syncopated Thriller: Dennis Potter's *The Singing Detective*', *Artforum*, May 1990, pp. 168–72.
Purser, Philip, 'Dennis Potter', *British Television Drama*, ed. George W. Brandt (Cambridge: Cambridge University Press, 1981), pp. 168–93.
Purser, Philip, Chapter on Potter in *Done Viewing* (London: Quartet, 1992).
Stead, Peter, *Dennis Potter*, Borderlines Series (Bridgend: Seren Books, 1993).
Wu, Duncan, Essay on Potter in *Six Contemporary Dramatists* (London: Macmillan, 1995).

Biography

Bosé, Mihir, 'Coffee without Cream' (on Grade and the PFH deal), Chapter 5, *Michael Grade: Screening the Image* (London: Virgin Books, 1992), pp. 103–121.
Gilbert, W. Stephen, *Fight and Kick and Bite: The Life and Work of Dennis Potter* (London: Hodder and Stoughton, 1995).
Moline, Karen, 'Someplace Where the Song Is for Real' (on Hoskins and *Pennies from Heaven*), Chapter 9, *Bob Hoskins: An Unlikely Hero* (London: Sidgwick and Jackson, 1986), pp. 72–80.
Paton, Maureen, Chapter on The Making of *Mesmer* in *Alan Rickman: The Unauthorized Biography* (London: Virgin Books, 1997).
Forthcoming: 'Official' Potter biography by Humphrey Carpenter, to be published by Faber and Faber, 1998.

Conferences

'The Passion of Dennis Potter', Session OS18: Papers and panel discussion, International Association of Philosophy and Literature 20th Anniversary Conference, George Mason University, Fairfax, Virginia, USA, 10 May 1996. International papers plus new essays on Potter to be published in forthcoming collection *The Passion of Dennis Potter* (eds.) V. Gras and J. Cook.

Courses

Note: the following is a list of known courses specifically on the subject of Dennis Potter which are currently taught in UK universities. Many other universities, however, cover Potter as part of wider 'Television' or 'Television Drama' modules:

'Clenched Fists: Potter, Politics and Culture', University College of Ripon and York St. John, Ripon Campus, Ripon, Yorkshire (Course leader: Dave Evans)
'Special Studies in Television: The Work of Dennis Potter', De Montfort University, Leicester (Course leader: John Cook)

Selected Internet web-sites

Note: with the growth of the Internet, it is now possible to find Potter alive and well in cyberspace. Some significant web-site addresses to check out are:

http://www.geocities.com./TelevisionCity/1956
http://www.oudenaarden.nl/potter
http://www.picpal.com/potter.html
http://www.ucrysj.ac.uk/potter/index.htm

Index

Major references to Potter's works are in **bold** type.